MOON

PACIFIC COAST
HIGHWAY
Road Trip

IAN ANDERSON

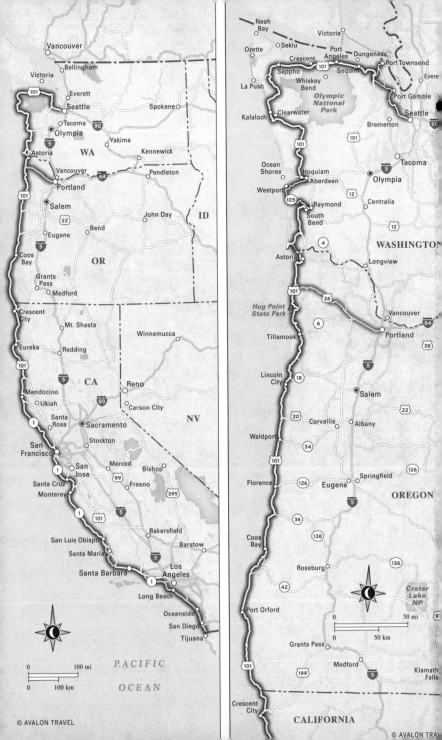

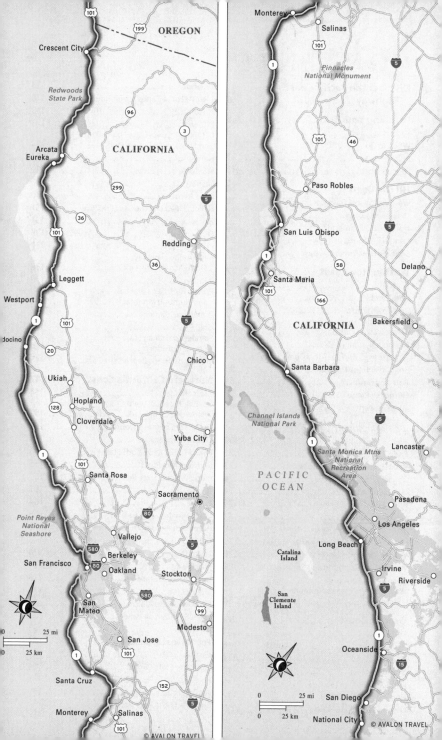

CONTENTS

DISCOVER
the Pacific Coast Highway

Y ou'll find the most colorful swath of open road in America along its western coast. The Pacific Coast Highway is 1,700 miles framed by golden sands and turquoise waters, bordered by emerald rainforests and basalt rock formations, and capped off with kaleidoscopic sunsets and indigo night skies.

This road trip stokes the imagination like few other journeys. The west was the last stop of the American frontier—its untamed wild roused fortune hunters and lured romance seekers to its shores. Today, the West Coast continues to ignite a creative spark that enthralls the entire world, be it through art, culture, or technology.

In the Northwest, cosmopolitan Seattle still holds on to the heart of a small town, while the industrious citizenry of Portland has carved out its own adaptation of modern Americana. In Southern California, the glamour and glitter of Los Angeles exudes sex appeal, while the laid-back beach culture of San Diego simply basks in the perfection of its weather. Iconic San Francisco sits in the middle, the cultured pearl of the West Coast and a beacon to visitors from every nation.

But for most of this drive, the untamed wild still beckons. From the preserved rainforests of Washington's mountainous Olympic Peninsula to the unspoiled cliffs of California's northern coast, the Pacific Coast Highway winds through a diversity of natural treasures. There are towering, ancient trees in the Redwood National Forest; massive sand dunes in Southern Oregon; and sea lions, whales, and dolphins breaching off the shores of Southern California.

Travel the entire coast and encounter the rest of the trove. Discover moonstone beaches, enigmatic basalt sea stacks, and remote lighthouses standing sentry over volatile seas. Visit resort towns, fishing villages, native reservations, and all but forgotten Victorian seaports. Dine on local-catch seafood, world-class fare, and ethnic culinary feasts. Sip on fine wine, fresh-roast coffee, and award-winning craft beer. You'll still end each day hungry for more.

The Pacific Coast Highway is an unlimited and unforgettable adventure. Are you ready to hit the road?

PLANNING YOUR TRIP

Regions

Washington Coast

Steeped in natural beauty, the **Olympic Peninsula** contains sparkling lakes, snowy mountain ridges, emerald **rainforests,** and driftwood-strewn shores. Its endless supply of fresh air and meandering hiking trails could fill an entire getaway. But a visit to the Northwest is not the same without a stopover in **Seattle,** a cosmopolitan city where fresh seafood reigns supreme and music fills every night.

Oregon Coast

With picturesque **arches** and **sea stacks,** and seemingly endless **sand dunes,** Oregon's coast often gives the sense of a prehistoric landscape, especially when the fog rolls in. Charming little seaside towns are often all that stand between the blue Pacific and endless green forest, each competing to serve the best bowls of warming clam chowder. For a taste of urban living, Oregon-style, head to **Portland** to soak up its independent spirit with some farm-to-table dining and craft beverages.

Northern California Coast

Much of California's north coast still feels like a frontier. You may drive through **giant redwoods**—in some cases literally—and lose yourself marveling at craggy, undeveloped coastlines. But then you'll cross the iconic Golden Gate Bridge into **San Francisco,** the frontier city that once stood as a beacon to adventurers and fortune seekers going west; now it offers the most famous sights, storied culture, and finest dining of the entire West Coast.

Central California Coast

Artists, writers, and poets have long found inspiration along California's central coast, where breathtaking pockets of unrefined natural beauty buffer a string of distinctive beach towns, each profiling its own unique sense of character. Funky **Santa Cruz** looks across a bay teeming with sea life at historic fishing center **Monterey,** which shares a peninsula with the elegant, upscale **Carmel-by-the-Sea.** To the south, Mediterranean-styled **Santa Barbara** soaks in sunshine, culture, and wine. And in between, the stunning and untouchable **Big Sur** provides a gorgeous setting only nature could dream up.

Southern California Coast

As it continues south, California's coastline adopts the care-free, **sun-drenched** beach culture best known to the world, mostly thanks to 100 years of films produced in **Hollywood.** Greater **Los Angeles** yields many thrills, including people-watching at the **Venice Beach Boardwalk** and celebrity-spotting in **Beverly Hills.** Further south, enjoy snorkeling in **La Jolla** followed by fish tacos and craft beer in **San Diego.** With an unparalleled sprawl of beaches stretching from **Malibu** to **Coronado,** SoCal offers unlimited recreation throughout an almost endless summer.

When to Go

The best time for this road trip is **late spring to early fall,** when the weather is best.

The window for good weather is shorter in **Washington** and **Oregon;** it's best **June through September** when it's warm and dry with average temperatures of 80°F.

Part of **California**'s allure is in its relatively **mild weather year-round.** While the northern coast rarely hits 70°F in the summertime and can be rainy and foggy,

Clockwise from top left: Sol Duc falls in Washington; coastal scenery in Northern California; cypress trees on Carmel Beach in Central California.

Clockwise from top left: the clock tower of the Santa Barbara County Courthouse; Fisherman's Wharf in San Francisco; the view of Seattle's skyline from Kerry Park.

the farther south you go, the warmer and sunnier it gets. In the San Francisco Bay Area, temperatures reach into the 70s and even 80s in summer and fall. Be prepared for the **chill of fog** in the evenings; even the warmest summer days often end with fog spilling over the Golden Gate into the city. From Santa Barbara south to San Diego, temperatures in the 80s are not unheard of even in January; summer temperatures can often hit the triple digits in inland Los Angeles.

If you drive the PCH in the **high summer season,** expect heavier **traffic** and **crowds.** Hotels and rental-car reservations go fast, so make your arrangements in advance. Rates are also higher during the summer. Port towns in Washington and Oregon can be hectic. Arrive early to the **ferry docks;** long lines form quickly and the wait can be two hours or more. Crowds and especially traffic intensify in California, especially on the freeways. Plan extra driving time and extra time along the way, especially at popular sights in big cities.

A **spring** or **fall** road trip will be less hectic, but the weather will be less reliable, especially in the Pacific Northwest, where you'll be certain to get some rain (and maybe even snow).

Before You Go

Getting There
Each region has a convenient **travel hub** in a metropolitan city: **Seattle** in Washington, **Portland** in Oregon, **San Francisco** in Northern California, **Los Angeles** and **San Diego** in Southern California. Smaller **regional airports** may also be helpful, including Eugene and North Bend in Oregon; Oakland and San Jose in Northern California; Monterey and Santa Barbara in Central California; and Burbank, Long Beach, and Santa Ana in Southern California.

Choose your travel hub based on which leg of the Pacific Coast Highway you

want to explore. If you want to drive the entire almost 1,700-mile route, it's convenient to **fly into Seattle** at the north end and **fly out of San Diego** at the southern end. You can also drive the route south to north; however, it's worth noting that driving north to south keeps the ocean on your right, making it easier to pull over and enjoy the scenery.

If you want to drive the entire coastal highway, you can return to your starting point via **I-5.** This roughly 1,300-mile route between Seattle and San Diego is **quicker (20 hours of driving)** but less scenic, with far fewer points of interest. You can also divert from the coast to I-5 at various points along the way to make up time.

Reservations
High-season travelers should plan ahead to visit **big-name attractions.** For example, if you have your heart set on visiting **Alcatraz** in San Francisco, purchase tickets at least two weeks in advance. You'll save money buying advance tickets for **Disneyland** online as well. Reservations are pretty much essential at **hotels** and **campgrounds,** especially in and around the popular resort towns, and at the limited number of lodges within Olympic National Park, which tend to sell out summer weekends several months in advance. Reserve a **rental car** ahead of time, too.

Passports and Visas
Coming to the United States from abroad? You'll need your **passport** and possibly a **visa.**

What to Pack
Be prepared for foggy, rainy weather on the northern section of the route and hot, sunny weather more likely the farther south you drive. Fog and the chill that comes with it are possible anywhere along the coast. Bring **layered clothing.** No matter what, bring (and use!) **sunscreen;** that cold fog doesn't stop the sun's rays from burning unwary beachgoers.

Driving Tips

Weather

The northern section of the Pacific Coast Highway endures **harsh weather** during **winter** and gusty winds almost year-round. There can be delays even in the warmer spring and summer months due to **heavy traffic** or **road work.** Most of the road is a **two-lane highway,** but plenty of sections allow for passing. It is just important to remember to take your time and enjoy the natural setting.

With the exception of Southern California, weather conditions change rapidly along the Pacific Coast. Be prepared for weather extremes from blustery rainstorms to hot sunny days. Highways can be closed abruptly with some sections impassable, typically due to **heavy rains** and **mudslides.** In the event of a road closure, be prepared to take alternative routes that may add hours of driving. **Winter snow** is a possibility in Washington and Oregon. Carry chains and be prepared to use them.

Wherever there's coast, there's a chance of **fog**—even sunny San Diego experiences fog so thick you can't see more than a car length ahead. When it comes up, keep your low beams on and drive *very* slowly.

Traffic

Expect **traffic delays** at major cities along the route; this is especially true of San Francisco, Los Angeles, San Diego, and Seattle, where afternoon rush hours begin midafternoon and extend into late evening.

To receive reports on **traffic and road conditions, call 511.** If your phone carrier does not support 511, call toll-free 800/977-6368. There are additional resources online: **Washington State Department of Transportation** (www.wsdot.com/traffic/trafficalerts), **Oregon Department of Transportation** (www.tripcheck.com), and the **California Department of Transportation** (www.quickmap.dot.ca.gov).

Fueling Up

Locating a **gas station** isn't hard throughout cities and towns en route; however, there are segments of the Pacific Coast Highway where nothing exists but trees, water, and local wildlife. Plan accordingly by knowing what time you will be arriving at your destination and whether there is a gas station available. Many stations in small towns (especially in Oregon) do not stay open late. Keep a full gas tank when you hit the road and don't let it drop below a quarter tank.

Clockwise from top left: purple flowers along the highway to Big Sur; a surfer at Huntington Beach; a hiking trail to Marymere Falls at Lake Crescent.

HIT THE ROAD

Check your tire pressure, change your oil, and fill up the tank. This world-class road trip will take you through nearly 1,700 miles of captivating scenery.

The full drive takes about **three weeks,** if you don't dawdle—plan on **3-5 hours of driving each day.** Take more time if you have it—there are enough destinations in this book to keep you busy for three months! But if not, consider flying into one of the coast's main **travel hubs** (Seattle, Portland, San Francisco, Los Angeles, or San Diego) and splitting the drive into **four- to seven-day** region-specific trips. Whichever section of this legendary highway you drive, the memories will last a lifetime.

For driving directions all along the way, see the *Getting There* sections in later chapters. All mileage and driving times are approximate and will vary depending on weather, traffic, and road conditions.

Washington in 4 Days

Days 1-2
SEATTLE
Spend two days in **Seattle,** a city of lakes and sounds. Stunning mountain views from every direction are best spied from the top of the soaring **Space Needle.** Explore rock-and-roll history at the Frank Gehry-designed **Experience Music Project (EMP).** Then ride the Monorail downtown to **Pike Place Market** for lunch, shopping, and people-watching. Spend the afternoon exploring the city's past at **Pioneer Square,** where a popular underground tour begins. Enjoy dinner in **Capitol Hill,** then maybe drinks and a band in **Fremont** before retiring to the **Paramount Hotel** downtown. For more ideas on how to spend your time in Seattle, see page 38.

Day 3
SEATTLE TO LAKE CRESCENT
139 miles / 224 kilometers / 4 hours
Cross Puget Sound on the **Seattle-Bainbridge Island Ferry** (depart from Pier 52). Take WA-305 North to WA-104 West, crossing the Hood Canal Bridge to connect with US-101. Spend the first half of your day exploring cute villages. Amble through **Port Gamble,** stop for lunch in **Port Townsend,** and go wildlife-viewing in sunny **Sequim.**

Spend the rest of your afternoon enjoying spectacular panoramic views while hiking along **Hurricane Ridge.** Then continue on US-101 to end your day in **Port Angeles.** Enjoy a hearty dinner before spending the night at charming **Colette's Bed & Breakfast.**

Day 4
LAKE CRESCENT TO LAKE QUINAULT
164 miles / 264 kilometers / 4 hours
Rise early to continue your journey on US-101. Stop at the sapphire waters of **Lake Crescent** for an easy hike to **Marymere Falls.** Follow this with another easy yet beautiful hike to **Sol Duc Falls,** a quick detour off the 101. Alternatively, skip the hikes and take a steamy dip in **Sol Duc Hot Springs.** Return to US-101, which will turn south as you round the peninsula. Plan on lunch in the old logging town of **Forks.**

After lunch, set out to experience the highlight of your day: the **Hoh Rain Forest,** 18 miles east when you reach Upper Hoh Road. Easy hikes on the **Hall of Mosses** and **Spruce Nature Trails** reveal a lush, canopied wonderland. Or stroll driftwood-strewn **Ruby Beach,** taking in views of its sea stacks.

Head south on US-101 to **Lake Quinault** and the **Quinault Rain Forest,** exploring more trails and seeing the world's largest spruce before checking in at historic **Lake Quinault Lodge** for a relaxing evening.

Best Beaches

Cannon Beach

Washington

- **Lake Crescent** (page 65) offers easy swimming and access to boats and paddle boards.

- **Rialto Beach** (page 73) offers sea stacks, tidepools, and, best of all, solitude.

Oregon

- **Cannon Beach** (page 113) is home to ever-popular, photogenic Haystack Rock.

- **Oswald West State Park** (page 117) is home to driftwood-laden and surfer-friendly Short Sands Beach.

Northern California

- **Black Sands Beach** (page 170), composed of crumbly volcanic rock, is the most accessible sight on the remote Lost Coast.

- **Stinson Beach** (page 194) is the favorite destination for San Franciscans seeking some surf and sunshine.

Central California

- **Carmel Beach** (page 248) features soft sand, blue water, and dogs roaming freely.

- **Pfeiffer Beach** (page 258) is the best place to watch the sun set along the Big Sur coastline.

- **Moonstone Beach** (page 263) is known for breathtaking views and surf-smoothed stones.

Southern California

- **Zuma Beach** (page 300), Malibu's classic beach party site, offers surfing, boogie boarding, and volleyball.

- **Huntington City Beach** (page 335), a.k.a. Surf City, USA, delivers waves, bikinis, volleyball nets, and a long bike path.

- **La Jolla Shores** (page 343) is a beautiful stretch of sand great for families and beginning surfers.

- **Black's Beach** (page 343) requires a little hiking, but the reward is a secluded Southern California beach backed by sandstone cliffs.

- **Coronado Beach** (page 356) is a family-friendly beach considered among the world's best, especially in front of the famous Hotel del Coronado, where lounge chairs and cocktails are available.

Oregon in 5 Days

Day 5
LAKE QUINAULT TO CANNON BEACH
146 miles / 236 kilometers / 3.5 hours
Get an early start, following US-101 south along Willapa Bay before taking four-mile Astoria Bridge across the Columbia River into Oregon.

Stop in **Astoria** for lunch before climbing the 164-step spiral staircase to the top of the **Astoria Column** for the perfect view of the river and coast. Check out the **Columbia River Maritime Museum** (one of the state's best). Explore **Fort Clatsop,** the centerpiece of sprawling **Lewis and Clark National Historical Park.**

Continue past the little towns of **Gearhart** and **Seaside** before arriving at artsy **Cannon Beach**—home to impressive **Haystack Rock.** Check in at enchanting **Stephanie Inn,** then finish the evening with a fine meal and local craft beer.

Days 6-7
EXCURSION TO PORTLAND
80 miles / 128 kilometers / 1.5 hours
From Cannon Beach, you can continue south down the coast toward Newport or head east on US-26 for an inland excursion to **Portland.**

Take two days to explore this unique city. Stop at famed **Powell's City of Books** and enjoy a one-of-a-kind treat at **Voodoo Doughnut.** Sip tea in the **Japanese Garden** (most authentic outside of Japan) and ramble along the manicured trails in **Washington Park.** Ride a bike along the banks of the **Willamette River** and drink some local **craft beer** before winding up downtown for dinner. End the day at the well-appointed **Sentinel** hotel. For more ideas on how to spend your time in Portland, see page 94.

To return to where you left off at the coast, take US-26 West back to **Cannon Beach.** Or to save time, depart US-26 on OR-6 West straight to **Tillamook** (74

miles/118 kilometers, 1.5 hours) and continue on US-101 South to Lincoln City, as described in Day 8.

Day 8
CANNON BEACH TO NEWPORT
125 miles / 202 kilometers / 4 hours
Set out early from Cannon Beach for a morning packed with memorable views. Begin just south of town at **Hug Point State Park** before exploring the beautiful beaches at **Oswald West State Park.** Continue south to the **Three Capes Scenic Route.** Try to spot migrating whales from the **Cape Meares** scenic viewpoint. Farther on, follow the trail at **Cape Lookout State Park** through the forest. Or wander mammoth-sized dunes at **Cape Kiwanda.**

Back on US-101, drive south past Tillamook to **Lincoln City,** a good stop for lunch. If you're here during June or October, head to the beach to watch colorful soaring kites. Otherwise, continue south, making stops at **Otter Crest Loop** for 360-degree views of the coast and **Devil's Punchbowl,** where sea and rock engage in an inconclusive battle.

Continue south to **Newport,** where you should bypass the tourist traps in favor of renowned **Oregon Coast Aquarium, Yaquina Bay Lighthouse,** and **Yaquina Head Lighthouse.** Head to quaint **Nye Beach** for dinner, followed by live music at **Nana's Irish Pub,** and a stay at the literary-themed **Sylvia Beach Hotel,** where a lack of electronics promotes reading and great conversations.

Day 9
NEWPORT TO GOLD BEACH
192 miles / 310 kilometers / 4.5 hours
Fill up your tank and get back on the road, driving between the forested mountains of the Coast Range and the Pacific Ocean. Just past the historic **Heceta Head** lighthouse, spectacular windswept sand takes shape along the stretch of **Oregon Dunes National Recreation Area,** which stretches 47 miles from Florence in the

Clockwise from top left: kayakers on Lake Crescent in the Olympic Peninsula; Portland's Japanese Garden; Seattle's iconic Pike Place Market sign.

Best Views

the view north from Hurricane Ridge

Washington

- The **Space Needle** (page 37) in Seattle was built for 360-degree views of Puget Sound, while the **Seattle Great Wheel** (page 34) offers views of the city skyline that include the Space Needle.

- **Hurricane Ridge** (page 62) rises over 5,757 feet from the Strait of Juan de Fuca, with views stretching from the Cascades to the Olympic Peninsula and beyond.

- **Neah Bay** (page 69) offers the most dramatic shoreline drive in the state.

Oregon

- **Ecola State Park** (page 114) has the most photographed view on the Oregon coast, featuring iconic **Haystack Rock** (page 113).

- **Cape Perpetua** (page 130) yields 150-mile views of the coast from a rustic, WPA-built observation point.

Northern California

- **Crescent Beach Overlook** (page 158) in Redwood National Park offers views of the seascape that are hard to beat.

- **Bodega Head** (page 188) offers rugged coastline views and occasional Pacific gray whales along their migration route.

- The **Marin Headlands** (page 196) have the best views of the San Francisco skyline and the Golden Gate Bridge, while the city's **Baker Beach** (page 205) offers the reverse view—bridge and headlands—from the opposite side.

Central California

- **Pfeiffer Beach** (page 258) showcases the best sunsets on the Big Sur coastline.

- **Julia Pfeiffer Burns State Park's Overlook Trail** (page 259) ends with a stunning view of McWay Falls cascading down the cliffside to a remote cove.

- **Gaviota Peak** (page 277) is at the end of a rugged three-mile trail that climaxes with stunning views of the Channel Islands.

Southern California

- **Point Dume State Beach** (page 300) has the best views of the Malibu coastline outside of a movie star's mega-mansion.

- **The Getty Center** (page 303) is a hilltop museum with unmatched views of the L.A. skyline and coastline.

- **Cabrillo National Monument** (page 355) sits on the highest point in San Diego, looking down on the city, its namesake bay, Coronado, Mexico, and a vast expanse of ocean.

north to North Bend in the south. Stop at **Old Town** in **Florence** for a bite to eat. Then put on a pair of goggles to surf the dunes riding an ATV.

Continue for another 125 miles, passing Lakeside, North Bend, and Coos Bay. Stop for photo ops in **Bandon,** with its dramatic views of boulders, sea stacks, and **Cape Blanco Light,** the oldest lighthouse in Oregon.

Stop for the night in **Gold Beach,** reserving a room at **Tu Tu Tun Lodge,** high above the Rogue River.

Northern California in 5 Days

Day 10
GOLD BEACH TO EUREKA
160 miles / 258 kilometers / 4 hours
Head south on US-101, crossing the Oregon/California border, driving through thick stands of giant redwoods. Stop in **Crescent City** for lunch before continuing on to the **Trees of Mystery** to ride the gondola and browse Native American art.

Exit US-101 to **Newton B. Drury Scenic Parkway** and explore **Prairie Creek Redwoods State Park.**

Return to US-101. After a few miles south, head west on Davison Road to **Gold Bluffs Beach.** Hike **Fern Canyon Trail,** marveling at the steep canyon dripping with green ferns—a vision of prehistoric times.

Continue south to liberal college town **Arcata** or nearby **Eureka.** Check out the bars in Arcata before crashing at a cheap chain hotel, or grab a good meal in Eureka and stay the night at **Abigail's Elegant Victorian Mansion.**

Day 11
ARCATA TO MENDOCINO
152 miles / 245 kilometers / 3 hours
Drive US-101 South, rounding the east edge of Arcata Bay and then curving inland to the **Avenue of the Giants,** which runs through magnificent redwoods. At the US-101 South/CA-1 split (just before Leggett), take CA-271 South to the admittedly cool tourist trap **Chandelier Drive-Thru Tree.**

Backtrack to CA-1, then head south through **Fort Bragg.** Continuing south, consider stops to explore the 47 acres of **Mendocino Coast Botanical Gardens** or the museum, marinelife exhibit, and lighthouse at **Point Cabrillo Light Station State Historic Park.**

Continue on to Mendocino, where you'll spend the rest of the day strolling through art galleries and shops. Book a room at the charming **MacCallum House,** where you can dine in the restaurant, enjoy a cocktail at the bar, or soak in a hot tub.

Day 12
MENDOCINO TO SAN FRANCISCO
170 miles / 272 kilometers / 4.5 hours
After breakfast in the garden at MacCallum House, simply enjoy the breathtaking stretch of coastline driving south, culminating with the rocky coves at **Sonoma Coast State Park.** Continue on CA-1 South to **Bodega Head** (watch for the sign!), the best spot for bird-watching and whale-watching, and home to **Spud Point Crab Company.** Grab fish sandwiches and clam chowder to go, then take them to Bodega Head trail to enjoy with panoramic views of the coast.

Follow CA-1 South to US-101 South. Stop in the Marin Headlands to enjoy the view of the iconic **Golden Gate Bridge** before crossing over it into San Francisco. Check into the Beatnik throwback **Hotel Boheme,** and walk into nearby **Chinatown** for noodles, dumplings, and other traditional dishes.

Days 13-14
SAN FRANCISCO
Start the morning with a **cable car** ride to **Fisherman's Wharf,** where you can cross the bay to tour the famous island prison

Clockwise from top left: a road sign on Avenue of the Giants; Bixby Bridge near Big Sur; the Golden Gate Bridge viewed from the Marin Headlands.

of **Alcatraz.** After you get your land legs back, stroll around the bayfront to the **Embarcadero** for lunch at the **Ferry Building.** Grab a coffee to go and spend the rest of the afternoon at **Golden Gate Park,** where you'll find the **de Young Museum** and **California Academy of Sciences.** Top off the day with an excellent dinner in the **Mission District.** For more ideas on how to spend your time in San Francisco, see page 202.

Central California in 3 Days

Day 15
SAN FRANCISCO TO BIG SUR
160 miles / 250 kilometers / 4 hours
Move out early and head down CA-1, rounding Monterey Bay. Choose stops along the way based on your interests. Stroll the boardwalk and ride the roller coaster in **Santa Cruz.** Tour **Monterey**'s famous aquarium. **Carmel** offers pristine white sand, cypress trees, and charming art galleries. All three towns have plenty of options for lunch.

The highway heading into **Big Sur** has some of the most scenic stretches in California. Be sure to snap some photographs, stopping or using pullouts only when it's safe. Enjoy astonishing views at the **Point Lobos State Reserve** and the **Bixby Bridge.** On the west side of CA-1, take Sycamore Canyon Road to **Pfeiffer Beach** to see impressive rock formations. Time your stop to enjoy the sunset.

Enjoy the view while you dine at **Nepenthe,** then retire to historic **Deetjens Big Sur Inn,** nestled in the redwoods.

Day 16
BIG SUR TO SAN LUIS OBISPO
117 miles / 188 kilometers / 3 hours
Set out early in the morning, stopping along the way at **Julia Pfeiffer Burns State Park** to hike the short trail to the

scenic overlook of McWay Falls. See the lighthouse and elephant seals at **Piedras Blancas.** Continue south to **San Simeon,** where you'll stop for lunch before touring the enchanting **Hearst Castle.**

At Morro Bay, CA-1 moves inland toward **San Luis Obispo,** a lively little college town, where the **Madonna Inn,** a roadside attraction, is worth a look around—or an overnight stay, depending on your appreciation for kitsch.

Day 17
SAN LUIS OBISPO TO SANTA BARBARA
105 miles / 170 kilometers / 2 hours
Continue south on US-101 to **Gaviota State Park,** where you can hike to Gaviota Peak for stunning views of the Channel Islands. Less ambitious beachgoers may prefer spending the morning at scenic **El Capitán State Beach.**

Continue south to **Santa Barbara** to enjoy lunch and window-shopping on **State Street.** Spend the afternoon diving into Santa Barbara's history and culture, visiting the **Old Mission Santa Barbara** or **Santa Barbara Museum of Art.** Then visit tasting rooms along the **Santa Barbara Urban Wine Trail** and stroll along the beach for sunset and dinner. Get a room at the Spanish-style **Brisas del Mar Inn,** just a short walk from the beaches.

Southern California in 4 Days

Day 18
SANTA BARBARA TO SANTA MONICA
85 miles / 136 kilometers / 2 hours
Take US-101 South until roughly five miles past Ventura, where CA-1 splits from US-101 and heads southwest into **Malibu,** a fantastic coastal drive passing by dreamy surf and million-dollar beach houses. Lovers of art and history should consider a stop at the **Getty Villa.**

Once you reach **Santa Monica,** visit the **Santa Monica Pier** for strolling and

Clockwise from top left: Alcatraz, San Francisco's notorious island prison; motorbike art along the highway passing through Moss Landing; Old Mission Santa Barbara.

Romantic Stopovers

colorful beachfront bungalows on Capitola Beach

These charming, lesser known destinations make great stopping points for those on a romantic journey.

Washington

* **Port Townsend** (page 48) is a Victorian seaport surrounded by water, with mountain views in either direction.

Oregon

* **Astoria** (page 106) was once one of the West's largest cities; now the town of 10,000 feels like a time capsule.

* **Newport** (page 124) is a touristy fishing town, but its quaint **Nye Beach** neighborhood feels a world apart, with quaint cafés and boutiques.

Northern California

* **Ferndale** (pages 169) is the most picturesque little town on the Lost Coast, comprising mostly Victorian buildings resembling gingerbread homes.

* **Mendocino** (page 178) boasts the best view of any small town in the United States—every restaurant, gallery, and boutique on Main Street looks out over a gorgeous bay.

* **Capitola** (page 234) sits just outside of funky Santa Cruz, offering a Venice, Italy-inspired beach town setting with cute shops and a friendly, unpretentious bar scene.

Central California

* **Carmel-by-the-Sea** (page 246) is a picture-perfect beach town, populated by upscale shopping, wineries, and dog-friendly everything.

* **Cambria** (page 262) offers cozy accommodations and stellar views along its Moonstone Beach, plus a social, village-like town center.

Southern California

* **Encinitas** (page 339) only feels like a small town relative to the rest of Southern California. But all the restaurants, shops, and entertainment you need are within walking distance of its gorgeous **Moonlight Beach.**

amusements, then head farther south to people-watch at the always funky **Venice Beach Boardwalk.** Grab dinner in Venice, or head back to Santa Monica before staying the night at the beachfront **Georgian Hotel.**

Day 19
LOS ANGELES

Wait for rush hour traffic to die down with a leisurely morning appreciating the art collections and view at **The Getty Center.** Then it's time for a classic L.A. drive up **Sunset Boulevard** into **Hollywood.** Wander the **Hollywood Walk of Fame** (corner of Gower Street and Hollywood Boulevard) and get an eyeful at the ornate **TCL Chinese Theatre.**

Enjoy some science along with views of the city from the **Griffith Observatory,** then head downtown to visit **The Broad** museum. Take your pick of the city's exciting dining options before getting a taste of Hollywood nightlife on the **Sunset Strip.** Families may want to plan on an extra day for an excursion to **Disneyland Resort.** For more ideas on how to spend your time in Los Angeles, see page 310.

Day 20
LOS ANGELES TO SAN DIEGO
130 miles / 210 kilometers / 3 hours

Any number of freeways south out of Los Angeles will eventually connect you to I-5 heading toward San Diego. If you run into traffic, push all the way to the Orange County coast to reconnect with CA-1, and catch some sun or waves at surf mecca **Huntington Beach.**

The coast highway too routes to I-5 heading into San Diego County, where Historic Route 101 reappears to pass slowly through several beautiful North County beach towns before reaching **Torrey Pines State Reserve,** one of the wildest stretches along the coastline north of **La Jolla.** Drop into **La Jolla Cove** for some kayaking or snorkeling, then dine at one of many incredible restaurants with a view in **La Jolla village** before continuing on to **San Diego,** to check into **Hotel Indigo.**

Day 21
SAN DIEGO

Start your day exploring **Balboa Park,** including the grand **Botanical Building.** Families will want to spend the morning ogling pandas and polar bears at world-famous **San Diego Zoo.** Sun-worshippers should head to **Coronado,** with its beachside shops and the legendary **Hotel del Coronado.** Craft beer fans will find plenty of spots to sip before sampling **Little Italy**'s impressive restaurant and cocktail scene for dinner. For more ideas on how to spend your time in San Diego, see page 353.

Clockwise from top left: Hollywood's Walk of Fame; rides on the Santa Monica Pier; Balboa Park in San Diego.

Washington Coast

At the most northern edge of the journey is Washington state, a scenic wonderland composed of some of the least-touched natural areas in the country.

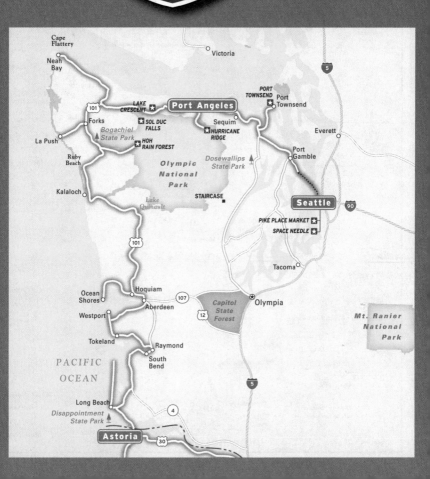

Washington Coast

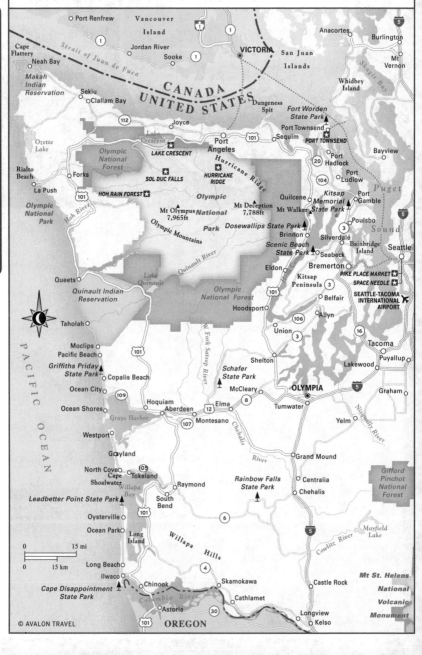

© AVALON TRAVEL

Highlights

★ **Pike Place Market:** Immerse yourself in the sights, sounds, and smells (both flowery and fishy) of the oldest continuously working market in the United States (page 34).

★ **Space Needle:** Built to celebrate the Space Age in 1962, the iconic tower is now synonymous with Seattle (page 37).

★ **Port Townsend:** Surrounded by the sea and snowcapped mountains, this attractive Victorian town makes for a charming getaway (page 48).

★ **Hurricane Ridge:** The most popular spot in Olympic National Park provides unmatched views of the gorgeous Strait of Juan de Fuca (page 62).

★ **Lake Crescent:** With cold depths measured at more than 1,000 feet, this lake is a place of beauty and mystery—and the only place in the world to fish for Beardslee trout (page 65).

★ **Sol Duc Falls:** A one-mile hike through old-growth forest leads to these year-round falls (page 67).

★ **Hoh Rain Forest:** Take a hike through this idyllic western section of the Olympic National Park to see gorgeous trees and majestic wildlife (page 74).

Here you can explore massive old-growth forests, rich river valleys, and an abundant coastline.

Starting at charming Port Townsend, US-101 bends west around the north end of the Olympic National Forest, passing near the most northwesterly tip of the contiguous United States. Heavy rains (12-14 feet a year) feed the temperate rainforests and form mist around the small towns that dot the coastline.

The harbor town of Port Angeles is the access point to the Olympic Discovery Trail—an old Milwaukee Railroad line that follows the waterfront—and the Olympic National Park. Explore more than 600 miles of hiking trails; discover 1,000 year-old trees that tower over rivers and glacier-fed lakes; or gaze at awe-inspiring views of the Olympic mountain range. The possibilities are truly limitless.

Tracing the edges of a landscape carved out by ancient glaciers and the Pacific Ocean, the highway follows the curves of the brilliant blue waters of Lake Crescent, then descends southwest through wooded lowlands and beaches toward the resort town near Lake Quinault and the maritime seaport of Grays Harbor.

The city of Seattle is a 35-minute ferry ride across Puget Sound, making it a convenient access point to the Olympic Peninsula, which offers interesting sights of its own.

Planning Your Time
Plan at least four days to hit the main sights and two weeks to explore and take it all in, while making a couple of side trips.

Outside of Seattle, the best places to visit include the waterfront town of Port Townsend and wilderness areas inside Olympic National Park, like Lake Crescent, Sol Duc, and Lake Quinault. To make sure you don't get stuck without a room in these places, book 4-6 months in advance. Towns like Port Angeles and Forks make convenient jumping off points for day trips to see the lakes, as well as to see Hurricane Ridge and Hoh Rain Forest, respectively.

It's roughly 330 miles from Seattle around the Olympic Peninsula and down to Long Beach on US-101. The Olympic Peninsula is a rural area connected by mostly two-lane highway, with long windy stretches between basic services, so fuel up and keep plenty of water, snacks, and an emergency kit in your vehicle.

Getting There
Car
Drivers enter from the north, over the Canadian border, east from Idaho, or south from Oregon. I-5 is the major north-south route, extending from the Canadian border in the north to the Mexican border in the south. I-90 is the best east-west route, but keep in mind that winter snow may close mountain passes.

Air
The **Seattle-Tacoma International Airport** (SEA, 17801 International Blvd., 800/544-1965 or 206/787-5388, www.portseattle.org/seatac) is the usual point of entry and is served by about two dozen airlines. Another option is **Portland International** (PDX, 7000 NE Airport Way, 877/739-4636, www.pdx.com), which is only a 2.5-hour drive from Seattle, over the Oregon border.

Train
Amtrak (King Street Station, 303 S. Jackson St., Seattle, 800/872-7245, www.amtrak.com) provides transport service throughout the country to the Northwest. The **Coast Starlight** connects Seattle, Portland, Sacramento, Oakland, and Los Angeles. Amtrak also runs the **Cascade Line** (800/872-7245,

Best Hotels

★ **Hotel Monaco:** This stylish boutique hotel comes with a prime Seattle location and an in-room pet goldfish (page 46).

★ **Fairmont Olympic Hotel:** Seattle's first choice in upscale lodging leads the way in elegance, convenience, and customer service (page 46).

★ **Manresa Castle:** This medieval (and haunted?) 1892 mansion makes guests feel like royalty (page 52).

★ **Lake Crescent Lodge:** Surrounded by fir trees, this historic lakeside retreat counts FDR among its many guests (page 66).

★ **Sol Duc Hot Springs Resort:** This retreat is built around its namesake bubbling mineral waters (page 68).

★ **Kalaloch Lodge:** The selling point of this lodge is access to nearby Ruby Beach (page 76).

★ **Lake Quinault Lodge:** This regal lodge benefits from its magnificent setting on the lake (page 77).

---

www.amtrakcascades.com), which runs between Eugene, Oregon, and Vancouver, British Columbia, with stops in Portland and Seattle. International visitors can buy an unlimited travel USA Rail Pass good for 15, 30, or 45 days.

Bus

Greyhound (503 S. Royal Brougham Way, Seattle, 800/231-2222, www.greyhound.com) offers special discounts to students and seniors with routes and stops sticking to major highways and cities.

BoltBus (648 SW Salmon St., 877/265-8287, www.boltbus.com) is the cheapest way to travel south from Vancouver, British Columbia, with stops in Seattle, Portland, and Eugene.

Fuel and Services

Services are limited inside Olympic National Park to minimize the environmental impact. Take advantage of the small towns that surround the park to stock up on supplies and fuel up. West of Port Townsend, you may count on finding gas stations only in Sequim, Port Angeles, Forks, and Lake Quinault.

To receive reports on **road conditions,** call **511.** If your phone carrier does not support 511, call toll-free 800/695-7623.

For **emergency assistance** and services call **911.**

Seattle

Best known for heavy rainfall, espresso drinks, homegrown rock music, and fresh oysters, **Seattle** (pop. 668,342) was a small shipping port for local timber that evolved into a big city with small town character. In recent years the tech industry has made a home here, prompting huge boosts to the population and economy, giving Seattle its share of growing pains, but also transforming it into one of most cosmopolitan cities in the American West.

Originally called Duwamps when founded by American settlers in 1851, the so-called Emerald City was soon after renamed Seattle, after the highly regarded tribal chief of the Duwamish people native to the region. Like Chief Seattle, the city's residents tend to espouse environmental preservation, as most are outdoorsy folk who greatly value the richly colored mountains, forests, and bodies of water surrounding the small metropolis. Brisk air pushing off the Puget Sound inspires the active and healthy lifestyle that makes Seattle one of America's fittest

Best Restaurants

★ **Salumi:** Italian hot and cold sandwiches are the best meals between bread in the entire Pacific Northwest (page 41).

★ **Shiro's:** Seattle's iconic sushi fixture takes advantage of a preponderance of fresh Northwest seafood (page 41).

★ **Espresso Vivace:** Seattle's espresso reputation hails from this café dedicated to the perfect pull (page 41).

★ **Altura:** This prix fixe dining experience serves Italian by way of the Pacific Northwest (page 42).

★ **Fountain Café:** Art lines the walls of this funky east-meets-west eatery in Port Townsend (page 50).

★ **The Oak Table Café:** This is the place to find a perfect cappuccino—not to mention Swedish pancakes—in Sequim (page 58).

★ **Toga's Soup House:** Soup and sandwiches are taken to the next level here—be sure to try the Dungeness crab panini (page 60).

cities, rousing appetites for the fine food and drink of local purveyors.

Getting There and Around
Air
Seattle-Tacoma International Airport (SEA, 17801 International Blvd., 800/544-1965 or 206/787-5388, www.portseattle.org/seatac) is the gateway to the Pacific Northwest. It's only a 30-minute drive north on **I-5** from Sea-Tac to downtown Seattle, unless you hit rush hour traffic, which seems to start earlier each year—best to make the drive prior to 4pm on weekdays. **WA-99** is a more scenic alternative drive that traverses the industrial district bounded by the Duwamish River and passes through the Alaskan Way Viaduct and the Battery Street Tunnel right into downtown Seattle.

Ferry
Ferries ride across the Puget Sound to the nearby islands of Bainbridge, Blake, and Vashon, as well as the Olympic Peninsula. The most convenient access point to the Washington coast is **Pier 52** (801 Alaskan Way, 888/808-7977 or 206/464-6400, www.wsdot.wa.gov/ferries, $18 per car one-way, $8 per passenger and walk-on, $4 children 6-18), by way of the **Seattle-Bainbridge Island Ferry.** It's a 35-minute glide across the open Puget Sound waters with comfortable seating, snacks, and restrooms on the main deck.

The **Edmonds-Kingston Ferry** (199 Sunset Ave. S., 888/808-7977 or 206/464-6400, www.wsdot.wa.gov/ferries, $18 per car one-way, $8 per passenger and walk-on, $4 children 6-18) is in quaint suburban Edmonds, a 20-minute drive north of Seattle on I-5; take exit 177 and follow the signs to the ferry terminal. The crossing takes 30 minutes and the ferry departs every 40 minutes.

Public Transit
Seattle is an easy city to get around, with most attractions concentrated in the walkable downtown area. **King County Metro Transit** (206/553-3000, www.kingcounty.gov/metro, $2.50-3.25 adults, $1.50 children 6-18) operates several lines throughout the city. The **Seattle Center Monorail** (5th Ave. and Pine St., www.seattlemonorail.com, 7:30am-11pm Mon.-Fri., 8:30am-11am Sat.-Sun., $2.25 adults, $1 children 5-12) links downtown with Seattle Center and the Space Needle. **Sound Transit light rail** (888/889-6368, www.soundtransit.org, 5am-1am Mon.-Sat., 6am-midnight

Downtown Seattle and Pioneer Square

MONORAIL

WESTLAKE AVE

5TH AVE

4TH AVE

OLIVE WAY

3RD AVE

2ND AVE

LENORA ST

VIRGINIA ST

1ST AVE

POST AL

PIKE PL

WESTERN AVE

STEWART ST

PINE ST

DOWNTOWN

PIKE ST

★ **PIKE PLACE MARKET**

UNION ST

★ **SEATTLE AQUARIUM**

99

Waterfront Park

★ **SEATTLE GREAT WHEEL**

PIER 56

PIER 55

Elliott Bay

PIER 50

PIER 48

2ND AVE

1ST AVE

★ **SEATTLE ART MUSEUM**

3RD AVE

POST AVE

WESTERN AVE

ALASKAN WAY

UNIVERSITY ST

● **FAIRMONT OLYMPIC HOTEL**

KIMPTON HOTEL MONACO SEATTLE

★ **SEATTLE CENTRAL LIBRARY**

SENECA ST

SPRING ST

MADISON ST

MARION ST

COLUMBIA ST

CHERRY ST

JAMES ST

3RD AVE

4TH AVE

5TH AVE

6TH AVE

MADISON ST

5

PIONEER SQUARE ★

YESLER WAY

PIONEER SQUARE

S WASHINGTON ST

99

S MAIN ST

KLONDIKE GOLD RUSH NATIONAL HISTORICAL PARK MUSEUM

SALUMI ▼

S JACKSON ST

1ST AVE S

2ND AVE S

3RD AVE S

4TH AVE S

S KING ST

0   200 yds

0   200 m

© AVALON TRAVEL

Inset map:

★ **FREMONT TROLL**

Union Bay

Queen Anne

Lake Union

Portage Bay

Washington Park

99

5

Kerry Park

Lake Union Park

EXPERIENCE MUSIC PROJECT

Volunteer Park

ALTURA

Capitol Hill

SEATTLE CENTER

SPACE NEEDLE

ESPRESSO VIVACE

Madison Park

E MADISON ST

WASHINGTON BLVD

SHIRO'S SUSHI

★

MAP AREA

PIKE PLACE MARKET

99

Sun., $2.25-3.25) connects all of downtown from Westlake Center to the International District.

Sights
Downtown
★ Pike Place Market

If it is possible to capture the essence of a city in one place, then **Pike Place Market** (Pike Pl. and Virginia St. between 1st Ave. and Western Ave., 206/682-7453, www. pikeplacemarket.org, 6am-1:30am daily) is Seattle's true soul. Famous for fish-throwing and the original Starbucks, it's a mecca of fresh produce, good food, and street entertainment. The main market is a micro-economy of 700 or so butchers and fishmongers, produce and flower vendors, artists and craftspeople, restaurateurs and entrepreneurs. It's lined with street-level stalls and an underground maze of unique shops that descends to the waterfront.

Waterfront Park

From Pike Place Market, you can easily walk down to **Waterfront Park** (1301 Alaskan Way, 206/684-4075, www.seattle.gov/parks), which offers beautiful views of Puget Sound along with benches and tables from which to admire them. If that's not close enough to the water, board one of the **Argosy Cruises** (Pier 55, 1101 Alaskan Way, 206/623-1445 or 800/642-7816, www.argosycruises.com, $27 adults, $13 children 4-12) that leave from Pier 55 for a one-hour spin around Elliott Bay.

At Pier 57, the **Seattle Great Wheel** (1301 Alaskan Way, 206/623-8600, www. seattlegreatwheel.com, 10am-11pm Sun.-Thurs., 10am-midnight Fri.-Sat., $14 adults, $9 children 3-11) is the best seat in the city—175 feet up in the sky. Opened in 2012, the newest city icon offers views that extend over the waterfront and out over Puget Sound and the surrounding islands and mountains.

Seattle's waterfront

Seattle Aquarium

Along the waterfront, the **Seattle Aquarium** (1483 Alaskan Way, 206/386-4320, www.seattleaquarium.org, 9:30am-5pm daily, $30 adults, $20 children 4-12) is the best way—short of donning scuba gear—to see the colorful underwater wildlife inhabiting Puget Sound's icy depths. Get your hands wet in tidepools and marvel at 350 species of aquatic animals on display, including harbor seals, sharks, giant Pacific octopuses, and sea otters. The 400,000-gallon Underwater Dome alone is worth the trip: Descend into a half-sphere to find scores of deep-sea creatures completely surrounding you.

Seattle Art Museum

The entrance to the **Seattle Art Museum (SAM)** (1300 1st Ave., 206/654-3100, www.seattleartmuseum.org, 10am-9pm Thurs., 10am-5pm Wed.-Mon., $20 adults, $13 children 13-19) is marked by a 48-foot kinetic sculpture, *Hammering Man,* that towers over the sidewalk as though he's about to smash his hammer into the concrete. The museum is renowned for its cultural displays of Native American, Asian, and African American art. The spacious, three-level building includes a café and gift shop.

Central Library

The spectacular Rem Koolhaus-designed glass and steel of the **Central Library** (1000 4th Ave., 206/386-4636, www.spl.org/locations/central-library, 10am-8pm Mon.-Thurs., 10am-6pm Fri.-Sat., noon-6pm Sun.) adds character to an otherwise traditional cityscape. The very modern architecture matches the library's other state-of-the-art features, such as the talking book repository outside and the automated book circulation system that ferries materials from floor to floor using conveyor belts. A must-see on a library visit is the Books Spiral, a long, gently sloping ramp that winds through four floors of materials. This innovative design allows the library's entire nonfiction collection to be accessed by anyone, without relying on stairs or elevators. The 10th floor holds the true reward: The view is spectacular, if not dizzying, and worth braving weekend crowds for.

Pioneer Square

South of the downtown core lies the **Pioneer Square Historic District** (between 4th Ave. and Alaskan Way S., from Yesler Way to King St.). Seattle's oldest neighborhood features 19th-century buildings nestled along modern art galleries, cafés, and nightclubs. Today, the square is the starting point of the **Bill Siedel's Underground Tour** (614 1st Ave., 206/682-4646, www.undergroundtour.com, 8:30am-7pm daily, $22 adults, $20 student 13-19, $10 children 7-12), an entertaining excursion through the original streets beneath the current city. It's also the location of the **Klondike Gold Rush National Historical Park Museum** (319 2nd Ave. S., 206/220-4240, www.nps.gov/

klgo, 10am-5pm daily, free), which traces Seattle's gold rush history through educational exhibits, films, historic photos, and activities. There's even a free walking tour (10am daily mid-June to Labor Day weekend).

At night, revelers come to enjoy the square's many restaurants, bars, and clubs, especially when the Mariners or Seahawks are playing. Safeco Field, the Mariners' home base, sits a few blocks south of Pioneer Square.

Capitol Hill

Home to some of Seattle's more eclectic denizens, the Capitol Hill district is located on a steep hill just east of central downtown. Bustling daytime activities flow into a rich nightlife that can extend into the early morning hours and occasionally spills onto the streets.

Once known as Broadway Hill, the neighborhood's main drag runs along Broadway between Roy Street and Olive Way. Walk the length of it to find all eight of the ***Dancers' Series: Steps.*** Installed by artist Jack Mackie in 1982, bronze footprints embedded in the sidewalk illustrate the footwork of famous dances, from mambo to tango. The year-round **Broadway Farmers Market** (Broadway Ave. E. and E. Pine St., 206/547-2278, www.seattlefarmersmarkets.org, 11am-3pm Sun.) draws shoppers looking for fresh vegetables, fruits, cheeses, and specialty treats.

Volunteer Park

New York has Central Park; San Francisco has Golden Gate Park; and Seattle has **Volunteer Park** (accessible from 4th or 5th Ave. E., 206/684-4075, www.seattle.gov/parks, 6am-10pm daily). Stroll the many trails framed in greenery to the conservatory, a glass building filled with rooms of blooming flowers and seasonal displays. A short walk to the other side of the park brings you to a spiral staircase leading to the 75-foot water tower, which has sweeping city views.

fresh catches on ice at Pike Place Market

Queen Anne Hill

Named for the architectural style of the mansions built on the hill by many of Seattle's founding elite, Queen Anne is bordered by Belltown (to the south), Lake Union (to the east), Lake Washington ship canal (to the north), and Magnolia (to the west). Along its picturesque residential streets you will find some of Seattle's most historic homes, and as Queen Anne is considered the highest hill in Seattle, you will also find some of the city's steepest streets.

Queen Anne is divided into two areas: upper Queen Anne, a quieter, more residential environment, and lower Queen Anne (also known as Uptown), the commercial heart of the district.

Kerry Park

A small, perfectly manicured lawn and a few benches are all you'll find in **Kerry Park** (corner of 2nd Ave. W. and W. Highland Dr., free), best known for its sweeping views of downtown Seattle, the

Space Needle, Mount Rainier, and the waterfront. It's a popular destination for photographers, locals, and tourists—especially at sunset.

Seattle Center

Adjacent to lower Queen Anne is the tourist mecca known as the **Seattle Center** (305 Harrison St., 206/684-7200, www.seattlecenter.com, 7am-9pm daily, free). Built for the 1962 World's Fair, it encompasses fairgrounds, the International Fountain, and a year-round arts and entertainment center, as well as the Space Needle and the Experience Music Project. It's also the location of the north terminal of the Seattle Monorail, which transports visitors between Seattle Center and downtown approximately every 10 minutes.

★ Space Needle

First sketched on a napkin by artist Edward E. Carlson in a coffee shop, the **Space Needle** (400 Broad St., 206/905-2100, www.spaceneedle.com, 8am-midnight daily, $19-29 adults, $13-18 children 5-12) dominated the 1962 Seattle World's Fair and has since become a celebrated Seattle icon enjoyed by locals and visitors alike. Traveling at a speed of 10 mph, the elevators glide 605 feet up to the observation deck, where panoramic, 360-degree views of the entire city and Puget Sound leave visitors breathless. With 25 lightning rods on its roof and elevators that reduce speed when winds reach 35 mph, the Needle was built to withstand the rough winds and thunderstorms that bless the Pacific Northwest.

Experience Music Project

The **Experience Music Project (EMP)** (325 5th Ave. N., 206/367-5483, www.mopop. org, 10am-5pm daily, $33 adults, $24 children 5-17) is also located in Seattle Center. The colorful, Frank Gehry-designed blob of a building is part rock-and-roll history museum (the space was initially envisioned as a showcase for

Two Days in Seattle

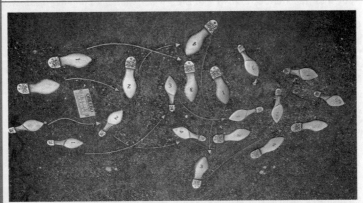

Learn some moves from Capitol Hill's sidewalks thanks to the *Dancers' Series: Steps* art installation.

Day 1

Spend the morning exploring **Pike Place Market** (page 34), the historic landmark where locals and tourists connect. Sample produce, try street food, browse the creative wares, and enjoy the quirky street performers. Cap off your visit with a ride to the top of the **Seattle Great Wheel** (page 34) to enjoy amazing views of Puget Sound.

Come down to earth to explore the underwater world of the **Seattle Aquarium** (page 35). If art is your passion, head a few blocks east to spend the afternoon at the **Seattle Art Museum** (page 35) instead.

End your day with dinner and a show at the **Pink Door** (page 41), where the cuisine may be accompanied by trapeze artists overhead.

Day 2

Begin your day in **Capitol Hill** (page 36), learning a few dance steps from the sidewalk and tasting a perfect coffee at **Espresso Vivace** (page 41). Then head south two miles to **Pioneer Square** (page 35), a historic neighborhood of 19th-century buildings. Take **Bill Siedel's Underground Tour** (page 35) or visit the **Klondike Gold Rush National Historical Park Museum** (page 35). Grab lunch to go from **Salumi** (page 41) and eat it while people-watching at nearby Occidental Square.

Leave the past behind and head a mile to the future at the **Seattle Center** (page 37), where the trip to the top of the **Space Needle** (page 37) is worthwhile for 360-degree views of Puget Sound. Aim for sunset in Queen Anne Hill's **Kerry Park** (page 37) for incredible, camera-ready views of Elliott Bay, Bainbridge Island, Mount Rainier, the Space Needle, and the city skyline. End your day with sushi at **Shiro's** (page 41) or oysters at **Elliott's Oyster House** (page 41).

Microsoft billionaire Paul Allen's Jimi Hendrix memorabilia), part interactive musical adventure, and part live music venue.

Fremont

Across the canal north of Queen Anne Hill, the neighborhood of Fremont is the traditional center of Seattle's counterculture. Calling itself "The People's Republic of Fremont," the sprawling urban neighborhood offers laid-back restaurants, bars, and coffeehouses, plus an eclectic assortment of unlikely public artworks, including a bronze **statue of Vladimir Lenin** (3526 Fremont Pl N.). Most famous is the **Fremont Troll** (Troll Ave. N. at N. 36th St.), a sculpture of a large troll lurking under the Aurora bridge, with a VW bug in its hand.

Recreation
Bicycling
Leg power and sweat are all you need to bicycle Seattle. The opportunities are numerous in and around the city. Rent a bike from **Seattle Cycling Tours** (714 Pike St., 206/356-5803, www.seattle-cycling-tours.com, 9:30am-4pm Tues.-Sun., $59/day) or **The Bicycle Repair Shop** (68 Madison St., 206/682-7057, www.thebicyclerepairshop.com, 8am-6pm Mon.-Fri., 10am-6pm Sat., noon-6pm Sun., $9-15/hour) and give the six-mile **Cheshiahud Lake Union Loop** around Lake Union a whirl. Interpretive signs along the trail provide insight into Seattle's Native American and maritime histories. There are plenty of grassy spots and picnic areas to stop for water breaks and snacks.

For a day ride that extends outside of Seattle, the **Burke-Gilman Trail** connects friendly, urban neighborhoods lined with restaurants, shops, and beautiful scenery. This is not a loop, so you will have to return the way you came. Begin at the south end of Golden Gardens Park on Puget Sound and bike to the Ballard Locks (about two miles), a popular site where salmon can be seen at the fish ladder during spawning season in August. The trail ends here, but a short ride on the road (NW Market St. to Shilshole Ave. to NW 45th St.) picks up the trail at Gasworks Park, a 19-acre public park that sits on the former Seattle Gas Light Company plant along Lake Union, and traverses the campus of University of Washington. You can turn back here

From top to bottom: Seattle's iconic Space Needle; a totem pole in the Pioneer Square neighborhood; Burnt Sugar and the Saturn Building in the Fremont neighborhood.

or continue east, passing crowds of picnickers and volleyball nets at several parks nestled along the path. The trail forks after crossing 96th Avenue NE: Veer left toward the Sammamish River Trail (which continues another 11 miles to Marymoor Park in Redmond) or take the right fork, which crosses the Sammamish River and ends the route at Riverside Drive.

Spectator Sports

The **Seattle Seahawks** (www.seahawks.com) make their touchdowns at **CenturyLink Field** (800 Occidental Ave. S., www.centurylinkfield.com, a 72,000-seat, open-air stadium that also plays host to the city's beloved **Seattle Sounders** (www.soundersfc.com) soccer team.

The **Seattle Mariners** (www.mlb.com/mariners) run the bases right next door at **Safeco Field** (1250 1st Ave. S., 206/346-4001), a state-of-the-art facility with seating for 47,000 fans, a retractable roof, kid zone, and several team shops and public services. Ticket costs vary from cheap to expensive, but no seat is a bad seat at this stadium. You don't have to live here to enjoy a Mariners' ballgame, but you do have to try the garlic fries.

Food
Downtown

Look for organic breakfast and lunch options at **Portage Bay Café** (391 Terry Ave. N., 206/462-6400, www.portagebaycafe.com, 7:30am-2:30pm daily, $12-18), or for a quicker bite with a little attitude, grab a Southern-style biscuit sandwich at **Biscuit Bitch** (621 3rd Ave., 206/623-1859, 7am-2pm Mon.-Fri., 8am-3pm Sat.-Sun., $5-10).

For fresh bread and baked treats, head to **Grand Central Bakery** (214 1st Ave. S., 206/622-3644, www.grandcentralbakery.com, 7am-5pm Mon.-Fri., 8am-4pm Sat., $6-15). While the cookies and assorted pastries are always sure to please, there are also delicious breakfasts and soup and sandwiches for lunch. The service

The Fremont Troll sculpture lives under a bridge.

is inviting and the environment is warm and natural.

A pair of small, lunchtime-only restaurants draw lines daily around Pioneer Square. With ★ **Salumi** (309 3rd Ave. S., 206/621-8772, www.salumicuredmeats. com, 11am-1:30pm Mon., 11am-3:30pm Tues.-Fri., $9-13), Seattle boasts one of the best sandwich shops in the nation. It's impossible to go wrong with the house salami, but the meatball sub and succulent *porchetta* (roast pork) prove worth any wait. Three blocks north, Seattleites flock to try the beautiful hand-made, organic pastas at **Il Corvo** (217 James St., 206/538-0999, www.ilcorvopasta.com, 11am-3pm Mon.-Fri., $9-10), with rotating sauces ranging from classic to creative.

To indulge in fresh, locally caught seafood with a gorgeous waterfront view, hit **Elliott's Oyster House** (Pier 56, 1201 Alaskan Way, 206/623-4340, www.elliottsoysterhouse.com, 11am-10pm daily, $9-38), which serves the freshest wild salmon and Dungeness crab, while giving shellfish lovers 40 different varieties of oysters.

Or, opt for 40 types of raw fish at legendary sushi bar ★ **Shiro's** (2401 2nd Ave., 206/443-9844, www.shiros.com, 5:30pm-10:30pm daily, $12-75)—order *omikase* (chef's choice) for an unforgettable experience.

Choose between a rooftop terrace or a comfortable dining room where trapeze artists may swing overhead while you eat Italian fare. That's the unique allure of the **Pink Door** (1919 Port Alley, Pike Place Market, 206/443-3341, www.thepinkdoor.net, 11:30am-11:30pm Mon.-Thurs., 11:30am-1am Fri.-Sat., 4pm-10pm Sun., $18-39). There's no sign, so look for the namesake pastel-painted entrance.

To really get into the tourist zone, grab small bites from the dozens of small shops around **Pike Place Market.** Lines will clue you in to the cult favorites, including Russian bakery **Piroshky Piroshky** (1908 Pike Pl., 206/441-6068, www.piroshkybakery.com, 8am-6pm Mon.-Thurs., 7:30am-8pm Fri.-Sun., $4-8), **Beecher's Handmade Cheese** (1600 Pike Pl., 206/956-1964, www.beechershandmadecheese.com, 9am-6pm daily, $6-12), and **Pike Place Clam Chowder** (1530 Post Alley, 206/267-2537, www.pikeplacechowder.com, 11am-5pm daily, $6-12).

Capitol Hill

With good reason, Seattle's earned a reputation for popularizing espresso drinks. But while a certain global chain has the furthest reach, the most influential of the bunch is ★ **Espresso Vivace** (532 Broadway E., 206/860-5869, www.espressovivace.com, 6am-11pm daily, $2-5), which has remained a small local chain for decades, earnestly devoted to perfecting the pulled shot.

That said, tourists do flock to the supposed "first Starbucks" store at Pike Place, which is not actually its original location. Fans of the chain should

look instead to the **Starbucks Reserve Roastery** (1124 Pike St., 206/624-0173, www.roastery.starbucks.com, 7am-11pm daily, $3-8), home of the brand's small-batch roasters, where it has erected a spacious ode to coffee in the form of a circular bar offering rotating, single-origin beans and every conceivable preparation method.

Like a cheap meal? Stubbornly low prices help **Dick's Drive-In** (115 Broadway E., 206/323-1300, www.ddir.com, 10:30am-2am daily, $1-3) retain its status as Seattle's favorite homegrown burger chain. At less than two bucks a burger, might as well add a milkshake.

Housed inside lower Capitol Hill's **Melrose Market,** nationally regarded **Sitka & Spruce** (1531 Melrose Ave., 206/324-0662, www.sitkaandspruce.com, 11:30am-2pm Mon.-Fri., 10am-2pm Sat.-Sun., 5pm-1pm Tues.-Thurs., 5pm-11pm Fri.-Sat., 5pm-9pm Sun.-Mon., $10-30) creates impeccable, ingredient-inspired dishes that change daily. Go next door to visit **Taylor's Shellfish** (1521 Melrose Ave., 206/501-4321, www.taylorshell-fishfarms.com, 11am-9pm Sun.-Thurs., 11am-10pm Fri.-Sat., $3-32), a casual spot for oysters and the regional delicacy geoduck clam (pronounced "gooey-duck").

★ **Altura** (617 Broadway E., 206/402-6749, www.alturarestaurant.com, 5:30pm-10pm Tues.-Thurs., 5pm-10pm Fri.-Sat., $137 prix fixe) serves fresh Pacific Northwest delectables with an Italian flare. It's fine dining at its best with a 10- to 15-course tasting menu prepared by talented chefs that celebrate seasonal cuisine. The wine selection is vast and the service is superb.

Nightlife
Bars and Clubs

A big club with an intimate atmosphere right in the heart of historic Pioneer Square, **Club Contour** (807 1st Ave., 206/447-7704, www.clubcontour.com, 3pm-2am Sun.-Thurs., 3pm-4am Fri.-Sat.) is the place for progressive dance music, DJ beats, and live entertainment. Its outdoor patio lets you appreciate warm summer nights while taking a break from the cozy dance floor. In Capitol Hill, **Q Nightclub** (1426 Broadway, 206/432-9306, www.qnightclub.com, 9pm-2am Wed.-Thurs., 10pm-3am Fri.-Sat.) features some of the world's top underground dance DJs.

There's never a dull moment at **Re-Bar** (1114 Howell St., 206/233-9873, www.rebarseattle.com, 7pm-1am Mon., 7pm-midnight Tues., 7pm-2am Thurs., 7pm-4am Fri.-Sat., 10pm-2:30am Sun.). They've got DJs, they've got burlesque, they've got karaoke, they've got glitter. Re-Bar's sparkle might grow on you—literally.

Three floors' worth of cocktail bar populate **Grim's Provisions & Spirits** (1512 11th Ave., 206/324-7467, www.grimseat-tle.com, 4pm-midnight Thurs., 4pm-2am Fri., 6pm-2am Sat.), ranging from lounge to speakeasy to pulsating dance floor.

Home of the famous "Gum Wall" in Pike Place Market, the intimate, brick-walled **Alibi Room** (85 Pike St. #410, 206/623-3180, www.seattlealibi.com, noon-2am daily) attracts a hip crowd for drinking, eclectic music, and dancing.

Seattle's a big craft beer city, and its rich brewing tradition begins with pioneer **Pyramid Alehouse** (1201 1st Ave. S., 206/682-3377, www.pyramidbrew.com/alehouse, 11am-9pm Sun.-Thurs., 11am-11pm Fri.-Sat.), which has been making beer since 1984, just across the street from the ballpark. Among the dozens of highly regarded smaller breweries all over town, the best known may be **Fremont Brewing Company** (1050 N. 34th St., 206/420-2407, www.fremontbrewing.com, 11am-9pm Sun.-Wed., 11am-10pm Thurs.-Sat.). To try a broader range of regional brews in one spot, head over to **Chuck's Hop Shop** (2001 E. Union St., 206/538-0743, www.chuckshopshop.com, 11am-midnight daily), which offers a massive variety in bottles and on tap, and a friendly patio on which to sip.

Seattle also leads the coast in craft distilling, with the top draws being whiskey specialist **Westland Distillery** (2931 1st Ave. S., 206/767-7250, www.westland-distillery.com, noon-7pm Tues.-Thurs., 11am-8pm Fri.-Sat.) and conveniently located **Copperworks Distilling Company** (1250 Alaskan Way, 206/504-7604, www. copperworksdistilling.com, noon-6pm Mon.-Thurs., noon-7pm Fri.-Sat., noon-5pm Sun.), next to Pike Place.

Staff will help wine lovers navigate the massive selection at **Purple Café & Wine Bar** (1225 4th Ave., 206/829-2280, www.purplecafe.com, 11am-11pm Mon.-Thurs., 11am-midnight Fri., noon-midnight Sat., noon-11pm Sun.), and if you're interested in Washington-produced wines visit Pike Place's **The Tasting Room** (1924 Post Alley, 206/770-9463, www.winesofwashington.com, noon-8pm Sun.-Thurs., noon-10pm Fri.-Sat.).

Live Music

Seattle has the highest per-capita music and dance attendance in the country, with 80 live music clubs and 15 symphony orchestras. Its venues are eclectic, offering everything from jazz, blues, and pop to the locals' favorite—rock. Pick up a copy of Seattle's free alt-weekly magazine The Stranger for current local club listings, or look to these classic venues for better-known performers.

The Crocodile Café (2200 2nd Ave., 206/441-4618, www.thecrocodile.com, 4pm-2am daily) is a "come as you are" venue with a stage that has seen the likes of big performers Nirvana and Mudhoney. There's a performance every night and great food downstairs in the café.

There is always something different happening at the **Triple Door** (216 Union St., 206/838-4333, www.tripledoor.net, 4pm-midnight daily) With everything from blues, jazz, pop, and funk, it's a microcosm of good tunes, drinks, and food, all under the roof of the old Embassy Theatre.

A Seattle "landmark," **The Showbox** (1426 1st Ave., 206/628-3151, www.showboxpresents.com) has been a fixture in the city's music scene for over 75 years, hosting bands like Dizzy Gillespie, Muddy Waters, Pearl Jam, and the Dave Matthews band. Sit back, have a drink, and enjoy up-and-comers or big-name acts belting it out on a phenomenal sound system and big stage.

Arts and Entertainment
Performing Arts

Built in the era of vaudeville and silent films, the exquisite **Paramount Theater** (911 Pine St., 206/682-1414, www.stgpresents.org) is Seattle's surviving theater royalty. This lavish, intricately decorated theater has been the backdrop to decades of performances and the home of a priceless Wurlitzer organ, which can be viewed as part of a theater tour.

There's not a bad seat in the house at **ACT (A Contemporary Theatre)** (700 Union St., 206/292-7676, www.acttheatre.org). Each of its five theater stages draws the audience in for an intimate experience with year-round contemporary productions.

Galleries

You've heard of the glass slipper, but have you heard of the glass house? It's the centerpiece of **Chihuly Garden and Glass** (305 Harrison St., 206/753-4940, www. chihulygardenandglass.com, 8:30am-8:30pm Mon.-Thurs., 8:30am-9:30pm Fri.-Sun., $29 adults, $18 children 5-12, $10 discount before 10am), an amazing gallery that pays tribute to the famous artist Dale Chihuly with an exhibition hall that includes eight galleries and three drawing walls, and a lush garden with four majestic sculptures. This glass house will overwhelm you.

Ghost Gallery (504 E. Denny Way, 206/832-6063, www.ghostgalleryart.com, 11am-7pm Wed.-Fri., 11am-6pm Sat.-Sun., free) isn't haunted by spirits, but it is hidden within a courtyard in the heart of the Capitol Hill neighborhood. Peruse local and national artist displays, a "petite works" room with miniature art, boutique wines, and a selection of handmade jewelry and vintage goods.

Follow the stairway under the ornate marquee by the **5th Avenue Theatre** (1308 5th Ave., 206/625-1900, www.5thavenue. org) to one of the best-kept secrets: the **Pedestrian Underground Concourse.** This isn't your typical art gallery. It's a three-block-long passage that chronicles the history of downtown Seattle through historical photos that line the walls.

At **Ancient Grounds** (1220 1st Ave., 206/749-0747, 7:30am-4:30pm Tues.-Fri., 10am-6pm Sat.) you can enjoy a caffè latte in a beautiful setting surrounded by Asian tapestries and Native American prints. Ooh and aah at the faces on the tribal masks while they ooh and aah right back at you.

Shopping
Downtown
Pacific Place (600 Pine St., 206/405-2655, www.pacificplaceseattle.com, 10am-8pm Mon.-Sat., 11am-7pm Sun.) has great eats, a big cinema, a skybridge, lots of moderately priced shops, and some expensive boutiques and specialty stores like Brookstone and Trophy Cupcakes. During the holidays, snow falls through the center of the mall as nightly performances echo the spirit of the holidays.

Every nook and cranny at **Laguna Pottery** (116 S. Washington St., 206/682-6162, www.lagunapottery.com, 10am-5:30pm Mon.-Wed. and Fri.-Sat., 10am-8pm Thurs., noon-4pm Sun.) is overflowing with rare and vintage pottery. It's a hidden gem tucked in the corner of Occidental Park in Pioneer Square.

If a stylish handbag, scarf, or jewelry is on your shopping list, visit **Fini** (86 Pine St., 206/443-0563, www.ilovefini.com, 10am-6pm Mon.-Sat., 10am-4pm Sun.)—you could spend all day trying to decide which best captures your personality!

A throwback shop where just about everything is nostalgic, **Golden Age Collectables** (1501 Pike Place Market, Ste. 401, 206/622-9799, www.goldenage-collectables.com, 9:30am-7pm daily) stocks kitschy items from lunch boxes to bobbleheads. Step inside to summon your inner nerd.

Souvenir and antiques shoppers are sure to find the perfect gift for that special someone at **Raven's Nest Treasure** (85 Pike St., Ste. B, 206/343-0890, www. ravenstreasure.com, 9:30am-6pm Tues.-Sat., 10:30am-5pm Sun.). It's a treasure trove of Native American art, intricate carvings, unique statues, and beautiful jewelry.

Capitol Hill
Big in space and selection, **Elliott Bay Book Company** (1521 10th Ave., 206/624-6600, www.elliottbaybook.com, 10am-10pm Mon.-Thurs., 10am-11pm Fri.-Sat., 10am-9pm Sun.) proves a great place to get lost among the shelves, browsing through new and old books.

Hip, funky, fabulous, and pink—there are all kinds of words to describe **Pretty Parlor** (119 Summit Ave. E., 206/405-2883, www.prettyparlor.com, 11am-7pm Mon.-Sat., noon-6pm Sun.). With a vast selection of clothing by local designers, this shop has fashionable apparel for women and men.

Melrose Market (1532 Minor Ave., 206/661-7979, www.melrosemarketse-attle.com, 11am-7pm daily) is the Pike Place Market of the Capitol Hill neighborhood. It's a community of shops encompassing the aroma of fresh flowers, local organic produce and craft vendors, and a 5,000-square-foot space for urban events.

Queen Anne Hill
The best place on Queen Anne Hill is **Four Winds Artful Living** (1521 Queen Anne Ave. N., 206/282-0472, 10:30am-6:30pm Tues.-Fri., 10:30am-5pm Sat., 11am-5pm Sun.-Mon.), an exotic import boutique with handmade silver jewelry,

candles and oils, leather handbags, home decor, and clothing.

Chocolopolis (1527 Queen Anne Ave. N., 206/282-0776, www.chocolopolis. com, 11am-7pm Tues.-Wed. and Fri.-Sat., 11am-9pm Thurs., 11am-6pm Sun.) is not a mythical place but a real paradise. The unique artisan chocolate bars are worth every delicious nibble.

Fremont

Plenty of small, independent boutiques populate funky Fremont, particularly along 35th Street and around Fremont Place. Curated fashions include local designers at the boutique **Show Pony** (702 N. 35th St., 206/706-4188, www.show-ponyboutique.com, 11am-7pm Mon.-Sat. and 11am-5pm Sun.). It's tough to walk past accessories and housewares shop **Burnt Sugar** (601 N. 35th St., 206/545-0699, www.burntsugar.us, 11am-6pm daily), partly due to the large rocket affixed to its storefront (possibly aiming for the planet atop the aptly named **Saturn Building** across the street).

To go deep into design history, spend some time browsing **Fremont Vintage Mall** (3419 Fremont Pl. N., 206/329-4460, www.fremontvintagemall.com, 11am-7pm Mon.-Sat., 11am-6pm Sun.).

Those with a sweet tooth will know bean-to-bar chocolatier **Theo Chocolate** (3400 Phinney Ave. N., 206/632-5100, www.theochocolate.com, 10am-6pm daily); its headquarters offers hand-crafted sweets unavailable elsewhere.

Events

One of the world's biggest entertainment festivals, **Bumbershoot** (Seattle Center, 305 Harrison St., www.bumbershoot. com, Labor Day weekend) does not disappoint, with over 100 musical acts, endless rows of food vendors, the Indie Market of handmade crafts, one-of-a-kind designs and fine arts, and loads of fun! Expect huge crowds, and walk, don't drive—it's always sunny for Bumbershoot!

Over 50 years, **Seafair** (Genesee Park & Playfield, 4316 S. Genesee St., www. seafair.com) has grown to an eight-week summer celebration of the Puget Sound lifestyle, with festivals, parades, a triathlon, and the roaming Seafair Pirates! And if that's not enough, the two main events are the Seafair Cup hydroplane races and the Blue Angels' air shows.

Expect nonstop music, food, and fun at the **Northwest Folklife Festival** (Seattle Center, 305 Harrison St., www. nwfolklife.org, Memorial Day weekend), a local tradition since 1972. There are plenty of family-friendly activities and a wonderful cultural art exhibit near the International Fountain Pavilion.

Accommodations
Under $150

Cheap doesn't have to lack style, and you'll find both at **City Hostel Seattle** (2327 2nd Ave., 206/706-3255, www.hostelseattle.com, $34 and up dorms, $100 and up private). With a location between the Space Needle and Pike Place Market as well as eccentric and artful motifs by local artists, it's been voted best hostel in the United States.

A well-known historical hotel, **Moore Hotel** (1926 2nd Ave., 206/448-4851 or 800/421-5508, www.moorehotel.com, $99 and up shared bath, $122 and up private bath) offers rooms with shared bathrooms located down the hall. For a little more money, you can get a room with a private bath.

$150-250

Nestled between Seattle's football and baseball stadiums, **Silver Cloud Stadium** (1046 1st Ave. S., 206/204-9800, www.silvercloud.com/seattlestadium, $189 and up) is near the Amtrak station, public transportation, and Pioneer Square.

Seattle has a good collection of elegant and trendy hotels that make for a memorable stay. **Paramount Hotel** (724 Pine St., 206/292-9500 or 800/426-0670, www. paramounthotelseattle.com, $199 and up) is in the center of downtown Seattle, just minutes away from the city's sights. Its lobby is decorated in dark woods and deep reds, and the rooms are tasteful and spacious.

A boutique hotel with modern panache, **Hotel Andra** (2000 4th Ave., 206/448-8600, www.hotelandra.com, $240 and up) is in the heart of downtown and perfectly set between Seattle's thriving retail hub and iconic attractions, a short walk from Pike Place Market. So is nearby **Mayflower Park Hotel** (405 Olive Way, 206/623-8700, www.mayflowerpark.com, $239 and up), though the 90-year-old landmark offers more timeless appeal.

Hotel Vintage (1100 5th Ave., 206/624-8000 or 800/853-3914, www.hotelvintageseattle.com, $176 and up) is a beautiful boutique hotel with a 24-hour fitness center and nightly hosted wine hour that features local wine partners.

Romance is in the details at ★ **Hotel Monaco** (1101 4th Ave., 206/621-1770, www.monaco-seattle.com, $204 and up), including spacious rooms, pillowtop beds, complimentary wine tasting, and an in-room pet goldfish. You can walk from the hotel to Pike Place Market, Pioneer Square, and the world-famous Seattle Public Library.

Over $250

The **Alexis Hotel** (1007 1st Ave., 206/624-4844 or 800/264-8482, www.alexishotel.com, $285 and up) is where you want to hang your hat. With their 300-thread-count sheets, you may never get out of bed. The rooms feature themed art and plush furnishings. Complimentary wine is offered in the afternoons at the Library Bistro, which also serves Northwest cuisine. A full spa is available when you want to relax after a day of shopping.

A hotel with modern tastes, **Hotel 1000** (1000 1st Ave., 206/957-1000, www.loewshotels.com/hotel-1000-seattle, $400 and up) is one of the most upscale places to stay in the downtown Seattle area. The rooms feature waterfall showerheads,

marbled bathrooms, and beautiful dark wood furnishings. One of the unique features of the hotel is its virtual golf course, where you can practice your swing.

Seattle's top-rated stay, ★ **Fairmont Olympic Hotel** (411 University St., 206/621-1700, www.fairmont.com/seattle, $409 and up) cuts no corners, offering luxury accommodations in a central location. Ornate, 1920s-era wood carvings adorn the public spaces, while mid-century décor, luxurious bedding, and modern technologies make rooms so comfortable you may not want to leave.

Information and Services

Seattle Visitor Center and Concierge Services (800 Convention Pl., 866/732-2695 or 206/461-5840, www.visitseattle.org, 9am-5pm Mon.-Fri. year-round, 9am-5pm daily in summer) provides accurate visitor information, and its location in the Washington State Convention Center lobby makes it easy to find.

Port Gamble

Settled on the shores of the Hood Canal River, **Port Gamble** (pop. 916) is a picturesque town reminiscent of a New England community with maple and elm trees lining the streets, and wooden water towers at the entrance to town. It was founded in 1853 by two Maine businessmen, William Talbot and Andrew Pope, who, along with partners Josiah Keller and Charles Foster, formed the Puget Mill Company to harvest lumber for the expanding West. The sand spit at the mouth of Gamble Bay proved to be the perfect location to log and ship timber, but it was already the site of an ancient S'Klallam village called Teekalet. Many of the S'Klallam had moved across the bay as more settlers arrived.

Though it's a tiny town (120 acres), Port Gamble warrants a stop to look out across the bay or to walk the original street laid over a century ago. The New

England architecture marks a period in time when familiarity was important to East Coast migrants looking for a better life. The town was constructed to make workers feel at home by reflecting the communities they left behind. The **Port Gamble Historic Museum** (32400 N. Rainier Ave., 360/297-8078, www.portgamble.com, 10am-5pm daily May-Sept., 11am-4pm Fri.-Sun. Oct.-Apr., $4 adults, $3 students, free children 6 and under) is filled with early-1800s photographs and town artifacts on the second floor of the General Store. There's no getting lost here: The town shops are all on a little two-block stretch on Rainier Avenue. The General Store is the last building on the right and sells a wide variety of merchandise and has a restaurant. Nearby shops include antiques stores, a trading company featuring local artisans, a gourmet shop, and a day spa.

The **Olympic Outdoor Center** (32379 Rainier Ave., 360/297-4659, www.olympicoutdoorcenter.com, 10am-6pm Mon.-Sat., 10am-5pm Sun. May-Sept., 10am-5pm Mon.-Sat. Oct.-Apr., bike $25/hour, kayak $17/hour) rents bicycles and kayaks and offers Salmon Habitat tours. The regal **St. Paul's Church** sits south of the shops, across the bend on a hill surrounded by meticulously manicured lawns and a white picket fence. You won't find hotels here, but a few cottages and B&Bs are on offer, including the **Port Gamble Guest Houses** (32440 Puget Ave. NE, 360/447-8473, www.portgambleguesthouse.com, $375 and up).

Getting There

Expect a trip of about 1 hour and 40 minutes from Seattle to Port Gamble. Take the ferry from Seattle Ferry Terminal to Bainbridge Island, then take WA-305 N. for 12.7 miles, WA-307 N. for 5.2 miles,

From top to bottom: a pair of wooden water towers in Port Gamble; vintage ads on an old building in downtown Port Townsend; totems at the Jamestown S'Klallam Tribal Community.

and WA-104 W. for 3.7 miles to reach Port Gamble. To avoid a ferry ride, take I-5 S. out of Seattle 21.6 miles to Tacoma, then take WA-16 W. 26.9 miles to Bremerton. Connect to WA-3 N. for about 25 miles, where it turns into WA-104 E. 1.3 miles before it reaches Port Gamble.

★ Port Townsend

With roots seeded in maritime culture, **Port Townsend** (pop. 9,255) has transformed itself into a sophisticated city of the arts. It's one of the last of the Victorian-era seaports, a classic town of ornate 19th-century mansions that flourished until the 1890s, when plans to extend the railroad failed and its booming economy dried up. The town was nearly abandoned until the development of artillery fortifications at Fort Worden and the paper mill moderately rekindled the economy. But it wasn't until the 1970s, when retirees and artists moved in and began restoring the town's historical attributes and creating trendy shops, art galleries, and restaurants, that Port Townsend returned to its former glory. Today, with its snowcapped mountain views, history and culture, and recreation opportunities, this attractive seaside town makes for an appealing getaway.

Getting There

Port Townsend rests on the northwestern tip of the Olympic Peninsula. Follow WA-104 west from Port Gamble. After crossing the Hood Canal Bridge, turn right onto WA-19 (Beaver Valley Rd.), which joins WA-20 after 14 miles and heads into Port Townsend. The drive from Port Gamble takes about 45 minutes. There are visible signs along the highway, but be aware that segments of the highway change to street names.

Sights

Port Townsend has a rich maritime heritage preserved by its continued marine trades industry and observed by its historical buildings and classic wooden boats. A good place to start is at the **Port Townsend Visitor Information Center** (2409 Jefferson St., 360/385-2722, www.enjoypt.com, 9am-5pm Mon.-Fri., 10am-4pm Sat., 11am-4pm Sun.) to pick up a tour map.

Fort Worden State Park

Perched above the northwest entrance of Puget Sound, **Fort Worden** (200 Battery Way, 360/344-4400, 8am-6pm daily) was commissioned in 1902 as part of the U.S. Army's "Triangle of Fire" harbor defenses. The government spent $7.5 million on its completion, with strategically constructed barracks designed to confuse the aim of gunners firing offshore and 41 artillery pieces that were never fired in battle. After 51 years of service, it was decommissioned and operated as a state detention center before becoming a state park. The **Coast Artillery Museum** (Bldg. 201, Fort Worden, 360/385-0373, www.coastartillery.org, 11am-4pm daily), barracks, and hangar once used for airships offer compelling insight into the fort's history. Much of the movie *An Officer and a Gentleman* was filmed here. Within the park's 434 acres, there are sandy beaches and views of the Olympic and Cascade Mountains. Hiking, kayaking, and biking are popular. Guided tours operate seasonally.

Rothschild House

Head uptown to get a good look at maritime life in the Victorian era by touring the **Rothschild House** (418 Taylor St., 360/385-1003, www.jchsmuseum.org, 11am-4pm daily May-Sept., $4 adults, $1 children under 12) and the remnants of the Kentucky Store. The store once sat on a pier that extended into Port Townsend Bay, where ships could directly load and unload their cargo, ranging from needles to anchors. The house's furnishings, from the mattresses

Port Townsend

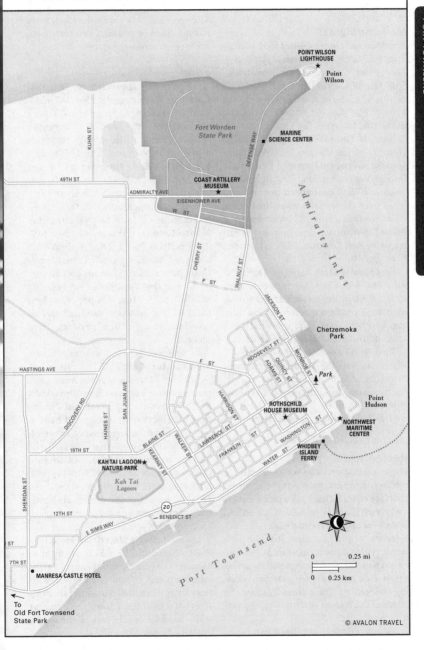

POINT WILSON
LIGHTHOUSE ★

Point
Wilson

*Fort Worden
State Park*

DEFENSE WAY

MARINE
SCIENCE CENTER ■

KUHN ST

49TH ST

ADMIRALTY AVE

COAST ARTILLERY
MUSEUM ★

EISENHOWER AVE

W ST

Admiralty Inlet

CHERRY ST

WALNUT ST

P ST

JACKSON ST

Chetzemoka
Park

HASTINGS AVE

F ST

ROOSEVELT ST

MONROE ST

QUINCY ST

ADAMS ST

Park

Point
Hudson

DISCOVERY RD

HAINES ST

SAN JUAN AVE

HARRISON ST

ROTHSCHILD
HOUSE MUSEUM ★

ST

BLAINE ST

WALKER ST

LAWRENCE ST

ST

WASHINGTON

ST

NORTHWEST
MARITIME ★
CENTER

19TH ST

FRANKLIN

WATER

ST

WHIDBEY
ISLAND
FERRY

SHERIDAN ST

KAH TAI LAGOON ★
NATURE PARK

KEARNEY ST

*Kah Tai
Lagoon*

12TH ST

(20)

ST

7TH ST

E SIMS WAY

BENEDICT ST

■ MANRESA CASTLE HOTEL

Port Townsend

N

0   0.25 mi

0   0.25 km

To
Old Fort Townsend
State Park

© AVALON TRAVEL

to the wallpaper, are originals. The family photo album preserves photos of sailing shipmasters.

Maritime Sights

The **Marine Science Center** (532 Battery Way E., 360/385-5582, www.ptmsc.org, 11am-5pm Wed.-Mon. summer, noon-5pm Fri.-Sun. spring, fall, and winter, $5 adults, $3 children 6-17) offers a chance to touch the interesting creatures that live in the cold waters of the Pacific.

Tour the **Point Wilson Lighthouse** (186 Harbor Defense Way, 360/385-3701, 1pm-4pm Sat. May-Sept.), named by Captain George Vancouver, who first sighted the point in 1792. The foghorn can be heard from over three miles away. Just three miles southeast, the 1888 **Marrowstone Point Lighthouse,** standing at the entrance to Port Townsend Bay, is not open to the public.

Fort Flagler State Park (10541 Flagler Rd., 360/385-1259, www.parks.state. wa.us, 6:30am-dusk summer, 8am-dusk winter, $2 donation) offers hiking, biking, and beach trails, plus a small museum housing coastal defense artifacts.

Visit **Northwest Maritime Center** (431 Water St., 360/385-3628, www.nwmaritime.org, 10am-5pm daily), a beautiful two-story building where they show you how wooden boats are built as well as hold informational classes and workshops.

Recreation

From water sports and walking trails to bird-watching and picnicking, there is no shortage of activities. Pack a picnic basket and watch the natural side of life unfold at **Kah Tai Lagoon Nature Park** (access at Kearney St. and Lawrence St.). The park borders the lagoon on 14th Street between Kearney and Haines Streets and is a protected sanctuary for waterfowl nesting and feeding. Trails meander along the edges of the lagoon and through the natural landscape.

To get your feet wet, head two miles north on Cherry Street to **Fort Worden State Park** (200 Battery Way), where you can swim, scuba dive, or play in the sand. The on-site Cable House Canteen store has all kinds of goodies, and restrooms are located across the street.

Food

Art lovers will appreciate ★ **Fountain Café** (920 Washington St., 360/385-1364, 11am-3pm and 5pm-9pm daily, $13-26), a funky eatery with eastern Mediterranean influences and art-lined walls set inside a historical building. The 1950s-style **Nifty Fifty's Soda Fountain** (817 Water St., 360/385-1931, www.niftyfiftyspt. com, $5-12) brings back the era of thick burgers and thick milkshakes. Located in the center of Haven Shipyard, the **Blue Moose Café** (311 Haines Pl., 360/385-7339, 6:30am-2pm Mon.-Fri., 7am-2pm Sat.-Sun., $8-20, no credit cards) serves fluffy pancakes and famous corned beef hash. The **Owl Sprit Café** (218 Polk St., 360/385-5275, 11am-7:30pm Wed.-Sat., $7-22) serves up soups, sandwiches, and tasty local favorites like "haystack" fried onions.

If seafood is what you crave, the **Silverwater Café** (237 Taylor St., 360/385-6448, www.silverwatercafe. com, 11:30am-3pm and 5pm-10pm daily, $12-26) takes Pacific Northwest cuisine to new heights with pan-seared halibut in a rich hazelnut cream sauce or jumbo prawns with cilantro ginger lime. All the Italian classics are at **Lanza's Ristorante** (1020 Lawrence St., 360/379-1900, www. lanzaspt.com, 5pm-9pm Tues.-Sat., $16-22). Its authentic dishes and intimate atmosphere make it a perfect place for couples.

Locals' favorite **Waterfront Pizza** (951 Water St., 360/385-6629, 11am-8pm Mon.-Fri., 11am-9pm Sat.-Sun., $4-20) attracts plenty of tourists as well, with tasty crispy crust slices selling from its streetside counter. Climb the adjacent stairs to order whole pies in the shop's upstairs dining room.

Nightlife and Entertainment

Though Port Townsend isn't a "club" town, it does have some good wine bars and pubs, including a few where weekend bands perform. The **Cellar Door** (940 Water St., entrance on Tyler St., 360/385-6959, www.cellardoorpt.com, 5pm-midnight Sun.-Tues., 5pm-2am Wed.-Sat.) is a casual wine and cocktail bar decorated in classic furnishings with diverse live music in the evenings. Every Friday and Saturday night **Sirens** (823 Water St., 360/379-1100, www.sirenspub.com, noon-midnight daily) welcomes local music and offers guests drinks and food. The **Uptown Pub** (1016 Lawrence St., 360/385-1530, noon-midnight Mon.-Sat., noon-9pm Sun.) has a laid-back atmosphere with pool tables, live music, and a dance floor.

Craft beer fans can get a few pints and play table tennis at the **Pourhouse** (2231 Washington St., 360/379-5586, noon-10pm Mon.-Tues., noon-11pm Wed.-Thurs., noon-midnight Fri.-Sat., noon-10:30pm Sun.), a taproom and beer garden with several local brews on tap. The peninsula's tastiest beer is made at award-winning **Propolis Brewing** (2457 Jefferson St., 360/344-2129, www.propolisbrewing.com, 2pm-8pm Wed.-Thurs., 2pm-9pm Fri., noon-9pm Sat., noon-6pm Sun.), which crafts farmhouse Belgian styles made with foraged local flora.

The small **Rose Theatre** (235 Taylor St., 360/385-1089, www.rosetheatre.com) screens new and classic movies, as well as arthouse cinema and filmed live theater, musical, and dance performances, with the option to dine and drink while you watch.

Shopping

Port Townsend is known for its antiques, art galleries, eclectic shops, and used bookstores. The **Port Townsend Antique Mall** (802 Washington St., 360/379-8069, 11am-5pm Sun.-Fri., 10:30am-5:30pm Sat.) is composed of several vendors stuffed to the brim with vintage and nautical collectibles.

Local artists are showcased and mingle with the public along Water Street in the downtown waterfront district during the popular **Gallery Walks** (5:30pm-8pm, first Sat. each month). **Forest Gems Gallery** (807 Washington St., 360/379-1713, www.forestgems.com, 10am-6pm daily) is a gallery of gorgeous, finely finished furniture carved from West Coast woods. Carefully navigate through this store and be mindful of the No Touching signs.

Despite the name, **The Green Eyeshade** (720 Water St., 360/385-3838, www.thegreeneyeshade.com, 10am-6pm daily) doesn't deal in cosmetics, but it does have lots of home decor items, handcrafted jewelry, and specialty gifts neatly laid out in this appropriately green building.

Jewelry is what you'll find at **Lila Drake Jewelry** (918 Water St., 360/379-2899, 10am-6pm daily), and you won't believe your eyes when you see their prices. There aren't many places where you can buy beautiful silver pieces for under $20.

Discover your inner writer on the corner of Water and Taylor Streets at **The Writers' Workshoppe and Bookstore** (820 Water St., 360/379-2617, 10am-5:30pm daily), a tiny bookstore filled with fantasy, horror, and fun stuff, like T-shirts, coffee mugs, and classic typewriters. Step into another world at **Phoenix Rising** (696 Water St., 360/385-4464, 10am-6pm daily) and browse a huge selection of spiritual books, crystals, music, and fairies. The staff is helpful, but the store gets pretty busy. Plan to spend a little extra time in this place.

The unique **Bergstrom's Antique & Classic Autos** (809 Washington St., 360/385-5061, 10am-5pm Thurs.-Sat. and Mon.) does offer cool vintage cars, but most of the converted garage is given to car-related antiques, games, memorabilia, models, and more.

If you're driving into Olympic National Park and wish to stock up on natural and unprocessed foods, make sure to stop at **The Food Co-op** (414 Kearney St., 360/385-2883, www.food-coop.coop, 8am-9pm daily) on the way out of town.

Events

Port Townsend hosts the largest **Wooden Boat Festival** (www.nwmaritime.org, Sept., one-day ticket $20/day, $40/weekend) in the world with more than 300 wooden vessels, hundreds of indoor and outdoor presentations, exhibitors, musical performances, children's activities, and more. It's a three-day event held at the Point Hudson Marina entrance.

The town has also been the set of popular movies like *An Officer and a Gentleman* and *Snow Falling on Cedars*. Independent filmmakers and cinema lovers flock here in September to attend the **Port Townsend Film Festival** (211 Taylor St., 360/379-1333, www.ptfilmfest.com, Sept., $15-40 per screening). There are five indoor and two outdoor theaters, numerous food venues, a cocktail lounge, and ongoing mingling with producers, directors, and actors.

Early October brings the very odd **Kinetic Sculpture Race** (www.ptkineticrace.org, Oct.), a themed contest of human-powered works of art that race over land and sea to the finish.

Accommodations

Embellished with antique furnishings and rich colors, ★ **Manresa Castle** (651 Cleveland St., 360/385-5750 or 800/732-1281, www.manresacastle.com, $100 and up) makes every guest feel like royalty with luxurious rooms in a haunted castle that overlooks Port Townsend Bay and the Cascade Mountains. Stay in room 305 to be visited by the mansion's original 1892 owner, Kate Eisenbeis.

Built in 1889, the **Palace Hotel** (1004 Water St., 360/385-0773, www.palace-hotelpt.com, $129 and up) is a beautifully restored boutique hotel with antique furnishings, high ceilings, and an old-world charm. Some rooms have a shared bath.

The **Bishop Victorian Hotel** (714 Washington St., 360/385-6122, www.bishopvictorian.com, $175 and up) is a turn-of-the-century building with 16 suites, each with its own cozy fireplace. It is right in the heart of the downtown historical district and is in walking distance of the waterfront.

While some towns have a few old homes turned into B&Bs, Port Townsend seems to burst at the seams with wonderful homes from its late-19th-century glory days. One lovely Victorian bed-and-breakfast, **The Old Consulate Inn** (313 Walker St., 360/385-6753, www.oldconsulate.com, $140 and up), overlooks Port Townsend from atop a high bluff, providing panoramic mountain and water views in comfortably elegant surroundings. The inn was built in 1889 by F. W. Hastings, son of Port Townsend's founding father, Loren B. Hastings, and served as the office of the German consul (hence the "Old Consulate" name) in the early part of the 20th century. Eight guest rooms all have private baths.

The **Port Townsend Inn** (2020 Washington St., 360/385-2211, www.porttownsendinn.com, $119 and up) has comfortable rooms without all the frills and a nice indoor pool and hot tub. **The Waterstreet Hotel** (635 Water St., 360/385-5467 or 800/735-9810, www.waterstotel.com, $50 and up) is in the renovated 1889 N.D. Hill Building. Rooms range from one-bed spaces with shared bath to suites with private decks overlooking the bay.

The **Point Hudson Resort** (101 Hudson St., 360/385-2828, $46 and up) is a private facility on the beach with full hookups for RVs. The **Jefferson County Fairgrounds** (4907 Landes St., 360/385-1013, www.jeffcofairgrounds.com, $17-25) provides year-round camping and RV parking without a reservation. It's a full-service facility with a bus stop located within the grounds.

Information and Services
The **Port Townsend Visitor Information Center** (2409 Jefferson St., 360/385-2722, www.enjoypt.com, 9am-5pm Mon.-Fri., 10am-4pm Sat., 11am-4pm Sun.) is a good resource for local events and activities. It is conveniently located right next to the Jefferson Transit Park-and-Ride, where you can catch a shuttle bus to downtown. Gasoline and small convenience stores are available within the town.

⚑ Eastern Peninsula: Dosewallips and Staircase

Leaving Port Townsend, WA-20 skirts Discovery Bay until it connects to US-101 at Discovery Junction. Taking US-101 west takes you around the Olympic Peninsula to the Pacific Coast. But if you wish to explore the eastern boundary of Olympic National Park, take US-101 south.

Dosewallips
About 50 minutes from Port Townsend, the 425-acre **Dosewallips State Park** (306996 US-101, 888/226-7688 or 360/796-4415, www.parks.state.wa.us/499/Dosewallips, 8am-10pm daily summer, 8am-5pm daily winter) is sandwiched between the saltwater of Hood Canal and the freshwater Dosewallips River. The park has a great viewing platform and large flats where clamming is popular seasonally (with a permit). The Dosewallips River originates in two forks, which join about five miles from the headwaters near Mt. Anderson. There are several legends about how the river got its name; the S'Klallam Native American oral history tells of the Doquebatl "Great Changer," who transformed a S'Klallam chief into a mountain at the river's source.

Like many rivers throughout the region, the Dosewallips once teemed with salmon, but human tinkering of the landscape by logging and farming ultimately destroyed the salmon habitat. Restoration efforts led by the Port Gamble S'Klallam Tribe, Wild Fish Conservancy, and the Hood Canal Coordinating Council are working to reconnect the river to its original delta to improve salmon habitat. The entire Dosewallips River Estuary is within Dosewallips State Park, where you can watch seasonal salmon spawning.

Less than a mile south of Dosewallips, the town of Brinnon is tiny, and you may miss it if you blink. Though there is a market, it lacks in selection and is costly. If you keep going, you'll have a chance to stop in Hoodsport (about a half hour south) for groceries and gas.

Recreation
Unmarked trails lead into the woods, but don't let this stop you from exploring. **Steam Donkey Loop Trail** (begins behind the park entrance) is an easy three-mile loop around the park through ferns and maple. It traverses many bridges onto the old Izett Railroad Grade before descending back to the main road. The **Rocky Brook Trail** is only accessible by hiking in since the road washed out over a decade ago, but the 229-foot waterfall that cascades from above is worth the trouble. The trail is very short and begins just after crossing Rocky Brook Bridge. Walk through wooded brush and green foliage before arriving at the spectacular waterfall.

Experienced mountain climbers will find **Mt. Anderson** (elevation 7,330 feet) and **Mt. Constance** (elevation 7,756 feet) both imposing and rewarding, with steep jagged cliffs, areas of crumbling rock, and commanding views of forest treetops, the Cascade Range, and various waterways.

Camping
Dosewallips Campground (360/565-3131, www.nps.gov, free) has several rustic walk-in campsites on both sides of the

highway. There are picnic and day-use facilities but no running water and only pit toilets.

Staircase

Roughly 30 miles southwest of Dosewallips, the **Staircase** area is the main entry into the southeastern portion of Olympic National Park. Although this is the "forgotten" corner of the park, that doesn't mean there isn't anything worth seeing or doing. This is the place for adventurous explorers, as trails penetrate deep into the primitive forest, fringing the Skokomish and Dosewallips Rivers, passing Pacific rhododendrons (the state flower), vibrant mossy old growth, waterfalls, and small alpine lakes.

Storms sometimes cause road closures. Always check weather and road reports before venturing into this part of the park.

Recreation

Hidden in the shadow of Mt. Lincoln and behind popular Lake Cushman, Staircase offers a myriad of nature trails. To enter the park, follow the signs to Lake Cushman and turn left at the end of the road, twisting along the dirt road to Staircase Ranger Station. There are no stairs, but there were when an 1890 expedition built a cedar stairway to get over the rock bluff. **Shady Lane Trail** marks the location. The path is a short 1.5-mile stroll through mossy undergrowth and grand vistas of Mt. Rose and the North Fork of the Skokomish River, passing a few bridges and an abandoned mine along the way. If you want a good look at rapids, a longer trail runs alongside the Skokomish River in a complete loop. The **North Fork Skokomish Trail** is about a four-mile trek to Flapjacks Lake; you can continue and make a complete 15-mile loop, passing a beautiful waterfall and rare views of the ragged Sawtooth Range of the Olympics. A steep three-mile climb to Wagonwheel Lake gains nearly 4,000

feet in subalpine forest, where bobcats, deer, and elk roam.

Camping

Staircase Campground (360/565-3131, www.nps.gov, spring-Oct., $20/night) is in a deeply wooded area away from the river but a great point for starting hikes into the Skokomish River Valley. There are no RV hookups. Toilets and drinking water are only available in the summer.

Olympic National Park

Olympic National Park stretches across much of the Olympic Peninsula's interior and coastline. You could spend eternity exploring Olympic National Park's breathtaking beauty and vast natural diversity; its sheer size is overwhelming (over 922,651 acres).

President Grover Cleveland designated these old-growth forests as a reserve in 1897. President Franklin Roosevelt established the area as a national park in 1938 to preserve its treasures for future generations. But it isn't just its intrinsic qualities that make this place memorable. It's the story that still lives within the landscape. Before the arrival of concrete and tire tracks, Native Americans forged the paths we still follow, hunting in the damp forests and fishing in the deep lake caverns. It was, and continues to be, a land embedded in tribal culture, exhibiting a spiritual understanding of the universe that unifies all living things. For those who arrived with the expanding American frontier, it was a place of opportunity, where the struggles and hardships of life were overcome by perseverance and hope.

There are three prominent ecosystems in the park: rugged coastline, snowcapped mountains, and temperate rainforests containing record-sized trees. Wildlife thrives and can be seen throughout the park, especially Roosevelt

Olympic National Park

elk, blacktail deer, bald eagles, and amazing butterflies (alongside wildflowers) in valley meadows and hillsides. Black bears roam the Quinault River valley.

Orientation

There are several access points into Olympic National Park. They are described as they appear, approaching from Seattle along US-101.

Eastern Olympic National Park

The little-visited eastern corner of the park, accessible from **Dosewallips** (see page 53) and **Staircase** (see page 54), is for adventurous travelers. Ancient stands of Douglas fir and cedar cloak the steep ridges of the wilderness valley. The wild waters of Skokomish River, awash with rainbow and bull trout, surge through the deep forest bed.

Northern Olympic National Park

The northern section of the park lies along the Strait of Juan de Fuca, one of the most beautiful places in the world. Frequent sightings of marine mammals, elk, deer, and even the occasional black bear make the region an animal haven. Not far from the town of Port Angeles is one of the most visited areas of the park: **Hurricane Ridge** (see page 62). Nearby, **Lake Crescent** (see page 65) is a deep, watery cavern popular for its Beardslee trout and for the shimmering cascades of **Marymere Falls.**

Western Olympic National Park

A lush green canopy of coniferous and deciduous species is found in the rainy western side of the Olympics. Mosses and ferns shroud the surface in shades of green as record-breaking trees cloak misty waterfalls, glacier-carved lakes, and an abundance of wildlife. This is where you'll find **Hoh Rain Forest** (see page 74) and **Lake Quinault** (see page 77), a favorite for outdoor activity.

Visiting the Park
Getting There

Olympic National Park is the center of the Olympic Peninsula, covering a 50-mile radius that includes most of the Pacific coastline. One major highway, **US-101,** loops around the park, following the northern edge of Lake Crescent to Lake Quinault's southwestern edge. The central portion of the park is completely roadless, so it is not possible to drive through the park. Off US-101, **access roads** wind deeper into the park's interior; however, you will eventually have to return to US-101 to exit the park.

The highway can be dangerous in extremely **windy** areas at Morse Creek. As you drive through Port Angeles, the **name of the highway changes** (to Golf Course Rd., Front St. and 1st St., and Lincoln Ave.), which can be confusing,

but well-placed signs help keep you on the right track.

Park Entrances

The coastal portion along the peninsula is accessible from US-101 at Kalaloch, La Push, Cape Alava, and Neah Bay. **Access roads** run from US-101 into the park's interior at Hurricane Ridge (17 miles south of Port Angeles), Elwha (11 miles west of Port Angeles), Sol Duc (12 miles west of Lake Crescent), Hoh Rain Forest (31 miles east of Forks), and Quinault. Two access points allow for exploration of the remote east side at the Staircase (9 miles west of US-101 in Hoodsport) and Quilcene (north of the Hood Canal Bridge).

Seasons

Olympic National Park is open year-round, 24 hours a day. Expect **snow** in the winter and **rain** in spring and fall. Pack reliable rain gear and a few extra pairs of socks. **July, August,** and most of **September** are the **driest and warmest** months, with temperatures reaching the mid-70s.

Some campgrounds and visitor facilities **close during winter,** including some interior roads. Fires and flooding contribute to the temporary shutdown of roads and services. Up-to-date information on weather and available facilities is available at the **Olympic National Park Visitor Center** (360/565-3130).

Permits and Regulations

Vehicle fees ($25 per private vehicle, $15 per motorcycle, $10 for visitors on foot or bicycle, free for children 15 and under) cover park entry. All passes are good for seven days. **Annual passes** are $50. **Wilderness permits** ($8 per person, per night) required for overnight backcountry hikers are available at the **Wilderness Information Center** (3002 Mount Angeles Rd., 360/565-3100, www.nps.gov/olym) in Port Angeles.

Dogs are allowed but not on most

trails or in the backcountry. Trailers must be 21 feet or less (15 feet at Queets Campground).

Food and Accommodations
In many parts of the park, it's best to bring your own food. The only restaurants within the national park boundaries are inside the park lodges. Bears, raccoons, and other critters are more than happy to clean up your campsite by eating all your goodies. Animal-resistant containers will keep your food safe, and many wilderness areas within the park require them.

Places to stay vary, as do rates. Many resorts fill up fast. Make reservations ahead of time.

Concessionaire **Aramark** (www.olympicnationalparks.com) runs four lodges in the park: **Lake Crescent Lodge** (416 Lake Crescent Rd., 360/928-3211 or 888/896-3818, May-Dec., $125 and up), **Log Cabin Resort** (3183 E. Beach Rd., 360/928-3325, late May-Sept., $80 and up), **Sol Duc Hot Springs Resort** (12076 Sol Duc Hot Springs Rd., 360/327-3583 or 866/476-5382, late-Mar.-Oct., $168 and up), and **Lake Quinault Lodge** (345 S. Shore Rd., 360/288-2900 or 800/562-6672, $229 and up).

Additional accommodations are available in towns near the park. Hurricane Ridge and Lake Crescent can be visited from Port Angeles; Hoh Rain Forest and Lake Quinault can be visited from Forks.

Camping
Campsites are available at 16 NPS-operated campgrounds in various areas of the park. Nearly all are first-come, first-served and do not take reservations. Kalaloch Campground takes individual reservations for the summer season, which can be made up to six months in advance. Sites can range from primitive to fairly modern and usually have picnic tables and a grill or a fire pit. Water, toilets, and garbage containers are found at most sites; however, you

have to go into town for laundry, showers, and hookups.

RV dump stations ($5-10 per use) are located at Fairholm, Hoh, Kalaloch, Mora, and Sol Duc campsites.

Camp concessions are open seasonally and sell wood. If there's no store or if it's outside operating hours, collecting dead wood in the campgrounds is permitted.

Jamestown S'Klallam Tribal Community

Twenty-five miles southwest of Port Townsend via WA-20 and US-101, the **Jamestown S'Klallam "Strong People" Tribal Community** looks out over Sequim Bay. Towering totem poles welcome visitors at the information kiosk pullout west of the highway. These carved masterpieces reflect the Coastal Salish Indian traditions and legacies. Listen to timeless legends as you journey along numerous totem poles to the **House of Myths** (set behind a native art gallery), where each totem is carefully carved. It's a fascinating, tribally guided tour known as **Tour of the Totems.** For scenic views or a leisurely stroll, follow the stairway at the west end of the pullout down to the **Olympic Discovery Trail,** a path that traces the former railroad corridors that were constructed between Port Angeles and Discovery Bay in the early 1900s. Two short bridges cross the Jimmycomelately Creek and Estuary, a stream that flows from the Olympic Mountains and into Sequim Bay. The logging and farming of the late 1800s nearly decimated the stream and salmon beds; the S'Klallam Tribe has led restoration efforts to revive salmon runs and protect the stream. In the summer, you can observe birds and wildlife and watch as chum salmon fight their way to spawning grounds.

There are no overnight accommodations, but a mile farther on US-101 in **Blyn** you'll find a restaurant inside the **Seven Cedars Casino** (270756 US-101,

360/683-7777, www.7cedarsresort.com, 9am-2am daily) with a weekend buffet. The casino's **Longhouse Market & Deli** (271020 US-101, 360/681-7777, 24 hours daily) provides an opportunity to fuel up on gasoline and snacks.

Sequim and the Dungeness Valley

Less than five minutes from the Jamestown S'Klallam Tribal Community on US-101, **Sequim** (pop. 6,737; pronounced "skwim") is a pleasantly dry patch on a peninsula famous for its rain. A typical year has 299 days of sunshine and just 17 inches of rain (comparable to rainfall in sunny Los Angeles). The agreeable climate has made this little town a popular retirement destination.

Sights

One block north of US-101 in Sequim, the **Museum and Arts Center** (175 W. Cedar St., 360/683-8110, www.sequimmuseum. com, 11am-3pm Wed.-Sat., 5pm-8pm first Fri. each mo., $2 donation) was built to store the 12,000-year-old tusks, bones, and artifacts unearthed at Sequim's famous Manis Mastodon Site, discovered in 1977 by Emanuel Manis, a retired farmer. Archaeologists discovered a prehistoric spear point in the rib cage of one of the mastodons, some of the earliest evidence that humans hunted these elephantine beasts. Other displays include several fine old cedar bark baskets, pioneer farming displays, and timber exhibits.

The aptly named **Dungeness Spit** (the word *dungeness* means "sandy cape") is a 5.5-mile-long stretch of sand (closed to horses on weekends and holidays Apr. 15-Oct. 15) that creates Dungeness Bay. The **Dungeness National Wildlife Refuge** (554 Voice of America Rd., 360/457-8451, $3 per group of up to four adults, free children under 16, sunrise to 30 min. before sunset daily) provides habitat for 250 species of birds on the nation's longest natural sand spit. As many as 30,000 birds rest at this saltwater lagoon during their migratory journeys.

Built in 1857, the **New Dungeness Lighthouse** (tip of the spit, 360/683-6638, www.newdungenesslighthouse.com) is managed by volunteers and offers tours, but you'll have to hike a total of 11 miles out and back to see it. It's a good idea to check the tide charts before starting out. For an overview of the area, hike the 0.5-mile trail from the parking lot to a bluff overlooking Dungeness Bay. Clamming, fishing, and canoeing are permitted in this protected wildlife refuge, but no camping, dogs, firearms, or fires.

The **Olympic Game Farm** (1423 Ward Rd., 360/683-4295 or 800/778-4295, www.olygamefarm.com, 9am-5pm Sun.-Fri., 9am-6pm Sat., $15 adults, $13 seniors and children 6-14), a vacation and retirement home for Hollywood animal stars, is a 90-acre preserve where over 200 animals, some of TV and movie fame, can be visited. Many of the Walt Disney nature specials were filmed here, along with parts of many feature movies. Follow the signs from Sequim five miles northwest to Ward Road.

Food

For the best French toast or Swedish pancakes, ★ **The Oak Table Café** (292 W. Bell St., 360/683-2179, www.oaktablecafe. com, 7am-3pm daily, $10-15) is where the locals go. The service is friendly, the cappuccinos perfect, and the prices will barely make a dent in your wallet.

For fast and well-prepared lunches, **Hi-Way 101 Diner** (392 W. Washington, 360/683-3388, 6am-8pm Mon.-Thurs., 6am-9pm Fri.-Sat., 7am-8pm Sun., $9-22) is a "fabulous fifties" family diner with the biggest local burgers. It's also a popular spot for breakfast. For locally sourced sandwiches, pizza, and sausage, check out small but tasty **Pacific Pantry** (229 S. Sequim Ave., 360/797-1221, 11am-7pm Mon.-Sat., $10-12).

Accommodations

Enjoy a room with a hot tub at **Sequim Bay Lodge** (268522 US-101, 800/622-0691, www.sequimbaylodge.com, $109 and up), conveniently located off US-101. It's not a glitzy hotel, but it's clean, comfortable, and surrounded by beautiful greenery.

Juan de Fuca Cottages (182 Marine Dr., 360/683-4433, www.juandefuca. com, $200 and up) offers suites and fully equipped housekeeping cottages overlooking Dungeness Spit.

Port Angeles

US-101 brings you 17 miles right into downtown Port Angeles via East 1st and Front Streets to Lincoln Street, about a 25 minute drive. **Port Angeles** (pop. 19,256) was built on a 2,700-year-old Native American village and is one of only two municipalities designated as a federal city by President Abraham Lincoln—the other being Washington, D.C. It was once a booming logging community, but the preservation of endangered spotted owls forced paper and logging mills to close, uprooting generations of workers. But thanks to its prime position between the Strait of Juan de Fuca and the magnificent mountains of Olympic National Park, Port Angeles has learned to cater to tourists, serving as a jumping-off point for trips both across the strait to Canada and to the natural splendor of nearby mountains, lakes, forests, and rivers.

Getting There and Around

US-101 brings you right into downtown Port Angeles via East 1st and Front Streets to Lincoln Street. The public bus service connects all local towns, making the area fairly simple to get around. **Clallam Transit** (360/452-4511 or 800/858-3747, www.clallamtransit. com, $1 single, plus $0.50 for additional zones, $3 day pass) offers service in and

Port Angeles

around Port Angeles, plus routes to Lake Crescent and Forks (route 14, $1.50), Neah Bay (route 14 to route 16), Sequim (route 30, $1.50), and the Bainbridge Island Ferry to Seattle (route 123, $10). **Olympic Bus Lines** (360/417-0700 or 800/457-4492, www.olympicbuslines. com) provides service to Seattle and Sea-Tac Airport ($49).

Sights

Due to the potential for floods, downtown Port Angeles was rebuilt on top of the original city in the early 1900s. **Port Angeles Historical Underground** (121 E. Railroad Ave., 360/452-2363, www. portangelesheritagetours.com, 2pm Mon.-Sat. year-round, 10am Mon.-Sat. May-Oct., $15 adults, $12 students, $8 children 6-12) offers a two-hour heritage tour through the past, uncovering the buildings lost beneath the city, including its original movie theater and a secret brothel.

The **Museum at the Carnegie** (207 S. Lincoln St., 360/452-6779, www.clallamhistoricalsociety.com, 1pm-4pm Wed.-Sat., donation $2 per adult, $5 per family) houses a modest collection of artifacts and exhibits on the town's logging history, as well as local Native American culture.

Ferries to Victoria, British Columbia

Port Angeles is a major transit point for travelers heading to or from Victoria, B.C., just 18 miles away across the Strait of Juan de Fuca. The MV *Coho* leaves Port Angeles for Victoria three times daily in summer (mid-May to mid-Sept.) and one-two times daily the rest of the year, except for a couple of winter weeks when the ferry is out for maintenance. The **Coho Ferry Terminal** (101 E. Railroad Ave., 360/457-4491, www.cohoferry.com, 1.5 hours, one-way $64 for car and driver, $18.50 adults, $9.25 children 5-11) is at the foot of Laurel Street in Port Angeles. Departure times are listed by date on the website. Vehicle space is at a premium on summer weekends; reservations can be made for an additional fee. The *Coho* lands in Victoria, within walking distance of many picturesque sights. A car is not entirely necessary for a day trip. You can pick up a map of Victoria at the visitors center near the ferry terminal in Port Angeles.

Recreation

The west-central route of the 30-mile **Olympic Discovery Trail** provides the perfect scenic stroll or bike ride on a maintained trail that begins at Port Angeles City Pier (Lincoln St. at W. Front St.) and extends across the Elwha River, along the coastal lowlands and Lake Crescent, to the top of Fairholm Hill.

Sound Bikes and Kayaks (120 E. Front St., 360/457-1240, 10am-6pm Mon.-Sat., 11am-4pm Sun., bikes $10/hour or $45/day, kayaks $15/hour or $50/day) rents out whatever you need to pedal or paddle your way around.

Food

★ **Toga's Soup House** (122 W. Lauridsen Blvd., 360/452-1952, www.togassouphouse.com, 7am-4pm Mon.-Fri., $5-14) does soup and sandwiches, but don't expect just grilled cheese! Don't leave without trying the Dungeness crab panini, an Alaska salmon sandwich, or one of their many homemade soups served in colorful bowls.

A bargain for the quality, **First Street Haven** (107 E. 1st St., 360/457-0352, 7am-3pm Mon.-Fri., 7am-4pm Sat., 8am-2pm Sun., $7-12) hits the spot! It's small but homey with delicious pastries and the perfect breakfast.

Right in front of the Red Lion Hotel downtown, **Kokopelli Grill** (203 E. Front St., 360/457-6040, www.kokopelli-grill.com, 11am-9pm Mon.-Thurs., 10am-10pm Fri.-Sat., 2pm-9pm Sun., $12-40) features Southwestern cooking in a warm, friendly space. Kitty-corner, the cleverly named **Turnip the Beat** (132 E. Front St., 360/797-1113, www.turnipthebeet.biz, 11am-8pm Sun.-Mon., 11am-11pm Tues.-Thurs., 11am-2am Fri.-Sat., $8-10) offers vegetarian and vegan sandwiches, salads, and wraps.

For a more upscale dinner, look down the street for **Michael's Seafood & Steakhouse** (117 E. 1st St., 360/417-6929, www.michaelsdining.com, 4pm-10pm Sun.-Thurs., 4pm-11pm Fri.-Sat., $15-60), in an underground location where the dress code is casual, the seafood is fresh, and the booths are cozy.

Nightlife and Entertainment

DJs turn up the volume for a younger crowd at **BarN9NE** (229 W. 1st St., 360/797-1999, www.barn9nepa.com, 2pm-2am daily).

Beer, pool, and an old jukebox are what's up at low-brow **Zak's** (125 W. Front St., 360/452-7575, 4pm-2am daily). Don't expect swank at **Front Street Alibi** (1605 E. Front St., Ste. A, 360/797-1500, 8am-2am daily)—just strong drinks, a DJ, a dance floor, and interesting dive bar characters.

Joshua's Restaurant & Lounge (113 Del

Guzzi Dr., 360/452-6545, 6am-9pm daily) serves live music along with its award-winning wines Thursday-Saturday nights.

A few blocks off the waterfront, **Next Door Gastropub** (113 W. 1st St., 360/504-2613, www.nextdoorgastropub.com, 11am-11pm Mon.-Thurs., 11am-midnight Fri.-Sat., 10am-10pm Sun., $11-26) hosts live music and comedy acts on weekends.

Shopping

Follow the sculptures that line the west side of Railroad Avenue to 1st Street, the city's shopping hub of antiques, books, and hobby shops.

The Landing Mall (115 E. Railroad Ave., 360/457-4407, www.thelanding-mall.com, hours vary daily) is a trilevel building, ideally situated next to the city pier on Railroad Avenue, with several art galleries, eateries, and specialty gift shops.

Step into the past at **Port Angeles Antique Mall** (109 W. 1st St., 360/452-1693, www.portangelesdowntown.com, 10am-5pm Mon.-Sat.) and **Brocante** (105 W. 1st St., 360/452-6322, 11am-6pm Mon.-Sat., 10am-5pm Sun.), where heirlooms ornament the interior with mystery and charm.

Get **InSpired!** (124 W. 1st St. #B, 360/504-2590, 10:30am-5:30pm Mon.-Fri., 10:30am-5pm Sat., noon-4pm Sun.) by the whimsical and spiritual with books, meditation supplies, and handcrafted soaps and lotions.

Unique gift items from jewelry to brass Buddhas make **Olympic Stained Glass** (112 N. Laurel St., 360/457-1090, 10am-5:30pm Mon.-Fri., 10am-5pm Sat.) a fun shop to browse.

Port Book and News (104 E. 1st St., 360/452-6367, 8am-7pm Mon.-Thurs., 8am-8pm Fri.-Sat., 9am-5pm Sun.), **Odyssey Bookshop** (114 W. Front St., 360/457-1045, 9am-7pm Mon.-Sat., 10am-5pm Sun.), and **Olympic Stationers** (112 E. Front St., 360/457-6111, 9am-5:30pm Mon.-Fri., 10am-5pm Sat.) all offer a wide selection of reading material.

Anime Kat (114 W. 1st St., 360/797-1313, www.animekat.com, 11am-7pm Tues.-Sat.) sells collectible card games, board game players, and anime figures.

The **Port Angeles Farmers Market** (133 E. Front St., The Gateway Plaza, 360/460-0361, 10am-2pm Sat.) brings home-grown businesses together to present organic foods and freshly baked goods to the public.

Events

One Saturday morning every August, Olympic National Park Hurricane Ridge Road is closed to motorists so cyclists may **Ride the Hurricane** (www.portangeles.org, 7am-noon, $50 registration, spectators welcome) and leisurely enjoy the scenic 24-36 miles.

Bring a chair or blanket to **Concerts on the Pier** (www.portangeles.org, 6pm-8pm Wed. during calendar summer), an outdoor festival of music for every melodic taste, from Irish folk and jazz to country and rock. Memorial weekends the city celebrates **Juan de Fuca Festival** (www.jffa.org, last weekend of May) with music and poetry performances all over town.

Accommodations

Hotels in Port Angeles are typically small budget motels or name-brand chains. On the cheap end are **Traveler's Motel** (1133 E. 1st St., 360/452-2303 or 866/452-2301, www.travelersmotel.net, $69 and up), the **Aircrest Motel** (1006 E. Front St., 360/452-9255, www.aircrest.com, $99 and up), and **Flagstone Motel** (415 E. 1st St., 360/457-9494, www.flagstonemotel.net, $100 and up). **Port Angeles Inn** (111 E. 2nd St., 360/452-9285 or 800/4210706, www.portangelesinn.com, $110 and up) offers a step up with kitchenette suites and bay views.

National chains include the **Quality Inn Uptown** (101 E. 2nd St., 360/457-9434 or 800/858-3812, www.quality-inn.com, $181 and up) and the **Best Western Olympic Lodge** (140 Del Guzzi

Dr., 360/452-2993 or 800/600-2993, www.olympiclodge.com, $200 and up). One block from the town center, the **Red Lion** (221 N. Lincoln St., 360/452-9215, www.redlion.com/portangeles, $199 and up) overlooks the Strait of Juan de Fuca.

For higher-end stays, a pair of B&Bs sit just east of the city and right on the waterfront. **Colette's Bed & Breakfast** (339 Finn Hall Rd., 360/457-9197, www. colettes.com, $255 and up) is a favorite choice for romantic getaways with luxurious suites, an outdoor sanctuary, and magnificent oceanfront views. Down the road, the **George Washington Inn** (939 Finn Hall Rd., 360/452-5207, www.georgewashingtoninn.com, $175-250) is a picturesque colonial building with a white picket fence surrounded by lavender.

Campgrounds and RV parks are sprinkled around Olympic National Park and not within the city.

Information and Services

The **Olympic Peninsula Visitors Bureau** (18 S. Peabody St., Ste. F, 360/452-2363, www.olympicpeninsula.org, 10am-4pm weekdays) is a good source for local attractions with a helpful staff, or stop by the **Port Angeles Chamber of Commerce** (121 E. Railroad Ave., 360/452-2363, www.cityofpa.com, 10am-4pm daily).

★ Hurricane Ridge

The most visited site in Olympic National Park, **Hurricane Ridge** rises over 5,757 feet from the Strait of Juan de Fuca, looking out over a snowcapped crescent of peaks. Picturesque meadows are populated by colorful wildflowers as well as mountain goats, deer, and Olympic marmots (found only in the Olympics).

The view is so vast that the U.S. military placed a lookout post here during World War II. Views to the north reveal

snowcapped Hurricane Ridge in Olympic National Park

the Strait of Juan de Fuca, Dungeness Spit, and Vancouver Island; dozens of glaciated and snowcapped peaks of the awe-inspiring Olympic Mountain range span across the south end; and to the east, Puget Sound, Hood Canal, and the Cascade Mountains stretch across the skyline.

The name comes from a Seattle Press Expedition in 1897. The winds blew so hard that the prospector declared the site Hurricane Ridge.

Getting There

Accessed via the Heart O' the Hills entrance, Hurricane Ridge is about 17 miles (40 minutes) south of Port Angeles and is reached by Hurricane Ridge Road, which turns off Mount Angeles Road at the Olympic National Park Visitor Center. During winter, the road shuts down Monday-Thursday, except holiday Mondays, and may be closed due to weather conditions at other times.

Call **Northwest Avalanche Center** (360/565-3131) for up-to-date road status information.

Recreation
Hiking
Visitors can follow Hurricane Ridge's well-worn network of trails. From spring to early fall, there are vistas to enjoy and an abundance of wildlife and wildflowers to see. Keep your eyes peeled to catch deer and elk grazing along the green-sloped meadow valleys. Mountain goats are often spotted traversing the trails, but chances are they've spotted you first. Marmots, chipmunks, and other furry critters run freely, playing in the grassy meadows while butterflies swoon about.

The easiest hike is **Hurricane Hill Trail,** which begins at the parking lot at the end of Hurricane Ridge Road. The trail is 3.2 miles round trip and leads to the top of the hill and 360-degree views of mountain peak vistas, Port Angeles, and the Strait of Juan de Fuca.

Hurricane Ridge also has a network of switchback trails accessed near the Hurricane Ridge Visitor Center. Start at the trailhead on the opposite end of the parking lot from the visitors center. The **Big Meadow Trail** (0.5 mile round-trip) is a short walk to the northern views of Hurricane Hill, the Strait of Juan de Fuca, and Vancouver Island. The **Cirque Rim Trail** (0.5 mile round-trip) leads through meadows of purple broadleaf lupine. The **High Ridge Trail** (one mile round-trip) may be the best of the easy hikes, offering panoramic views. It also leads to a spur trail that continues to a narrow crest aptly named **Sunrise Point.** The **Klahhane Ridge Trail** (five miles round-trip) is a difficult but beautiful climb among colorful flowers and butterflies, mountain goats, and deer.

Winter Sports
During winter months, Hurricane Ridge becomes a cross-country and downhill skier dreamland. The **Hurricane Ridge**

Winter Sports Club (848/667-7669, www. hurricaneridge.com, rentals 10am-4pm Sat.-Sun. and holiday Mon.) operates two rope tows and a Poma lift, opening in December and continuing until the end of March. It is the westernmost ski area in the contiguous United States, averaging 400 inches of snowfall a year. The sports facility is on a hill above the Hurricane Ridge Visitor Center, where you can obtain information.

Food and Accommodations

There are no options for lodging within Hurricane Ridge. The closest accommodations are 17 miles north in the town of Port Angeles, which has a wide range of B&Bs, motels, and RV parks.

Twelve miles north of Hurricane Ridge, **Heart O' the Hills** (Hurricane Ridge Rd., 360/565-3130, www.nps.gov, $20) offers 105 campsites in the old-growth forest year-round.

Food and beverage concessions, much like what you'd find at a ski resort, are located at the **Hurricane Ridge Visitor Center** (Hurricane Ridge Rd., 360/565-3131, www.nps.gov/olym, 9am-7pm daily in summer, 10am-4pm Sat.-Sun. late Dec.-Apr.).

Information and Services

Information is available at the **Hurricane Ridge Visitor Center,** which also houses exhibits, a gift shop, and a café. The center offers guided walks and outdoor programs (late June) and provides details on the surrounding winter-use area for skiing and sledding.

The **Olympic National Park Visitor Center** (3002 Mt. Angeles Rd., 360/565-3130, 9am-4pm daily May-Sept., 10am-4pm daily Oct.-Apr.) offers maps; trail brochures; campground, weather, and road information; and wildlife-viewing locations. **Park entrance fees** run about $25 per car, or you can purchase a yearly pass for $50. Weather dependent, the road generally opens to uphill traffic at 9am and closes to uphill traffic at 4pm.

Lake Crescent shimmers on the Olympic Peninsula.

The **Wilderness Information Center** (3002 Mt. Angeles Rd., 360/565-3100, www.nps.gov/olym, 7:30am-6pm daily late June-Labor Day; 7:30am-6pm Sun.-Thurs., 7:30am-7pm Fri.-Sat. rest of the year) is directly behind the Olympic National Park Visitor Center and provides trail and safety information and up-to-date weather reports. It issues camping permits, handles campground reservations (where necessary), and rents animal-proof containers ($3).

★ Lake Crescent

A sparkling sapphire set amid high-forested mountains that seem to touch the sky, **Lake Crescent** is more than a place of beauty—it is a place of mystery. The cold depths of Lake Crescent and its ancient past have formed many of the myths that surround it. In 1970, surveys estimated the lake depth at around 624 feet, the maximum range of the instruments used,

but recent measurements show depths in excess of 1,000 feet, shedding some light on its Loch Ness aura. The lake, named for its sickle shape, is also famous for its Beardslee trout, a 14-pound fish found only at Lake Crescent.

In the lore of the local S'Klallam and Quileute peoples, Lake Crescent is the site of a conflict between two tribes that ended in destruction when the god Mountain Storm King (4,534 feet to the east of the lake) broke off part of his head and hurled it at the warriors, killing them all and splitting the lake in two, creating the upper Lake Sutherland.

Getting There

US-101 skirts the southern shore of alluring Lake Crescent, just 20 miles (35 minutes) west of Port Angeles. The closest ranger station is Storm King. Accessing Lake Crescent from Hurricane Ridge by car requires driving out of the park and getting back on US-101. The drive is about 40 miles (1 hour and 10 minutes).

Recreation
Hiking
The 90-foot Marymere Falls is a spectacular marvel, accessed via the **Marymere Falls Trail,** which starts at the Storm King Ranger Station, about 0.2 mile up from Lake Crescent Lodge. A flat path leads over Barnes Creek via footbridge, and from there stairs climb to the falls viewing area (0.85 mile), where the sheer force of the falls creates a cool, thick mist. A complete two-mile loop can be done by taking the **Crescent Lake Lodge Trail.**

At 2.2 miles one-way, the **Mount Storm King Trail** at the Marymere Falls Trail split takes you to an elevated (over 3,000 feet) view of the lake.

The well-known **Spruce Railroad Trail** (4 miles) is accessed from East Beach Road or Camp David Jr. Road at the opposite ends of the lake. The trail follows a World War I rail bed built to extract large Sitka spruce for aircraft, but the war ended prior to its completion. Starting from the Spruce Railroad Trailhead on East Beach Road, the trail eases upward a half-mile to its crest, then descends to the lakeshore to Devil's Punchbowl Bridge. Across the bridge are open views of Mount Storm King rising from the southern shore. Continuing along the north shore, the trail passes two old railroad tunnels that are closed to visitors due to dangerous conditions. The journey continues with views of the lake and Aurora Ridge emerging from behind the lodge. Inland, the trail ascends and meets Camp David Jr. Road to the west side of the lake.

Water Sports

The lake's true depth is ultimately unknown, but its beauty is famous. You can rent a canoe, kayak, or paddleboard ($20/hour, $60/day) at three locations around the lake: **Fairholm General Store** (221121 US-101, 360/928-3020, 9am-7:30pm daily May-Oct.) at the west end; **Log Cabin Resort** (Piedmont Rd., off US-101, 360/928-3325, www.olympicnationalparks.com, 8am-7pm daily mid-May-Sept.) on the north; and **Lake Crescent Lodge** (416 Lake Crescent Rd., 360/928-3211, www.lakecrescentlodge.com, 8am-one hour before dusk daily, May-mid.-Oct.) on the south shore. Lake Crescent Lodge also offers two-hour, guided kayaking tours ($55 single, $75 double).

Boat launches are located at the east end. Motorboats are prohibited on the west side, which is reserved for swimmers. Lake Crescent is extremely cold due to its depth. Life jackets and protective clothing are suggested.

Two miles east of Lake Crescent, **Lake Sutherland** is warmer as it is shallower. It hosts several water sports activities. Swimming is popular, as are sailing, windsurfing, waterskiing, tubing, and Jet Skiing.

East Beach Picnic Area (on E. Beach Rd., 0.7 mile west of US-101 at east end of Lake Crescent) is set on a grassy meadow overlooking Lake Crescent. It's a popular swimming spot with six picnic tables and vault toilets.

Lake Crescent is a catch-and-release recreational lake, with trout and salmon. Lake Sutherland is a premier spot for kokanee sockeye salmon and cutthroat and rainbow trout. **Bob's Piscatorial Pursuits** (Forks, 866/347-4232, www.piscatorialpursuits.com, Sept.-May) offers fishing trips around the peninsula. Along with a license, pick up a Washington Catch Record Card to fish for salmon. Any catches must be reported to the Washington Department of Fish & Wildlife (https://fishhunt.dfw.wa.gov). Fishing regulations vary throughout the park, so always check with the National Park Service for information first. Licenses are available from sporting goods and outdoor supply stores around the peninsula.

Food and Accommodations

Built in 1916, ★ **Lake Crescent Lodge** (416 Lake Crescent Rd., 360/928-3211 or 888/896-3818, www.olympicnationalparks.com, May-Dec., $125 and up) is a rustic lakeside retreat engulfed by hemlock and fir trees and offering inspiring sunset views. President Franklin D. Roosevelt, who stayed here in 1937, is one of the many guests who have rested at the lodge over the years. Sit on the porch for fine views of the mountains and Lake Crescent, or lounge in front of the big fireplace on a cool evening. The lodge has all sorts of accommodations, including lodge rooms (bath down the hall), cottages (some with fireplaces), and modern motel units. The on-site restaurant, appropriately named **The Lodge** (416 Lake Crescent Rd., 360/928-3211, 7am-10pm late-Apr.-early Jan., $14-46), offers casual lakeside dining for breakfast, lunch, and dinner. Large bay windows look out over the lake and feature gorgeous sunset views. Some of the menu favorites are wild salmon, filet mignon, glacier crab melt, grilled turkey sandwich, and an unforgettable clam chowder.

Log Cabin Resort (3183 E. Beach Rd., 360/928-3325, www.olympicnational-parks.com, late May-Sept., $80 and up cabins, $40 RVs), at the northeast end of the lake, is three miles from US-101. Lodging is available in rustic cabins, motel rooms, and waterfront A-frame chalets. Many of the buildings have stood here since the 1920s.

Fairholme Campground (western shore of Lake Crescent, www.nps.gov, May-Oct., $20/night, National Park Pass required) has 88 campsites for tents and 21-foot RVs, and it has a boat launch. Campsites are first-come, first-served.

Information and Services

Storm King Ranger Station (360/928-3380) is usually open in summer with information and books for sale, and it has accessible year-round restrooms.

Campgrounds have adjacent picnic areas with tables, limited shelters, and restrooms, but no cooking facilities. Drinking water is available at ranger stations, interpretive centers, and inside the campgrounds. Pets and bicycles are not permitted on trails, except on the Spruce Railroad Trail.

Sol Duc

South of Lake Crescent, the isolated **Sol Duc Valley** conceals hot springs, waterfalls, and alpine meadows, along with some of the best views of Mount Olympus. Nearly 50 miles of dense forest and rugged terrain separate the upper Sol Duc River (also spelled Soleduck, meaning "shimmering waters") from the Pacific Ocean and the high mountain ridges that lie to the north and south. Frequented for its superb fishing, the Sol Duc is home to several species of salmon and trout.

Getting There

Thirty miles east of Port Angeles and nine miles east of Lake Crescent Lodge, Sol Duc Hot Springs Road turns southeast off US-101, running nearly 14 miles alongside the Sol Duc River to culminate at the Sol Duc trailhead. The Eagle Ranger Station (open in summer) is the closest National Park Service outpost.

Sights and Recreation

Hiking river trails past waterfalls and relaxing in hot springs top the list of activities along the Sol Duc River, while steelhead and coho salmon run in the spring and fall.

It's important to check with the Olympic National Park Visitor Center on the correct fees and permits necessary. Backcountry wilderness permits are required for mountaineers.

Sol Duc Hot Springs

These bubbling mineral waters are captured in a spa-like outdoor pool area at the **Sol Duc Hot Springs Resort** (12076 Sol Duc Hot Springs Rd., 360/327-3583 or 866/476-5382, www.olympicnational-parks.com, 9am-8pm daily late Mar.-May and Sept.-Oct., 9am-9pm daily Jun.-Aug., $15 adults, $10 children 4-12). Relax and soak in the three mineral pools with approximate temperatures of 99°F, 101°F, and 104°F. There is a freshwater pool as well. Guests at the resort get free access to the pools, and day-use access is available for nonguests.

★ Sol Duc Falls

From Sol Duc Hot Springs Resort, a one-mile hike through old-growth western hemlocks and Douglas firs leads to well-known **Sol Duc Falls.** Along the way, you'll pass the 70-foot Salmon Cascades, where salmon fight their way upstream in late summer and fall. The falls themselves make for a pretty sight as the river navigates the change in terrain. For a longer stroll, instead of going back the way you came, take the three-mile Lover's Lane Trail (with or without your sweetheart), along the south side of the river, to return to the hot springs.

Fishing

Trout and salmon from nearby streams flow into the Sol Duc River, attracting fishing enthusiasts; fly-fishing is a favorite pastime too. Along with a license, pick up a Washington Catch Record Card to fish for salmon. Any catches must be reported to the Washington Department of Fish & Wildlife (https://fishhunt.dfw.wa.gov). Fishing regulations vary throughout the park, so always check with the National Park Service for information. Licenses are available from sporting goods and outdoor supply stores around the peninsula.

Food and Accommodations

In addition to the springs, ★ **Sol Duc Hot Springs Resort** (12076 Sol Duc Hot Springs Rd., 360/327-3583 or 866/476-5382, www.olympicnationalparks.com, late-Mar.-Oct., $168 and up) has a restaurant, grocery store, and gift shop, plus cabins (some with kitchenettes). An RV campground is also available; reservations are advised.

Inside Sol Duc Hot Springs Resort, **The Springs Restaurant** (12076 Sol Duc Hot Springs Rd., 360/327-3583, $14-34) serves Northwest cuisine, and the **Poolside Deli** (360/327-3583, $5-20) has lots of snacks, sandwiches, and cold drinks. There's also an espresso bar for a pick-me-up.

Sol Duc Campground (360/327-3534, $21 walk-in, $21 per site) is open year-round and has 82 sites right along the river and a short walk away from the hot springs. Campsite reservations are available for summer stays.

Information and Services

Eagle Ranger Station (12 miles south of US-101 on Sol Duc Hot Springs Rd., 360/327-3534) is usually open in summer. **Sol Duc Hot Springs Resort** (12076 Sol Duc Hot Springs Rd., 360/327-3583 or 866/476-5382, www.olympicnationalparks.com) has a small store with snacks and basic personal items.

the Sol Duc River

The **Fairholm General Store** (221121 US-101, 360/928-3020, www.fairholm-store.com, 9am-7:30pm May-Oct.) sells groceries and gasoline, and offers boat rentals. The store is easily found on the west side of Lake Crescent. Restroom facilities are also available.

Campgrounds have adjacent picnic areas with tables, limited shelters, and restrooms, but no cooking facilities.

Drinking water is available at ranger stations, interpretive centers, and inside the campgrounds.

Pets and bicycles are not permitted on trails.

◆ WA-113 to WA-112: Neah Bay and Cape Flattery

Off US-101, WA-113 leads to WA-112 and the twin towns of **Clallam Bay** and **Sekiu** (SEE-kyoo), which are just a mile apart

on the Strait of Juan de Fuca. These two towns offer basic services but not much else. Heading west from Sekiu on WA-112 is one of the most dramatic shoreline drives in Washington: The narrow road winds along cliff faces and past extraordinary views. At the end of the road, in virtual isolation, the 44-square-mile **Makah Indian Reservation** (www.makah. com) sits on Cape Flattery at the northwesternmost point of the contiguous United States. A **recreation permit** ($10-15 per car) is required to enter the reservation; it can be purchased at the Makah Cultural and Research Center, Makah Marina, Washburn's General Store, or Neah Bay Charter & Tackle.

Getting There
US-101 meets WA-113 N. 15.4 miles east of Sol Duc Rd., at Sappho (12.3 miles north of Forks). Take WA-113 9.8 miles to reach WA-112 W., which passes Clallum (at 5.9 miles) and Sekiu (at 8.2 miles) along its 26.5 mile drive to Neah Bay.

Sights
In 1970, a powerful storm and the resulting tidal erosion unearthed an ancient Makah fishing village that had long been buried. Thousands of artifacts dating back 1,600-2,000 years were discovered, including harpoons, hooks, baskets, mats, cedar rope, paddles, carvings, and even full longhouse structures. Many of these artifacts are displayed at the **Makah Cultural and Research Center** (WA-112 and 1800 Bayview Ave., 360/645-2711, www.makah.com, 10am-5pm daily, reservations required, $5 adults, $4 seniors and students). Private tours of the museum and the archaeological site can be arranged.

Recreation
Scenic hiking trails trace the coastline, offering gorgeous views. To reach the trailhead, follow the WA-112 until it ends, then turn left on Fort Street. After two blocks, turn right on 3rd Avenue and

head southwest on Cape Flattery Road, which loops counter-clockwise around the reservation for 8 miles before becoming Cape Loop Road and ending up at the trailhead. The **Cape Flattery Trail** is one of the most beautiful scenic hikes on the Makah Reservation. A 0.75-mile boardwalk leads down to the rocky coastline with views of the 1858 Cape Flattery Lighthouse on Tatoosh Island. A dump lies along the route, so beware of unpleasant odors, especially on a warm summer day. Four observation decks offer breathtaking views of the Olympic Coast National Marine Sanctuary, which harbors a diverse collection of marinelife and wildlife, including over 239 species of birds. The trail continues around the cape in a 16-mile loop, passing a small waterfall on the way back to Neah Bay.

The **Ozette Triangle** is a remarkable day trip that connects the **Cape Alava Trail** to **Sand Point Loop.** Take WA-112 west to Sekiu. The road descends and winds its way toward Lake Ozette. Turn left on the Hoko-Ozette Road and take it to the end. Head to the Ozette Ranger Station, where restrooms and water are available, to reach the trailhead. Take the Cape Alava Trail through hemlock, cedar, and Sitka stands to a bridge. The trail climbs to a crest with views of a long abandoned homestead at Ahlstroms Prairie. At Cape Alava, enjoy views of Cannonball Island and Ozette Island offshore, where you may also see whales. Head south to the circular red-black symbol. To the right, ancient Makah petroglyphs can be seen carved into the large rock, Wedding Rock, depicting images of marine mammals. Continue on to Sand Point, then return three miles following the trail through the forest to Lake Ozette along nine-mile Sand Point Loop.

Food and Accommodations

The few restaurants in Neah Bay are more casual and personal than they are

a rocky coast on the strait of Juan de Fuca, near Neah Bay

touristy, though every place seems to have a view of the bay. Fry bread tacos and pies are the specialty at cozy **Pat's Place** (1111 Bay View Ave., noon-6pm Tues., Wed., and Fri., noon-5:30pm Thurs. and Sun., $4-8). Fry bread isn't native to the Makah, but the recipes been shared among native reservations. Nearby, **Linda's Wood Fired Kitchen** (1110 Bay View Ave., 360/640-2192, noon-7pm Tues.-Sun., $3-10), also cozy, uses its oven both to make pizza and to grill fresh local catch.

Camping

Stay overnight at **Ozette Campground** (21083 Hoko Ozette Rd., 360/963-2725, $20), where tents and RVs are welcome, or head back to Neah Bay and relax in a beachfront cabin. Contact the **Olympic National Park Visitor Center** (3002 Mount Angeles Rd., 360/565-3100, www.nps.gov) for backcountry camping reservations, permits, and trail conditions.

Forks

The westernmost incorporated city in the Lower 48, **Forks** is the economic center and logging capital of the western Olympic Peninsula—a big handle for this little town with one main drag. Since the spotted-owl controversy began, logging in this area has been severely curtailed on Forest Service lands, and Forks went into something of a depression as loggers searched for alternative means of earning a living. In recent years the town has diversified, emphasizing the clean air, remote location, and abundance of recreational possibilities within a few miles in any direction at Olympic National Park or the Pacific Coast beaches. Tourism here has seen a boost thanks to author Stephanie Meyer, who chose Forks as the setting for her best-selling *Twilight* books.

Getting There

To reach Forks, take US-101 from Lake Crescent (36 miles, 45 minutes) or Sol Duc Hot Springs Road (27.5 miles, 30 minutes). From Neah Bay, take WA-112 E. to WA-113 S. (26.5 miles) to US-101 (10 miles), which travels 12.3 miles to Forks; it'll take 1 hour and 10 minutes.

Sights

The **Forks Timber Museum** (1421 S. Forks Ave./US-101, 360/374-9663, www.forkstimbermuseum.org, 10am-4pm Mon.-Fri., 11am-4pm Sun., 10am-5pm Mon.-Sat. summer, $3 adults, free children under 12) has historical exhibits that include a steam donkey, a logging camp bunkhouse, old logging equipment, and various pioneer implements. The real surprise is a large 150-year-old canoe that was discovered by loggers in 1990. Out front is a memorial to loggers killed in the woods, along with a replica of a fire lookout tower.

While there's no dedicated *Twilight* museum for fans of the popular vampire series, tours are available with advance notice through **Leppell's Flower and Gifts** (130 Spartan Ave., 360/374-6931), with a two-hour morning tour (10am, $30) and a three-hour afternoon tour including the beach at La Push (1pm, $45).

Or, visit the **Forks Chamber of Commerce Visitor Center** (1411 S. Forks Ave., 360/374-2531 or 800/443-6757, www.forkswa.com, 10am-4pm Mon.-Sat., 11am-4pm Sun.) for a map of *Twilight* points of interest, including Bella's old Chevy pickup, and take a self-guided tour.

Food

Loggers stop for coffee and doughnuts at the **Forks Coffee Shop** (241 S. Forks Ave., 360/374-6769, 5:30am-8pm daily, $4-10), where friendly waitresses serve dependable food three meals a day. **The In Place** (320 S. Forks Ave., 360/374-4004, 6am-9pm daily, $5-17) makes hot sandwiches and great mushroom bacon burgers. They also serve pasta, steak, and seafood dinners.

Accommodations

Motels make up the bulk of places to stay in Forks, like the bare-bones **Forks Motel** (351 S. Forks Ave., 360/374-6243, www.forksmotel.com, $95 and up). Or, pay a little extra for a red-and-black *Twilight*-themed room at **Pacific Inn Motel** (352 S. Forks Ave., 360/374-9400 or 800/235-7344, www.pacificinnmotel.com, from $104 and up), which also offers clean, standard-issue rooms.

Located off South Forks Avenue, **Dew Drop Inn** (100 Fern Hill Rd., 360/374-4055 or 888/433-9376, www.dewdropinnmotel.com, $114 and up) has one- and two-bed rooms, each with a private balcony or patio.

Designated the "Cullen House," **Miller Tree Inn** (654 E. Division, 360/374-6806, www.millertreeinn.com, $170 and up) is a bed-and-breakfast with seven guest rooms (private or shared baths) in a beautiful three-story 1914 homestead set on a shady lot on the edge of town. The back deck has a large hot tub.

Second Beach, La Push

Information and Services

In addition to *Twilight* information, the **Forks Chamber of Commerce Visitor Center** (1411 S. Forks Ave., 360/374-2531 or 800/443-6757, www.forkswa.com, 10am-4pm Mon.-Sat., 11am-4pm Sun.) is a great resource for other area information.

The **Forks Recreation Information Center** (551 N. Forks Ave., 360/374-7566, 8:30am-12:30pm and 1:30pm-5:30pm daily in summer, Mon.-Fri. only the rest of the year) is housed in the transportation building in Forks. Stop here for recreation information, maps, and handouts, and to take a look at the big 3-D model of the Olympic Peninsula.

✦ WA-110: La Push and Rialto Beach

At the north end of Forks, the WA-110—a.k.a. La Push Road—splits west off US-101. Take it 14 miles till it ends to wind up at the coastal village of **La Push** (pop. 2,000), home of the Quileute tribe. In mid-July the tribe hosts **Quileute Days,** with a traditional fish bake, canoe races, and fireworks. La Push is also known for being a Twilight locale, and for its three scenic beaches.

Or, go nine miles and turn right onto Mora Road to head instead to Rialto Beach, which sits, desolate, across the Quillayute River mouth from La Push. You can walk along the beach for miles without anyone around.

Recreation

You'll see **First Beach** when you hit the coast driving on La Push Road. But watch for signs to find the trailheads for a hike to the arch and stacks of wood-strewn **Second Beach** (0.75 mile) or **Third Beach** (1.4 miles). Camping is allowed at each for those with a **wilderness permit** (360/565-3100, www.nps.gov/olym).

Food and Accommodations

There's only one restaurant in La Push: **River's Edge** (41 Main St., 360/374-0777, 8am-8pm daily, $6-12) serves clam chowder, some local seafood, and sandwiches. Six miles east, a fast food counter and food market may be found at **Three Rivers Resort** (7764 La Push Rd., 360/374-5300, www.threeriversresortandguideservice.com, 8am-7pm daily summer, 9am-7pm daily winter, $6-15), just outside of Forks.

Two miles before Rialto, **Mora Campground** (360/374-5460, www.nps.gov, $20) offers a quiet place from which to explore the shore's driftwood, sea stacks, and tidepools. Surfers and kayakers love the powerful waves. Nature enthusiasts enjoy watching bald eagles and brown pelicans sail across the sky.

The **Quileute Oceanside Resort** (330 Ocean Front Dr., 360/374-5267, www.quileuteoceanside.com, $69 and up) offers several accommodation options, from simple cabins to deluxe duplexes. There are also two full-hookup RV parks and 20 beach campsites.

Information and Services

For a tide chart or local hiking information, the **Mora Ranger Station** (360/374-5460, www.nps.gov) is staffed daily June-August.

Bogachiel State Park

Six miles south of Forks on US-101, **Bogachiel State Park** (185983 US-101, 360/374-6356, www.parks.wa.gov) encompasses 123 acres on the usually clear Bogachiel River. (*Bogachiel* means "muddy waters" in the language of the local Quileute people.) Enjoy the short nature trail through a rainforest, or swim, paddle, or fish in the river—famous for its summer and winter steelhead, salmon, and trout. The park has bare-bones to full-utility **campsites** ($12-45, $19 for RV hookups) and is open year-round.

Right on the opposite side of the highway from the park entrance is Undi Road, which leads east five miles (the last two are gravel) to the **Bogachiel River Trailhead.** The trail follows the lush, infrequently visited valley of the Bogachiel River east for two miles through national forest land until reaching the edge of Olympic National Park, where the trail continues all the way up to **Seven Lakes Basin** (27 miles) or **Sol Duc Hot Springs** (27 miles). The lower section of trail in the rainforest is a lovely place for a day hike. Mountain bikers are allowed on the trail as far as the edge of the national park, but it's a pretty soggy ride.

★ Hoh Rain Forest

Olympic National Park is famous for the lush rainforests that carpet the western flanks of the mountains. The best known and most visited is **Hoh Rain Forest,** where annual rainfall averages over 10 feet. Vibrant foliage paints the dense landscape in an epic display of enormous

the Hall of Mosses Trail in Hoh Rain Forest

Sitka spruce and Douglas fir trees that tower into the sky. Some of the towering conifers are over 200 feet tall and up to 10 feet wide. Mist lingers between the trees and along the banks of streaming rivers. Damp beds of moss suck up moisture and spread across the ground and onto trees. Lacy ferns carpet the forest floor, and some even survive in the tops of the big-leaf and vine maples. Wandering into the Hoh Rain Forest is an adventure into another world, or so it would seem.

Getting There
One of the park's most famous sights is also one of its most remote. Fourteen miles south of Forks along US-101, the paved Upper Hoh Road heads east 19 miles into the Hoh Rain Forest. The drive from Forks takes about an hour.

Sights
A revered mountain of mystical creatures, **Mount Olympus** (7,828 feet) is the centerpiece of the Olympic Peninsula.

Though it's not the tallest mountain in western Washington, it does have a majestic allure that makes it a giant among higher peaks. In 1778, the British explorer John Meares said of the mountain, "If that not be the home where dwell the gods, it certainly is beautiful enough to be, and I therefore will call it Mount Olympus." But the mountain already had a name: The Quileute people called it Oksy.

Mount Olympus is the first peak that storms encounter, resulting in high accumulations of snow and rain. Nestled around Olympus are several glaciers. The largest, Blue Glacier, covers over 5.31 kilometers; the longest, Hoh Glacier, is over two miles long. The mountain gets about 12 feet of rain each year along its west side and nearby valleys, which aids the growth of the temperate forest. Along the eastern side is a rain shadow that receives only 25 inches every year, creating a drier climate.

Recreation
Hiking
Three short interpretive trails lead through the lush, spikemoss-draped forests behind the visitors center. A paved wheelchair-accessible **mini-trail** (truly mini at 0.1 mile total) is directly behind the center, and the **Hall of Mosses Trail** offers an easy 0.8-mile loop. **Spruce Nature Trail** covers a 1.25-mile loop that crosses a crystalline spring-fed creek and then touches on the muddy, glacially fed Hoh River.

More adventurous folks can head out on the **Hoh River Trail,** an 18-mile path that ends at Blue Glacier and is used to climb Mount Olympus. Hikers heading into the wilderness need to pick up permits at the visitors center or the **Wilderness Information Center** (3002 Mount Angeles Rd., 360/565-3100, www. nps.gov) in Port Angeles.

Climbing
Mountain and ice climbing is a popular

activity around Mount Olympus due to its triple peaks and glaciated surface. In good weather, climbing conditions are spectacular. But due to the heavily crevassed glaciers, winter months are considered very dangerous, and weather changes occur without warning with heavy fog making it difficult to navigate. Climbing the mountain requires experience and tools such as rope, ice axe, crevasse rescue gear, and crampons. The most ventured trail to the dome of the mountain is a flat 13-mile trail along the Hoh River. Massive trees cluster together, some in diameter of 20 feet. The trail ascends to Glacier Meadows, where you can begin the ascent across Blue Glacier and onward to the summit. Guided expeditions are available through **Mountain Madness** (3018 SW Charlestown St., Seattle, 206/937-8389, www.mountainmadness.com, $1,350).

Permits are required, and group climbers must camp at designated group camping sites. Information on trailhead shuttles, camping, and backcountry permits is available at the **Wilderness Information Center** (3002 Mount Angeles Rd., Port Angeles, 360/565-3100, www.nps.gov).

Accommodations

Not far away from the visitors center, the **Hoh Rain Forest Campground** (18113 Upper Hoh Rd., 360/374-6925, www.nps.gov, open year-round, $20/night) has 88 forested campsites nestled in the old-growth rainforest along Hoh River. Running water, toilets, and dump station are available.

There are **no restaurants or food options** in the Hoh Rain Forest area. Forks, about 30 miles away or a one-hour drive, offers more options for accommodations and food.

Information and Services

The **Hoh Rain Forest Visitor Center** (Upper Hoh Rd., 360/374-6925, www.nps.gov/olym, 9am-5pm daily) offers interpretive exhibits and summertime guided walks and campfire programs. Stop by for brochures, information, books, and educational exhibits on the life of the forest and the climate.

Ruby Beach and Kalaloch

US-101 rejoins the coast at **Ruby Beach,** just south of the mouth of the Hoh River, about 27 miles from Forks and 14 miles from Upper Hoh Road. You quickly become aware that this part of Washington's coastline—from the state's northwestern corner at Neah Bay to the Quinault Reservation—is a picture of how the Pacific Coast looks in brochures and calendar photos: pristine beaches, pounding waves, trees sculpted by relentless sea breezes.

A very popular trail leads down to a beautiful sandy shoreline dotted with red pebbles (sadly not actual rubies), with piles of driftwood and the flat top of **Destruction Island** several miles offshore. The island is capped by a 94-foot lighthouse.

South of Ruby Beach, the highway cruises along the bluff, with five more trails dropping to shoreline beaches, creatively named Beach 6, Beach 5, and so on, to Beach 1. A massive western red cedar tree stands just off the highway near Beach 6.

Accommodations and Camping

Nine miles south of Ruby Beach, the ★ **Kalaloch Lodge** (157151 US-101, 360/962-2271 or 866/662-9928, www.thekalalochlodge.com, $215 and up) consists of a main lodge, cabins, and a motel. The only TV is in the common area sitting room. Some of the cabins have kitchens and offer waterside views. Make reservations far ahead for the nicest rooms or the bluff cabins; a year ahead of time is recommended for peak season (July-Aug.). The lodge also has a café, gift shop, and lounge. The on-site **Creekside Restaurant** (157151 US-101, 360/962-2271, ext. 4007, www.thekalalochlodge.com, $15-38) has a great menu selection that ranges from French toast and omelets to burgers and king salmon.

The National Park Service's **Kalaloch Campground** (360/565-3130 or 877/444-6777, www.recreation.gov, $22) sits on a bluff overlooking the beach. It takes reservations for summer only.

Information and Services

Across from the lodge is the Park Service's **Kalaloch Visitor Information Center** (156954 US-101, 360/962-2283, www.nps.gov, May-Sept.), where you'll find natural history books, maps, pamphlets, and tide charts.

Lake Quinault

Surrounded by steep mountains and dense rainforest, **Lake Quinault** is bordered on the northwest by Olympic National Park and on the southeast by Olympic National Forest; the lake itself and land to the southeast are part of the Quinault Reservation and subject to Quinault regulations. Located at the southwestern edge of Olympic National Park, Lake Quinault is a hub of outdoor activity during the summer months. This very scenic, tree-rimmed lake is surrounded by cozy lodges, and hiking trails provide a chance to get a taste of the rainforest that once covered vast stretches of the Olympic Peninsula.

The **Quinault Rain Forest** is one of three major rainforests that survive on the peninsula. Here the annual average rainfall is 167 inches, resulting in enormous trees, lush vegetation, and moss-carpeted buildings. During the rainy winter months, bring your heavy rain gear and rubber boots, not just a nylon poncho and running shoes. If you're prepared, a hike in the rain provides a great chance to see this soggy and verdant place

at its truest. July and August are the driest months, but even then it rains an average of three inches. Typical Decembers see 22 inches of precipitation.

Getting There

US-101 borders Lake Quinault, which is approximately 70 miles (about 1.5 hours) south of Forks and 35 miles south of Kalaloch. To reach the Quinault Rain Forest Ranger Station, take the North Shore Road turnoff; to reach the U.S. Forest Services Ranger District Office, take the South Shore Road turnoff.

Recreation
Hiking

The Quinault area is a hiker's paradise, with trails for all abilities snaking through a diversity of terrain. A good hike for those traveling with small children begins at North Fork Campground, following the **Three Lakes Trail** for the first mile to **Irely Lake.** The aptly named half-mile **Maple Glade Rain Forest Trail** begins at the Park Service's Quinault Rain Forest Ranger Station on North Shore Road and traverses a glade of maples.

Another easy jaunt is the **Cascading Terraces Trail,** a one-mile loop that begins at the Graves Creek Campground on the South Shore Road. From the same starting point, the **Enchanted Valley Trail** takes you through a wonderful rainforest along the South Fork of the Quinault River. Day hikers often go as far as Pony Bridge, 2.5 miles each way, but more ambitious folks can continue to Dosewallips, a one-way distance of 28 miles.

Food and Accommodations

Built in 1926 over a period of just 10 weeks, the rambling ★ **Lake Quinault Lodge** (345 S. Shore Rd., 360/288-2900 or 800/562-6672, www.olympicnationalparks.com, $229 and up) occupies a magnificent setting of grassy lawns bordering Lake Quinault. This is how a lodge should look, with a darkly regal interior and a big central fireplace surrounded by comfortable couches and tables. Accommodations include a variety of rooms in the main lodge and in newer buildings nearby and include an indoor pool and sauna. Some of the rooms have kitchenettes. Call two months ahead to be sure of space in midsummer. The **Roosevelt Dining Room** (345 S. Shore Rd., 360/288-2900, 7:30am-9pm daily summer, 7:30am-8pm daily winter, $18-34) in the lodge offers panoramic views of the mountains and lake, as well as menu items that will please, especially their homemade marionberry cobbler. Get groceries at the **Mercantile** (352 S. Shore Rd.) across the road, which also sells pizzas, burgers, milkshakes, espresso, and sandwiches.

Rain Forest Resort Village (516 S. Shore Rd., 360/288-2535 or 800/255-6936, www.rainforestresort.com, $135 and up) has cabins with fireplaces (and some with kitchens). The resort also has a good **restaurant and lounge,** a general store, laundry, RV hookups, and canoe rentals. The world's largest Sitka spruce is on the resort grounds. This thousand-year-old behemoth is more than 19 feet in diameter and 191 feet tall.

Camping

Choose from a number of public campgrounds in the Quinault Lake area. The Forest Service maintains three campgrounds on South Shore Road, east of US-101: **Falls Creek** (2.5 miles east, 360/288-2900, late May-mid-Sept., $25/vehicle plus $7 for additional vehicle, $20/walk-in); **Gatton Creek** (3 miles east, 360/288-2900, late May-mid-Sept., $20, walk-in only, no water); and **Willaby** (1.8 miles east, $25, water), which has a boat ramp.

Olympic National Park campgrounds are more scattered. The spacious 30-site **Graves Creek** (19.1 miles east, 360/565-3131, www.nps.gov, open year-round, $20) is accessed by slow, unpaved

roads. Same with the primitive **North Fork Campground** (16.4 miles east, mid-May-late Sept., $10), which does not have running water. Not recommended for RVs.

Park RVs at the private **Rain Forest Village Resort** (S. Shore Rd., 360/288-2535 or 800/255-6936, www.rainforestresort.com, $35), the only campground with showers.

Information and Services

The **U.S. Forest Services Ranger District Office** (353 S. Shore Rd., 360/288-2525, 8am-4pm daily Memorial Day-Labor Day, Mon.-Fri. the rest of the year) is next door to Quinault Lodge on the south side of the lake. They have informative handouts and offer guided nature walks and talks at the lodge in the summer.

Stop by the Olympic National Park's **Quinault Rain Forest Ranger Station** (5.8 miles up N. Shore Rd., Thurs.-Mon. June-Labor Day (funding dependent), open intermittently the rest of the year) for brochures, maps, and information on the park. The area around the station is a good place to see Roosevelt elk, especially in early summer and after September.

WA-109 to WA-115: Ocean Shores

Sixteen miles south of Quinault, WA-109 hooks west from US-101 around the northern edge of North Bay, winding up at a forested bluff. There, at the southern tip of Lang Lake, WA-115 (milepost 16) continues south to **Ocean Shores.** This six-mile stretch of wide, sandy beaches backed by grassy dunes attracts resort-goers to build sandcastles, fly kites, surf, and, of course, sunbathe.

Recreation

Explore the beach by horseback with a friendly guide from **Honey Pearl Ranch**

Horseback Riding (32 Humptulips Valley Rd., 360/209-0332, www.honeypearlranch.com, $25/hour, 10am-4pm daily). If the thought of sand between your toes doesn't appeal to you, put on a pair of golf shoes at **Ocean Shores Golf Course** (500 Canal Dr. NE, 360/289-3357, www.oceanshoresgolf.com), an 18-hole championship course.

Food and Accommodations

Quinault Beach Resort and Casino (78 WA-115, 360/289-9466 or 888/461-2214, www.quinaultbeachresort.com, $139 and up) offers spacious rooms, oceanfront views, a spa, and fine dining—plus RV parking ($5 and up). Get a good, affordable meal at **Alec's by the Sea** (131 E. Chance A La Mer NE, 360/289-4026, 11:30am-8pm Sun.-Thurs., 11:30am-9pm Fri.-Sat., $12-26). They have a big menu selection with great burgers, grilled steaks, pasta, salads, and steamed clams. Get a full kitchen suite at **Canterbury Inn** (643 Ocean Shores Blvd. NW, 360/289-9586, www.canterburyinn.com, $110 and up).

Information

For local information, **Ocean Shores Chamber of Commerce Visitor Information Center** (120-B W. Chance A La Mer, 360/289-2451, www.osgov.com, 9am-5pm Mon.-Fri., 10am-4pm Sat.-Sun.) provides brochures for all sorts of local activities, including area maps.

Grays Harbor: Aberdeen and Hoquiam

About 45 miles (1 hour) south of Lake Quinault, **Aberdeen** (pop. 16,255) and **Hoquiam** (HO-qwee-um, pop. 8,389) are twin cities on the easterly tip of Grays Harbor, separated by the Hoquiam River.

Between the sleepy towns, Aberdeen is better known to Washingtonians for being the home town of Seattle grunge icon Kurt Cobain, of the band Nirvana.

Grays Harbor Historical Seaport (500 N. Custer St., 360/352-8611, www.historicalseaport.com) celebrates the area's maritime past with its full-scale replica of *Lady Washington,* the first American ship to sail around South America to reach the western coast of North America. When not visiting other ports, it and the *Hawaiian Chieftain,* which also calls Aberdeen home, are open for tours ($3 donation) and excellent two- to three-hour sailing trips ($49 and up).

The 26-room mansion of the son of a wealthy lumber magnate is now the **Polson Museum** (1611 Riverside Ave., 360/533-5862, www.polsonmuseum.org, 11am-4pm Wed.-Sat., noon-4pm Sun., $4 adults, $2 students, $1 under 12) in Hoquiam. The museum houses all sorts of memorabilia: a magnificent old grandfather clock, a fun model railroad, a model of an old logging camp, a two-man chainsaw, and even an old boxing bag. The adjacent park holds a rose garden, historical logging equipment, and a blacksmith shop.

❧ WA-105: Westport and Tokeland

Westport (pop. 2,018) once called itself "The Salmon Capital of the World," and it remains one of the most active ports in Washington. Charter services and commercial fishing and crabbing boats line the waterfront alongside the expected shops selling saltwater taffy, kites, and souvenir kitsch. Chain-smoking fishermen drive beat-up old pickups through town, and local life revolves around the crab cannery and seafood markets. This area is popular for sportfishing but also offers long beaches, good surfing, and reasonably priced lodging.

Across the Chehalis River, south of Aberdeen, US-101 meets WA-105 S., which travels 21 miles (30 minutes) to Westport, and 33 miles (45 minutes) to Tokeland. About 20 miles southeast of Tokeland, WA-105 S. reconnects to US-101 in Raymond.

Sights and Recreation

Two towers overlook the water. A tall observation tower provides a fine vantage point to view freighter activity, scenery, sunsets, or an occasional whale, while a lower ramp tower looks into the marina. In front of this is a small memorial to fishermen lost at sea.

Westport Light State Park (1595 Ocean Ave., 360/268-9717, www.parks.wa.gov, 8am-10pm daily summer, 8am-8pm daily winter), about a mile south of Westhaven off WA-105 (continue straight when WA-105 goes left), is accessible on foot from Westhaven via a 1.3-mile paved boardwalk. The classic **lighthouse** inside the park—tallest on the West Coast—was built in 1898 and is visible from an observation platform on Ocean Avenue. The lighthouse originally stood much closer to the water, but the accretion of sand has pushed the beachfront seaward. The building is closed to the public.

The day-use only park covers 626-acres of peninsula separating the Pacific from Gray's Harbor, with sandy shores both on the ocean, and a crescent shaped harbor-side beach called Half Moon Bay. The beaches are popular among kite-flyers, rock-hounds, surfers, sea kayakers, and divers, with ocean perch offering the best shore fishing.

On WA-105, two miles south of Westport, **Twin Harbors State Park** (3120 WA-105, 360/268-9717 or 888/226-7688, www.parks.wa.gov, 8am-5pm daily, yurts $49-69) has campsites, a 0.75-mile sand dune nature trail, picnic areas, and a playground. This is one of the most popular oceanside campgrounds, especially when razor clam harvesting is allowed (usually March and October).

Take a charter boat to find the best **fishing,** not to mention having your fish cleaned and ready to cook by the time you get back to shore. Wander along Westhaven Drive to check out the various charter companies, or get a listing of boats from the visitors center. The charter services all charge about the same amount ($140-160), so when you call for reservations be sure to check whether the price includes bait and tackle, cleaning, and sales tax. Note, however, that most departures are at the frightfully early hour of 6am, with a return around 3:30pm.

Many of the charter operators also provide **whale-watching trips** (March-May, $35-45) when the gray whales are heading north from their winter quarters off Baja California. The passenger ferry to Ocean Shores is an inexpensive way to watch for whales that periodically wander into Grays Harbor.

Food and Accommodations

Harbor Resort Motel (871 Neddie Rose Dr., 360/268-0169, www.harborresort. com, $79 and up) has rooms with kitchenettes and cottages sleeping up to five. The cottages have private decks over the water. All rooms are decorated with antique furniture and nautical memorabilia. Many rooms have views over the harbor and marina.

In the tiny town of **Tokeland,** about 16 miles south of Westport off WA-105, is the **Tokeland Hotel** (100 Hotel Rd. at Kindred Rd., 360/267-7006, www.tokelandhotel.com, $89 and up). Built in 1885, it's said to be the oldest resort hotel in Washington and is now on the National Register of Historic Places. The spacious front lawn, brick fireplace, and jigsaw puzzles provide an air of relaxation.

Because of the early morning departure of fishing charters, several local Westport cafés are already open at 5am, including the very popular café at the **Inn of the Westwind** (2119 N. Nyhus St., 360/268-1315, 5:30am-2pm daily,

4:30am-2pm daily in salmon season, $9-18).

Buy freshly shucked oysters to go from **Brady's Oysters** (3714 Oyster Pl. E., 360/268-0077, www.bradysoysters. com, 9am-7pm daily). They were the first to grow oysters on suspended lines, a method that many claim produces a more delicately flavored oyster.

Information

Westport-Grayland Chamber of Commerce Visitors Center (2985 N. Montesano St., 360/268-9422 or 800/345-6223, www.westportgrayland-chamber. org) provides maps, brochures, and tour and charter information.

Willapa Bay: Raymond and South Bend

East and south from Tokeland, Washington's coastline wraps around Willapa Bay, a 25-mile-long inlet protected by the Long Beach Peninsula. It is believed to be the cleanest and least developed estuary on the West Coast of the Lower 48 states. Locals posit that these waters produce the best-tasting oysters in the nation (a claim disputed by folks in Grays Harbor). WA-105 and US-101 skirt Willapa's scenic marshy shoreline, and tree farms carpet the surrounding hills.

From Aberdeen, US-101 continues south for 25 miles (35 minutes) to the town of **Raymond.** Drive slowly through Raymond, in part to avoid a local speed trap, in part to take notice of metal sculptures positioned sporadically through town. If you feel like stopping, the **Dennis Company** (146 5th St., 360/942-2427, www.denniscompany.com, 7:30am-6pm Mon.-Fri., 8am-5:30pm Sat., 9am-5pm Sun.) is a big, old-fashioned dry goods store that features historical photos and a mural—said to be the largest in Washington—covering one wall of the building and depicting the early days of logging. Across the street is a display of antique logging and farm equipment in front of the **Northwest Carriage Museum** (314 Alder St., www.nwcarriagemuseum. org, 10am-4pm daily, $8 adults, $5 6-18) Hikers and cyclists will enjoy the 3.5-mile **Rails to Trails** paved path that follows the river from Raymond to South Bend.

Just four miles west of Raymond, **South Bend** calls itself "The Oyster Capital of the West." You can give some—or a lot—of them a try at **River View Dining** (618 W. Robert Bush Dr., 360/875-6155, 10am-8pm daily, $3-40). At **Robert Bush Park** (1101 W. Robert Bush Dr.), named for a hometown Medal of Honor-winning Navy corpsman, is a giant oyster shell purporting to be the world's largest.

Follow the signs up the hill to the 1910 **Pacific County Courthouse.** This "gilded palace of reckless extravagance," as it was called, was built in 1910 at the then-extravagant cost of $132,000. The immense stained-glass dome and mosaic-tile flooring are worth a look, but not everything is as it appears: The marble columns are actually concrete painted to look like marble. A county jail inmate painted the columns and the decorative panels inside. The courthouse's grounds—complete with a stocked duck pond—offer views of the hills and the town below.

Long Beach Peninsula

The **Long Beach Peninsula** is a 28-mile-long strip of sand that locals call the "World's Longest Beach." Whether or not that claim is technically true, this is one *very* long stretch of sand, and a favorite getaway for folks from Seattle and Portland.

US-101 hits the southern end of the Long Beach Peninsula and junctions with WA-103 (a.k.a. Pacific Hwy.), which climbs north to Leadbetter Point State Park at the tip of the peninsula. From south to north, the settlements on the peninsula are Ilwaco, Seaview, the

town of Long Beach, Klipsan Beach, and Ocean Park on the Pacific Ocean side. On the Willapa Bay side are Nahcotta and Oysterville.

Sights and Recreation

Contrary to expectations, the 28 miles of sandy beach on Long Beach Peninsula are not safe for swimming. Not only are there dangerous undertows and riptides, but rogue waves can occur, and there are no lifeguards. For kite enthusiasts, the beach at **Long Beach** is a delight. The walkable downtown offers little shops and souvenir joints.

It may be campy, but you definitely don't want to miss **Marsh's Free Museum** (409 Pacific Ave., 360/642-2188, www.marshfreemuseum.com, 9am-6pm Mon.-Fri., 9am-5pm Sat.-Sun.), a huge souvenir shop in downtown Long Beach. Inside is a delightful collection of the tasteless and bizarre, much of it from old amusement parks, traveling shows, and attics. You'll find an impressive collection of glass fishing balls, the world's largest frying pan, a vampire bat skeleton, and a two-headed calf. Drop a nickel for a flapper-era peep show, pay a dime to test your passion factor on the "throne of love." And don't miss "Jake the Alligator Man," stuck in a back corner inside a glass aquarium.

The northern tip of Long Beach Peninsula is capped by two publicly owned natural areas. **Leadbetter Point State Park** (360/642-3078, www.parks.state.wa.us) has a 1.5-mile trail through the evergreen forest, connecting its two parking lots. From the north lot, you can enter **Willapa National Wildlife Refuge** and walk through stunted lodgepole pine forests to beachgrass-covered sand dunes along the Pacific Ocean.

This area is also a very important

From top to bottom: the entrance to Forks Timber Museum; metal sculptures decorate the town of Raymond; the "world's largest oyster" in South Bend.

The Discovery Trail

Sculptures commemorating the Lewis and Clark expedition are found all along the Discovery Trail.

The Discovery Trail (17 miles round-trip) on the Long Beach Peninsula traces the footsteps of the Lewis and Clark expedition after their West Coast arrival in 1805. The trail joins the towns of Long Beach on the north end of the peninsula and Ilwaco, near the mouth of the Columbia River to the south. Many bike and hike the trail to enjoy its sandy dunes, tall grasses, and marshes filled with dragonflies. Migrating trumpeter swans draw bird-watchers. Wooden boardwalks provide elevated views of migrating gray whales in spring and fall.

The trail's interpretive markers provide an opportunity to appreciate both the area's beauty and its historic significance.

Standing beside the shore, *Clark's Tree,* a bronze sculpture by Stanley Wanlass, commemorates the pine tree that Clark inscribed with the words, "William Clark. Nov. 19, 1805. By land from the U. States." Another sculpture appears two miles along the trail, where a basalt monolith is inscribed with excerpts from Clark's journal. A 10-foot metal sturgeon, created by artist Jim Demetro, lies at the foot of a life-sized Clark, who gazes downward.

The trail does not continue to Cape Disappointment or to the Lewis and Clark Interpretive Center, but it is worth a side trip to gain a better perspective of the expedition. The Discovery Trail reaches its end at the Port of Ilwaco.

sanctuary for waterfowl, particularly during spring and fall migrations. Bird-watchers will see thousands (and sometimes hundreds of thousands) of black brant, Canada geese, dunlin, plover, sandpipers, and other birds during these times. The northern end of Willapa National Wildlife Refuge is closed to all entry April-August to protect the threatened snowy plover that nests on the dunes here. Fires and camping are not allowed.

Accommodations

Friendly with a funky sense of nostalgia, Seaview's **Sou'wester Lodge** (3728 J Pl., 360/642-2542, www.souwesterlodge. com, $113 and up) is an offbeat haven for those who appreciate a place with simple comforts. The accommodations include rooms in the stately three-story lodge built in 1892 as a summer estate by Henry Winslow Corbett, a wealthy timber baron, banker, and U.S. senator from Oregon. Outside are beach cottages and even a hodgepodge of 1950s-era trailers. Tent and RV spaces are also available.

Seaview's acclaimed **Shelburne Inn** (4415 Pacific Way, 360/642-2442 or 800/466-1896, www.theshelburneinn. com, $149 and up) is an elegant 1896 Victorian building. The oldest continuously used lodging place in Washington, the inn is packed with tasteful antiques, stained-glass windows (from an old English church), and original artwork, but no televisions. A full country breakfast is included; for many, it's the highlight of their stay. Beware of the ghost who is rumored to wander the third floor on some nights.

Information

Get information at the **Long Beach Peninsula Visitors Bureau** (3914 Pacific Way, Seaview, 360/642-2400 or 800/451-2542, www.funbeach.com, 9am-6pm Mon.-Sat.) at the junction of US-101 and WA-103.

⬦ WA-100: Cape Disappointment State Park

Located 2.5 miles southwest of Ilwaco on Washington's southernmost point, **Cape Disappointment State Park** (244 Robert Gray Dr., Ilwaco, 360/642-3078, www.parks.wa.gov, 6:30am-dusk) is the Long Beach Peninsula's most scenic state park. The name originated in 1788, when British fur trader John Meares was searching for the fabled Northwest Passage. He had heard tales of an enormous river near here from a Spaniard, Bruno Heceta, who had noted it in 1775. Meares failed to find the river, hence the disappointment that gives the cape its name.

In the 1,882-acre park, you'll find a museum dedicated to Lewis and Clark, century-old military fortifications,

Southern Washington coastline, near Cape Disappointment.

historic lighthouses, old-growth forests, white beaches, and dramatic vistas across the mouth of the Columbia River. There are also excellent **campsites** (reservations 888/226-7688, $12-31 tents, $30-42 RVs).

The must-see **Lewis and Clark Interpretive Center** (244 Robert Gray Dr., 360/642-3029, www.parks.wa.gov, 10am-5pm Wed.-Sun., $5 adults, $2.50 7-17) is a fascinating introduction to the duo's historic 1804-1806 expedition. Exhibits detail their trip up the Missouri River, over the Rockies, and then down the Columbia River. You'll learn about the various participants, the unusual air gun they used to impress local indigenous people, how they constructed dugout canoes, and the everyday experiences in their winter camp at Fort Clatsop. Expansive windows look out on Cape Disappointment Lighthouse, the Columbia River, and the mighty Pacific. You're certain to see ships plying the waters offshore.

Cape Disappointment Lighthouse is the Northwest's oldest, built in 1856. It offers great vistas across the mouth of the Columbia. Follow the quarter-mile trail from the interpretive center or a steep quarter-mile path from the Coast Guard Station to reach it.

More than 230 ships were wrecked or sunk on the Columbia bar before jetties were constructed to control the sand. The longest of these, **North Jetty,** reaches a half mile out from the end of the cape and is a popular place to fish for salmon, rock cod, perch, and sea bass. Although the jetties succeeded in stabilizing the shifting Columbia bar, they also caused sand dunes to accumulate north of here and worsened an undertow that makes for dangerous swimming conditions.

Tiny **Waikiki Beach** is a favorite local spot for picnics and swimming in the summer (but no lifeguard). You can follow a trail uphill from Waikiki to the Lewis and Clark Interpretive Center, and then on to Cape Disappointment Lighthouse.

Oregon Coast

Dramatic and diverse scenery dominates the shores of Oregon, making it one of the most photographed coastlines in the country.

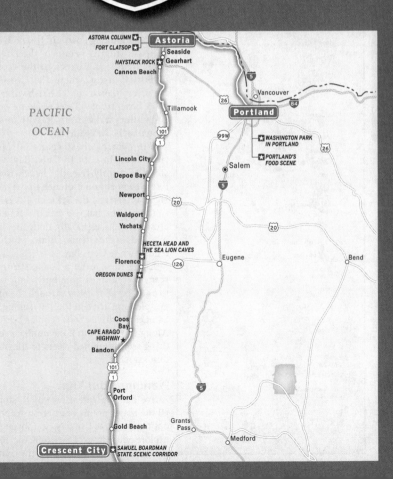

ASTORIA COLUMN
FORT CLATSOP
Astoria
Seaside
HAYSTACK ROCK Gearhart
Cannon Beach

PACIFIC
OCEAN

Tillamook

Vancouver

Portland

WASHINGTON PARK
IN PORTLAND
PORTLAND'S
FOOD SCENE

99W

Salem

Lincoln City
Depoe Bay
Newport
Waldport
Yachats
HECETA HEAD AND
THE SEA LION CAVES
Florence
OREGON DUNES

Eugene

Bend

Coos
Bay
CAPE ARAGO
HIGHWAY
Bandon

Port
Orford

Gold Beach   Grants
Pass
Crescent City SAMUEL BOARDMAN   Medford
STATE SCENIC CORRIDOR

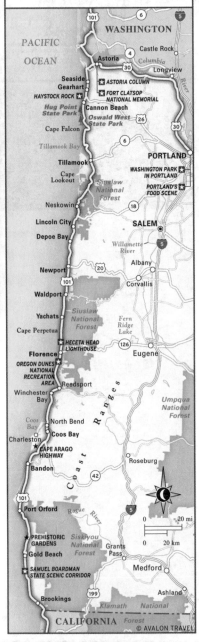

Coastal Oregon

Resort towns and historical villages occasionally pop up between windswept beaches, evergreen forests, vast sand dunes, massive rock arches, and towering sea cliffs.

Oregon's north coast stretches from the swift-flowing Columbia River at Astoria, one of the oldest American settlements west of the Rockies, to the rich dairy lands of Tillamook County. Scattered among the scenes of ship crossings and grazing cows are fragments of the past, from the ruins of the famous *Peter Iredale* shipwreck to the replica of Fort Clatsop, where the Corps of Discovery waited out the harsh winter of 1805. Beachfront villages welcome weekend visitors and vacationers with unique shops, cafés, and galleries.

The central coast spans 60 miles from Lincoln City to Coos Bay, with stops in family-friendly beach towns like Newport and Florence in between. Heceta Head and the Sea Lion Caves lure in the masses, but you can still find less crowded spots, especially along the shifting sands of the Oregon Dunes, which extend down to Coos Bay.

Along the southern coast, stunning scenery continues from one scenic cape to another, all the way through the most eye-pleasing drive in the state, along the Samuel Boardman State Scenic Corridor. Along the way, you'll encounter everything from untamed rivers to life-sized dinosaurs.

Planning Your Time

A five-day trip will allow you to stop at all the major points of interest. Another option is to take five days to thoroughly explore one section of the coast: the north coast, Astoria to Pacific City; the central

Highlights

★ **Washington Park in Portland:** At this sprawling park, you can stop and smell the roses, check out panoramic views of the city, and get a taste of Japan all in one go (page 97).

★ **Portland's Food Scene:** Portland has led the West Coast in locally sourced, detail-oriented cuisine for decades (page 98).

★ **Astoria Column:** Climbing its 164 steps offers views from the Cascades south to Tillamook Head (page 106).

★ **Fort Clatsop:** The centerpiece of Lewis and Clark National Historical Park is a reconstruction of the explorers' encampment during the grueling winter of 1805-1806 (page 108).

★ **Haystack Rock:** This icon of the Oregon coast attracts seabirds, marinelife, and photo-happy road-trippers (page 113).

★ **Heceta Head and the Sea Lion Caves:** At 150 feet above the ocean, a photogenic lighthouse stands watch

over the sea lion habitat below (page 131).

★ **Oregon Dunes:** The artistry of these crests of sand—some as high as 500 feet—inspired Frank Herbert's iconic sci-fi novel (page 135).

★ **Samuel Boardman State Scenic Corridor:** This gorgeous drive encapsulates the beauty of the Oregon coast (page 144).

Best Hotels

★ **Sentinel:** Luxury comes at an affordable price at this ideally located hotel in downtown Portland (page 105).

★ **Hotel Vintage:** This landmark Portland hotel blends historical significance with modern-day elegance (page 106).

★ **Cannery Pier Hotel:** Astoria's best hotel extends out onto the Columbia River for incomparable views (page 112).

★ **Stephanie Inn:** This enchanting Cannon Beach hotel is great for a romantic getaway (page 117).

★ **Sylvia Beach Hotel:** The literary decor of this Newport hotel, with rooms dedicated to authors like Jane Austen, makes it perfect for curling up with a good book (page 129).

★ **Landmark Inn:** The hilltop location of this hotel in Florence affords it not only great views but also proximity to restaurants and shopping (page 135).

★ **Edwin K. B&B:** This elegant 1914 home now hosts guests and treats them to five-course breakfasts (page 135).

coast, Lincoln City to Florence; or the south coast, Reedsport to Brookings.

Although all towns along the coastline offer lodging, food, and fuel, larger towns and resort destinations such as Astoria, Cannon Beach, Newport, Florence, and Bandon have more travel-friendly options.

The Pacific Coast Highway through Oregon is well maintained. Numerous twists and sharp turns hugging the edges of high cliffs provide phenomenal views and treacherous driving. Allow extra time to safely navigate the roadway.

Getting There
Car

Interstate-5 (I-5), the major north-south artery of the West Coast, connects Oregon to Washington in the north and California in the south. The most viable highway for inbound travelers from the east is I-84, connecting Oregon to Idaho. I-84 extends west all the way to Portland.

The great Columbia River is the border between Oregon and Washington, linked together by the Astoria-Megler Bridge in the north coast town of Astoria and by the I-5 Bridge in Portland.

The central coast can be approached from Eugene via OR-126, which travels east to the seaside town of Florence.

The south coast is easily accessed from Medford via US-199 south. The highway dips into Northern California and then curves up to the Oregon coast town of Brookings.

Air

Two international airports provide the main entry to the state. **Portland International** (PDX, 7000 NE Airport Way, 877/739-4636, www.pdx.com) offers regular nonstop flights. The other option is Seattle's **Seattle-Tacoma International Airport** (SEA, 800/544-1965 or 206/787-5388, www.portseattle.org/seatac), which is only a 2.5-hour drive from Portland, over the Washington border.

A few smaller regional airports offer limited domestic service. **Eugene** (EUG, 28801 Douglas Dr., 541/682-5544, www.flyeug.com), also known as Mahlon Sweet Field, provides service to a variety of metropolitan cities. Tiny **Southwest Oregon Regional Airport/North Bend** (OTH, 1100 Airport Ln., www.cooscountyairportdistrict.com) is the gateway to the

Best Restaurants

★ **Tasty & Alder:** Downtown Portland's wood-fire restaurant more than lives up to its name (page 99).

★ **Pok Pok:** This affordable street Thai restaurant may be Portland's most celebrated (page 100).

★ **Apizza Scholls:** This humble beer and vintage arcade place is hailed as one of America's best pizza spots (page 100).

★ **Fort George Brewery & Public House:** Enjoy world-class beer, elevated pub fare, and a river view upstairs from a favorite regional brewery (page 110).

★ **Cannon Beach Café:** This Parisian-style eatery is the place for a fine meal in Cannon Beach (page 115).

★ **Tillamook Cheese Factory:** The cheese is good, but Tillamook's incredibly smooth, creamy ice cream is the number one reason to stop here (page 118).

★ **Tables of Content:** Make new friends over delicious family-style meals at Sylvia Beach Hotel's restaurant (page 128).

★ **Waterfront Depot:** Located in an old train station, this fine dining establishment in Florence has charm to spare (page 133).

coast, with limited flights to Denver, Portland, and San Francisco. **Rogue Valley International/Medford Airport** (1000 Terminal Loop Pkwy., 541/776-7222, www.jacksoncountyor.org/airport) is the southernmost Oregon stop, located in Medford, connecting to major West Coast cities from Seattle through Los Angeles.

Train

Amtrak Coast Starlight (800 NW 6th Ave., 800/872-7245, www.amtrak.com) train connects Portland with Seattle, San Francisco, Los Angeles, and San Diego. Amtrak also runs the **Cascade Line** (800/872-7245, www.amtrakcascades.com), which runs between Eugene, Oregon, and Vancouver, British Columbia, with stops in Portland and Seattle. International visitors can buy an unlimited travel USA Rail Pass, good for 15, 30, or 45 days.

Bus

Greyhound buses (550 NW 6th Ave., 800/231-2222 or 503/243-2361, www.greyhound.com) provide service nationwide, and often work in tandem with Amtrak. Stations are located in downtown areas.

BoltBus (728 NW Everett St., 877/265-8287, www.boltbus.com) is the cheapest way to travel south from Vancouver, British Columbia, with stops in Seattle, Portland, and Eugene.

Fuel and Services

All **gas stations** in Oregon are **full service** by law; just pull up to a pump and an attendant will fill your tank for you. Oregon makes the top 10 list of most expensive states for gasoline—so expect to pay a little more.

There are 85 parks along US-101 with public facilities, as well as rest stops (some have coffee) and roadside pullouts.

To receive reports on **road conditions,** call **511.** If your phone carrier does not support 511, call toll-free 800/977-6368.

For **emergency assistance** and services, call **911.**

OREGON COAST

Downtown Portland

Portland

Rallying behind the unofficial slogan "Keep Portland Weird," Oregon's largest city embodies its state's prideful independent streak. Even in the mass media age, a healthy mix of entrepreneurial spirit, progressive values, and creative self-expression has helped **Portland** (pop. 639,863) maintain a grassroots culture unlike any other city in America. It has long attracted adventurous spirits—usually people who appreciate the city's originality as well as its many green, outdoor spaces.

Despite being 80 miles inland from the Pacific, Portland has plenty of waterfront. It's flanked to the north by the Columbia River—also the state border with Washington—and split down the center by the Willamette River, where 11 bridges connect the city's east and west sides. Portland's urban center resides around downtown, Old Town-Chinatown, and the Pearl District, all found in the compact southwest (SW) and northwest (NW) quadrants (delineated by Burnside Street). The city's quirky homegrown character, famously lampooned by the popular TV show *Portlandia,* may best be experienced exploring neighborhoods like Belmont, Hawthorne, and Division, in the sprawling southeast (SE).

Public parks abound in Portland, along the rivers, throughout the surrounding forest, and heading into snowcapped Mount Hood to the east. They make hiking and biking a fruitful endeavor, even if you don't stray far from urban areas. And it behooves you to work up an appetite. Portland has a fantastic food and beverage scene, including nationally renowned restaurants, award-winning craft beer, and world-class coffee. Portland also has more bookstores and movie theaters per capita than any other U.S. city—you may often drink coffee in the former, beer in the latter.

Getting There and Around

The drive direct from Seattle to Portland on I-5 takes about three hours (175 miles), without traffic. Coming from the Olympic Peninsula and Washington coast highway, three routes connect US-101 to I-5 to access the city: US-12 east from Aberdeen (56 miles); WA-6 east from Raymond (50 miles); and WA-4 east out of Nemah (60 miles).

Air

Portland International (PDX) (7000 NE Airport Way, 877/739-4636 or 503/460-4234, www.pdx.com) is within 10 miles of downtown. The **MAX Light Rail system** connects to downtown; purchase your ticket from the kiosks located on the airport station platform and take the red line.

Public Transit

Getting around spirited Portland is a breeze thanks to an efficient, connected, multi-transportation system. **TriMet** (503/238-7433, www.trimet.org) serves most of the metro area with bus ($2.50 for 2 hours, $5 all day) and light-rail lines (every 15 minutes 5am-midnight daily, $2.50 adults, $1 seniors), which also connect with the **Portland Streetcar** (503/823-2900, www.portlandstreetcar. org, $2).

Parking

SmartPark (503/790-9302, www.portlandoregon.gov, $1.60/hour, $7 for 4 hours, rates subject to change) operates the most affordable parking garages in the city. Find them downtown at SW 10th and Yamhill, SW 4th and Yamhill, SW 3rd and Alder, SW 1st and Jefferson, and NW Naito and Davis.

Driving to the Coast

To get to the Oregon coast from Portland, take I-405 North from West Burnside Street to I-5 North; exit 36 connects with US-30 West. Route 30 follows the trail taken by the Lewis and Clark expedition.

Two Days in Portland

Find pristinely sculpted serenity in Portland's Japanese Garden.

Day 1

Invest a little time to stand in line for sweet treats at iconic **Voodoo Doughnut** (page 99), only a short stroll from **Old Town-Chinatown** (page 96) and its serene **Lan Su Chinese Garden** (page 97). Make your way east following a pleasant riverwalk at **Tom McCall Waterfront Park** (page 95), moving south to find the stern-wheeler *Portland* and a tour of the **Oregon Maritime Museum** (page 95).

Head east into downtown and the historic **Pioneer Courthouse Square** (page 95) at the corner of SW Broadway and Yamhill to catch the whimsical noon forecast of the *Weather Machine.* If skies are clear, eat lunch like the locals do: Head to SW 10th Avenue and Alder Street and grab a tasty bite from downtown's largest collection of **food carts** (page 99).

Then head back north toward the **Pearl District** (page 96) to spend the afternoon shopping, particularly browsing the endless aisles at **Powell's City of Books** (page 96). Bring your new purchases back to your room at the **Sentinel** (page 105) to read and relax before a memorable dinner at nearby **Tasty & Alder** (page 99), then cross the street to ponder over a thousand fine spirits at **Multnomah Whiskey Library** (page 101).

Day 2

Start with a healthy Scandinavian breakfast at **Café Broder** (page 100) to fuel a long morning exploration of Portland's green west side. First, follow the street signs off West Burnside to **Pittock Mansion** (page 98), worth a stop for its French-Renaissance architecture and panoramic views. Then it's off to **Washington Park** (page 97), where 160-plus acres and multiple attractions can occupy your time. Choose the **Oregon Zoo** (page 97), the **International Rose Test Garden** (page 97), or the gorgeous and meditative **Japanese Garden** (page 98).

Once you've earned an appetite, head southeast for pizza and arcade games at **Apizza Scholls** (page 100), then spend the late afternoon exploring hipster Portlandia, being sure to try the city's favorite ice cream at **Salt & Straw** (page 100) or most celebrated coffee at **Stumptown Coffee Roasters** (page 98). Cap your time on the east side with dinner including the famous fish sauce wings at **Pok Pok** (page 100) before settling down for craft beer at Portland's classic **Horse Brass Pub** (page 101). If you have the energy, see which bands are playing at rock venues **Doug Fir Lounge** (page 102) or **Crystal Ballroom** (page 102).

A two-lane road replaces the four-lane highway after about 25 miles, passing through sawmill towns, forested corridors, and alder trees. Following along the Columbia River and past the Lewis and Clark Wildlife Refuge, the highway arrives in Astoria. This 97-mile drive will take around 2 hours.

Sights
Downtown

Portland is walkable, with compact blocks and narrow streets that are easily navigated via car, bike, and public transportation. Most of the city's municipal building and hotels are concentrated here, including brand-name and indie retailers. During the holidays, "pop-up" shops appear, adding another dimension to the city's original character.

Pioneer Courthouse Square

Smack in the center of downtown is **Pioneer Courthouse Square.** Affectionately referred to as "Portland's living room," it's a magnet for locals and visitors alike, featuring an elaborate fountain, bronze statue, and outdoor chess tables. Every day at noon lights flash and trumpets blare as the 33-foot-tall *Weather Machine* releases a cloud of mist followed by a series of objects that pop out from the top: the sun for clear weather, a heron for cloudy weather, and a dragon for rainy weather. The **Pioneer Courthouse** (700 SW 6th Ave.) itself is the oldest federal building in the Northwest. The square is also a venue for annual events, speeches, and political demonstrations.

Portland Art Museum

A hallmark to the city's visual arts culture, the **Portland Art Museum** (1219 SW Park Ave., 503/226-2811, www.portlandartmuseum.org, 10am-5pm Tues.-Sun., 10am-8pm Thurs.-Fri., $20 adults, children under 18 free) has been around since 1892, making it the oldest museum in the Pacific Northwest. Its vast collection takes visitors on a journey around the world and through time, spanning ancient to modern art. Notable exhibits include Vincent van Gogh's "The Ox-Cart" and an extensive treasury of Native American artifacts.

Oregon Maritime Museum

If seagoing vessels make you weak in the knees, climb aboard the stern-wheeler *Portland,* the last operating stern-wheel steamboat in the United States. Moored on the Willamette River at downtown's Waterfront Park, it's been converted into the **Oregon Maritime Museum** (198 SW Naito Pkwy., 503/224-7724, www.oregonmaritimemuseum.org, 11am-4pm Mon., Wed., and Fri., $7 adults, $4 children 13-18), which preserves artifacts and memorabilia of the Northwest's seafaring past. There's a children's corner with nautical objects, a library with over 22,000 photographs that catalogue the region's maritime history, and a gift shop to take a piece of the past home with you.

Tom McCall Waterfront Park

Running a mile and a half along the west bank of the Willamette River, **Tom McCall Waterfront Park** (Naito Pkwy. between SW Harrison St. and NW Glisan St., 503/823-7529, www.portlandoregon.gov/parks, 5am-midnight daily) proves a popular stretch for people to walk, bike, or skate, passing under several bridges and a cherry tree grove. It also provides a venue for food, drink, and music festivals throughout the year.

Oregon Museum of Science and Industry

Science comes to life at OMSI, the **Oregon Museum of Science and Industry** (1945 SE Water Ave., 503/797-4000, www.omsi.edu, 9:30am-5:30pm Tues.-Sun., $14 adults, $9.75 children). Four levels brim with hundreds of interactive exhibits that challenge and entertain. Test your brainpower through hands-on lab exhibits, or watch a laser light show in the

planetarium. There's even a real submarine to explore: The USS *Blueback* (SS-581) is the U.S. Navy's last non-nuclear, fast-attack submarine. It was the sub used in the movie *The Hunt for Red October*.

Pearl District

Located on Portland's northwest side, between West Burnside Street to the south and the Willamette River to the north, the historical Pearl District has transformed from its industrial, working-class roots into a neighborhood of trendy shops and eateries, art galleries, walking parks, and upscale condominiums.

With three public parks, there is plenty of open space to stroll or read a book. **Jamison Square**'s simulated tidal pool fountain attracts families and people-watchers. **Tanner Springs Park** provides a walking trail and an opportunity to appreciate the renewed wetlands and creek. The largest park, **Field's Park,** lets dogs run free.

Powell's City of Books

The landmark **Powell's City of Books** (1005 W. Burnside St., 800/878-7323, www.powells.com, 11am-9pm daily) earns its name, with more than 1.5 million new and used books taking up residence in an entire city block. If you've finished the books you're traveling with, you may trade them at the front for store credit. Consult the bookstore's color-coded map to navigate Powell's thousands of shelves, or simply get lost browsing and let the right books find you.

Old Town-Chinatown

Portland's oldest neighborhood is sandwiched between the Pearl District to the north and downtown to the south. It encompasses the official historic districts of Skidmore-Old Town and Chinatown/

From top to bottom: Tom McCall Waterfront Park; the gate to Chinatown; Powell's City of Books.

Japantown. If the neon reindeer sign doesn't make it obvious that you've entered Old Town territory, you'll know for certain when you reach the 19th-century buildings lovingly converted into hip shops and notable eateries.

Lan Su Chinese Garden

An incredible replication of Ming Dynasty landscaping, the **Lan Su Chinese Garden** (239 NW Everett St., 503/228-8131, www.lansugarden.org, 10am-7pm daily mid-Mar.-Oct., 10am-4pm daily Nov.-mid-Mar., $10 adults, $7 children 6-18, $28 family) guides visitors through an oasis of prismatic landscapes, covered walkways, and pavilions, built by 65 artisans from Suzhou, China. The centerpiece of the garden is artificially constructed Lake Zither. Everywhere you look, there are trees, bamboo, orchids, and fragrant gardenias, with over 400 different species of plantlife in all.

Forest Park

Forest Park (NW Thurman St. and Leif Erikson Dr., 503/823-2525, www.portlandoregon.gov/parks, 5am-10pm daily) sits elevated above the city in the northwest, where its 5,000 acres make it one of the largest urban forests in the United States. It features 80 miles of biking, equestrian, and hiking trails, including the 30-mile **Wildwood Trail** (11028-11192 NW Germantown Rd.), which culminates in Washington Park.

★ Washington Park

In 1871, the City of Portland purchased undeveloped wilderness just west over the main highway (known as I-405). By the 1880s, German immigrant Charles M. Meyers had transformed the untamed land into a park, modeled by memories of his homeland. Today, visitors flock to **Washington Park** (4001 SW Canyon Rd., 503/823-2525, www.portlandonline.com, free, parking $1.60/hour, $4/day Oct.-Mar., $6.40/day Apr.-Sept.) for its sprawling 5,100 acres of trees, trails, and lively attractions. At its entrance stands a 34-foot granite memorial honoring the Lewis and Clark expedition (1804-1806) that traveled from St. Louis, Missouri, to the Pacific Coast. A nearby bronze statue of Sacajawea (Shoshone) holding her son Jean-Baptiste commemorates her significant role in aiding the explorers.

The park is easy to find. Get here via the MAX Light Rail red or blue line, or TriMet bus 63. A free shuttle loops throughout the park every 15 minutes on weekends and daily during the summer.

Oregon Zoo

Washington Park's east end is home to the **Oregon Zoo** (4001 SW Canyon Rd., 503/226-1561, www.oregonzoo.org, 9am-4pm daily spring-fall, 10am-4pm daily winter, $15 adults, $10 children 3-11), where endangered Asian elephants and African lions roam habitat grounds, and busy beavers can be seen chewing on river branches. Climb aboard the Zoo Railway for a scenic ride through the animal park.

Portland Children's Museum

At the west end of Washington Park, the **Portland Children's Museum** (4015 SW Canyon Rd., 503/223-6500, www.portlandcm.org, 9am-5pm daily, $10.75) inspires creative and interactive displays. But don't just stop at the exhibits; go outside and play on the outdoor eco-playground, which gives every child a chance to flex their sensory muscles.

International Rose Test Garden

Portland first became infatuated with roses when Georgiana Brown Pittock, wife of publisher Henry Pittock, founded the Portland Rose Society with a group of friends in 1889. The love affair continues today at the **International Rose Test Garden** (400 SW Kingston Ave., 503/823-3636, www.portlandoregon.gov/parks, 7:30am-9pm daily), a fragrant wonderland of more than 550 colorful varieties. Free public tours are offered at 1pm in the summer (Memorial Day weekend-Labor Day weekend).

Japanese Garden

The northern end of Washington Park includes the meditative **Japanese Garden** (611 SW Kingston Ave., 503/223-1321, www.japanesegarden.com, noon-7pm Mon., 10am-7pm Tues.-Sun., $15 adults, $10.50 children 6-17). Natural elements create the five distinct garden styles. Arbors, pagodas, bridges, ponds, and stone walkways complement the 5.5-acre landscape. Stop at any of the numerous benches to take in the serenity; close your eyes and listen to the trickling of the nearby streams. A gift shop and teahouse operate throughout the year, and private tours are offered for groups of 10 or more (reservations required).

Pittock Mansion

Rising 1,000 feet from its perch above the city skyline, the century-old **Pittock Mansion** (3229 NW Pittock Dr., 503/823-3623, www.pittockmansion.org, 11am-4pm daily fall-spring, 10am-5pm daily summer, closed Jan., $10 adults and $7 children 6-18) boasts breathtaking panoramic views. A marvel of French-Renaissance architecture, it is a monument to Portland's transformation from a small lumber town into a prosperous city. A stroll through the 46-acre grounds reveals fragrant gardens, miles of hidden hiking trails, and commanding views of the city and snowcapped Cascade Mountain Range.

Recreation
Hiking

Above the city in the Northwest, 5,000 acres make **Forest Park** (NW Thurman St. and Leif Erikson Dr., 503/823-2525, www.portlandoregon.gov/parks, 5am-10pm daily) a hiker's dream. Do a section of the 30-mile **Wildwood Trail** (11028-11192 NW Germantown Rd.), which culminates in Washington Park.

In Washington Park, the 3.9-mile **Washington Park Loop Hike** may be started at the Sacajawea Statue Trailhead (2600 SW Lewis Clark Way) or Hoyt Arboretum (4000 SW Fairview Blvd.). Either way leads you through forest and past the park's attractions, including the Rose Test Garden, Portland Japanese Garden, and Oregon Zoo.

Not far away, the **Pittock Mansion Hike** skirts the border of Forest Park and Washington Park, going 2.5 miles through forest each way from lower Macleay Park (2998 Northwest Upshur St.) to the Pittock Mansion (3229 NW Pittock Dr.).

Spectator Sports

When it comes to major sports teams, the city's longtime pride is NBA team the **Portland Trail Blazers** (www.nba.com/blazers), which plays at **Moda Center** (1 N. Center Ct. St., 503/235-8771, rose-quarter.com/venue/moda-center). More recently, **The Portland Timbers** (www.timbers.com) quickly won over Major League Soccer fans with a 2015 championship, its 5th as a franchise. They play matches at **Providence Park** (1844 SW Morrison St., 503/553-5400, www.providenceparkpdx.com).

★ Food

Portland's restaurant and craft beverage scene has set the tone for much of the West Coast, led by small businesses in pursuit of high-quality ingredients and focused on detail-oriented preparation. It's quite a rewarding place to eat and drink!

Downtown

A pioneer in global, direct trade sourcing as a means of finding the world's best coffee beans, Portland's **Stumptown Coffee Roasters** (128 SW 3rd Ave., 1026 SW Stark St., 3356 SE Belmont St., 4525 SE Division St., 855/711-3385, www.stumptowncoffee.com, 7am-7pm daily) has locations all around town (and also in New York). "There's no place like home" or a home-style breakfast to start the day right at **Mother's Bistro & Bar** (212 SW Stark St., 503/464-1122, www.mothersbistro.com, 7am-9pm Tues.-Thurs., 7am-9pm Fri., 8am-10pm Sat., 8am-2:30pm Sun., $8-20). For Mom's meatloaf and gravy and chicken dumplings, stop in for lunch or dinner. Kids will love **Slappy Cakes** (4246 SE Belmont St., 503/477-4805, www.slappycakes.com, 8am-2pm Mon.-Fri., 8am-3pm Sat.-Sun., $10-13), a popular pancake spot that lets you flip your own sweet masterpieces on a grill-installed table.

Bunk Sandwiches (211 SW 6th Ave., 503/328-2865, 8am-3pm Mon.-Fri., 9am-3pm Sat.-Sun., $8-11) specializes in satisfying meat and bread combinations; try the pulled pork or grilled Tillamook cheddar. Few can resist the spicy (or not) chicken and rice bowls at **Nong's Khao Man Gai** (1003 SW Alder St., 971/255-3480, www.khaomangai.com, 10am-4pm Mon.-Sat., $9-14).

Perfectly grilled meats and vegetables make ★ **Tasty & Alder** (580 SW 12th Ave., 503/621-9251, www.tastynalder.com, 9am-10pm Sun.-Thurs., 9am-11pm Fri.-Sat., $15-44) a downtown favorite, and the restaurant's small and large plates only get better thanks to its exquisitely flavorful sauces.

Want something to go? Head to SW 10th Avenue and Alder Street, where downtown's famous **food carts** serve up tasty afternoon bites.

Pearl District

Enjoy a mouthwatering pastry while streetcars glide by the big bay windows of **Lovejoy Bakers** (939 NW 10th Ave., 503/208-3113, 6am-6pm daily, $10-25), just north of Jamison Square. It's also a great stop for delicious sandwiches.

With locations throughout Portland, **Laughing Planet** (721 NW 9th Ave. #175, 1720 SW 4th Ave., 3320 SE Belmont St., 503/505-5020, www.laughingplanetcafe.com, 11am-9pm daily, under $10) takes healthy to delicious heights and makes it quick and affordable. Choose from fat-free burritos, cheesy quesadillas, and zesty bowls of exotic flavors from around the world.

Vegetarian, vegan, gluten-free, or raw—whatever your specialty diet, it's accommodated by **Prasad** (925 NW Davis St., 503/224-3993, www.prasadpdx.com, 7:30am-8pm Mon.-Fri., 9am-8pm Sat.-Sun., $8-12), which puts a focus on healthy ingredients.

Park Kitchen (422 NW 8th Ave., 503/223-7275, www.parkkitchen.com, 5pm-9pm daily, $14-65) has become a beacon for creative food. Pile up the shared plates, or dive into the $65 per person "chef's supper" to be treated to a sampling of the restaurant's seasonal best.

Old Town-Chinatown

A morning staple, the **Bijou Café** (132 SW 3rd Ave., 503/222-3187, www.bijoucafepdx.com, 7am-2pm Mon.-Fri., 8am-2pm Sat.-Sun., under $11) whips up famous oyster hash and delicious sausage and eggs daily. Right next door, the city's famous **Voodoo Doughnut** (22 SW 3rd Ave., 503/241-4704, www.voodoodoughnut.com, 24 hours daily, $1-12) produces uniquely colorful varieties of cake, raised, and vegan doughnuts and crullers—including a few X-rated doughnut shapes.

Red Robe Tea House & Café (310 NW Davis St., 503/227-8855, www.redrobeteahouse.com, 11am-8pm Mon.-Fri., noon-8pm Sat., $7-15) serves good Asian-American fusion dishes in a setting reminiscent of contemporary China. The selection of traditional Chinese teas is exceptional. The owner often performs traditional tea ceremonies.

An Old Town fixture, world-famous **Dan & Louis Oyster Bar** (208 SW Ankeny St., 503/227-5906, www.danandlouis.com, 11am-9pm Mon.-Thurs., 11am-10pm Fri.-Sat., noon-9pm Sun., $17-26) has been serving its trademark seafood favorites for more than 100 years. Choose from pan-seared scallops or lightly breaded oysters or entrées like sockeye salmon or good old-fashioned steak.

Southeast

SE Division Street has grown into a dining destination all its own, but the short city blocks sprawling throughout the southeast's many neighborhoods feature plenty of homegrown deliciousness for foodies to explore.

Start the day with the pristine Scandinavian dishes of **Café Broder** (2508 SE Clinton St., 503/736-3333, www.broderpdx.com, 8am-3pm daily, $10-14), usually with a choice between pork belly, smoked trout, and seasonal vegetables, and pick up a side of the spherical Danish pancakes, æbleskivers.

You might not expect a partially outdoor Thai street food restaurant to rank among Portland's best, but that's the case with ★ **Pok Pok** (3226 SE Division St., 503/232-1387, www.pokpokpdx.com, 11:30am-10pm daily, $10-25). Its award-winning chef promotes family-style northern Thai cuisine, and it's impossible to go wrong, but you don't want to leave without trying the fish sauce wings.

For some of the best pizza you've ever had, make a pilgrimage to ★ **Apizza Scholls** (4741 SE Hawthorne Blvd., 503/233-1286, www.apizzascholls.com, 5pm-9:30pm daily, 11:30am-2:30pm Sat.-Sun., $20-26). Born out of a former bakery, its pies start with terrific dough, then topped by gourmet ingredients. Grab a pint of local beer and play on the restaurant's vintage 1980s arcade games while you wait.

Adopting old-school European techniques, **Olympia Provisions** (107 SE Washington St., 503/954-3663, www.olympiaprovisions.com, 11am-10pm Mon.-Fri., $11-18) crafts beautiful charcuterie, including salami, sausage, pâté, and a classic variety of cured meats. Try them on a cheese board or in a sandwich, or pick up picnic supplies to go.

Portland's ice cream favorite, **Salt & Straw** (3345 SE Division St., 838 NW

the colorful fare at Portland's Voodoo Doughnut

23rd Ave., 126 SW 2nd Ave., 503/208-2054, www.saltandstraw.com, 11am-11pm daily, $4-8) has expanded to L.A. and San Francisco, but its local locations still provide the best places to pick up fresh scoops of its sweet, salty, and/or fruity ice creams.

Nightlife
Bars and Clubs

Built into a brick second-story loft, **Multnomah Whiskey Library** (1124 SW Alder St., 503/954-1381, 4pm-midnight Mon.-Thurs., 4pm-1am Fri.-Sat.) lives up to its name, with shelves lining the walls with a thousand different bottles of whiskey and more than 600 other globally sourced spirits. By the glass, the cheapest pour goes for $5, the most expensive for $834, but most fall in the $14-45 range. Pick your poison from a leather-bound book, or get expert advice from your bartender to assemble a tasting flight.

Craft breweries abound in Portland, most of them very good. The biggest attraction may be **Deschutes Public House** (210 NW 11th Ave., www.deschutesbrewery.com, 503/296-4906, 11am-11pm Sun.-Thurs., 11am-midnight Fri.-Sat.), serving beers made on-site as well as from its original central Oregon location. Farther northwest, **Breakside Brewery** (1570 NW 22nd Ave., 503/444-7597, www.breakside.com, 11am-11pm Sun.-Thurs., 11am-midnight Fri.-Sat.) has made a reputation for always pushing forward with new recipes and bold flavors. In southeast, sour specialist **Cascade Brewing** (939 SE Belmont St., 939 SE Belmont St., www.cascadebrewingbarrelhouse.com, noon-11pm Sun.-Thurs., noon-midnight Fri.-Sat.) stands peerless in the Pacific Northwest in producing fruited, barrel-aged beers.

To sample a wider range of local beers, visit one of the city's top taphouses. Just across the Burnside Bridge from downtown, the cash-only **Apex** (1216 SE Division St., 503/273-9227, www.apexbar.com, 11:30am-2:30am daily) offers an outdoor beer garden and 50 handles to choose from. Farther east, you'll find the regional classic **Horse Brass Pub** (4534 SE Belmont St., 503/232-2202, www.horsebrass.com, 11am-2:30am daily). The British-style pub has brought English ales to Portland since the 1970s and subsequently became a pioneering craft beer hub, supporting local breweries since their inception. Along with over 50 beers, it offers excellent fish-and-chips and the best Scotch eggs on the West Coast.

A cool little basement bar in Old Town, **Shanghai Tunnel** (211 SW Ankeny Ave., 503/220-4001, 5pm-1:30am daily) is always busy during happy hour. Though it's dimly lit with hanging Chinese paper lanterns, it isn't a dingy dungeon. The drinks are cheap, and the food is pretty darn good; try the udon noodles.

Chic sophistication with a modern Euro-flair, **Vault Martini** (226 NW 12th Ave., 503/224-4909, www.vaultmartinibar.com, 4am-midnight Sun.-Wed., 4pm-1am Thurs., 4pm-2am Fri.-Sat.)

has a fantastic drink menu using house-infused vodka to craft 99-plus takes on the martini. Two blocks down the street, **Teardrop Lounge** (1015 NW Everett St., 503/445-8109, www.teardroplounge.com, 4pm-12:30am Sun.-Thurs., 4pm-2am Fri.-Sat) caters to a trendy crowd with a nice selection of snazzy cocktails and light snacks.

For dancing, try **Holocene** (1001 SE Morrison St., 503/239-7639, www.holocene.org, 8:30pm-2:30am Wed.-Thurs., 9pm-2:30am Fri.-Sat.). The floors light up at **Spin Room at Dirty** (35 NW 3rd Ave., 503/227-1898, 9pm-2am Thurs.-Sat. and Mon., no cover), as do the walls. And the ceiling. DJs keep its young clientele drinking and dancing. Upscale gay club **CC Slaughters Nightclub and Lounge** (219 NW Davis St., 503/248-9135, www.ccslaughterspdx.com, 3pm-2am daily) has it all: cheap drinks; phenomenal DJs; go-go dancers; a huge dance floor; and, the best part, no cover charge.

Noble Rot (Leed-Platinum building, 111 E. Burnside St., 503/233-1999, 5pm-10pm daily) offers amazing sunset and night-sky views, best for enjoying wine, beautiful cocktails, and delicious small bites incorporating vegetables from the surrounding rooftop garden.

Live Music

The iconic **Crystal Ballroom** (1332 W. Burnside St., 503/225-0047, www.crystal-ballroompdx.com, ticketed events) rules the downtown live music scene, hosting iconic musical talents (the Grateful Dead and James Brown played here back in the day) that fill its historic, century-old ballroom with the sounds of indie rock, pop, soul, and hip-hop. **Lola's Room** downstairs showcases smaller acts.

A historical vaudeville theater dating to the 1920s, **Aladdin Theater** (3017 SE Milwaukie Ave., 503/234-9694, www.aladdin-theater.com) also features big-name acts from the world of music and comedy.

More intimate stages featuring local and touring indie rock bands include **Doug Fir Lounge** (830 E. Burnside St., 503/231-9663, www.dougfirlounge.com), a stylish music venue built into the basement of the Jupiter Hotel, and **Mississippi Studios** (3939 N. Mississippi Ave., 503/288-3895, www.mississippistudios.com), a former Baptist church converted into a performance space known for its acoustics.

Arts and Entertainment
Performing Arts
Portland'5 Centers for the Arts (www.portland5.com, 503/248-4335) is a performance center that incorporates five venues in three buildings. The 2,776-seat **Arlene Schnitzer Concert Hall** (1037 SW Broadway Ave.), a restored late-1920s Italian Renaissance landmark, hosts the Oregon Symphony amid a rich variety of musical and theatrical performances. The courtyard-style **Winningstad Theatre** (Hatfield Hall building, 1111 SW Broadway Ave.) arranges floor seating, balconies, and the stage according to the creative whims of the performance, an innovative approach to set-design that ultimately shapes the experience of the audience for the better. The 1917 **Keller Auditorium** (222 SW Clay St.) has a capacity of 2,992 and hosts the Portland Opera, the Oregon Ballet Theatre, and touring Broadway shows like The Book of Mormon and Hamilton. Each of the 880 seats at the Edwardian-style **Newmark Theater** (1111 SW Broadway Ave.) is the best in the house; none is farther than 65 feet from the stage. Many of the city's cultural events and modern dance performances take place here. The last of the five is the **Brunish Theatre** (1111 SW Broadway Ave.), which hosts private events.

In the Pearl District's historic Portland Armory, the 600-seat **Gerding Theater** (128 NW 11th Ave., 503/445-3700, www.psc.org) features classic and modern plays staged by theater company Portland

Center Stage, as well as popular musicals like *West Side Story* and *Dreamgirls*.

Galleries

In the Pearl District, **Blue Sky Gallery** (122 NW 8th Ave., 503/225-0210, www. blueskygallery.org, noon-5pm Tues.-Sun.) features emerging and established photographers. An on-site reading room provides printed books of shows over the past 20 years.

Focused on emerging artists who demonstrate "a conceptual edge," **PDX Contemporary Art** (925 NW Flanders St., 503/222-0063, www.pdxcontempo-raryart.com, 11am-6pm Tues.-Sat.) nevertheless remains friendly and accessible. Artist-operated **Blackfish Gallery** (420 NW 9th Ave., 503/224-2634, www.black-fish.com, 11am-5pm Tues.-Sat.) features a steady rotation of works produced in the Pacific Northwest.

Shopping

A big perk to shopping in Portland (or anywhere in Oregon for that matter) is that there's no sales tax.

Downtown

Find department stores, international re-tailers, boutiques, and specialty shops on the west end of downtown.

Radish Underground (414 SW 10th Ave., 503/928-6435, www.radishunder-ground.com, 11am-7pm Mon.-Sat., noon-6pm Sun.) specializes in timeless quality clothing, jewelry, and artwork from local, independent designers and artists.

Open just one day a week, **Arthur W. Erickson, Inc. Fine Arts & Unusual Antiques** (1030 SW Taylor St., 503/227-4710, www.arthurwerickson.com, 11am-5pm Wed.) specializes in indigenous arts and artifacts, including basketry and pottery, beadwork and jewelry, rugs and blankets. Although it's allegedly male-oriented, everyone should enjoy brows-ing the unique assortment of furniture, home goods, and gifts at **Boys Fort** (902 SW Morrison St., 503/567-1015, www.

boysfort.com, 11am-6pm Mon.-Sat., noon-6pm Sun.).

On the east side of the Willamette, **Music Millennium** (3158 E. Burnside St., 503/231-8926, www.musicmillennium. com, 10am-10pm Mon.-Sat., 11am-9pm Sun.) is the oldest record store in the Pacific Northwest. It specializes in hard-to-find titles and underground music, and hosts in-store performances.

Union Way Arcade is a pedestrian al-leyway that extends from downtown's Ace Hotel on SW Stark Street to Powell's City of Books in the Pearl District. Notable venues include designer clothier **Steven Alan** (1029 SW Stark St., 971/277-9585, www.stevenalan.com, 11am-7pm Mon.-Sat., 11am-6pm Sun.) and clas-sic beauty boutique **Spruce Apothecary** (1022 W. Burnside St., 503/206-4022, www.spruceapothecary.com, 11am-6pm Mon.-Sat., 11am-5pm Sun.).

Pearl District

The Pearl District is a shopaholic's swank dream, with brand-name retailers and boutiques, most on or around West Burnside Street.

The big draw is **Powell's City of Books** (1005 W. Burnside St., 503/228-4651, www.powells.com, 11am-9pm daily), oc-cupying an entire city block with 3,500 different sections.

The clothing lines at **Rachelle M. Rustic House of Fashion** (132 NW 12th Ave., 971/319-6934, www.rachellem. com, 10am-6pm Sun.-Wed., 10am-7pm Thurs.-Sat.) reflect current fashion trends that meet every lifestyle and budget. Nearby, the products at **Thea's Vintage Living** (1204 NW Glisan St., 503/274-0275, www.theasvintageliving.com, 10am-6pm Mon.-Sat., 11am-5pm Sun.) date from the 1800s to mid-20th century, with an eclectic blend of furniture, acces-sories, and jewelry.

Old Town-Chinatown

One of Portland's most intriguing places, **Hoodoo Antiques & Design** (122 NW

Couch St., 503/360-3409, www.hoodoo-antiques.com, 11am-4:30pm Fri.-Sun.) has eccentric and alluring curiosities clustered together throughout the store, creating an otherworldly aura. Browse vintage furnishings and unique art and decor from around the world.

Stop at the **Pendleton Home Store** (220 NW Broadway, 503/535-5444, www.pendleton-usa.com, 10am-5:30pm Mon.-Sat.) for Oregon-made wool blankets and clothing. Two blocks west, **Orox Leather Co.** (450 NW Couch St., 503/954-2593, www.oroxleather.com, 10am-5pm Mon.-Sat.) crafts quality leather products like sandals, wallets, and bags.

Southeast

Portland's premier craft beer retailer, **Belmont Station** (4500 SE Stark St., 503/232-8538, www.belmont-station.com, 10am-10pm Mon.-Sat., 11am-9pm Sun.) keeps 1,500 mostly regional beers in stock in cans and bottles, plus a few on draft for on-premise consumption in the shop's bar and patio areas.

For a different sort of brew, try **Townshend's Teahouse** (3531 SE Division St., 503/236-7772, www.townshendstea.com, 9am-10pm daily), which serves and sells more than a hundred types of high-grade loose-leaf tea.

The Portland zeitgeist thrives at women's fashion boutique **Donna & Toots** (3574 SE Division St., 503/241-5570, www.donnaandtoots.com, 11am-6pm daily), which features affordable, eclectic fashions, including unique hand-sewn designs by the owner herself.

Events

The nation's largest weekly open-air market actually takes place both days each weekend March-December, at the **Portland Saturday Market** (2 SW Naito Pkwy., 503/222-6072, www.portlandsaturdaymarket.com, 10am-5pm Sat., 11am-4:30pm Sun., free), which welcomes shoppers rain or shine. Rows of booths line Waterfront Park south of Burnside

Bridge. Browse unique handcrafted arts and crafts from jewelry and home decor to cannabis paraphernalia. There are also food vendors and live music.

The **Portland Rose Festival** (503/227-2681, www.rosefestival.org, late May-early June, $15-30) originated in 1907, following the successful 1905 Lewis and Clark Exposition, which celebrated the centennial of the expedition. The civic festival begins with the glorious 4.3-mile **Grand Floral Parade** that begins inside the Memorial Coliseum and continues through downtown. The festival also includes a waterfront carnival, sing-off concerts, and an evening Starlight Parade.

Beneath the St. Johns Bridge, Cathedral Park's spacious lawns fill up for the annual three-day **Cathedral Park Jazz Festival** (8676 N. Crawford St., mid-July, free), the longest-running free jazz festival west of the Mississippi. The last full weekend of July, the region's best beer makers set up at Waterfront Park for the **Oregon Brewers Festival** (www.oregonbrewfest.com). Admission is free, but to drink requires buying a $7 mug, and tastes cost a dollar apiece.

Accommodations
Under $150

Portland has two conveniently located hostels. **Hawthorne Hostel** (3031 Hawthorne Blvd., 503/236-3380, www.portlandhostel.org, dorm bed $28 and up, private room $66 and up) is an eco-friendly crash pad with 34 beds, including two private rooms and two co-ed dorm rooms. **Northwest Portland Hostel** (425 NW 18th Ave., 503/241-2783, www.nwportlandhostel.com, dorm bed $25 and up, private room $69 and up) is housed in three adjacent historical buildings centrally located near popular restaurants and cafés and the city's vibrant nightlife.

$150-250

The impeccably restored **Heathman Hotel** (1009 SW Broadway, 503/241-4100

North Coast

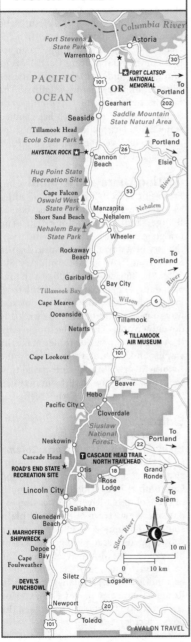

and 800/551-0011, $169 and up) is where the *50 Shades of Grey* characters, Ms. Steele and Mr. Grey, frequently meet for a drink at the bar (try the 50 Shades Cocktail).

Part of a boutique hotel chain, **Ace Hotel** (1022 SW. Stark St., 503/228-2277, www.acehotel.com, $200 and up) picks up on the Portland vibe with vintage furniture, original art, complimentary bicycles, and even Stumptown coffee. It's in the Pearl District, close to Powell's City of Books and a stone's throw away from the Portland streetcar.

Rich in art, architecture, and history, the ★ **Sentinel** (614 SW 11th Ave., 503/224-3400, www.sentinelhotel.com, $156 and up) is a timeless treasure. Housed in two historic downtown buildings (the east wing was completed in 1909, and its west wing in 1926), it offers elegant rooms and reasonably priced comfort.

Located across the street from the legendary Crystal Ballroom, the **Crystal Hotel** (303 SW 12th Ave., 503/972-2670, www.mcmenamins.com/crystalhotel, $155 and up) brings its rock-and-roll vibe and history to life through the decor in each of its 51 rooms. Richly painted walls highlight the artistry of the headboards, while black velvet drapery and animal print accents add a little Mick Jagger swagger. The hotel features a saltwater soaking pool, an upscale café that serves Northwest foods, and an adjoining bar with sidewalk seating that serves pub fare.

For a rockin' east-side stay, you'll find cool digs at the **Jupiter Hotel** (800 E. Burnside St., 503/230-9200, www.jupiterhotel.com, $180 and up)—just be aware it's upstairs from the **Doug Fir Lounge** concert venue, so it's not a place to stay when in search of peace and quiet.

Over $250

Conveniently located **Hotel Monaco Portland** (506 SW Washington St., 503/222-0001, www.monaco-portland.

com, $250 and up) is only a short walk away from Tom McCall Waterfront Park and downtown shopping. Large suites employ artful, eclectic decorative styles with whimsical accents. Extra-special amenities include a hosted wine reception, spa service, complimentary bicycles, and even goldfish companions on request.

In the heart of downtown, ★ **Hotel Vintage** (422 SW Broadway, 503/228-1212 and 800/263-2305, www.vintage-plaza.com, $320 and up) is a restored landmark building that blends Pacific Northwest history with modern suaveness for a memorable stay.

With a history dating back to 1915, the lovely **Hotel DeLuxe** (729 SW 15th Ave., 503/219-2094, www.hoteldeluxeportland.com, $200 and up) still projects old-fashioned glamour. It's an easy walk to Providence Park and the Pearl District.

Information and Services

The **Travel Oregon Visitor Information Center** (701 SW 6th Ave., Pioneer Courthouse Square, 503/275-8355 and 877/678-5263) is the best resource for local information and itinerary suggestions.

Astoria

The oldest American city west of the Rocky Mountains, **Astoria** (pop. 9,521) was founded in 1811 by fur-trade tycoon John Jacob Astor. The town protected the tenuous American claim to the Pacific Coast until the opening of the Oregon Trail brought substantial settlement. By the turn of the 20th century, Astoria was still Oregon's second-largest city, gaining additional notoriety with the construction of the Astoria Bridge, which connects the states of Washington and Oregon.

Today, Astoria is a tiny enclave of historic haunts, fishing vessels, craft breweries, and grand views of where the Columbia River meets the Pacific Ocean. Its late-Victorian-period homes showcase the Queen Anne architectural style, which have made it a picturesque backdrop for Hollywood movies like *The Goonies* (1985). Astoria supports an active commercial fishing fleet. Dozens of tugboats guide tankers and container ships around treacherous sandbars. The most notorious is the three-mile-wide Columbia River Bar, which has claimed some 2,000 large ships. One such shipwreck is the Liverpool sailing ship *Peter Iredale*, still visible at low tide.

Getting There and Around

From Portland, US-30 travels 95 miles to meet US-101 at the famous Astoria Bridge, about a two-hour trip. The bridge marks the northern boundary of the city of Astoria. The historic Astoria Riverfront Trolley (480 Industry St., 503/861-5365, www.old300.org, noon-6pm daily, $1 per boarding or $2 all day), lovingly dubbed "Old 300," is the quickest way to get around outside the walkable downtown area. The conductor narrates the town's history as the trolley makes its way around. On foot, you may follow the **Astoria Riverwalk,** a 5.1-mile paved trail that runs along the waterfront between the Port of Astoria and 40th Street.

Sights
★ Astoria Column

Rising 125 feet, the **Astoria Column** (1 Coxcomb Dr., 503/325-2963, sunrise-sunset daily, parking $2) sits atop Coxcomb Hill, overlooking the mouth of the Columbia River, showcasing expansive views from the coastal plain south to Tillamook Head and on to the snowcapped Cascade Range. On a clear day you can see Mount St. Helens to the east. Constructed in 1926, the column was modeled after Trajan's Column in Rome. A mural encases the exterior wall, recording influential events in the town's history.

Pick up a toy wooden airplane at the

Astoria and Vicinity

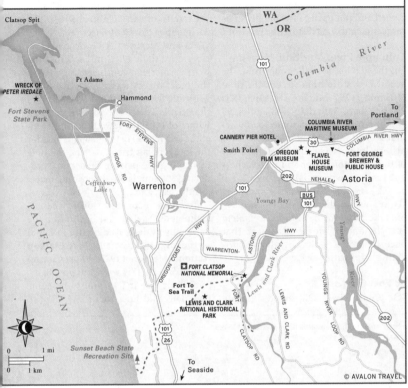

gift shop near the base of the column, then climb the 164-step spiral staircase to send it soaring from the top!

Flavel House

The **Flavel House** (441 8th St., 503/325-2203, www.cumtux.org, 10am-5pm daily May-Sept., 11am-4pm daily Oct.-Apr., tours $6 adults, $2 children 6-17) is a Queen Anne mansion built in 1886 by a sea captain who made millions operating the first pilot service to guide ships across the Columbia River Bar. He built the house for his very young wife (at the time of their wedding, she was 14 to his 30), and they filled it with three children. The restored mansion is elegantly furnished and features 14-foot ceilings and

beautiful Douglas fir wood throughout. The visitors center behind the house features exhibits, including a video presentation, and a gift shop.

Oregon Film Museum

Housed in the old Clatsop County Jail, the **Oregon Film Museum** (732 Duane St., 503/325-2203, www.oregonfilmmuseum.org, 11am-4pm daily Oct.-Apr., 10am-5pm daily May-Sept., $6 adults, $2 children 6-17) celebrates Astoria's contributions to the film industry, which date back to 1908. Get your own mug shot or wander the jail, which is famously depicted in the opening jailbreak scene of *The Goonies* (1985). You can even shoot your own film using Goonie-type sets.

Fans of the film may want to drive by the **Goonies House** (368 38th St.), where main character Mikey lived. It's privately owned and not open to the public, so be respectful and don't disturb the residents.

Columbia River Maritime Museum

On the north side of the waterfront, the acclaimed **Columbia River Maritime Museum** (1792 Marine Dr., 503/325-2323, 9:30am-5pm daily, $14 adults, $5 children 6-17) displays some 30,000 artifacts of fishing, shipping, and military history. Interactive exhibits tell the story of the Columbia River and its treacherous sandbar, which claimed over 2,000 vessels, enough to earn it the name the "Graveyard of the Pacific." Docked behind the museum, the *Lightship Columbia* is a National Historic Landmark that once served as a floating lighthouse, providing ships with safe navigation.

★ Fort Clatsop

"Ocian in view! O! the joy" wrote Captain William Clark in his journal on November 7, 1805, when he first sighted the Pacific Ocean while standing at the mouth of the Columbia River. The 33-member Corps of Discovery, led by Clark and Meriwether Lewis, had traveled more than 4,000 miles across the North American continent to establish the most direct water route from the Missouri River to the unknown land of the Pacific. They waited out the grueling winter of 1805-1806 two miles upstream at the self-made Fort Clatsop (named for the local Indian tribe), passing the time by making 332 pairs of moccasins, producing 30 pounds of salt, creating maps, hunting elk, and fighting fleas.

Today, a reconstruction of the encampment (the second built after the original was destroyed by fire in 2005) is the highlight of the **Fort Clatsop National Memorial** (92343 Fort Clatsop Rd., 503/861-2471, www.nps.gov, 8am-5pm daily Labor Day-mid-June, 8am-6pm daily mid-June-Labor Day, $5 peak

a boat outside the Columbia River Maritime Museum

season, $3 Labor Day-mid-June), as well as the focal point of the multiple sites that make up **Lewis and Clark National Historical Park.** This 1,500-acre park sits six miles southwest of Astoria and three miles east of US-101 on the Lewis and Clark River. A nearby visitors center houses historical items from the expedition and hosts costumed reenactments and historical demonstrations. Visitors can also trace the route the Lewis and Clark expedition took from Fort Clatsop to the Pacific Ocean, on the 6.5-mile **Fort to Sea Trail,** which crosses coastal rivers, lakes, and wondrous sand dunes.

Fort Stevens State Park

Ten miles south of Astoria, **Fort Stevens State Park** (100 Peter Iredale Rd., 503/861-1671 or 800/551-6949, $5 day-use) boasts 4,300 acres of hiking, camping, beachcombing, and exploration of a historic military fort. But the best-known attraction is the wreck of the 275-foot British schooner *Peter Iredale,* which

ran ashore on October 25, 1906, en route from Mexico to the Columbia River. All of the ship's crew members were rescued, but efforts to recover the ship were unsuccessful, and it was abandoned on the narrow Clatsop Spit near Fort Stevens. Today, its skeletal remains appear on the beach at low tide.

Sunset Beach State Recreation Site

Stroll the boardwalk at **Sunset Beach State Recreation Site** (503/861-2471, www.oregonstateparks.org) for incredible views of Cape Disappointment and Ecola State Park. The beach is accessed from Sunset Beach Road via US-101, and just north of the road's western terminus is the western trailhead of the historic 6.5-mile **Fort to Sea Trail,** which traces the steps of Lewis and Clark.

Food

T Paul's Supper Club (360 12th St., 503/325-2545, www.tpaulssupperclub. com, 11am-9pm Mon.-Thurs., 11am-10pm Fri.-Sat., $12-26) adds a little swank to its easygoing atmosphere. The menu is laden with tempting choices like crab ravioli and mac-and-cheese.

Enjoy a chic waterfront dining experience at **Clemente's Café and Public House** (175 14th St. #180., 503/325-1067, 11am-10pm Tues.-Sat., $11-30), which features seasonal menus based on local catches and harvests.

For something quick and easy, head to the **Blue Scorcher Bakery Café** (1493 Duane St., 503/338-7473, www.bluescorcher.com, 7am-4pm daily, $3-8). It doubles as a bakery that sells fresh breads and pastries and a café that serves soups and light fare.

Join the long line outside the 48-foot boat across from the Columbia Maritime Museum, the home of **Bowpicker Fish & Chips** (1634 Duane St., 503/791-2942, www.bowpicker.com, 11am-6pm Wed.-Sun., $9-11). It's worth the wait for their famous lightly battered albacore tuna served with thickly cut steak fries.

Popular **Columbian Cafe** (1114 Marine Dr., 503/325-2233, www.columbianvoo-doo.com, 8am-2pm Wed.-Fri., 9am-2pm Sat.-Sun., $14-18) is a good choice for fresh seafood, with large portions and reasonable prices.

Pick up the best smoked salmon to go at commercial fish packers **Josephson's Smokehouse** (106 Marine Dr., 503/325-2190, 9:30am-5:30pm Mon.-Sat., 10am-5pm Sun., $12-18), a family-owned company for over 90 years.

Good food and fantastic views draw them in at the **Bridgewater Bistro** (20 Basin St., 503/325-6777, www.bridgewaterbistro.com, 11:30am-9pm Mon.-Thurs., 11:30am-10pm Fri.-Sat., 11am-9pm Sun., $17-36) on the Columbia River waterfront. The menu ranges from burgers to wild salmon and roasted duck.

Elegant **Carruthers Restaurant** (1198 Commercial St., 503/975-5305, 4pm-10pm Tues.-Thurs., 4pm-11pm Fri.-Sat., $18-30) dishes fine food in a historical atmosphere.

Nightlife and Entertainment

Craft beer thrives in Astoria. For a great beer and a great meal, head to ★ **Fort George Brewery & Public House** (1483 Duane St., 503/325-7468, www.fortgeorgebrewery.com, 11am-11pm Mon.-Thurs., 11am-midnight Fri.-Sat., noon-11pm Sun.) for some dank ales and roasty stouts. The brewery offers three beer-slinging venues: a casual pub downstairs, a river-view pizza restaurant upstairs, and the Lovell Taproom, best accessed around the corner from 14th Street, where you'll find the deepest cuts of the award-winning brews.

Over on the riverwalk, **Buoy Beer Company** (1 8th St., 503/325-4540, www.buoybeer.com, 11am-10pm Sun.-Thurs., 11am-midnight Fri.-Sat.) is housed in a cannery built in 1924, with a window in the floor looking down on the seals who like to rest below. A tasting room in front caters to dedicated beer drinkers, while the full-service restaurant overlooking the water serves unique eats like bison burgers.

Kick back and relax at the **Wet Dog Cafe & Astoria Brewing House** (144 11th St., 503/325-6975, 11am-10pm Mon.-Fri., 8am-10pm Sat.-Sun., happy hour 3pm-6pm Mon.-Fri.), just west of the Maritime Museum, or the **Rogue Public House** (100 39th St., 503/325-5964, 11am-9pm daily), inside the former Bumble Bee Tuna cannery on Pier 39. Both offer handcrafted ales and lagers and tasty happy hour menu specials.

The self-proclaimed "oldest watering hole in the oldest American settlement west of the Rockies," **Astoria Portway Tavern** (422 W. Marine Dr., 503/325-2651, www.portway-astoria.com, 11am-11pm Mon.-Tues., 11am-1am Wed.-Thurs., 11am-1:30am Fri.-Sat., noon-9pm Sun.) is a dive-y pub decorated with life preservers and rumored to have a resident ghost. The riverwalk's **Inferno Lounge** (77 11th St., 503/741-3401, 4pm-midnight Tues.-Thurs., 2pm-midnight Fri.-Sun.) serves cocktails with a priceless view and a swanky old-school sense of glamour.

In its heyday, the 1920s **Liberty Theater** (1203 Commercial St., 503/325-5922, www.libertyastoria.org) welcomed celebrities like Duke Ellington, Jack Benny, and presumably Al Capone. The impressive venue includes a Chinese lantern-style chandelier made of paper and cotton, and large Venetian paintings. Enjoy plays, concerts, and the occasional apparition.

Shopping

The wonderful thing about shopping in Oregon is that there's no sales tax. Browse and shop along Commercial Street, which is lined with diverse retail stores.

Terra Stones (951 Commercial St., 503/325-5548, 10am-6pm daily) carries unique art and gifts, jewelry-making supplies, and a large selection of beautiful beads. A block east, **A Gypsy's Whimsy Herbal** (1139 Commercial St., 503/338-4871, 11am-6pm Tues.-Sat.) is a mecca for organic herbs, teas, and metaphysical treasures. Head across the street for one-of-a-kind home decor and handcrafted gifts at **Foxgloves** (1124 Commercial St., 503/468-0700). A couple doors down, **Finn Ware** (1116 Commercial St., 800/851-3466 or 503/325-5720, www.finnware.com, 10am-5pm Mon.-Sat., noon-4pm Sun.) boasts stylish Norwegian products and authentic sauna aromatherapy accessories imported from Finland.

The two-story **Phog Bounders Antique Mall** (892 Marine Dr., 503/338-0101, www.phogbounders.com, 10am-5:30pm daily) brims with nostalgic items from bygone eras. Two blocks west, **Vintage Hardware** (1162 Marine Dr., 503/325-1313, www.astoriavintagehardware.com, 10am-5pm Mon.-Sat., noon-4pm Sun.) is stocked with old-world wonders, from beautifully preserved furnishings to rare salvaged architecture.

From May to October, the **Astoria Sunday Market** (12th St., 503/325-1010, 10am-3pm Sun.) hosts regional artists, music, fresh produce, and culinary delights!

Events

With performances at venues throughout Astoria, **Fisher Poets Gathering** (www.fisherpoets.org, last weekend of Feb., 5pm-11pm, $15) commemorates Astoria's maritime roots through art, music, and literature. The **Astoria Music Festival** (1271 Commercial St., 503/325-9896, www.astoriamusicfestival.org, June) highlights classical music and opera along with modern dance and ballet. The **Astoria Scandinavian Midsummer Festival** (Clatsop County Fairgrounds, 92937 Walluski Loop, 503/325-6136, 3rd weekend in June, $8 adults, $3 children 6-12) celebrates that rich immigrant

From top to bottom: the *Peter Iredale* wreck at Fort Stevens State Park; the 125-foot-Astoria Column; the reconstructed stockade fence of Fort Clatsop.

heritage with a parade, traditional music, dance, crafts, and foods.

Downtown's **Second Saturday Art Walk** (www.astoriadowntown.com, 5pm-8pm 2nd Sat. each month, free) celebrates Astoria's growing arts community with work by local artists and live entertainment. Maps are available at the **Astoria Chamber of Commerce** (111 W. Marine Dr., 503/325-6311, www.oldoregon.com).

Accommodations

Extending 600 feet out into the Columbia River, the ★ **Cannery Pier Hotel** (10 Basin St., 503/325-4996, www.cannerypierhotel.com, $199 and up) is a rarity. Enjoy magnificent views of passing ships from your own private balcony. Complimentary guest services include breakfast, wine-tasting, and day-use bicycles.

The **Crest Motel** (5366 Leif Erickson Dr., 503/325-3141, www.astoriacresthotel.com, $99 and up) overlooks the great Columbia River. Historical and stylish **Hotel Elliott** (357 12th St., 503/325-2222, www.hotelelliott.com, $150 and up) is close to the riverwalk.

You may never want to leave homey **Clementine's** (847 Exchange St., 503/325-2005, www.clementines-bb.com, $98 and up), which boasts comfortable rooms and an amazing breakfast.

A charming boutique hotel in the heart of downtown, the **Commodore Hotel** (258 14th St., 503/325-4747, $69 and up cabin, $149 and up suite) blends right in to the old-time feel of historic Astoria. It is walking distance from the Fort George Brewery and the Maritime Museum. It also offers European-style rooms with shared bathroom facilities or private bathroom suites. Go for a walk or run on the Astoria Riverwalk trail only a half block away.

The **Norblad Hotel and Hostel** (443 14th St., 503/325-6989, www.norbladhotel.com, $34 dorm, $79 and up private suite) is a clean, affordable hostel in the center of town, with laundry facilities.

Information and Services

The **Astoria Chamber of Commerce** (111 W. Marine Dr., 503/325-6311, www.oldoregon.com, 9am-5pm Mon.-Fri., 10am-5pm Sat.) provides a wide range of visitor information on local activities, restaurants, and accommodations.

Gearhart

Barely 15 miles (20-30 minutes) south of Astoria on US-101, **Gearhart** (pop. 1,562) seems like a quiet and uncrowded town. Its claim to fame is the culinary legacy of its former resident chef, TV personality, and cookbook author James Beard. You can get a taste of Beard's famous crab cakes and other tasty Northwest cuisine at the **Pacific Way Bakery & Cafe** (601 Pacific Way, 503/738-0245, www.pacificwaybakery-cafe.com, bakery 7am-1pm Thurs.-Mon., café 11am-3:30pm and from 5pm Thurs.-Mon.), an eclectic place with an adjoining bakery that whips up delicious pastries and coffee.

Seaside

Less than three miles farther along US-101 South, the resort town of **Seaside** (pop. 6,685) is Oregon's oldest playground by the sea, with wide and sandy beaches that are popular for beach biking, volleyball, kite flying, sandcastles, and evening bonfires. Its first guesthouse was built in 1870 by Ben Holladay, a prominent land developer and railroad builder who envisioned an elegant summer resort. But Seaside had already played host to a famous party some 65 years earlier: the Lewis and Clark Corps of Discovery. A bronze statue of Meriwether Lewis and William Clark (and Lewis's dog Seaman) marks the end of the Lewis and Clark Trail—which now overlooks the beach at the end of the small town's main drag, Broadway.

The walkable **Seaside Promenade** runs

Cannon Beach

firehousegrill.org, 8am-3pm Thurs.-Mon., $7-12).

Affordable two-star hotels sit within easy walking distance of the beach. Or book a room at the **Gilbert Inn** (341 Beach Dr., 800/507-2714, $80 and up), a classic Victorian built in 1892. Much of the original decor remains, including the parlor fireplace and groove ceilings.

The **Seaside Visitors Bureau** (7 N. Roosevelt Dr., 503/738-3097 or 888/306-2326, 9am-5pm Mon.-Sat., noon-4pm Sun.) is the best source for local information.

Cannon Beach

Cannon Beach (pop. 1,705) is one of the most picturesque destinations on the coast. Dozens of art galleries as well as charming restaurants and boutique shops line downtown's main drag, known as Hemlock Street. Walk along the long, sandy beach or just enjoy the view from the door of your beachfront suite; there are plenty of lodging choices. But no matter where you stay, Cannon Beach offers more awe-inspiring views than imaginable, making *National Geographic*'s list of "one of the world's 100 most beautiful places."

Getting There and Around

From the north, Cannon Beach is a short drive south from Seaside on US-101 (17 miles, 15 minutes); it may also be directly accessed from Portland, by taking US-26 west (80 miles, 1.5 hours).

Sunset Empire Transit District (503/861-7433 or 866/811-1001, www.ridethebus.org, $1, runs hourly) operates the Cannon Beach Shuttle (route 20, route 21 weekends), which runs a loop connecting Cannon Beach and Seaside.

Sights
★ Haystack Rock

Claimed as the third-tallest seashore formation in the state, the 235-foot-high

along Broadway, starting at the beach and continuing across the Necanicum River a couple blocks away. Its shops and arcades sell the likes of saltwater taffy, frozen desserts, cheap seafood, and pub fare. Best bets are morning bites and coffee at **Bagels by the Sea** (210 S. Holladay Dr., 503/717-9145, 6:30am-3pm daily, $5-7), which also serves lunch. Or get breakfast and burgers at the **Firehouse Grill** (841 Broadway, 503/717-5502, www.

Haystack Rock is also Cannon Beach's claim to fame, setting it apart from the other quaint seaside towns along this stretch of coastline. It's home to nesting seabirds in the summer, and year-round to marine creatures that dwell in the tidepools that form around its base. These creatures are protected as part of the Oregon Islands National Wildlife Refuge, which means look but don't touch, not even the rock. It's best approached while strolling south along the beach from town, but to grab a quick photo, follow a set of public stairs leading down from Hemlock Street at Arbor Lane. While it's one of Oregon's most popular photo ops, it's actually not the only Haystack Rock along the coast—there are two other formations by that name at Cape Kiwanda and Bandon.

Ecola State Park

Just after Christmas Day in 1806, the Lewis and Clark Corps of Discovery scaled the rugged headlands and pushed through the thick shrubs and trees south to where a beached whale lay in what is now **Ecola State Park** (84318 Ecola State Park Rd., 503/436-2844, www.oregon-stateparks.org, dawn-dusk daily, $5 per car). Today, it's a photographer's dream, with astonishing views. To the north, you can see Tillamook Rock Lighthouse, which guided its last ship in 1957. To the south, Haystack Rock and Cannon Beach rest in the shadow of Neahkahnie Mountain. The entire park encircles Tillamook Head, which rises 1,200 feet above the sea.

Cannon Beach History Center & Museum

Cannon Beach History Center & Museum (1387 S. Spruce St., 503/436-9301, www. cbhistory.org, 11am-5pm daily, donation) houses a collection of artifacts and memorabilia. A gift and book shop is on-site.

the coastline near Cannon Beach

Food

Get the day started with a morning cup of joe at **Sleepy Monk Coffee Roasters** (1235 S. Hemlock St., 503/436-2796, www.sleepymonkcoffee.com, 8am-2pm Mon., Tues., and Thurs., 8am-4pm Fri.-Sun.). At night, the same space becomes the intimate and elegant **Irish Table** restaurant (503/436-0708, 5:30pm-9pm Fri.-Tues., $25-30). Next door, **Cannon Beach Hardware and Public House** (1235 S. Hemlock St., 503/436-4086, www.cannonbeachhardware.com, 10am-10pm Thurs.-Tues., $10-20) started out as, and continues to be, a hardware store. But over the years it's morphed into a craft beer bar and counter restaurant as well, and become a local favorite.

Crepe Neptune (175 E. 2nd St., 503/436-9200, www.crepeneptune.com, 9am-4pm Mon., Tues., and Fri., 9am-6pm Sat., 9am-5pm Sun., $5-10) specializes in generously stuffed savory or sweet French-style pancakes. **Lazy Susan Café** (126 N. Hemlock St., 503/436-2816, www.lazy-susan-cafe.com, 8am-3pm Wed.-Mon., $6-18) features delicious specialty omelets and endless coffee.

★ **Cannon Beach Café** (1116 S. Hemlock St., 503/436-1392, www.cannonbeachcafe.com, 11am-3pm and 5pm-9pm Thurs.-Sun., $15-30) is a little gem inside the Cannon Beach Hotel. The menu has Parisian flair, and the service will make you feel like family.

Ecola Seafoods (208 N. Spruce St., 503/436-9130, www.ecolaseafoods.com, 10am-9pm daily summer, 10am-7pm daily spring and fall, 10am-6pm daily winter, $12-24) has been serving the best locally caught fish and shellfish for more than 37 years.

Castaways' Tini Tiki Hut (316 Fir St., 503/436-4444, 5pm-9pm daily, $11-30) is a little place with big Caribbean tastes like jerk chicken and jambalaya.

Nightlife and Entertainment

For beers, **Bill's Tavern & Brewhouse** (188 N. Hemlock St., 503/436-2202, 11:30am-10pm daily) offers a friendly neighborhood spirit and flavorful brews. Less than a mile south, regional craft beer mainstay **Pelican Brewing** (1371 S. Hemlock St., 503/908-3377, www.pelicanbrewing.com, 11am-10pm Sun.-Thurs., 11am-11pm Sat.-Sun.) operates a well-lit pub and restaurant.

Sate your palate with superb Northwest wines at **The Wine Bar at Sweet Basil's Cafe** (271 N. Hemlock St., 503/436-1539, www.cafesweetbasils.com, 4pm-10pm Wed.-Sun.), which hosts Saturday-night courtyard concerts.

The **Coaster Theatre Playhouse** (108 N. Hemlock St., 503/436-1242, www.coastertheatre.com) stages a wide range of musicals and plays; there's not a bad seat in the house.

Shopping

Much of the charm of downtown Cannon Beach is due to the many local artists, galleries, and boutiques that are grouped

into little courtyard plazas in the main shopping district along Hemlock Street.

Every piece of handcrafted jewelry made at **Golden Whale** (194 N. Hemlock St., 503/436-1166, www.goldenwhalejewelry.com, 10am-5pm daily) is unique, imaginative, and affordable.

Upstairs in Sandpiper Square, **Primary Elements Gallery** (232 N. Spruce St., 503/436-0220, www.primaryelementsgallery.com, 9am-6pm) has beautiful sculptures, woodcarvings, ceramics, and furniture. **Cannon Beach Treasure Co.** (148 N. Hemlock St., 503/436-1626, www.cannonbeachtreasure.com, 10am-5pm daily) peddles artifacts salvaged from beneath the sea alongside one-of-a-kind artwork and jewelry. Expect the unexpected at **The Butler Did It** (124 N. Hemlock St., 503/436-2598, 11am-5pm daily), a whimsical little shop with kitchen accessories and vintage decor.

A few blocks south, **La Luna Loca** (107 N. Hemlock St., 503/436-0774, 10am-6pm daily) showcases artistry imported from around the world with colorful, comfortable, and fun clothing and jewelry.

Steidel's Art (116 S. Hemlock St., 503/436-1757, www.steidelsart.com, call for hours) enchants with colorfully brushed artworks and statuary. **DragonFire Studio and Gallery** (123 S. Hemlock St., Ste. 106, 503/436-1533, www.dragonfirestudio.com, 10am-5pm daily) makes exceptional yet affordable art pieces in media ranging from paint to fiber to metal. In the same building, **Dena's Shop on the Corner** (123 S. Hemlock St., 503/436-1275, www.denasshop.com, 10am-6pm Mon.-Sat., 10am-5pm Sun.) offers stylish and affordable women's clothing and accessories.

Cannon Beach Surf (1088 S. Hemlock St., 503/436-0475, www.cannonbeachsurf.com, 8am-5pm Sun.-Fri., 8am-6pm Sat.) carries everything for the beach: surfwear, sunglasses, even board rentals and surf lessons.

Browse artisanal products alongside local fresh fruits and vegetables at the **Cannon Beach Farmers Market** (163 E. Gower Ave., 503/436-8044, www.cannonbeachmarket.org, 1pm-5pm Tues. mid-June-Sept.).

Recreation

In Ecola State Park, the **Clatsop Loop Trail** (2.5 miles) begins at Indian Beach and travels to the southern end of Tillamook, allowing you to trace the steps of the Corps of Discovery. You'll pass interpretive signs as well as salmonberries, large Sitka spruces, and salal shrubs along the pathway. Wildlife is easy to spot, especially during winter and spring when whales make their way along the coastline.

Located on the south end of Cannon Beach, **Tolovana State Recreation Site** (503/436-2844, www.oregonstateparks. org) has lots of sandy oceanfront space for recreation.

Trot through the surf on horseback with **Sea Ranch Stables** (415 Fir St., 503/436-2815, www.searanchrv.com, $80-140). Riders are guided along a southbound trail to Haystack Rock or northbound to Cove Beach. Riders must be at least seven years old, and reservations must be made in person.

Events

One of the oldest sandcastle contests in Oregon is **Sandcastle Day** (207 N. Spruce St., 503/436-2623, www.cannonbeach. org), held annually in early June. Teams compete for cash, but you don't have to put your hands in the sand to have fun; watch as wondrous creations take shape before your eyes!

The annual **Stormy Weather Arts Festival** (207 N. Spruce St., 503/436-2623, www.cannonbeach.org, free) is a three-day affair in November featuring exhibits and gallery shows, an auction, musical performances, and a special evening concert.

Accommodations

It's no surprise to find an enchanting hotel like ★ **Stephanie Inn** (2740 S. Pacific St., 800/633-3466, www.stephanieinn.com, $269 and up) in a magical place like Cannon Beach. It's the perfect getaway for couples and for special occasions, with afternoon wine-tasting, pampered services, and perfect views of Haystack Rock. The closest property to the rock is oceanfront **Hallmark Resort & Spa** (1400 S. Hemlock St., 503/436-1566, www.hallmarkinns.com, $118 and up), which offers ocean views, pet-friendly rooms, and free beach-cruiser rentals.

The Ocean Lodge (2864 S. Pacific St., 503/436-2241, 888/777-4047, www.theoceanlodge.com, $219 and up) combines laid-back charm and quality service. The romantic **Inn at Cannon Beach** (3215 S. Hemlock St., 800/321-6304, www.innatcannonbeach.com, $135 and up) is the perfect starting point for sunset strolls on the beach.

Just one block from the beach, **McBee Motel Cottages** (888 S. Hemlock St., 503/436-1392, www.mcbeecottages.com, $114 and up) is a refurbished vintage motor inn that welcomes guests and their pets.

Information and Services

The best source of complete information is the **Cannon Beach Visitor Center** (207 N. Spruce St., 503/436-2623, www.cannonbeach.org, 9am-5pm daily) in the heart of downtown Cannon Beach.

Hug Point State Park

Just five miles south of Cannon Beach, **Hug Point State Park** (800/551-6949) has beautiful, forested picnic areas, a magical seasonal waterfall, and mysterious caves carved into its towering cliffs. It's a good alternative to ever-popular Cannon Beach. But what's hidden beneath the waves makes it a must-see: Old Stagecoach Road. Before the highway was built, carriages traveled along the shoreline, dashing between the incoming waves. At low tide, head north of the parking lot to see the rutted road left by these early pioneers, which is some 800 feet long.

Oswald West State Park

Ten miles south of Cannon Beach, the scenic coastline rises high above the ocean below, cutting into the mountains. The views are dominated by legendary **Neahkahnie Mountain,** which some say local Native Americans named "place of gods," no doubt for its transcendent views. But the mountain is also known for its hidden treasure, supposedly buried by the captain of a Spanish galleon that was shipwrecked at its base. Captain and crew hauled the treasure up the south side of Neahkahnie and concealed it in an unknown location. Though many have searched, no treasure has ever been found.

Neahkahnie is contained within the 2,484-acre rainforest of **Oswald West State Park** (Arch Cape, 800/551-6949). Here you can wander in the shade of cedar and spruce, ferns and salmonberry, or walk the half-mile trail beneath the highway to **Short Sands Beach,** a premier surfing destination.

A 13-mile segment of the **Oregon Coast Trail** winds through the entire park. In the spring, it's an unforgettable hike through wildflowers and old-growth forest that culminates at the Neahkahnie summit for striking views of the coastline below.

Oswald West includes a well-sheltered **campground** (spring-fall, $15) with 29 campsites. Five miles south, **Nehalem Bay State Park** (34600 Gary St., 503/368-5154 or 800/551-6949, open year-round, $45-55) has a large campground with yurts and hot showers.

Tillamook

Over the next 28 miles, US-101 curves inland past wetlands and dairy lands along Tillamook Bay (pronounced "TILL-uh-muk"; the name is a Salish word meaning "land of many waters"). Grazing cows come into view as you near the town of **Tillamook** (pop. 5,183), known for its cheese-making.

It's worth a stop to watch how the curd is transformed into the many cheese varieties at the ★ **Tillamook Cheese Factory** (4175 N. US-101, 503/815-1300, 8am-6pm daily Labor Day-mid-June, 8am-8pm daily mid-June-Labor Day, free self-guided tours) but even more fun is sampling the results, and especially the factory's incredible ice cream. A mile south, the **Blue Heron French Cheese Company** (2001 Blue Heron Rd., 503/842-8281, www.blueheronoregon. com, 8am-6pm daily) gives you a taste of their famous Blue Heron Brie. Their **Blue Heron Deli** (11am-4pm daily, $7-10) is perfect for lunch, with freshly baked bread and homemade soups and salads.

The **Tillamook Air Museum** (6030 Hangar Rd., 503/842-1130, www.tillamookair.com, 10am-5pm daily, $9.75 adults, $6.50 children 7-16, $2.75 children 1-6) is housed in a former blimp hangar that's one of the world's largest wooden structures, spanning seven acres. Its rare warbird collection includes MiG fighters, a twin-tailed P-38, and an F-14 Tomcat.

People drive for miles to enjoy the Belgian-style beers produced by **De Garde Brewing** (6000 Blimp Blvd., 503/815-1635, www.degardebrewing. com, 3pm-7pm Thurs.-Fri., noon-7pm Sat., 11am-5pm Sun.).

◆ OR-131: Three Capes Scenic Route

Between Tillamook and Lincoln City, US-101 strays inland, losing sight of the Pacific Ocean. To continue along the coast, head west on OR-131 and follow signs that point the way to the **Three Capes Scenic Route,** a worthy 35-mile side trip that strings together three captivating bluffs: Cape Meares, Cape Lookout, and Cape Kiwanda. The highway will take you through dairy land and second-growth forest. To enjoy the dramatic beauty of these capes, you'll need to get out of the car and hike along their trails.

Cape Meares

On the south end of Tillamook Bay, **Cape Meares** (named for John Meares, a British explorer) forms a steep bluff where the historic Cape Meares Lighthouse and Sitka spruce trees sit atop its wind-beaten rock. The most famous Sitka spruce is the strangely twisted **Octopus Tree,** which rises some 105 feet. Believed to be several hundred years old, it has no central trunk and possibly owes its curious octopus-like shape to early Native Americans, who may have used the tree to hold ceremonial canoes. A scenic viewpoint overlooks the sea and rocky beach below. Whales can be seen in the spring and winter, along with sea lions and nesting sea birds.

A few miles south of Cape Meares, the coastal hamlets of **Oceanside** and **Netarts** provide opportunities to stop for gas and refreshments.

Cape Lookout

Roughly eight miles past Netarts, you'll reach **Cape Lookout.** Seventeen miles of trails wander through a forest of hemlock, alder, and fir trees, and along the sandy coastland. The campground at **Cape Lookout State Park** (13000 Whiskey Creek Rd., 503/842-4981, www.oregon-stateparks.org, $21-98) offers tent sites, yurts, and cabins with hot showers. The **Cape Lookout Trail** offers two branches: The **South Trail** (3.6 miles round trip, 2.5 hours) heads down to a sandy beach and hidden cove, and the **North Trail** (4.6

Three Capes Scenic Route

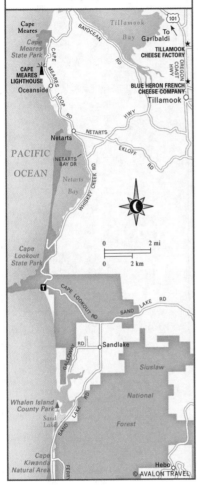

Cape Kiwanda

The route turns inland before winding south to **Cape Kiwanda,** notorious for some of the wildest surf in the state. Surfers, windsurfers, and kite flyers enjoy the shore winds, while hang gliders take advantage of the gusts from above. At its north end, a towering six-story-high sand dune juts out over the cape. A mile offshore, a second **Haystack Rock** (the more commonly known is in Cannon Beach) rises 327 feet from the seafloor.

Pacific City

South of Cape Kiwanda, the beach stretches eight miles toward the Nestucca Spit (which you'll have to cross) and on to the southernmost oceanfront settlement of **Pacific City** (pop. 1,035). You can grab a bite at the **Grateful Bread Bakery** (34805 Brooten Rd., 503/965-7337, 8am-9pm Thurs.-Mon., $10-21), choosing between vegan and gluten-free dishes, sandwich wraps, breakfast scrambles, burgers, and local seafood.

Just past Pacific City, the route connects with US-101 at Lincoln City.

Lincoln City

Lincoln City (pop. 8,722) lies 44 miles south of Tillamook, along the most developed section of US-101, a very busy and at times congested highway. Five fishing and logging towns were combined to form Lincoln City in the 1960s, which accounts for its larger size compared to most neighboring coastal towns.

Before early settlements infiltrated the region, it was inhabited by the Salish Indians, which included the Tillamook, Nehalem, and Siletz. Local rivers teemed with salmon, and homesteaders fished for extra income. By the 1920s, the numbers of fish had diminished and many turned to logging, which became the lifeblood of the town's economy, until it too dried up in the 1980s.

Today, Lincoln City has become a

miles round trip, 3 hours) takes you to the tip of the cape.

Continuing south, the loop briefly enters the Siuslaw National Forest, then enters an expanse of sweeping sand dunes as well as the Sand Beach estuary. This ecological wonder includes woodlands, grasslands, wetlands, and dune sedgelands and serves as home to salmon, shorebirds, deer, otters, and even bears and cougars.

home to retirees and a destination for tourists seeking its beautiful 7.5-mile beach. From fall to spring caches of spherical blown-glass floats can be spotted, reminiscent of the floats used by Japanese immigrants who, like so many, made their living on the sea.

Getting There and Around

Continue south via US-101 for 44 miles, passing through the small towns of Manzanita, Nehalem, and Wheeler to Lincoln City. The mostly two-lane highway becomes clogged with traffic just before entering the town.

Sights
Glass Floats

Lincoln City's main attraction is its beach, a mecca for beachcombing, kite flying, and sand-play. But its most intriguing sights are the colorful blown-glass floats seen above the tide line and below the beach embankment from mid-October through Memorial Day. These elegant glass orbs, emblematic of Northwestern coastal culture, are part of "Finders Keepers," a city-sponsored event where artist-signed and numbered floats are buried in the sand to be discovered and kept as souvenirs. If you find one, call the visitors center (www.oregoncoast.org/glass-floats, 800/452-2151 or 541/996-1274) and register your float to receive a certificate of authenticity.

You can also watch the 2,000-year-old art of glassblowing at the **Alder House III Glassblowing Studio** (611 Immonen Rd., 541/996-2483, www.alderhouse.com, 10am-5pm daily May-Oct.) or blow your own colorful spheres at **Jennifer L. Sears Glass Art Studio** (4821 SW US-101, 541/996-2569, www.jennifersearsglassart.com, $65-145 per float, 10am-6pm daily).

J. Marhoffer Shipwreck

In 1910, a gas explosion on board the wooden steam schooner **J. Marhoffer** set the 175-foot ship ablaze before it smashed into the craggy basalt lava rocks at Boiler

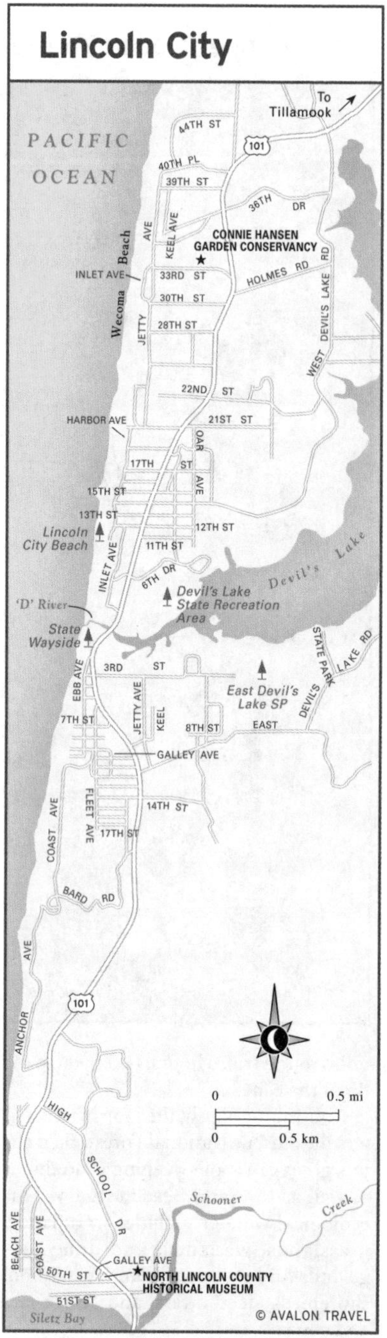

Lincoln City

PACIFIC OCEAN

To Tillamook

CONNIE HANSEN GARDEN CONSERVANCY

Lincoln City Beach

'D' River State Wayside

Devil's Lake State Recreation Area

Devil's Lake

East Devil's Lake SP

STATE PARK

Schooner Creek

Siletz Bay

NORTH LINCOLN COUNTY HISTORICAL MUSEUM

0   0.5 mi
0   0.5 km

© AVALON TRAVEL

Bay. The ship's boiler and driveshaft drifted ashore and are still visible at low tide. A large chunk of rusted steel sticks up from the bluff above, blown there by the force of the explosion and firmly embedded in the ground.

Connie Hansen Garden Conservancy

Enchanting pathways meander along lush greenery and colorful blooms at the **Connie Hansen Garden Conservancy** (1931 NW 33rd St., 541/994-6338, www.conniehansengarden.com, dawn-dusk daily, free). A San Francisco artist who moved to Lincoln City in 1973 created it over a 20-year period—an amazing accomplishment considering the salt air and sandy soil. In the summertime, it bursts with color as everything is in bloom, including roses and rhododendrons. Rare trees and shrubbery can be seen throughout the year. Tours are available by appointment, scheduled a minimum of two weeks in advance.

North Lincoln County Historical Museum

Local history and culture are preserved at the **North Lincoln County Historical Museum** (4907 SW US-101, 541/996-6614, www.northlincolncountyhistoricalmuseum.org, noon-5pm Wed.-Sun. June-Aug., noon-5pm Wed.-Sat. Sept.-May, free), with 19th- and 20th-century exhibits on the lives of early pioneers and homesteaders, and an amazing display of glass fishing floats.

Food

Start the day with a hearty breakfast at **The Otis Cafe** (1259 Salmon River Hwy., 541/994-2813, www.otiscafe.com, 7am-8pm daily, under $10), where large portions and affordable prices go hand in hand. Gourmet pizza, housemade sausage, and other locally sourced fare is served at **Hearth & Table** (660 US-101, 541/614-0966, 11am-8pm Tues.-Sat., under $10).

Hwy 101 Burger (5045 S. US-101, 541/418-2305, www.hwy101burger.com, 11am-8pm Sun.-Thurs., 11am-9pm Fri.-Sat., $6-11) serves good old-fashioned burgers, thick and juicy, double or even quadruple. **The Nelscott Café** (3237 SW US-101, 541/994-6100, www.nelscottcafe. com, 9am-3pm Thurs.-Mon., $8-13) makes its burgers a little interesting with tasty sides like homemade pickle chips. If you stop in for breakfast, don't pass up the best stuffed French toast on the coast.

Blackfish Café (2733 NW US-101, 541/996-1007, www.blackfishcafe.com, 11:30am-3pm and 5pm-9pm daily, $16-30) is known for its signature clam chowder, fish-and-chips, and breaded oysters. **J's Fish & Chips** (1800 SE US-101, 541/994-4445, 11:30am-8pm daily, $6-12) shucks then simmers clams in a creamy broth, and lightly coats and fries halibut to perfection.

Intimate dining with views of the Pacific makes **The Bay House** (5911 SW US-101, 541/996-3222, www.thebayhouse.org, 5pm-9pm Wed.-Sun., $29-76) a local favorite. Every dish is a culinary masterpiece, paired with fine wines for the ultimate in fine dining.

Creekside dining on the patio of **Wildflower Grill** (4250 NE US-101, 541/994-9663, www.thewildflowergrill. com, 7am-9pm Tues.-Sat., 7am-4pm Sun.-Mon., $10-16) includes breakfast, seafood, sandwiches, and comfort food options.

Nightlife and Entertainment

The Nauti Mermaid Bar & Bistro (1343 NW US-101, 541/614-1001, 11am-2:30am Mon.-Sat., 11am-midnight Sun.) is a friendly neighborhood bar with mixed drinks, beer on tap, pool tables, and lottery games. **Old Oregon Tavern** (1604 NE US-101, 541/994-8515, 7am-2:30am daily) is a popular dive bar with cheap drinks, bar grub, and a big-screen TV. Across the street, **Maxwell's at the Coast** (1643 NW US-101, 541/994-8100, www.maxwellslincolncity.com, 8am-2:30pm

Mon.-Thurs., 8am-3am Fri., 6am-3am Sat., 6am-2:30am Sun.) has pool tables, darts, golf, and karaoke.

At **Game Over Arcade Bar and Grill** (2821 NW US-101, 541/614-1150, www. gameover-arcade.com, 1pm-midnight Mon.-Thurs., 1pm-2am Fri., 10am-2am Sat., 10am-midnight Sun.), a pocketful of quarters is all you need for a good time. It's for adults only (kids at heart), serving beer and wine amid the rows of old-school arcade games and pinball machines.

Entertainment abounds at **Chinook Winds Casino Resort** (1777 NW 44th St., 888/244-6665, www.chinookwinds-casino.com, 24 hours daily), from slots, video poker machines, and table games to concerts and comedy acts. Situated above the fairways of the Chinook Winds golf course, **Aces Sports Bar & Grill** (541/994-8232) entertains with NFL games, UFC Pay-per-View, and the Pac-12 Network played on 14 screens.

Shopping

Along US-101 is a collection of galleries and souvenir and specialty shops, such as **101 Coastal Creations** (4840 SE US-101, 541/614-1525, 11am-5pm Wed.-Mon.), which specializes in blown glass, fine art, and handcrafted jewelry. **Cap'N Gulls Gift Place** (120 SE US-101, 541/994-7743, 9:30am-6pm daily) stocks glass floats, wind chimes, clothing, and specialty gifts. The **Lincoln City Surf Shop** (4792 SE US-101, 541/996-7433, www.lcsurfshop. com, 9am-7pm daily) offers surf, skim, and wetsuit rentals. Browse handcrafted jewelry made from Pacific Northwest gems at **Rock Your World** (1423 NW US-101, 541/351-8423, 11am-6pm daily summer, 11am-5pm Sun.-Thurs., 11am-6pm Fri.-Sat.).

Prehistoric (1425 NW US-101., 541/614-1294, www.prehistoricoregon. com, 8:30am-5pm daily) deals in fossils, minerals, and meteorites, including things like dinosaur teeth and insects trapped in amber.

Lincoln City Farmers and Crafters Market (540 NE US-101, 541/867-6293, www.lincolncityfarmersmarket.org, 9am-2pm Sun.) offers locally grown produce, baked goods, prepared foods, and handcrafted items from inside the Lincoln City Cultural Center during the cold months or outdoors when the sun is shining.

Tanger Outlet Center (1500 SE Devils Lake Rd., 541/996-5000, 10am-8pm Mon.-Sat., 10am-6pm Sun.) encompasses more than 50 discount name-brand stores that will satisfy quality tastes without empting your wallet.

Recreation

Most people come to Lincoln City for a day at the beach. The favored access points are at the north and south ends of the city. The prettiest stretch of beach is on the north end of town at **Road's End State Wayside** (off US-101 on Logan Rd., 541/994-7341, www.oregonstateparks. org, 5am-10pm). The cool sandy shore has interesting rock features and tidepools that reveal bright starfish and sea anemones at low tide.

A short drive north off Three Rocks Road, **Knights Park** marks the lower trailhead (open year-round, free) to the **Cascade Head Trail,** a moderate four-mile journey through old-growth fir and spruce, across streams and bridges, and butterfly meadows. Viewpoints extend down the coastline, exposing the Salmon River Estuary, Cape Foulweather, and Devil's Lake.

On the northeast side of US-101, **Devil's Lake State Park** (541/994-2002 and 800/551-6949, www.oregonstate-parks.org, $5 per vehicle) offers summer recreation, including fishing, boating ($10 moorage), and waterskiing. Boat launches are located on the west shore of the lake near the campground ($17-21 tents, $44 yurts, $27-31 RVs) and on the southern end at East Devil's Lake day-use park (205 NE East Devils Lake Rd.). **Blue Heron Landing Rentals** (4006

NE West Devils Lake Rd., 541/994-4708, www.blueheronlanding.net, 9am-7pm Mon.-Sat., 10am-7pm Sun.) rents canoes and kayaks ($19/hour, $57/day) and carries bait supplies and other fishing equipment.

To the south, across US-101, **Siletz Bay** is an estuary populated by many bird species, including great blue herons, hawks, and egrets. The sandy peninsula jutting out into the bay is the **Salishan Spit,** which provides both an easy and scenic 8.1-mile hike, passing spruce trees, crumbling sandstone ridges, and hundreds of lounging seals. The trailhead is accessed at Gleneden Beach State Park, off US-101 on Wesler Street.

Boiler Bay is popular with surfers despite its jagged lava-rimmed bay and strong currents; it is not a place for beginners. Sea life is abundant, with whales seen off the bay year-round. At low tide, rich tidepools are revealed, as is the wreckage of the *J. Marhoffer.*

Events

Kites vie for sky space at Lincoln City's summer and fall **Kite Festivals** (D-River Wayside, late June and early Oct.). The weekend events feature demonstrations, kite-making activities, and some of the biggest, most colorful kites in the world.

Accommodations

Affordable yet charming, **Palace Inn and Suites** (550 SE US-101, 541/996-9466, www.thepalaceinn.com, $50 and up) has 51 spacious guest rooms in walking distance from the beach, restaurants, and shopping. The **Historic Anchor Inn** (4417 SW US-101, 541/996-3810, www.historicanchorinn.com, $109 and up) surrounds you with 1940s nostalgia and nautical paraphernalia, and offers an on-site massage therapist. The **Inn at Wecoma** (2945 NW US-101, 541/994-2984 and 800/452-8981, www.innatwecoma.com, $84 and up) offers a hearty breakfast, spacious rooms, and special accommodations for pets. The **Looking Glass Inn** (861 SW

51st St., 541/996-3996 and 800/843-4940, www.lookingglass-inn.com, $119 and up) sits on a driftwood-strewn beach, offering views of the Siletz River and Bay. Guest rooms include all the comforts of home.

Every room at **Inn at Spanish Head** (4009 SW US-101, 800/452-8127 or 541/996-2161, www.spanishhead.com, $160 and up) offers floor-to-ceiling windows with unobstructed ocean views. You'll never miss a sunset at the **Nelscott Manor** (3037 SW Anchor Ave., 541/996-9300 or 800/972-6155, www.onthebeachfront.com, $129 and up), which offers five oceanfront suites with whirlpool tubs.

Information and Services

Detailed information is available by contacting the **Lincoln City Visitor and Convention Bureau** (801 SW US-101 #401, 800/452-2151 or 541/996-1274, www.lincolncity.org, 8am-5pm Mon.-Fri.), on the fourth floor of the City Hall building.

Depoe Bay

Twelve miles south of Lincoln City, the tiny village of **Depoe Bay** (pop. 1,448) boasts the "smallest harbor in the world," but its reigning title as the "Whale Watching Capital of the Oregon Coast" is more worthy of braggadocio. From March through December a pod of gray whales takes up residence offshore. But whales are not the only attraction blowing sea water into the air. Depoe Bay's coastline is riddled with lava beds that occasionally shoot water nearly 60 feet into the sky once enough pressure has built up. A huge seawall runs along the entire length of downtown, where the ocean always remains in view.

Gracie's Sea Hag Restaurant & Lounge (58 US-101, 541/765-2734, www.theseahag.com, 7am-9:30pm daily, $15-32) is worth a stop for its homemade chowder. Gracie herself has become a local celebrity for playing "bottle music" behind the bar. There's more traditional live music Thursday-Sunday. Stay the night at the **Inn at Arch Rock** (70 NW Sunset St., 800/767-1835 or 541/765-2560, www.innatarchrock.com, $89 and up), which offers spectacular views and easy access to the beach. Or, go big at **Whale Cove Inn** (2345 US-101, 541/765-4300, www.whalecoveinn.com, $341 and up), where each suite includes a private deck, an outdoor hot tub, and a view of the aptly named cove.

Otter Crest Loop: Cape Foulweather and the Devil's Punchbowl

During his voyage of discovery to the Sandwich Islands, Captain James Cook (circa 1778) first landed at **Cape Foulweather,** a basalt cliff that rises 500 feet above the Pacific, overlooking Otter Rock and Yaquina Head.

Two miles south of Depoe Bay, a sign on US-101 marks the turn-off to Otter Crest Access Loop Road, a twisting three-mile section of the old coastal highway, where the already rugged coastal bluffs become even more dramatic. It winds its way to the Otter Crest State Scenic Viewpoint, where there's a parking lot. Watch the crashing surf along the shore, sea lions basking in the sun, and migrating whales and ships passing on the horizon. The never-ending views are unforgettable. **The Lookout** (milepost 232.5, US-101, 541/765-2270, 10am-4pm Wed.-Sun.) is a small interpretive center and gift shop atop the bluff that is protected as a historic landmark.

At the south end of the loop, the churning surf surges against a wave-sculpted basin appropriately named the **Devil's Punchbowl.** North of the Punchbowl, tidepools are revealed when the water recedes. To the south is a viewpoint with picnic tables. Still farther south is **Mo's**

West (122 1st St., Otter Rock, 541/765-2442, www.moschowder.com, 11am-3pm Sun.-Fri., 11am-8pm Sat., $9-18), where a hot cup of famous chowder hits the spot!

Newport

Nearly 13 miles south of Depoe Bay sits the largest town on the Oregon coast, **Newport** (pop. 10,393), founded in the 1860s largely due to the demand for its sweet Yaquina Bay oysters. Summer tourists wander the shops, galleries, and attractions along the bayfront and pack into the Oregon Coast Aquarium. In the distance, fishing boats bait the waters for the day's bounty, while sea lions lounge on the docks.

On the north side of town, charming **Nye Beach** was one of the first resort destinations on the coast. Old, 19th-century cottages remain as a testament to the town's early roots, scattered among neoteric hotels, vintage shops, and quaint cafés.

Getting There and Around
Newport sits at the junction of US-101 and US-20, 25 miles (40 minutes) south of Lincoln City. Lincoln County provides daily bus service with the **Newport City Loop** (541/265-4900, www.co.lincoln.or.us, $1).

Sights
Bayfront
On the east side of US-101, Newport's **Historic Bayfront** is a tourist hub with saltwater taffy shops, souvenir stores, and overpriced attractions. **Mariner Square** (250 SW Bay Blvd., 541/265-2206, www.marinersquare.com, 11am-4pm Mon.-Fri., 10am-4pm Sat.-Sun., later hours in the summer, $15 adults, $8 children 5-12) marks the entrance to **The Wax Works, Ripley's Believe It or Not!,** and the **Undersea Gardens,** where Oregon's largest collection of local marinelife can be seen swimming through a kelp forest.

Newport

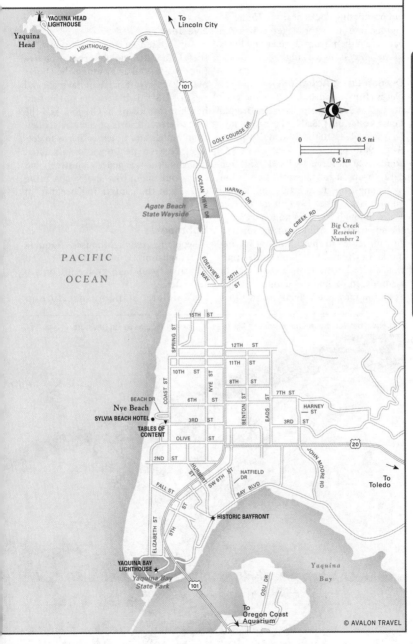

YAQUINA HEAD
LIGHTHOUSE

Yaquina
Head

LIGHTHOUSE DR

To
Lincoln City

101

GOLF COURSE DR

OCEAN VIEW DR

HARNEY DR

Agate Beach
State Wayside

BIG CREEK RD

Big Creek
Resevoir
Number 2

PACIFIC

OCEAN

EDENVIEW WAY

20TH ST

0   0.5 mi
0   0.5 km

15TH ST

SPRING ST

12TH ST

10TH ST

NYE ST

11TH ST

8TH ST

BENTON ST

EADS ST

7TH ST

BEACH DR

COAST ST

6TH ST

HARNEY
ST

Nye Beach
SYLVIA BEACH HOTEL

3RD ST

3RD
ST

TABLES OF
CONTENT

OLIVE ST

2ND ST

HURBERT ST

SW 9TH ST

HATFIELD
DR

BAY BLVD

JOHN MOORE RD

20

To
Toledo

FALL ST

9TH ST

HISTORIC BAYFRONT

ELIZABETH ST

YAQUINA BAY
LIGHTHOUSE

Yaquina Bay
State Park

101

OSU DR

Yaquina
Bay

To
Oregon Coast
Aquarium

© AVALON TRAVEL

Tickets can be purchased at Mariner Square per attraction or at a discount for all three. The loitering sea lions sprawled out on floating docks near the Undersea Gardens are one of the biggest draws. You can watch them from the pier and listen to their incessant barking.

Oregon Coast Aquarium

Get a slimy handshake from the resident giant Pacific octopus at the **Oregon Coast Aquarium** (2820 SE Ferry Slip Rd., 541/867-3474, 10am-5pm daily June-Aug., 9am-6pm daily Sept.-May, $23 adults, $20 children 13-17, $15 children 3-12), brought to the world's attention by its one-time main attraction: Keiko, an orca, star of the 1993 hit movie *Free Willy*. Though Keiko is no longer here, the aquarium is still one of the top marine museums in the country, featuring outdoor exhibits of sea lions, tufted puffins, and other shorebirds cavorting in a simulated rockbound habitat, as well as an indoor aquatic aviary tunnel that allows for undersea viewing of sharks. The museum offers visual and interactive information on Pacific Coast ecosystems.

Nye Beach

Easily missed (if you don't know it's there), the little neighborhood of **Nye Beach** is tucked away along the shores of the Pacific, just north of Bayfront and west of US-101. It was one of the first beach resort towns in Oregon, and the first to erect all sorts of getaway abodes, from motels and hotels to B&Bs to cottages. Nye is a great town to walk about (there is a car-free pedestrian street) and check out the quirky shops, charming cafés, and the captivating oceanfront views.

Lighthouses

Newport has two lighthouses—Yaquina Bay Lighthouse, built in 1871, and Yaquina Head Lighthouse, lit only a year later.

The oldest standing structure in

In Oregon, the PCH crosses many bridges, like this one crossing Yaquina Bay in Newport.

Newport, **Yaquina Bay Lighthouse** (846 SW Government St., 541/265-5679, noon-4pm daily) sits above the mouth of the Yaquina River. It illuminated its oscillating light for only three years before it was decommissioned. The light tower sits above a two-story house, not the usual design for a watchtower, but it did serve as a residence and a guiding light to offshore vessels. In 1996, it was lovingly restored and its white light relit, now shining steadily from dusk to dawn. Visitors are welcome to explore the lighthouse on their own. Private tours can be arranged with Sylvia White (541/270-0131, fee may apply).

On the north side of town, **Yaquina Head Lighthouse** (750 NW Lighthouse Dr., 541/574-3100, parks and outdoor nature areas outside lighthouse 8am-5pm daily, $7 parking pass, good for three days) rises 93 feet from its basalt perch and is Oregon's tallest lighthouse. A tour guide dressed in 1800s attire paints a picture of the past and shares old tales as you

ascend the 114 spiraling steps to the top for a breathtaking view. Tours operate every hour (noon-3pm Thurs.-Tues.). It's first-come, first-served and space is limited, so get there early. Even if you miss the tour, the 100-acre site offers visitors unprecedented views, an interpretive center, a gift shop, the Tidepool Loop Trail leading through an old quarry, and abundant marinelife and wildlife.

Food

The original **Mo's** (622 SW Bay Blvd., 541/265-2979, www.moschowder.com, 11am-8pm Sun.-Thurs., 11am-9pm Fri.-Sat., $4-22) started serving its famous clam chowder here over 70 years ago and now boasts seven locations, including a roomier **Annex** just across the street (657 SW Bay Blvd.). Some locals prefer the **Chowder Bowl at Nye Beach** (728 NW Beach Dr., 541/265-7477, www.newportchowderbowl.com, 11am-8pm daily, $5-22). All three offer much more than chowder in sourdough bread bowls, including seafood, chili, and burgers.

Relatively upscale **Saffron Salmon** (859 SW Bay Blvd., 541/265-8921, 11:30am-2:30pm Fri.-Sun., 5pm-8:30pm Thurs.-Tues., $14-28) offers fresh and local seafood with a view of the Yaquina Bay Bridge, while **Local Ocean Seafoods** (213 SE Bay Blvd., 541/574-7959, www.localocean.net, 11am-9pm Sun.-Thurs., 11am-9:30pm Fri.-Sat., $16-30) does so in a contemporary setting.

The tiny district of Nye Beach dishes up some excellent grub! From its bright yellow exterior, **Cafe Stephanie** (411 NW Coast St., 541/265-8082, 7:30am-2pm daily, $8-14) is hard to pass up, and you won't want to miss their pastries galore, banana French toast, and omelets. **Panini Bakery** (232 NW Coast St., 541/272-5322, 7am-7pm daily, $3-20) makes fresh pizza in a wood-fired oven and sells it by the slice. They also make great baked goods and the best lattes in town. Bright and cheery **Nye Beach Café** (526 NW Coast St., 541/574-1599, 7am-3pm daily., $8-12) offers a mix of fresh, healthy fare, with gluten-free options and clam chowder of its own.

On the southwest side of US-101, family-friendly **Georgie's Beachside Grill** (744 SW Elizabeth St., at Hallmark Resort, 541/265-9800, www.georgies-beachsidegrill.com, 7:30am-9pm daily, $10-33) serves up fresh seafood, steak, pasta, and vegan dishes with a gorgeous ocean view.

Delicious, family-style dinners are well worth the price at the Sylvia Beach Hotel restaurant ★ **Tables of Content** (267 NW Cliff St., 541/265-5428, www.sylviabeachhotel.com/restaurant, 6pm seating, $28), but it's the opportunity to meet and share stories with fellow travelers that makes for a most memorable evening.

Nightlife and Entertainment

Artsy Nye Beach has a dynamic nightlife. **Nana's Irish Pub** (613 NW 3rd St., 541/574-8787, www.nanasirishpub.com, 11am-9pm Sun.-Thurs., 11am-10pm Fri.-Sat.) is a spirited meeting place with live music every Monday night (and sometimes weekends) with everything from traditional Irish music to rock-and-roll. At upbeat, bohemian **Café Mundo** (209 NW Coast St., 541/574-8134, 11am-10pm Thurs.-Sat., 11am-3pm Sun.), the art is unique, the cocktails are perfect, and the music (jazz and folk) is always free.

Two dozen handles of craft beer pour at the **Taphouse at Nye Creek** (515 NW Coast St., 541/272-5545, www.taphouse-atnye.com, 11am-10pm Sun.-Fri., 11am-11pm Fri.-Sat.), along with pizza and sandwiches. Oregon's famed **Rogue Ales** brewery has been brewing across the bridge, in South Beach, since 1989. Pass between its tall, stainless-steel tanks to access its **Rogue Ales Public House** (2320 SE Marine Science Dr., 541/867-3660, www.rogue.com, 11am-8pm Sun.-Thurs., 11am-9pm Fri.-Sat.) for food and tastings.

Newport Performing Arts Center

(777 W. Olive St., 541/265-2787, www.coastarts.org, box office 9am-5pm Mon.-Fri.) hosts musical entertainment, Shakespearean plays, Broadway musicals, and dance productions year-round.

Shopping

The Historic Bayfront is lined with art galleries and unique gift shops. Located near the Undersea Gardens, **The Wind Drift Gallery** (414 SW Bay Blvd., 541/265-7454, www.oregoncoastgalleries.net, 10am-5:30pm daily) is filled with wind chimes, jewelry, home decor, and knickknacks. Next door, you'll find natural stone jewelry, exquisite glass art, and other crafts from Northwest artists at **Breach the Moon Gallery** (434 SW Bay Blvd., 541/265-9698, www.oregoncoastgalleries.net, 10am-6pm daily). The art at **Latta's Fused Glass** (669 Bay Blvd., 541/265-9685, www.lattasfusedglass.com, 10am-5pm daily) ranges from whimsical to sophisticated; every vase, plate, and platter has its own personality.

On a sea cliff west of US-101, Nye Beach has its own mix of stylish boutiques and quirky shops. **For ArtSake Gallery** (258 NW Coast St., 541/574-9070, www.forartssakegallery.com, 10am-5pm daily) displays paintings, pottery, leather handbags, jewelry, and glass art. Make your own jewelry with help from **Nye Cottage Beads** (208 NW Coast St., 541/265-6262, www.nyecottage.com, 10am-5pm daily), a little nook draped in wall-to-wall strands of color. At charming **Tu Tu Tu** (222 NW Coast St., 541/265-8065, 10am-5pm Thurs.-Sat., Mon., 11am-4pm Sun.), kitchen and cooking supplies include oyster-shucking hardware.

Pirates and sea creatures are scattered throughout clusters of colorful antique and specialty gift shops at **Aquarium Village** (3101 SE Ferry Slip Rd., 541/867-6531, www.aquariumvillage.org, 8am-4:30pm Mon.-Fri.). There's also a climbable pirate ship for kids.

Recreation

On the south side of Yaquina Head, **Agate Beach** is a hot spot for surfers with good breaks at mid- to high tide. The beach is easily accessed from the Agate Beach parking lot, right past **Ossies Surf Shop** (4860 N. Coast Hwy., 541/574-4634, www.ossiessurfshop.com, 10am-6pm Mon.-Sat., 10am-5pm Sun.), which offers surf lessons, gear rentals, and kayak tours.

Crabbing and clamming around Yaquina Bay are also popular. Butter, cockle, and littleneck clams can all be found on the mudflats at **Sally's Bend,** accessed from Yaquina Bay Drive at low tide. Bring a shovel, bucket, and rubber boots. Red rock crabs are caught off the Abbey Street and Bay Street piers on the Newport Historic Bayfront. The required license can be purchased at local tackle shops, like **Harry's Bait & Tackle** (404 SW Bay Blvd., 541/265-2407), which also rents equipment ($25 deposit).

Events

The **Seafood and Wine Festival** (1 Lee's Wharf, 800/262-7844, www.seafoodandwine.com, Feb., $16-40) is a gathering focused on culinary delights plucked from the sea, Pacific Northwest wines, and lovely artwork.

Writers, poets, playwrights, and songwriters perform at the monthly **Writers' Series** (777 NW Beach Dr., 541/563-6263, www.writersontheedge.org, 7pm third Sat. monthly, $8) in Nye Beach.

Accommodations

Sylvia Beach isn't a beach but the name of the founder of famed Paris bookshop Shakespeare and Company. Like the shop, the unique and memorable ★ **Sylvia Beach Hotel** (267 NW Cliff St., 541/265-5428, www.sylviabeachhotel.com, $135 and up) also proves a must-see for book-lovers, with the decor for each of its 21 rooms taking inspiration from a particular author: Agatha Christie, Mark Twain, and J. K. Rowling, for example.

Among the truly creative rooms, some have a deck, a bathtub, and/or a view, but there's no TV or no Wi-Fi. There is a cozy reading library overlooking the ocean—at Nye Beach.

For more traditional hotel amenities nearby, the **Inn at Nye Beach** (729 NW Coast St., 541/265-2477 or 800/480-2477, www.innatnyebeach.com, $250 and up), atop a bluff connected by a staircase to the beach below, has you covered. Enjoy great views, room service, and fresh scones. For a little less, **The Whaler Motel** (155 SW Elizabeth St., 541/265-9261, www.whalernewport.com, $154 and up) offers ocean-view rooms and an indoor pool.

At the scenic north end of town, **Agate Beach Motel** (175 NW Gilbert Way, 541/265-8746 or 800/755-5674, www.agatebeachmotel.com, $174 and up) offers ocean-view cottage units with full kitchens, private decks, and easy beach access.

The romantic **Hallmark Resort** (744 SW Elizabeth St., 855/391-2484, www.hallmarkinns.com, $189 and up) has ocean-view rooms with patios, cozy fireplaces, and spa tubs for two.

Information and Services

For further information on Newport attractions or for a complete list of hotels, contact the **Greater Newport Chamber of Commerce** (555 SW Coast Hwy., 541/265-8801, www.newportchamber.org, 8:30am-5pm Mon.-Fri.).

Waldport

As US-101 continues along wooded coast another 16 miles, it comes to low-key **Waldport** (pop. 2,163), a relaxed alternative to its tourist-hungry neighbors. Much of the town's economy still relies on fishing. The town's most popular activity is watching fishing boats, waterfowl, and seals out in the Alsea Bay. **Alsea Bay Bridge Interpretive Center** (620 NW Spring St., 800/551-6949, 10am-4pm

Thurs.-Sun.) offers clamming and crabbing demonstrations, bridge walk tours, and information on the local Alsea tribe.

Vintage **Cape Cod Cottages** (4150 SW Pacific Coast Hwy., 541/563-2106, www.capecodcottagesonline.com, $76 and up), located on a quiet sandy beach, offers one- and two-bedroom rentals with full kitchens. Four miles south of the Alsea bridge, **Beachside State Recreation Area** (541/563-3220) has a good-sized campground with all the amenities, including a coin-operated laundry.

Yachats

Eight miles south of Waldport, the charming, tiny village of **Yachats** (pop. 742; pronounced "YA-hots") is an idyllic retreat in a remarkable natural setting at the mouth of the Yachats River and in the shadow of Cape Perpetua. You're more likely to find peace and quiet than crowds of beachgoers.

Along the beautiful one-mile loop around **Ocean Road State Natural Area,** you can see a spouting basalt blowhole and spot migrating whales. In and around town, there are artist galleries and gift shops, as well as a **Sunday Farmers Market** (4th St. next to Yachats Commons, 541/961-3295, www.yachatsfarmersmarket.webs.com, 9am-2pm Sun. mid-May-mid-Oct.).

Overleaf Lodge & Spa (280 Overleaf Lodge Ln., 541/547-4880 or 800/338-0507, $221 and up) looks out over the sea, offering sweeping views and relaxing spa treatments. **ONA Restaurant and Lounge** (131 US-101 N., 541/547-6627, 11am-8:30pm daily, $12-37) is perfect for a romantic dinner, with views of the Yachats River and the Pacific Ocean.

Cape Perpetua

Just outside Yachats, **Cape Perpetua** is a steep bluff rising above the Pacific Ocean,

Central Oregon Coast

© AVALON TRAVEL

over 800 feet at its highest point. On a clear day, you can see nearly 70 miles of coastline from its ridge. It also includes 26 miles of hiking trails that meander through old-growth forests of Douglas fir, western hemlock, and spruce, including the 600-year-old Giant Spruce, which measures more than 185 feet tall.

As you enter, stop at the **visitors center** (2400 US-101, 541/547-3289, www.fs.usda.gov, 10am-4:30pm daily, $5/car) for hiking and driving tour maps. It also features an observation deck, natural history and cultural exhibits, a theater, and a small bookstore.

The driving tour will lead you to the summit. Once you've taken in the view, you can follow the half-mile loop **Whispering Spruce Trail,** which travels through the grounds of a Word War II Coast Guard station, built in 1933 by the Civilian Conservation Corps.

Down on the beach, you can make your way to Devil's Churn, Spouting Horn, and Thor's Well, basalt rock formations that spray seawater 50 feet into the air in strong surf.

Along the banks of Cape Creek, the **Cape Perpetua Campground** (2200 US-101, 877/444-6777, www.recreation.gov, $26) is surrounded by trees. There are picnic tables, drinking water, and flush toilets, but no showers or hookups.

★ Heceta Head and the Sea Lion Caves

Nearly 14 miles south of Yachats you'll find one of the most visited and photographed lighthouses in the United States perched at the top of 1,000-foot-high Heceta Head. Built in 1893, it was named for a captain of the Royal Spanish Navy who made note of the headland in his journal when exploring the region. The masonry tower stands 56 feet tall and its light shines 21 miles out to sea—farther than any other on the Oregon coast.

The former light-keeper's house is today known as **Heceta House** (92072 US-101, 541/547-3696 or 866/547-3696, www.hecetalighthouse.com, free), which acts as an *interpretive center* (noon-5pm Mon.-Thurs. Memorial Day-Labor day) and a quaint **bed-and-breakfast** ($215 and up). Free guided tours are offered regularly during the summer and by appointment the rest of the year. Stories of strange activities and unexplained occurrences at Heceta House have collected over the years, winning it a place on lists of the 10 most-haunted houses in the United States. Public parking is located at the Heceta Head Lighthouse State Scenic Viewpoint ($5 per vehicle).

Just south of the lighthouse, the surge of the sea crashes into the vast **Sea Lion Caves** (91560 US-101, 541/547-3111, www.sealioncaves.com, $14 adults, $8 children 5-12, 9am-6pm daily), one of the largest known sea caves in the world and a dwelling place for thousands of Steller sea lions. You can ride the elevator down into the cavern and witness these enormous mammals (males can weigh over a ton, while females reach 600-800 pounds). Fall and winter are the best times to see them. When the sun comes out, you can see them playing in the ocean and basking on rocks from viewpoints along US-101.

Florence

Midway between the Oregon coastal cities of Newport and Coos Bay, **Florence** (pop. 8,800) sits at the mouth of the Siuslaw River (pronounced "sigh-YOU-slaw"). It's an eclectic city of old and new, defined by its historical structures, natural setting, and commercial industries. The Siuslaw Indians originally lived around the estuary of the Siuslaw River and taught early pioneers how to collect food and fish its waters. Eventually "industry" took over with commercial fishing and timber mills, as the demand for wood increased throughout the West.

Getting There and Around

Florence sits on US-101, 49 miles (1 hour, 10 minutes) from Newport along a stretch of highway that hugs the coastline, offering open views of the ocean. Services and sights are spread out, so a car or bus service is best to get around.

The **Rhody Express** (541/902-2067, www.ltd.org/rhody. 10am-6pm Mon.-Fri., $1 one-way, $2 day pass) is the public transportation service within the community, and operates a South (Dune Village, Old Town, Three Rivers Casino) and North (Grocery Outlet, Fred Meyer) loop in a 70-minute circuit. There are several stops along its route, each clearly visible.

Sights

Along Bay Street's three blocks, you'll find cafés, seafood restaurants, and all kinds of interesting boutiques and galleries with treasures to uncover. But the more interesting and somewhat curious wonders are found just south of Old Town.

Old Town

On the southern end of Florence, **Old Town** is nestled into the Port of Siuslaw. It's easy to miss from the highway and there is only one sign pointing the way, but that doesn't mean it's not worth stopping. It's a welcoming fishing village, established in 1893, with narrow streets,

historical buildings, and a meandering boardwalk. There's a lot to explore along Laurel and Bay Streets, where artful shops and eateries are found. Follow the brick path past the gazebo to the ferry landing overlook, a great spot for birdwatchers and for photos of the Siuslaw River Bridge.

Siuslaw River Bridge

Ferry boats were the link across the Siuslaw River until 1936, when the **Siuslaw River Bridge** was completed. Designed by Conde McCullough in the bascule style, the bridge has two 154-foot concrete tied arches and four art deco-style obelisks. Walking west on Bay Street brings you under the bridge to the **Interpretive Center** and viewing platform, which provides unobstructed views of the bridge and estuary. Walkways wander past benches where you can rest and take in the landscape, while interpretive signs give the history and geology of the site.

Heceta House, the oft-photographed lighthouse on Heceta Head

Siuslaw Pioneer Museum

Historical photographs and 19th-century artifacts fill **Siuslaw Pioneer Museum** (278 Maple St., 541/997-7884, www.siuslawpioneermuseum.com, noon-4pm daily, $4 adults, free children under 16), located in a renovated 1905 schoolhouse building. Upstairs, memorabilia from the Civil War and World Wars I and II share space with Native American relics, while downstairs exhibits focus on the logging, fishing, and maritime industries.

Darlingtonia State Natural Site

A visit to **Darlingtonia State Natural Site** (5400 Mercer Lake Rd., 541/997-3851, www.oregonstateparks.org, daylight hours) might leave you uneasy once you realize what lives here: a carnivorous plant! No, it isn't Audrey II from the musical *Little Shop of Horrors;* it's a cobra lily, a rare, hooded plant, also known as *Darlingtonia californica.* From the parking lot, a boardwalk trail with views of the Oregon Dunes leads to this botanical wonder that lures insects with sweet nectar from the opening beneath its yellowish-green leaves.

Jessie M. Honeyman Memorial State Park

Three miles south of Florence, **Jessie M. Honeyman Memorial State Park** (84505 US-101, 800/551-6949, www.oregonstateparks.org, $5 day-use, $21 camp, $44 yurt) springs to life with vibrant rhododendrons in late April to the middle of May. But the park's main attractions are rows and rows of shifting **sand dunes** that stretch two miles along the coast. The Oregon Dunes National Recreation Area adjoins the west side of the park.

Food

Start the day at **Fresh Harvest Café** (3056 US-101, 541/997-4051, www.freshharvestcafe.com, 7am-2pm daily, $5-15), whether you hanker for pancakes and egg dishes or terrific crepes.

Housed in an old railroad station, ★ **Waterfront Depot** (1252 Bay St., 541/902-9100, www.thewaterfrontdepot.com, 4pm-10pm daily, under $12-28) serves great seafood and steaks in its dining room and outdoor patio, with picturesque views.

Big Dogs Donuts & Deli (1136 US-101, 541/997-8630, 5am-3pm Mon.-Sat., 5am-noon Sun., $1-9) is inside an old yellow gas station, but don't judge the food by the building. The fresh doughnuts are legendary, and they know how to make a great sandwich, too.

For tastes with a little added spice, try family-owned **Rosa's Mexican Restaurant** (2825 US-101, 541/997-1144, 10:30am-9pm Mon.-Sat., $8-16), where the chips and salsa are homemade and the service is delightful.

Nature's Corner Café & Market (185 US-101, 541/997-0900, www.naturescornercafe.com, 7am-6pm Mon.-Sat., 7:30am-3pm Sun., $4-21) serves everything organic and sometimes gluten-free, with everything from breakfast burritos and blueberry pancakes to fish tacos and burgers.

La Pomodori Ristorante (1415 7th St., 541/902-2525, www.lapomodori.com, 11:30am-2pm Tues.-Fri., 5pm-8pm Tues.-Sat., $6-22) fuses traditional Italian cooking with Northwest flavors. The pasta dishes and crab cakes are delicious, and the garlic bread is unbelievable.

Local sourcing of meat, seafood, and organic veggies makes for plenty of great dishes to pair with regional craft beer and cider at **Homegrown Public House** (294 Laurel St., 541/997-4886, www.home-grownpub.com, 11am-8pm Tues.-Thurs., 11am-9pm Fri.-Sat., $9-27).

Colorful Asian bistro **Spice** (1269 Bay St., 541/997-1646, www.spiceinflorence.com, 4pm-8pm Tues.-Sat., $15-35) serves a variety of savory Eastern dishes and Northwest favorites. Try the house favorite Shellfish Madness—so much seafood that it needs two bowls!

Nightlife and Entertainment

For over 50 years, the **Beachcomber Pub** (1355 Bay St., 541/997-6357, 7am-midnight daily) has been a fixture in Old Town Florence, with over 100 bottled beers, a great selection of beers on tap, and live bands every Friday and Saturday night.

Despite its unassuming appearance, **Travelers Cove** (1362 Bay St., 541/997-6845, 9am-8pm Mon.-Fri., 9am-9pm Sat.-Sun., extended weekend hours) is a local favorite because of its well-priced drinks, eclectic musical entertainment, and the lively deck above the river.

Three Rivers Casino (5647 OR-126, 877/374-8377, www.threerivers.com, 24 hours daily) is packed with over 700 Vegas-style slots, video games, and table games.

Enjoy an evening of theatrical delight attending a play or musical at the **Florence Playhouse** (208 Laurel St., 541/997-1675), in Old Town on Laurel and 1st Streets, just steps away from the Siuslaw River.

Shopping

Most shopping is in Old Town.

If you love beautiful things, stop by **Bonjour Boutique** (1336 Bay St., 541/997-8194, www.bonjourboutiqueonline.com, 10am-6pm Sun.-Fri.) to explore exquisite clothing, jewelry, and gifts from around the world.

When they named it **All About Olives** (1367 Bay St., 541/997-3174, www.all-aboutolives.us, 10am-5pm daily), they weren't kidding. This little shop is stuffed with unique and exotic varieties, as well as olive oils, balsamic vinegars, tapenades, and, best of all, free samples!

Periwinkle Station (1308 Bay St., 541/902-7901, 10am-6pm Mon.-Sat., 11am-5pm Sun.) offers vintage games, lunch boxes, and books. Gaming is also the focus of **Wizard of Odds** (1341 Bay St., 541/902-0602, www.odds-n-ends.com, 10am-6pm daily), but in this case it involves sculpted pewter and resin dragons and fairies.

You'll find a unique mix of candy in the front and regionally produced crafts and jewelry in the back of longtime Florence shop **Wind Drift Gallery** (1395 Bay St., 541/997-7993, www.oregoncoast-galleries.net, 10am-5:30pm daily).

Florence Antiques (494 US-101, 541/997-8104, 10am-5pm daily) offers a treasure trove of fine china, art, and furniture.

Recreation

Inside Jessie M. Honeyman Memorial State Park are two natural freshwater lakes. **Cleawox Lake,** which occupies the park's west side, is a great place to swim, kayak, or canoe. At the larger **Woahink Lake,** on the east side, boating, water-skiing, and windsurfing are the popular activities. There are also camping and bathroom facilities, and an on-site store with souvenirs and snacks is open Memorial Day weekend through Labor Day.

Eight miles north of Florence, **C&M Stables** (90241 US-101 N., 541/997-7540, www.oregonhorsebackriding.com, $65-150) provides horseback riding tours along the beach.

Located just north of Three Rivers Casino, **Ocean Dunes Golf Links** (3345 Munsel Lake Rd., 541-997-3232, www.threeriverscasino.com/golf, $83-99 pp) is an 18-hole course with a par of 71 and a slope of 124.

Events

Florence holds the annual **Rhododendron Festival** (27th St. and Oak St., 541-997-3128, www.florencechamber.com, $10-15) in Old Town the third weekend in May. It's the second-oldest flower festival in Oregon, showcasing a parade of flower-covered floats, a street fair, car show, and carnival.

Accommodations

Set on a hilltop with panoramic views of the river and sand dunes, the ★ **Landmark Inn** (1551 4th St., 541-997-9030, www.landmarkmotel.com, $85 and up) is spacious, comfortable, and convenient to shopping and restaurants. The warm, family-friendly **Old Town Inn** (170 US-101, 800-301-6494 or 541-997-7131, www.old-town-inn.com, $104 and up) is also well located, minutes away from popular sights and activities.

The elegantly restored 1914 ★ **Edwin K. B&B** (1155 Bay St., 541-997-8360, www.edwink.com, $165 and up) has six spacious rooms with private baths. A five-course breakfast is served in the formal dining room. **Driftwood Shores** (88416 1st Ave., 541-997-8263 or 800-422-5091, www.driftwoodshores.com, $130 and up) boasts magnificent oceanfront views. Rooms come with a full kitchen or refrigerator and microwave. Amenities include an on-site swimming pool, a restaurant, and a bar.

Surrounded by the sandy seascape and wooded trails, **Three Rivers Casino & Hotel** (5647 OR-126, 877-374-8377, www.threeriverscasino.com, $109 and up) offers elegant rooms, free RV parking, and an electric car charging station.

Information and Services

The best source of information about the area is the **Florence Area Chamber of Commerce** (290 US-101, 541-997-3128, 9am-5pm Mon.-Fri., 10am-2pm Sat.).

★ Oregon Dunes

South of Florence, wind-sculpted sand dunes soar up to 500 feet above sea level, surrounded by clusters of trees, marshes, and beaches. This is the nearly 50-mile stretch of the **Oregon Dunes National Recreation Area,** the largest expanse of coastal sand dunes in North America. Formed by the weathering of inland mountains and volcanic eruption, these dunes are a testament to nature's artistry. "Tree islands" remain as a reminder that before deposits of sand piled high onto the shore, a large forest covered the area. Travelers make pilgrimages here to see these ever-changing anomalies for themselves. Author Frank Herbert's famous science fiction novel *Dune* was inspired by these mountains of sand.

The geography is best explored at the dunes' midpoint, just south of the small town of **Reedsport,** about 22 miles (30 minutes) south of Florence on US-101. Permits, required for day use, hiking, and camping, are available at the **Reedsport Visitor Center** (2741 Frontage Rd., 541-271-3495, 8am-4:30pm Mon.-Fri.).

Recreation

Just off US-101, the **Oregon Dunes Overlook** is the trailhead for several loop hikes that lead through marshes, tree islands, forests, and dunes to the sea. The **John Dellenback Dunes Trail** is a moderate 2.7-mile trek that begins at Eel Creek Campground and continues through evergreens and freshwater lakes before ending on the beach. The 3.5-mile loop to **Tahkenitch Creek** offers diverse flora and glimpses of wildlife.

For a guided tour or to rent a dune buggy, head a few miles south of Florence to **Sandland Adventures** (85366 US-101 S., 541/997-8087, www.sandland.com, 9am-5pm daily summer, varying winter hours, closed Jan.-Feb.) or **Sand Dunes Frontier** (83960 US-101., 541/997-3544, www.sanddunesfrontier.com, 9am-6pm daily). Tours generally cost up to $50, while dune buggy rentals run about $45 an hour.

For an even more exhilarating experience, try sandboarding down the dunes at Florence's **Sand Master Park** (5351 US-101, 541/997-6006, 10am-5pm Mon.-Tues. and Thurs.-Sat., noon-5pm Sun., $10-25). It's much like surfing—although you don't get wet!

Food and Accommodations

In the midst of the dunes, the line of motels and burger joints in the town of **Reedsport** seems a little surreal. **Maple Street Grille** (165 Maple St., 541/997-9811, 11:30am-8pm Thurs.-Tues., $16-26) cooks up good, old-fashioned dishes like pot roast, fried chicken, burgers, and mac-and-cheese. Just north of Reedsport, **Gardiner Guest House** (401 Front St., 541/271-4005, $75-95) offers a convenient stay in an elegant restored Victorian.

A number of campgrounds offer access points to the local dunes. **Eel Creek Campground** (72044 US-101, milepost 222, 541-271-6000, www.recreation.gov, $20), which offers flush toilets and drinking water, is the starting point of a moderate 2.7-mile trek through evergreens and freshwater lakes that ends on the beach.

Umpqua Lighthouse State Park

You can explore a mosaic of open sand dunes, ocean beach, freshwater lakes, and old-growth coniferous forests at **Umpqua Lighthouse State Park** (505 Lighthouse Rd., 800/452-5687, www.oregonstateparks.org, year-round, $7

sand dunes along John Dellenback Dunes Trail

day-use). The park was originally designated to preserve the forested basin of the small freshwater Lake Marie, which lies between the headland and dune ridge formations. Swimming and fishing are popular activities. A one-mile hiking trail loops around Lake Marie, and a spur trail extends westward to an overlook at the edge of the forest above the sand dunes.

The **campground** (800/452-5687, 8am-5pm Mon.-Fri., $19 camping, $41 cabin or yurt) at Lake Marie has 44 campsites for both tents and RV; there are also yurts and log cabins. Showers are free and are centrally located near the restrooms.

The **Umpqua River Lighthouse** (1020 Lighthouse Rd., 541/271-4631, 10am-5pm daily., $5 adults, $4 students and seniors) is adjacent to the park, an easy 0.6-mile hike from the campground, and offers panoramic views of the ocean, perfect for spotting California gray whales. The lighthouse was first constructed in 1857 along the Umpqua River, but strong winds and mountain runoff in 1861 caused severe damage, and a few years later it collapsed. Rebuilt in 1864, the tower rises over the entrance of the Umpqua River with a focal plane of 165 feet above sea level. Guided tours are provided through the **Umpqua River Lighthouse Museum** (541/271-4631, www.umpquavalleymuseums.org, 10am-4:30pm daily May-Oct., call for winter hours, free), located in the historic Coast Guard Station. There is no direct access to the dunes from Umpqua Lighthouse State Park.

Coos Bay

Nearly 50 miles south of Florence, thriving commercial harbor **Coos Bay** (pop. 16,292) is home to the largest coastal deep-draft harbor between Puget Sound and San Francisco. It has the largest population on the Oregon coast. Several Native American tribes lived and fished along the bay for thousands of years, including Confederated Tribes of Coos, Lower Umpqua, and Siuslaw Indians, and the Coquille Indians. In 1853, American settlers called the town Marshfield. Over a hundred years later, the name was changed to Coos Bay.

Downtown is the Old Marshfield district. You can tour the historical waterfront or walk along the **Coos Bay Boardwalk.**

Sharkbites Cafe (240 S. Broadway, 541/269-7475, www.sharkbites.cafe, 11am-9pm Mon.-Sat., $10-20) makes the best fish tacos in town, part of a menu that also includes award-winning fish-and-chips, seafood sandwiches, and juicy burgers.

If you can swing a room at the **Edgewater Inn** (275 E. Johnson Ave., 541/267-0423, www.edgewaterinns.com, $105 and up), you'll find that the view and locale are worth it! It's Coos Bay's only waterfront motel, located just one block off US-101 and only minutes from sand dunes, ocean beaches, and Shore Acres State Park. Other lodging options include chain motels and bed-and-breakfasts.

Cape Arago Highway: Shore Acres State Park

Three miles west of Coos Bay on Newmark Ave., the Cape Arago Highway skirts the coastline for little more than 14 miles, adding an extra hour of driving, but providing access to beaches, sea caves, viewpoints, and uncrowded parks.

The crowning jewel of the south coast, **Shore Acres State Park** (89039 Cape Arago Hwy., 541/888-3732 www.oregonstateparks.org, 9am-dusk daily, $5 dayuse) sits high above the ocean swells on a wave-battered bluff. The park combines natural and artificially constructed features that pleasantly inspire those who make the journey. Wild spruce and pine trees encapsulate the meticulously manicured gardens with plant and flower varieties from around the world. There is an observation tower, and paved trails descend directly below to **Simpson Beach.** A winding path leads to more seascape vistas, marinelife, and a secluded cove.

The highway culminates at **Cape Arago State Park** (541/888-3778, $5 day-use). First sighted by Europeans during Sir Francis Drake's expeditions in the 1500s, Cape Arago is a good place to spot migrating whales and other marine mammals. A north trail leads to offshore views of sea lions and seals at Shell Island (part of the Oregon Islands National Wildlife Refuge, closed Mar.-June), beachcombing, and fishing. The south trail takes you to a sandy beach and tidepools flowing with marinelife.

To return to US-101, you must backtrack six miles on Cape Arago Highway. Turn right on Seven Devils Road to head south for roughly six miles; then turn left on West Beaver Hills Road to continue

Southern Oregon Coast

south for another six miles to connect to US-101.

Bandon

Roughly 30 miles south of Coos Bay, **Bandon** (pop. 3,134) boasts a warmer, almost Mediterranean climate along its remote and stunning coastline. A Native American village called Na-So-Mah existed here along the banks of the Coquille (ko-KWEL) River some 3,500 years ago. Euro-American settlers arrived in the 1850s and renamed the site Averill. The name changed again to Bandon, which felt more like home to a later wave of immigrants from Bandon, Ireland.

Bandon's economy is centered on wood products, fishing, tourism, and agriculture. It is also Oregon's cranberry capital. In autumn, you can see cranberries floating at the top of flooded bogs, south of town, awaiting harvest. An average of 30 million pounds are harvested each year.

Old Town's blocks are lined with galleries, craft shops, and fine restaurants. A boardwalk runs along the waterfront, linking the town with the old lighthouse, and is often busy with visitor foot traffic during warmer months. Bandon's biggest feature is its natural wind-formed monoliths. To get the full monty, drive scenic **Beach Loop Road,** a two-plus-mile waterfront route that passes a series of offshore monoliths (the most famous is **Face Rock**), with access to a couple of photogenic viewpoints.

Getting There and Around

Bandon is on US-101 south of Coos Bay. From the south, take I-5 north to OR-42. **Coastal Express** buses (541/412-8806 and 800/921-2871, www.currypublictransit. org, $4 per city segment) travel US-101 through Bandon, Coos Bay, and North Bend.

Sights
Face Rock

One mile south of Old Town, **Beach Loop** runs along a ridge overlooking a fantastic cluster of coastal monoliths and jagged Bandon Islands. The largest, **Face Rock**, is easily identified by its human-like features. Its seemingly stoic silhouette gazes skyward, surrounded by the crashing of white-foamed waves and the wailing of gale winds. Both scientific theory and Native American storytelling explain the origins of the monoliths. The geologic story is riddled with volcanic eruptions, earthquakes, and erosion. The Coquille legend tells of the Indian princess Ewanua, who took her dog and pet raccoons down to the beach for a swim in the moonlight. The evil ocean spirit Seatco turned them all to stone. If you close your eyes and listen, you can hear Ewanua's voice in the wind.

The best place to see the face of the Indian princess is by following Beach Loop Road to **Face Rock State Scenic Viewpoint,** about a quarter-mile south of Old Town. A hiking trail leads down to the beach, where you can explore the rock and intertidal sea life, including starfish, sea anemones, and sea slugs at low tide. Beware of the tide as it rises, or you'll be swimming back to shore.

Bandon Historical Society Museum

In 1936, a wildfire swept through the region and laid waste to the downtown business district, destroying hundreds of shops and homes. This devastating event is preserved in the **Bandon Historical Society Museum** (270 Fillmore St. SE, 541/347-2164, www.bandonhistorical-museum.org, 10am-4pm daily, $3 adults, free children under 12). Other exhibits touch on the Native American culture of the Coquille people, whose legends and names are embedded in the landscape, as well as the later maritime and cranberry industries that fueled the town's economy.

Coquille River Lighthouse

At the mouth of the Coquille River, the small **Coquille River Lighthouse** (56487 Bullards Beach Rd., 800/551-6949, 11am-5pm daily, $41 yurt) is the only Oregon lighthouse to be struck by a ship, when in 1903 an abandoned schooner smashed into it during a storm. During the devastating 1936 fire, the lighthouse was spared, touched only by ash. It was used as a temporary shelter for local hospital patients.

Westcoast Game Park Safari

Seven miles south of Bandon, the 129-acre **Westcoast Game Park Safari** (46914 US-101, 541/347-3106, www.westcoastgameparksafari.com, 10am-5pm daily, $17.50 adults, $10 children 7-12, $7 children 2-6) is home to exotic animals that you can see, pet, and, in some cases, actually hold. Several resident animals roam freely, mingling with visitors. The park houses endangered species, such as the snow leopard, as part of the park's captive breeding program. All of the animals have been rescued—some from other zoos that can no longer take care of them.

Food

Get a hearty, affordable breakfast or brunch at the **Minute Café** (145 N. 2nd St. SE, 541/347-2707, 5:30am-7pm Thurs.-Mon., 5:30am-3pm Tues.-Wed., $6-15). If French croissants and pastries are more your style, **Bandon Baking Co & Deli** (160 2nd St. SE, 541/347-9440, www.bandonbakingco.com, 8am-4pm Tues.-Sat., $3-11) is a delicious choice. They also serve specialty sandwiches and hearty soups.

For fresh waterfront grub right on the boardwalk, stop at **Bandon Fish Market** (249 1st St. SE, 541/347-4282, www.bandonfishmarket.com, 11am-7pm daily, $8-20). Or go for fish tacos, clam steamers, or Dungeness crab at **Tony's Crab Shack** (155 1st St., 541/347-2875, www.tonyscrabshack.com, 10:30am-7pm daily, $6-40).

The upscale **Lord Bennett's Restaurant and Lounge** (1695 Beach Loop Rd., 541/347-3663, www.lordbennett.com, 10am-2pm Sun., 5pm-9pm daily, $12-32) has spacious seating and gorgeous sunset views.

Watch the sun set over the Coquille River and lighthouse from **The Loft Restaurant & Bar** (315 1st St. SE, 541/329-0535, www.theloftofbandon.com, 5pm-9pm Tues.-Sat., $18-38), with the best views in town. The menu offers creative dishes with fresh, local ingredients.

Nightlife and Entertainment

Cheap, strong drinks draw a crowd at the no-frills **Arcade Tavern** (135 Alabama Ave. SE, 541/329-0526, 10am-2am daily), a place with friendly service and decent bar fare.

Unwind with a glass of pinot noir and an appetizer at the charming **Alloro Wine Bar & Restaurant** (375 2nd St. SE, 541/347-1850, www.allorowinebar.com, 11am-9pm daily); grab pizza and local beer at **Bandon Brewing Company** (395 2nd St. SE, 541/347-3911, www.bandonbrewingco.com, 11am-8pm Mon.-Thurs., 11am-9pm Fri.-Sat., noon-8pm Sun.); or seek out craft cocktails and cheese boards at **Speakeasy 33** (323, Grand Ave. SE, 541/329-0389, www.speakeasy33bar.com, 4pm-11pm Wed.-Sun.).

Located downstairs in the lodge at Bandon Dunes Golf Resort, **The Bunker** (57744 Round Lake Dr., 541/347-5737, www.bandondunesgolf.com, 7pm-midnight daily) is a dapper man cave where you can shoot pool, play poker, smoke cigars, or have a glass of scotch.

Shopping

In Old Town, **Big Wheel Farm Supply & General Store** (130 Baltimore St. SE, 541/347-3719, www.bandonbythesea.com/bigwheel.htm, 9am-5:30pm Mon.-Sat., 10am-5pm Sun.) offers a selection of T-shirts, myrtlewood gifts, and local jams. Perhaps best of all, it's the home of the **Fudge Factory,** which produces 26 varieties of the tasty treat. Upstairs, the **Bandon Driftwood Museum** (free) showcases both sculpted tree roots and fertilizer displays, epitomizing Bandon's back-to-the-land, hippie ethos. A block away, **2nd Street Gallery** (210 2nd St. SE, 541/347-4133, www.secondstreetgallery.net, 11am-5pm daily) displays sophisticated art, crafts, and original jewelry.

Devon's Boutique (92 2nd St. SE, 541/347-8092, www.devonsboutique.com, 10am-5pm Tues.-Sun.) makes chic, unique, and comfortable apparel available for women.

Kimberly's Book Nook (49044 US-101, 541/260-1343, 11am-4pm Wed.-Mon.) offers a mosaic of used books, while **WinterRiver Books** (170 2nd St. SE, 541/347-4111, www.winterriverbooks.com, 10am-6pm daily) stocks new titles and specialty items like Nepali singing bowls.

Shops along US-101 are also worth a look. **Bandon Glass Art Studio** (240 US-101, 541/347-4723, www.bandonglassart.com, irregular hours) is a remarkable gallery of intricately blown glass. The beautifully packaged, delicious jams and jellies at **Misty Meadows Jams** (48053 US-101, 888/795-1719, www.oregonjam.com, 9am-5pm daily) make perfect gifts.

Recreation

Explore the beach and view wildlife along the easy **Coquille Point Interpretive Trail,** a paved pathway winding over the headland, marked by a series of interpretive panels on local wildlife, history, and Coquille Indian sites. Access to the trail is at the Kronenberg County Park parking area, west of Beach Loop Drive.

Protecting a tidal salt marsh, the **Bandon Marsh National Wildlife Refuge** (W. Riverside Dr., 541/347-1470, www.fws.gov/refuge/bandon_marsh, sunset-sunrise daily, free) draws thousands of feather-gazers each year. Herons, falcons, and waterfowl can be seen from an elevated viewing platform on the west side of Riverside Drive.

Just two miles north of Bandon, **Bullards Beach State Park** (52470 US-101, 541/347-2209, www.oregonstateparks.org, open year-round, $5 parking, $5 hiking) is a large, year-round park with 192 campsites ($28/night) and 13 yurts ($41/night), nestled in a forest of shore pines. Horse trails provide access to the beach and dunes for equestrian campers

From top to bottom: a fish sculpture made from recycled beach toys in Bandon; a dinosaur sculpture at Prehistoric Gardens; scenery along the Samuel Boardman State Scenic Corridor.

($19/night). A public boat launch area includes a fish-cleaning station, bathrooms, and picnic tables. It gets crowded during chinook salmon season (late summer-early fall).

The elite **Bandon Dunes Golf Resort** (57744 Round Lake Dr., 541/347-4380 or 888/345-6008, www.bandondunes-golf.com, $110-300 greens fee) is set among massive dunes and pine trees, and is noted for its Scottish-style links. Surrounded by beautiful vistas, the affordable **Bandon Crossings Golf Course** (87530 Dew Valley Ln., 541/347-3232, www.bandoncrossings.com, 8am-7pm daily, $29-99 greens fee) lets you play 18 holes in Bandon's "banana belt," which provides gentler weather for play.

Events

They say "the fresher the cranberry, the higher the bounce!" As Oregon's cranberry capital, Bandon does a lot of berry bouncing! The annual **Cranberry Festival** (Old Town, 541/347-9616, www.bandon. com/cranberry-festival, second weekend in Sept.) celebrates the harvest with food, games, and craft booths. Activities include a parade, the Cranberry Bowl football game, a cranberry-eating contest, and a petting zoo.

Accommodations

Find relaxation at the serene **Bandon Dunes Golf Resort** (57744 Round Lake Dr., 888/345-6008, www.bandondunes-golf.com, $220 and up), in the midst of sand dunes and forest. Options include single rooms, suites, and secluded multi-cottages. Guests receive discounts at the golf courses.

La Kris Inn (940 Oregon Ave. SE, 541/347-3610, www.lakrisinn.com, $70 and up) is cheap, clean, and close to shops and eateries. The scenic **Bandon Inn** (355 US-101, 541/347-4417, www.bandoninn. com, $110 and up) overlooks Old Town Bandon, the Coquille River, and the Pacific Ocean.

Two family-owned motels offer comfort and value. **Table Rock Motel** (840 Beach Loop Dr., 541/347-2700 or 800/457-9141, www.tablerockmotel.com, $70 and up) is situated high on a bluff that overlooks the Pacific Ocean. Amenities include pillow-top mattresses, and the motel offers kitchenettes and pet-friendly rooms. On Coquille Point, **Bandon Beach Motel** (1090 Portland Ave. SW, 541/347-9451 or 866/945-0133, www.bandon-beachmotel.com, $85 and up) is just steps away from tidepools, unique rock formations, and wildlife. Some rooms have fireplaces and patios; all have ocean views.

B&Bs are sprinkled along the Coquille waterfront. **The Sea Star Guest House** (370 1st St. SE, 541/347-9632 or 888/693-4497, www.seastarbandon.com, $80 and up) offers rooms decorated in maritime themes. The tasteful **Lighthouse Bed & Breakfast** (650 Jetty Rd. SW, 541/347-9316, www.lighthouselodging.com, $140 and up) provides both wonderful breakfasts and exceptional service.

Information and Services

For detailed information on local sights and visitor services, contact the **Bandon Chamber of Commerce** (300 2nd St. SE, www.bandon.com, 541/347-9616, 10am-4pm daily).

Port Orford, Cape Blanco, and Humbug Mountain

US-101 moves inland along the 25-mile stretch between Bandon and Port Orford. Here, cranberry bogs, dairy and sheep farms, grasslands, and forest groves make up the changing landscape.

On your way to Port Orford, you'll want to detour off US-101 onto Cape Blanco Road to explore the westernmost point in the state. Jutting 1.5 miles out into the Pacific Ocean, **Cape Blanco** was named by early Spanish explorers for its white-shelled cliff face.

To get a full appreciation of the cape's dense woodlands, sandy beaches, rock formations, driftwood, and views, hike the Oregon Coast Trail south from the Sixes River to the mouth of the Elk River (8.5 miles round-trip). Depending on the time of year, the Elk River can be too treacherous to walk across, so use caution.

Circa 1870, **Cape Blanco Light** (91100 Cape Blanco Rd., tours 10am-3:15pm Wed.-Mon. Apr.-Oct., $2 adults, free children) is Oregon's oldest lighthouse. A mile away, **Hughes Historic House** (91816 Cape Blanco Rd., tours 10am-3:30pm Wed.-Mon. Apr.-Oct., donation) is an 11-room, Victorian home built in 1898 by pioneers Patrick and Jane Hughes.

Continuing south on US-101, **Port Orford** (pop. 1,159) also has a rich history that includes fishing, mining, logging, and a notorious battle. Captain William Tichenor arrived in June 1851 and left nine armed men to establish a European settlement right in the middle of Qua-to-mah Indian village. The newcomers were understandably not welcome. When conflict ensued, the men took refuge on a large rock at the edge of the beach, where they were besieged for two weeks before fleeing in the dark of night. Tichenor returned, better armed, with 70 men and succeeded in founding his settlement. The Qua-to-mah village was lost, but the rock, dubbed **Battle Rock,** still remains. Today, Port Orford has a collection of galleries, gift shops, cafés, and B&Bs.

Port Orford Wetland Interpretive Walkway (on the west side of US-101, 541/332-8055) is a 160-foot interpretive boardwalk that extends over a freshwater marsh. Viewing platforms provide an unhindered view of the wetlands' ecosystem, which supports birds, mammals, and amphibians. Interpretive signs explain the function of wetlands as a natural filtering system for runoff

water before it flows into nearby lakes. The trailhead is accessed from 18th and Idaho Streets at a small parking lot.

Six miles south of Port Orford, US-101 rises into the lush rainforest before meeting the east edge of **Humbug Mountain.** At 1,756 feet in elevation, it's the highest peak on the coast. Adventurers can summit the mountain by way of a three-mile trail that begins at the highway near **Humbug State Park Campground** (541/332-6774, $17), which offers 101 campsites and shower facilities.

Prehistoric Gardens

About 12 miles from Port Orford, amid a lush rainforest of dewy mosses, large ferns, and imposing trees, lies one of the most unusual tourist traps on the Oregon coast: the **Prehistoric Gardens** (36848 US-101, 541/332-4463, www.prehistoricgardens.com, 9am-6pm daily summer, 10am-5pm spring/fall, $12 adults, $8 children 3-12). Here, vibrantly colored dinosaurs stand seemingly frozen in time within their jungle-like setting. They are the creation of amateur paleontologist E. V. Nelson, who sculpted his first of about two dozen life-sized replicas in 1953. Some stand at 40 feet high. While it's no *Jurassic World,* the mix of paleontology and kitsch is hard to beat. It's a must-see for anyone under the age of 10.

Gold Beach

Named for the gold once mined near the mouth of the Rogue River, **Gold Beach** sits about 28 miles south of Port Orford. Today it draws visitors seeking a different kind of treasure: salmon and steelhead.

Jerry's Rogue Jets (29985 Harbor Way, 541/247-4571 or 800/451-3645, www.roguejets.com, 10am-6pm daily May-Oct., $50-95) has taken passengers upriver since 1958. The trip makes a 1.5-hour stop at **Agness,** a tiny town about 36 miles upstream, where lunch and dinner are served at a mountain lodge (food is not included in the tour price).

You'll find plenty of affordable motels right along US-101. For a more memorable stay, head for **Tu Tu Tun Lodge** (96550 North Bank Rogue, 541/247-6664 or 800/864-6357, www.tututun.com, $175 and up). Right on the banks of the Rogue River, the lodge is rustic yet luxurious and, best of all, peaceful. Expect comfortable rooms and a great restaurant, which serves breakfast, lunch, and five-course dinners.

★ Samuel Boardman State Scenic Corridor

A little over 13 miles south of Gold Beach, you'll find the **Samuel Boardman State Scenic Corridor,** a small ribbon of land between the highway and sea—and perhaps the most scenic drive on the entire Oregon coast. Allow extra driving time to stop for photo ops. Rugged cliffs tumbling dramatically to the violent sea, deep-water bays, endless sea stacks, and surreal rock arches are just some of the sights on this 12-mile segment of US-101. There are several parking areas and viewpoints, some with walking paths that connect to other lookouts.

The north end features the natural contours of **Arch Rock** just offshore; secluded **Secret Beach,** which is accessible by way of a steep trail; and the sandy beach at **Thunder Rock Cove.** Look for the small green **Thomas Creek Bridge** (the tallest bridge in Oregon at 345 feet) sign on the highway. At the south end is a turnout and viewpoint.

At the south end, the landscape shifts. The rocky cliffs are less steep, and conifer forests give way to a patchwork of woodlands and grassy bluffs. The most notable

Arch Rock in Samuel Boardman State Scenic Corridor

stop is **Whaleshead Beach,** named for the sea stack that resembles the head of a whale. When waves crash into the rock, its seawater sprays as if spurting from the whale's blowhole. A viewpoint with parking lot is located on US-101 about seven miles north of the town of Brookings. It's a good spot for pictures or for gazing out at the horizon. A trail heads down to the beach, but be cautious; it's steep.

There is no fee to park or walk the trails, and there are no facilities except for a few picnic areas.

Brookings: Harris Beach State Park

Just a few more miles after the Corridor ends, you'll find **Brookings** (pop. 6,526), the southernmost town on the Oregon coast, is only five miles north of the California border. It offers warm, ocean breezes, unspoiled beaches, and saltwater

fishing. Paddle a kayak on the mouth of Chetco River to catch freshwater and saltwater fish, or paddle around exploring hidden coves and giant sea rocks; if you're lucky, you might behold the enormity of a passing whale.

In late spring and fall, colorful blooming azaleas blanket the 36-acre **Azalea Park** (640 Old County Rd., 541/469-1103, www.brookings.or.us, dawn-dusk daily), a popular gathering place for picnics, leisurely strolls, weddings, and summer concerts, like the annual **American Music Concert Series** (every other Sun. June-mid-Sept., free). If you enjoy beachcombing and evening sunsets, stay at **Lowden's** Beachfront (14626 Wollam Rd., 541/469-7045 and 800/453-4768, www.beachfrontbb.com, $109 and up), a beachfront B&B with direct access to a crescent-shaped beach of sand and driftwood.

Harris Beach State Park is just north of Brookings on US-101, adjacent to the Oregon Welcome Center. You'll find sandy beaches, rugged outcroppings, tidepools, and sea stacks. Just offshore, **Bird Island,** a National Wildlife Sanctuary, is a breeding ground for rare bird species. The park **campground** (800/551-6949, www.oregonstateparks.org, campsites $20 camping, $43 yurt) is open year-round and has flush toilets and hot showers.

A short drive southbound on US-101 brings you to the California border, where you'll enter Redwood National Park.

Northern California Coast

California's remote northern coastline showcases charming coastal towns, breathtaking seascapes, and strands of towering redwoods, all leading up to the main attraction—the city of San Francisco.

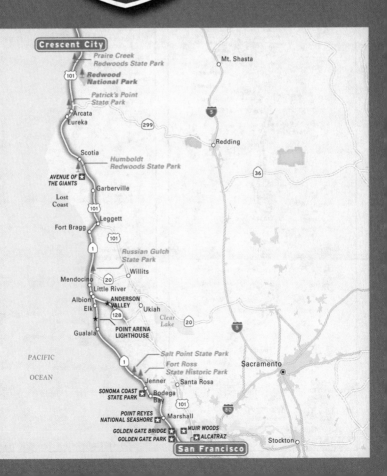

Crescent City

Praire Creek
Redwoods State Park

Mt. Shasta

101

Redwood
National Park

Patrick's Point
State Park

Arcata

Eureka

299

Redding

Scotia

Humboldt
Redwoods State Park

**AVENUE OF
THE GIANTS**

36

Garberville

Lost
Coast

101

Leggett

Fort Bragg

101

1

Russian Gulch
State Park

Willits

Mendocino

20

Little River

Albion

**ANDERSON
VALLEY**

Elk

128

Ukiah

Clear
Lake

20

Gualala

**POINT ARENA
LIGHTHOUSE**

Salt Point State Park

1

Fort Ross
State Historic Park

Sacramento

PACIFIC

OCEAN

Jenner

Santa Rosa

**SONOMA COAST
STATE PARK**

Bodega
Bay

101

**POINT REYES
NATIONAL SEASHORE**

Marshall

GOLDEN GATE BRIDGE

MUIR WOODS

GOLDEN GATE PARK

ALCATRAZ

Stockton

San Francisco

Northern California - North

STOUT MEMORIAL GROVE
Klamath Mountains
OCEAN WORLD
POINT SAINT GEORGE
Crescent City
South Beach
Crescent Beach
Enderts Beach
Crescent Beach
Overlook
Jedediah Smith Redwoods State Park
Del Norte County
Six Rivers
National
Forest
Smith River

PACIFIC OCEAN

Lake Earl

TREES OF MYSTERY
Klamath
NEWTON B. DRURY SCENIC PARKWAY
FERN CANYON
Prairie Creek Redwoods State Park
BIG TREE
LADY BIRD JOHNSON GROVE
Stone Lagoon
Orick
Big Lagoon
Agate Beach
WEDDING ROCK
PATRICK'S POINT
TALL TREES GROVE
SUMEG VILLAGE
Patrick's Point State Park
Trinidad
Redwood National Park
Klamath River

Humboldt County

COAST RANGES

Arcata

Humboldt Bay National Wildlife Complex
Eureka
HUMBOLDT BOTANICAL GARDEN
QUESO KINGS GRILLED CHEESE BAR
Fortuna
Ferndale
Scotia
Owl Creek Ecological Reserve
Mad River
299
36

Bear River
MATTOLE ROAD
Humboldt Redwoods State Park
Weott
AVENUE OF THE GIANTS
SHRINE DRIVE THRU TREE
Mattole River
PUNTA GORDA LIGHTHOUSE
King Range National Conservation Area
Lost Coast
Redway
Garberville
101

© AVALON TRAVEL

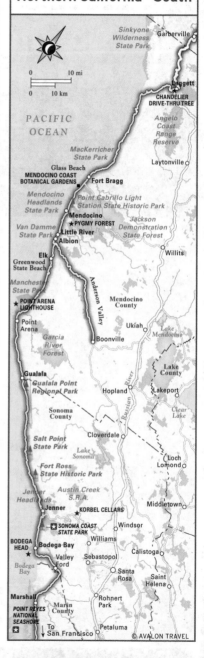

Northern California - South

Sinkyone Wilderness State Park
Garberville

PACIFIC OCEAN

Leggett
CHANDELIER DRIVE-THRU TREE
Angelo Coast Range Reserve
Laytonville

MacKerricher State Park
Glass Beach
MENDOCINO COAST BOTANICAL GARDENS
Fort Bragg
Mendocino Headlands State Park
Point Cabrillo Light Station State Historic Park
Mendocino
PYGMY FOREST
Little River
Albion
Van Damme State Park
Jackson Demonstration State Forest
Willits

Elk
Greenwood State Beach
Mendocino County
Manchester State P.
POINT ARENA LIGHTHOUSE
Point Arena
Garcia River Forest
Anderson Valley
Boonville
Ukiah
Lake Mendocino

Gualala
Gualala Point Regional Park
Hopland
Lake County
Lakeport
Clear Lake

Sonoma County
Salt Point State Park
Lake Sonoma
Cloverdale
Loch Lomond

Fort Ross State Historic Park
Austin Creek S.R.A.
Russian River
Middletown

Jenner Headlands
Jenner
KORBEL CELLARS
SONOMA COAST STATE PARK
Windsor
Williams
BODEGA HEAD
Bodega Bay
Valley Ford
Sebastopol
Calistoga
Bodega Bay
Santa Rosa
Saint Helena
Marshall
POINT REYES NATIONAL SEASHORE
Marin County
Rohnert Park
To San Francisco
Petaluma

© AVALON TRAVEL

Highlights

★ **Avenue of the Giants:** This aptly named scenic drive parallels US-101 for 31 miles through Humboldt Redwoods State Park and the last remaining stands of virgin redwoods (page 172).

★ **Sonoma Coast State Park:** This park offers 17 miles of rocky points and sandy cove beaches, viewable from cliff-top vantage points (page 186).

★ **Point Reyes National Seashore:** Home to tule elk, desolate beaches, dairy and oyster farms, one of the oldest West Coast lighthouses, and scores of remote wilderness trails, Point Reyes is one of the most diverse parks in the Bay Area (page 191).

★ **Muir Woods:** Stand among trees nearly 1,000 years old and 200 feet tall in one of the nation's earliest national monuments (page 196).

★ **Golden Gate Bridge:** Nothing beats the view from one of the most famous and fascinating bridges in the country. Pick a fogless day for a stroll or bike ride across the span (page 197).

★ **Alcatraz:** Spend the day in prison . . . at this historically famous, former maximum-security penitentiary in the middle of the bay (page 199).

★ **Golden Gate Park:** This huge urban park attracts millions of visitors annually with its amazing museums, gardens, and recreational fields (page 203).

Between the dense green forests and the azure ocean silhouetting craggy Pacific shores, it's a breathtaking drive. You can make an entire day of just pulling over at viewpoints to gape.

You'll pass through Crescent City, Eureka, and some of the oldest old-growth forests at Humboldt Redwoods State Park before US-101 breaks away from the coast at Leggett. Here, CA-1 picks up the route, passing through the urbane town of Mendocino, briefly diverging from the coast to the town of Valley Ford before rejoining the sea near the mouth of Tomales Bay.

The highway runs by the unspoiled Sonoma Coast, beautiful 71,028-acre Point Reyes National Seashore, and Muir Woods before merging with US-101 to cross the famed bridge to San Francisco, where diverse cultures and rich history combine to forge the West Coast's most beloved metropolis.

Planning Your Time

Allow five days for exploration of the main sights along the northern coast, and a week to make the most of what Northern California's beaches, national forests, and historic cities have to offer.

Accommodations along the northern redwood coast are rustic but not hard to find. The towns from Fort Bragg south to San Francisco, including Mendocino, Bodega Bay, Point Reyes, and Stinson Beach, are popular getaways for city-dwellers; expect the charm and prices to rise accordingly.

It's just over 350 miles from Crescent City to San Francisco. If you plan to follow US-101 to CA-1, which hugs the coastline, navigate carefully around the bends and turns, planning extra driving time for scenic viewing and photo stops. Gas stations are well placed along the highway and within towns and cities.

Getting There

Car

From the north, US-101 provides a direct path from Oregon to Northern California, connecting to the northern coast and Eureka to the south. US-199 begins north of Crescent City and travels northeast to Grants Pass, Oregon. The junction of US-101 and US-199 is one of only two junctions of two U.S. routes in California.

US-101 and CA-1 (also known as Hwy-1, California 1, Shoreline Highway, Pacific Coast Highway, and PCH) are the best north-south routes, providing a phenomenal scenic drive along most of California's Pacific coastline. CA-1 at times runs parallel to US-101. Its southern end is at I-5 near Dana Point and its northern end is at US-101 near Leggett.

Air

The major Northern California airport is **San Francisco International Airport** (SFO, 650/821-8211, www.flysfo.com), about 15 miles south of the city center. **Del Norte County Regional Airport** (707/464-7288), also known as Jack McNamara Field, is three miles northwest of Crescent City, in Del Norte County, with service provided by SkyWest Airlines to Eureka/Arcata, Sacramento, and San Francisco.

Train or Bus

Amtrak (800/872-7245, www.amtrak.com, $135 and up) offers service on the **Coast Starlight** to Seattle, Portland, Sacramento, Oakland, and Los Angeles. International visitors can buy an unlimited travel USA Rail Pass, good for 15, 30, or 45 days.

Greyhound (800/231-2222, www.greyhound.com) offers special discounts to students and seniors with routes and stops sticking to major highways and cities.

Best Hotels

★ **Abigail's Elegant Victorian Mansion:** With an astonishing collection of antiques, this Eureka hotel is as Victorian as it gets (page 168).

★ **Inn at Newport Ranch:** A private redwood forest meets ocean cliffs at this unique lodge north of Fort Bragg (page 178).

★ **St. Orres:** This remote 90-year-old property offers relaxation and spa services at the border of Mendocino and Sonoma Counties (page 184).

★ **Olema Druids Hall:** This restored 1885 meeting hall is a perfect base for exploring Point Reyes National Seashore (page 194).

★ **Hotel Boheme:** Decor from the best of the Beat era ensures a very San Francisco experience (page 214).

★ **Argonaut Hotel:** This boutique hotel has it all: history, classic style, and a prime San Francisco location (page 214).

Fuel and Services

Gas stations are all self-service and easily accessed off US-101 and CA-1. Service is sparser within national parks.

To receive reports on **road conditions**, call **511.** If your phone carrier does not support 511, call toll-free 800/977-6368.

For **emergency assistance** and services, call **911.**

Crescent City

Established as a trading port for miners of California's gold rush, the state's northernmost city gets its name from the windy, crescent-shaped stretch of sand extending south from its harbor. Twenty miles from the Oregon border, routine onshore flow delivers cool weather to **Crescent City** (pop. 6,670), while offshore geography makes it America's tsunami capital. More than 30 tidal waves have been recorded since 1933, the largest caused by a 9.2 Alaskan earthquake in 1964 that destroyed much of the old city.

Following a destructive 2011 wave, Crescent City's harbor was rebuilt, and its marina was engineered to be tsunami proof and supportive of local fishing. The same underwater terrain that makes the small, sleepy town prone to waves proves a boon to fans of deep-sea fishing.

Sights

The sands of Crescent City are wide, flat expanses that invite strolling, running, and just sitting to contemplate the endless crashing Pacific. **South Beach,** located, as advertised, at the south end of town, is perfect for a romantic stroll, so long as you're bundled up. Farther south, **Crescent Beach** and **Enderts Beach** offer picnic spots and tidepools.

Wild, lonely **Point St. George** (at the end of Washington Blvd.) epitomizes the glory of California's northern coast. Walk out onto the cliffs to take in the deep blue sea, wild salt- and flower-scented air, and craggy cliffs and beaches. On a clear day, you can see all the way to Oregon. Short, steep trails lead across wild beach prairie land down to broad, flat, nearly deserted beaches. In spring, wildflowers bloom on the cliffs, and swallows nest in the cluster of buildings on the point. On rare and special clear days, you can almost make out the St. George Reef Lighthouse, alone on its perch far out in the Pacific.

A great family respite is **Ocean World** (304 US-101 S., 707/464-4900, www. oceanworldonline.com, 8am-8pm daily summer, 9am-7pm daily winter, $13 adults, $8 children 3-11). Tours of the small sea park depart about every 15 minutes and last about 40 minutes. Featured

Best Restaurants

★ **Brick & Fire Bistro:** Eureka's best meal is wood-oven pizza made with hundred-year-old sourdough starter (page 166).

★ **Mayan Fusion:** Traditional Mexican flavors find their way into delicious American dishes in Fort Bragg (page 177).

★ **River's End:** Enjoy a fine meal with a fine view where the Russian River meets the Pacific Ocean (page 185).

★ **Spud Point Crab Company:** This little seafood counter shop in Bodega Bay claims to have the best clam chowder in town—more like the best in the state (page 189).

★ **Hog Island Oyster Co.:** Try the famous local oysters at their Marshall location, which gives you the option to shuck them yourself (page 191).

★ **Burma Love:** Take a rare opportunity to try beautifully presented Burmese cuisine in one of San Francisco's most underrated restaurants (page 208).

★ **The Mill:** Catch on to a distinctly West Coast trend by snacking on the gourmet toast of this hipster bakery (page 209).

attractions are the shark petting tank and the 500,000-gallon aquarium.

Food and Accommodations

A top stop for the night is the popular **Curly Redwood Lodge** (701 S. Redwood Hwy., 707-464-2137, www.curlyredwoodlodge.com, $60-79), built entirely from a single sawn-up redwood tree. It isn't pet-friendly, but it is spacious and comfortable.

The **Good Harvest Café** (575 US-101 S., 707/465-6028, 7am-9pm Mon.-Sat., 8am-9am Sun., $7-10) offers a good range of options, from diner food to fish tacos and seafood linguine.

⊕ US-199: Jedediah Smith Redwoods State Park

Known to locals as **Jed Smith** (US-199, 707-465-7335, www.parks.ca.gov, day-use and camping year-round, $8 per vehicle), this redwood park sits along the Smith River nine miles east of Crescent City, right next door to the immense Smith River National Recreation Area (US-199

west of Hiouchi). The state park visitors center sits on the east side of the park, doubling as the Hiouchi Information Center.

Sights

The best redwood grove in all of this old growth is **Stout Memorial Grove.** The coastal redwood trees are, as advertised, stout—though the grove was named for a Mr. Frank Stout, not for the size of the trees. Somehow spared the loggers' saws, these are some of the biggest and oldest trees on the north coast. The old giants make humans feel small. Its far-north latitude makes the grove harder to reach than many others, meaning there are often fewer tourists here.

Hiking

The trails running through the trees make for wonderful summer hiking that's cool and shady. Many trails run along the river and the creeks, offering a variety of ecosystems and plenty of lush scenery to enjoy. Just be sure that wherever you hike, you stay on the established trails. If you wander into the forest, you can stomp on the delicate and shallow redwood root

Oregon Border to Patrick's Point

systems, unintentionally damaging the very trees you're here to visit.

The **Simpson Reed Trail** (one mile, easy) takes you right from US-199 (six miles east of Crescent City) down to the banks of the Smith River.

To get a good view of the Smith River, hike the **Hiouchi Trail** (two miles, intermediate). From the visitors center and campgrounds, cross the Summer Footbridge, then follow the river north. The Hiouchi Trail then meets the Hatton Loop Trail, which heads west from the river another 1.5 miles into the forest, where it ends in a .3 mile loop.

The **Mill Creek Trail** (7.5 miles roundtrip, difficult) is a longer and more aggressive trek. A good place to start is at the Summer Footbridge. The trail then follows the creek down to the unpaved Howland Hill Road.

If it's redwoods you're looking for, take the **Boy Scout Tree Trail** (5.2 miles, difficult). It's more of a trek out to the trailhead along an unpaved road, but rumor has it that's part of the beauty of this hike.

Camping

The **Jedediah Smith campground** (US-199, Hiouchi, 800/444-7275, www.reserveamerica.com, $35 per night, $5 hike-in primitive sites) clusters near the river, with most sites near the River Beach Trail (immediately west of the visitors center). There are 106 RV and tent sites. Facilities include plenty of restrooms, fire pits, and coin-op showers. Reservations in advance are advised, especially for summer and holiday weekends.

Information and Services

Jed Smith has a **visitors center** (US-199, one mile west of Hiouchi, 707-458-3496, 9am-5pm daily summer, subject to staffing winter), where you can get park information and purchase souvenirs and books. Ask for a schedule of nature programs and guided hikes.

Del Norte Coast Redwoods State Park

Five miles south of Crescent City, **Del Norte Coast Redwoods State Park** (US-101, accessible via Mill Creek Rd., 707/465-7335, www.parks.ca.gov) encompasses a variety of ecosystems, from eight miles of wild coastline to second-growth redwood forest to virgin old-growth forests. One of the largest in this system of parks, Del Norte is a great place to "get lost" in the backcountry with just your backpack and fishing rod, ready to camp and ply the waters of the meandering branches of Mill Creek.

Camping

Seven miles south of Crescent City, the **Mill Creek Campground** (800-444-7275, www.reserveamerica.com, $35) has 145 sites to accommodate tents and RVs. Facilities include restrooms and hot showers.

Trees of Mystery

Ten miles south of Del Norte, you'll spot the gigantic wooden **Paul Bunyan** and his blue ox, Babe, from US-101. The **Trees of Mystery** (15500 US-101 N., 707/482-2251, www.treesofmystery.net, 8am-7pm daily June-Aug., 9am-5pm daily Sept.-May, $15 adults, $8 children 6-12) roadside attraction has been providing good cheesy fun for generations. Enjoy the original Mystery Hike as well as the Skytrail gondola ride through the old-growth redwoods and the palatial gift shop. At the left end of the gift shop rests a little-known gem: the Native American museum. Artifacts from tribes across the country and native to the redwood forests grace several crowded galleries.

Just south of the Trees of Mystery, you'll find the northernmost of three drive-through trees. **Klamath Tour Thru Tree** (430 CA-169, 707/482-5971, $5 per vehicle) is over 725 years old.

ancient redwood trees at Jedediah Smith Redwoods State Park

Prairie Creek Redwoods State Park

A gorgeous scenic cutoff through the redwoods, the **Newton B. Drury Scenic Parkway** (about 10 miles south of Trees of Mystery, cuts off US-101) features old-growth trees lining the roads, a close-up view of the redwood forest ecosystem, and a grove or trailhead about every hundred yards or so. Turn off the highway at the **Big Tree Wayside.** The namesake tree is only a short walk from the parking area, and several trails radiate from the little grove.

At the junction of the south end of the Newton B. Drury Scenic Parkway and US-101, **Prairie Creek Redwoods State Park** (127011 Newton B. Drury Pkwy., 707/488-2039, www.parks.ca.gov) boasts large campgrounds and shady hiking trails through redwoods. Just beyond the entrance, the visitors center includes a small interpretive museum describing the history of the California redwood forests. A tiny bookshop adjoins the museum, well stocked with books describing the history, nature, and culture of the area. Many ranger-led programs originate at the visitors center.

One of the cool things that make a drive to Prairie Creek worth the effort is the herd of **Roosevelt elk** that live there. The big guys with their huge racks hang out at—where else?—the Elk Prairie. This stretch of open grassland lies right along the highway. The best way to find the viewing platform is to watch for the road signs pointing you to the turnoff. The best times to see the elk out grazing in the field are early morning and around sunset. Please stay in the viewing area and let the elk enjoy their meals in peace.

Perhaps the single most famous hiking trail along the redwood coast is the 0.7-mile **Fern Canyon Trail** to Gold Bluffs Beach (trailhead at parking lot two miles off US-101 on Davison Rd.). This hike takes you through a narrow canyon carved by Home Creek. Ferns, mosses, and other water-loving plants grow thick up the sides of the canyon, creating a beautiful vertical carpet of green that made the perfect setting for Steven Spielberg's *Jurassic Park 2* and *The Return of the Jedi.*

A longer and tougher loop can take you from the visitors center on a more serious foot tour of the park. Start out on the **James Irvine Trail,** but don't follow it all the way to the coast. Instead, make a right onto the **Clintonia** and cut across to **Miner's Ridge.** The hike runs a total of about six miles.

Redwood National Park

Twenty million years ago, colossal giants thrived in the cool, continuously damp environment found only on the northernmost coast of what is today California. These conditions haven't changed, as the colossal giants are still here—we call them redwoods. Nobody really knows why these trees grow to such towering heights, and it may be this mystery, along with the area's magnificent beauty, that draws more than 400,000 people each year to Redwood National and State Parks. At one time, close to two million acres of old-growth redwoods blanketed California's northern coast. Alas, massive logging left little more than 45 percent of the area's old-growth coast redwoods, half found in the Redwood National and State Parks system.

In 1968, **Redwood National Park** was established to protect some 131,983 acres of redwood forest, of which 60,268 acres make up the adjacent Smith, Del Norte, and Prairie Creek Redwoods State Parks. The trees preserved in the Redwood National Park section are not the oldest; they're second- or third-growth timber. However, these reddish-brown beauties still possess a magical sway that inspires awe among visitors.

Visiting the Park

Spanning a length of 50 miles from the Oregon border to the north and the Redwood Creek watershed near Orick, California, to the south, Redwood National Park is located on the northernmost coast of California. The cool, moist air created by the Pacific Ocean maintains the trees' moist habitat even during summer droughts.

Seasons

Redwood National Park is always open, welcoming visitors year-round. Visitors to the park should be prepared for all types of weather by dressing in layers to accommodate temperature changes. Wear durable walking shoes or hiking boots with grip soles to avoid slipping on moist trails, logs, or rocks. Good rain gear and a water bottle are imperative.

Temperatures stay between the mid-40s to low-60s (Fahrenheit) with cooler, sometimes snowy winters. Warmer months bring moist fog that collects where the cold ocean and dry land meet, creating a damper interior. Rain averages 60-80 inches annually, with October-April as the rainier months. However, weather cannot always be predicted.

The best time of year for hiking and outdoor activities is in summer. Cooler months (Dec.-Jan. and Mar.-Apr.) offer favorable opportunities to see migrating gray whales along the coast.

Weather can cause changes in both campground and trail access. Check for revised schedules before arrival.

Fog and strong winds can create difficult driving conditions and road closures. Closures to US-101 may result in detours up to four hours. Check for updated highway reports with the **California Department of Transportation** (www. quickmap.dot.ca.gov).

Park Entrances

Many visitors are surprised to discover that there are no formal entrance stations, or even entrance fees, at Redwood National Park. In fact, US-101 (known in these parts as the Redwood Highway) runs the entire length of the park.

Visitors Centers

There are two information centers and three visitors centers. All centers provide National Park passport stamps.

The northernmost, **Crescent City Information Center** (1111 2nd St., 707/465-7335, 9am-5pm daily spring-fall, 9am-4pm daily winter) provides an array of useful materials, including maps and brochures, and has several great exhibits and live video feeds from the Castle Rock National Wildlife Refuge. Less than 10 miles northeast of Crescent City, **Hiouchi Information Center** (US-199, 707/458-3496, 9am-5pm daily summer, subject to staffing winter) has ranger-led activities, exhibits, and public facilities.

The visitor centers offer public facilities, as well as information, exhibits, and bookstores. The northernmost, 16 miles east of Crescent City, is **Jedediah**

Smith Visitor Center (1440 US-199, 707/458-3496, Wed.-Sun. 9am-4pm, 9am-5pm daily summer). **Prairie Creek Visitor Center** (127011 Newton B. Drury Scenic Pkwy., 707/488-2039, 9am-5pm daily, 9am-5pm daily summer) is at the south end of Newton B. Drury Scenic Parkway in Prairie Creek Redwoods State Park. The southernmost facility is the **Thomas H. Kuchel Visitor Center** (US-101, 707/465-7765, www.nps.gov/redw/planyourvisit/visitorcenters.htm, 9am-5pm spring-fall, 9am-4pm daily winter), which also offers beach access.

Permits and Regulations

There are no entrance fees for Redwood National Park. However, a $5 day-use fee is charged at the three adjoining state parks: Prairie Creek Redwoods State Park, Del Norte Coast Redwoods State Park, and Jedediah Smith Redwoods State Park.

A $5 permit for backcountry camping is required and is available year-round from the Crescent City Information Center or the Thomas H. Kuchel Visitor Center, as well as seasonally from Hiouchi Information Center.

A free permit is required for the Tall Trees Grove access road and can be obtained at the Thomas H. Kuchel Visitor Center and Hiouchi Information Center (summer only). Please note that these permits are limited to only 50 per day and are issued on a first-come, first-served basis.

Special-use permits may be required for group events, commercial activities, and research projects. An application must be completed (call 707/465-7307 for more information).

Camping

The Redwood National and State Parks offer developed campgrounds and backcountry camping. Fees are $35 at all campgrounds. **Reservations** (800/444-7275, www.reserveamerica.com) during the summer months are advised and should be made at least 48 hours in advance. However, Gold Bluffs Beach Campground never accepts reservations and is first-come, first-served.

Jedediah Smith Campground (nine miles northeast of Crescent City on US-199, 800/444-7275, www.reserveamerica.com, $35) is in Crescent City within an old-growth redwood grove on the banks of scenic Smith River, offering recreational activities from swimming to fishing, along with extensive hiking trails. The 86 campsites accommodate tents or RVs (hookups not available) and the campground has full facilities with hot showers, fire pits and barbecues, food lockers, and a campfire center.

Mill Creek Campground (seven miles south of Crescent City on Mill Creek Rd., 800/444-7275, www.reserveamerica.com, $35) in Crescent City offers 143 tent sites amid large maple and alder trees and young redwoods.

Elk Prairie Campground (127011 Newton B. Drury Pkwy., 800/444-7275, www.reserveamerica.com, $35) in Orick offers easy access to 70 miles of hiking and biking trails, numerous opportunities for wildlife viewing, and seasonal ranger-led hikes, all among ancient giant redwoods. There are 75 sites for tents or RVs (no hookups). The campground also offers hot showers, bathroom facilities, picnic tables, fire pits, barbecues, and food lockers.

Gold Bluffs Beach Campground (Davison Rd., 800/444-7275, www.reserveamerica.com, $35) is in Orick near secluded beaches, hiking and biking trails, and viewing of wildlife such as Roosevelt elk. There are campsites for tents or RVs (no hookups). Facilities include solar showers, restrooms, wind shelters, picnic tables, fire pits, barbecues, and food lockers.

Fires are allowed only in designated fire rings and grills provided by the parks. Dead and downed wood may be collected for burning (limit of 50 pounds) from within a quarter-mile of backcountry camps on national parkland. Wood collection is prohibited in developed campgrounds. State parklands allow up to 50 pounds of driftwood per person per day. It is imperative that you check with one of the local visitors centers to ensure that you are fully informed of permissible campfire activity.

Animal-proof food canisters are available free of charge at the **Redwood National State Park Information Center** (1111 2nd St., 707/465-7335) in Crescent City.

Food and Supplies

There are no grocery stores or restaurants within the parks. You will find restaurants, full-service grocery stores, and a couple co-ops in the nearby communities of Klamath (five miles north), Orick (three miles north), Crescent City (five miles southwest), Trinidad (17 miles south), McKinleyville (25 miles south), Arcata (31 miles south), and Eureka (39 miles south).

Sights

It's all about the trees! There are plenty to see along US-101 from behind the wheel, but some of the most incredible sights are a short walk away. Rising an average of 300 feet, the **Stout Memorial Grove** (accessed via the east end of Howland Road and from Jedediah Smith Campground by way of a seasonal summer bridge) contains the tallest trees within the Jedediah Smith region. It's an easy 0.5-mile walk among sword ferns that carpet the forest floor, and the flow of the nearby Smith River is entrancing.

No doubt the giant coast redwoods are the cynosures of Redwood National and State Parks, but there is also an abundance of wildlife and stunning viewpoints. Possibly the best spot to spy migrating whales in the winter is from **Crescent Beach Overlook,** less than two miles past Crescent Beach within the Del Norte section of the parks. The cliffside platform offers dominating views of the seascape that are simply hard to beat. A short trail leads down the bluffs to **Enderts Beach,** where driftwood, seashells, and the best tidepools are aplenty. The trail is part of the larger 70-mile-long Coastal Trail, which is a good way to explore—feet willing.

Farther south in Prairie Creek Redwoods State Park lies a beautiful natural landmark and popular destination, **Fern Canyon:** Water streams down its 50-foot steep walls, draped with thick emerald ferns. It's no wonder the site was used as a filming location for movies such as *The Lost World: Jurassic Park* and the BBC's *Walking with Dinosaurs,* as the canyon exudes a prehistoric aura. Wear waterproof shoes or expect to get your feet wet!

To see **Big Tree,** a 304-foot-high redwood measuring 21 feet in diameter, follow Newton B. Drury Scenic Parkway. It's a short 100-yard walk from the Prairie Creek Visitor Center, and it's worth the 30-minute drive off US-101. Nearby, the **Ah Pah Trail** (.6 mile) provides a glimpse into the past logging era, with interesting trailside exhibits.

A mile north of Orick on Bald Hills Road (watch for a sign at the junction of US-101) are two well-known groves: the regal **Lady Bird Johnson Grove,** where gathered giants create a cathedral-esque canopy, and **Tall Trees Grove,** whose star attraction is the soaring Howard Libbey Tree. The Lady Bird Johnson Grove is named in honor of the former first lady (wife of President Lyndon B. Johnson) in recognition of her efforts to help preserve America's natural beauty, which ultimately led to the bill that created Redwood National Park. But what really makes the trees here special is that in comparison to other groves, these trees are highlanders—sitting 1,200 feet above sea level.

To visit Tall Trees Grove, stop by Thomas H. Kuchel Visitor Center to pick up a free permit and combination to unlock the gate that leads to some of the most massive trees on the planet. There is a limit of 50 cars per day, and if you're one of the lucky ones (trailers and RVs are not permitted), it's a 45-minute drive to the trailhead up the narrow unpaved Bald Hills Road. The trail drops about 800 feet in elevation before arriving at Tall Trees Grove (two miles) and the 367.8-foot former reigning giant, **Howard Libbey Tree.** Although larger redwoods have been discovered, Libbey continues to be popular among visitors due to its accessibility and to the locations of rival giants never being revealed for their protection.

Beneath the lush green canopy, majestic **Roosevelt elk** roam the northern redwood region; their noble antlers are observable in late summer through winter. In the 1920s, only 15 elk could be found here, but today, they are a common sight thanks to the protection of critical habitat. Safe viewing areas can be navigated by car at Elk Prairie along Newton B. Drury Scenic Parkway (34 miles south of Crescent City) and Elk Meadow via Davison Road (three miles north of Orick). Another good viewpoint is less than five miles up the road from Elk Meadow at Gold Bluffs Beach. However, there is a day-use fee and trailers are not allowed, as this portion of the road is unpaved. As a gentle reminder, please *do not* approach Roosevelt elk. These wild animals need no introduction, and are perfectly hospitable—but from afar. It is also imperative that drivers respect speed limits and be attentive to wildlife along the roads and highways, as Roosevelt elk (and other forest critters) do not yield to drivers or look both ways.

Recreation

Before you set foot on a trail, it is always a good idea to pick up a map at any of the visitors centers. Backcountry hikers are encouraged to speak with the rangers to answer questions or just to pick their brains for good route advice.

More than 200 miles of trails weave through old-growth forests, colorful meadows, prairies, and primeval beaches. Northern trails that start along US-199 near Hiouchi and end at the Klamath River include **Leiffer-Ellsworth Loop Trail,** a 2.6-mile loop in Jedediah Smith Redwoods State Park. The trailhead is off Walker Road, less than a half mile from the US-199 junction. Head clockwise along Leiffer Loop to the Ellsworth Loop split-off, which bends around the south edge of Leiffer Loop. A less-traveled path, it passes through vine maple, California hazel, and red huckleberries before climbing 200 feet on a densely wooded hillside to flatter land near the Smith River. Expect spectacular views and very little foot traffic.

Saddler Skyline Trailhead is in Del Norte Coast Redwoods State Park between campsites 7 and 8 in the Mill Creek Campground. It's a 1.5-mile moderate hike with some steep grades and switchbacks. The trail is filled with numerous brush, wild ginger, huckleberry, California blackberry, and wildlife.

For an exhilarating adventure, **Little Bald Hills Trail** is a vigorous bike trail (and it's horse friendly) located in Jedediah Smith Redwoods State Park, offering a 3.3-mile primitive ride to the campsite and 4.8 miles to the park boundary. The trailhead is on the east end of Howland Hill Road. The trek is steep, rising 1,800 feet in elevation through a changing scenery of lush lowland redwoods, various shrubs, flowered meadows, and a few small ocean views before coming to the park boundary. Head back or continue through the Smith River National Recreation Area to Paradise Trail and on to South Fork Road; it's all downhill.

Although the redwoods are best known for towering trees, the nearly continuous **Coastal Trail** offers a 70-mile journey along seaside bluffs, where on a clear day you can look out over endless blue waters, perhaps spotting spouting gray whales. Sea creatures hide in secluded tidepools and driftwood collects below the jagged sea cliffs. There are several access points, such as Hidden Beach in Redwood National Park.

The **Hidden Beach** section of the Coastal Trail is 7.8 miles long, ascending approximately 1,390 feet above sea level. The trailhead is off US-101 at the north end of the Lagoon Creek parking lot, just before the Trees of Mystery attraction (via south). The trail is somewhat primitive as it climbs along spruce-covered bluffs; there are no redwoods on the Coastal Trail. At the first divide, a short loop curves to the left following the edge of a lagoon (and the humming of the highway), or continue to the right toward a more scenic journey without highway interruption. Blackberries, bushels of ferns, tall red alder, and spruce border the pathway, offering peeks of the ocean, before you arrive at a nice open viewpoint. The trail culminates through a grassy hillside that gives way to views of the rushing Klamath River.

One of the best mid-spring to early summer hikes is on the Redwood National and State Parks' southern trail in Prairie Creek Redwoods State Park. The **Rhododendron Trail** is a colorful 6.8-mile wonderland filled with trees, bushes, red huckleberries, blackberries, and beautiful blooms of bright pink and red rhododendrons. It is the perfect landscape, favored among painters and photographers. There are several access points from trails that traverse the pathway (Cathedral Trees Trail, the Brown Creek Trail, and South Fork Trail), but the main trailhead is just off the east side of Newton B. Drury Scenic Parkway.

Patrick's Point State Park

15 miles south of Orick, **Patrick's Point State Park** (4150 Patrick's Point Dr., 25 miles north of Eureka, 707/677-3570, www.parks.ca.gov/patrickspoint, $8 per vehicle, $35-45 camping) is a rambling coastal park with campgrounds, trails, beaches, landmarks, and history. It's not the biggest of the many parks along the north coast, but it ranks among the best. The climate remains cool year-round, making it perfect for hiking and exploring, if not for ocean swimming. It's easy to get around Patrick's Point because it is tiny in comparison to the other parks. Request a map at the gate and follow the signs along the often-nameless park roads.

Sights

Prominent among the landmarks is the park namesake **Patrick's Point,** which offers panoramic Pacific views after a brief hike from a convenient parking lot. Another popular spot is **Wedding Rock,** adjacent to Patrick's Point in a picturesque cove. People truly do hike the narrow trail out to the rock to get married—you might even see a newly married couple stumbling along, holding hands on their way back from their ceremony.

Perhaps the most fascinating area in all of the park is **Sumeg Village.** This recreation of a native Yurok village is based on an actual archaeological find that lies east of the "new" village. Visitors can crawl through the perfectly round hobbit-like hole-doors into semi-subterranean homes, meeting places, and storage buildings. Or check out the native plant garden, a collection of local plants the Yurok people used for food, basketry, and medicine. Today, the local Yurok people use Sumeg Village as a gathering place for education and celebrations, and request that visitors tread lightly and do not disturb this tranquil area.

For those who want to dip a toe in the ocean rather than just gaze at it from afar, Patrick's Point encompasses a number of accessible beaches. The steep trail leading down to **Agate Beach** deters few visitors. This wide stretch of coarse sand bordered by cliffs shot through with shining quartz veins is perfect for lounging, playing, and beachcombing. The semiprecious stones for which it is named really do cluster here. The best time to find good agates is in the winter, after a storm.

Recreation
Only six miles of trails thread their way through Patrick's Point. Choose from the **Rim Trail** (1.7 miles, easy), which will take you along the cliffs for a view of the sea and, if you're lucky, migrating whales. On the other hand, tree-lovers might prefer the **Octopus Tree Trail** (.2 mile, easy), which shows its walkers a great view of an old-growth Sitka spruce grove.

Camping
The campgrounds at Patrick's Point meander through the park. It can be difficult to determine the difference between **Agate Beach, Abalone,** and **Penn Creek,** so be sure to get good directions from the rangers when you arrive. Most campsites are pleasantly shaded by the groves of trees; all include a picnic table, a propane stove, and a food storage cupboard. You'll find running water and restrooms nearby, plus showers.

Information and Services
You can get a map and information at the **Patrick's Point State Park Visitors Center** (707/677-1945, usually 9am-4:30pm daily), immediately to the right when you get to the entry gate. Information about nature walks and campfire programs is posted on the bulletin board.

Arcata

After Crescent City, the Pacific Coast Highway quietly passes 78 miles of rural forest until it reaches two small cities on Arcata Bay. First is the pretty little town of **Arcata** (pop. 17,974). Home to Humboldt State University, it's known for its entrenched hippie culture. Today, that's more about progressive politics and a vibrant arts and music scene than tie-dyed T-shirts and psychedelia. Its rich natural surroundings include Arcata Marsh & Wildlife Sanctuary.

Getting There and Around
The best routes are from US-101, which runs north to south right through Arcata, and CA-299, which runs east to west.

If arriving by bus, **Amtrak** and **Greyhound** are both located at the **Arcata Transit Center** (925 E St., 707/825-8934).

A small airport, **Arcata-Eureka Airport** (3561 Boeing Ave., 707/839-5401) is in McKinleyville, just six miles north of Arcata on US-101. Airline service is limited.

Walking and biking are the best modes of transportation. Bike rentals are available at **Revolution Bicycle** (1593 G St., www.revolutionbicycle.com, 9am-6pm Mon.-Fri., 9am-5pm Sat., 9am-4pm Sun., $25 per half day).

Two local bus lines operate around the city: The **Arcata and Mad River Transit** city line (707/822-3775, www.arcatatransit.org, $2.50 day-pass) operates within Arcata, while **Redwood Transit System** (707/443-0826, http://www.redwoodtransit.org, $4.90 day pass) links to other towns in the area.

Sights
Serving as the center of town, **Arcata Plaza** (844 H St., 707/822-4500, www.arcatamainstreet.com) is a grassy square built around a statue of America's 25th president, William McKinley. It's surrounded by shops, bars, and restaurants, and plays home to community gatherings, music, and more.

Arcata also has the oldest movie theater in the United States. Built in 1914, **The Minor Theatre** (1001 H St., 707/822-3456, www.minortheatre.com, $6-9.50 per ticket), shows all the newest releases. The Great Houdini performed his daring magic acts on the small theater stage; a trap door he used for his shows is still there.

Patrick's Point to the Lost Coast

Trinidad
Patrick's Point State Park

PACIFIC OCEAN

Humboldt Bay NWR

CENTRAL AVE

MURRAY RD

OLD RAILROAD GRADE RD

101

299

ARCATA PLAZA/ MINOR THEATRE

Arcata Community Forest

Arcata

★ ARCATA MARSH & WILDLIFE SANCTUARY

NEW NAVY BASE RD

Arcata Bay

255

Samoa

101

Eureka

SEE "EUREKA" MAP

HUMBOLDT BOTANICAL GARDEN

101

South Bay

Eel River Wildlife Area

Humboldt Bay NWR

QUESO KINGS GRILLED CHEESE BAR

Headwaters Forest Ecological Reserve

211   101   Fortuna

0   25 mi
0   25 km

© AVALON TRAVEL

Recreation

Arcata Bay is the northern half of Humboldt Bay and part of the 300-acre Samoa Dunes Recreation Area, where you can hike or kayak. There are no fees to enter this area. Launch kayaks from the Arcata ramp or Hookton Slough in Humboldt Bay National Wildlife Refuge.

Fishing is also popular on Arcata Bay (New Navy Base Rd.), and many come seeking Pacific and California halibut. Mad River lies just north of Arcata, where steelhead, trout, king, and silver salmon are caught at the mouth of the river. The Mad River has also become known for its excellent winter steelhead, due to the **Mad River Fish Hatchery** (1660 Hatchery Rd., 707/822-0592, www.wildlife.ca.gov/Fishing/Hatcheries/Mad-River, 7am-3pm daily). Contact the **California Department of Fish and Game** (707/445-6493, www.wildlife.ca.gov/Fishing) for current regulations and license requirements.

The world-famous **Arcata Marsh & Wildlife Sanctuary** (569 S. G St., 707/826-2359, www.arcatamarshfriends.org, 9am-5pm Tues.-Sun., 1pm-5pm Mon., free) is a wetland preserve for over 150 bird species and other wildlife. Bird-watchers can enjoy walking trails, an interpretive center, and blinds (the best way to stay hidden).

Food

A healthy and tasty choice is the **Wildflower Café and Bakery** (1604 G St., 707/822-0360, www.wildflowercafebakery.com, 9am-3pm and 5:30pm-9:30pm Thurs.-Sun., 9am-3pm Mon.-Wed., $8-13), specializing in fresh and delicious vegetarian meals for breakfast, lunch, and dinner, with gourmet espresso and delicious house breads. Rumored to be the inspiration for the Krusty Krab, the eponymous hero's workplace in the cartoon *SpongeBob Squarepants,* **Stars Hamburgers** (1535 G St., 707/826-1379, 11am-8pm Mon.-Thurs. and Sat., 11am-9pm Fri., noon-6pm Sun., $5-7) occupies a simple square shack that serves up craveable burgers, including vegetarian options.

Nightlife

Serving locally brewed craft beers, **Humboldt Brews** (856 10th St., 707/826-2739, www.humbrews.com, 11:30am-midnight Sat.-Thurs., 11:30am-2am Fri.) also shows broadcast sporting events and hosts local bands. The unique **Cafe**

Mokka (495 J St., 707/822-2228, www.cafemokkaarcata.com, noon-11pm Sun.-Thurs., noon-1am Fri.-Sat.) offers a place to unwind over coffee and meditate in a tranquil Finnish country sauna and soaking tub.

The bar scene around Arcata Plaza can get lively when the university students come out, with several spots slinging drinks. Best bet is to start (or finish) at **The Alibi** (744 9th St., 707/822-3731, www.thealibi.com, 8am-2am daily), a lively venue with fabulous martinis and live bands.

Shopping

Discover beautiful beads from around the world and unique jewelry at **Heart Bead** (830 G St., 707/826-9577, www.heartbead.com, 10am-6pm Mon.-Sat., noon-5pm Sun.).

Northtown Books (957 H St., 707/822-2834, www.northtownbooks.com, 10am-7pm Mon.-Thurs. and Sat., 10am-9pm Fri., noon-5pm Sun.) is a well-stocked independent bookstore with a wide range of genres. For used and rare books, **Tin Can Mailman** (1000 H St., 707/822-1307, www.tincanbooks.com, 10am-6pm Mon.-Thurs., 10am-7pm Fri.-Sat., noon-6pm Sun.) is a short walk away. Both are great bookstores.

Gear up with everything you need to explore the local rivers, trails, and beaches at **Adventure's Edge** (650 10th St., 707/822-4673, www.adventuresedge.com, 9am-6pm Mon.-Sat., 10am-5pm Sun.).

On Saturdays, the **Farmer's Market** (Arcata Plaza, 10am-2pm Sat. Dec.-Mar., 9am-2pm Sat. Apr.-Nov.) is bustling with locals and out-of-towners shopping for fresh organic foods, artisan breads, and handcrafted art.

Events

The annual **Arcata Main Street's Oyster Festival** (Main Street Plaza, June, www.arcatamainstreet.com/oyster-festival) has fast become a tradition, as avant-garde culinary enthusiasts prepare oysters in every imaginable, but delicious, way.

On the second Friday of every month the phenomenon known as **Arts! Arcata** (shops around Arcata Plaza, www.arcatamainstreet.com/arts-arcata, 6pm-9pm, free) brings the community together with 60 visual artists and live musicians at 30 participating locations to celebrate love of the arts.

Arcata is the starting point for the "Triathlon of the Art World," the **Kinetic Grand Championship** (www.kineticgrandchampionship.com, Memorial Day weekend), when zany human-powered amphibious works of art take to the roads, beaches, and yes, Humboldt Bay. The three-day race continues south along the coast, through to Ferndale, with a museum commemorating past years' designs found in Eureka.

Accommodations

Familiar hotel chains are the most common in Arcata, ranging from cheap, no-frills motels to two-star mainstays, led by **Days Inn and Suites Arcata** (4975 Valley West Blvd., 707/822-4861, www.daysinnarcata.com, $90-170), which provides an indoor swimming pool and pet-friendly rooms.

The centrally located **Hotel Arcata** (708 9th St., 707/826-0217 or 800/344-1221, $97-110) is right on the plaza, close to shopping and sightseeing. It's a budget stay, but pet friendly, and offers guests passes to a nearby gym with a pool and sauna.

For a little local color, a beautifully kept 1888 Victorian B&B, **The Lady Anne Inn** (902 14th St., 707/822-2797, www.ladyanneinn.com, $115-220), sits on a hilltop overlooking Humboldt Bay, a short walk from both town and university.

Information and Services

The **Arcata Chamber of Commerce** (1635 Heindon Rd., 707/822-3619, www.arcatachamber.com, 9am-4pm Mon.-Fri.) operates the **California Welcome Center (CWC)**

to provide valuable information and services to every traveler.

Eureka

Eight miles on the other side of Arcata Bay, the town of **Eureka** (pop. 27,226) began as a seaward access point for the remote gold mines of Trinity County, to the east. Almost immediately, settlers realized the worth of the redwood trees surrounding them and started a logging industry. In the late 19th century, lumber barons built a wealth of lovely Victorian homes and downtown commercial buildings. Today, lumber is still a major industry in Eureka, but tourism is another draw. People come to enjoy the waterfront wharf and charming, walkable downtown. Active outdoors lovers can fish, whale-watch, and hike, while history buffs can explore museums and mansions.

Getting There and Around

Eureka is a short ride by vehicle from Arcata via southbound US-101. From San Francisco, it is a spectacular, scenic, six-hour drive north through Sonoma, Mendocino, and Humboldt Counties to reach Eureka.

The **Arcata-Eureka Airport** (3561 Boeing Ave., 707/839-5401) is 10 minutes north of Eureka and is served by three air carriers: Delta, Horizon Air, and United.

There's no train station, but **Amtrak Thruway** buses connect Eureka to the Capitol Corridor train at Martinez, northeast of San Francisco, from a stop at 6th and C Streets. For national bus rides, there's a different stop to catch a **Greyhound** (1603 4th St., 800/231-2222, www.greyhound.com). Local bus service within Eureka is provided by **Eureka Transit Service** (133 V St.,

From top to bottom: Sumeg Village in Patrick's Point State Park; the Paul Bunyan statue at Trees of Mystery; the Carson Mansion in Eureka.

Eureka

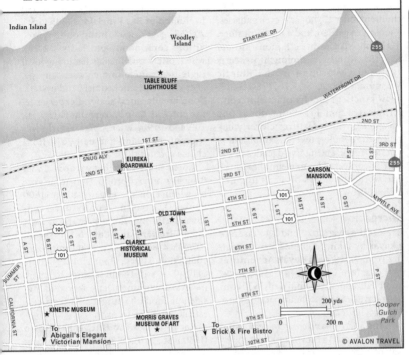

www.eurekatransit.org, $3.95 day pass), while **Redwood Transit System** (707/443-0826, http://www.redwoodtransit.org, $4.90 day pass) links to other towns in the area.

Sights

Decorative Victorian-era buildings adorn **Old Town** (from 1st St. to 3rd St. between D St. and M St.), creating an alluring village-esque feel for shopping, dining, or just taking a stroll. At the end of 2nd Street sits one of the most written-about and photographed mansions, the **Carson Mansion** (143 M St., no tours). A masterpiece of Queen Anne architecture, it is considered the grandest Victorian home in America, with renditions of the mansion found in amusement parks, including Disneyland's train station clock tower.

Take in the fresh air at the nearby **Eureka Boardwalk** (Waterfront between C St. and F St.) and the views across the water of the marina on **Woodley Island** (385 Startare Dr.); the **Table Bluff Lighthouse**, which was moved to the island in 1987; and *The Fisherman,* a memorial statue commemorating mariners lost at sea. Across a small channel adjacent to Woodley Island sits **Indian Island** (or Duluwat Island), where the indigenous Wiyot people lived at an ancestral village known as Tolowot.

The town's rich history is proudly displayed at the **Clarke Historical Museum** (240 E St., 707/443-1947, www.clarkmuseum.org, 11am-4pm Wed.-Sat., donations accepted), with changing exhibits and rooms dedicated to vibrant Native American cultures, gold rush pioneers, the lumber and ranching empires, and farming and seafaring life.

The **Morris Graves Art Museum** (636 F St., 707/442-0278, www.humboldtarts.org, noon-5pm Wed.-Sun., $5 adults, free children under 17) houses seven galleries, a sculpture garden, and a museum store.

Humboldt County's famous annual Kinetic Grand Championship race is captured year-round in the **Kinetic Museum** (518 A St., 707/786-3443, www.kineticgrandchampionship.com, 2:13pm-6:32pm Fri.-Sun., donations accepted), which features cleverly engineered, people-powered, amphibious vehicles representing five decades of the quirky contest. The museum keeps the odd workshop hours of race's founder, Hobart Brown.

Recreation

Explore the rivers, bay, and lagoons from a **kayak** by taking a guided tour or renting from **Humboldt Kayak Adventures** (601 Startare Dr., 707/443-5157, www.humboats.com, 9am-5pm daily, $30 two-hour kayak, $45 two-hour paddleboard, $45 two-hour canoe).

A fun and romantic way to get around and experience the town of Eureka is by way of horse and carriage via **Old Town Carriage Co.** (2nd St. and F St., Old Town by the gazebo, 646/591-2058, $28 for 20-25 minutes).

Stroll through a beautiful garden covered with varied shades of green and vibrant flowers at the **Humboldt Botanical Gardens** (7351 Tompkins Hill Rd., College of the Redwoods Campus, 707/442-5139, www.hbgf.corg, 10am-4pm Wed.-Sun., $8 adults, $5 children 6-17, $5 dogs), where you can also explore trails that lead to surprising views of the bay and surrounding lands.

Food

In the downtown historical quarter, **Ramone's Bakery** (209 E St., 707/445-2923, www.romanesbakery.com, 7am-6pm Mon.-Fri., 8am-5pm Sat., 8am-4pm Sun., $8-18) offers a great start to the day with baked goods like pumpkin scones and buttermilk coffeecake, herb breads, and espresso.

For a sampling of local flavor, drop in to **Humboldt Bay Provisions** (205 G St., 707/672-3850, www.humboldtbayprovisions.com, noon-9pm daily, $2-20), which offers small plates featuring local ingredients including cheese, sausage, beer and wine, smoked fish, and oysters. For a broader local seafood experience, the pub-like **Cafe Waterfront** (102 F St., 707/443-9190, www.upstairsatthewaterfront.com, 9am-9pm daily, $10-18), a choice spot for the season's best.

Local craft beer heavy **Lost Coast Brewery** moved production to a large brewhouse on the edge of town (1600 Sunset Dr.), but the century-old downtown building where it started, **Lost Coast Brewery and Cafe** (617 4th St., 707/445-4480, www.lostcoast.com, 11am-10pm Mon.-Thurs., 11am-11pm Fri.-Sun., $11-30), is still the best place to drink its award-winning beers, served alongside pub food like burgers, Philly cheesesteaks, and fish tacos.

Locals flock to ★ **Brick & Fire Bistro** (1630 F St., 707/268-8959, www.brickandfirebistro.com, 11:30am-2:30pm Mon. and Wed.-Fri., 5pm-9pm Wed.-Sun., $11-15), and it's been featured on foodie television shows, so it's wise to make reservations to ensure a dinnertime seat in this small Italian restaurant that uses a century-old sourdough starter to cultivate pizza dough. It all cooks in a wood-fired brick oven with assorted high quality toppings—you can't go wrong.

Since the 1890s, the **Samoa Cookhouse** (908 Vance Ave., Samoa, 707/442-1659, www.samoacookhouse.net, 7am-8pm daily, $16) has been a Eureka institution even though it's technically located in the little town of Samoa (take CA-255 over the water to get there). Red-checked tablecloths cover long rough tables to re-create a logging-camp dining hall atmosphere. Meals are served family-style from huge serving platters. Diners sit on benches and pass the hearty fare down in turn. Think big hunks of roast beef, mountains of mashed potatoes, and piles of cooked vegetables.

Inside the Loleta Cheese Factory, about 13 miles south of Eureka, grilled cheese bar **Queso Kings** (10am-7pm Mon.-Fri., 9am-5pm Sat.-Sun.) offers inarguably the best way to sample local cheeses—as the gooey center of a crispy grilled cheese sandwich, featuring creamy cheese blends, gourmet meats, and fresh vegetables.

Nightlife

The **Pearl Lounge** (507 2nd St., 707/444-2017, www.pearleureka.com, 5pm-2am daily) has it all: microbrews, organic beer, wine, live music, and a dance floor. One block down, the **SpeakEasy** (411 Opera Alley, 707/444-2244, 4pm-11pm Sun.-Thurs., 4pm-1am Fri., 4pm-midnight Sat.) is a New Orleans-inspired bar located in a 120-year-old building that hosts live blues music, burlesque shows, and craft cocktails.

A good Irish pub to stop in for Guinness, **Gallagher's** (139 2nd St., 707/442-1177, www.gallaghers-irishpub.com, 11am-9pm daily) has a friendly atmosphere with fun musical acts.

A stylish wine-and-beer-only venue, **2 Doors Down** (1626 F St., 707/268-8989, www.2doorsdownwinebar.com, 4:30pm-9:30pm daily) serves savory tapas and small Italian dishes to accentuate your drink.

Shopping

Old Town is a vibrant shopping area where you can find almost anything, from antiques and books to gift boutiques and souvenirs.

Collectibles from the 1920s to the 1950s are at **Annex 39** (610 F St., 707/443-1323, noon-5:30pm Tues.-Sat.), right next to the old Eureka Theater.

Browse at beautiful **Eureka Books** (426 2nd St., 707/444-9593, www.eurekabooksellers.com, 10am-6pm daily), which offers new, used, and rare books, along with an extraordinary selection of vintage photographs, prints, and maps, or at **Booklegger** (402 2nd St., 707/445-1344, 10am-5:30pm Mon.-Sat., 11am-4pm Sun.), which carries over 50,000 volumes of literature in all genres.

Eureka has a few fantastic places for unique gifts. **Many Hands Gallery** (438 2nd St., 877/445-0455, www.manyhandsgallery.net, 10am-9pm Mon.-Sat., 10am-6pm Sun.) is a museum store featuring art and gifts from countries around the world and the art of 50 local artists. **Humboldt Herbals** (300 2nd St., 707/442-3541, www.humboldtherbals.com, 10am-6pm Mon.-Sat., 11am-5pm Sun.) offers more than 400 organic, culinary, and medicinal herbs; bulk organic teas; locally crafted herbal products; aromatherapy; natural body care; and books and gifts. **Talisman Beads** (214 F St., 707/443-1509, www.talismanbeads.us, 11am-6pm Mon.-Sat., 11am-5pm Sun.) is a remarkable treasure trove of beautiful Czech glass, Swarovski, African trade, sterling beads, and so much more.

Events

Eureka's most unusual event is the **Kinetic Grand Championship** (www.kineticgrandchampionship.com, Memorial Day weekend), a race that starts in Arcata, continues through Eureka, and ends in Ferndale. Competitors create colorful, often ridiculous, human-powered locomotive sculptures. Be prepared for dinosaurs, donkeys, dung beetles, and other sublimely silly things. The sculptures cross pavement, sand, water, and mud over the course of the three-day race. While other towns now have their own kinetic sculpture races, the north coast is the origin of the event, and this remains the grand championship of them all. For a great view, try to get a spot to watch Dead Man's Drop or the Water Entry.

Arts Alive (Old Town and downtown, 6pm-9pm first Sat. of the month) is a popular en masse art browse, where lovers of art and artists mingle on the first

Saturday of every month. About 80 galleries, museums, theaters, and cafés in Eureka's Old Town stay open late.

Accommodations

★ **Abigail's Elegant Victorian Mansion** (1406 C St., 707/444-3144, www.eureka-california.com, $135-145) is as Victorian as it gets. Originally built by one of the founders of Eureka, the inn has retained many of the large home's original fixtures. The owners took pains to learn the history of the house and town, and have added appropriate decor to create a truly Victorian mansion, right down to the vintage books in the elegant library. Each of the three rooms comes with its own story and astonishing collection of antiques. All rooms have private baths, though the bathroom might be just across the hall. Children are not encouraged at this romantic inn, but they can be accommodated.

Historical **Cornelius Daly Inn** (1125 H St., 707/445-3638 and 800/321-9656, www.dalyinn.com, $130-185) is draped in elegance with original turn-of-the-20th-century antiques and lovely Victorian gardens.

A re-created Victorian manor, **Carter House Inn** (301 L St., 800/404-1390, www.carterhouse.com, $190-235) has spacious rooms and an intimate fine dining restaurant that serves complimentary breakfast to guests.

Information and Services

For further information, contact the **Eureka! Humboldt County Convention and Visitors Bureau** (322 1st St., 707/443-5097 or 800/346-3482, 9am-5pm Mon.-Fri.).

⬥ CA-211 to the Lost Coast

The Lost Coast stretches across 80 miles. Its rugged isolation, volcanic black sand, and wandering feral pathways attract backwoods meanderers, sandy-footed adventurers, and rugged explorers looking to be absorbed into its mysteries and untouched beauty.

The Lost Coast enigma is the work of the **King Range**, which rises 4,088 feet within a few miles of the coast and cuts it off from the main highway system; the state declared it impenetrable in the early 20th century. And the King Range is still rising at about 10 feet every 1,000 years. However, the Pacific Ocean is continually eroding its base, creating 700-foot cliffs, toppled trees, and miles of black-sand beaches.

The north section of the King Range is an exhilarating canvas of green meadows, spring wildflowers, and wind-blown shores, but even more inspiring are the central and southern reaches claimed by the **King Range National Conservation Area** and **Sinkyone Wilderness State Park.** These two areas also offer the best options for hiking and camping. In King Range NCA, the Lost Coast Trail from **Mattole Campground** traverses some of the coastline's best features, from the old abandoned **Punta Gorda Lighthouse** to abundant wildlife to rugged vistas to the famous **Black Sands Beach.** The entire Lost Coast Trail is a rugged, 25-mile backpacking trip, which takes 3-4 days to complete.

Getting There

This side trip along the Lost Coast is roughly **100 miles,** but it's slow going along winding, sometimes rough coastal roads. Plan on at least **four hours** of driving, not including stops.

From US-101, head south on CA-211 toward Ferndale. You'll continue via Mattole Road, reaching the coast at Black Sands Beach. It takes another three hours of driving along the King Range to reach Shelter Cove, which also offers coastal access. Head east to rejoin US-101 at Garberville.

A few tiny towns provide services not that far past Ferndale. **Petrolia** has a general store with the bare essentials and gasoline, and the slightly larger town of **Shelter Cove** offers a couple of small inns and basic food services within a rural setting. But it is the remoteness that makes hiking and camping on this part of California's coastline remarkable.

Ferndale

Ferndale (pop. 1,372) was built in the 19th century by Scandinavian immigrants who came to California to farm. Little has changed since the immigrants constructed their fanciful gingerbread Victorian homes and shops. A designated historical landmark, Ferndale is all Victorian, all the time. Just ask about the building you're in and you'll be told all about its specific architectural style, its construction date, and its original occupants. Main Street's shops, galleries, inns, and restaurants are all set into scrupulously maintained and restored late-19th-century buildings. Even the public restrooms in Ferndale are housed in a small Victorianesque structure.

Sights

The **Ferndale Museum** (515 Shaw Ave., 707/786-4466, www.ferndale-museum. org, 11am-4pm Wed.-Sat., 1pm-4pm Sun. Feb.-Sept., $1) is a block off Main Street and tells the story of the town. Life-sized dioramas depict period life in a Victorian home, and antique artifacts bring history to life. Downstairs, the implements of rural coast history vividly display the reality that farmers and craftspeople faced in the pre-industrial era.

To cruise further back into the town's history, consider wandering out into the **Ferndale Cemetery** (on Ocean St.). Well-tended tombstones and mausoleums wind up the hillside that backs the town.

Food

Popular among locals, the small and casual breakfast and lunch counter **Lost Coast Cafe & Bakery** (468 Main St.,

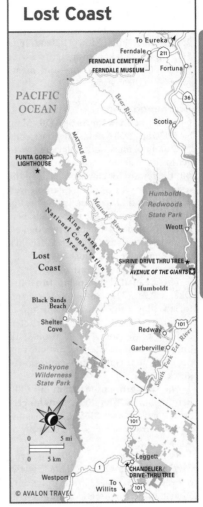

Lost Coast

707/786-5330, Thurs.-Sat. 10:30am-4pm, Sun.-Mon. 10:30am-3pm, $6-12) offers surprisingly tasty vegan soups, salads, and sandwiches, with the chalkboard menu changing often. For something quick on weekend mornings, try the pecan cinnamon roll and other sweet and savory baked goods at **Humboldt Sweets** (614 Main St., 707/786-4683, Fri.-Sun. 8am-5pm; $4-9).

To sit down and enjoy table service,

it's got to be farm-to-table restaurant **Farmhouse on Main** (460 Main St., 707/786-9222, Thurs.-Sun. 11:30am-2pm, 5pm-7:30pm, Mon. 11:30am-2pm; $11-30), which takes advantage of a wide range of produce grown—and meats raised—in the region.

Accommodations

Guests of the **Shaw House B&B** (703 Main St., 707/786-9958, www.shawhouse.com, $129 and up) must walk a block or two to get to the heart of downtown Ferndale. But the reward for staying outside of the town center is a spacious garden well worth a stroll of its own. In the heat of the afternoon, huge shade trees and perfectly positioned garden benches make a lovely spot to sit and read a book, hold a quiet conversation, or just enjoy the serene beauty of garden and town.

The beautiful **Victorian Inn** (400 Ocean Ave., 707/786-4949, www.victorianvillageinn.com, $189 and up) is a vintage 1890 building constructed of local redwoods. The 13 rooms, all uniquely decorated, feature antique furnishings, luxurious linens, and pretty knickknacks.

The **Gingerbread Mansion Inn** (400 Berding St., 707/786-4000, www.gingerbread-mansion.com, $165 and up) has antiques, luxurious linens, and turn-down service.

Redwood Suites (332 Ocean Ave., 707/786-5000 or 888/589-1863, www.redwoodsuites.com, $145 and up) is only a block off Main Street, and suites with full kitchens are available.

Mattole Road

One of the few drivable routes to view the Lost Coast is via **Mattole Road.** Starting in Ferndale, this narrow, mostly paved two-lane road affords views of remote ranchland, unspoiled forests, and a few short miles of barely accessible cliffs and beaches. In good weather, the vista points from Mattole Road are spectacular. Lighthouse Road turns off Mattole Road south of Petrolia and runs west to Mattole, the northern end of the Lost Coast Trail.

Black Sands Beach

One of the most amazing and unusual—and accessible—sights on the Lost Coast is the ominous **Black Sands Beach**, composed of crumbly volcanic rock. It's roughly 20 miles south of Ferndale along Mattole Road. The dark sands of this wide beach also serve as the south end of the Lost Coast Trail.

Shelter Cove

Located on less than six square miles where the King Range meets the Pacific Ocean, **Shelter Cove** (pop. 592) hugs a secluded stretch of the California coast that looks like "the land that time forgot."

It was first inhabited by the Sinkyone Indians, possibly to escape the summer heat of the interior valleys. Then Spanish ships and seal traders arrived, and later ranchers settled into the area. A thriving tanbark industry followed, a wharf was built to ship the bark, and the little village quickly grew.

When the steep terrain surrounding Shelter Cove proved too difficult for highway builders to penetrate during the early 20th century construction of State Route 1 (referred to as California 1, Highway 1, and the Pacific Coast Highway), the long segment of what is now the Lost Coast was abandoned, and so was Shelter Cove when the tanbark industry met its end soon after.

The forsaken shoreline was deemed "The Lost Coast," but it wasn't truly forgotten. Three brothers who spent their summers here returned to see the village revived. The Machi brothers saw an opportunity for new industry development and tourism, promoting Shelter Cove as a vacation destination and fishing as its bread and butter. City dwellers came from all over, including San Francisco

Humboldt Roadside Attractions

As you're driving along Redwood Highway through Humboldt County, kitschy roadside attractions may catch your eye. They're not more than curiosities, really, but they can make for a fun 5- to 30-minute diversion.

On the southern end of Avenue of the Giants, look for the **Living Chimney Tree** (1111 Ave. of the Giants, free), a nearly 80-foot redwood that survived a fire but wound up burned hollow, so it's possible to stand inside its trunk.

A little over six miles south of Garberville, the **Legend of Bigfoot** (2500 US-101, 707/247-3332, 8am-7pm daily, free) is mainly a souvenir shop surrounded by wood carvings. There are bears, elves, gnomes, and a fantastical carved treehouse called Bear's Hollow—plus a life-sized Bigfoot, of course.

Less than two miles farther south, in Piercy, the twin trunks of the 1,800-year-old **Grandfather Tree** (779 US-101, 707/247-3413, free) measure 55 feet around, and it looms nearly 270 feet tall over its own wood carvings and a gift shop. Next door, **One Log House** (705 US-101, 707/247-3717, www.oneloghouse.com, 5am-8pm daily summer, 9am-5pm daily winter, free) is a single-room mobile home made from the hollowed-out trunk of a 2,000-year-old redwood.

A few miles farther, **Confusion Hill** (75001 US-101, 707/925-6456, www.confusionhill.com, 9am-6pm daily May-mid-Sept., 9am-5pm daily mid-Sept.-Apr.) offers a pair of entertaining attractions: the dizzying, off-kilter **Gravity House** ($5 adults, $4 children 4-12) and the scenic 30-minute **Mountain Train Ride** ($10 adults, $7.50 children 4-12).

(230 miles), and they never stopped coming.

Today, Shelter Cove is a community of fisherfolk, builders, and retirees. A nine-hole golf course encircles the single-run-way Shelter Cove Airport at the heart of the commercial district. Most of the land belongs to the King Range National Conservation Area, which is managed by the Bureau of Land Management.

From Shelter Cove, head east to rejoin US-101 at Garberville (see page 173).

Food and Accommodations
The **Cove Restaurant** (10 Sea Dr., 707/986-1197, 5pm-9pm Thurs.-Sun., $6-20) is the best choice for a meal. If you'd like to stay the night, head for the cliff-top **Inn of the Lost Coast** (205 Wave Dr., 707/986-7521 or 888/570-9676, www.innofthelostcoast.com, $225 and up). Stock up on supplies at the small **general store** (7272 Shelter Cove Rd., 707/986-7733, 7:30am-7:30pm daily).

Humboldt Redwoods State Park

Surprisingly, the largest strand of un-logged redwood trees anywhere in the world isn't on the coast and it isn't in the Sierra. It's right here in Humboldt, bisected by US-101, about 35 miles south of Eureka. Come to this park to hike beneath 300-foot old-growth trees that began their lives centuries before Europeans knew California existed.

While it's more than worth the time to spend a weekend in the Humboldt Redwoods, you can also spend as little as an hour or two here. A drive through the Avenue of the Giants with a stop at the visitors center and a quick nature walk or picnic can give you a quick taste of this lovely south end of the coastal redwood region.

Visitors Center
The **visitors center** (17119 Ave. of the Giants/CA-254, 707/946-2263, www.humboldtredwoods.org, 10am-4pm

daily) for the park rests along the Avenue of the Giants, between the towns of Weott and Myers Flat. Start here if you're new to the region or need hiking or camping information.

★ Avenue of the Giants

The most famous stretch of redwood trees in the state, the **Avenue of the Giants** (look for signs on US-101 to turn-offs, www.avenueofthegiants.net) parallels US-101 and the Eel River between Fortuna and Garberville. Visitors come from all over the world to gawk in wonder at the sky-high old-growth redwoods that line the pavement. Campgrounds and hiking trails sprout among the trees off the road.

The **Shrine Drive-Thru Tree** (13078 Ave. of the Giants, 707/943-1975, 6am-8pm daily, closed winter, $5 per vehicle) is near the town of Myers Flat at the southern end of the park. It's said that in the late 1800s teamsters pulled their coaches through the tree.

The avenue's highest traffic time is July and August, when you can expect a bumper-to-bumper, stop-and-go traffic jam for almost the whole of the 31-mile stretch of road. If crowds aren't your thing, try visiting in the spring or fall, or even braving the rains of winter to gain a more secluded redwood experience.

Hiking

With all that fabulous forest, it's hard to resist parking the car and getting out to enjoy the world of the big trees up close and personal.

Many visitors start with the **Founders Grove Nature Loop Trail** (0.5 mile, easy), at mile marker 20.5 on the Avenue of the Giants. This flat nature trail gives sedate walkers a taste of the big old-growth trees in the park. Sadly, the one-time tallest tree in the world (the Dyerville Giant) fell.

Right at the visitors center, you can enjoy the **Gould Grove Nature Trail** (0.5 mile, easy), a wheelchair-accessible

massive redwoods along the Avenue of the Giants

interpretive nature walk that includes signs describing the denizens of the forest.

Camping

Few lodging options are really close to Humboldt Redwoods State Park other than the campgrounds in the park itself. Car and RV campers will find a few options. The pleasant but not very private **Burlington Campground** (707/946-1811, www.reservecalifornia.com, $35 with one vehicle) is adjacent to the visitors center and is equipped with bathrooms and showers. Seasonal **Albee Creek** (Mattole Rd., five miles west of Ave. of the Giants, 707/946-2472, www.reservecalifornia. com, $35 with one vehicle) has sites under redwoods and is very popular. The large and slightly more private **Hidden Springs Campground** (five miles south of the visitors center, Ave. of the Giants, 707/943-3177, www.reservecalifornia.com, $35 with one vehicle) is close to the Eel River. Reservations are strongly recommended

for campsites, as this region is quite popular with weekend campers.

Garberville

Considered the gateway to both the Avenue of the Giants and the Lost Coast, the town of **Garberville** (pop. 913) sits about seven miles below Avenue of the Giants and provides a few places to eat and sleep for those exploring redwood country.

Food

Enjoy a fresh, organic breakfast at the **Woodrose Café** (911 Redwood Ave., 707/923-3191, www.thewoodrosecafe. com, 8am-2pm daily, 5pm-9pm Wed.-Fri., $9-18) or homemade bagels and espresso at **Bon Bistro & Bakery** (867 Redwood Dr., 707/923-2509, 7am-3pm Mon.-Fri., 8am-2pm Sat.-Sun., $3-12).

The restaurant at the **Benbow Inn** (445 Lake Benbow Dr., 800/355-3301, www.benbowinn.com, 8am-3pm and 5pm-9pm daily) matches the lodgings for superiority in the area. It serves upscale California cuisine and features an extensive wine list with many regional wineries represented. The white-tablecloth dining room is exquisite, and the expansive outdoor patio overlooking the water is the perfect place to sit as the temperature cools on a summer evening.

Accommodations

The place to stay in the Humboldt Redwoods area is the **Benbow Inn** (445 Lake Benbow Dr., 707/923-2124 or 800/355-3301, www.benbowinn.com, $195-660). A swank resort backing onto Lake Benbow, this inn has it all: a gourmet restaurant, an 18-hole golf course, and a woodsy atmosphere that blends perfectly with the idyllic redwood forest surrounding it. Rooms glow with polished dark woods and jewel-toned carpets and decor. Wide king and comfy queen beds beckon to guests tired after

a long day of hiking in the redwoods or golfing beside the inn.

The best deal is **Motel Garberville** (948 Redwood Dr., 707/923-2422, www.motelgarbervillecalifornia.com, $80-90). At **Best Western Humboldt House Inn** (701 Redwood Dr., 707/923-2771, www.humboldthouseinn.com, $126-160), the rooms are clean and comfortable, the pool is sparkling and cool, and the location is convenient to restaurants and shops in Garberville. Most rooms have two queen beds, making this motel perfect for families and couples traveling together on a budget.

Leggett

About a half hour from Garberville, the town of **Leggett** (pop. 122) is notable as the location of the southernmost of the drive-thru trees. The **Chandelier Drive-Thru Tree** (67402 Drive-Thru Tree Rd., 707/925-6464, www.drivethrutree.com, 8:30am-dusk daily, $5 per car) is at the junction of CA-1 and US-101. The tree opening is about six feet wide and a little over six feet high. And, of course, there's a gift shop. Leggett marks the point at which CA-1 splits off US-101 going south (and merges with US-101 going north).

You may also stop for burgers at the funky **Peg House** (69501 US-101, 707/925-6444, 7:30pm-8pm daily, $5-15), a restaurant counter and convenience store with outdoor seating and a stage for live music in the summer.

Fort Bragg

CA-1 makes its way to the coast from Leggett and after 43 miles reaches **Fort Bragg** (pop. 7,287), about 133 miles from Eureka. Now a California Historical Landmark, it was established as a pre-Civil War military garrison that was abandoned in the 1860s, after which it became a lumber and commercial fishing

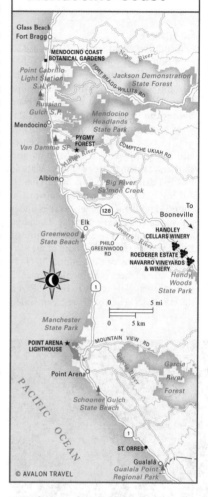

Mendocino Coast

town, leaving the tourist trade to its upscale neighbor, Mendocino.

But since the 2002 closing of the Georgia Pacific lumber mill, Fort Bragg has worked to reclaim its coastline appeal and push in a more tourist-friendly destination. It's converted the 425-acre industrial site where its old mill once stood into a couple of miles of coastal trail connecting a scenic sequence of craggy points, coves, and colorful sea glass beaches.

That connects to **MacKerricher State Park** to the north, while on the southern end of town lie **Mendocino Coast Botanical Gardens** and **Point Cabrillo Light Station State Historic Park,** where trails and stunning views abound!

Getting There and Around

State Route 1 (CA-1), California's Pacific Coast Highway, turns into Main Street as it passes through Fort Bragg. CA-20 heads east to west, running for several miles alongside and south of the Skunk Train route from Willits.

Several local lines offer bus service through the **Mendocino Transit Authority** (707/462-1422 or 800/696-4682, www.4mta.org, fare from $1.50 to $23 one way), which also offers connecting services south to Bodega and Santa Rosa.

Sights

The **Mendocino Coast Botanical Gardens** (18220 CA-1 N., 707/964-4352, www.gardenbythesea.org, 9am-5pm daily Mar.-Oct., 9am-4pm daily Nov.-Feb., $15 adults, $8 children 6-14) is a vast expanse of land bearing an astonishing variety of vegetation. Stretching 47 acres down to the sea, these gardens offer literally miles of walking and hiking through careful plantings and wild landscapes. The gardens' map is also a seasonal guide, useful for folks who aren't sure whether it's rhododendron season or whether the dahlia garden might be in bloom. Butterflies flutter and bees buzz, and good labels teach novice botany enthusiasts the names of the plants they see.

Whether you're into scenery or history, nautical or otherwise, you won't want to miss a visit to the **Point Cabrillo Light Station State Historic Park** (45300 Lighthouse Rd., 707/937-6123, www.pointcabrillo.org, sunrise-sunset daily, $5). This 300-acre nature preserve, just south of Fort Bragg, features two museums, a marinelife exhibit, and walking trails. The beautiful **Point Cabrillo Light Station** has been functioning for more than 100 years. It was built in part to facilitate the movement of lumber and other supplies south to San Francisco to help rebuild the city after the massive 1906 earthquake. The site is currently being managed by a volunteer organization, the Point Cabrillo Lightkeepers Association. The trail that leads to the lighthouse from the parking lot is about 0.5 mile downhill, but remember you'll have to walk uphill to the parking lot.

Ride through the redwoods and into areas inaccessible by car on the **Skunk Train** (100 W. Laurel St., 707/964-6371, www.skunktrain.com, $24-84 round-trip adults, $15-42 children $10 dogs), a line that runs 40 miles from Fort Bragg on the coast to Willits, traversing 30 bridges and trestles and two deep mountain tunnels. The name came from the pungent odor given off by the rail-bus. It's one of the best ways to see the local coast terrain, if not by foot.

Beaches

On the north edge of town, multicolored glass sparkles in the sand beneath the sun at **Glass Beach,** left over from its past as a garbage dump. Residents threw their trash over the cliffside to be burned in piles. After several decades, the pounding waves wore down the discarded broken bottles and jars into the pieces of small, smooth glass that have given the beach its name. Glass Beach is on the southern end of **MacKerricher State Park** (24100 MacKerricher Park Rd., 707/937-5804, www.parks.ca.gov, 6am-10pm daily), a pristine stretch of coastline that contains beaches, wildlife habitat, dunes, coves, tidepools, wetlands, forest, and Lake Cleone.

Recreation

Go **abalone diving** or **kayak** the many caves and arches off the coast. You can rent gear and get all the information you need at **Sub-Surface Progression Dive Shop** (18600 CA-1 N., 707/964-3793,

www.subsurfaceprogression.com, 9am-5pm daily). Or observe over 150 species of birds at **Mendocino Coast Botanical Gardens** (18220 CA-1 N., 707/964-4352, www.gardenbythesea.com, 9am-5pm daily, 9am-4pm daily Nov.-Feb., $15 adults, $6 children 6-14).

Whale-watching is one of Fort Bragg's most popular attractions during the winter and spring, when gray and humpback whales migrate along the coast. They can be seen from several offshore points, especially at **MacKerricher State Park** (24100 MacKerricher Park Rd., 707/937-5804, www.parks.ca.gov, 6am-10pm daily) and **Point Cabrillo Light Station State Historic Park** (13800 Point Cabrillo Dr., 707/937-6123, www.pointcabrillo.org, sunrise-sunset daily). Whale-watching charter boats, such as **Anchor Charter Boats** (32260 N. Harbor Dr., 707/964-4550, www.anchorcharter-boats.com, 6am-10pm daily, $40 pp), are located in Noyo Harbor.

Food

The **North Coast Brewing Company** (444 N. Main St., 707/964-3400, www.northcoastbrewing.com, 11:30am-9pm Sun.-Thurs., 11:30am-10pm Fri.-Sat.) opened in 1988, and its Red Seal Ale and Old Rasputin stout hold a place in craft beer lore. The brewery's taproom makes a comfortable place to check out the latest beers while grabbing a classic brewpub meal.

Cheap but great waffles and homemade goodies are at **Headlands Coffeehouse** (120 E. Laurel St., 707/964-1987, www.headlandcoffeehouse.com, 7am-10pm Mon.-Sat., 7am-5pm Sun., $4-8). Vegetarian breakfast and lunch options are part—not all—of the menu at popular **Café One** (753 N. Main St., 707/964-3309, 7:30am-2:30pm daily,

From top to bottom: the Chandelier Drive-Thru Tree in Leggett; Glass Beach in Fort Bragg; St. Orres resort in Gualala is centered around a 90-year-old redwood lodge.

$9-16), while **Egghead's Restaurant** (326 N. Main St., 707/964-5005, 7am-2pm daily, $10-18) has been serving an enormous menu of breakfast, lunch, and brunch items to satisfy diners for more than 30 years. The menu includes every imaginable omelet combination and Flying-Monkey Potatoes, derived from the *Wizard of Oz* theme that runs through the place.

For fresh seafood, **Silver's at the Wharf** (32260 N. Harbor Dr., 707/964-4283, www.wharf-restaurant.com, 11am-9:30pm Sun.-Thurs., 11am-10pm Fri.-Sat., $15-33) serves cuisine from the sea along the Noyo River. Hankering for pizza and beer? Try the small but lively gathering spot **Piaci Pub & Pizzeria** (120 W. Redwood Ave., 707/961-1133, www.piacipizza.com, 11am-9:30pm Mon.-Thurs., 11am-10pm Fri.-Sat., 4pm-9:30pm Sun., $11-30).

★ **Mayan Fusion** (418 N. Main St., 707/961-0211, www.mayanfusionftbragg.com, 11am-9pm daily, $12-30) offers a unique and exceptionally tasty Mexican infusion that includes tapas, tamales, and steak or seafood entrées served with cheesy mashed potatoes.

Nightlife and Entertainment

Fort Bragg is not without its dive bars. Local favorite **Tip-Top Lounge** (321 N. Franklin St., 707/964-5448, 9am-2am daily) boasts cheap drinks, a pool table, and a jukebox. The **Welcome Inn** (148 E. Redwood Ave., 707/964-5491, 8am-2am daily) has a cool vibe and atmosphere, including several pool tables and shuffleboard.

Silver's at the Wharf (32260 N. Harbor Dr., 707/964-4283, www.wharf-restaurant.com, 11am-9:30pm daily) doubles as a sports bar setting with a large-screen TV, a couple cozy couches, and a fantastic view of the Noyo River.

Offering a wide range of theater experiences, from musicals to operas to concerts, **Gloriana Musical Theater** (210 N. Corry St., 707/964-7469, www.gloriana.org) brings talented artists and actors together for fantastic performances that the whole family can enjoy.

Shopping

Rubaiyat Beads (222 E. Redwood Ave., 707/961-0222, www.rubaiyatbeads.com, 10am-5pm daily) is the place to discover beads, tribal jewelry, ethnic textiles, incense, and sacred treasures from around the world.

Be blown away by **Glass Fire Gallery** (18320 CA-1 N., 707/962-9420, www.glassfiregallery.com, 11am-6pm Tues.-Sat., noon-5pm Sun.), where gorgeous blown-glass vessels, sea jellies, sculptures, and jewelry are displayed, or explore **Sacred Woods** (32281 N. Harbor Dr., 707/964-3507, www.sacredwoods.noyo.com, 10am-5pm daily), a garden collection of amazing sculptures and beautiful outdoor furniture from Thailand and Indonesia to the north coast.

Tons of used books and vintage records are found at **Windsong Used Books & Records** (324 N. Main St., 707/964-2050, 10am-5:30pm Mon.-Sat., 10am-4pm Sun.), which also has some gift items like candles, incense, and artwork. **The Bookstore & Vinyl Cafe** (137 E. Laurel St., 707/964-6559, 10am-5:30pm Mon.-Sat., 11am-3pm Sun.) is small but has a good selection of new and used books, with a great upstairs section filled with used records.

Stop by the **Lost Surf Shack** (319 N. Franklin St., 707/961-0889, www.lostsurfshack.com, 10am-6pm daily) for great beachwear. Surfers will love that they have everything to surf the waves, including board rentals.

For unique fashion items and gifts, go to **Toto Zaida** (401 N. Main St., 707/964-8686, 11am-5pm Mon.-Sat.) or stop by **Tangents** (368 N. Main St., 707/964-3884, 9am-6pm daily), a mix of exotic and cool-funk fashion, including a nice selection of one-of-a-kind ethnic gifts.

Events

Taste local microbrews and wines and browse arts and crafts during the **Fort Bragg Whale Festival** (707/961-6300), held every third weekend in March, or celebrate the days of lumberjacks at **Paul Bunyan Days** (www.paulbunyandays.com, Labor Day weekend), which features a parade, logging show, and square dancing.

Accommodations

What really makes the **Beachcomber Motel** (1111 N. Main St., 707/964-2402, www.thebeachcombermotel.com, $110-270) worthwhile, besides its lower-than-B&B prices, is that it's right on the beach, offering many rooms with ocean views. Rooms are clean, with few amenities, but guests just need to walk out the back door to be on the sand.

The best bang for your buck is the **Grey Whale Inn** (615 N. Main St., 707/964-0640, www.greywhaleinn.com, $110-150) on the northern end of town, which isn't fancy but is comfortable and conveniently located with good-sized rooms.

A popular little B&B in the heart of downtown, **Country Inn** (632 N. Main St., 707/964-3737, www.beourguests.com, $105-180) has a laid-back aura, friendly hosts, and a hot tub to unwind in at the end of a long day.

The **Weller House Inn** (524 Stewart St., 707/964-4415, www.wellerhouse.com, $120-200) is a restored 1886 mansion with a gorgeous ballroom and luxurious amenities.

About a 15-minute drive north of Fort Bragg, there are only a handful of luxury lodgings at the ★ **Inn at Newport Ranch** (31502 CA-1, 707/962-4818, www.theinnatnewportranch.com, $250-375), despite the property extending more than 2,000 acres! The main lodge and cabins stand on the foundation of what once was the bustling logging town of Newport, sitting atop grassy ocean bluffs—part of the inn's mile of coastline trail. Most of the property extends east of the highway, rising into redwood forest and intersected by hiking, ATV, and horse-riding trails. Guests may plan activities over complimentary breakfast in the lodge, then discuss the day's exploits over an optional family-style dinner in the evening, before retiring to therapeutic hot tubs and a star-filled sky.

Information and Services

The best source of information is the **Fort Bragg-Mendocino Coast Chamber of Commerce** (215 S. Main St., 707/961-6300, www.mendocinocoast.com, 10am-5pm Mon.-Fri.).

Russian Gulch State Park

Some of the most popular hiking trails in coastal Mendocino County wind through **Russian Gulch State Park** (CA-1, two miles north of Mendocino, 707/937-5804, www.parks.ca.gov, dawn to dusk, $8), 9 miles south of Fort Bragg. Russian Gulch has its own **Fern Canyon Trail** (three miles round-trip), winding into the second-growth redwood forest filled with lush green ferns. At the four-way junction, turn left to hike another 0.75 mile to the ever-popular 36-foot waterfall. Be aware that you're likely to be part of a crowd visiting the falls on summer weekends. To the right at the four-way junction, you can take a three-mile loop for a total hike of six miles that leads to the top of the attractive little waterfall. If you prefer the shore to the forest, hike west rather than east to take in the lovely wild headlands and see blowholes, grasses, and even trawlers out seeking the day's catch.

Mendocino

Set on a bluff overlooking the ocean, the picturesque town of **Mendocino** (pop. 894) is a favorite for romantic weekend getaways, with quaint

Mendocino

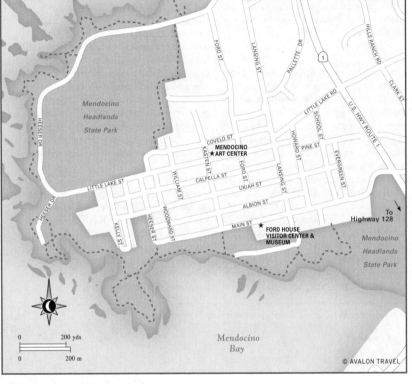

bed-and-breakfasts, art galleries, and local, sustainable dining. Art is especially prominent in the culture; from the 1960s onward, aspiring artists have found supportive communities here, 10 miles from Fort Bragg.

Sights

The town of Mendocino has long been an inspiration and a gathering place for artists of many varieties, and the **Mendocino Art Center** (45200 Little Lake St., 707/937-5818 or 800/653-3328, www. mendocinoartcenter.org, 10am-5pm daily, donation) is the main institution that gives these diverse artists a community, provides them with opportunities for teaching and learning, and displays the work of contemporary artists for the benefit of both the artists and the general public. Since 1959 the center has offered artist workshops and retreats. Today it has a flourishing schedule of events and classes, five galleries, and a sculpture garden. You can even drop in and make some art of your own. Supervised "open studios" in ceramics, jewelry making, watercolor, sculpture, and drawing take place throughout the year.

Mendocino Headlands State Park (Mendocino, 707/937-5804, www.parks. ca.gov, day-use only, free) occupies the waterfront land that surrounds the town of Mendocino. A few trails weave through the grassy bluffs and take you to cliffside water views or down to the beach. At the south end of the park, the historical **Ford House Museum and Visitor Center** (45035 Main St., 707/937-5397, www.mendoparks.org, 11am-4pm daily) has information about the town of Mendocino.

Food

One of the most appealing and dependable places to get a good meal any day of the week is the **Mendocino Café** (10451 Lansing St., 707/937-6141, www.mendocinocafe.com, 11am-9pm daily, $16-30). The café has good, simple, well-prepared food, a small children's menu, a wine list, and a beer list. Enjoy a Thai burrito, a fresh salmon fillet, or a steak in the warm, well-lit dining room. Or sit outside: The café is in the gardens of Mendocino Village, and thanks to a heated patio, you can enjoy outdoor dining any time of day.

Café Beaujolais (961 Ukiah St., 707/937-5614, www.cafebeaujolais.com, 11:30am-2:30pm Wed.-Sun., 5:30pm-9pm daily, $24-42) is a standout French-California restaurant in an area dense with great upscale cuisine. This charming out-of-the-way spot is a few blocks from the center of Mendocino Village in an older, creeper-covered home. Despite the white tablecloths and fancy crystal, the atmosphere is casual at lunchtime and gets only slightly more formal at dinner. The giant salads and delectable entrées are made with organic produce, humanely raised meats, and locally caught seafood. Beware: Portions can be enormous, but you can order them half-size. Reservations are available on the website.

Shopping

Having Mendocino Bay as a backdrop makes browsing shops in Mendocino Village particularly delightful. Gardens and flowers abound among charming galleries, bookstores, and boutiques, which occasionally find interesting ways to incorporate one of the town's old-fashioned wooden water towers.

Spectacular views are found all along the Mendocino County coast.

Panache (45120 Main St., 707/937-1234, www.thepanachegallery.com) displays and sells beautiful works of art in all sorts of media. You'll find paintings and jewelry, sculpture and art glass. Much of the artistic focus reminds viewers of the sea crashing just outside the large multi-room gallery.

Nothing makes a weekend getaway more enjoyable than a delicious book. Pick one up at the **Gallery Book Shop** (319 Kasten St., 707/937-2665, 9:30am-6pm Sun.-Thurs., 9:30am-9pm Fri.-Sat.).

Accommodations

Places to stay in Mendocino tend to be smaller, often luxury, properties. For lower-priced options, try Fort Bragg, about 10 miles and 20 minutes north.

Fun and funky, the **Sweetwater Inn and Spa** (44840 Main St., Mendocino Village, 800/300-4140, www.sweetwater-spa.com, $135-330) recalls the days when Mendocino was a starving artists' colony rather than a yuppie weekend retreat. A redwood water tower was converted into a guest room, joined by a motley collection of detached cottages that guarantee guests great privacy. Every room and cottage has its own style—you'll find a spiral staircase in the water tower, a two-person tub set in a windowed alcove in the Zen Room, and fireplaces in many of the cottages. Thick gardens surround the building complex, and a path leads back to the Garden Spa.

With several properties in addition to the main hotel in Mendocino Village, **MacCallum House** (45020 Albion St., 800/609-0492, www.maccallumhouse.com, $150-350) is the king of luxury on the Mendocino coast. Choose from private cottages with hot tubs, suites with jetted baths, and regular rooms with opulent antique appointments. The woodwork gleams and the service pleases. Note that a two-night minimum is required on weekends, and a three-night minimum goes into effect for most holidays.

For a perfect vantage point for sunset over the Pacific, stay at the **Sea Rock Bed & Breakfast Inn** (11101 Lansing St., 707/937-0926 or 800/906-0926, www.searock.com, $225-325). Located away from the Main Street area, the cottages, junior suites, and suites sleep 2-4 people each. The inn's breakfast room serves complimentary quiche and fresh fruit every morning.

The **Stanford Inn** (44850 Comptche Ukiah Rd., 707/937-5615 or 800/331-8884, www.stanfordinn.com, $230-500) is one of the largest accommodations in the Mendocino area. This resort hotel sits up away from the beaches, surrounded by redwood forest. Gardens surround the resort (in fact, there's a nursery on the property), perfect for an after-dinner stroll. The location is convenient to hiking and only a short drive to Mendocino Village and the coastline. Guest rooms have the feel of an upscale forest lodge, with beautiful honey-color wood-paneled walls, pretty furniture, and puffy down comforters.

Little River and Albion

Little River (pop. 117) is about three miles south of Mendocino on CA-1. Albion (pop. 168) is also along CA-1, about eight miles south of Mendocino and almost 30 miles north of Point Arena. Find a state park and several plush places to stay in this area.

Van Damme State Park

At Van Damme State Park (8001 CA-1, three miles south of Mendocino, 707/937-5804, www.parks.ca.gov, free), take a walk to the park's centerpiece, the Pygmy Forest, on the wheelchair-accessible loop trail (0.25 mile, easy). Here, you'll see a true biological rarity: mature yet tiny cypress and pine trees perpetually stunted by a combination of always-wet ground and poor soil-nutrient conditions. You can get to the Pygmy Forest from this park's Fern Canyon Trail (six miles one-way, difficult) or drive Airport Road to the trail parking lot (opposite the county airport) directly to the loop.

Kayak Mendocino (707/813-7117, www. kayakmendocino.com) launches 1.5-hour Sea Cave Nature Tours (9am, 11:30am, 2pm, $60 pp) from Van Damme State Park. No previous experience is necessary, as the expert guides provide all the equipment you need and teach you how to paddle your way through the sea caves and around the harbor seals.

Camping (800/444-7275, www.reserve-california.com, $35) is available in Van Damme State Park, and reservations are strongly encouraged.

Food and Accommodations

The Little River Inn (7901 CA-1 N., Little River, 707/937-5942, www.littleriverinn. com, $175-225) appeals to coastal vacationers who like a little luxury. It has a nine-hole golf course and two lighted tennis courts, and all its recreation areas overlook the Pacific, just across the highway. The sprawling grounds surround a white Victorian house and include a spa, restaurant, and charming sea-themed bar.

The luxurious Glendeven Inn (8205 CA-1 N., 707/937-0083 or 800/822-4536, www.glendeven.com, $215-415) is situated in an old farmhouse with ocean views. The hosts will help you settle in with a complimentary wine and hors d'oeuvres hour in the late afternoon, and they wake you in the morning with a three-course made-to-order breakfast, delivered to your guest room exactly when you want it.

The Albion River Inn (3790 CA-1 N., 707/937-1919 or 800/479-7944, www.albionriverinn.com, $195-355) is a gorgeous and serene setting for an away-from-it-all vacation. A full breakfast is included in the room rates, but pets and smoking are not allowed, and there are no TVs.

The Ledford House Restaurant (3000 CA-1 N., Albion, 707/937-0282, www. ledfordhouse.com, 5pm-9pm Wed.-Sun., $18-32) is beautiful even from a distance; you'll see it on the hill as you drive up CA-1. With excellent food and nightly jazz performances, it's truly special.

◆ CA-128: Anderson Valley

To follow the Anderson Valley wine trail, head southeast on CA-128, about three miles south of Albion. The wine trail continues for roughly 60 miles (45 minutes) to Boonville. From Boonville, you can reverse the route to return to CA-1 or continue another 60 miles (90 minutes) to rejoin US-101 at Cloverdale.

Handley Cellars (3151 CA-128, 707/895-3876, www.handleycellars.com, 10am-5pm daily) offers a tasting of hand-crafted wines you probably won't see in your local grocery store.

The largest winery in the area is Navarro (5601 CA-128, Philo, 707/537-9463, www.navarrowine.com, 8am-6pm

Anderson Valley

To Hwy 1

128

Navarro

Navarro

HANDLEY CELLARS WINERY

HOLMES RANCH RD

ROEDERER ESTATE

PHILO - GREENWOOD RD

River

NAVARRO VINEYARDS

Hendy Woods State Park

128

A n d e r s o n

RAYS RD

Philo

0   2 mi

ANDERSON VALLEY WAY

0   2 km

V a l l e y

Boonville

ANDERSON VALLEY BREWING CO

To Cloverdale and Alexander Valley

To Ukiah

128

BOONVILLE-UKIAH RD

253

© AVALON TRAVEL

Mon.-Fri., 10am-5pm Sat.-Sun.), which offers a range of tasty wines as well as some interesting specialty products, such as *verjus* (the pressed juice of unripened grapes).

In a valley full of great wineries, **Roederer Estate** (4501 CA-128, 707/895-2288, www.roedererestate.com, 11am-5pm daily, tasting fee) creates some of the best sparkling wines in the state. Be sure to ask for a taste of Roederer's rarely seen still wines—you might find something wonderful.

For visitors who prefer a cold beer to a glass of wine, **Anderson Valley Brewing Company** (17700 Boonville Rd., 707/895-2337, www.avbc.com, 11am-6pm Sat.-Thurs., 11am-7pm Fri., closed Tues.-Wed. in winter) serves up a selection of microbrews that changes each year and each season. The warehouse-sized beer hall has a bar, tables, and a good-sized gift shop.

Elk

About 10 miles (15 minutes) south of Albion on CA-1, the town of **Elk** (pop. 208) used to be called Greenwood, after the family of Caleb Greenwood, who settled here in about 1850. Details of the story vary, but it is widely believed that Caleb was part of a mission to rescue survivors of the Donner Party after their rough winter near Truckee.

Greenwood State Beach (CA-1, 707/937-5804, www.parks.ca.gov, visitors center 10am-4pm Wed.-Sun. Mar.-Nov.) is an intriguing place to visit. From the mid-19th century until the 1920s, this stretch of shore was a stop for large ships carrying timber to points of sale in San Francisco and sometimes even China. The visitors center displays photographs and exhibits about Elk's past in the lumber business. It also casts light on the Native American heritage of the area and the natural resources that are still abundant.

A short **hike** demonstrates what makes this area so special. From the parking lot, follow the trail down toward the ocean. You'll soon come to a fork; to the right is a picnic area. Follow the left fork to another picnic site and then, soon afterward, the beach. Turn left and walk about 0.25 mile to reach Greenwood Creek. Shortly past it is a cliff, at which point you have to turn around and walk back up the hill. Even in the short amount of time it takes to do this walk, you'll experience lush woods, sandy cliffs, and dramatic ocean overlooks.

Queenie's Roadhouse Café (6061 CA-1, 707/877-3285, www.queeniesroad-housecafe.com, 8am-3pm Thurs.-Mon.) is the place to go to fill up on American basics. The food is hot, the atmosphere is friendly, and the location is perfect—in the center of town and across the street from the ocean.

Point Arena Lighthouse

About 20 miles south of Elk is the **Point Arena Lighthouse** (45500 Lighthouse Rd., 707/882-2809 or 877/725-4448, www.pointarenalighthouse.com, 10am-4:30pm daily summer, 10am-3:30pm daily winter, $7.50 adults, $1 children 5-12). Although its magnificent Fresnel lens no longer turns through the night, it remains a Coast Guard light and fog station. But what makes this beacon special is its history. When the 1906 earthquake hit San Francisco, it jolted the land all the way up the coast, severely damaging the Point Arena Lighthouse. When the structure was rebuilt two years later, engineers devised the aboveground foundation that gives the lighthouse both its distinctive shape and additional structural stability.

Docent-led tours up to the top of the lighthouse are well worth the trip, both for the views from the top and for the fascinating story of its destruction and rebirth through the 1906 earthquake as told by the knowledgeable staff.

Gualala

With a population of 585, **Gualala** (pronounced "wa-LA-la") feels like a metropolis along the CA-1 corridor in this region. It's about 15 miles south of Point Arena. While it's not the most charming coastal town, it does have some of the services other places may lack.

If you're hungry when you hit town, try **Trinks Café** (39140 CA-1 S., 707/884-1713, www.trinkscafe.com, 7am-4pm Mon.-Sat., 8am-4pm Sun., 5pm-8pm Wed. and Fri. $12-22).

Surrounded by beautiful gardens, **North Coast Country Inn** (34591 CA-1, 707/884-4537 and 800/959-4537, www.northcoastcountryinn.com, $200-245) provides a country-style experience with rustic decor and fireplaces.

Gualala Point Regional Park (42401 CA-1 S., 707/565-2267, http://parks.sonomacounty.ca.gov, $32 per night winter, $35 per night Memorial Day to Thanksgiving) has great year-round **camping.**

Established around a unique, hand-built, 90-year-old redwood lodge, the resort at ★ **St. Orres** (36601 CA-1 S., 707/884-3303, www.saintorres.com, $95 and up rooms, $140 and up cottages and cabins) covers 50 acres of forest, featuring cabins, cottages, beach access, and spa services in addition to the main hotel and fine-dining restaurant.

Salt Point State Park

About 19 miles south of Gualala, **Salt Point State Park** (25050 CA-1, Jenner, 707/847-3221, www.parks.ca.gov, sunrise-sunset, day use $8 per vehicle) stretches for miles along the Sonoma coastline and provides easy access to more than a dozen sandy state beaches. You don't have to visit the visitors center to enjoy this park and its many beaches—just follow the signs along the highway to the turnoffs and parking lots. To scuba dive or free dive, head for **Gerstle Cove,** accessible from the visitors center just south of Salt Point proper. The cove was designated one of California's first underwater parks, and divers who can deal with the chilly water have a wonderful time exploring the diverse undersea wildlife.

Fort Ross State Historic Park

There is no historical early American figure named Ross who settled here. "Ross" is short for "Russian," and this park commemorates the history of Russian settlement on the north coast. In the 19th century, Russians came to the wilds of Alaska and worked with native Alaskans to develop a robust fur trade, killing seals, otters, sea lions, and land mammals for their pelts. The hunters chased the animals as far as California. Eventually, a group of fur traders came ashore on what is now the Sonoma coast and developed a fortified outpost that became known as **Fort Ross** (19005 CA-1, Jenner, 707/847-3286, www.parks. ca.gov, sunrise-sunset daily, parking $8, camping $35), located 8 miles south of Salt Point State Park. The area gradually became not only a thriving Russian American settlement but also a center for agriculture and shipbuilding and the site of California's first windmills. Learn more at the park's large visitors center, which provides a continuous film and a roomful of exhibits.

You can also take a long, level walk into the reconstructed fort buildings and see how the settlers lived. The only original building still standing is the captain's quarters—a large, luxurious house for that time and place. The other buildings, including the large bunkhouse, the chapel, and the two cannon-filled blockhouses, were rebuilt using much of the original lumber used by the Russians.

Sonoma Coast

Jenner

Twelve winding miles south from Fort Ross State Historic Park, and about 87 miles from Mendocino, **Jenner** (pop. 136) is on CA-1 at the Russian River. It's a beautiful spot for a quiet getaway or a paddle in a kayak. **Goat Rock State Park** (Goat Rock Rd., 707/875-3483, www. parks.ca.gov, day-use $8) is at the mouth of the Russian River. Harbor seals breed and frolic here, and you may also see gray whales, sea otters, elephant seals, and other sea life. Pets are not allowed, and swimming is prohibited.

Both the food and the views are memorable at ★ **River's End** (11048 CA-1, 707/865-2484 ext. 111, www.ilovesunsets.com, 5pm-9pm Thurs.-Tues., noon-3:30pm Sat.-Sun., $25-50). The restaurant is perched above the spot where the Russian River flows into the Pacific, and it's a beautiful sight to behold over, say, oysters or filet mignon. Prices are high, but if you get a window table at sunset, you may forget to think about it.

The cliff-top perch of the **Timber Cove Resort** (21780 CA-1 N., 707/847-3231, www.timbercoveresort.com, $195-325) provides a spectacular view of the rugged Sonoma coast, making it one of the best places to stay.

★ Sonoma Coast State Park

Seventeen miles of coast are within **Sonoma Coast State Park** (707/875-3483, www.parks.ca.gov, day use $8 per vehicle). The park's boundaries extend from Bodega Head at the south up to the Vista Trailhead, four miles north of Jenner. As you drive along CA-1, you'll see signs for various beaches, most of them boasting gorgeous views, like Goat Rock, where an upper parking lot offers a great view of surfers braving the cold waves below. Although they're lovely places to walk, fish, and maybe sunbathe on the odd hot day, it is not advisable to swim here. If you go down to the water, bring your binoculars and your camera. The cliffs, crags, inlets, whitecaps, mini islands, and rock outcroppings are fascinating in any weather, and their looks change with the shifting tides and fog.

◈ CA-116: The Russian River & Bohemian Highway

The Russian River meets the coast at Jenner. Turning inland onto CA-116 allows for a nice riverside drive. About 10 minutes from the coast, **Duncans Mills** offers a small assortment of galleries and restaurants in a picturesque 19th-century

Goat Rock State Park in Jenner

township. Fifteen minutes farther along, there are a few wineries and restaurants in the **Guerneville** area, but most people come here to float, canoe, or kayak the gorgeous river. In addition to its busy summertime tourist trade, Guerneville is also a very popular gay and lesbian resort area. The rainbow flag flies proudly here, and the friendly community welcomes all.

CA-116 passes through the aptly named **Forestville** and eventually ends in **Santa Rosa**, 30-plus miles inland from Jenner, at US-101, which can get travelers to San Francisco much more quickly than the winding but more beautiful CA-1. Or, you may turn right before Guerneville, at the small resort area of **Monte Rio,** where CA-116 connects to the winding Bohemian Highway, which follows Salmon Creek south through the forest, past more wineries and the woodsy burgs of **Occidental** and **Freestone,** before joining CA-1 south of **Bodega Bay.**

Sights

Korbel Cellars (13250 River Rd., Guerneville, 707/824-7000, www.korbel.com, 10am-5pm daily), the leading producer of California sparkling wines, maintains a winery and tasting room on the Russian River, where visitors get to sample far more than the ubiquitous Korbel Brut that appears each New Year's. The facility also has a full-service gourmet deli and picnic grounds for tasters who want to stop for lunch.

Recreation

In summer, the waters of the Russian River are usually warm and dotted with folks swimming, canoeing, or simply floating tubes serenely downriver amid forested riverbanks and under blue skies. **Burke's Canoe Trips** (8600 River Rd., Forestville, 707/887-1222, www.burkescanoetrips.com, Memorial Day-mid-Oct., $68) rents canoes and kayaks on the Russian River. The put-in is at Burke's beach in Forestville; paddlers then canoe downriver 10 miles to Guerneville, where a courtesy shuttle picks them up. Burke's also offers overnight campsites for tents, trailers, and RVs.

On the north bank, **Johnsons Beach & Resort** (16215 1st St., 707/869-2022, www.johnsonsbeach.com, 10am-6pm daily May-Oct.) rents canoes, kayaks, pedal boats, and inner tubes for floating the river. There is a safe kid-friendly section of the riverbank that is roped off for small children; parents and beachcombers can rent beach chairs and umbrellas for use on the small beach.

The fastest way to explore the forest is with **Sonoma Canopy Tours** (6250 Bohemian Hwy., Occidental, 888/494-7868, www.sonomacanopytours.com, tour times vary daily, $99 weekdays, $109 weekends), which sends you on zipline tours zooming through the treetops, including occasional nighttime tours.

Food and Accommodations

Guerneville offers a few nice little inns, like the intimate sanctuary **Applewood Inn** (13555 CA-116, 707/869-9093, www. applewoodinn.com, $225 and up), with fine dining and a spa, or the solar-powered **Sonoma Orchid Inn** (12850 River Rd., 707/869-4466, www.sonomaorchidinn.com, $149 and up), which features a homey fireplace lounge, hot tub, and communal gourmet breakfast.

In Forestville, you'll find luxury in a rustic setting at the **Farmhouse Inn** (7871 River Rd., 707/887-3300, www.farmhouseinn.com, $500 and up), including a Michelin-starred restaurant.

On the Bohemian Highway, local craft beer and elevated pub fare may be enjoyed at the far out **Barley and Hops Tavern** (3688 Bohemian Hwy., Occidental, 707/874-9037, www.barleynhops.com, 4pm-9pm Mon.-Thur., 1pm-9:30am Fri.-Sun., $12-21), while locals line up for coffee and organic scones, biscotti, or loaves at **Wild Flour Bread** (140 Bohemian Hwy, Freestone, 707/874-2938, www.wildflourbread.com, 8am-6:30pm Fri.-Mon., $6-16).

Bodega Bay

Ten miles past Jenner, **Bodega Bay** (pop. 1,027) is popular for its coastal views, whale-watching, and seafood, but it's most famous as the filming locale of Alfred Hitchcock's *The Birds*.

The best sight you could hope to see is a close-up view of Pacific gray whales migrating with their newborn calves. The whales head past January-May on their way from their winter home off Mexico back to their summer home in Alaska. If you're lucky, you can see them from the shore. **Bodega Head,** a promontory just

From top to bottom: totems in Gualala Point Regional Park; the mouth of the Russian River; the Cypress Tunnel in Point Reyes National Seashore.

north of the bay, is a place to get close to the migration route. To get to this prime spot, travel on CA-1 about one mile north of the visitors center and turn west onto Eastshore Road; make a right at the stop sign, and then drive three more miles to the parking lot. On weekends, volunteers from **Stewards of the Coast and Redwoods** (707/869-9177, ext. 1., www.stewardsofthecoastandredwoods.org) are available to answer questions. Contact them for organized whale-watching tours or to learn more about their various educational programs.

Food and Accommodations

Bodega Bay Lodge (103 CA-1, 707/875-3525, www.bodegabaylodge.com, $239 and up) is one of the more luxurious places to stay in the area. It is a large resort with long rows of semidetached cabins. The facility also has a spa, a pool, a fitness center, two fine restaurants, and a library. The lodge's restaurant, **Drakes Sonoma Coast Kitchen** (103 CA-1, 707/875-3525, www.bodegabaylodge.com, 7:30am-11am and 6pm-9pm daily, $22-38) offers elegant coastal dining featuring local wine, cheese, produce, meat, and seafood. There's a fireside lounge overlooking the bay and even some outdoor seating for warmer days.

One of the best restaurants in the area is **Terrapin Creek** (1580 Eastshore Dr., 707/875-2700, www.terrapincreekcafe.com, 4:30pm-9pm Thurs.-Mon., $27-36), where they make creative use of the abundance of fresh seafood available.

Exploring Bodega Head is worthwhile if only to visit ★ **Spud Point Crab Company** (1910 Westshore Rd., 707/875-9472, www.spudpointcrab.com, 9am-5pm daily, $7-15), home of this coast's best clam chowder, plus crab cake, tuna, and smoked fish sandwiches. Order to go from the small counter, and take it to picnic at one of many breathtaking scenic overlooks along the Sonoma Coast.

Under 10 miles southeast of Bodega Bay on CA-1 is the town of **Valley Ford** (pop. 147). One of the few remaining 19th-century buildings houses the **Valley Ford Hotel** (14415 CA-1, 707/876-1983, www.vfordhotel.com, $115 and up) and its quirky roadhouse restaurant **Rocker Oysterfeller's** (www.rockeroysterfellers.com, 5pm-8:30pm Thurs.-Fri., 3pm-8:30pm Sat., 10am-8:30pm Sun., $13-34).

⚑ CA-12: Sonoma and Napa

There's nothing like a drive through the Sonoma and Napa countryside, especially when there are grape-bearing vines that beckon a stop at a winery along the way. This side trip covers 60 miles (90 minutes of driving time), but plan for a full day, especially if you will be wine-tasting. Also plan on a designated driver to remain sober and safe on the road.

From Bodega Bay, take Highway 12 East (CA-12) to London Ranch Road in Sonoma County, where the historic **Benziger Family Winery** (1883 London Ranch Rd., Glen Ellen, 888/490-2739, www.benziger.com, 10am-5pm daily) sits alongside Jack London State Historic Park. The family vineyard was the first in the United States to go completely "green." Climb aboard the Biodynamic Vineyard Tram for a 45-minute tour ($25) to learn about the ecofriendly vineyard, then journey through the fermentation facility and crush pad and explore a hidden cave filled with treasured wine barrels, followed by a tasting of four wines.

Return to CA-12, head east, then hang a left at West Napa Street (watch for Sonoma signs), which turns into Old Winery Road. Just five minutes from Sonoma's famous plaza square, **Buena Vista Winery** (18000 Old Winery Rd., 800/926-1266, www.buenavistawinery.com, 10am-5pm daily) is the oldest commercial wine producer in the state of California and a historic landmark. The Press House is open for tasting

North Bay

year-round and offers a chance to taste new releases, or if you'd rather, you can sample older wines in the library. There is also a Barrel Tour and Tasting (11am-2pm daily).

Backtrack via CA-29 South to CA-12 West/CA-121 South (follow signs for Sonoma) to the oldest family-owned winery, **Gundlach Bundschu** (2000 Denmark St., 707/938-5277, 11am-4:30pm daily Nov.-Apr., 11am-5:30pm daily May-Oct., tours $40-85). Owned and operated by six generations since 1858, Gundlach Bundschu focuses on creating pinot noir, gewürztraminer, and chardonnay ultra-premium wines from its hand-farmed, 320-acre vineyard at the crossroads of the Sonoma Valley. Sample a selection of wines from the tasting room courtyard or enter the wine cave nearby through a tunnel, exiting into a view overlooking the vineyards and gorgeous lake.

Take the first right onto CA-12 West/CA-121 South to **Domaine Carneros** (1240 Duhig Rd., Napa, 707/257-0101, www.domainecarneros.com, 10am-5:30pm daily, $40 tour, $30 tasting pp) to taste award-winning sparkling wines or pinot noirs. Get a behind-the-scenes look at the magic of *méthode champenoise* sparkling winemaking with an intimate tour, or simply relax and enjoy a glass of wine while savoring the sweeping view of the south end of Napa Valley.

Take CA-12 East/CA-121 North to Henry Road in Napa County, winding through fields of wildflowers until you at last reach the entrance to **Artesa Vineyards & Winery** (1345 Henry Rd., Napa, 707/254-2126, www.artesawinery.com, tasting room 10am-5pm daily, $45 tours at 11am and 2pm daily). Continue up the long driveway to the winery, built on the hillside. The facility is much like a modern museum, with lots of hanging art, light-colored walls, and wood floors. Guided tours of the winemaking facility include a sparkling wine greeting and a reserve tasting of five wines at the end of the tour. Although Artesa's collection of wines is vast, they are most known for their estate pinot noir, which received high marks from *Wine Enthusiast*.

Return to the coast via CA-116 or Skillman Lane to CA-1 South in Marin County at Tomales.

Marshall

From Bodega Bay, the Pacific Coast Highway meanders inland, then after 23 miles returns to the coast at the little Tomales Bay community of **Marshall** (pop. 394). A quick stop for tourists heading to the Point Reyes Peninsula, Marshall was built on the dairy industry in the 1850s but has since become a major center for oysters and clams. **The Marshall Store** (19225 CA-1, 415/663-1339, www.themarshallstore.com, 10am-4pm Mon.-Fri., 10am-5pm Sat.-Sun. Oct.-Apr., 10am-5pm Mon.-Fri., 10am-6pm Sat.-Sun. May-Sept., $11-20) prepares them nearly 100 ways, and ★ **Hog Island Oyster Co.** (20215 Shoreline Hwy., 415/663-9218, www.hogislandoysters.com, 9am-5pm daily, $11-16) has built a small restaurant empire on the flavor of its sweetwater oysters, farmed and served here. There's even a boat-shaped bar where you may choose to shuck them yourself.

For an upscale lodging and dining experience on the quiet bay, **Nick's Cove & Cottages** (23240 CA-1, 415/663-1033, www.nickscove.com, 11am-9pm daily, $18-38 restaurant, $350 and up cottages) serves local oysters with high-end steaks and seafood, plus a wide variety of wines and microbrews.

★ Point Reyes National Seashore

About 20 miles from Marshall, the **Point Reyes National Seashore** (1 Bear Valley Rd., 415/464-5100, www.nps.gov/pore, dawn-midnight daily) stretches for miles between Tomales Bay and the Pacific, north from Stinson Beach to the tip of the land at the end of the bay, about 37 miles north of San Francisco. The area boasts acres of unspoiled forest and remote, almost untouched beaches. The protected lands shelter wildlife. In the marshes and lagoons, a wide variety of birds—including three different species of pelicans—make their nests. The pine forests shade shy deer and larger elk. Expect cool weather even in the summer, but enjoy the lustrous green foliage and spectacular scenery that result.

The Point Reyes area includes three tiny towns that provide services for the area: Olema, Point Reyes Station, and Inverness. You'll pass a few inns, restaurants, and shops in each. **Olema** (pop. 245) was once the main settlement in West Marin. Its name stems from the Miwok Indian word for "little coyote." The town grew around an old stagecoach road, leading to a Wild West era of card rooms, rough saloons, and obscene establishments. When the narrow-gauge railroad was laid to the north, it bypassed Olema for **Point Reyes Station** (pop. 848), which flooded with early settlers fired up by the gold rush. A few miles northwest of Port Reyes Station, the sleepy residential outpost of **Inverness** (pop. 1,304) is a destination for people trying to escape the big-city noise via romantic B&Bs and rental cottages amid its tranquil hills and beaches. Innumerable trails showcase glorious scenic and wildlife views.

Getting There and Around

Point Reyes Station is along CA-1, which runs directly through downtown as Main Street. North of Olema, US-101 intersects with CA-1 via Sir Francis Drake Boulevard.

Transportation to Point Reyes from nearby San Rafael is available through route 68 of the **West Marin Stagecoach** (415/226-0855, www.marintransit.org, $2).

stairway to Point Reyes Lighthouse

Sights and Recreation

Located in Point Reyes Station, the **Bear Valley Visitor Center** (1 Bear Valley Rd., 415/464-5100, 10am-5pm Mon.-Fri., 9am-5pm Sat.-Sun.) is a popular starting point for visitors and offers nature trails and interpretive exhibits. It is also the access point to **Earthquake Trail,** which leads to a 16-foot crack in the ground caused by the 1906 shaker that is etched in the minds of San Franciscans. Another path connects to **Kule Loklo,** a reconstruction of a Miwok village.

It's a leisurely 25-minute drive to **Mount Vision** for sweeping views of the national seashore. (Follow Sir Francis Drake Boulevard, then make a left onto Mt. Vision Road.)

Continue on Sir Francis Drake Boulevard and turn on Drakes Beach Road to reach **Kenneth C. Patrick Visitor Center** (1 Drakes Beach Rd., 415/669-1250, 9:30am-4:30pm Sat.-Sun. winter only) and the **Tule Elk Preserve,** where a large herd of elk can often be seen roaming freely in the mist.

Continue to the end of Sir Francis Drake Boulevard to reach **Point Reyes Lighthouse** (27000 Sir Francis Drake Blvd., 415/669-1534, 10am-4:30pm Fri.-Mon.). The jagged rocky shores of Point Reyes make for great scenery but dangerous maritime navigation. The lighthouse was constructed in 1870 and still stands today, accessed by descending a windblown flight of 300 stairs. It's worth the descent (and the uphill climb back). The Fresnel lens and original machinery all remain in place, but the tumultuous ocean views are the highlight. It's also the best place to view seasonal migrations of gray whales, which journey south in January, then back north in late March and early April, often with newborn calves. From the lighthouse, a short hike past **Chimney Rock** reveals resident elephant seals. Migrating birds along the seashore bring **bird-watchers** during fall and spring. Along the road to the lighthouse, you'll pass by the photographer favorite **Cypress Tree Tunnel** (17400 Sir Francis Drake Blvd.), an orderly grove of the beautiful trees standing sentry to the approach of a retired telegraph station.

Food

Start the morning at the divine **Bovine Bakery** (11315 CA-1, 415/663-9420, www.bovinebakeryptreyes.com, 6:30am-5pm Mon.-Fri., 7am-5pm Sat.-Sun., $3-8), with deliciously sweet delights and organic coffee.

Station House Café (11180 CA-1, 415/663-1515, www.stationhousecafe.com, 8am-3:30pm and 5pm-9pm Thurs.-Tues., $16-32) is both casual and upscale. Since 1974, long before "organic" and "local" were foodie credos, the Station House Café has been dedicated to serving food with ingredients that reflect the agrarian culture of the area. It's more comfort food than haute cuisine, and you'll find lots of familiar dishes and fantastic takes on old classics. The oyster stew is not to be missed.

For great deli sandwiches, **Whale of a Deli** (997 Mesa Rd., 415/663-8464, 9:30am-7pm daily, $7-10) offers all kinds of meat and cheese combinations, including Mexican food and pizza. The all-Italian menu at **Osteria Stellina** (11285 CA-1, 415/663-9988, www.osteriastellina.com, 11:30am-2:30pm and 5pm-9pm daily, $16-32) includes classic pasta dishes and pizza. You'll find beer, music, and good, old-fashioned fun at the **Old Western Saloon** (11201 CA-1, 415/663-1661, 10am-2am daily), established in 1906.

An 1876 building houses the **Sir and Star at the Olema** (10000 Sir Francis Drake Blvd., Olema, 415/663-1034, www.sirandstar.com, 5pm-9pm Wed.-Sun., under $22-85), with a memorable prix fixe or à la carte menu and a rustic motif. Sample fresh Tomales Bay oysters and dip into the extensive wine list at the **Farm House Restaurant** (10005 CA-1, 415/663-1264, www.thelodgeatptreyes.com, 11:30am-9pm daily, $14-36), part of the Lodge at Point Reyes.

The **Saltwater Oyster Depot** (12781 Sir Francis Drake Blvd., 415/669-1244, 5pm-9pm Mon. and Thurs.-Fri., noon-9pm Sat.-Sun., $16-28), on the southwest banks of the bay, is a good place to sample the local shellfish and thoughtful cuisine. Sample some local wines or margaritas while you're at it.

Shopping

Vita Collage (11101 CA-1, 415/663-1160, www.vitacollage.com, 11am-5pm Sun. and Wed.-Fri., 11am-6pm Fri., 10:30am-5:30pm Sat.) features fine jewelry, leather purses, and distinctive accessories. For unique gifts of ethnic arts and crafts, **Zuma** (11265 CA-1, 415/663-1748, www.zuma.com, 10am-5pm daily) brings items from around the world to one place. Gifts for the equestrian are at **Cabaline** (11313 CA-1, 415/663-8303, www.cabaline.com, 10am-6pm Mon.-Sat., 10am-5:30pm Sun.), which offers clothing, horse-grooming tools, books, and toys for kids.

For something truly one-of-a-kind, stop by **Shaker Shops West** (5 Inverness Way, 415/669-7256, www.shakershops.com, 10:30am-5pm Fri.-Sat.), creators of fine Shaker furniture and handicrafts.

Accommodations

The best place to stay, ★ **Olema Druids Hall** (9870 Shoreline, 415/663-8727, www.olemadruidshall.com, $295 and up) is a beautifully restored 1885 meeting hall turned luxury inn. The beautiful **Olema Cottages** (9970 Sir Francis Drake Blvd., 415/663-1288, www.olemacottages.com, rooms $170 and up) are surrounded by open space and pasture views. Another option is the 22-room **Lodge at Point Reyes** (10021 CA-1, 800/404-5634, http://www.thelodgeatptreyes.com, rooms $225 and up).

Just off Limantour Road, eight miles from Point Reyes Station and 10 miles from the beach, the **Point Reyes Hostel** (1390 Limantour Spit Rd., 415/663-8811, www.norcalhostels.org/reyes, $29 and up dorms, $105 and up private rooms) is spare but comfortable, with a communal kitchen and three lounge areas. It is steps away from fantastic hiking and lush natural scenery.

Stinson Beach

Twenty-two miles from Olema, the primary attraction at **Stinson Beach** (pop. 632) is the tiny town's namesake: a broad 3.5-mile-long sandy stretch of coastline that's unusually (for Northern California) congenial to visitors. Although it's as plagued by fog as anywhere else in the San Francisco Bay Area, on rare clear days Stinson Beach is the favorite destination for San Franciscans seeking some surf and sunshine.

Recreation

To get out on the water, swing by **Stinson Beach Surf and Kayak** (3605 CA-1, 415/868-2739, www.stinsonbeachsurfandkayak.com, 9:30am-6pm Sat.-Sun.), which will set you up with a surfboard, kayak, boogie board, or stand-up paddleboard. Wetsuits, which you will certainly need, are available. Surf lessons also available, including notes on the etiquette of paddling around wildlife.

Food

A few small restaurants dot the town; most serve seafood. Among the best is the **Sand Dollar Restaurant** (3458 CA-1, 415/868-0434, www.stinsonbeachrestaurant.com, 3pm-9pm Mon.-Fri., 11am-9pm Sat.-Sun., $14-27), formed nearly a century ago by fusing together three barges. It features live jazz and bluegrass.

Accommodations

Sandpiper Lodging (1 Marine Way, 415/868-1632, www.sandpiperstinsonbeach.com, $165 and up) has six guest rooms and four cabins, and you can choose between motel accommodations with comfortable queen beds, private baths, and gas fireplaces or the four individual redwood cabins, which offer additional privacy, bed space for families, and full kitchens.

The **Stinson Beach Motel** (3416 CA-1, 415/868-1712, www.stinsonbeachmotel.com, $110 and up) features eight vintage-y, beach-bungalow-style guest rooms that sleep 2-4 guests each. Some guest rooms have substantial kitchenettes; all have private baths, garden views, TVs, and blue decor. The motel is a great spot to bring the family for a beach vacation.

❦ Panoramic Highway: Mount Tamalpais

To see the whole Bay Area in a single day, take Panoramic Highway east from Stinson Beach a few miles into **Mount**

Tamalpais State Park (801 Panoramic Hwy., Mill Valley, 415/388-2070, www.parks.ca.gov/mttamalpais, 7am-sunset daily, day-use parking $8). Known as Mount Tam, this park boasts stellar views of the San Francisco Bay Area—from Mount St. Helena in Napa down to San Francisco and across to the East Bay. The Pacific Ocean peeks from around the corner of the western peninsula, and on a clear day you can just make out the foothills of the Sierra Nevada mountains to the east. This park is the Bay Area's backyard, with hiking, biking, and camping opportunities widely appreciated for both their beauty and easy access. There are over 100 miles (160 kilometers) of trails. Ample parking, interpretive walks, and friendly park rangers make a visit to Mount Tam a hit even for less outdoorsy travelers.

Although overnight backpacking isn't allowed, standard camping is available at the **Pantoll Ranger Station** (3801 Panoramic Hwy., 415/388-2070, 7am-sunset daily) and the historic 1920s Bootjack Campground. The ranger station can also set you up with maps and other information for your visit.

To reach Pantoll Ranger Station from Stinson Beach, take a right (east) on Panoramic Highway at the T intersection with CA-1 just south of town. The ranger station is about five miles inland on Panoramic Highway.

Muir Beach

Prone to mudslides, CA-1 may be closed south of Stinson Beach. If that's the case, detour on Panoramic Highway as it loops inland and returns to the Coast Highway at **Muir Beach** (pop. 275). It's abundant with wildlife and picturesque scenery from colorful monarch butterflies fluttering through pine trees to fish splashing up rocky Redwood Creek. There are trails along the sandy beach, where boogie boarders and kayakers play in the crashing waves. A short hike on the trail to the left of the entrance leads to the top of a cliff, offering a spectacular view.

Food and Accommodations

A favorite follow-up for summertime beachgoers is grabbing a pint from the tavern at the **Pelican Inn** (10 Pacific Way, 415/383-6000, www.pelicaninn.com, $224 and up) and enjoying it out front on the lawn. In winter, the cozy dining room has a true country pub feel. Each of the seven small guest rooms comes with a private bath and full English-style breakfast, but no TV or phone.

★ Muir Woods

Established in 1908 and named for naturalist and author John Muir, **Muir Woods National Monument** (1 Muir Woods Rd., 415/388-2596, www.nps.gov/muwo, 8am-sunset daily, $10 adults, free children 15 and under) comprises acres of staggeringly beautiful redwood forest nestled in Marin County. More than six miles of trails wind through the redwoods and accompanying Mount Tamalpais area, crossing verdant creeks and the lush forest. These are some of the most stunning and accessible redwoods in the Bay Area.

Begin your exploration at the **Muir Woods Visitor Center** (1 Muir Woods Rd., 9am-5:30pm daily, closing hours vary). In addition to maps, information, and advice about hiking, you'll also find a few amenities.

Muir Woods boasts many lovely trails that crisscross the gorgeous redwood forest. First-time visitors should follow the wheelchair- and stroller-accessible **Main Trail Loop** (one mile). Leading from the visitors center on an easy and flat walk through the beautiful redwoods, this trail has an interpretive brochure (pick one up at the visitors center) with numbers along the trail that describe the flora

and fauna. Hikers can continue the loop on the **Hillside Trail** (2-mile loop) for an elevated view of the valley.

Getting There

Muir Woods is about 10 miles from Stinson Beach. Muir Woods Road comes off CA-1 about 6.5 miles south of Stinson Beach. Take Muir Woods Road for about 2.5 miles to reach the park entrance. To get back to CA-1, you don't need to go back the way you came. From the Muir Woods parking lot, turn left (east) onto Muir Woods Road, and in about 1.5 miles, it will hit Panoramic Highway, where you'll take a right. In about a mile, there will be a left turn to get back onto CA-1, which merges into US-101 through the rest of Marin County and over the Golden Gate Bridge.

Get to the Muir Woods parking areas early. They fill fast, especially on holidays and weekends. To avoid the traffic hassle, ride the **Muir Woods Shuttle** (415/455-2000, www.marintransit.org, May-Oct., $5 adult, free children 15 and under), which leaves from various points in southern Marin County, including the Sausalito ferry terminal.

Marin Headlands

The **Marin Headlands** lie north of San Francisco at the north end of the Golden Gate Bridge. The land here encompasses a wide swath of virgin wilderness, former military structures, and a historic lighthouse.

Going south, to access the Marin Headlands, take the Sausalito exit, which is the last exit before the Golden Gate Bridge. If you do nothing else in the headlands, visit the vista point on Conzelman Road. From the exit, make a left onto Alexander Avenue and then turn right (going uphill) on Conzelman Road. You'll see a few parking spaces on the left, usually filled up with multiple cars waiting; grab a spot if you can, and make the walk out to arguably the best view of the Golden Gate Bridge.

Start your exploration of the Marin Headlands at the **visitors center** (948, Fort Barry, Sausalito, 415/331-1540, www. nps.gov/goga, 9:30am-4:30pm daily), located in the old chapel at Fort Barry. It contains historical and natural history displays, a small gift shop, and details on hiking and biking routes.

Golden Gate Bridge National Recreation Area

A patchwork area that stretches from northern San Mateo County to southern Marin County, the **Golden Gate National Recreation Area** encompasses San Francisco Bay, welcoming more than 13 million visitors a year. The park offers visitors a monumental collection of attractions, such as the infamous Alcatraz and the Presidio of San Francisco. It is also home to 1,273 plant and animal species, and has a half dozen operational and shuttered military fortifications that go back through the centuries of California's history, from the Spanish conquistadors to the California Gold Rush to the still active Cold War-era Nike missile sites. There are miles of trails, as well as the 1855 Point Bonita Lighthouse.

★ Golden Gate Bridge

This icon of California is 1.7 miles across and joins southern Marin County to the city of San Francisco. Named after the gap in land that allows entry to San Francisco Bay from the Pacific, the **Golden Gate Bridge** is painted in magnificent "international orange." CA-1 blends with US-101 until you cross the bridge, and then splits off at the CA-1/19th Avenue exit. This route takes you through the Presidio of San Francisco and Golden Gate Park, but it's actually mostly a corridor through a few of the city's outer neighborhoods. To get to the heart of San Francisco, stay on US-101 as

it follows Lombard Street and then Van Ness Avenue.

Note that the best places to view the Golden Gate Bridge are from the Marin Headlands and Baker Beach.

San Francisco

The beautiful city by its eponymous bay, **San Francisco** (pop. 864,816) is famous for its ethnic diversity, liberal politics, and chilling, dense fog. Urban explorers can enjoy San Francisco's great art, world-class music, unique theater and comedy, and a laid-back club scene, not to mention the food. Many come to the city solely for its vibrant and innovative restaurant scene. Despite its reputation as being on the cutting edge of technology, San Francisco is not a city without history: Some of its most famous sights—Fisherman's Wharf, Alcatraz, Coit Tower—are reminders of its storied past.

Getting There and Around
Air
It's easy to fly into the San Francisco region. There are three major airports. Among them, you should be able to find a flight that fits your schedule. **San Francisco International Airport (SFO)** (www.flysfo.com) is 13 miles south of the city proper. **Oakland Airport (OAK)** (www.flyoakland.com) is 11 miles east of the city but requires crossing the bay, via either the Bay Bridge or public transit. **Mineta San José Airport (SJC)** (www.flysanjose.com) is the farthest away, roughly 47 miles to the south. These last two airports are less than an hour away by car, with car rentals available. Some San Francisco hotels offer complimentary airport shuttles as well.

Public Transit
For getting around in dense and crowded downtown San Francisco, it's best to use public transportation. **BART** (www.bart.gov), or Bay Area Rapid Transit,

connects San Francisco to other cities in the Bay Area, as well as to San Francisco International Airport. There are only eight BART stops within San Francisco proper, and aside from going to or from the airport ($9 to/from downtown), BART is most convenient for getting to the Mission District from downtown.

Within the city, **San Francisco Municipal Railway** (Muni, 415/701-2311 or 311 within San Francisco, www.sfmta.com or www.511.org, 6am-midnight daily with limited overnight service) runs a system of buses, light-rail, three cable cars, and one historic streetcar. Muni can get you almost anywhere in San Francisco, but for destinations beyond downtown, it's debatable whether it's better to take a lumbering Muni vehicle or drive and deal with the hassle of parking. Fares are $2.75 to ride anything except the cable cars for 90 minutes. Cable cars are $7 per ride. Unlimited ride Visitor Passports (one day $21, three days $32, seven days $42) are available and are valid on all Muni vehicles, including cable cars, but they are not valid on BART.

Cable cars may be one of San Francisco's most recognizable icons, but they are not necessarily a great way to get around. While they are no slower than a bus, waiting to get on a cable car, especially on weekends, can take longer than the ride itself. Powell-Mason cable cars get you to Fisherman's Wharf in 30 minutes (not counting the wait); Powell-Hyde cable cars provide the scenic route; and the California line is the most historic and runs east to west, going over Nob Hill.

Ride-share services such as **Uber** (www.uber.com) and **Lyft** (www.lyft.com) have become common throughout the city, summoning cars for hire via smartphone app.

Sights
Union Square

Bordered by Geary, Powell, Post, and Stockton Streets, **Union Square** was

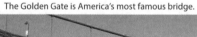

The Golden Gate is America's most famous bridge.

named after the pro-Union rallies that took place there during the Civil War. Today, it is the city's premier shopping district, with one of the largest collections of retail stores, department stores, art galleries, and bars in the western United States. At the center of Union Square stands a statue of Victoria, goddess of victory, a monument that commemorates Admiral George Dewey's 1898 victory at Manila Bay during the Spanish American War. Views of the square are best from Harry Denton's Starlight Room in the Sir Francis Drake Hotel.

Chinatown

A neighbor to North Beach, **Chinatown** is centered on Grant Avenue and Stockton Street. Established in 1848, it's the oldest Chinese district in the United States. The Chinese immigrants of that era were essential in building the Transcontinental Railroad. Chinatown remains an influential part of ethnic Chinese immigrant culture today.

The district is marked by the **Dragon Gate,** the only authentic Chinatown Gate in North America, located on Grant Avenue at Bush Street. More tourists pass under its green-tiled roof than pass over the Golden Gate Bridge. Once here, visitors become immersed in the many shops, temples, and dragon parades and celebrations.

North Beach

North Beach is San Francisco's Little Italy, dense with old-world cafés, restaurants, and delicatessens, but it was once an actual beach, filled in with landfill for warehouses, fishing wharves, and docks. In the late 1800s, thousands of Italians made the area their home. They are credited with saving the neighborhood during the 1906 fire by draping houses with blankets soaked in wine from the barrels in their cellars.

North Beach is also the birthplace of the Beat Generation. Many of the most famous Beat writers lived here, including Jack Kerouac, Allen Ginsberg, Gregory Corso, Neal Cassady, and poet Lawrence Ferlinghetti, who founded City Lights Bookstore, now a historic landmark. The **Beat Museum** (540 Broadway St., 415/399-9626, www.kerouac.com, 10am-7pm daily) features a collection of their works, including books and original manuscripts.

Fisherman's Wharf

Fisherman's Wharf encompasses the northern waterfront area from Ghirardelli Square or Van Ness Avenue east to Pier 35 (Kearny Street). It is one of the city's busiest tourist attractions, likely attributed to its location on Pier 39, fresh seafood from the floating Forbes Island restaurant, and, of course, being the launching point of ferries headed to Alcatraz.

★ Alcatraz

Nicknamed "The Rock," **Alcatraz** (415/981-7625, www.alcatrazcruises.

San Francisco

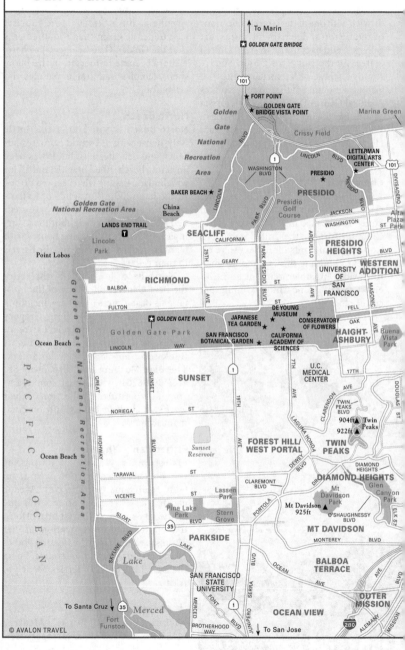

© AVALON TRAVEL

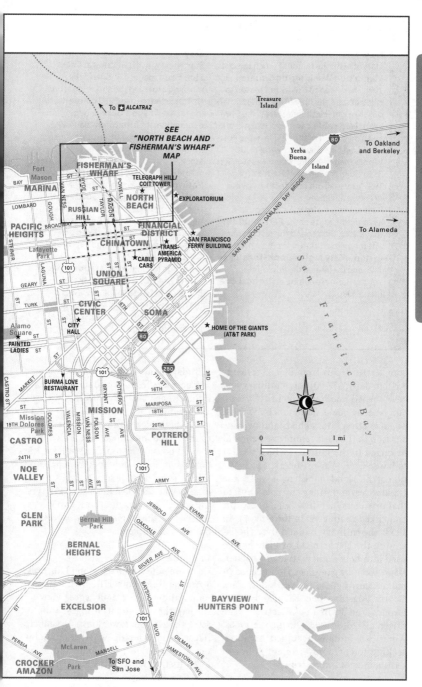

To ★ ALCATRAZ

Treasure
Island

*SEE
"NORTH BEACH AND
FISHERMAN'S WHARF"
MAP*

To Oakland
and Berkeley

FISHERMAN'S
WHARF

Fort
Mason

MARINA

TELEGRAPH HILL/
COIT TOWER

Yerba
Buena
Island

★EXPLORATORIUM

NORTH
BEACH

To Alameda

LOMBARD

RUSSIAN
HILL

PACIFIC
HEIGHTS

BROADWAY

FINANCIAL
DISTRICT

Lafayette
Park

CHINATOWN

TRANS-
AMERICA
PYRAMID

★SAN FRANCISCO
FERRY BUILDING

★CABLE
CARS

UNION
SQUARE

S a n

GEARY

TURK

CIVIC
CENTER

F r a n c i s c o

SOMA

Alamo
Square

CITY
HALL

★ HOME OF THE GIANTS
(AT&T PARK)

PAINTED
LADIES

B a y

BURMA LOVE
RESTAURANT

MISSION

MARIPOSA

Mission
19TH Dolores
Park

POTRERO
HILL

CASTRO

0   1 mi

NOE
VALLEY

0   1 km

GLEN
PARK

Bernal Hill
Park

BERNAL
HEIGHTS

SILVER AVE

BAYVIEW/
HUNTERS POINT

EXCELSIOR

GILMAN AVE

CROCKER
AMAZON

McLaren
Park

To SFO and
San Jose

JAMESTOWN AVE

Two Days in San Francisco

Day 1

Start off with the famous French toast at **Mama's on Washington Square** (page 207). Then head to Union and Mason to climb aboard the only historical landmark on wheels in the United States: The **San Francisco cable car** (page 198) will offer you a quick tour of the city. Take the Powell-Mason Line down to **Fisherman's Wharf** (page 199). Continue west to Pier 33 to catch the ferry to **Alcatraz** (page 199). Tours sell out fast, so reserve your tickets in advance.

If your escape from Alcatraz built up an appetite, graze at the **Ferry Building** (page 203), then spend the rest of your afternoon exploring North Beach. Be sure to stop at **City Lights Bookstore** (page 212), and for dinner, dig into photoworthy Burmese cuisine at **Burma Love** (page 208).

Day 2

Start the day with pancakes at **Sears Fine Food** (page 206). Spend the morning browsing the shopping around **Union Square** (page 211) before heading for the **Dragon Gate** to begin your exploration of **Chinatown** (page 199). Once you've worked up an appetite, stop in **House of Nanking** (page 206) for lunch.

After lunch, head to **Golden Gate Park** (page 203). There are 1,017 acres to explore, including gardens, museums, lakes, picnic areas, and trails. Choose between the **California Academy of Sciences** (page 203), the **de Young Museum** (page 205), or the **Japanese Tea Garden** (page 203).

Splurge for dinner at **Farallon** (page 206) or keep it cheap with a Mission Burrito at **El Farolito** (page 208). End the night with cocktails at a historic saloon or dancing to the latest beats at **Mezzanine** (page 210).

com, ferries depart from Pier 33 8:45am-6:30pm daily, $37-90) was a military fortress turned maximum-security prison, and is today one of San Francisco's most popular attractions. The island became a prison in the 19th century while it still belonged to the military, which used it to house Civil War prisoners. The isolation of the island in the bay, as well as the frigid waters and strong currents, ensured that prisoners had little hope of escape, and risked death even in the attempt. In 1934, the military handed over the island to the Department of Justice, who used it to house a new style of prisoner: Depression-era gangsters. Honored maximum-security guests included Al Capone, George "Machine Gun" Kelly, and Robert Stroud ("the Birdman of Alcatraz"). The prison closed in 1963. During the 1960s, American Indians occupied Alcatraz, seeking to end a government policy of termination of Indian tribes.

Today, many of the buildings are gone. The barracks from its prior existence as a military base, the cell house, lighthouse, and a handful of other buildings remain.

A visit to Alcatraz involves a ferry ride to the island and an audio tour around the cell house. The tour lasts at least 2.5 hours, but tickets only specify departure times from Pier 33, so you can stay as long as you like until the last boat leaves the island. Buy tickets at least two weeks in advance; they often sell out, especially on summer weekends.

Coit Tower

Crowning the top of Telegraph Hill, **Coit Tower** (1 Telegraph Hill Blvd., 10am-5pm daily) offers a 360-degree view of the bay, the city, and its bridges. Built in 1933, the 210-foot tower looks very much like a fire hose nozzle (whether or not by design is a subject of debate and local lore). Its interior features New Deal-era fresco murals. It's surrounded by 4.89-acre **Pioneer Park.**

Embarcadero

The skyscrapers of the Financial District create most of the San Francisco skyline, which extends out to the waterfront, locally called the **Embarcadero.** Hotels tend toward expensive tall towers, and the shopping here caters to folks with plenty of green. There's also a wealth of restaurants and bars, and foodie heaven at the Ferry Building.

Ferry Building

The restored 1898 **San Francisco Ferry Building** (1 Ferry Bldg., 415/983-8030, www.ferrybuildingmarketplace.com, 10am-7pm Mon.-Fri., 8am-6pm Sat., 11am-5pm Sun.) stands at the end of the Financial District at the edge of the water. Inside the handsome structure, it's all about the food, from fresh produce to high-end wine to cheese and gourmet eateries. Sample from local favorites like Cowgirl Creamery, Acme Bread Company, and Blue Bottle Coffee. For immediate gratification, a few incongruous quick-and-easy restaurants offer reasonable eats.

You can also actually catch a ferry here. Boats come in from Larkspur, Sausalito, Tiburon, Vallejo, and Alameda each day. Check with the **Blue and Gold Fleet** (www.blueandgoldfleet.com), **Golden Gate Ferry** (www.goldengateferry.org), and **Bay Link Ferries** (www.baylinkferry.com) for information about service, times, and fares.

Exploratorium

The innovative **Exploratorium** (Pier 15, 415/528-4444, www.exploratorium.edu, 10am-5pm Sat.-Thurs., 6pm-10pm for 18 years and older Thurs., 10am-9pm Fri., $30 adults, $25 children 13-17, $20 children 4-12) makes science the most fun thing ever for kids; adults are welcome to join in, too. Learn about everything from frogs to the physics of baseball, sound, and seismology.

★ Golden Gate Park

Golden Gate Park (main entrance at Stanyan St. at Fell St., McLaren Lodge visitors center at John F. Kennedy Dr., 415/831-2700, www.golden-gate-park.com) was built on sand dunes in the late 1800s.

Today, in addition to walking and bike trails, the park encompasses gardens, cultural arts, and scientific museums. The **Japanese Tea Garden** is a place of solace to sit and sip tea while gazing at the remarkable 100-year-old trees and five acres of picturesque scenery. The **Conservatory of Flowers** offers a stroll through a Victorian greenhouse filled with vibrant flowers from all over the world, while the **San Francisco Botanical Garden at Strybing Arboretum** displays native blooms and plant life.

California Academy of Sciences

The **California Academy of Sciences** (55 Music Concourse Dr., 415/379-8000, www.calacademy.org, 9:30am-5pm Mon.-Sat., 11am-5pm Sun., $36 adults, $31 children 12-17, $26 children 4-11) is a triumph of the sustainable scientific principles it exhibits. From its grass-covered roof to its underground aquarium, the award-winning design by architect Renzo Piano exemplifies environmental ideals. Visitors can wander through the steamy Rainforests of the World exhibit, contained inside a 90-foot glass dome, or travel through an all-digital outer space in the high-tech Morrison Planetarium. More studious nature lovers can spend hours examining exhibits like the 87-foot-long blue whale skeleton. The Steinhart Aquarium includes a display of coral reef, tidepool, and swamp habitats, as well as a well-loved colony of African penguins. Kid-friendly, often interactive exhibits offer endless opportunities for learning.

North Beach and Fisherman's Wharf

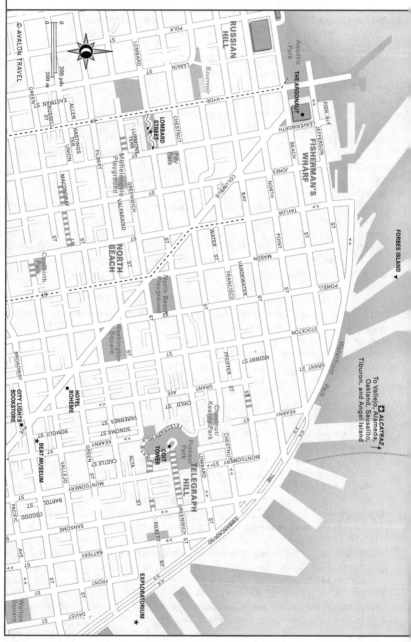

© AVALON TRAVEL

RUSSIAN HILL

THE ARGONAUT

FISHERMAN'S WHARF

FORBES ISLAND ▼

★ ALCATRAZ
To Vallejo, Alameda,
Oakland, Sausalito,
Tiburon, and Angel Island

NORTH BEACH

Washington Square

Michelangelo Playground

North Beach Playground

Fay Park

Coolbrith Park

Pioneer Park

TELEGRAPH HILL

COIT TOWER

Chestnut/Kearny Park

HOTEL BOHÈME

BEAT MUSEUM

CITY LIGHTS BOOKSTORE

EXPLORATORIUM ★

Walton Square

de Young Museum

In Golden Gate Park, follow the artificial fault-line in the sidewalk to the **de Young Museum** (50 Hagiwara Tea Garden Dr., 415/750-3600, http://deyoung.famsf.org, 9:30am-5:15pm Tues.-Sun., $15 adults, free children 17 and under), which showcases American art dating to the 17th century, international contemporary art, and art from the Americas, the Pacific, and Africa. The museum stays open until 8:30pm on Fridays April-August.

The Presidio

The Presidio (Montgomery St. and Lincoln Blvd., 415/561-4323, www.nps.gov/prsf, visitors center 10am-5pm daily, trails dawn-dusk daily, free) is a sweeping stretch of land running along the San Francisco Headlands down to the Golden Gate. Established as a military installation by the Spanish in 1776, it was taken over by the U.S. Army in 1848 and became a national park in 1994. The Presidio had a role in every Pacific-related war from the Civil War through Desert Storm.

As you explore the huge park, you can visit the pioneering aviation area **Crissy Field,** Civil War-era fortifications at **Fort Point,** and the **Letterman Digital Arts Center** (Chestnut St. and Lyon St., www.lucasfilm.com), built on the site of a former army hospital. More recent additions include art installations by Andy Goldsworthy, who works with natural materials.

Alamo Square

Just a few blocks northeast of Golden Gate Park, **Alamo Square Park** (Hayes St. and Steiner St., 415/218-0259, www.sfrecpark.org, 5am-midnight daily) features walking paths, playgrounds, and an off-leash dog park. But it's best known for a hilltop view of the **Painted Ladies,** a famous block of Victorian row houses painted in a rainbow of distinctive colors and backed by an idyllic view of San Francisco's skyline. This view was featured in the opening credits of popular 90s TV show *Full House.*

The Castro

The Castro (Castro St. between Market St. and 19th St.) has stood as an international beacon of gay rights and community since the 1960s. Comprising proudly gay-owned shops, bars, and restaurants amid elegant Victorian structures, the neighborhood's street life is infused with plenty of colorful, playful, and diverse character, championing tolerance and often embracing its flamboyant reputation with a party or three.

Recreation

Beaches

Ocean Beach is found where Golden Gate Park ends. The cold water and strong currents make it dangerous for swimming but popular among surfers who find the big waves worth the risk. Most visitors enjoy the beautiful seascape from the sand. It's a great place for a picnic or a bonfire. From time to time, debris from the 1800s shipwreck the *King Philip* reappears at low tide.

Below the cliffs on the Presidio's western shoreline, **Baker Beach** stretches a mile, offering magnificent views of Golden Gate Bridge and the Marin Headlands. **China Beach** is a tiny cove that got its name from the Chinese fishermen who anchored their small vessels nearby to camp on the beach. It lies between Baker Beach and Lands End and is part of the Golden Gate National Recreation Area. It offers a picnic area, sunbathing, and spectacular views of the Golden Gate. On the northwestern end of the city, the **Lands End** trail reveals hillsides of cypress and wildflowers, and the beautiful shoreline. It provides access to the old Sutro Baths, other beaches, and an observation site at the **visitors center** (680 Point Lobos Ave., 415/426-5240, www.nps.gov/goga, 9am-5pm daily, donation).

The closest views of the Golden Gate Bridge in the city are from **Fort Point** (end of Marine Dr., 415/556-1693, www. nps.gov/fopo, 10am-5pm Fri.-Sun., free), a National Historic Site at the bridge's southern end. Although the Civil War-era brick fort never saw action, there are tours and on-site reenactments.

Bicycling

Get around on a bike to see the parks, especially Golden Gate Park, which offers about a two-mile ride. On Sundays you can pedal around without traffic interruption when the city closes off the eastern half of JFK Drive in Golden Gate Park. **Golden Gate Park Bike and Skate** (3038 Fulton St., 415/668-1117, www.goldengateparkbikeandskate.com, 10am-6pm Mon.-Fri., 10am-7pm Sat.-Sun. summer, 10am-5pm Mon.-Fri., 10am-6pm Sat.-Sun. winter, $5/hour, $20/day skates, $5/hour, $25/day bikes) rents, not surprisingly, bikes and skates.

Bike the 22-mile **Tiburon Loop,** which starts in San Rafael and goes through the Cal Park Hill Tunnel (no cars). The route offers glimpses of wildlife and gorgeous views of Richardson Bay and Angel Island. **Avenue Cyclery** (756 Stanyan St., 415/387-3155, www.avenuecyclery.com, 10am-6pm daily, $30/day) rents bikes just outside Golden Gate Park.

Spectator Sports

Local baseball fans love their **San Francisco Giants,** who play Major League home games during the summer at **AT&T Park** (24 Willie Mays Plaza at 3rd St. and King St., 415/972-2000 and 877/473-4849, www.sanfrancisco.giants.mlb.com). Home games at AT&T Park swell restaurants, buses, and trains in the area to beyond capacity. Meanwhile, the NFL's **San Francisco 49ers** play through the fall at **Levi's Stadium** (4900 Marie P DeBartolo Way, Santa Clara, 415/464-9377, www.49ers.com). Recent NBA champions the **Golden State Warriors** will make their home in the **Chase Center** (3rd St. and South St.) beginning in the fall of 2019.

Food
Union Square

Make reservations in advance if you want to dine at the legendary **Farallon** (450 Post St., 415/956-6969, www.farallonrestaurant.com, 4:30pm-9:30pm Mon.-Thurs., 4:30pm-10pm Fri.-Sat., 4:30pm-9pm Sun., $32-50). Seafood dominates the pricey menu, and the under-the-sea theme carries over into the decor—complete with jellyfish chandeliers.

Opened by Denmark's famous gypsy brewer, Mikkeller Bar (34 Mason St., 415/984-0279, www.mikkellerbar.com, noon-midnight Sun.-Wed., noon-2am Thurs.-Sat., $12-17) offers sausage and other pub fare perfect for complementing its world-class craft beer tap list.

Sears Fine Food (439 Powell St., 415/986-0700, www.searsfinefood.com, 6:30am-10pm daily, $12-30) is a good option for breakfast, with their famous dollar-sized pancakes. With many locations throughout the city, **Blue Bottle Coffee** (115 Sansome St., 510/653-3394, www.bluebottlecoffee.com, 6:30am-7pm Mon.-Fri., 7:30am-3:30pm Sat.-Sun.) is the best known among San Francisco's many artisan coffee roasters.

Chinatown

You'll find restaurants covering many Chinese culinary traditions throughout Chinatown, so when choosing, go with the style of food, and maybe spice level, you hope to experience.

The playfully brusque service of **House of Nanking** (919 Kearny St., 415/421-1429, www.houseofnanking.net, 11am-9pm Mon.-Fri., noon-9pm Sat.-Sun., $9-14) makes it a tourist favorite, along with dishes that epitomize America's palate for Chinese food. If you seek the numbing pepper and hot spice of Szechuan cuisine, the classic is **Z&Y Restaurant** (655 Jackson St., 415/981-8988, www.zandyrestaurant.com, 11am-9:30pm Sun.-Thurs., 11am-10:30pm Fri.-Sat., $11-30). For dim sum, try the nation's oldest dim sum restaurant,

1920 **Hang Ah Tea Room** (1 Pagoda Pl., 415/982-5686, www.hangah1920.com, 10:30am-9pm daily, $3-9 small dishes).

The dry fried chicken wings are famous at clamorous **San Tung** (1031 Irving St., 415/242-0828, 11am-3pm and 5pm-9:30pm Thurs.-Tues., $7-16), while noodle dishes and rice porridge reign supreme at storied late-night spot **Sam Wo** (713 Clay St., 415/989-8898, www.samworestaurant.com, 6pm-midnight Wed.-Thurs., 6pm-3am Fri.-Sat., 11am-4pm Wed.-Mon., $8-12). The restaurant, which opened in 1907 following the earthquake, is no longer at its original location, once frequented by Beat poets, but community activists pushed to ensure the neighborhood didn't lose one of its oldest restaurants.

Any time of day, cap a meal by indulging in custard-filled confections or sugary lotus seed paste moon cakes at **Golden Gate Bakery** (1029 Grant Ave., 415/781-2627, 8am-8pm daily, $10).

North Beach

For a hearty breakfast, head to North Beach and look for the big green awning with little pink hearts at **Mama's on Washington Square** (1701 Stockton St., 415/362-6421, www.mamas-sf.com, 11am-3pm Tues.-Sun., $8-13.50), which serves 10 types of French toast, to-die-for eggs Benedict, and the best Monte Cristo.

No North Beach visit is complete without an authentic Italian meal, and the food at **Trattoria Contadina** (1800 Mason St., 415/982-5728, www.trattoria-contadina.com, 5pm-9pm Mon.-Thurs., 5pm-9:30pm Fri., 4pm-9:30pm Sat.-Sun., $19-37) attracts crowds. So does **Original Joe's** (601 Union St., 415/775-4877, www.originaljoessf.com, 11:30am-10pm Mon.-Fri., 10am-10pm Sat.-Sun., $17-50), and its meatballs, prime rib, and

From top to bottom: the island prison of Alcatraz; riding a cable car; the entrance to Chinatown.

other decadent dishes have been attracting them since 1937.

Fisherman's Wharf and Marina

Landmark fish counter **Swan Oyster Depot** (1517 Polk St., 415/673-1101, 10:30am-5:30pm Mon.-Sat., $11-50) serves the city's freshest shellfish, from its raw bar, in cocktail form, smoked, steamed, or stewed. The city's famous sourdough specialist, **Boudin Bakery** (160 Jefferson St., 415/928-1849, www.boudinbakery.com, 8am-10pm Sun.-Thurs., 8am-10:30pm Fri.-Sat.), offers a massive, tourist-friendly bakery counter restaurant (serving grilled cheese and other sandwiches) at Fisherman's Wharf, where it keeps its mother dough, which has been the bread's starter since 1849.

Mission District

San Francisco's Mission District doesn't feature many attractions, but it does offer great food destinations, especially its street-style Mexican food.

Longtime local favorite **La Taqueria** (2889 Mission St., 415/285-7117, 11am-9pm Tues.-Sat., 11am-8pm Sun., $4-11) has become a chef's favorite for flavorful tacos and burritos both, while nearby **El Farolito** (2779 Mission St., 415/824-7877, 10am-3am Mon.-Wed. and Sat., 10am-3:30am Thurs.-Fri., 10am-midnight Sun., $7-15) best represents the neighborhood's namesake burrito style, the Mission Burrito, notable for its giant, steamed flour tortilla flexible enough to contain everything—meat, cheese, sour cream, avocado, salsa, beans, and rice—wrapped in foil.

Combining influences of Chinese, Indian, and Thai cuisine, Burmese food is a rare find in the United States, but in San Francisco it's become one of the city's most cherished tastes. ★ **Burma Love** (211 Valencia St., 415/861-2100, www.burmalovesf.com, 11:30am-3pm daily, 5pm-10pm Sun.-Thurs., 5pm-10:30pm Fri.-Sat., $11-28) represents the local **Burma Superstar** family of restaurants.

the Painted Ladies as seen from Alamo Square Park

Absolutely start with its signature dish, a fermented green-tea-leaf salad, but expect dazzling flavors and beautiful presentation from every menu item.

Alamo Square

How did San Francisco turn toast into a foodie trend? Find out at hipster bakery ★ **The Mill** (736 Divisadero St., 415/345-1953, www.themillsf.com, 7am-9pm daily, $5-10), which tops thick slices of toasted bread with seasonal ingredients, served alongside delicious, locally roasted coffee from Four Barrel Coffee.

Nightlife

San Francisco nightlife covers every taste. Several historical waterholes, from pre-Prohibition to the Beatnik era, still welcome locals and tourists, while dance and live music venues fuel plenty of late nights.

Bars and Clubs

Dating back to 1851, the **Old Ship Saloon**

(298 Pacific Ave., 415/788-2222, www.oldshipsaloon.com, 11am-2am Mon.-Fri., 3pm-2am Sat.-Sun.) is made out of a ship's hull that ran aground during a storm off Alcatraz. In the Mission, an old polished mahogany bar recalls the days of the Wild West at **Elixir** (3200 16th St., 415/552-1633, www.elixirsf.com, 3pm-2am Mon.-Fri., noon-2am Sat.-Sun.), the city's second-oldest saloon, dating back to 1858.

A few other historical venues to grab a drink at include **The Saloon** (1232 Grant St., 415/989-7666, noon-1:30am daily), which dates to 1861, while the nearby Comstock **Stop Saloon** (155 Columbus Ave., 415/617-0071, www.comstocksaloon.com, 4pm-midnight Sun.-Mon., 4pm-2am Tues.-Thurs. and Sat., noon-2am Fri.) turns a saloon that opened in 1907 into a gorgeous venue for craft cocktails. At **Shotwell's** (3349 20th St., 415/648-4104, www.shotwellsbar.com, 4:30pm-2am Mon.-Sat., 4:30pm-1am Sun.), which first opened in 1891 as a grocery store saloon with a back room for beer drinking, you can drink local microbrews and play pinball.

Most of America's top craft brewers point to **Anchor Brewing** (1705 Mariposa St., 415/863-8350, www.anchorbrewing.com, 9:30am-7pm Mon.-Fri., 10:30am-7pm Sat.-Sun., tours by reservation) as a major influence—it's been making excellent beer since 1896.

For quiet conversation, **Hotel Biron** (45 Rose St., 415/703-0403, www.hotelbiron.com, 5pm-2am daily) is the perfect date spot, and features rotating artwork and an immense wine list. A couple other great wine bars are **Café Nook** (1500 Hyde St., 415/447-4100, www.cafenook.com, 7am-9pm Mon.-Fri., 8am-9pm Sat.-Sun.), a charming little café by day and cozy wine bar by night, and the **Hidden Vine** (408 Merchant St., 415/674-3567, www.thehiddenvine.com, 4pm-10pm Mon., 4pm-midnight Tues.-Sat.), a unique place with redbrick walls and an outdoor bocce ball court.

Ruby Skye (420 Mason St., 415/693-0777, www.rubyskye.com, 9pm-2am Thurs., 9pm-4am Fri.-Sat.) stands out as the city's most popular dance club, with Victorian style, a swanky lounge graced by celebrities, and a killer sound system appreciated by top DJs.

San Francisco boasts a world-famous underground house music scene, with parties all over town almost nightly. Two best bets for exploring local sound may be found near the Mission District at **Mezzanine** (444 Jessie St., 415/625-8880, www.mezzaninesf.com) and the multi-level **Public Works** (161 Erie St., 415/496-6738, www.publicsf.com). Keep an eye on their respective calendars for events.

The local gay bar and club scene is just as world famous, with favorite destinations being wine- and cocktail-savvy **Blackbird** (2124 Market St., 415/503-0630, www.blackbirdbar.com, 3pm-2am Mon.-Fri., 2pm-2am Sat.-Sun.) and popular pick-up joint **Powerhouse** (1347 Folsom St., 415/552-8689, www.powerhousebar.com, 4pm-2am daily).

Live Music

Though the Beat Generation of Jack Kerouac and Allen Ginsberg has faded, **Vesuvio Café** (255 Columbus Ave., 415/362-3370, www.vesuvio.com, 6pm-2am daily) continues to pay tribute to its jazz, art, and poetry roots, while **Caffe Trieste** (601 Vallejo St., 415/392-6739, www.caffetrieste.com, 6:30am-10pm Sun.-Thurs., 6:30am-11pm Fri.-Sat.) hosts poets, composers, and artists over some of the finest coffee in San Francisco.

For more than 100 years, the **Hotel Utah Saloon** (500 4th St., 415/546-6300, www.hotelutah.com, 11am-2am daily) has attracted all kinds of people, from gamblers and gold seekers to politicians and celebrities. Today, it plays host to indie rock bands, singer-songwriters, and the longest-running open mics in town.

Rita Hayworth got her start at **Bimbo's 365 Club** (1025 Columbus Ave., 415/474-0365, www.bimbos365club.com), a supper club and speakeasy that opened in 1931. Today, everyone from up-and-coming indies to big headliners takes the stage.

The counterculture of 1960s San Francisco elevated two local music venues to legendary status. **The Fillmore** (1805 Geary St., 415/346-6000, www.thefillmore.com) hosted classic acts like Jimi Hendrix, Pink Floyd, and the Velvet Underground, and continues to draw top performers. It also played host many times to local icons The Grateful Dead, who also maintained a residence at the more intimate **The Warfield** (982 Market St., 415/345-0900, www.thewarfieldtheatre.com). They also played at what may be the city's most elegant venue, the ornate, 1907 **Great American Music Hall** (859 O'Farrell St., 415/885-0750, www.slimspresents.com).

Arts and Entertainment

San Francisco virtually oozes with culture, claiming great playwrights Sam Shepard and Tom Stoppard, and boasting avant-garde theater and internationally recognized symphony, opera, and ballet companies, not to mention the finest of classical and contemporary art galleries and museums.

Performing Arts

With a long and distinguished history, the prestigious **American Conservatory Theatre** is housed in the **Geary Theater** (415 Geary St., 415/834-3200, www.act-sf.org) and showcases diversely unique theater productions that are inspiring and thought-provoking.

Marvel at the magnificence and intricate beauty of the **Orpheum Theatre** (1192 Market St., 888/746-1799, www.shnsf.com), a dramatic, 12th-century Spanish-style palace with a vaulted ceiling and richly colored decor. It's been the setting for vaudeville, silent films, motion pictures, musical comedy, and other theatrical entertainment since it first opened in 1926. The illustrious **Golden Gate Theater** (1 Taylor St., 888/746-1799, www.shnsf.com, $35), which made its debut in 1922 during the vaudeville era with headliners like the Marx Brothers, presents Broadway shows like *Billy Elliot* and *Chicago*.

Other theaters include the **Curran Theatre** (445 Geary St., 415/358-1220, www.sfcurran.com), which hosts many traveling Broadway shows, and the **Lorraine Hansberry Theatre** (777 Jones St., 415/345-3980, www.lhtsf.org), which features productions written by African American playwrights.

Galleries

Tucked away on the second floor of the Eureka Bank building, the **North Beach Museum** (1435 Stockton St., 415/391-6210, 9am-4pm Mon.-Thurs., 9am-6pm Fri., free) features changing displays and photo exhibits of the Chinese and Italian communities in the late 19th and early 20th centuries. The **Chinese Culture Center** (750 Kearny St. #3, 415/986-1822, www.c-c-c.org, 10am-4pm Tues.-Sat., $5 suggested donation) offers exhibitions of traditional and contemporary art, performances of Chinese opera and dance, tours, and workshops.

View artwork from emerging local artists at the **49 Geary Art Galleries** (49 Geary St., 888/470-9564, 9:30am-5:30pm Tues.-Fri., 10:30am-5:30pm Sat.). Visit **Robert Koch Gallery** (49 Geary St., 415/421-0122, www.kochgallery.com, 11am-5:30pm Tues.-Sat.) for photography. The **Haines Gallery** (49 Geary St. #540, 415/397-8114, www.hainesgallery.com, 10:30am-5pm Tues.-Sat.) showcases emerging and internationally established artists from all over the world.

Shopping

San Francisco has a large collection of retail stores, department stores, boutiques, galleries, and tourist shops, making it a premier city to shop. In Union Square you'll find many high-end retail shops; Chinatown is a destination for antiques and unique objects; North Beach caters to an eclectic crowd; while Fisherman's Wharf gives tourists mementos of the city to take home.

Union Square

Looking to make an impression? Maison Goyard (118 Grant Ave., 415/523-8200, www.goyard.com, 10am-6pm Mon.-Sat., noon-5pm Sun.) is an ultra-luxury brand of French handbags and luggage that most fine-tote carriers know by the signature, stenciled fabric with the distinctive chevron print. These babies are carried on many A-list arms, but be warned: They don't run cheap. And neither do the fine antiques at **333 Peking Arts Oriental Antiques & Furniture** (535 Sutter St., 415/433-6780, 10:30am-5:30pm Mon.-Sat.), where collectibles from the Han and Ming dynasties, including terra-cotta statues, porcelain figures, snuff bottles, and jade statues, are mesmerizing. **Farinelli Antiques** (311 Grant Ave., 415/433-4823, 9am-9pm Mon.-Sat., 10am-7pm Sun.) displays a breathtaking selection of 19th- and 20th-century European dining room sets, rare pianos, fine porcelain by Meissen and Sèvres, more than 100 chandeliers, marble and bronze statues, silk Persian carpets, rare jade and ivory . . . need we go on?

Craft beer enthusiasts may find a terrific selection to buy and drink at **City Beer Store** (1168 Folsom St., 415/503-1033, www.citybeerstore.com, noon-10pm daily). If whiskey is your passion, you've come to the right place when you step into **Scottish Imports Hector Russell** (360 Sutter St., 415/989-5458). The shop sells more than 400 kinds of whiskeys, and if you take your whiskey the traditional Scottish way, the store imports and rents authentic hand-stitched kilts.

Aside from its many specialty shops, Union Square plays home to internationally known, upscale department stores.

Chinatown

Dragon House (455 Grant Ave., 415/781-2351, 10am-6pm) sells authentic antiques and Asian fine arts, including jewelry that dates back 2,000 years. It's worth a stop at **Peter Pap Oriental Rugs** (470 Jackson St., 415/956-3300 and 888/581-6743, 10am-5pm Mon.-Fri., 10am-4:30pm Sat.) just to run your fingers over the silken works of art.

Superior Trading Company (837 Washington St., 415/982-8722, www.superiortrading.com, 9:30am-6pm daily) boasts the largest quantity of Oriental herbs and ginseng, with imports from China, Hong Kong, and Korea, while **Vital Tea Leaf** (1044 Grant Ave., 415/981-2388, 11am-7pm daily) offers a world of loose tea leaves, with expert advice and tastings to help you sort through scores of flavorful options.

North Beach

No San Francisco shopping experience is complete without a visit to **City Lights Bookstore** (261 Columbus Ave., 415/362-8193, www.citylights.com, 10am-midnight daily), an iconic literary hub made famous by Beat poets and authors. It still hosts relevant literary events and has an excellent collection of the written word.

An eclectic clothing store, **AB Fits** (1519 Grant Ave., 415/982-5726, www.abfits.com, 11:30am-6:30pm Tues.-Sat., noon-6pm Sun.) specializes in European and Asian designer jeans, seemingly made to fit each unique body.

Leather jackets and handmade sweaters are at **Knitz and Leather** (1429 Grant Ave., 415/391-3480, 11am-7pm Mon.-Sat., noon-5pm Sun.), which offers unique designs and styles.

If sparkly is what catches your eye, **Macchiarini Creative Design & Jewelry** (1544 Grant Ave., 415/982-2229, 11am-6pm Tues.-Sat., noon-6pm Sun.) creates handmade jewelry that's modern, with tribal and African influences.

For something decorative for the home, **Biordi Arts** (412 Columbus Ave., 415/392-8096, www.biordi.com, 11am-5pm Mon.-Fri., 9:30am-5pm Sat.)

San Francisco's North Beach

imports handmade and painted majolica pottery from central Italy.

Fisherman's Wharf

Souvenir hunters will not be disappointed shopping at Fisherman's Wharf. **Only In San Francisco** (Pier 39 Concourse #107, 415/397-0143, www.pier39.com, 8:30am-10:30pm daily) is a souvenir superstore with gifts and memorabilia. The **Cable Car Store** (39 Pier #231, 415/989-2040, www.cablecarstore.com, 10am-9pm daily) is a hot spot for anyone wanting to take a piece of San Francisco home with them. From cable car music boxes to magnets, T-shirts and sweatshirts to barking sea lions, it's all here.

Events

The **North Beach Festival** (Grant Ave. and Vallejo St., 800/310-6563, June, free) celebrates the neighborhood's Italian heritage with live music, poetry readings, dancing, arts and crafts booths, and gourmet foods.

Chinatown's annual **Autumn Moon Festival** (Grant Ave. and Broadway, www.moonfestival.org, early Sept., free) continues the ancient Chinese tradition of celebrating the harvest moon, with colorful parades, local bazaars, entertainment, and divine moon cakes.

San Francisco has the biggest and arguably best **Pride Festival** (Civic Center Plaza, www.sfpride.org, June, free) in the nation, celebrating the city's groundbreaking, history-making lesbian, gay, bisexual, and transgender community. It kicks off with a well-attended parade down Market Street, ending at City Hall.

Accommodations

San Francisco is an expensive city, and room prices are no exception. The bulk of the hotels are either around Union Square or in the Fisherman's Wharf area. Staying around Union Square is convenient, with good access to public transportation, but will cost you—not only for the room, but for parking as well. Fisherman's Wharf proper is not much cheaper, and although the views may be more scenic, transit options are more limited than around Union Square. The lower-priced motels lining Lombard Street, west of Van Ness, often come with parking, but the location is inconvenient to most points of interest.

Under $150

For a budget room, Hostelling Internationals has three locations worth a look. **Fisherman's Wharf Hostel** (240 Fort Mason, 415/771-7277, www.sfhostels.org, $40 and up dorm, $110 and up private) has the advantage of beautiful views, owing to its perch on the north end of the city. Reservations far in advance are recommended. Its **Downtown Hostel** (312 Mason St., 415/788-5604, www.sfhostels.org, $35 and up dorms, $94 and up private) is conveniently located at Union Square, while the nearby **City Center Hostel** (685 Ellis St., 415/474-5721, www.sfhostels.org, $33 and up dorms, $90 and up private) offers a little more quiet and comfort in return for being less central.

$150-250

Just outside Chinatown, the comfortable **Grant Plaza Hotel** (465 Grant Ave., 800/472-6899 or 415/434-3883, www.grantplaza.com, $159 and up) is close to many attractions and features colorful stained-glass windows and tasteful decor.

Free parking makes **Beck's Motor Lodge** (2222 Market St., 415/621-8212, www.becksmotorlodge.com, $219 and up) a reasonable option for road trippers. Though not central to downtown, it's near both Castro and Mission Districts.

An upscale hotel with a Japanese theme, **Hotel Kabuki** (1625 Post St., 415/922-3200, www.jdvhotels.com, $229 and up) offers guests a relaxing stay with koi ponds, a Zen garden, and an on-site spa. Just off Union Square, **Hotel Rex** (562 Sutter St., 415/433-4434, www.jdvhotels.com, $229 and up) is named for a local literary hero, poet Kenneth Rexroth, sometimes called the father of the Beats, and the hotel decor adopts a literary theme.

Renovated with an eclectic mix of literary and visual motifs drawn from the Beat era, ★ **Hotel Boheme** (444 Columbus Ave., 415/433-9111, www.hotelboheme.com, $235 and up) is an inviting and memorable experience for guests.

San Francisco's first boutique hotel, **Hotel Union Square** (114 Powell St., 415/397-3000, www.hotelunionsquare.com, $170 and up) offers small affordable rooms in addition to deluxe suites. Built over 100 years ago, it offers a fusion of art deco, beautiful brick walls, original 1915 Egyptian-motif mosaic murals, and classic San Francisco hospitality.

Over $250

Experience the **Clift Hotel** (495 Geary St., 415/775-4700, www.morganshotelgroup.com, $269 and up), a hip hotel with trendy furnishings in walking distance to shopping and the Muni bus stops.

The unique ★ **Argonaut Hotel** (495 Jefferson St., 415/563-0800, www.argonauthotel.com, $307 and up) has it all: history, classic style, prime location, elegant rooms, and superb service.

The iconic **Palace Hotel** (2 New Montgomery St., 415/512-1111, www.sfpalace.com, $400 and up) has remained a landmark for accommodations in San Francisco, with such timeless creations as the Garden Court's stained-glass dome, elegant decor and rooms, and revered restaurants.

No list of San Francisco hotels would be complete without a representative from Nob Hill. **The Fairmont San Francisco** (950 Mason St., 415/772-5000, www.fairmont.com/san-francisco, $433 and up) is often the choice of presidents and diplomats, and it is the picture of classic luxury.

Information and Services

The **San Francisco Visitor Information Center** (Hallidie Plaza Lower Level, 900 Market St., www.sftravel.com, 9am-5pm Mon.-Fri., 9am-3pm Sat.-Sun. May-Oct., closed Sun. Nov.-Apr.) is centrally located just outside the Powell Street BART and Muni station. Free city maps, brochures, and sightseeing guides are available, as well as advice from knowledgeable locals.

CA-1 through San Francisco

In San Francisco, CA-1 does not run along the coast. It follows 19th Avenue south through some of the most gridded streets in the city until it joins I-280 near the border between San Francisco and its neighbor to the south, Daly City. CA-1 splits off from I-280 a few miles south, and you start getting glimpses of the ocean as you head toward Pacifica.

To drive along the coast in San Francisco, you would need to take the Great Highway, which starts at the very western end of Geary Avenue. It follows Ocean Beach until just past the San Francisco Zoo, when it hits CA-35, also known as Skyline Boulevard. Take CA-35 south for about five miles, where it meets up with CA-1.

Pacifica

About 15 miles south of San Francisco, the coastal community **Pacifica** (pop. 39,062) is best known to locals for its large and festive bowling alley **Sea Bowl** (4625 CA-1, 650/738-8190, www.seabowl.com, 10am-midnight Mon.-Thurs., 10am-12:30am Fri., 9am-1am Sat., 9am-midnight Sun.). For travelers, it has one of the closer RV parks to San Francisco. **San Francisco RV Resort** (700 Palmetto Ave., 650/355-7093 or 800/822-1250, www.sanfranciscorvresort.com, $74 and up) can accommodate most RV sizes, and many sites have hookups.

Montara State Beach

Montara State Beach (2nd St. and CA-1, Montara, www.parks.ca.gov, 650/726-8819, 8am-sunset daily) is one of the most beautiful beaches in this area. It is as popular with tide-poolers, surfers, and anglers as it is with picnickers and beachcombers. The beach also remains relatively uncrowded compared to many of the other beaches to the south. It has a tendency to get windy, and there is limited parking. It is off CA-1 about 20 miles south of San Francisco.

Moss Beach

Located 23 miles south of San Francisco, **Moss Beach** (3,103) is one of several residential towns that line the coast. There is little here besides stunning scenery, a few small businesses, and the Fitzgerald Marine Reserve.

For tide-pooling near San Francisco, the **Fitzgerald Marine Reserve** (200 Nevada Ave., 650/728-3584, www.co.sanmateo.ca.us, sunrise-sunset daily) is the place to go. The 32-acre reserve extends from the Montara Lighthouse south to Pillar Point and is considered one of the most diverse intertidal zones in the Bay Area. On its rocky reefs, you can hunt for sea anemones, starfish, eels, and crabs—there's even a small species of red octopus. The reserve is also home to egrets, herons, an endangered species of butterfly, and a slew of sea lions and harbor seals that enjoy sunning themselves on the beach's outer rocks. For the best viewing, come at low tide (tide logs are available at most local bookstores, but for a quick reference, check out www.protides.com) and on weekdays, as this is a popular destination for families. For a more leisurely and drier experience, numerous trails crisscross the windswept bluffs and wind through sheltering groves of cypress and eucalyptus trees.

The **Moss Beach Distillery** (140 Beach Way, 650/728-5595, www.mossbeachdistillery.com, noon-8pm Mon.-Thurs., noon-8:30pm Fri.-Sat., 11am-8pm Sun., $15-38) has been featured on *Unsolved Mysteries* and *Ghost Hunters* and written up in countless publications not for its food but for its famous ghost: the Blue Lady. Rumor has it that a beautiful young woman walked the cliffs of Moss Beach from her home to a coastside speakeasy then known as Frank's Place, now Moss Beach Distillery, to meet her lover, a handsome piano player who worked in the bar. The Blue Lady, whose name has never been discovered, perished one night on the cliffs under suspicious circumstances, and her ghost is said to haunt the building. The restaurant offers something of a cross between traditional American food and California cuisine. Portions are large and service is friendly, if occasionally slow during peak times.

Half Moon Bay

Located about 30 miles south of San Francisco on CA-1, **Half Moon Bay** (pop. 12,697) is a charming small town with several shops and art galleries. Many of the local businesses line Main Street a block east of the CA-1 bypass. Half Moon Bay enjoys a beautiful natural setting and earns significant income from tourism, especially during the world-famous pumpkin festival each October.

Recreation

The beaches of Half Moon Bay draw visitors from over the hill and farther afield all year long, despite the chilly fog during the summer. Perhaps the most famous beach in the area is one that has no name. At the end of West Point Avenue in the neighboring town of Princeton is the Pillar Point Marsh and a long stretch of beach that wraps around the edge of the point. This beach is the launch pad for surfers paddling out to tackle the infamous **Mavericks Break** (Pillar Point Marsh parking lot, past Pillar Point Harbor). Formed by unique underwater topography, the giant waves are the site of the **Titans of Mavericks Surf Contest** (www.titansofmavericks.com). The competition is always held in winter, when the swells reach their peak, and left until the last minute to ensure that they are the biggest of the year. When perfect conditions present themselves, the best surfers in the world are given 48 hours' notice to make it to Mavericks to compete. Unfortunately, you can't see the breaks all that well from the beach, but there are dirt trails that crisscross the point, where breathtaking views can be had. Walk up West Point Avenue past the yellow gate and catch any number of dirt trails heading west toward the bluffs. But for those eyeing the big waves, beware: Mavericks is not a beginner's break, especially in winter, and the giant surf can be deadly, even for pros.

Food

The quality of food in Half Moon Bay is superb. **Pasta Moon** (315 Main St., Ste. C, 650/726-5125, www.pastamoon.com, 11:30am-2pm and 5:30pm-9pm Mon.-Thurs., 11:30am-2pm and 5:30pm-9:30pm Fri., noon-3pm and 5:30pm-9pm Sat.-Sun., $19-40) serves updated Italian cuisine with an emphasis on fresh, light dishes. Their wood-fired pizzas are particularly good and affordable, as are any of the pasta dishes, made with housemade noodles.

For seafood, **Sam's Chowder House** (4210 N. Cabrillo Hwy., 650/712-0245, www.samschowderhouse.com, 11:30am-9pm Mon.-Thurs., 11:30am-9:30pm Fri., 11am-9:30pm Sat., 11am-9pm Sun., $22-30) offers everything from a stiff drink at the bar to light appetizers and champagne on the deck, to steaming plates of whole lobster, seafood paella, and seared tuna served in the ample yet cozy dining room.

When all you need is a quick bite or a casual lunch, the **Moonside Bakery & Café** (604 Main St., 650/726-9070, www.moonsidebakery.com, 7am-5pm daily, $10-15) can fix you up with breakfast pastries and espresso or sandwiches and wood-fired pizzas for lunch.

Events

The biggest annual event in this small agricultural town is the **Half Moon Bay Art & Pumpkin Festival** (www.pumpkinfest.miramarevents.com). Every October, nearly 250,000 people trek to Half Moon Bay to pay homage to the big orange squash. The festival includes live music, food, artists' booths, contests, activities for kids, an adult lounge area, and a parade. Perhaps the best-publicized event is the pumpkin weigh-off, which takes place before the festivities begin. Farmers bring their tremendous squash on flatbed trucks from all over the country to determine which is the biggest of all. The winner gets paid per pound, a significant prize when the biggest pumpkins weigh over 1,000 pounds.

Accommodations

Half Moon Bay offers several lovely bed-and-breakfasts, like the elegant and affordable **Pacific Victorian Bed and Breakfast** (325 Alameda Ave., 888/929-0906, www.pacificvictorian.com, $165 and up), which is only a block and a half from the beach.

On the higher end, the **Ritz-Carlton Half Moon Bay** (1 Miramontes Point Rd., 650/712-7000, www.ritzcarlton. com, $500 and up) looms large over the Pacific and resembles a medieval castle. Inside, guests enjoy the finest of modern amenities. The Ritz-Carlton has a top-tier restaurant (Navio), a world-class day spa, and posh guest rooms that really are worth the rates. Golf at the Ritz is second to none in the Bay Area.

Information and Services

Visit the **Half Moon Bay Chamber of Commerce** (235 Main St., 650/726-8389, www.halfmoonbaychamber.org, 9am-5pm Mon.-Fri., 10am-3pm Sat.-Sun.), in the red house just after you turn on Main Street from CA-92. The chamber also doubles as a visitors center, where you can find maps, brochures, and a schedule of events.

Central California Coast

The scenic coastline between San Francisco and Los Angeles marries the sparkle of Southern California beaches with the rolling green hills and towering forests of the north.

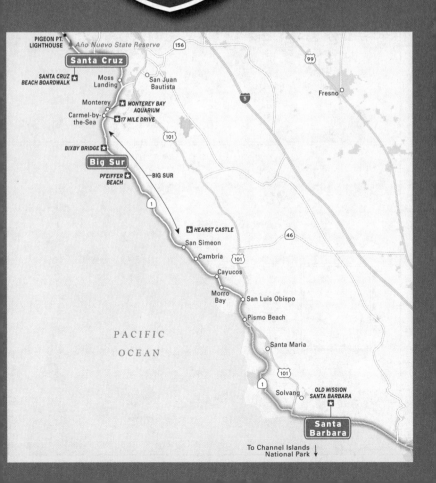

PIGEON PT. LIGHTHOUSE
Año Nuevo State Reserve
156
Santa Cruz
99
SANTA CRUZ BEACH BOARDWALK
Moss Landing
San Juan Bautista
Fresno
Monterey
MONTEREY BAY AQUARIUM
5
Carmel-by-the-Sea
17 MILE DRIVE
101
BIXBY BRIDGE
Big Sur
PFEIFFER BEACH
BIG SUR
1
HEARST CASTLE
46
San Simeon
Cambria
101
Cayucos
Morro Bay
San Luis Obispo
Pismo Beach
PACIFIC OCEAN
Santa Maria
101
1
OLD MISSION SANTA BARBARA
Solvang
Santa Barbara
To Channel Islands National Park

Central California Coast

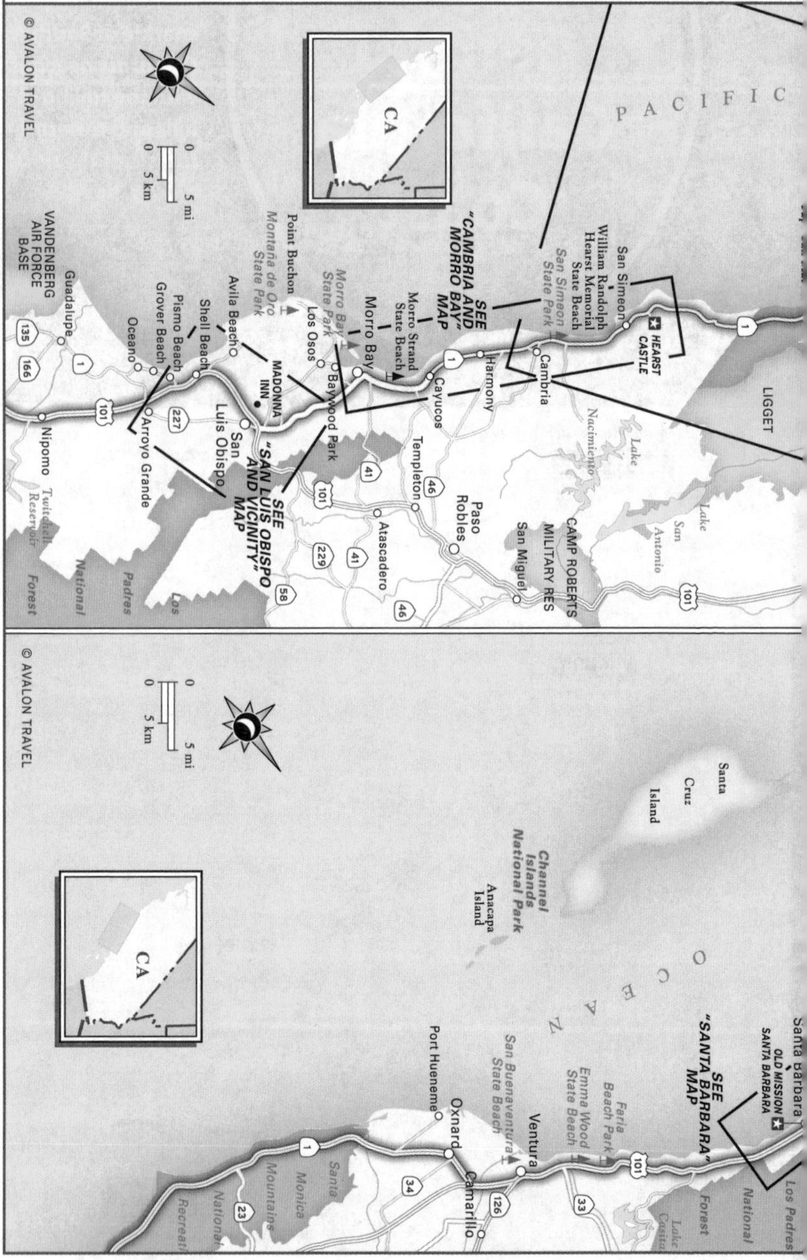

PACIFIC

CA

0   5 mi
0   5 km

VANDENBERG
AIR FORCE
BASE

Guadalupe

135

166

1

Nipomo

101

Oceano

Arroyo Grande

227

Pismo Beach

Grover Beach

Shell Beach

Avila Beach

San Luis Obispo

MADONNA
INN

Los Osos

Baywood Park

Point Buchon

Montaña de Oro
State Park

Morro Bay
State Park

Morro Bay

Morro Strand
State Beach

Cayucos

Harmony

Cambria

"SEE
CAMBRIA AND
MORRO BAY"
MAP

San Simeon

William Randolph
Hearst Memorial
State Beach

San Simeon
State Park

★ HEARST
CASTLE

LIGGET

"SEE
SAN LUIS OBISPO
AND VICINITY"
MAP

41

Templeton

46

Atascadero

229

41

58

46

101

Paso
Robles

San Miguel

CAMP ROBERTS
MILITARY RES

Lake
Nacimiento

Lake
San
Antonio

101

Twitchell
Reservoir

National

Forest

Padres

Los

© AVALON TRAVEL

0   5 mi
0   5 km

CA

Santa
Cruz
Island

Channel
Islands
National Park

Anacapa
Island

O C E A N

Port Hueneme

Oxnard

Camarillo

126

34

23

1

Santa

Monica

Mountains

National

Recreation

33

101

Ventura

San Buenaventura
State Beach

Emma Wood
State Beach

Faria
Beach Park

Santa Barbara

OLD MISSION ✚
SANTA BARBARA

"SEE
SANTA BARBARA"
MAP

Los Padres

National

Forest

Lake
Casitas

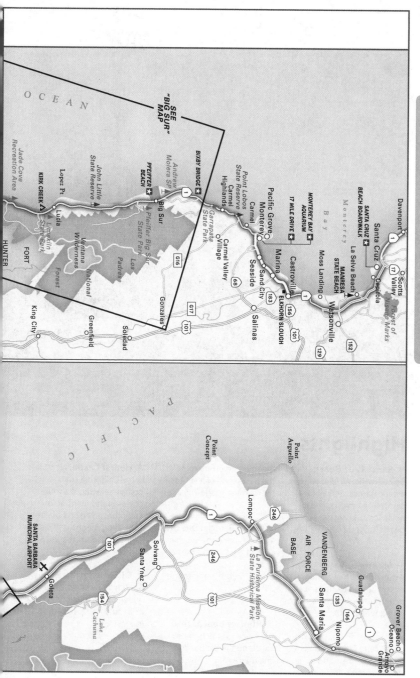

OCEAN

SEE "BIG SUR" MAP

Jade Cove Recreation Area

KIRK CREEK

Lopez Pt.

John Little State Reserve

Andrew Molera SP

PFEIFFER BEACH

BIXBY BRIDGE

Point Lobos State Reserve

Carmel Highlands

Pacific Grove

MONTEREY BAY AQUARIUM

17 MILE DRIVE

Davenport

Santa Cruz

SANTA CRUZ BEACH BOARDWALK

La Selva Beach

Capitola

Scotts Valley

Coast of Many Marks

HUNTER

FORT

Lucia

Limekiln St. Park

Big Sur

Pfeiffer Big Sur State Park

Ventana Wilderness

Los Padres National Forest

Carmel Valley

Carmel

Carmel Valley Village

Garrapata State Park

Monterey

Seaside

Sand City

Marina

Castroville

Moss Landing

MANRESA STATE BEACH

Watsonville

M o n t e r e y   B a y

King City

Greenfield

Soledad

Gonzales

Salinas

ELKHORN SLOUGH

G16

68

183

156

G17

101

101

129

152

P A C I F I C

Point Concepcion

Point Arguello

Lompoc

VANDENBERG AIR FORCE BASE

La Purisima Mission State Historical Park

Solvang

Santa Ynez

Santa Maria

Guadalupe

Nipomo

Grover Beach

Oceano

Arroyo Grande

SANTA BARBARA MUNICIPAL AIRPORT

Goleta

Lake Cachuma

246

246

135

166

154

101

101

1

1

1

1

17

Highlights

★ **Santa Cruz Beach Boardwalk:** A roller coaster, arcade games, and all the carnival food you can eat make for a classic day at the beach (page 227).

★ **Monterey Bay Aquarium:** The vast array of sea life and exhibits at this mammoth aquarium is astonishing (page 236).

★ **17 Mile Drive:** Home to the Lone Cypress and more than a dozen other sights, the toll road offers some of the best views of a very scenic road trip (page 245).

★ **Bixby Bridge:** Due to its location along the seaside cliffs of Big Sur, this is one of the most photographed bridges in the world (page 256).

★ **Pfeiffer Beach:** This is the place to watch the sun set along the Big Sur coastline (page 258).

★ **Hearst Castle:** No visit to the California coast is complete without a tour of this grand mansion on a hill, conceived and built by publishing magnate William Randolph Hearst (page 261).

★ **Old Mission Santa Barbara:** It's known as the queen of the missions for its beauty and lush setting (page 278).

Culturally, the central coast embodies laid-back California, but its geography and climate frequently draw comparisons to Mediterranean shores—with bigger waves and better sunsets.

CA-1 twists along the wild, rugged coast from bohemian Santa Cruz to Monterey, buoyed by rich marinelife and a renowned aquarium. The stunning stretch from Carmel to Big Sur boasts views of the Pacific bounded by jagged coastline and rock formations, descending south into remote beachfronts so ideal, publishing magnate William Randolph Hearst settled in the region to build his opulent, no-expenses-spared Hearst Castle.

From here, CA-1 and US-101 engage in a dance of merges and splits through farmlands that flourish from the cool climate, producing a bounty of crops, especially strawberries, artichokes, and, most recently, wine grapes. Put on the wine maps by the 2004 film *Sideways,* this wine country now competes with the best of them, with nearly 100,000 acres of grape-bearing vines, culminating in beloved vacation destination Santa Barbara, a.k.a. the American Riviera.

Planning Your Time

Plan five days to a week to explore the central coast. It's easy to run yourself ragged trying to see and do everything. Instead, pick what interests you the most and leave everything else as an opportunity for an enhanced travel experience, should time allow.

Towns all along the coastline offer lodging, food, and fuel. Cities such as Santa Cruz, Monterey, San Luis Obispo, Santa Barbara, and Ventura offer more options, but smaller beach towns and resorts such as Carmel, Cambria, and Pismo Beach may be more charming. Scenic Big Sur offers an interesting mix of campgrounds and upscale resorts.

It is just under 75 miles south from San Francisco to Santa Cruz via US-101, and 95 miles north from Los Angeles to Santa Barbara via US-101. If you plan to leave US-101 where California's Highway 1 (CA-1) diverges, the drive will prove much more scenic, but longer.

Getting There
Car
The central coast is accessible by car via the scenic, two-lane CA-1, which winds along the entire stretch of the coastline.

US-101 is the primary highway that connects San Jose, Salinas, Paso Robles, San Luis Obispo, Santa Maria, Santa Barbara, Ventura, and on southward. Built along the railroad corridor, the highway at times runs concurrent with CA-1, specifically through Ventura and Santa Barbara Counties.

Much of CA-1 is a two-lane road with winding turns around the coast. Some stretches are fairly isolated, and it is always wise to make sure your tank is full before getting back on the road.

Air
Coastal international airports to access the central coast region from the south include **Los Angeles International Airport** (LAX, 1 World Way, 855/463-5252, www.lawa.org/lax).

The major Northern California airport is **San Francisco International Airport (SFO)** (780 S. Airport Blvd., 650/821-8211, www.flysfo.com), on San Francisco Bay about 15 miles south of the city center.

Regional air service includes **Monterey Regional Airport (MRY)** (200 Fred Kane Dr. #200, 831/648-7000, www.montereyairport.com), **San Luis Obispo Airport (SBP)** (901 Airport Dr., 805/781-5205, www.sloairport.com), and **Santa Barbara Municipal Airport (SBA)**

Best Hotels

★ **West Cliff Inn:** The Italianate grand dame of Santa Cruz offers lavish amenities and commanding ocean views (page 233).

★ **Seven Gables Inn:** Every room has a view at this Pacific Grove inn, considered one of the most romantic in America (page 244).

★ **Tradewinds Carmel:** Impeccable design makes this one of the most glamorous hotels on the coast (page 250).

★ **Post Ranch Inn:** This rustic yet luxurious resort blends right into the cliffside along Big Sur (page 258).

★ **Madonna Inn:** The famed road-trip stopover is kitschy, over the top, and excessively pink (page 272).

★ **Simpson House Inn:** Opulent rooms, a formal English garden, and evening wine-tastings are features of this Santa Barbara B&B (page 287).

(500 James Fowler Rd., 805/683-4011, www.santabarbaraca.gov).

Train

Amtrak (800/872-7245, www.amtrak.com, $135 and up) offers service on the **Coast Starlight** to Seattle, Portland, Sacramento, Oakland, and Los Angeles. The **Pacific Surfliner** provides service from San Luis Obispo to Santa Barbara, Los Angeles, and San Diego. International visitors can buy an unlimited travel USA Rail Pass, good for 15, 30, or 45 days.

Bus

Greyhound (800/231-2222, www.greyhound.com) offers special discounts to students and seniors with bus routes and stops sticking to major highways and cities.

Fuel and Services

Gas stations are easy to find within beachfront towns, and the farther south you travel, the easier it gets. However, don't expect 24-hour service. If you pull into Big Sur at midnight with an empty tank, you'll find yourself stranded.

To receive reports on **road conditions,** call **511.** If your phone carrier does not support 511, call toll-free at 800/427-7623.

For **emergency assistance** and services, call **911.**

San Gregorio

Forty miles south of San Francisco, or about an hour's drive, the tiny town of **San Gregorio** (pop. 214) is a picture of rolling rangeland, neat patches of colorful crops, and century-old homes, including a one-room schoolhouse and an old brothel. Its beating heart is the **San Gregorio General Store** (7615 Stage Rd., 650/726-0565, www.sangregoriostore.com, 10:30am-6pm Mon.-Thurs., 10:30am-7pm Fri., 10am-7pm Sat., 10am-6pm Sun.). Open since 1889, the San Gregorio General Store has an eclectic book section, cast-iron cookery, oil lamps, and raccoon traps. In the back of the store are coolers stocked with juice, soda, bottled water, and deli sandwiches made in the back kitchen. The real centerpiece is the bar, serving beer, wine, and spirits to ranchers and farmers out for a coffee break in the mornings and locals just getting off work. On the weekends the store is packed by mostly out-of-towners, and the live music keeps things moving. The deep picture windows out front make it a comfy place to watch the

Best Restaurants

★ **Duarte's Tavern:** The olallieberry pie alone is worth a stop at this classic, James Beard-recognized road stop in tiny Pescadero (page 225).

★ **The Forge in the Forest:** This Carmel legend has been serving up perfect dishes for decades (page 248).

★ **Nepenthe:** The menu is short and tasty, but the real feast is the amazing view from the outdoor deck (page 253).

★ **Madeline's:** An exquisite menu and an intimate setting make for a Parisian repast in Cambria (page 263).

★ **La Super-Rica Taqueria:** A favorite of legendary chef Julia Child, this taco shop's secret is its hand-made tortillas (page 283).

★ **Stella Mare's:** French country dining and amazing desserts are on the menu in this historical Santa Barbara home (page 284).

afternoon pass by with a cold beer. The San Gregorio General Store lives up to its name: You can even buy stamps or mail a letter at the full-service post office next door.

At the intersection of CA-84 and CA-1, **San Gregorio State Beach** (650/726-8819, www.parks.ca.gov, 8am-sunset daily, $10 per car) stretches farther than it seems. Once you're walking toward the ocean, the small-seeming cove stretches out beyond the cliffs that bound it to create a long stretch of beach perfect for contemplative strolling. San Gregorio is a local favorite in the summer, despite the regular appearance of thick, chilly fog over the sand. Brave beachgoers can even swim and bodysurf here, although you'll quickly get cold if you do so without a wetsuit. Picnic tables and restrooms cluster near the parking lot, but picnicking may be hampered by the wind.

Pescadero

Pescadero (pop. 624) is a tiny dot on the coastline, about 8 miles south of San Gregorio on CA-1, with one main street, one side street, several smallish farms, and, of course, the legendary Duarte's Tavern.

Pescadero State Beach (CA-1, north of Pescadero Rd., 650/726-8819, www.parks.ca.gov, 8am-sunset daily) is the closest beach to the town of Pescadero. It's a great spot to walk in the sand and stare out at the Pacific, but near-constant winds make it less than ideal for picnics or sunbathing. It does have some facilities, including public restrooms.

Food

★ **Duarte's Tavern** (202 Stage Rd., 650/879-0464, www.duartestavern.com, 7am-8pm daily, $12-25) has been honored by the James Beard Foundation as "An American Classic," and once you walk through the doors you'll see why. The rambling building features sloping floors and age-darkened wooden walls. The food is good, the service friendly, and the coffee plentiful. And while almost everybody comes to Duarte's eventually for a bowl of artichoke soup or a slice of olallieberry pie, it is really the atmosphere that is the biggest draw. Locals of all stripes—farmers, farmhands, ranchers, and park rangers— sit shoulder to shoulder with travelers from "over the hill," sharing conversation and a bite to eat, particularly in the dimly lit bar. The greatest assets are the outdated jukebox and excellent Bloody Marys, garnished with a pickled green bean.

Pigeon Point Lighthouse

A few miles south of Pescadero is **Pigeon Point Lighthouse** (210 Pigeon Point Rd., at CA-1, 650/879-2120, www.parks.ca.gov/pigeonpoint, 8am-sunset daily). First lit in 1872, Pigeon Point is one of the most photographed lighthouses in the United States. Sadly, visitors find the lighthouse itself in a state of disrepair, and recent earthquakes have made climbing to the top unsafe. Yet the monument stands, its hostel still shelters travelers, and visitors still marvel at the incomparable views from the point. Winter guests can look for migrating whales from the rocks beyond the tower.

For a budget place to stay in this area, try the **Pigeon Point Hostel** (210 Pigeon Point Rd., at CA-1, 650/879-0633, www.norcalhostels.org/pigeon, dorms $28-32, private rooms $82-113). This Hostelling International hostel has simple but comfortable accommodations, both private and dorm-style. Amenities include three kitchens, free Wi-Fi, and beach access. But the best amenity of all is the cliff-top hot tub, which makes this hostel more than special.

Año Nuevo State Reserve

7 miles south of Pigeon Point Lighthouse, **Año Nuevo State Reserve** (1 New Years Creek Rd., 650/879-2025, www.parks.ca.gov/anonuevo, 8:30am-sunset daily, $10 per car) is world-famous as the winter home and breeding ground of the once-endangered elephant seals. The reserve also has extensive dunes and marshland. The beaches and wilderness are open year-round. The elephant seals start showing up in late November and stay to breed, birth pups, and loll on the beach until early March. Visitors are

Flowers bloom along the Central California coast.

not allowed down to the elephant seal habitats on their own and must sign up for a guided walking tour with Reserve America (800/444-4445, www.reserve-california.com). Once you see two giant males crashing into one another in a fight for dominance, you won't want to get too close. Book your tour at least a day or two in advance because the seals are popular with both locals and travelers.

Santa Cruz

Sitting on a point where redwood forest meets the north tip of the crescent-shaped Monterey Bay, **Santa Cruz** (pop. 64,465) fronts the coast but faces south, looking 22 miles across the bay at the north-facing town of Monterey. Santa Cruz decidedly casts itself as the younger of the two towns, known for its funky college vibe, standout surf, and carnival-like Boardwalk. Folks here have mastered the art of chillin' in the sun.

Getting There and Around

Both US-101 and CA-1 provide access into Santa Cruz by car. The most picturesque route is 50 miles along CA-1 South through San Mateo County from Half Moon Bay to Santa Cruz.

Amtrak trains and Greyhound run to or near the downtown Santa Cruz Metro Center. The nearest major airports are in San Jose and San Francisco.

Santa Cruz is a walking and bicycling town. It's only a 20-minute walk from downtown to the beach. With 262 sunny days per year, why drive? If you do, find plenty of car parking through **Santa Cruz Metro** (920 Pacific Ave., 831/425-8600, www.scmtd.com, $6 day-pass), including downtown and outer areas.

Sights
★ Santa Cruz Beach Boardwalk

The **Santa Cruz Beach Boardwalk** (400 Beach St., 831/423-5590, www.beach-boardwalk.com, 11am-10pm Sun.-Thurs., 11am-11pm Fri.-Sat., ride hours vary by season, rides closed weekdays in winter, parking $15), or just "the Boardwalk" as it's called by the locals, has a rare appeal that beckons to young children, teenagers, and adults of all ages.

The amusement park rambles along each side of the south end of the Boardwalk; entry is free, but you must buy either per-ride tickets ($4-7) or an unlimited-rides wristband ($37). The Great Dipper boasts a history as the oldest wooden roller coaster in the state, still giving riders a thrill after all this time. In summer, a log ride cools down guests hot from hours of tromping around. The Boardwalk also offers several toddler and little-kid rides.

At the other end of the Boardwalk, avid gamesters choose between the lure of prizes from the traditional midway games and the large arcade. Throw baseballs at things, try your arm at Skee-Ball, or take a pass at classic or newer video games. The traditional carousel actually has a brass ring to grab.

Santa Cruz

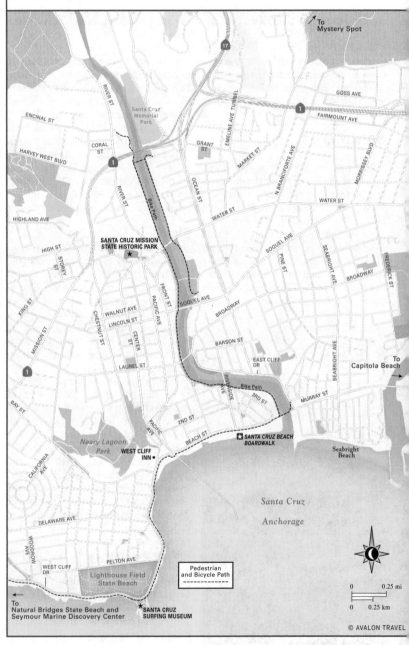

To
Mystery Spot

GOSS AVE

FAIRMOUNT AVE

17

Santa Cruz
Memorial
Park

RIVER ST

ENCINAL ST

CORAL
ST

1

HARVEY WEST BLVD

GRANT
ST

EMELINE AVE TUNNEL

MARKET ST

N BRANCIFORTE AVE

MORRISSEY BLVD

RIVER ST

HIGHLAND AVE

WATER ST

WATER ST

SOQUEL AVE

SEABRIGHT AVE

FREDERICK ST

Bike Path

SANTA CRUZ MISSION
STATE HISTORIC PARK

HIGH ST

STOREY
ST

PINE ST

BROADWAY

FRONT ST

SOQUEL AVE

KING ST

WALNUT AVE

CHESTNUT ST

LINCOLN ST

PACIFIC AVE

CENTER
ST

BROADWAY

MISSION ST

LAUREL ST

BARSON ST

EAST CLIFF
DR

SEABRIGHT AVE

To
Capitola Beach

1

BAY ST

RIVERSIDE AVE

Bike Path

3RD ST

MURRAY ST

Neary Lagoon
Park

WEST CLIFF
INN

PACIFIC AVE

2ND ST

BEACH ST

SANTA CRUZ BEACH
BOARDWALK

Seabright
Beach

CALIFORNIA
AVE

Santa Cruz

Anchorage

DELAWARE AVE

WOODROW
AVE

PELTON AVE

WEST CLIFF
DR

Lighthouse Field
State Beach

Pedestrian
and Bicycle Path
- - - - - - - -

0   0.25 mi

0   0.25 km

To
Natural Bridges State Beach and
Seymour Marine Discovery Center

SANTA CRUZ
SURFING MUSEUM

© AVALON TRAVEL

After you've worn yourself out playing games and riding rides, you can take the stairs down to the broad, sandy beach below the Boardwalk. It's a great place to flop down and sun yourself, or brave a dip in the cool Pacific surf. Granted, it gets crowded in the summertime.

Looking for something tasty to munch on or a drink to cool you off? You can definitely find it at the Boardwalk. An old-fashioned candy shop sells sweets to the sweet, while the snack stands offer corn dogs, burgers, fries, lemonade, and other traditional carnival food.

Santa Cruz Surfing Museum

West of the Boardwalk, on Lighthouse Field State Beach, is the world's first surfing museum. Housed in the Mark Abbott Memorial Lighthouse, the **Santa Cruz Surfing Museum** (Lighthouse Point, 701 W. Cliff Dr., 831/420-6289, www.santacruzsurfingmuseum.org, 10am-5pm Thurs.-Tues. July 4-Labor Day, noon-4pm Thurs.-Mon. rest of the year) relates the history of surfing through a collection of surfboards from different times and other ephemera of surf culture. From the cliffs adjacent to the museum, you'll find a close overhead view of surfers shredding the famous **Steamer Lane** break.

Seymour Marine Discovery Center

"Ms. Blue," one of the largest blue whale skeletons, rests across from **Seymour Marine Discovery Center** (100 McAllister Way, 831/459-3800, www.seymourcenter.ucsc.edu, 10am-5pm Tues.-Sun., $8 adults, $6 children), where tours and exhibits let you dive into the latest ocean discoveries and where shark-petting is encouraged.

Santa Cruz Mission State Historic Park

Founded by the Franciscans in 1791, **Santa Cruz Mission State Historic Park** (144 School St., 831/425-5849, 10am-4pm Thurs.-Sat. and Mon., noon-4pm Sun.) puts history buffs at the site of the oldest building in the city. This is the only remaining original building of the Mission Santa Cruz settlement. It's free to tour the mission, which has several good exhibits on local Native American life.

Recreation

The Santa Cruz Wharf is known for fishing and viewing marinelife, while local parks and beaches offer many opportunities for surfing, bird- and butterfly-watching, kayaking, biking, golfing, and hiking.

Both **Lighthouse Field State Beach** (740 W. Cliff Dr., 831/429-2850, 7am-sunset daily), well known to surfers for its great wave riding and the adjacent Surfing Museum, and **Natural Bridges State Beach** (2531 W. Cliff Dr., 831/423-4609, 8am-sunset daily, $10 parking), known for its natural sea arch, attract **birders and butterfly watchers** that gather for a rare glimpse of the black swift and colorful monarch butterflies, as well as to see offshore sea lions and the migrating whale population. Natural Bridges State Beach's remaining mudstone bridge (there were once three, but two collapsed) was carved out by the Pacific Ocean through wind and water erosion. Arches are formed out of collapsed caves, the mouth becoming a gateway to the open sea.

Rent a kayak or paddleboard from **Kayak Connection** (413 Lake Ave. #103, 831/479-1121, www.kayakconnection.com, 10am-5pm daily, $35 and up) to get a closer look at marine mammals or just a different perspective off the beach, or go scuba diving with **Aqua Safaris Scuba Center** (6896-A Soquel Ave., 831/479-4386, www.aquasafaris.com, 10am-6pm daily) and explore the world below the surface.

Take a three-mile walk or bike ride on **West Cliff Drive,** a path along the Pacific Ocean that provides a wonderful vantage point to see all the beachfront and offshore activity, or navigate the bike paths on either side of the San Lorenzo River, which runs parallel to Pacific Avenue. Conveniently located bicycle rentals may be found at **Pacific Ave Cycles** (320 Pacific Ave., 831/471-2453, www.pacificavecycles.com, 10am-4:30pm daily, $10/hour, $35/day), right by the bike park off from the Boardwalk, or **Spokesman Bicycles** (231 Cathcart St., 831/429-6062, www.spokesmanbicycles.com, 10am-6pm Mon.-Sat., noon-5pm Sun., $10/hour, $30/four hours), just a few blocks from downtown.

Golf at the historic **Pasatiempo Golf Club** (20 Clubhouse Rd., 831/459-9169, www.pasatiempo.com, 7am-6pm daily, up to $250 greens fees, $120 replay), designed by world-renowned golf architect Alister MacKenzie. The club offers a beautiful course, daily tee times, a Tap Room, and the MacKenzie Bar & Grill, where you can have a bite to eat and kick back and relax after a long day on the green.

Food

One of the West Coast's most celebrated coffee roasters, Verve Coffee (1540 Pacific Ave., 831/600-7784, www.verve-coffee.com, 6:30am-9pm daily, $4-7) has coffee bars in Los Angeles and Tokyo, but this hometown shop is the roaster's finest. For freshly baked goods, check out the European-style **Buttery** (702 Soquel Ave., 831/458-3020, www.butterybakery.com, 7am-7pm daily, $4-8) or the original **Bagelry** (320 Cedar St., 831/429-8049, www.bagelrysantacruz.com, 6:30am-5:30pm Mon.-Fri., 7am-5:30pm Sat., 7:30am-4pm Sun., $4-9), local mecca of the perfect bagel.

Zoccoli's (1534 Pacific Ave., 831/423-1711, www.zoccolis.com, 8am-6pm Mon.-Sat., 10am-6pm Sun., $7-9) is an Italian deli serving a wide array of sandwiches, along with soup and salad. If you're after burgers and shakes, hit up **Betty's Eat Inn** (1222 Pacific Ave., 831/600-7056, www.bettyburgers.com, 11am-9:30pm Sun.-Thurs., 11am-10:30pm Fri.-Sat., $7-12).

the Santa Cruz Beach Boardwalk

Part of the area's retro Betty Burger chain, this location offers entrées in addition to sandwiches.

It's tough not to use the word affordable when describing local mainstay **Charlie Hong Kong** (1141 Soquel Ave., 831/426-5664, www.charliehongkong. com, 11am-11pm daily, $6-10), but the tasty Asian noodle and rice bowl specialist finds a way to please just about every diet, including omnivore, vegetarian, vegan, gluten free, and locovore.

El Palomar (1336 Pacific Ave., 831/425-7575, www.elpalomarsantacruz.com, 11am-9pm Mon.-Wed., 11am-10pm Thurs., 11am-10:30pm Fri., 10am-10:30pm Sat., 10am-9pm Sun., $7-27) draws a line with Mexican food favorites like burritos and tacos.

For the finer things, **Soif** (105 Walnut Ave., 831/423-2020, www.soifwine.com, 5pm-9pm Sun.-Thurs., 5pm-10pm Fri.-Sat., $16-30) offers a sophisticated ambience and contemporary dishes.

Nightlife

Several bars and lounges congregate in downtown, covering a range of both drink and music tastes, most without a cover charge. At the far end of the wharf, **Vino Prima** (55 Municipal Wharf, 831/426-0750, www.vinoprimawines. com, 2pm-8pm Mon.-Thurs., 2pm-10pm Fri., noon-10pm Sat., noon-8pm Sun.) pours California boutique wines and even has a mimosa bar!

Your ticket to NFL games and cocktails, **Ideal Bar & Grill** (106 Beach St., 831/423-5271, www.idealbarandgrill. com, 11am-2am Mon.-Fri., 8am-2am Fri.-Sat.) has two big-screen TVs, a menu of classic cocktails, and live music on Friday and Saturday nights. For a good old-fashioned pub, go to **Parish Publick House** (841 Almar Ave., 831/421-0507, www. theparishpublick.com, 11am-2am daily), which has a great selection of draft beers and whiskey, savory fish-and-chips, and foot-stompin' music.

Surf bar **The Reef** (120 Union St., 831/459-9876, 11am-10pm Sun.-Wed., 11am-11pm Thurs.-Sat.) hosts jazz jams and open mics. Enjoy live music, pub grub, and the outdoor patio at the **Seabright Brewery** (519 Seabright Ave. #107, 831/426-2739, www.seabright-brewery.com, 11:30am-11:30pm daily), or hang out at **Blue Lagoon** (923 Pacific Ave., 831/423-7177, www.thebluelagoon. com, 4pm-2am daily) for beer and cocktails and live rock-and-roll.

Mellow with a dash of hip, **515 Kitchen & Cocktails** (515 Cedar St., 831/425-5051, www.515santacruz.com, 5pm-midnight Mon.-Tues., 5pm-1:30am Tues.-Fri., 10am-1:30am Sat., 10am-midnight Sun.) serves creative cocktails. Low lighting, music, and craft cocktails at **Red Restaurant and Bar** (200 Locust St., 831/425-1913, www.redrestaurantand-bar.com, 5pm-1:45am daily) form an intimate setting. Santa Cruz's best-kept secret, **Bocci's Cellar** (140 Encinal St., 831/427-1795, www.bocciscellar.com, 10:30am-2am daily) attracts locals and tourists not only because it's a historical landmark (circa 1800s), but because it has some of the best wine, food, and musical entertainment around.

Arts and Entertainment

An eclectic city of art and entertainment, Santa Cruz's diversity gives it that uniquely captivating edge. Watch a Shakespearean production at the **Sinsheimer-Stanley Festival Glen** (UCSC Theater Arts Center, 1156 High St., 831/459-2159, $36-48 adults, $16 children under 18), an unforgettable venue in a grove of massive redwoods beneath the starry sky.

Feel like a good movie and popcorn? **Nickelodeon Theatre** (210 Lincoln St., 831/426-7500, www.landmarktheatres. com, $10.50 general, $6 matinee) shows all the major blockbuster films, including foreign and indie productions. Don't pass up the snack bar's award-winning organic popcorn and locally made treats.

One of the oldest museums in the state of California, the **Santa Cruz Museum of Natural History** (1305 E. Cliff Dr., 831/420-6115, www.santacruzmuseum. org, 11am-4pm Tues.-Fri., 10am-5pm Sat.-Sun., $4 adults, free children under 18) is where Ohlone Native American artifacts are preserved and where visitors can learn about local flora and fauna. In the heart of downtown, **Museum of Art & History** (705 Front St., 831/429-1964, www.santacruzmah.org, 11am-5pm Tues.-Sun., $10 adults, $8 students) is a small facility with three floors of galleries, changing exhibits, and a gift shop.

Santa Cruz has a couple of ticketed entertainment venues that feature class-act musicians. At **Kuumbwa Jazz Center** (320 Cedar St., 831/427-2227), local talent and internationally acclaimed jazz acts play to a packed house in a concert setting with food and drinks available. **Moe's Alley** (1535 Commercial Way, 831/479-1854, www.moesalley.com) offers live performances from jazz and blues to reggae and salsa in a laid-back scene.

Shopping

Every Wednesday, the **Santa Cruz Community Farmers' Market** (corner of Cedar St. and Lincoln St., 831/454-0566, www.santacruzfarmersmarket. org, Wed. 1:30pm-5:30 winter, 1:20pm-6:30pm spring-fall) showcases the central coast's agricultural diversity with organic specialties that include sweet strawberries, artichokes, crafted goat cheeses, and vegetables.

To shop for souvenirs or local vintage wines, take a stroll along the **Santa Cruz Wharf** (21 Municipal Wharf, 831/420-5725, www.santacruzwharf.com, 5am-2am daily).

Surfers can find a huge selection of surfboards, sunglasses, and the famous O'Neill wetsuits at **O'Neill Surf Shop** (110 Cooper St. #100D, 831/469-4377, www. oneill.com, 10am-9pm Sun.-Thurs., 10am-10pm Fri.-Sat.).

Get a good book from **Bookshop Santa Cruz** (1520 Pacific Ave., 831/423-0900, www.bookshopsantacruz.com, 9am-10pm Sun.-Thurs., 9am-11pm Fri.-Sat.) to enjoy on the beach while working on your tan.

To see artwork by local artisans, visit **Artisans Gallery** (1368 Pacific Ave., 831/423-8183, www.artisanssantacruz. com, 10:30am-6:30pm daily.) downtown, which features wall art, jewelry, ceramics, metal work, and woodworking. Stop at **Dell Williams Jewelers** (1320 Pacific Ave., 831/423-4100, www.dellwilliams. com, 10am-5:30pm Mon.-Sat.) for classic to contemporary jewelry.

Foodies should visit **The True Olive Connection** (106 Lincoln St., 831/458-6457, www.trueoliveconnection.com, 10am-6pm daily), a family-owned retail boutique with over 35 delicious extra-virgin olive oils from around the world and 25 balsamic vinegars from Modena, Italy. Next door, let your hair down and go nuts over 120 different kinds of nuts, dried fruits, and other natural treats at **Nut Kreations** (104 Lincoln St., 831/431-6435, www.nutkreations.com, 11am-6pm Sun.-Thurs., 11am-8pm Fri.-Sat.).

Events

The second-largest gathering of "Woodies" in the world, **Woodies on the Wharf** (www.santacruzwoodies.com, late June, free) features more than 200 vintage and classic station wagons, celebrating these beauties with music, food, prizes, and good old-fashioned fun.

It just wouldn't be right if Santa Cruz wasn't host to some of the most recognized surf contests, such as the **O'Neill Coldwater Classic** (Steamer Ln., www.oneill.com, late Oct., free), an event that draws international boarders to Steamer Lane, a popular surfing spot in the West Cliff. **SCLU Longboard Invitational** (www.santa-cruz-longboard-union.com, free) rounds up nearly 200 longboarders from across the state each Memorial Day weekend to compete in the longest-running longboard surf contest. Hang out with the best surfers around, get some sun, and see who will win the title!

November hosts the **Santa Cruz Film Festival** (Del Mar and Rio Theaters, www.santacruzfilmfestival.com), which showcases independent films from all over the world.

The premier way to see the best art in Santa Cruz, **Open Studios Art Tour** (831/475-9600 ext. 17, www.artscouncilsc.org) displays the works of more than 300 artists during the first three weekends in October. An events guide ($10) and the Open Studios Art Tour app ($5) are handy tools that provide a glimpse of an artist's work and exhibit location.

Accommodations

For a romantic getaway, the old-world charm of the Italianate grand dame, ★ **West Cliff Inn** (174 W. Cliff Dr., 831/457-2200, www.westcliffinn.com,

From top to bottom: Pigeon Point Lighthouse; a surfer in Santa Cruz; the tiny Santa Cruz Surfing Museum.

$210-310), embodies a lavish experience with gas fireplaces, deep soaking tubs, and commanding ocean views.

It just feels right to stay at a hostel in Santa Cruz. You can avail yourself of the **HI-Santa Cruz Hostel** (321 Main St., 831/423-8304, $25-28 dorms, $60-75 private rooms), with dorm beds in an immaculate 1870s cottage. There are also private rooms and cheaper rooms that share a bathroom.

Reasonably priced places include the **Beachview Inn** (50 Front St., 831/426-3575, www.beach-viewinn.com, $115 and up) and the **Seaway Inn** (176 W. Cliff Dr., 831/471-9004, $110-270); both offer clean, comfortable rooms and are close to the beach, wharf, and Boardwalk. Just three blocks from downtown and close to the warm sand and crashing waves, the **Carousel Beach Inn** (110 Riverside Ave., 831/425-7090, www.carousel-beach-inn. com, $100 and up) is just steps away from the excitement of the Boardwalk's rides and amusements.

For a room with a spectacular view, you really can't go wrong at **Beach Street Inns & Suites** (125 Beach St., 831/423-3031, www.beachstreetinn.com, $180 and up); most of their rooms overlook Monterey Bay. Amenities include an on-site gourmet café and free guest parking, which is a nice bonus in a location across from the Boardwalk.

A quaint little gem is the **Adobe on Green B&B** (103 Green St., 831/469-9866, www.adobeongreen.com, $140 and up), with boutique accommodations and organic breakfasts in a quiet atmosphere. Stroll the garden grounds of **Babbling Brook** (1025 Laurel St., 831/427-2437, $200 and up); the rooms are decorated in the French country style and feature featherbeds and fireplaces. Adorned in hardwoods, Tiffany lamps, and open hearths, the **Darling House** (314 W. Cliff Dr., 831/458-1958, www.darlinghouse. com, $175 and up) is a 1910 oceanfront mansion with stunning views and grand rooms with private baths.

Walking distance to everything, **Pacific Blue Inn** (636 Pacific Ave., 831/600-8880, www.pacificblueinn. com, $190-290) offers environmentally friendly lodgings in a quiet courtyard hotel with free parking and bikes!

Information and Services

The **Santa Cruz Conference & Visitor Center** (303 Water St., Ste. 100, 831/425-1234, www.santacruz.org, 9am-4pm Mon.-Fri., 11am-3pm Sat.-Sun.) provides brochures, maps, and useful information to point you in the right direction.

Capitola

About 10 minutes south of Santa Cruz, the smaller community of **Capitola** (pop. 10,180) sits just far enough removed from the larger town to carve out a small beach-town feel all its own. A wood and iron train trestle marks the entrance to the small coastal village, recognizable by the brightly colored beach cottages sitting at the base of a small wharf, across Soquel Creek from the shops and bars of the bustling U-shaped Esplanade.

Note that paid parking within the village has a three-hour maximum, unless you carry a special permit offered by a local hotel (see www.cityofcapitola.org for info). Options farther from the beach allow parking for up to 12 hours.

Driftwood gathers where the creek splits **Capitola Beach** (The Esplanade, 831/475-6522, www.capitolasoquelchamber.com, sunrise-sunset) in two, where it's fronted by a beginner-friendly surf break. You may rent beach gear, including chairs, umbrellas and surf boards at **Capitola Beach Company** (131 Monterey Ave., 831/462-5222, www.capitolabeachcompany.com, 10am-6pm daily).

Gift boutiques and art galleries comprise many of the small shops around the Esplanade, including **Craft Gallery** (209 Capitola Ave., 831/475-4466, 10am-6pm daily), which showcases pottery, clocks, candles, sea glass, sandcastles, and jewelry boxes; and the ocean-polished baubles of **Village Sea Glass** (201 Monterey Ave., Ste. A, 831/464-3005, www.villageseaglass.com, 11am-5pm Wed.-Mon.).

At night, Capitola boasts a popular beach bar scene, as locals and visitors comingle as they bounce between several bars and restaurants along the Esplanade. Outside the village, the local craft beer scene has come into its own, led by the world-class Belgian-inspired farmhouse styles of **Sante Adairius Rustic Ales** (103 Kennedy Dr., 831/462-1227, www.rusticales.com, 3pm-8pm Tues.-Thurs., noon-8pm Fri.-Sat.). While that closes relatively early, the tasting continues at **Beer Thirty** (2504 S. Main St., 831/477-9967, www.bthirty.com, noon-10pm daily), a craft bottle shop and beer garden with tasty regional beers on tap to go with table tennis and other games.

The most central stay to the Esplanade is within the homey rooms of **Capitola Hotel** (210 Esplanade, 831/476-1278, www.capitolahotel.com, $225 and up). Or stay across the Soquel River, right on Capitola Beach, at the all-suites **Capitola Venetian Hotel** (1500 Wharf Rd., 831/476-6471, www.capitolavenetian.com, $169 and up).

Moss Landing

21 miles and 30 minutes south of Capitola, marked by the mammoth smokestacks of a power plant, **Moss Landing** (pop. 204) is home to **Elkhorn Slough** (1700 Elkhorn Rd., 831/728-2822, www.elkhornslough.org, 9am-5pm Wed.-Sun., trail fee), a large wetland area full of birds and otters. One of a few remaining wetland areas of its kind on the central coast, it's home to nine species of fish and over 200 species of waterfowl. While you can access the wetlands and bird habitats from CA-1 in Moss Landing, to get to the visitors center you must drive several miles into the agricultural backcountry. But once you're there, knowledgeable and dedicated rangers can provide you with all the information you need to spot your favorite birds and animals, plus find a few you've never seen before.

❧ CA-156: Castroville and San Juan Bautista

CA-156 passes through Monterey, San Benito, and Santa Clara Counties, overlapping US-101 for eight miles between Prunedale and San Juan Bautista. Considered to be the quickest route (along with US-101) from San Francisco Bay to the Monterey Peninsula, its westernmost two-mile stretch runs through the town of **Castroville** (pop. 6,481), culminating at the CA-1 interchange.

Aside from the 1947 Artichoke Queen, a title bestowed on a young woman then named Norma Jean Baker (better known to history as Marilyn Monroe), Castroville's claim to fame is growing the biggest artichokes. **The Giant Artichoke,** a resident 20-foot sculpture that has hovered over Merritt Street since the early 1960s, is a tribute to the town's farming talents and "artichoke thumb." Nearby, the **Giant Artichoke Restaurant** (11261 Merritt St., 831/633-3501, 7am-9pm daily) sells fried artichokes and other tasty green-layered creations.

The town lies three miles from the Pacific Ocean and 10 miles from Salinas in Monterey County. There is no direct access from CA-156 West to CA-1 North. Motorists heading west on CA-156 will need to exit at the CA-183 interchange to access CA-1. It is important to note that this is a highly traveled road that experiences delays due to congestion, and accidents are well documented along its meager length.

About 20 miles east of Castroville, past the US-101 junction with CA-156, is **San Juan Bautista** (pop. 1,975). This small town feels frozen in time—the buildings look like they could feature in an old western, and the state historic park at the center of town maintains four buildings from the 1800s. The town's most famous sight is one that never really existed. **Mission San Juan Bautista** (406 2nd St., 831/623-4528, www.oldmission-sjb.org, 9:30am-4:30pm daily, free) features prominently in Alfred Hitchcock's *Vertigo,* but the bell tower so central to the plot was fabricated for the movie.

Monterey

Originally inhabited by Native Americans who fished here, Monterey Bay became a fishing hub for the European settlers in the 19th century as well. Author John Steinbeck later immortalized its unglamorous fish-canning industry in his novel *Cannery Row.* It wasn't until the 20th century that the city began to lean toward gentrification. The bay became a wildlife preserve, the Monterey Bay Aquarium opened, and tourism became the mainstay of the local economy. Today, **Monterey** (pop. 28,454) is the big city on the well-populated southern tip of its namesake bay, 43 miles (about an hour) south of Santa Cruz (half that time from Moss Landing). It's plenty cosmopolitan, but a little more approachable than its high-class neighbor, Carmel.

The best days in Monterey are picture perfect: It's no wonder so many artists have been inspired to paint this land- and seascape. Wandering the twisting coastline, you'll see boats, kayaks, and otters playing along the bay. A bike and walking path connects all the major sights, making it easy and pleasant to visit them all in a day, without a car.

Getting There and Around

CA-1 runs through Monterey, providing access southward from Santa Cruz and northward through Big Sur. Southbound on US-101, at Prunedale, travel west on CA-156 to CA-1 South to Monterey.

The **Amtrak** (www.amtrak.com) Coast Starlight train stops in Salinas (30 minutes away) en route between Seattle, Washington, and Los Angeles, California. A free bus shuttles travelers from Salinas to the Monterey Transit Plaza.

Monterey Peninsula Airport (200 Fred Kane Dr., 831/648-7000, www.montereyairport.com) offers regular flights from San Francisco, Los Angeles, Phoenix, Las Vegas, and San Diego. Service providers include United, American, Alaska, and Allegiant Air.

Local bus service is provided by **Monterey-Salinas Transit** (888/678-2871, www.mst.org), with the towns of Carmel and Pacific Grove en route, as well as popular wineries. The Salinas **Greyhound** (www.greyhound.com) station also provides link service to Monterey.

Monterey's downtown operates trolleys that run every 10-15 minutes during the summer, holidays, and weekends (10am-7pm); however, many local area attractions, restaurants, and hotels are in walking distance.

Sights
★ Monterey Bay Aquarium

The first aquarium of its kind in the country, the **Monterey Bay Aquarium** (886 Cannery Row, 831/648-4800, www.montereybayaquarium.org, 9:30am-6pm daily Memorial Day weekend-Labor Day weekend, 10am-5pm daily rest of year, $50 adults, $30 children 3-12) is still unique in many ways. From the very beginning, the aquarium's mission has been conservation. It has taken custodianship of the Pacific coastline and waters in Monterey County down to Big Sur, playing an active role in the conservation of at-risk wildlife in the area. Many of the animals in the aquarium's tanks were rescued; those that survive may eventually be returned to the wild. All the exhibits

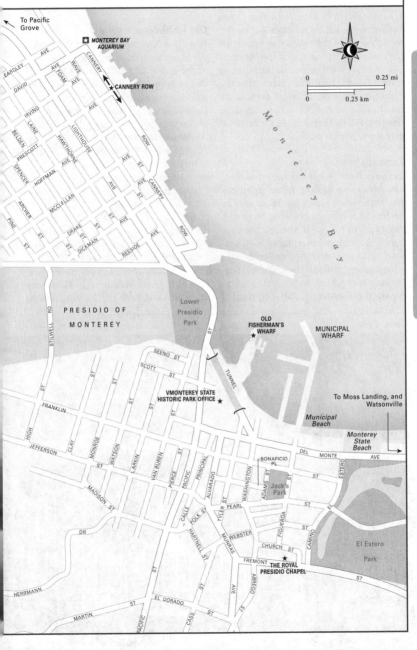

Monterey

To Pacific Grove

MONTEREY BAY AQUARIUM

CANNERY ROW

0   0.25 mi

0   0.25 km

EARDLEY

AVE

DAVID

WAVE

FOAM

AVE

CANNERY

IRVING

LANE

BELDEN

LIGHTHOUSE

HAWTHORNE

AVE

PRESCOTT

SPENCER

HOFFMAN

AVE

AVE

CANNERY

ARCHER

McCLELLAN

ST

PINE

DRAKE

AVE

ST

ST

DICKMAN

REESIDE

ROW

Monterey Bay

PRESIDIO OF

MONTEREY

Lower Presidio Park

STILWELL RD

ST

OLD FISHERMAN'S WHARF

MUNICIPAL WHARF

SEENO ST

SCOTT ST

ST

ST

TUNNEL

VMONTEREY STATE HISTORIC PARK OFFICE

To Moss Landing, and Watsonville

FRANKLIN

ST

Municipal Beach

HIGH

CLAY

MONROE

WATSON

LARKIN

VAN BUREN

PIERCE

PACIFIC

PRINCIPAL

ALVARADO

WASHINGTON

ADAMS

Monterey State Beach

JEFFERSON

ST

BONAFICIO PL

DEL MONTE AVE

ESTERO

MADISON ST

CALLE

POLK ST

TYLER

PEARL

Jack's Park

FIGUEROA

ST

CAMINO

EL

DR

HARTNELL ST

MINNAS

WEBSTER

ST

El Estero Park

HERRMANN

FREMONT

CHURCH ST

THE ROYAL PRESIDIO CHAPEL

ABREGO

ST

MARTIN

PACIFIC

EL DORADO

CASS

ST

ST

you'll see in this mammoth complex feature only local sea life.

The largest tank in the aquarium is a 1,200,000-gallon tank in the Open Sea galleries, which features one of the world's largest single-paned windows. In the peaceful jellyfish room, the balloon-like creatures drift through illuminated water. The highlight for many visitors, and often the most crowded area, is the sea otter experience. You can watch from two levels of windows to see the otters at play above water or below.

Cannery Row

Cannery Row (www.canneryrow.com) has American author John Steinbeck and his novel to thank for its name. The six blocks still resemble what Steinbeck described in his novel, though the canneries are long gone, replaced with seafood restaurants, shops, galleries, and wine-tasting rooms. The colorful, corrugated metal buildings remain, as do the overhead crossovers that connected

them to the nearby railway, which once transported Monterey sardines across the state.

Old Fisherman's Wharf

Watch sea lions and otters play in the harbor as working trawlers unload the catch of the day at **Old Fisherman's Wharf** (1 Old Fisherman's Wharf, www.monterey-wharf.com), a good place to embark on a glass-bottom boat tour or whale-watching excursion, or to eat and shop. Nearby, the **Wharf Marketplace** (290 Figueroa St., 831/649-1116, www.thewharfmarketplace.com, 7am-7pm daily) sits at the historic Standard Pacific Railroad Passenger Station, a pioneer in providing locally grown foods. It's the place to go for a firsthand look at the bounty produced by the surrounding farmlands.

Monterey State Historic Park

Probably the most concentrated historical area in Monterey is **Monterey State Historic Park** (20 Custom House

Cannery Row

Plaza, 831/649-7118, www.parks.ca.gov/mshp). The park encompasses the **Old Town Historic District,** a collection of old buildings and intriguing features, such as the whalebone sidewalk in front of the **Old Whaling Station** (391 Decatur St., 831/375-5356). One of the most interesting ways to explore the grounds is to follow the two-mile **Path of History,** marked by yellow plaques in the sidewalk. It offers a self-guided cell phone tour (831/998-9458) that leads to 55 historical sites, including adobes and the Royal Presidio Chapel, the oldest structure in Monterey. Maps and guidebooks are available at **Pacific House Museum** (10 Custom House Plaza, 831-649-7118, 10am-3pm Thurs.-Sun., free), where you can also see interactive exhibits chronicling the past of early Native American life. Learn about the town's booming whaling era, displayed in the **Museum of Monterey** (5 Custom House Plaza, 831/372-2608, www.museumofmonterey.org, 10am-5pm Sun.-Thurs., 10am-6pm Fri.-Sat., free), detailed through exhibits and old photographs.

Royal Presidio Chapel

A striking example of 18th-century Spanish colonial architecture, the **Royal Presidio Chapel** played a pivotal role as an outpost for the Spanish military in North America and is considered the most significant building in early California. The chapel is now known as the **Cathedral of San Carlos Borromeo** (500 Church St., 831/373-2628, www.sancarloscathedral.org, 2nd and 4th Mon. 10am-noon and 1:15pm-3:15pm, Wed. 10am-noon, Fri. 10am-3pm, Sat. 10am-2pm, Sun. 1pm-3pm, free) and is an active place of worship. Although the current structure was built in 1794, recent archaeology has revealed two previous structures, the oldest dating back to 1770, buried on the grounds and establishing the site as the earliest Christian place of worship in the state of California. To the south of the chapel bell tower—which includes the oldest non-indigenous sculpture in the state, *Our Lady of Guadalupe*—granite and rock footings of the 1770 stone chapel still lie beneath the dirt unseen. The ornate stone-cut doors of the east chapel entryway were once the original doors to the baptistery, demolished in 1868.

Follow the path that leads to the San Carlos School and the rectory of San Carlos Cathedral. To the right of the cathedral lies a statue of the Virgin Mary, and at the back of the building is a California landmark, the Junípero Oak, where missionary Junípero Serra declared California a Spanish territory in 1770.

Recreation

Cruise the bay and observe local marinelife, from sea lions to otters to migrating whales, on a tour provided by a charter company, such as **Princess Monterey Whale Watching** (96 Fisherman's Wharf #1, 831/372-2203 and

831/205-2370, www.montereywhale-watching.com, 8am-8pm daily, $45), or go deep-sea fishing for albacore, halibut, or sea bass with **J&M Sport Fishing** (66 Fisherman's Wharf, 831/372-7440 and 800/251-7440, www.jmsportfishing.com, 7am-5pm daily, $80 adults, $50 children 12 and under). **Monterey Bay Sailing** (78 Fisherman's Wharf #1, 831/372-7245, www.montereysailing.com, 9am-9pm daily, $39 and up) offers sailing cruises and rentals. Get on board the **Little Mermaid Glass Bottom Boat Tours** (101-199 Fisherman's Wharf, 831/372-7151) for a window seat into the sea.

Land lovers can hike the waterfront **Monterey Bay Coastal Recreation Trail,** an 18-mile paved adventure, from Castroville to Pacific Grove, which follows the same route as the old Southern Pacific Railway, connecting the Monterey Bay Aquarium, Cannery Row, the Museum of Monterey, and Fisherman's Wharf. Go by bike from **Cannery Row Rentals** (601 Wave St.,

750 Cannery Row, 831/655-2453, $8-39), with two Cannery Row locations offering rentals and tours.

If the life of a grape from vine to bottle sounds more intriguing, **Ag Venture Tours** (831/761-8463, www.agventure-tours.com, $50 and up) specializes in wine-tasting, sightseeing, and agricultural education tours. The tasting room at **Sovino Wine Bar & Merchant** (241 Alvarado St., 831/641-9463, 3pm-11pm daily) lets you simply relax and sample wines from throughout California.

Food

In downtown Monterey, the selection of restaurants is more down to earth than those in the Fisherman's Wharf/Cannery Row area.

A chili egg puff stuffed with three cheeses, incredible omelets, and outrageously divine banana nut pancakes are the reasons **Rosine's** (434 Alvarado St., 831/375-1400, www.rosinesmonterey. com, 8am-9pm Sun.-Thurs., 8am-10pm

Old Fisherman's Wharf

Fri.-Sat., $8-24) should be your first morning stop in the historical center.

For fresh-off-the-boat seafood, head to **Monterey's Fish House** (2114 Del Monte Ave., 831/373-4647, 11:30am-2:30pm, 5pm-9:30pm daily, $12-21), west of downtown. Excellent house-brewed beer goes with burgers and smoked meat sandwiches at **Alvarado Street Brewery** (426 Alvarado St., 831/655-2337, www.alvaradostreetbrewery.com, 11:30am-10pm Sun.-Thurs., 11:30am-11pm Fri.-Sat., $14-30).

Romantic **Epsilon** (422 Tyler St., 831/655-8108, www.epsilonrestaurant.com, 11am-2pm Mon.-Fri., 5pm-9pm Tues.-Sun., 5pm-9:30pm Tues.-Sun., $15-25) is a cozy Greek restaurant serving fantastic flavors of the Mediterranean. Another great date spot, **Alvarado Fish and Steak House** (481 Alvarado St., 831/717-4468, www.alvaradofishandsteakhouse.com, 5pm-10pm daily, 11:30am-10pm Tues. and Thurs.-Fri., $10-30) serves freshly caught seafood and choice steaks in an elegantly inviting atmosphere. **Montrio** (414 Calle Principal, 831/648-8880, www.montrio.com, 4:30pm-10pm daily, $16-30) is another entry in elegantly casual Monterey dining. The crab cakes are legendary.

The best place on the wharf is **Old Fisherman's Grotto** (39 Fisherman's Wharf, 831/375-4604, www.oldfishermansgrotto.com, 11am-10pm daily, $16-40). For over 50 years, the Shake family has run the wharf's premier restaurant as one of the most-sought-out eateries, serving top seafood dishes, Angus steaks, and award-winning wines in style and with a beautiful view.

Cannery Row has a number of restaurants offering waterfront dining. **The Sardine Factory** (701 Wave St., 831/373-3775, www.sardinefactory.com, 5pm-9:30pm daily, $28-60) first opened in 1968 and helped to revitalize the Cannery Row area. World leaders and celebrities have enjoyed the seafood dishes here, served in elegant surroundings.

Nightlife

Alvarado Street is a concentrated area of lively bars and pubs like **Lallapalooza** (474 Alvarado St., 831/645-9036, www.lalla-palooza.com, 4pm-11pm Sun.-Wed., 4pm-midnight Thurs.-Sat.), with an endless list of martinis. Don't miss dinner, cocktails, and live jazz at **Cibo Ristorante Italiano** (301 Alvarado St., 831/649-8151, www.cibo.com, 5pm-midnight daily). Taste artisanal cocktails in a vintage Parisian-style bar at **Hotel 1110** (1110 Del Monte Ave., 831/655-0515, www.hotel1110.com, 4pm-9pm Sun.-Thurs., 4pm-10pm Fri.-Sat.), which stays open late and has a rooftop lounge that overlooks the ocean.

You just can't beat a good British pub, and Monterey has a couple. **Crown & Anchor** (150 W. Franklin St., 831/649-6496, www.crownandanchor.net, 11am-1am daily) is where over 20 of the best international brews hang out, all in good company, and the **Britannia Arms**

(444 Alvarado St., 831/656-9543, www. britanniaarmsofmonterey.com, 11am-2am daily) is a place where nothing goes better with a good ale than live music and soccer.

On Cannery Row, **Blue Fin** (685 Cannery Row, 831/717-4280, www.blue-finbilliards.com, 11am-2am daily) lets you let your hair down with live DJs, tournament pool tables, and karaoke, while nearby, **Sly McFly's** (700 Cannery Row, 831/649-8050, www.slymcflysmonterey.com, 11:30am-12:30am Sun.-Thurs., 11:30am-1:30am Fri.-Sat.) is filled with the rhythms of jazz and blues.

In the Lighthouse District, **Carbone's** (214 Lighthouse Ave., 831/643-9169, www.lighthousedistrict.net, 3pm-2am daily) is a good old-fashioned neighborhood bar with pool, foosball, darts, live bands, and friendly people.

Arts and Entertainment

There are two **Monterey Museum of Art** locations (559 Pacific St., 831/372-5477, www.montereyart.org, 11am-5pm Thurs.-Mon., $10 adults, free 18 and under). One is in the heart of Old Monterey, which houses eight galleries filled with early American paintings, photography, and contemporary art. The other is in **La Mirada** (720 Via Mirada, 831/372-3689) but is only open for special events.

For soothing classics, **Monterey Symphony** (2560 Garden Rd., Ste. 101, 831/646-8511, www.montereysymphony. org) performs the works of the great composers and their contemporaries with both public appeal and intellectual merit.

A world-class concert and live theater venue, **The Golden State Theatre** (417 Alvarado St., 831/649-1070, www.golden-statetheatre.com) presents comedy, musicals, and more in a medieval-style castle.

Get a good laugh at Cannery Row's number one comedy club and bar, **Planet Gemini** (2110 N. Fremont St., 831/241-6805, www.planetgemini.com, 8pm-2am daily), featuring nationally known comedians and major stars! An intimate theater, **Bruce Ariss Wharf Theater** (Fisherman South Wharf #1, 831/649-2332) has become an icon for presenting classic plays and musicals to Monterey Bay and is one of the most respected supporters of the arts.

Races and other motor vehicle events take place throughout the year at **Laguna Seca Raceway** (1021 Monterey Salinas Hwy., 831/242-8200, www.mazdaraceway.com), including those pitting vintage cars from vastly distinct eras against each other.

Shopping

Shops line Fisherman's Wharf and Cannery Row, while independent stores dot Alvarado Street downtown.

For the souvenir shopper, Fisherman's Wharf has several variety stores. **Balesteri's Wharf Front** (6 Fisherman's Wharf #1, 831/375-6411, 10am-7pm Mon.-Thurs., 10am-8pm Sat.-Sun.) sells ocean-themed gifts and jewelry, while **Pirates Cove Gifts & Things** (42 Fisherman's Wharf #1, 831/372-6688) has all kinds of fun pirate novelties, knick-knacks, and clothing. Stop by the big pink building, better known as the **Harbor House Gifts** (1 Fisherman's Wharf #1, 831/372-4134), for truly unique gifts or just to see the world's largest hand-blown Venetian Murano glass chandelier.

For something that sparkles, **Monterey Bay Silver Company** (95 Fisherman's Wharf #1, 831/373-1515) shines up beautifully jeweled wearables; **Splash** (95 Fisherman's Wharf #1, 831/373-3434) lets you show off Swarovski crystal fashion jewelry; and **Morning Star Pearl** (95 Fisherman's Wharf #1, 831/373-8105) strands together lovely pearls for that special someone.

Cutting-edge resort wear and fashion jewelry at **California Classics** (750 Cannery Row, 831/324-0528) or color-changing apparel and accessories at **Del Sol** (660 Cannery Row, Ste. 109, 831/375-4786) both make shopping the Cannery a unique experience. For those cool coastal evenings, **Pacific Coast Clothing & Gifts Company** (685 Cannery Row, 831/375-9822) keeps you warm with outerwear.

Two floors of antiques are packed into an old 1920s cannery building at **Cannery Row Antiques** (471 Wave St., 831/655-0264, www.canneryrowantiquemall.com, 10am-5:30pm Mon.-Fri., 10am-6pm Sat., 10am-5pm Sun.), or head to Alvarado Street, where **LeBlanc Gallery** (271 Alvarado St., 831/372-7756, www.leblancgallery.com, 10am-6pm daily) features sculptures, fountains, and beautiful wind chimes, while the local artist-owned **Venture Gallery** (260 Alvarado St., 831/372-6279, www.venturegallery.com, 10am-6pm daily) offers all original paintings, sculptures, ceramics, pottery, and jewelry by Monterey artisans.

Events

Get inspired by the largest mammals of the sea at the annual **Whalefest Monterey** (1 Old Fisherman's Wharf, www.montereywharf.com, Oct.) and get acquainted with the wonderful work of Monterey Bay marine groups, including the Monterey Bay National Marine Sanctuary. Celebrate the past at the **History Fest** (831/655-2001, www.historicmonterey.org, early Oct., free), which showcases Monterey's role in California's early history with art and cultural activities at Monterey's historical locations, including Custom House Plaza, Historic Monterey, the Presidio of Monterey, the Royal Presidio Chapel, and Cannery Row. Tap your foot to the beat of the **Monterey Jazz Festival** (2004 Fairground Rd., www.montereyjazzfestival.org, Sept., $20 and up), one of the oldest jazz fests around, showcasing over 500 artists performing on eight stages spread over 20 acres.

The best poets, performers, and artisans come together every winter for the three-day **Cowboy Poetry and Music Festival** (831/649-5080, www.montereycowboy.com, Nov., $10 and up), featuring a Western dance night, art sale, "cowboy" church service, and many other festivities.

An eclectic mix of competitive events in the water and on the shore, **Monterey Beach Sportsfest** (831/383-8520, www.montereybeachsf.com, Oct., free) happens every October to celebrate wellness of the sea. It boasts a beer garden, food, lots of beach fun, and exciting sport competitions.

Accommodations

Lodgings in Monterey can be expensive, as it's a popular vacation spot, especially for weekending San Franciscans.

The **Monterey Hostel** (778 Hawthorne St., 831/649-0375, www.montereyhostel.org, $32 and up dorms, $59 and up private) offers inexpensive accommodations within walking distance of the major attractions of Monterey, but the dorm rooms can be pretty crowded.

A cute, small, budget motel, the **Monterey Bay Lodge** (55 Camino Aguajito, 831/372-8057, www.montereybaylodge.com, $135 and up) brings a bit of the Côte d'Azur to the equally beautiful coastal town of Monterey. With small rooms decorated in classic yellows and blues, the lodge makes a good base for the budget-minded when traveling in the Monterey region.

Upscale guest rooms at a reasonable price and all the comforts of home make **Hotel Abrego** (755 Abrego St., 844/857-8500, www.hotelabrego.com, $125 and up) a convenient place to put your feet up. Around the corner, **Casa Munras Hotel & Spa** (700 Munras Ave., 831/375-2411, www.hotelcasamunras.com, $159 and up) pampers guests in an adobe hacienda once owned by a 19th-century Spanish don. Next to the bay on Cannery Row, **Monterey Plaza Hotel and Spa** (400 Cannery Row, 877/862-7552, www.montereyplazahotel.com, $249 and up) combines elegant European architecture, dramatic coastal views, and refined style for a supremely memorable stay.

A waterfront resort, **Portola Hotel &**

Spa (2 Portola Plaza, 888/222-5851, www. portolahotel.com, $161 and up) is in the center of shopping, dining, and outdoor activities in Old Monterey. A boutique B&B, **Old Monterey Inn** (500 Martin St., 831/375-8284 and 800/350-2344, www. oldmontereyinn.com, $239 and up) features lavish rooms and suites on an estate surrounded by lush English gardens.

Information and Services
The **Monterey Visitors Center** (401 Camino El Estero, 800/555-6290, www. seemonterey.com, 9am-5pm daily) provides local information, maps, and brochures.

Pacific Grove

10 minutes west of Monterey, on the northern tip of the Monterey Peninsula, **Pacific Grove** (pop. 15,624) has earned the nickname Butterfly Town, U.S.A., due to the kaleidoscope of monarch butterflies that cluster in eucalyptus trees around the quaint seaside community each October after their migration south.

Sights
See the migrant butterflies at the **Monarch Grove Sanctuary** (250 Ridge Rd., 831/648-5716, dawn-dusk daily, free). Sanctuary docents are on-site noon-3pm daily to assist with monarch viewing and answer questions about the butterflies. There's no fee to get in, but donations are appreciated.

To learn more about the monarch butterflies as well as the birds, wildlife, plants, and geology of the area, visit the **Pacific Grove Museum of Natural History** (165 Forest Ave., 831/648-5716, www.pg-museum.org, 10am-5pm Tues.-Sun., $9 adults, $6 children 4-18).

Pacific Grove is the site of the oldest continuously operating lighthouse on the West Coast: **Point Pinos Lighthouse** (80 Asilomar Ave., 831/648-3176, www. pointpinoslighthouse.org, 1pm-4pm Thurs.-Mon., $2 adults, $1 children).

A community gallery, **Pacific Grove Art Center** (568 Lighthouse Ave., 831/375-2208, www.pgartcenter.org, noon-5pm Mon.-Sat., 1pm-4pm Sun., free) works to enhance art appreciation and encourage creative thinking, housing a large variety of art forms and exhibits.

Food and Accommodations
Pacific Grove's small-town feel extends to its eateries. A local favorite is **Peppers Mexicali Cafe** (170 Forest Ave., 831/373-6892, www.pepperspg.com, 11:30am-9pm Mon. and Wed.-Thurs., 11:30am-10pm Fri.-Sat., 4pm-9pm Sun., $14-20), where you'll see workers on their lunch breaks enjoying the fajitas and other south-of-the-border fare.

The Fishwife (1996 1/2 Sunset Dr., 831/375-7107, www.fishwife.com, 11am-9pm Sun.-Thurs., 11am-9:30pm Fri.-Sat., $12-23) serves seafood for lunch and dinner.

Unassuming Pacific Grove has landmark places to stay: **Asilomar** (800 Asilomar Blvd., 831/372-8016 or 888/635-5310, www.visitasilomar.com, $145 and up) was designed by architect Julia Morgan. A National Landmark, the **Centrella Inn** (612 Central Ave., 831/372-3372, www.centrellainn.com, $168 and up) oozes Victorian romance and charm, enchanting guests with luxurious bedding, antique decor, and the natural beauty of the nearby seashore.

Spectacular views come with every guest room at ★ **Seven Gables Inn** (555 Ocean View Blvd., 831/372-4341, www. thesevengablesinn.com, $229 and up), considered to be "One of the 10 Most Romantic Inns in America" by American Historic Inns. This boutique hotel features more than views: ornately lavished rooms, a complimentary full breakfast, afternoon wine and cheese, and the fragrant scent of surrounding gardens carried on the breeze.

★ 17-Mile Drive

Hugging the coastline between Pacific Grove and Pebble Beach, **17-Mile Drive** ($10/vehicle, cash only, no motorcycles) offers an introduction to some of the most beautiful and representative land and seascapes on the central coast. But don't get too excited yet—long ago, the locally all-powerful Pebble Beach Corporation realized what a precious commodity they held in this road and began charging a toll. The good news is that when you pay your fee at the gatehouse, you'll get a map of the drive that describes the parks and sights that you will pass as you make your way along the winding coastal road. These include the much-photographed Lone Cypress, the beaches of Spanish Bay, and Pebble Beach's golf course and resort. Stop at the many turnouts to take photos of the stunning ocean and the iconic cypress trees. You can picnic at many of the formal beaches, most of which have basic restroom facilities and ample parking lots. The only food and gas to be had are at the Inn at Spanish Bay and the Lodge at Pebble Beach. If you're in a hurry, you can get from one end of the 17-Mile Drive to the other in 20 minutes, but that would defeat the main purpose of taking 17-Mile Drive, which is to go slowly and stop often to enjoy the beauty of the area.

There are five entrance gates to 17-Mile Drive where you can pay the toll and receive the brochure (listed from north to south): **Pacific Grove Gate** (17-Mile Dr. just past CA-68), **Country Club Gate** (Forest Lodge Rd. at Congress Ave.), **S.F.B. Morse Gate** (Morse Dr. at CA-68), **Highway 1 Gate** (17-Mile Dr. at junction of CA-1 and CA-68), and **Carmel Gate** (N. San Antonio Dr. at 2nd Ave.).

From top to bottom: the colorful beachfront bungalows on Capitola Beach; Point Pinos Lighthouse in Pacific Grove; a shop in Carmel.

ⓕ CA-146: Pinnacles National Park

A 23-million-year-old geological phenomenon spewed into existence by a volcanic eruption that occurred 195 miles south in Southern California, **Pinnacles National Park** lies along the San Andreas Fault. Debris and erosion have formed the massive pillars and walls over time, but this majestic mountain's crowning glory is its two talus caves, composed from the large boulders that have fallen down into random piles.

The park was designated in January 2013, and it hosts several healthy populations of smaller animals, including bobcats, bats, the endangered California condor, and the highest bee variety in the world. Miles of hiking trails traverse the edges of an abundance of diverse habitat, offering ample wildlife viewing. Hike to **Balconies Cave** (9.4 miles round-trip) via Chalone Creek on the **Bench and Old Pinnacles Trails.** You can explore the cave (a flashlight is required) and marvel at the views of the largest rock formations in the park. Or, opt for the shorter **Balconies Cliffs-Cave Loop** (a flashlight is required), which, after crossing up to Balconies Cave, heads down to the Old Pinnacles Trail and through the cave. You may get wet, as wading may be necessary during winter months.

Other features of the park include **Bear Gulch Cave,** which is closed mid-May through mid-July to protect the park's colony of bats as they raise their young. The **campground** (reservations 877/444-6777, www.recreation.gov, $23 tents, $36 RVs) is near the east entrance and is open to tents and RVs. It is outfitted with picnic tables, electrical hookups, water, showers, bathrooms, a swimming pool (Apr.-Sept.), and a **store** (831/389-4538, 3pm-5pm Sun.-Thurs., 2pm-5pm Fri., 10am-4pm Sat.).

There are two entrances to the park, one to the west off US-101 at Soledad and the other to the east on CA-146.

The **Pinnacles National Park Visitor Center** (5000 CA-146, 831/389-4485, www.nps.gov/pinn/planyourvisit, 9am-5pm daily, $10 parking fee) provides information on ranger-led programs, hiking trails, and rock-climbing routes, and it has several displays on the geologic history of the region.

Carmel

It's not unusual to find English cottages, Spanish motifs, and other European accents in this adorable village perched on the cliffs above the Pacific. It's worth a stop just to walk the cottage-lined streets and meander in and out of its art galleries (the highest number per capita in the United States). **Carmel** (pop. 3,891) is also dog lover's central: Many hotels, shops, and even some restaurants allow them inside. It's worth staying longer to explore the golf courses and beach parks that surround the town.

Getting There and Around

CA-1 provides access to Carmel four miles south from Monterey or 15 miles north from Big Sur.

Amtrak (www.amtrak.com) runs a bus service to Carmel with stops to and from Monterey, as well as the Coast Starlight train, which provides coastline service.

The closest airline is **Monterey Peninsula Airport** (200 Fred Kane Dr., 831/648-7000, www.montereyairport.com), which provides flights from San Francisco, Los Angeles, Phoenix, Denver, and Salt Lake City, via United, American, US Airways, and Allegiant Air.

Carmel and its surrounding beaches are easily explored on foot. There is usually two-hour free parking. Bicycling is available, with visitors being reminded of the winding roads consisting of little to no shoulder space.

Local transit service is provided by

Carmel

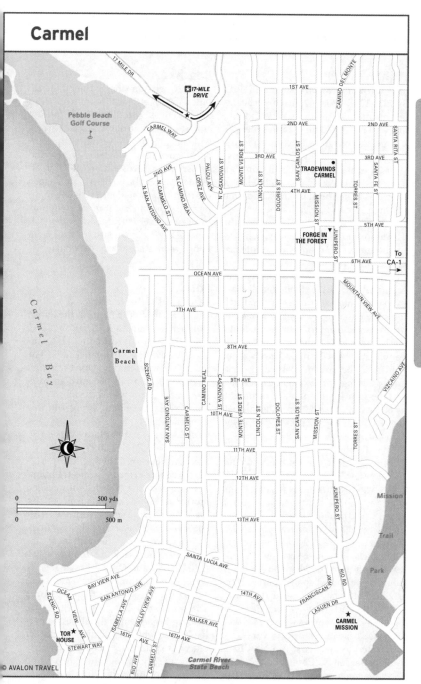

CARMEL

Monterey-Salinas Transit (888/678-2871, www.mst.org) between Carmel and Monterey.

Sights

The **Carmel Mission** (3080 Rio Rd., 831/624-1271, 9:30am-7pm daily, 9:30am-5pm winter, $6.50 adults, $2 children), just west of CA-1, a mile south of central Carmel, is considered the most beautiful mission of the 21 California missions. Formally named Mission San Carlos Borroméo del Río Carmelhe, it served as home, headquarters, and final resting place of Father Junípero Serra, the Franciscan priest who founded the 21 California missions. Today, he is entombed under the chapel floor, southeast of the altar; the site is marked with an inscription. Explore the mission and museums, which house exhibits and displays of Spanish colonial liturgical art and artifacts; the elaborate travertine marble and bronze Serra memorial cenotaph; and a Native American cemetery. Plan to dress conservatively as Catholic Masses occur regularly. The gardens—where on weekends wedding parties alight from limos to take family photos—are beautiful, as is the facade with its photogenic bell tower. This is the mission to visit if you visit only one.

The famous stone home of poet Robinson Jeffers, the **Tor House** (26304 Ocean View Ave., 831/624-1813, www.torhouse.org, hourly tours starting 10am-3pm Fri.-Sat., $12 adults, $7 children under 12) is the abode where Jeffers wrote all his most beloved poetical works—*The Women at Point Sur, Medea,* and others. Jeffers, who lived here between 1914 and 1962, built much of what you see out of boulders he hauled up by hand from the beach. Both the house and the tower, known as Hawk Tower, reflect the genius of the man whose ashes were spread with his wife's beneath a nearby yew tree.

Created by the artist Jim Needham, **Gravity Garden** (97 Corona Rd., 831/625-3099, open daily, free) is an intriguing garden of sculpture rock, some stacked up to nine feet, without the use of supporting structures or bolts.

Beaches

Friendly pets can run free along the 1.5 miles of **Carmel Beach** (bottom of Ocean Ave.). The **Scenic Bluff Path** follows along Scenic Road above Carmel Beach, which begins at 8th Avenue and meanders through rare Monterey cypress and landscaped gardens to Carmel Point, offering spectacular views of the rugged coastline. **Carmel River State Beach** offers bird-watchers the perfect opportunity to observe feathery residents at Carmel River Lagoon. Just north of Point Lobos, **Monastery Beach** is a popular diving area.

Food

Perfect dishes have attracted visitors and locals to ★ **The Forge in the Forest** (Junipero St. and 5th Ave., 831/624-2233, www.forgeintheforest.com, 11:30am-11pm daily, $14-34) for decades. The menu is overwhelming. Don't miss out on the stuffed portobello with crab, rosemary, and Cajun spices; the lobster linguini with tarragon; or award-winning clam chowder.

Breakfast at **Katy's Place** (Mission St. and 6th Ave., 831/624-0199, www.katysplacecarmel.com, 7am-2pm daily, $12-22) is a self-described "Carmel tradition" that can get quite crowded on weekend mornings. With a range of menu options, you're sure to find your favorite, whether you love eggs Benedict or Belgian waffles.

For a rare hole-in-the-wall local dining experience, seek out **Tommy's Wok** (Mission St. and Ocean Ave., 831/624-8518, www.tommyswokcarmel.com, 11:30am-2:30pm and 4:30pm-9:30pm Tues.-Sun., $10-20). All the veggies are fresh and organic, and the dishes taste reliably good whether you dine in or order takeout to enjoy elsewhere.

If you're just looking for a good burger, **R.G. Burgers** (201 Crossroads

Wine-Tasting: Carmel

More than a dozen tasting rooms scattered throughout the village of Carmel showcase the wines of the agricultural region to its east. The local chamber of commerce offers a **Wine Tasting Passport** (Carmel Plaza, 2nd floor, on Ocean Ave. between Junipero and Mission, www.carmelchamber.org, 10am-6pm, $100), which may be purchased in person at the chamber office or ahead of time online. The passport offers four tastes at each of 10 tasting rooms of your choosing—each within walking distance of one another. Note that most of the tasting rooms operate between 11am and 6pm.

Blvd., 831/626-8054, www.rgburgers. com, 11am-8:30pm Sun.-Thurs., 11am-9pm Fri.-Sat., $10-15) is the best. Their shakes and sandwiches aren't bad either! For pizza with a perfect crust, **Allegro Gourmet Pizzeria** (Big Sur Barn, 3770 The Barnyard, 831/626-5454, www.allegrogourmetpizzeria.com, 11:30am-9pm Mon.-Thurs., 11:30am-9:30pm Fri.-Sat., noon-9pm Sun., $10-25) offers fabulous gourmet pizza and a wide selection of classic Italian entrées.

For Mediterranean-inspired cuisine, dine at **Cafe Stravaganza** (241 Crossroads Blvd., 831/625-3733, www. cafestravaganza.com, 8am-9pm daily, $14-25), which serves generous portions and gourmet pizza you can't resist! Stylish and romantic, **PortaBella** (Ocean Ave., 831/624-4395, 11:30am-10pm Sun.-Thurs., 11:30am-9:30pm Fri.-Sat., $26-36) has an undeniable ambience and fantastic dishes inspired by the Mediterranean countryside.

Nightlife

Carmel has a few traditional bars and pubs along with its handful of wine and cocktail bars.

Sade's (Lincoln St. between Ocean Ave. and 7th Ave., 831/624-0787, 11am-2am daily) offers cocktails in a casual, friendly atmosphere. Located inside the Cypress Inn, **Terry's Lounge** (7th Ave. and Lincoln St., 831/624-3871, www.carmelterrys.com, noon-11pm Sun.-Thurs., noon-midnight Fri.-Sat.) is a relaxing venue for drinks and live music. Referred

to as one of Carmel's "Hidden Gems" by *Monterey Peninsula*, **Brophy's Tavern** (San Carlos St., 831/586-5566, www.brophystavern.com, 11am-11pm daily) offers a pub menu, which includes their popular Philly cheesesteak, beer, and drink specials.

For exceptional margaritas and a festive atmosphere, stop by **Baja Cantina & Grill** (7166 Carmel Valley Rd., 831/625-2252, 11:30am-midnight Mon.-Fri., 10am-midnight Sat.-Sun.) and have a cocktail on the heated patio, or grab a beer and watch a sporting event.

Andre's Bouchee Bistro and Wine Bar (Mission St. and 7th Ave., 831/626-7880, www.andresbouchee.com, 5:30pm-9:30pm daily) is a chic French restaurant that features a nice little wine bar with an exceptional selection. **Mundaka** (7th Ave. and San Carlos St., 831/624-7400, 5pm-9:30pm daily) offers wine, music, and Spanish-style tapas.

With over-sized chairs, a mahogany bar, and two large flat-screen TVs, **Fuse Lounge** (3665 Rio Rd., 831/624-1841, www.carmelmissioninn.com, 5pm-10pm daily) is a fusion of sophistication and casual ambience, featuring specialty cocktails, wine, and great live music.

Shopping

Carmel Plaza (Ocean Ave. and Mission St., 831/624-0138, www.carmelplaza.com, 10am-6pm Mon.-Sat., 11am-5pm Sun.) is a shopping must for elegant and fashionable items. A boutique with a Euro flare, **Pamplemousse** (Ocean Ave. between

Mission St. and San Carlos St., 831/624-1259, www.pamplemousseboutique.com, 10am-6pm Mon.-Sat., 11am-5pm Sun.) is an elegant find, offering contemporary clothing, accessories, and jewelry. **The Club** (Ocean Ave. between San Carlos St. and Dolores St., 831/625-1645, www.theclubcarmel.com, 10am-6pm daily) is a premier designer clothing and accessories boutique. For the finest cashmere, **Carmel Cashmere & Co.** (San Carlos St. and 6th Ave., 831/624-0595, www.carmelcashmere.com, 10am-5:30pm Tues.-Sat.) sells the purest high-quality cashmere in fashion and blankets. If your four-legged best buddy needs some new duds or a new toy for the beach, hop to **Diggidy Dog** (Mission St. between Ocean Ave. and 7th Ave., 831/625-1585, www.diggidydog.com, 10am-6pm Mon.-Thurs., 10am-7pm Fri.-Sat., 11am-5pm Sun.).

Exquisitely unique, the **Cayen Collection** (NW Mission St. between 5th Ave. and 6th Ave., 831/626-2722, www.cayenjewelers.com, 10am-6pm Mon.-Sat., 11am-5pm Sun.) will make you want to drape yourself in jewels. There is just too much beauty in this one shop.

The Cheese Shop (Ocean Ave. and Mission St., Carmel Plaza, 831/625-2272, www.thecheeseshopinc.com, 10am-6pm Mon.-Sat., 11am-5:30pm Sun.) is filled with every deliciously cheesy gourmet treat and sophisticated wine imaginable.

Ooh and aah your way through **Conway of Asia** (Dolores between Ocean Ave. and 7th Ave., 831/624-3643, www.conwayofasia.com, 10am-6pm Mon.-Sat., 11am-5pm Sun.), a world imports shop filled with beautiful antiques and contemporary Hindu, Buddhist, and Christian statuary, paintings, artifacts, furniture, carpets, and architectural antiquities.

Events

The annual **Carmel Mission Fiesta** (Carmel Mission Courtyard, Rio Rd. and Lasuen Dr., 831/624-8322, fall, free) celebrates the tradition of community with Mexican food, live music, and handmade arts and crafts.

From mermaids to castles and everything imaginable, Carmel's **Sand Castle Contest** (south of 10th Ave., 831/620-2020, Sept./Oct.) is an amazing event that takes over the shore each fall.

Accommodations

Accommodations in Carmel tend toward the quaint or luxurious.

Egyptian cotton linens, luxurious goose-down feather beds, silk pillows, spa tubs, Japanese *tansu* wet bars and vanities, and antique and custom furniture from Bali and China are just a few reasons why ★ **Tradewinds Carmel** (Mission St. at 3rd Ave., 831/624-2776, www.tradewindscarmel.com, $250 and up) has been called one of the most glamorous hotels in *Architectural Digest* and voted as one of the world's top inns by *Coastal Living*, but isn't it better to experience the best for yourself?

Lobos Lodge (Monte Verde Ave. and Ocean Ave., 831/624-3874, www.loboslodge.com, $255 and up) sits right in the midst of downtown Carmel-by-the-Sea, making it a perfect spot from which to dine, shop, and admire the endless array of art in this upscale town. Each of the 30 rooms and suites offers a gas fireplace, a sofa and table, a bed in an alcove, and enough space to stroll about and enjoy the quiet romantic setting. Do be aware that Lobos Lodge bills itself as an adult retreat. While families with children can stay here, expect to pay extra for more than two guests in your room, and there is little in the way of child-friendly amenities.

The historical **Pine Inn** (Ocean Ave. and Monte Verde Ave., 831/624-3851, www.pineinn.com, $189 and up) offers elegant, boutique accommodations in downtown within walking distance to the ocean.

A pet-friendly B&B, **Carmel Country Inn** (Dolores St., 831/625-3263 and

800/215-6343, www.carmelcountryinn.com, $245 and up) features intimate studios and large suites with luxury baths, along with a daily breakfast buffet.

An exquisite mansion built in 1905, **La Playa Carmel** (8th Ave. and Camino Real, 831/624-6476 and 800/582-8900, www.laplayahotel.com, $380 and up) offers a historical experience of elegant gardens and intimate patios and courtyards just steps from Carmel Beach.

A resort of splendor set among acres of bountiful beauty, **Carmel Valley Ranch** (1 Old Ranch Rd., 855/687-7262, www.carmelvalleyranch.com, $475 and up) indulges guests with a cozy in-room fireplace, breakfast in bed, hot tubs throughout the property, an 18-hole golf course, access to hundreds of miles of hiking trails, mountain-top yoga, and so much more.

Information and Services

The **Carmel Chamber of Commerce & Visitor Center** (Ocean Ave. between Junipero and Mission, 831/624-2522 and 800/550-4333, www.carmelchamber.org, 10am-5pm daily) is the best resource for local visitor information.

Point Lobos State Reserve

Three miles south of Carmel-by-the-Sea, **Point Lobos State Reserve** (62 CA-1, 831/624-4909, www.parks.ca.gov/pointlobos, 8am-sunset or 7pm, whichever is earlier, daily, $10 per car) is known as one of the most beautiful parks in the state park system, offering hikes through forestland and along the beach, scuba diving (831/624-8413) off the shore, picnic spots, and nature study. The dramatic scenery, resident marine and shore life, and one of the last groves of Monterey cypress in existence are just a few of the natural attractions. Take a walk through unique ecosystems and observe the indigenous wildlife while strolling through the rugged landscape. Binoculars will help you see creatures offshore (such as otters!).

A small whaling cabin, first used by Portuguese whalers from the Azore Islands in 1861, is located at the southeast end of Whalers Cove. When whaling oil dropped in the 1880s due to kerosene lamps, the local industry dwindled but was briefly revived in 1897 when a Japanese company moved in; that operation lasted only a few years. The cabin is now the **Whalers Cabin Museum** (831/624-4909, 9am-5pm daily), which houses documents and equipment as well as old try pots used to boil whale blubber and the skeletal fragments of a 100-year-old fin whale.

Limits on the number of visitors in the park mean that there may be a line to get in. Try to arrive early to avoid the wait. Be aware that from July through September fog often dims the summer sun at Point Lobos, even midday. Spring and fall are the best times to visit, weather-wise.

Big Sur

The natural scenery and breathtaking vistas make **Big Sur** (pop. 839) one of the highlights of the entire Pacific Coast Highway. The rugged yet peaceful area contains boundless wilderness and 90 miles of staggeringly beautiful coastline. CA-1 twists around mountains and clings to rocky cliffs as it navigates the rugged coast between Carmel and San Simeon.

Practicalities

The Big Sur region is sparsely populated and can feel remote. Less than 300 hotel rooms exist here, there are only three gas stations, and no supermarkets or fast-food restaurants. There is essentially one road in and one road out: CA-1 (California State Route 1, also known as Highway 1). The highway can be treacherous due to its winding character, but

Big Sur

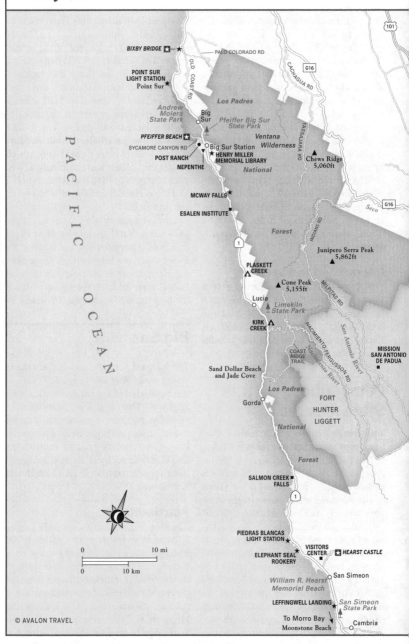

BIXBY BRIDGE

PALO COLORADO RD

OLD COAST RD

CACHAGUA RD

G16

101

POINT SUR
LIGHT STATION
Point Sur

Andrew
Molera
State Park

Los Padres

Big
Sur

Pfeiffer Big Sur
State Park

PFEIFFER BEACH

SYCAMORE CANYON RD

Big Sur Station

Ventana
Wilderness

TASSAJARA RD

Chews Ridge
5,060ft

POST RANCH

HENRY MILLER
MEMORIAL LIBRARY

NEPENTHE

National

PACIFIC

MCWAY FALLS

ESALEN INSTITUTE

Seco

G16

Forest

Junipero Serra Peak
5,862ft

1

PLASKETT
CREEK

Cone Peak
5,155ft

MILPITAS RD

Lucia

Limekiln
State Park

San Antonio River

KIRK
CREEK

NACIMIENTO-FERGUSSON RD

Nacimiento River

OCEAN

COAST
RIDGE
TRAIL

San Antonio River

MISSION
SAN ANTONIO
DE PADUA

Sand Dollar Beach
and Jade Cove

Los Padres

FORT

Gorda

HUNTER

National

LIGGETT

Forest

SALMON CREEK
FALLS

1

PIEDRAS BLANCAS
LIGHT STATION

VISITORS
CENTER

HEARST CASTLE

ELEPHANT SEAL
ROOKERY

San Simeon

William R. Hearst
Memorial Beach

San Simeon
State Park

LEFFINGWELL LANDING

To Morro Bay
Moonstone Beach

Cambria

0   10 mi

0   10 km

© AVALON TRAVEL

PCH: Under Construction

California's undeveloped coastline can be as scary as it is beautiful. In a state that's prone to earthquakes, wildfires, and landslides, it's always important to know what road conditions lie ahead.

For example, in 2016, wildfires consumed sections of the forest near Big Sur, leaving hillsides exposed to unusually heavy winter rains. These rains created massive mudslides that took out a bridge to the north of town and buried a section of the PCH south of town. Consequently, 26 miles of Big Sur were inaccessible for most of 2017.

To prevent your epic road trip from becoming an epic failure, always check current road conditions before you start driving. **Current PCH conditions** can be found on the Caltrans website (www.dot.ca.gov) or by calling the Caltrans Highway Information Network (800/427-7623).

especially when fog sets in and visibility drops.

The biggest concentration of travel necessities, such as lodging, food, and gas, is in the town of Big Sur, about 25 miles, or an hour, south of Carmel. Otherwise, places to rest and fill up are few and far between until you reach Cambria.

Most options for food are provided by hotels and resorts, and many close by 9pm. Prices can be quite high for what you get (you won't find cheap here).

Accommodations are limited for an area that draws an estimated three million visitors each year, which explains the high room rates. There is little to no cell phone reception, and in some cases, no television network providers. **Big Sur Campground and Cabins** offers a wide range of camping options that put you right on the Big Sur River. There is no shortage of things to do, and the **Big Sur Chamber of Commerce** (47500 CA-1, 831/667-2100, www.bigsurcalifornia.org, 9am-1pm Mon., Wed., and Fri.) has everything needed to help you decide.

Getting There and Around

Big Sur is a remote area accessible only by CA-1 via US-101 South to CA-156 West to CA-1 or visa US-101 North to CA-1. When roads are open, the easiest way to get there is by car, but gas stations are scarce (and expensive), so remember to fill up before entering the Big Sur region.

Monterey-Salinas Transit (888/678-2871, www.mst.org) route 22 runs from downtown Monterey to Nepenthe in Big Sur, and stops at several area state parks. Or take the convenient **Central Coast Day Tripper** (831/657-9442 and 831/241-2526), which runs along the Big Sur and Monterey Peninsula.

Bicycling CA-1 is common but can be dangerous due to the many turns and lack of shoulder space.

The nearest airport, **Monterey Regional Airport** (200 Fred Kane Dr. #200, 831/648-7000, www.montereyairport.com), is about 30 miles away.

Food

Most food options are inside resorts, hotels, and inns. Reservations are pretty much the norm or at least a necessity during peak season, and many places stop seating by 9pm.

★ **Nepenthe** (48510 CA-1, 831/667-2345, www.nepenthebigsur.com, 11:30am-9pm daily, $15-46) offers a short but tasty menu of meats, fish, and plenty of vegetarian dishes, but the real feast is the sweeping view—be sure to ask for a table outdoors. Located below Nepenthe, the seasonal **Cafe Kevah** (48510 CA-1, 831/667-2344, 9am-4pm daily, $8-18) offers a similar sampling of food at slightly lower prices. The view of the Pacific steals the show here, too.

Big Sur has some good breakfast spots. **Big Sur Bakery & Restaurant** (47540 CA-1,

831/667-0520, www.bigsurbakery.com, 8am-9pm daily, $8-26) offers all the regular morning favorites, including baked goodies. If you prefer a view with your morning meal, **Big Sur Lodge Restaurant & Espresso House** (47225 CA-1, 831/667-3111, www.bigsurlodge.com, 8am-9:30pm daily, $11-32) is on the banks of the Big Sur River with views of redwoods.

Lucia Lodge (62400 CA-1, 831/667-2391 and 866/424-4787, www.lucialodge.com, 11am-8pm Mon.-Fri., 11am-9pm Sat.-Sun., $21-38) has excellent fish-and-chips. If you want a good burger, **Redwood Grill** (47200 CA-1, 831/667-2129, 11:30am-9pm daily, $12-26) serves buffalo burgers, salmon burgers, veggie burgers, and, of course, beefy burgers.

North of Big Sur Village, **Fernwood Bar & Grill** (47200 CA-1, 831/667-2129, www.fernwoodbigsur.com, 11:30am-9pm daily, $13-18) is a local hangout for meeting friends for a drink, playing table tennis, and listening to good music.

Accommodations

Campgrounds and hotels/resorts are the overnight options in Big Sur. Many do not have cell phone service, and reservations are required.

Just south of Lucia and Limekiln State Parks, **Kirk Creek Campground** (CA-1, 805/434-1996 and 877/444-6777, www.recreation.gov, $35 per night) is a reservation-only campsite located in Los Padres National Forest, offering campsites right on a bluff overlooking the ocean. Trails lead down to the dog-friendly beach, bluffs that overlook the beach, and coves in the area. Cross the highway from the campground to access the Vicente Flats Trailhead, which leads into the Ventana Wilderness. There are bathrooms but no running water. At **Big Sur Campground and Cabins** (47000 CA-1, 831/667-2322, www.bigsurcamp.com, $60-75 tents, $130-175 tent cabins, $195-430 cabins) you have a choice between campsites, tent cabins, and rustic cabins, in a quiet setting along the Big Sur River, which offers

the coastline in Big Sur

swimming, inner-tubing, or just drifting with the gentle flow.

Big Sur River Inn (46840 CA-1, 831/667-2700 and 800/548-3610, www.bigsurriverinn.com, $150 and up) offers 20 cabin-style guest rooms, a full-service restaurant, and a heated pool. About a mile south of Big Sur River Inn, **Fernwood Resort** (CA-1, 831/667-2422, www.fernwoodbigsur.com, campsites $60-80, cabins $250, motel rooms $150 and up) includes a 12-room motel, a small grocery-cum-convenience store, a restaurant, and a tavern that is, relatively speaking, the local nighttime hot spot. Farther down the small road, you'll find the campgrounds, which include tent cabins as well as tent and RV sites.

Deetjens Big Sur Inn (48865 CA-1, 831/667-2377, www.deetjens.com, $105-270) is a rustic inn set among beautiful gardens, the redwoods, and the Castro Canyon waterfall. Overlooking the Pacific Ocean, **Ventana Inn & Spa** (48123 CA-1, 831/667-2331 and 800/628-6500, www.ventanabigsur.com, luxury camping $325 and up, rooms $475 and up) is a luxurious resort offering suites, villas, cottages, and luxury camping, or "glamping," sites, combining a high-end stay with stunning scenery.

Information and Services

Big Sur Chamber of Commerce (47500 CA-1, 831/667-2100, www.bigsurcalifornia.org, 10am-7pm Sun.-Fri.) provides local area information and travel brochures. For outdoor recreational information, **Big Sur Ranger Station** (47555 CA-1, 831/667-2315, 9am-4pm daily) offers maps, important area information, and services.

Check out **CalTrans** weather reports by calling the free hotline (888/836-0866), especially to avoid getting caught driving in morning fog.

Be aware that cell service is not reliable along the remote area of the coast. Gasoline is also limited, and those few stations that operate along the highway can be extremely expensive.

Garrapata State Park

Just off CA-1, seven miles south of Carmel, **Garrapata State Park** (on CA-1, 831/649-2836, www.parks.ca.gov) often goes unnoticed. It is marked with a single sign on the west side of the road, between mile markers 63 and 67, and features pristine coastline, colorfully diverse flora and fauna, and trails that run from the beaches and into groves of redwood. The Rocky Ridge Trail offers commanding views of the Pacific and Santa Lucia Mountains, as well as views of sea lions, sea otters, and gray whales.

The area was once the home of the Ohlone and Rumsien tribes and then became the residence of cows and sheep owned by Ezequiel Soberanes in the early 1900s, and later the Doud family. These names still live on within the park in Soberanes Point and Doud River.

★ Bixby Bridge

Eleven miles north of Big Sur Village, **Bixby Bridge** is an iconic landmark, spanning 713 feet in length. Like many bridges along CA-1, Bixby Bridge is a single-span concrete deck arch design, but it is considered one of the highest in the world. Concrete was chosen instead of steel because it was cheaper and reduced maintenance costs; the fact that concrete blended with the color and composition of the natural rock cliff made it all the more desirable.

Construction began in 1931; its many laborers were prisoners hoping to shave some time off their sentences. It was completed a year later.

Today the bridge is considered one of the most photographed due to its attractive design and, of course, its location. You can snap a photo from the north side of the bridge at the pull-off.

Andrew Molera State Park

The first "Big Sur" park you'll encounter is **Andrew Molera State Park** (CA-1, 20 miles south of Carmel, 831/667-2315, www.parks.ca.gov, day-use $10). Once home to small camps of Esselen Native Americans, then a Spanish land grant, this chunk of Big Sur eventually became the Molera ranch. Today, the **Molera Ranch House Museum** (831/667-2956, http://bigsurhistory.org/museum.html, 11am-3pm Thurs.-Sun. mid-June-Labor Day, free) displays stories of the life and times of Big Sur's human pioneers and artists as well as the wildlife and plants of the region. Take the road toward the horse tours to get to the ranch house.

The park has numerous hiking trails that run down to the beach and up into the forest along the river; many of these are open to biking and horseback riding as well. Most of the park trails lie to the west of the highway. The beach is a one-mile walk down the easy, multi-use **Trail Camp Beach Trail.** From there, climb on

Bixby Bridge

the **Headlands Trail,** a 0.25-mile loop, for a beautiful view from the headlands. To get a better look at the Big Sur River, take the flat, moderate **Bobcat Trail** (5.5 miles round-trip) and perhaps a few of its ancillary loops. You'll walk right along the riverbanks, enjoying the local microhabitats. Just be sure to look out for bicycles and the occasional horse and rider. For an even longer and more difficult trek up the mountains and down to the beach, take the eight-mile **Ridge Bluff Loop.** You'll start at the parking lot on the Creamery Meadow Beach Trail, then make a left onto the long and fairly steep Ridge Trail to get a sense of the local ecosystem. Then turn left again onto the Panorama Trail, which runs down to the coastal scrublands, and finally out to the Bluffs Trail, which takes you back to Creamery Meadow.

At the park entrance, you'll find bathrooms but no drinkable water and no food concessions. If you're camping here, be sure to bring plenty of your own water for washing dishes as well as drinking. If you're hiking for the day, pack in bottled water and snacks.

Pfeiffer Big Sur State Park

The biggest, most developed park in Big Sur is **Pfeiffer Big Sur State Park** (47225 CA-1, 26 miles south of Carmel, 831/667-2315, www.parks.ca.gov, day-use $10). It's got the **Big Sur Lodge,** a restaurant and café, a shop, an amphitheater, a softball field, plenty of hiking-only trails, and lovely redwood-shaded campsites. This park isn't situated by the beach; it's up in the coastal redwoods forest, with a network of roads that can be driven or biked up into the trees and along the Big Sur River.

Pfeiffer Big Sur contains **Homestead Cabin,** once the home of part of the Pfeiffer family, the first European immigrants to settle in Big Sur. Day-trippers and overnight visitors can take a stroll through the cabins of the Big Sur Lodge, built by the Civilian Conservation Corps during the Great Depression.

For a starter walk, take the easy 0.7-mile **Nature Trail** in a loop from Day Use Parking Lot 2. Grab a brochure at the lodge to learn about the park's plant life as you walk the trail. For a longer stroll, head out on the popular **Pfeiffer Falls Trail** (1.5 miles round-trip). You'll find stairs on the steep sections and footbridges across the creek, then a lovely platform at the base of the 60-foot waterfall, where you can rest and relax midway through your hike. For a longer, more difficult, and interesting hike deeper into the Big Sur wilderness, start at the Homestead Cabin and head to the **Mount Manuel Trail** (10 miles round-trip, difficult). From the Y intersection with the Oak Grove Trail, it's four miles of sturdy hiking to Mount Manuel, one of the most spectacular peaks in the area.

This is one of the few Big Sur parks to offer a full array of services. Before you head out into the woods, stop at the Big Sur Lodge restaurant and store complex to get a meal and some water, and to load up on snacks and sweatshirts. Between the towering trees and the summer fogs, it can get quite chilly and somewhat damp on the trails.

★ Pfeiffer Beach

Some of the most dramatic views in Big Sur are seen at **Pfeiffer Beach** (accessed via Sycamore Canyon Rd., about 0.25 mile south of Big Sur), one of the most photographed spots, especially at sunset.

The stunning brilliance of **Keyhole Arch** at Pfeiffer Beach possesses a mystical power that captures the imaginations of those who see it. Professional and amateur photographers from all over the world try time and again to preserve the piercing beam of glory that radiates the cavern void, like a small door opening to heaven, just before the setting sun in the weeks surrounding winter solstice. The arch measures 20 feet by 20 feet and was not formed by human hands but by nature. The conditions for the awe-inspiring event are dependent on the sun's positioning directly behind the opening, a clear sky, and when the tide has aligned to a high enough position to reflect the natural light of ocean waters.

Hidden on an isolated stretch of CA-1 in Big Sur, and down an unmarked one-lane road (Sycamore Canyon Rd.), Pfeiffer Beach is not the easiest to find, but you'll kick yourself later if you miss out on its impressive rock formations, sea caverns, and unusual purple sands, and most assuredly if you pass on the opportune moment to witness the natural phenomenon at Keyhole Arch.

Post Ranch Inn and Ventana

Two luxury properties sit essentially across the street from one another at the south end of Big Sur. ★ **Post Ranch Inn** (47900 CA-1, 800/527-2200, www.post-ranchinn.com, $825-1,225) is perched on the cliffs of Big Sur on the west side of CA-1. The unique design of the resort makes the structures seem like they are

McWay Falls at Julia Pfeiffer Burns State Park

a part of the natural landscape, flowing around the curves, rather than leveling them off. Spa, yoga, and a rustic atmosphere are just a few of its perks.

On the other side of CA-1, **Ventana** (48123 CA-1, 831/667-2331 or 800/628-6500, www.ventanainn.com, $600-2,450) is a place where the panoramic ocean views begin in the parking lot. Picture home-baked pastries, fresh yogurt, in-season fruit, and organic coffee delivered to your room in the morning, then imagine enjoying that sumptuous breakfast outdoors on your own private patio overlooking a wildflower-strewn meadow that sweeps out toward the blue-gray waters of the ocean. And that's just the beginning of an unbelievable day at the Ventana.

The guest rooms range from the "modest" standard rooms with king beds, tasteful exposed cedar walls and ceilings, and attractive green and earth tone appointments, all the way through generous and gorgeous suites to multi-bedroom

houses. You'll reach your room by walking along the paved paths, which are crowded by lush landscaping, primarily California native plants that complement the wild lands of the trails behind the main hotel buildings.

Dining at the elegant **Sur House** restaurant is one way to get a bit of Ventana's luxury without committing to the price of a room.

Henry Miller Memorial Library

Henry Miller lived and wrote in Big Sur for 18 years, and one of his works is titled for the area. Today the **Henry Miller Memorial Library** (48603 CA-1, 831/667-2574, www.henrymiller.org, noon-8pm daily) celebrates the life and work of Miller and his brethren in this quirky community center/museum/coffee shop/gathering place. The library is easy to find as you drive either north or south on CA-1—look for the hand-painted sign and funky fence decorations. What you won't find is a typical lending library, bookshop, or slicked-up museum. Instead, you'll wander the lovely sun-dappled meadow, soaking in the essence of Miller's life here; come inside and talk to the docents about the racy novels Miller wrote; and maybe sit back with a cup of coffee to meditate on life, art, and isolated gorgeous scenery. The library offers a glimpse into Big Sur as an artists' colony that has inspired countless works by hundreds of people.

Julia Pfeiffer Burns State Park

One of the best-known and easiest hikes in all of the Big Sur region sits in **Julia Pfeiffer Burns State Park** (CA-1, 37 miles south of Carmel, 12 miles south of Pfeiffer Big Sur State Park, 831/667-2315, www.parks.ca.gov, $10/vehicle). The **Overlook Trail** runs only two-thirds of a mile round-trip, along a level wheelchair-friendly boardwalk. Stroll under CA-1, past the Pelton wheelhouse, and out to the observation deck and the stunning view of **McWay Falls.** The medium-sized waterfall cascades year-round off a cliff and onto the beach of a remote cove, where the water wets the sand and trickles out into the sea. The water of the cove gleams bright cerulean blue against the just-off-white sand of the beach. Anyone with an ounce of love for the ocean will want to build a hut right there beside the waterfall. But you can't—in fact, the reason you'll look down on a pristine and empty stretch of sand is that there's no way down to the cove that's even remotely safe.

The tiny Pelton wheel exhibit off the Overlook Trail describes what a Pelton wheel is and what it does. No other museums make their homes here, though there's a small visitors center adjacent to the parking lot.

If you want to spend all day at Julia Pfeiffer Burns State Park, drive north from the park entrance to the Partington Cove pullout and park along the side of the highway. On the east side of the highway, start out along the **Tanbark Trail** (6.4 miles round-trip, difficult). You'll head through redwood groves and up steep switchbacks to the top of the coastal ridge. Be sure to bring your camera to record the stunning views before you head back down the fire road to your car.

Esalen Institute

Visitors journey from all over the state and beyond to the **Esalen Institute** (55000 CA-1, 831/667-3000, www.esalen.org), sometimes called "The New Age Harvard." It's a forerunner and cutting-edge player in ecological living; a space to retreat from the world and build a new and better sense of self.

One of the biggest draws of the institute sits down a rocky path right on the edge of the cliffs overlooking the ocean. The clothing-optional bathhouse includes a motley collection of mineral-fed hot tubs looking out over the ocean—you can choose the Quiet Side or the Silent Side to sink into the water and contemplate the Pacific Ocean's limitless expanse, meditate on a perfect sunset or arrangement of stars, or (on the Quiet Side) get to know your fellow bathers.

Esalen is also the home of the California massage technique. If you are not staying at the retreat, a **massage** ($165 for those staying off-site) at Esalen will give you access to the baths for an hour before and after your treatment. You can also try to get one of the 20 **public access spots** (reservations 831/667-3047, $25) that are available nightly 1am-3am.

Piedras Blancas

75 miles from Big Sur and atop a rugged point, **Piedras Blancas Light Station** (15950 CA-1, 805/927-7361, www.piedrasblancas.org, Tues., Thurs., and Sat. 9:45am, $10 adults, $5 children) first illuminated its light in 1875 to guide mariners along the rocky California coast. The lighthouse was built on indigenous land that was later claimed by Mission San Miguel, about 50 miles inland, and was eventually passed to the U.S. Coast Guard in 1937. Today, visitors can tour the lighthouse and explore the cultural and natural history.

About two miles south of the lighthouse, the **Northern Elephant Seal Rookery** (four miles north of Hearst Castle entrance on CA-1, 805/924-1628, www.elephantseal.org) is a spot where elephant seals have gathered since the 1990s. In the winter months, the seals come here to breed, and in the summer months they molt. Winter is the best time to view the males, females, and newborn pups. There is a large parking area with viewing spot signs, along with a boardwalk where a guide is available 10am-4pm to provide information and answer questions.

San Simeon

Driving from north to south, **San Simeon** (pop. 462) marks the end of the Big Sur coast, about 80 miles south of Carmel. Although the most dramatic parts of the California coast are behind you, there are still plenty of sights to behold, including one of the most famous: Hearst Castle. In fact, the tiny town of San Simeon was founded to support the construction efforts up the hill at Hearst Castle. The town dock provided a place for ships to unload tons of marble, piles of antiques, and dozens of workers.

Sights
★ Hearst Castle

There's nothing else in California quite like **Hearst Castle** (750 Hearst Castle Rd., 800/444-4445, www.hearstcastle. org, 9am-close daily). Newspaper magnate William Randolph Hearst conceived of the idea of a grand mansion in the Mediterranean style, on the land his parents bought along the central California coast. His memories of camping on the hills above the Pacific led him to choose the spot on which the castle now stands. He hired Julia Morgan, the first female civil engineering graduate from UC Berkeley, to design and build the house for him. She did a brilliant job with every detail, despite the ever-changing wishes of her employer. By way of decoration, Hearst assisted in the relocation of hundreds of European medieval and Renaissance antiquities, from tiny tchotchkes to whole gilded ceilings. William Randolph also adored exotic animals, and created one of the largest private zoos in the nation on his thousands of central coast acres. Though most of the zoo is gone now, you can still see the occasional zebra grazing peacefully along CA-1 to the south of the castle, acting as heralds to the exotic nature of Hearst Castle ahead.

The visitors center is a lavish affair with a gift shop, restaurant, café, ticket booth, and movie theater. Here you may view the much-touted film *Hearst Castle—Building the Dream,* which offers an overview of the construction and history of the marvelous edifice, and of William Randolph Hearst's empire. Shuttles going up the hill to the castle board here; no private cars are allowed on the roads up to the castle proper. In order to get on the shuttle, you will need a ticket for a tour, which can be purchased at the visitors center, as long as spaces are available. Advance tickets (http://hearst.reservecalifornia.com) are recommended, and tours may be purchased up to 56 days prior to your visit.

There are four tours, each focusing on different spaces and aspects of the castle: Grand Rooms Tour, Upstairs Suites Tour, Cottages & Kitchen Tour, and the Evening Tour. The day tours ($25 adults, $12 children) are 45 minutes, and after the tour, you can walk around parts of the castle, such as the gardens and pools, before the shuttle back. The Evening Tour ($36 adults, $18 children), which is seasonal, is 100 minutes long, with volunteers dressed in 1930s fashion.

Beaches

The **William Randolph Hearst Memorial State Beach** (750 Hearst Castle Rd., San Simeon, 805/927-2020, www.parks. ca.gov/hearstsansimeonsp, dawn-dusk daily) is just across from the entrance to Hearst Castle, and offers beautiful coastline views off a 1,000-foot wooden pier, surrounded by sandy beaches. Fishing is permitted off the pier without a license, but limits are enforced. There are plenty of picnic areas and hiking and kayaking opportunities. The park also encompasses the **Coastal Discovery Center** (San Simeon, 805/927-6575, www.montereybay.noaa.gov, 11am-5pm Fri.-Sun. and holidays, free), which offers educational and interactive exhibits that highlight the cultural and natural history of the area.

Food and Accommodations

San Simeon has a few places to stay that are convenient for visiting Hearst Castle. The **San Simeon Lodge** (9520 Castillo Dr., 805/927-4601, www.sansimeonlodge.net, $70-160) is a 60-unit motel near Hearst Castle and the beach. It's a very good value, though the accommodations are simple and basic. **Best Western Cavalier Oceanfront Resort** (9415 Hearst Dr., 805/927-4688, www.cavalierresort.com, $150-280) was built in 1965 and makes for a comfortable stay. Of the 90 available, the best rooms face directly to the ocean, and each room has binoculars for admiring the landscape.

The **San Simeon Beach Bar & Grill** (9520 Castillo Dr., 805/927-4604, www.sansimeonlodge.net, 7am-10pm Sun.-Thurs., 7am-1am Fri.-Sat.) has a pool table, TVs, and live music.

Cambria

Located roughly 10 miles south of Hearst Castle, **Cambria** (pop. 6,032) owes much of its prosperity to that giant attraction. But this small beach town becomes surprisingly spacious when you start exploring it. Plenty of visitors come here to ply Moonstone Beach, peruse the charming downtown area, and just drink in the laid-back, art-town feel.

Getting There and Around

Traveling south on CA-1, Cambria sits directly south of San Simeon. If traveling southbound via US-101, take CA-46 west. From the south, take the San Luis Obispo exit onto CA-1 Morro Bay/Hearst Castle and continue to Cambria.

The closest **Amtrak** station is in Paso Robles (800 Pine St., 800/872-7245, www.amtrak.com), about 30 miles east, and another is 35 miles south in San Luis Obispo (1011 Railroad Ave.).

San Luis Obispo Regional Transit Authority (179A Cross St., 805/781-4472, www.slorta.org, $1.50 one-way) runs between Morro Bay to Hearst Castle, stopping in Cayucos and Cambria via Route 15.

Sights

While William Randolph Hearst built one of the most expensive homes ever seen in California, local eccentric Arthur Harold Beal (a.k.a. Captain Nit Wit or Der Tinkerpaw) got busy building the cheapest "castle" he could. **Nitt Witt Ridge** (881 Hillcrest Dr., 805/927-2690, $10, by appointment only) is the result of five decades of scavenging trash and using it as building supplies to create a multi-story home like no other on the coast. Today, you can make an appointment with owners Michael and Stacey O'Malley to take a tour of the property. (Please don't just drop in.)

One of Cambria's oldest homes, the Guthrie-Bianchini House is the site of the **Cambria Historical Museum** (2251 Center St., 805/927-2891, http://cambriahistoricalsociety.com/museum.html, 1pm-4pm Fri.-Sun., 10am-1pm Mon., free). Built in 1870, the house was later sold to Benjamin Franklin, rumored to be a relative of the Benjamin Franklin who helped draft the Declaration of Independence and the U.S. Constitution, among a number of other historic acts. Today, it preserves exhibits on Cambria's treasures of the past, including an oar from the lifeboat of the *S.S. Montebello,* which was sunk off the coast of Cambria on December 23, 1941.

A National Historic Registry Landmark, **The Old Santa Rosa Chapel** (2353 Main St., 805/927-1175, www.santarosachapel.com, 10am-3pm Fri.-Mon., free) is one of the oldest churches in the county. It rests on a hilltop among a pine and oak forest near an old pioneer cemetery. Although the chapel's final Mass was in 1963, this pristine white church built of pine draws couples for wedding

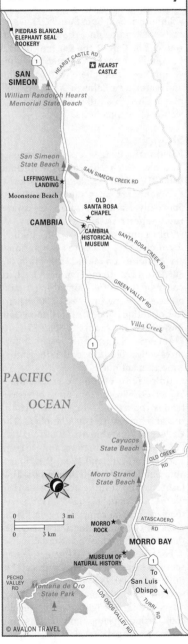

Cambria to Morro Bay

PIEDRAS BLANCAS
ELEPHANT SEAL
ROOKERY

HEARST CASTLE RD

HEARST
CASTLE

SAN
SIMEON

William Randolph Hearst
Memorial State Beach

San Simeon
State Beach

SAN SIMEON CREEK RD

LEFFINGWELL
LANDING

Moonstone Beach

OLD
SANTA ROSA
CHAPEL

CAMBRIA

CAMBRIA
HISTORICAL
MUSEUM

SANTA ROSA CREEK RD

GREEN VALLEY RD

Villa Creek

PACIFIC

OCEAN

Cayucos
State Beach

OLD CREEK
RD

Morro Strand
State Beach

0   3 mi

0   3 km

MORRO
ROCK

ATASCADERO
RD

MORRO BAY

MUSEUM OF
NATURAL HISTORY

To
San Luis
Obispo

PECHO
VALLEY
RD

Montaña de Oro
State Park

LOS OSOS VALLEY RD

TURRI RD

© AVALON TRAVEL

ceremonies, families for special celebrations, and curious visitors interested in the town's early settlement roots.

Recreation

For breathtaking views of seascapes, wildlife, and tidepools, stroll the **Moonstone Beach Boardwalk,** which follows along the cliffs; stairs take you down to the beach. Although you won't find moonstone here, you will find plenty of agates, and possibly jasper and California jade. On the northern end of Moonstone Beach, **Leffingwell Landing** (San Simeon-Monterey Creek Rd.) offers spectacular views for the amateur or professional photographer, and is a wonderful area to explore tidepools and marinelife.

Fiscalini Ranch Preserve (CA-1 to Windsor, past Shamel Park, 805/927-2856, www.ffrpcambria.org) offers one of the most popular trails, **Bluff Trail,** which is a continuation of the California Coastal Trail and offers awe-inspiring ocean views from almost every direction. It is a fairly easy walk, including both a paved pathway and boardwalk. Bikes are allowed on specified trails only, and pets must be leashed.

Food

Fine dining Parisian-style is what ★ **Madeline's** (788 Main St., 805/927-4175, 5pm-9pm daily, $22-46) is all about. An exquisite menu, local boutique wines, and an intimate setting make it the perfect evening out.

A quirky garden setting and expansive ocean views make for memorable meals at **Centrally Grown** (7432 Exotic Garden Dr., 805/927-3563, www.centrallygrown. com, 8am-9pm daily, $22-40), from casual breakfasts on the ground floor through full table service in the dining room upstairs.

For the authentic flavors of Mexico, try **Medusa's Real Mexican Food** (1053 Main St., 805/927-0135, www.medusas-cambria.com, 7am-8pm Mon.-Sat., under $10) or **Las Cambritas** (2336 Main St.,

805/927-0175, 11:30am-9pm daily, $11-24), which has all the spicy south-of-the-boarder dishes you love, plus mixed drinks and exceptional service.

Dragon Bistro (2150 Center St., 805/927-1622, 11am-9pm daily, $12-20) offers good Chinese food, large portions, and great prices. **The Sow's Ear** (2248 Main St., 805/927-4865, www.thesowsear.com, 5pm-9pm daily, $19-31) does its best to create the proverbial "silk purse" dining experience, with upscale comfort foods and dim, romantic lighting.

A very popular stop, **Sea Chest Restaurant & Oyster Bar** (6216 Moonstone Beach Dr., 805/927-4514, 5:30pm-9pm Wed.-Mon., $18-42) is one of the best seafood restaurants around and offers beautiful waterfront views. The dining room fills up fast. It's cash only.

Nightlife and Entertainment

Enjoy draft beer, pool, and $3 hot dogs at **Mozzi's Saloon** (2262 Main St., 805/927-4767, www.mozzissaloon.com, 1pm-2am daily), in a historical building reminiscent of the cowboy days. For a good cocktail or specialty drink, go to **Moonstone Beach Bar & Grill** (6550 Moonstone Beach Dr., 805/927-3859, www.moonstonebeach.com, 11am-3pm and 5pm-9pm Mon.-Sat., 9am-3pm and 5pm-9pm Sun.), or for a full bar and one of the best Bloody Marys around, drop by **West End Bar and Grill** (774 Main St., 805/927-5521, www.westendcambria.com, 10am-2am Mon.-Fri., 8am-2am Sat.-Sun.), a hub for meeting up with friends for a drink or watching a game on one of four TVs.

For music and $1 pints, **The Cambria Pub & Steakhouse** (4090 Burton Dr., 805/927-0782, www.thecambriapub.com, 11am-midnight daily) brings in a good-sized happy hour crowd. For eclectic entertainment, **Cambria Pines Lodge** (2905 Burton Dr., 805/927-4200, www.cambriapineslodge.com, 5pm-9pm daily) offers music including folk, rock, jazz, and even karaoke.

Immerse yourself in the dramatic and the comedic at **Pewter Plough Playhouse** (824 Main St., 805/927-3877, www.pewterploughplayhouse.org, showtimes 7:30pm Fri.-Sat., 3pm Sun., $22), which casts outstanding stage productions year-round. The **Cafe-Piano Bar** (no cover) is just off the lobby of the theater, providing an intimate atmosphere with soft lights and featuring a Baldwin "parlor grand" piano. There is a full wine bar and a selection of premier beers.

Shopping

Filled with vintage treasures from over 30 dealers, **Rich Man Poor Man Antique Mall** (2110 Main St., 805/203-5350, www.richmanpoormanantiques.com, 10am-5pm daily) features furniture, glassware, rugs, tapestries, art, and jewelry, all within a unique two-floor, loft building. A couple other places to shop antiques are **Antiques on Main** (2338 Main St., 805/927-4292, 10am-5pm daily), where you're bound to find something to take home after browsing over 10,000 square feet of antique goods, and **Hidden Gate Antiques** (2261 Main St., 805/975-5140, 11am-4pm Thurs.-Sun.), which features collectible 18th- and 19th-century American antiques.

Dolce Yogurt & Boutique (801 Main St., 805/927-2638, 11am-6pm) offers delicious yogurt and women's fine clothing and accessories in one place. **The Gallery of Wearable Art** (4009 West St., 805/927-1005, www.gowacambria.com, 11am-5pm Mon. and Wed.-Sat., 11am-4pm Sun.) dresses you in one-of-a-kind fashions and unique accessories. **The Place** (2336 Main St., 805/927-1195, www.theplacecambria.com, 10am-6pm) is *the* place for classic clothing and accessories that are comfortable and affordable.

For specialty gifts and distinctive souvenirs, **A Matter of Taste in Cambria** (4120 Burton Dr., 805/927-0286, www.amatteroftastecambria.com, 10am-5pm daily) offers culinary delights for the gourmet cook, including jams and sauces, baking mixes, serving dishes, kitchen gadgets, and cookbooks. **Exotic Nature** (2535 Village Ln., 805/927-8423 and 888/562-7903, www.exoticnature.com, 11am-3pm Mon.-Thurs., 10am-4pm Fri.-Sat.) is a wonder of gift options that include custom scented lotions, aromatherapy, soaps, candles, and clothing. For beautifully created jewelry, **Hauser Brothers Goldsmiths** (2060 Main St., 805/927-8315, www.hausergold.com, 11am-6pm Mon.-Sat.) has been making it more than four decades, offering "Joel's Collection" and other fashionable treasures.

Events

Over 420 lively and whimsical scarecrows decorate the streets of Cambria's West and East Villages every October during **Cambria Scarecrow Festival** (805/395-2399, www.cambriascarecrows.com), a unique month-long event unlike anything else in the United States, with pie-eating contests, fun tours, and more.

Accommodations

A favorite even among the many inns of Cambria, the **Olallieberry Inn** (2476 Main St., 805/927-3222, www.olallieberry.com, $155-210) sits in a charming 19th-century Greek Revival home and adjacent cottage. Each of the nine rooms features its own quaint Victorian-inspired decor with comfortable beds and attractive appointments. A full daily breakfast (complete with olallieberry jam) rounds out the comfortable experience.

Hotels line the road running along Moonstone Beach, and all of the following embrace the nighttime chill by providing in-room fireplaces for optimally romantic conditions. Stylish **Cambria Beach Lodge** (6180 Moonstone Beach Dr., 805/927-4624, www.cambriabeachlodge.com, $120-300) offers an updated take on the roadside

From top to bottom: the polished stones of Cambria's Moonstone Beach; Elephant Seals at the Piedras Blancas Elephant Seal colony; Bishop Peak, San Luis Obispo.

motel, providing complimentary bikes and beachy decor. **Cambria Landing Inn & Suites** (6530 Moonstone Beach Dr., 805/927-1619, www.cambrialanding.com, $150-260) adds ocean views and private balconies. The small, sophisticated **El Colibri Boutique Hotel & Spa** (5620 Moonstone Beach Dr., 805/924-3003, www.elcolibrihotel.com, $140-260) immerses guests in luxury with spa therapies and exclusive wines combined with rejuvenating rooms and atmosphere. Finally, the cozy beach cottages of **Fireside Inn** (6700 Moonstone Beach Dr., 805/927-8661, www.firesideinncambria.com, $130-250) offer private terraces, jet tubs, and warm fireplaces.

Moonstone Cottages (6580 Moonstone Beach Dr., 805/927-1366, www.cambriainns.com, $240-380) offers the perfect hideaway to enjoy a sunset from a quaint cottage, with lofted ceilings and Cape Cod-style furnishings. Set along the shores of the central coast, **Pelican Inn & Suites** (6316 Moonstone Beach Dr., 805/927-1500, www.pelicansuites.com, $140-280) offers a quiet retreat with tailored guest services and comfortable accommodations.

Information and Services
Cambria Chamber of Commerce and Visitor Center (767 Main St., 805/927-3624, www.cambriachamber.org, 9am-5pm Mon.-Fri., noon-4pm Sat.-Sun.) offers extensive area information and visitor services.

Cayucos

Fifteen miles south of Cambria, most of what the little resort town of **Cayucos** (pop. 2,592) offers revolves around its beach: swimming, surfing, kayaking, and skin diving are popular, and there's a pier for rock fishing and surf fishing year-round at Estero Bay.

Most of the restaurants are located along Ocean Avenue. **Schooners** (171

massive Morro Rock in Morro Bay

N. Ocean Ave., 805/995-3883, www. schoonerswharf.com, 11am-9pm Sun.-Thurs., 11am-9pm daily, $12-26) is a great spot for seafood. Just in front of the beach, **Ruddell's Smokehouse** (101 D St., 805/995-5028, www.smokerjim.com, 11am-6pm daily, $6-10) offers smoked fish in sandwiches, salads, or stuffed into spongy flour tortillas for delicious, quick eats. Private vacation rentals abound in Cayucos, but more traditional accommodations include the central, beachfront, and pet-friendly **Shoreline Inn** (1 N. Ocean Ave., 805/995-3681, www.cayucosshore-lineinn.com, $125-200) and the charming **On the Beach Bed & Breakfast** (181 N. Ocean Ave., 805/995-3200, www.californiaonthebeach.com, $150-250), with ocean views and easy access to the beach.

Morro Bay

Six miles south, **Morro Bay** (pop. 10,648) is part of a coastal California that seems

to be vanishing. It's not fancy or pretentious here, and hasn't been overbuilt with trendy shops and hotels. The atmosphere is languid; visitors can stroll along the Embarcadero to the call of sea lions, browsing the small shops and snacking on saltwater taffy. You're just as likely to see veteran fisherfolk walking around town as tourists.

The defining geographical feature of Morro Bay is the impressive ancient volcanic and sacred Chumash Indian site called **Morro Rock,** an unmistakable round formation rising out of the bay. You cannot climb on it since it's home to endangered peregrine falcons. The **Museum of Natural History** (20 State Park Rd., 805/772-2694, 10am-5pm daily, $3 adults, free children under 16) has a great location in the back bay, near the marina, with a view of the rock. It's a small, kid-friendly museum, with touch exhibits about sand, waves, and animals and a good assortment of stuffed birds, like the peregrine falcon, and a massive albatross dangling from the ceiling. There's also a full-sized skeleton of a minke whale on the outside deck overlooking the bay.

Frankie and Lola's (1154 Front St., 805/771-9306, www.frankieandlolas. com, 6:30am-2:30pm daily, $8-14) serves breakfast and lunch in a small, deliberately low-key space. It is one of the few places to open early, should you need breakfast before you leave town. You can see the rock while you enjoy the creative food, like French toast that is dipped in crème brûlée and mixed with whole nuts. For the largest tacos you've ever seen, hit local favorite **Taco Temple** (2680 Main St., 805/772-4965, www.tacotemple.com, 11am-9pm daily, $14-30), especially the fresh local catch—do not try to tackle a burrito on your own! Otherwise, for seafood, try **The Galley** (899 Embarcadero, 805/772-7777, www.galleymorrobay.com, 11am-2:30pm and 5pm-8pm daily, $18-38), which offers dishes like pan-seared scallops and simple presentations of swordfish, ahi tuna, and ono.

Morro Bay is a good place to shop for vintage finds, thanks to a high concentration of antique shops. Most are found along Morro Bay Boulevard, east of Main Street, or head north on Main Street to explore the charming art deco structure housing **Morro Bay Antiques** (1612 Main St., 805/225-1620, www.morrobayantiques.com, 10am-5pm daily).

Morro Bay is a relaxing place to spend the night. The **Sundown Inn** (640 Main St., 805/772-7381, www.sundownmotel.com, $75-100) is a budget choice, with few amenities except for a coffeemaker in the room and a Wi-Fi signal. The rooms are standard size and minimally decorated, but clean and comfortable. The conveniently located eight-room **Estero Inn** (501 Embarcadero, 805/772-1500, www.esteroinn.com, $140-200) has well-appointed rooms.

San Luis Obispo

Going 14 miles south from Morro Bay, CA-1 turns inland and merges with US-101 at **San Luis Obispo** (pop. 47,536), known as SLO to locals. Though the sleepy community often lives up to its nickname, it's also a university town—home to the California Polytechnic University, San Luis Obispo (Cal Poly)—and students contribute to a lively evening vibe. Most of the action takes place in a compact downtown district, particularly along Higuera Street, where restaurants and bars feature back patios along the banks of the charming, tree-lined San Luis Obispo Creek.

Getting There and Around

Access by car is from US-101/CA-1, which runs through town. The two highways merge from points north at San Luis Obispo, then split apart again to the south, in Pismo Beach.

San Luis Obispo County Regional Airport (901 Airport Dr., 805/781-5205) is a commercial airport with flights to Los Angeles, San Francisco, and Phoenix. Car rentals are available.

The **Amtrak** station is in downtown (1011 Railroad Ave., 800/872-7245, www.amtrak.com), with service from Seattle to Los Angeles via Coast Starlight, and to Santa Diego on the Pacific Surfliner.

San Luis Obispo Regional Transit Authority (179 Cross St., 805/781-4833, www.slorta.org, $1.50 one-way) operates bus routes throughout the region, including to Paso Robles, San Simeon, Cambria, Morro Bay, and Pismo Beach.

Most everything in SLO's downtown area is within walking distance, and in cases where walking is not preferred, county bus lines run consistently throughout town.

Sights

Just west of US-101 at the foot of town, the **Madonna Inn** (100 Madonna Rd., 805/543-3000, www.madonnainn.com) is a remarkable example of what architecturally minded academic types like to call vernacular kitsch. Created by local contractor Alex Madonna, who died in 2004, the Madonna Inn offers over 100 unique rooms, each decorated in a wild barrage of fantasy motifs. Bright pink honeymoon suites are known as "Just Heaven" and "Love Nest." The "Safari Room" is covered in fake zebra skins above a jungle-green shag carpet. The name of the "Cave Man Room" speaks for itself (Yabba dabba doo!). *Roadside America* rates the Madonna Inn as "the best place to spend a vacation night in America." Even if you can't stay, at least stop for a look at the gift shop, which sells postcards of the different rooms. Guys should head down to the men's room, where the urinal trough is flushed by a waterfall.

Built in 1772, **Mission San Luis Obispo de Tolosa** (751 Palm St., 805/781-8220, www.missionsanluisobispo.org, 9am-5pm daily summer, 9am-4pm daily winter, $2 donation) is the fifth California mission founded by Junípero Serra, and

San Luis Obispo and Vicinity

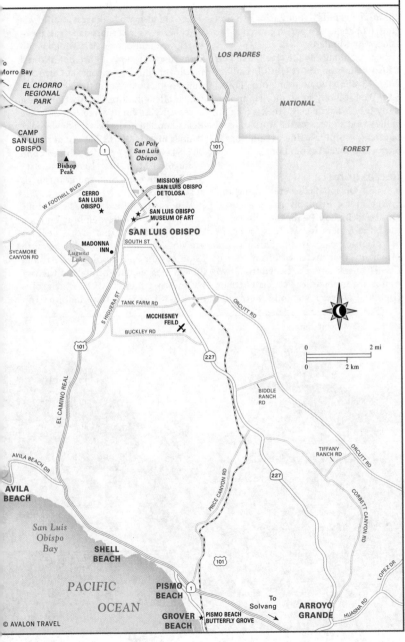

LOS PADRES

To Morro Bay

EL CHORRO REGIONAL PARK

CAMP SAN LUIS OBISPO

NATIONAL

Bishop Peak

Cal Poly San Luis Obispo

FOREST

1

101

MISSION SAN LUIS OBISPO DE TOLOSA

W FOOTHILL BLVD

CERRO SAN LUIS OBISPO

SAN LUIS OBISPO MUSEUM OF ART

SAN LUIS OBISPO

SYCAMORE CANYON RD

MADONNA INN

Laguna Lake

SOUTH ST

S. HIGUERA ST

TANK FARM RD

ORCUTT RD

MCCHESNEY FEILD

BUCKLEY RD

101

227

EL CAMINO REAL

BIDDLE RANCH RD

0   2 mi

0   2 km

AVILA BEACH DR

TIFFANY RANCH RD

ORCUTT RD

AVILA BEACH

227

CORBETT CANYON RD

San Luis Obispo Bay

SHELL BEACH

PRICE CANYON RD

PACIFIC

OCEAN

PISMO BEACH

To Solvang

ARROYO GRANDE

LOPEZ DR

HUASNA RD

GROVER BEACH

PISMO BEACH BUTTERFLY GROVE

1

101

is the only L-shaped mission in the state. An adjacent museum chronicles the daily lives of the Chumash tribal and Spanish colonial periods. Today, the mission church operates as a parish church of the Diocese of Monterey.

Located alongside the creek, **San Luis Obispo Museum of Art** (1010 Broad St., 805/543-8562, www.sloma.org, 11am-5pm Wed.-Mon. year-round, 11am-5pm daily July 5-Labor Day, free) is a small gallery that showcases the work of local painters, sculptors, fine-art photographers, and special exhibitions.

Recreation

San Luis Obispo has several hiking and biking areas. Probably the most well known is **Bishop Peak,** the highest of the Nine Sisters (or Morros), a chain of volcanic peaks in the Santa Lucia Mountains that stretch east from Morro Bay. The peak can be accessed from two trailheads, from either Patricia Drive or Highland Drive. It's about a four-mile hike round-trip with several switchbacks through open oak woodlands, and up the west and east summits of the peak. There are plenty of oak trees, California blackberry, sage scrub, chaparral, monkeyflower, and poison oak, which you'll want to avoid. Bicycles are not allowed on the trail but are welcome at **Cerro San Luis,** another member of the Nine Sisters, which offers multiple biking trails, best accessed via Marsh Street or Carriage Road. Located in the heart of downtown, **Wally's Bicycle Works** (209 Bonetti Dr., 805/544-4116, www.wallysbikes.com, 10am-6pm Mon.-Fri., 10am-5pm Sat., $35-40/day) offers bike and gear rentals at good prices.

Vineyards sprawl across San Luis Obispo's Edna Valley, embracing cool, coastal conditions that prove ideal for growing favorite oenophile varietals such as pinot noir and chardonnay. Around 30 wineries operate throughout the valley, mostly around CA-227, which splits off US-101 around the Madonna Inn

the eccentric Madonna Inn

and rejoins the larger highway south of Pismo Beach. Standouts include the century-old yellow schoolhouse tasting room surrounded by vineyards at **Baileyana** (5828 Orcutt Rd., 805/269-8200, www. baileyana.com, 10am-5pm daily), which offers wines including pinot noir rosé and alternative whites; and **Sextant Wines** (1653 Old Price Canyon Rd., 805/542-0133, www.sextantwines.com, 10am-4pm Mon.-Fri., 10am-5pm Sat.-Sun.), housed in the old mercantile building of the Township of Old Edna, which offers a conceptual and sometimes literal blend of fruit grown in SLO and farther north in the warmer climate around Paso Robles.

Food

House-roasted coffee goes with café breakfasts, salads, and sandwiches at **Kreuzberg Coffee** (685 Higuera St., 805/439-2060, www.kreuzbergcalifornia. com, 7:30am-10pm daily, $5-10), the sort of large, central coffee shop that doubles as a community hub. After 6pm, light

pub-style fare is served, along with wine and beer, often accompanied by live entertainment in the shop and/or a small performance space in the back.

The central coast takes pride in its contribution to American barbecue: the ranch hand cut of sirloin known as tri-tip. Fans flock from every direction for the tri-tip sandwiches at **Firestone Grill** (1001 Higuera St., 805/783-1001, 11am-10pm Sun.-Wed., 11am-11pm Thurs.-Sat., $6-13), which serves chewy rolls topped by thin slices of tender, slow-cooked beef and barbecue sauce.

A popular stop, **Jaffa Café** (1308 Monterey St., 805/543-2449, www.jaffacafe.us, 10:30am-9pm Mon.-Fri., 11am-9pm Sat.-Sun., $8-14) whips up phenomenal Mediterranean dishes, including gyros, falafels, kebab, and excellent hummus! A hip spot with freshly baked goods, **Splash Cafe** (893 Higuera St. and 1491 Monterey St., 805/773-4653, 7am-9pm Sun.-Wed., 7am-9:30pm Thurs.-Sat., $7-10) serves award-winning clam chowder.

A pioneer of farm-to-table cuisine in the area, **Big Sky Café** (1121 Broad St., 805/545-5401, 7am-8pm Mon.-Thurs., 7am-9pm Fri., 8am-9pm Sat., 8am-8pm Sun., $15-25) takes advantage of its proximity to farming, ranching, and fishing to provide vegetarian, pescatarian, and meat dishes.

A hot spot for locals and an iconic dining experience, **Novo Restaurant and Lounge** (726 Higuera St., 805/543-3986, www.novorestaurant.com, 11am-9pm Mon.-Thurs., 11am-10pm Fri.-Sat., 10am-9pm Sun., $18-36) features a riverside patio, a flavorful array of international dishes, an endless selection of wine, and a full bar.

Elegant with a touch of old-world sophistication, **Koberl at Blue** (998 Monterey St., 805/783-1135, www.epkoberl.com, 4pm-midnight daily, $25-50) is downtown and features "wine country cuisine to complement the central coast's wine region," including wonderful vegetarian dishes and delectable desserts.

Nightlife

Pub life thrives in SLO, including the creekside patio and live entertainment of **The Frog & Peach Pub** (728 Higuera St., 805/595-3764, www.frogandpeachpub.com, noon-2am daily); exceptional imported beers are more the focus at **Spike's Pub** (570 Higuera St., 805/544-7157, www.spikespub.com, 3pm-2am Mon.-Sat., 11am-midnight Sun.). Also creekside, **SLO Brew** (736 Higuera St., 805/543-1843, www.slobrew.com, 11:30am-2am Tues.-Sat., 11:13am-midnight Sun.-Mon.) pairs its house-brewed beer with rock, country, blues, funk, and cover band concerts most nights.

Luis Wine Bar (1021 Higuera St., 805/762-4747, www.luiswinebar.com, 3pm-11pm Sun.-Thurs., 3pm-midnight Fri.-Sat.) has a relaxing atmosphere and an extensive wine list from San Luis Obispo County and the entire central coast. Creekside wine bar **Luna Red** (1023 Chorro St., 805/540-5243, www.lunared-slo.com, 11:30am-9pm Mon.-Thurs., 11:30am-midnight Fri., 9am-midnight Sat., 9am-9pm Sun.) is a trendy place in a Spanish-style building with fine wines, cocktails, and tapas. Don't miss the **Silver Bar Cocktail Lounge** (100 Madonna Rd., 805/784-2432, www.madonnainn.com, 10am-midnight Mon.-Sat., 9am-11pm Sun.), inside the Madonna Inn. It's decorated with *Alice in Wonderland* wing-back chairs, pink retro bar stools, and a blooming fuchsia carpet.

Shopping

A mix of local and national retailers populate the five blocks comprising downtown, primarily along Monterey and Marsh Streets, and the main drag on Higuera. Every Thursday night, downtown becomes a community party with the immensely popular **Downtown SLO Farmers/ Market** (Higuera St. between Osos and Nipomo, 805/541-0286 www.downtownslo.com/farmers-market, 6pm-9pm), which features plenty of local produce, terrific local barbecue, activities for children, and live music.

Cool, hip clothing is at **Ambiance** (737 Higuera St., 805/540-3380, www.shopambiance.com, 10am-8pm Mon.-Sat., 11am-7pm Sun.), with jewelry and accessories for every occasion. **HepKat Clothing & Beauty Parlor** (785 Higuera St., 805/547-0777, www.hepkatclothing.com, 10am-7pm Sun.-Wed., 10am-9pm Thurs.-Sat.) is a fashion-forward boutique that doubles as a beauty salon.

Central coast artists and artisans sell their wares in **The Gallery at the Network** (778 Higuera St., Ste. B, 805/788-0886, www.galleryatthenetwork.com, 11am-6pm Mon.-Sat., 11am-5pm Sun.), ranging from contemporary works to decorative pieces. More local goods may be found at **The Crushed Grape** (491 Madonna Rd. #1, 805/544-4449, www.crushed-grape.com, 9:30am-5:30pm Mon.-Sat.), including a host of gourmet foods, gift baskets, and wines.

An open-air market, **Avila Valley Barn** (560 Avila Beach Dr., 805/595-2816, www.avilavalleybarn.com, 9am-5pm daily) provides another opportunity for gift shopping, gourmet foods, and even hayrides. Stop by **The Secret Garden Herb Shop** (740 Higuera St., Ste. A, 805/544-4372, www.organicherbshop.com, 11am-6pm daily) and choose from rows and rows of fragrant organic teas.

Accommodations

San Luis has a number of good places to stay, with reasonable rates that drop considerably after the summertime peak season. First on the list is the famed ★ **Madonna Inn** (100 Madonna Rd., 805/543-3000, www.madonnainn.com, $210-500), a whimsical hotel with kitschy vibes, eccentric taste, and an excessively "pink" café.

Avenue Inn Downtown San Luis Obispo (345 Marsh St., 805/543-6443, $110-250) also offers affordable rates and is in walking distance to downtown restaurants and shopping. **La Cuesta Inn** (2074 Monterey St., 805/543-2777, $130-200) has large rooms, free continental breakfast, and free DVD rentals, a steal for the price.

Several hotels offer charming accommodations for a bit more cash. These include **Petit Soleil Bed & Breakfast** (1473 Monterey St., 805/549-0321, www.petitsoleilslo.com, $180-240), a charming European-style bed-and-breakfast that offers elegant morning meals and complimentary evening wine-tasting; and **Apple Farm** (2015 Monterey St., 805/544-2040, www.applefarm.com, $180-280), an upscale country hotel with rooms that are smaller than average but cozy and tastefully decorated.

Or, live like a rock star at the **SLO Brew Lofts** (738 Higuera St., 805/543-1843, www.slobrew.com/the-lofts, $250-350). Located in the center of downtown, the brick wall lofts above the SLO Brew beer and music venue trade the quiet life for kitchens and amenities like vinyl records, musical instruments, and MTV-like decor.

Information and Services

San Luis Obispo Visitor Center (895 Monterey St., 805/781-2777, www.slochamber.org, 10am-5pm Sun.-Wed., 10am-7pm Thurs.-Sat.) is a good resource for brochures and maps and provides information on available discounts for restaurants and events.

Pismo Beach

After passing through San Luis Obispo, US-101/CA-1 heads south back toward the coast, where CA-1 splits off from US-101 at **Pismo Beach** (pop. 8,198), 13 miles south. This low-key, easygoing, touristy beach town is like a time machine that stops in 1960s California. Expect friendly people and great waves. Located at the end of lively Pomeroy Street, the pier is the focal point of the beach, with plenty of restrooms, food, and parking nearby.

Sights

Pismo Beach Butterfly Grove (CA-1 just south of North Pismo State Beach Campground, 805/773-7170, www.monarchbutterfly.org, docents available 10am-4pm daily Nov.-Feb., free) sees the return of monarch butterflies each November-February, when tens of thousands of butterflies migrate to this small grove of eucalyptus trees near the beach to mate. On average there are about 30,000 of these silent winged creatures, and the trees are often transformed into brilliant shades of orange after the butterflies' 2,000-mile journey to get here. This is the largest of the four gathering spots for the monarchs in California. Docents give talks about the butterflies and their unique but short lives.

Food

Splash Cafe (197 Pomeroy, 805/773-4653, www.splashcafe.com, 8am-8:30pm Sun.-Thurs., 8am-9pm Fri.-Sat., $7-10) is the place to go for cheap eats by the beach. This is classic Pismo—bright, airy, and rambunctious, with plastic chairs and tables and crudely painted walls with old surfing photos and other surfing paraphernalia. They are best known for their thick, chunky, and creamy clam chowder. The fish-and-chips and fish tacos are also worth trying. Burgers and shakes are also served. It does get crowded, so plan to get there early. There are also two locations in San Luis Obispo.

The oft-crowded **Cracked Crab** (751 Price St., 805/773-2722, www.crackedcrab.com, 11am-9pm Sun.-Thurs., 11am-10pm Fri.-Sat., $20-50) is *the* place to crack open crab, lobster, and other shellfish in a cafeteria-style environment. Old black-and-white photos of fishing days gone by line the walls. Perhaps it's the plastic bibs that give it away, but this is a hands-on joint. They will dump the shellfish right on your table so you can get to work.

For creative Latin American cuisine and gorgeous sunset views, dine at the **Ventana Grill** (2575 Price St., 805/773-0000, http://ventanagrill.com, 10am-9pm Sun., 11am-9pm Mon.-Thurs., 11am-10pm Fri.-Sat., $15-30). It's worth a visit for the margarita selection alone.

Two miles south of downtown Pismo, just off CA-1, a pair of passenger train cars have been converted to the narrow but fun Rock & Roll Diner (1300 Railroad St., 805/473-2040, www.rockandroll-diner.com, 8am-8:30pm Sun.-Thurs., 8am-9pm Fri.-Sat., $10-25), offering a 1950s-era diner menu and decor from breakfast through dinner, with a little pit barbecue for kicks.

Accommodations

A few lower-priced chain hotels dot Pismo Beach and the surrounding communities of Avila Beach and Grover Beach. For a splurge, the **Dolphin Bay Resort and Spa** (2727 Shell Beach Rd., Pismo Beach, 800/516-0112, www.thedolphinbay.com, $340-650) has one of the best locations on the entire central coast, perched just yards from the cliffs that drop dramatically down to the Pacific Ocean. The one-bedroom suites, at nearly 1,000 square feet, have full kitchens, fireplaces, and flat-screen plasma TVs, and bikes are provided for all guests.

Foxen Canyon Road: Santa Maria Valley

After CA-1 splits off from US-101 in Pismo Beach, the drive south along either highway is largely inland until it reaches Gaviota near Santa Barbara. Since you won't be missing any coastal scenery, you could take a detour even farther inland to the Santa Maria Valley to sample wines in the region made famous by the movie *Sideways*. Running roughly parallel to US-101, **Foxen Canyon Road** is

Pismo Beach

a back road hugging the foothills, with multiple wineries along the way.

From the north on US-101, take the East Betteravia Road exit and head east about three miles until it turns into Foxen Canyon Road. From this point, Tepusquet Road, where Kenneth Volk Winery is located, is about 10 miles away. From the south, take the Alisos Canyon Road turnoff from US-101, about 25 miles north of the CA-1/US-101 split in Gaviota. Take Alisos Canyon Road 6.5 miles and turn left onto Foxen Canyon Road. Foxen Canyon Road eventually turns into East Betteravia Road and connects back to US-101.

Located on a little road off Foxen Canyon Road, award-winning **Kenneth Volk Vineyards** (5230 Tepusquet Rd., 805/938-7896, www.volkwines.com, 10:30am-4:30pm Thurs.-Mon.) offers all the strange wines you've never tried. In addition to the standard offerings like chardonnay and cabernet sauvignon, Kenneth Volk is a champion of heirloom varieties like cabernet pfeiffer, négrette, verdelho, and aglianico. You won't regret the long trek to get to the tranquil 12-acre property along the Tepusquet Creek, surrounded by oak and sycamore trees.

Set in an old barn, **Rancho Sisquoc** (6600 Foxen Canyon Rd., 805/934-4332, www.ranchosisquoc.com, 10am-4pm Mon.-Thurs., 10am-5pm Fri.-Sun.) makes a beautiful spot for a picnic. The wood-sided tasting room is rustic but comfortable, and the surrounding setting—a vast field with low hills in the distance—is perfect for some quiet wine-enhanced relaxation.

Foxen Winery (7600 Foxen Canyon Rd., 805/937-4251, www.foxenwinery. com, 11am-4pm daily) is known for its rustic wood tasting room: It looks like a rundown shed. But the wines are a far cry from rustic. In addition to the usual suspects, the winery is one of the few to produce the underappreciated chenin blanc. Foxen's longstanding reputation goes back six generations, and its 10 acres are the only dry-farmed vineyard in the area, meaning that irrigation is not used.

If you get a carnivorous craving between Pismo Beach and Foxen Canyon Road, stop by **Jocko's** (125 N. Thompson, Nipomo, 805/929-3686, 8am-10pm Sun.-Thurs., 8am-11pm Fri.-Sat., $15-34). They're known for their oak-grilled steaks and their no-frills decor. The steaks and grilled meats are all prime quality, cooked and seasoned by people who know how to grill. On weekends, and often on weeknights as well, there are notoriously long waits. Make reservations, though that doesn't mean you won't still wait.

La Purisima Mission

48 miles from Pismo, **Mission La Purisima Concepcion de Maria Santisima** (2295 Purisima Rd., Lompoc, 805/733-3713, www.lapurisimamission.org, self-guided tours 9am-5pm daily, free

one-hour guided tours daily at 1pm, $6 per vehicle) is one of the best of the 21 California missions to visit. Its extensive restoration and wide grounds evoke the remoteness of the landscape during the mission period.

The mission was founded on December 8, 1787, but was destroyed by an earthquake in 1812. The fathers then rebuilt the mission in a different spot, and it is that mission that a quarter of a million visitors enjoy today as a state historic park. Sitting inside 2,000 acres are trails for simple hikes and walks, and when you visit you can examine the five-acre garden that shows native and domestic plants typical of a mission garden, including fig and olive trees and a wide variety of plants like sage and Spanish dagger. Animals typical of the times, such as burros, horses, longhorn cattle, sheep, goats, and turkeys, are displayed in a corral in the main compound.

Wandering through the sleeping quarters, the weaving shop, candle-making room, chapel, and many other rooms on display, you can get a feel for daily life in the mission. You can also see few conical Chumash huts. This is one of the few missions that do not have church services, since it's now a state park.

La Purisima is easily accessible from CA-1: In Lompoc, take Purisima Road east to the mission.

⬥ CA-246: Buellton and Solvang

About 50 miles south of Pismo, the town of **Buellton,** a block west of US-101 at the Solvang exit, holds one of California's classic roadside landmarks, **Andersen's Pea Soup Restaurant** (376 Ave. of the Flags, 805/688-5581, www.peasoup-andersens.net, 7am-10pm daily, $10-14), advertised up and down the coast. The **Hitching Post** (406 CA-246 E., 805/688-0676, www.hitchingpost2.com, 4pm-9:30pm Mon.-Fri., 3pm-9:30pm Sat.-Sun.,

La Purisima Mission

$25-50) restaurant gained fame in the wine-loving road-trip movie *Sideways*.

Four miles east of Buellton and US-101 is America's most famous mock-European tourist trap, the Danish-style town of **Solvang** (pop. 5,385). Set up by a group of Danish immigrants in 1911 as a cooperative agricultural community, Solvang found its calling catering to passing travelers. The compact blocks of windmills, cobblestone streets, and old-world architecture charm road-trippers and busloads of tourists with a Hans Christian Andersen museum, a Little Mermaid statue, and, more recently, regional winery tasting rooms. **The Elverhoj Museum of Art & History** (1624 Elverhoj Way, 805/686-1211, www.elverhoj.org, 11am-4pm Wed.-Sun., $5 suggested donation) chronicles the cultural influence of the Danish people.

Just east of Solvang's windmills and gables, the brooding hulk of **Old Mission Santa Inés** (1760 Mission Dr., 805/688-4815, 9am-5pm daily, $5 guided tours) stands as a sober reminder of the region's Spanish colonial past. Built in 1804, it was once among the more prosperous of the California missions, but now it is worth a visit mainly for the gift shop selling all manner of devotional ornaments.

Pop singer Michael Jackson's Neverland Ranch lies in the foothills of the Santa Ynez Valley, southeast of Solvang via the truly scenic CA-254, which loops inland and continues south to Santa Barbara.

Allow 2-4 hours to wander the area, depending whether you stop in one of Solvang's tourist trap restaurants for Danish puffed pancakes, called Æbleskivers.

Gaviota State Park

About 62 miles from Pismo, CA-1 rejoins US-101 at Las Cruces, near the north end of **Gaviota State Park** (US-101, 33 miles west of Santa Barbara, 805/968-1033, www.parks.ca.gov, 7am-sunset daily, $10), which includes a beach, hiking trails, and hot springs. The trailhead to **Gaviota Peak** (six miles round-trip) is at the parking area. The trail is mostly rugged and wide leading upward, and the views of the ocean and the Channel Islands are fantastic. The trail that leads to the hot springs is shorter, only a mile, but there are still some beautiful scenic views along the way. Surfers and kayakers use a boat hoist on the west end of the beach to access the Santa Barbara Channel waters. At Gaviota Beach, US-101 turns east, hugging the coastline.

Refugio State Beach

10 miles from Gaviota State Park, **Refugio State Beach** (10 Refugio Beach Rd., Goleta, 805/968-1033, www.parks.ca.gov, dawn-sunset daily, $10) is a state park with a small strip of grass that abuts the

water. It offers excellent coastal fishing, snorkeling, and scuba, as well as hiking, biking trails, and picnic sites, with 1.5 miles of flat shoreline. Palm trees planted near Refugio Creek give a distinctive look to the beach and camping area. Refugio is 20 miles west of Santa Barbara on US-101 at Refugio Road.

El Capitán State Beach

Just 3 miles southeast from Refugio State Beach, **El Capitán State Beach** (off US-101, 17 miles west of Santa Barbara, 805/968-1033, www.parks.ca.gov, dawn-sunset daily, $10) offers visitors a sandy beach, rocky tidepools, and stands of sycamore and oak trees along El Capitán Creek. It's a perfect setting for swimming, fishing, surfing, picnicking, and camping. A stairway provides access from the bluffs to the beach area. Amenities include RV hookups, pay showers, restrooms, hiking and bike trails, a fabulous beach, a seasonal general store, and an outdoor arena. Many of the camping sites offer an ocean view. If you take US-101 north about 15 minutes from downtown Santa Barbara you will see the El Capitán signs. At the bottom of the exit, turn left and go under the bridge. The road will take you right into the park.

Santa Barbara

It's called the American Riviera, with weather, community, and sun-drenched beaches reminiscent of the Mediterranean coast. In truth, **Santa Barbara** (pop. 91,930) is all California. It has all the amenities of a big city, but the pace of life slows down just enough to make for a relaxing stay. In fact, many California natives consider it their favorite vacation spot. In town, you'll find world-class museums, shopping, and dining. Fabulous four-star resorts cluster along the beaches.

Getting There and Around

Santa Barbara by vehicle is accessed via US-101, approximately 95 miles south of San Luis Obispo. Take the Garden Street exit to go downtown and Cabrillo Boulevard for access to local beaches.

Santa Barbara Municipal Airport (500 Fowler Rd., 805/683-4011, www.santabarbaraca.gov) is the gateway for visitors via air travel with daily flights from Los Angeles (LAX), San Francisco, Las Vegas, Phoenix, Denver, and other destinations. Car rentals are available from all major service providers.

The Santa Barbara **Amtrak** station (209 State St., 800/872-7245, www.amtrak.com) is located in a historical landmark building and provides service from San Luis Obispo to San Diego on the Pacific Surfliner, and from Seattle to Los Angeles on the Coast Starlight.

The **Greyhound station** (224 Chapala St., 800/231-2222, www.greyhound.com) is adjacent to the train station, providing service several times a day from Santa Barbara and Carpinteria to LAX, as well as other options. Car rental service providers are conveniently located near the Amtrak and Greyhound stations.

The **Santa Barbara Metropolitan Transit District** (805/963-3364, www.sbmtd.gov) runs buses throughout the city, including the neighboring cities of Goleta and Montecito. SBMTD's route 11 bus links the airport with downtown Santa Barbara. A shuttle bus (9am-6pm daily fall-spring, 9am-10pm daily summer, $0.50) runs every 15 minutes along State Street between downtown Sola Street and along the waterfront; bus route 22 takes you right to the Museum of Art, Old Mission Santa Barbara, and more.

Walking, biking, and even inline skating are popular along the waterfront, and there are businesses that rent gear.

Sights
★ Old Mission Santa Barbara
Old Mission Santa Barbara (2201 Laguna

St., 805/682-4713, www.santabarbara-mission.org, 9am-5pm daily, self-guided tours $9 adults, $4 children 5-17), with its coral pink facade, is considered the prettiest of all the California missions, albeit one of the least authentic. A self-guided tour takes you through the interior courtyard, where a center fountain is encircled by palm trees, and the cemetery where a beautiful Moreton Bay fig tree planted around 1890 still stands. From there it is a few steps into the church. It has the most decorated of the mission interiors, with lots of vibrant stenciling surrounding the doors and altar and a complete painted wainscoting. Large paintings flank both walls. Near the formal entrance, a small gated room houses the only original altar and tabernacle in the California mission chain, dating from 1786. After leaving the church, you'll enter the museum section, which houses old photographs and artifacts from the early services.

Chumash Painted Cave

Mysterious red, black, and white images are concealed in a small sandstone cave at **Chumash Painted Cave State Historic Park** (CA-154, right on Painted Cave Rd., 805/733-3713, www.parks.ca.gov, dawn-sunset, free). Launch your expedition and navigate the steep path leading to the cave entrance, where Delphian-like images date to the 1600s and earlier. Although the images are known to be the artistry of ancient Chumash ancestors, the subjects depicted in the rock art are open to speculation and interpretation. Many believe the petroglyphs, created using mineral pigments, depict Chumash cosmology, possibly representing a solar eclipse that happened November 24, 1677, but some images are thought to date back 1,000 years or more. The cave was discovered in the 1870s. The iron gate that blocks passage was placed at the cavern mouth in 1908 for the purpose of preservation.

The cave is accessed from the very narrow and winding Painted Cave Road (north) off of CA-154, about 11 miles (18 kilometers) northwest of Santa Barbara. Look to the left side of the road for the cave. There is a small parking shoulder with an interpretive sign about the site. Flash cameras will harm the images and are prohibited.

Stearns Wharf

Stearns Wharf (intersection of State St. and Cabrillo Blvd., www.stearnswharf.org) is Santa Barbara's most visited landmark. Santa Barbara has no natural harbor, and the wharf was built in 1871 to allow ships to off-load supplies for the bourgeoning town. The current iteration is a favorite for tourists. Frankly, there are a lot of typical tourist shops selling seashells, small, personalized license plates, and gift items you can find most anywhere, but if you walk to the end, you get some of the best views back to the city. There are no railings at the end of the wharf, so keep an eye on little ones.

In addition to the views, there are a few restaurants, an ice cream store, and the **Ty Warner Sea Center** (211 Stearns Wharf, 805/962-2526, www.sbnature.org, 10am-5pm daily, $8.50 adults, $6 children 2-12). A branch of the Santa Barbara Museum of Natural History, this two-story building is devoted to giving you a better understanding of how our oceans work. There are touch tanks on the lower level and staff to answer questions.

El Presidio de Santa Bárbara State Historic Park

Founded on April 21, 1782, **El Presidio de Santa Bárbara State Historic Park** (123 E. Canon Perdido St., 805/965-0093, www.sbthp.org, 10:30am-4:30pm daily, $5 adults, children under 17 free, admission includes Casa de la Guerra) can rightfully be called the birthplace of Santa Barbara. The presidio was the last in a chain of four military fortresses built by the Spanish along the coast of California. The whitewashed buildings were constructed of sun-dried adobe bricks laid upon foundations of sandstone boulders. Timbers

Santa Barbara

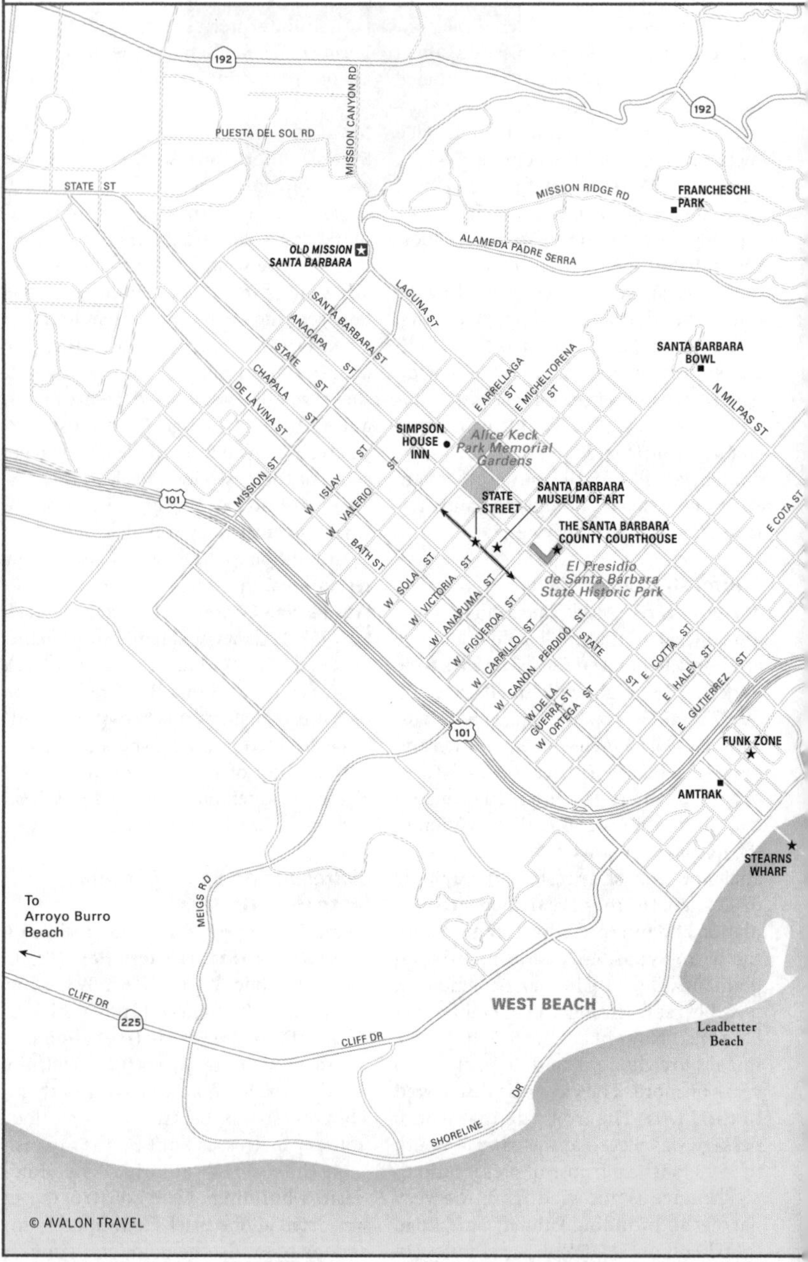

192

MISSION CANYON RD

PUESTA DEL SOL RD

192

STATE ST

MISSION RIDGE RD

FRANCHESCHI PARK

ALAMEDA PADRE SERRA

OLD MISSION SANTA BARBARA

LAGUNA ST

SANTA BARBARA ST

SANTA BARBARA BOWL

ANACAPA ST

STATE ST

CHAPALA ST

DE LA VINA ST

E ARRELLAGA ST

E MICHELTORENA ST

N MILPAS ST

SIMPSON HOUSE INN

Alice Keck Park Memorial Gardens

SANTA BARBARA MUSEUM OF ART

MISSION ST

W ISLAY ST

VALERIO ST

STATE STREET

THE SANTA BARBARA COUNTY COURTHOUSE

E COTA ST

101

W BATH ST

El Presidio de Santa Bárbara State Historic Park

W SOLA ST

VICTORIA ST

ANAPUMA ST

FIGUEROA ST

W VICTORIA ST

W CARRILLO ST

PERDIDO ST

STATE ST

E COTTA ST

W CANON ST

E COTTA ST

E HALEY ST

W DE LA GUERRA ST

ORTEGA ST

E GUTIERREZ ST

W ORTEGA ST

FUNK ZONE

101

AMTRAK

STEARNS WHARF

To Arroyo Burro Beach

MEIGS RD

CLIFF DR

225

CLIFF DR

WEST BEACH

Leadbetter Beach

DR

SHORELINE

© AVALON TRAVEL

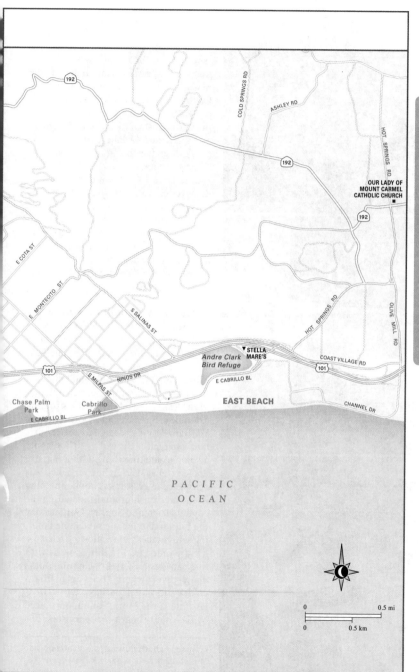

from Los Padres forest supported roofs of red tile. The buildings of the presidio form a quadrangle enclosing a central parade ground. Today, only two sections of the original presidio quadrangle remain: El Cuartel (the second-oldest building in California, dating from 1782), the family residence of the soldier assigned to guard the western gate into the Plaza de Armas; and the Canedo Adobe, named after the presidio soldier to whom it was deeded when the presidio became inactive. El Cuartel is small, with tiny doors and windows reflective of the time, but the massively thick walls still stand as they have for more than 200 years, with only cosmetic touch-ups to the plaster that covers the original adobe bricks. The presidio is just a block off State Street downtown and can easily be worked into your downtown sightseeing plans.

Santa Barbara County Courthouse

Covering an entire city block, the still-functioning **Santa Barbara County Courthouse** (1100 Anacapa St., 805/882-4520, www.sbcourts.org, 8am-5pm Mon.-Fri., 10am-5pm weekends and holidays., free docent-led tours 10:30am and 2pm Mon.- Fri., 2pm Sat.-Sun.) is a stunning example of Spanish and Moorish design. William Mooser designed this courthouse to replace the earlier 1872 version, a colonial-looking thing with a massive domed cupola. When the courthouse was completed in 1929, it was unlike anything in the city. Lush grounds, including the copious lawn and Sunken Gardens, lay the foundation for the sandstone building with arabesque windows, archways, hand-painted wood ceilings, walls with intricate designs, and pueblo tile inlays nearly everywhere flashing brilliant colors and native designs. Of particular note is the Mural Room, once used by the county board of supervisors. The

From top to bottom: windmills in Solvang; Old Mission Santa Barbara; Santa Barbara County Courthouse.

huge room is covered in a mural depicting the early Chumash Indians and following the history of the area leading up to California statehood. All tours of the building meet in the Mural Room and are approximately one hour.

The clock tower, known as **El Mirador,** juts out of the top of the courthouse, making it one of the tallest structures in the city, though the tower is a mere 85 feet tall. But it is here that you'll get the best views of downtown, the mountains, and the ocean from a downtown perspective—it's a must for photo ops.

Santa Barbara Museum of Art

See the power of the visual arts at the **Santa Barbara Museum of Art** (1130 State St., 805/963-4364, www.sbmuseart.org, 11am-5pm Tues.-Sun., $10 adults, $6 children, free children 6-17, free Thurs. 5pm-8pm). Santa Barbara has one of the most impressive art museums and best collections for a community of its size and showcases pieces in many styles and from various eras. Their notable Asian holdings contain more than 2,600 objects representing 4,000 years of history and include Japanese woodblock prints and the 19 Chinese robes that started the collection.

Recreation

Long, flat **Leadbetter Beach** (402 E. Ortega St., 805/564-5418, www.santabarbaraca.gov, 24 hours) is the best in Santa Barbara. Sheer cliffs rise from the sand, trees dot the point, and the beach is protected by the harbor's breakwater, making it ideal for swimming.

Named because it is east of Stearns Wharf, **East Beach** (Cabrillo Blvd. at S. Milpas St., sunrise-10pm daily) is all soft sand, with a dozen volleyball nets, a snack bar, a children's play area, and a bike path.

Known locally as Hendry's, dog-friendly **Arroyo Burro Beach** (Cliff Dr. and Las Positas Rd., sunrise-10pm daily) is a popular spot for surfers and kayakers.

Far removed from downtown, it's very popular with locals.

Santa Barbara is also home to numerous private and public golf courses. **Hidden Oaks** (4760 Calle Camarada, 805/967-3493, www.hiddenoaksgolfcoursesb.weebly.com 8:30am-8pm, $12 weekdays, $14 weekends) and **Twin Lakes** (6034 Hollister Ave., 805/964-1414, www.twinlakesgolf.com, 7am-7pm daily, $15) are both affordable nine-hole courses. The **Santa Barbara Golf Club** (3500 McCaw Ave., 805/687-7087, www.santabarbaraca.gov, 6am-8:30pm daily, $40 and up) and the world-class **Rancho San Marcos** (4600 CA-154, 805/683-6334, www.rsm1804.com, 7am-5:30pm daily, $40-80) offer the complete 18-hole golf experience.

Food

There are pancakes and other breakfast standards, but a build-your-own-hash option makes a breakfast favorite of **Dawn Patrol** (324 State St., 805/962-2889, www.dawnpatrolsb.com, 7:30am-2pm daily, $6-13), which sources mostly local ingredients.

People line up daily to see why culinary icon Julia Child frequented the cash-only ★ **La Super-Rica Taqueria** (622 N. Milpas St., 805/963-4940, 11am-9pm Thurs., Sun., and Mon., 11am-9:30pm Fri.-Sat., $4-10), giving plenty of time to watch soft corn tortillas being made by hand through the kitchen window for a long list of street tacos.

Vegans and vegetarians will find happiness at **Natural Café & Juice Bar** (508 State St., 805/962-9494, www.thenaturalcafe.com, 11am-9pm Sun.-Thurs., 11am-9:30pm Fri.-Sat., $8-12), along with outdoor sidewalk dining.

Locally beloved **McConnell's Fine Ice Creams** (728 State St., 805/324-4402, www.mcconnells.com, 11:30am-10pm Sun.-Thurs., 11:30am-11pm Fri.-Sat., $5-12) scoops out creative rotating flavors two at a time, to get you closer to trying them all.

Expect a wait at **Arigato Sushi** (1225 State St., 805/965-6074, 5:30pm-10pm Sun.-Thurs., 5:30pm-10:30pm Fri.-Sat., $20-40), but the best sushi in town is worth it. Fresh seafood with an unpretentious dash of sophistication keeps the dining room busy at **Enterprise Fish Company** (225 State St., 805/962-3313, 11:30am-10pm Sun.-Thurs., 11:30am-11pm Fri.-Sat., $16-28).

A Funk Zone favorite, **Lark** (131 Anacapa St., 805/284-0370, www.thelarksb.com, 5pm-10pm Tues.-Sun., $16-38) wows instagramming foodies with trending ingredients and boatloads of creativity. An upscale establishment inside a historic 1872 house, ★ **Stella Mare's** (50 Los Patos Way, 805/969-6705, www.stellamares.com, 11:30am-9pm Tues.-Thurs., 11:30am-10pm Fri., 10am-10pm Sat., 10am-9pm Sun., $12-32) offers the perfect table for two for romantic, French country-style dining. For something light, share one of their delicious small plates. Under no circumstances should you pass on desserts like chocolate ganache-filled cream puffs and lavender and vanilla crème brûlée.

Downey's Restaurant (1305 State St., 805/966-5006, www.downeyssb.com, 5:30pm-9pm Tues.-Thurs. and Sun., 5:30pm-9:30pm Fri.-Sat., $30-40), one of the best restaurants in town, and the local favorite **Wine Cask** (813 Anacapa St., 805/966-9463, www.winecask.com, 11:30am-2pm Tues.-Fri., 5:30pm-9pm Tues.-Thurs., 5:30pm-10pm Fri.-Sat., $24-95) both feature excellent California cuisine and perfect wine pairings. Reservations are recommended.

Nightlife

Many of the bars and nightclubs are on or around the main drag of State Street, much of which caters to college students from the nearby university.

Bars with strong, cheap drinks are **Joe's Cafe** (536 State St., 805/966-4638, www.joescafesb.com, 7:30am-10pm daily), which packs a pretty potent punch.

Stearns Wharf

Wine-Tasting: Santa Barbara

Catering to the affections of crushed-grape aficionados, the **Santa Barbara Urban Wine Trail** (www.urbanwine-trailsb.com) leads to about 25 premium tasting rooms, all within blocks of downtown and the beach. Most are open 10am-6pm, with some last pours offered as late as 8pm. Most belong to the Santa Barbara County Vintners' Association, whose membership is made up of only licensed growers with a winery facility in the Santa Barbara County and at least 75 percent annual production in Santa Barbara County. Seventeen tasting rooms are located in Santa Barbara's up-and-coming **Funk Zone neighborhood** (www.funkzone. net), which offers plenty to see and do beyond wine, including galleries and shops.

Voted the "best" Santa Barbara happy hour, **Sandbar Mexican Restaurant and Tequila Bar** (514 State St., 805/966-1388, www.sandbarsb.com, 11am-2am daily, 3pm-7pm happy hour Sun.-Fri.) features superb drinks, half-off appetizers, and a lively outdoor patio.

Well-known pubs are **The James Joyce** (513 State St., 805/962-2688, www.sbjamesjoyce.com, 10am-2am daily), a traditional Irish watering hole with weekend bands, and **Dargan's Irish Pub & Restaurant** (18 E. Ortega St., 805/568-0702, www.dargans.com, 11:30am-2am Mon.-Sat., 11:30am-midnight Sun.), which serves some good Irish stew, Guinness, and Irish music.

Play a few rounds of pool or sit back with a beer or glass of wine and listen to rock bands at **Elsie's Tavern** (117 De La Guerra, 805/963-4503, noon-2am Mon.-Fri., 4pm-2am Sat.-Sun.). Jazz and soul bills are mixed in at **SOhO Restaurant and Music Club** (1221 State St., 805/962-7776, www.sohosb.com, restaurant 11am-6pm, shows nightly, $10 and up).

To dance the night away, **Wildcat Lounge** (15 W. Ortega St., 805/962-7970, www.wildcatlounge.com, 4pm-2am daily) is "the" dance club in Santa Barbara and offers a full bar. **MR8X** (409 State St., 805/957-4111, www.m8rxsb.com, 6pm-10pm Wed.-Fri., plus noon-8pm Sun. during NFL season) packs a nightclub into a historic landmark building dating back to 1889.

Serving light food and cocktails, **Blush Restaurant & Lounge** (630 State St., 805/957-1300, www.blushsb.com, 4:30pm-11pm Wed.-Thurs., 4:30pm-2am Fri., 10am-2am Sat., 10am-10pm Sun.) has a chic modern feel, with signature drinks and a primo happy hour. **Les Marchands Wine Bar & Merchant** (131 Anacapa St., Ste. B, 805/284-0380, www.lesmarchandswine.com, 11am-10pm

Mon.-Thurs., 11am-11pm Fri., 10am-11pm Sat., 10am-10pm Sun.) offers a vast selection of wine by the glass and excellent international beer and cider.

Arts and Entertainment

A couple of the vintage theaters along State Street host musical and theatrical events, as well as film. Nearly a century old, the 1924 **Granada Theatre** (1214 State St., 805/899-2222, www.granadasb.org) brings touring Broadway shows, stand-up comedy, world music, dance, and more. The **Arlington Theatre** (1317 State St., 805/963-4408) features the Santa Barbara International Film Festival as well as big-name performers. It's worth the price of admission to admire its 1931 Spanish colonial and Mission Revival architecture, which features a covered courtyard with a fountain. Elaborate Spanish balconies, staircases, and houses are built out from the walls, creating the illusion of a Spanish colonial town.

Catch a fabulous musical comedy, theatrical play, or musical performance at the **Ensemble Theatre Company** (33 W. Victoria St., 805/965-5400, www.etcsb.org, $25 and up).

Exclusively filled with original works, the Santa Barbara Art Association's **Gallery 113** (1114 State St. #8, 805/965-6611, www.gallery113sb.com, 11am-5pm Mon.-Sat., 1pm-5pm Sun.) hosts numerous exhibitions.

Legendary bands and musicians perform in a relatively intimate outdoor amphitheater, **Santa Barbara Bowl** (1122 N. Milpas St., 805/962-7411, www.sbbowl.com); recent headliners include Willie Nelson, Brian Wilson, John Legend, and Radiohead.

Shopping

Plenty of open-air shopping centers house the usual retail chains, but **La Arcada** (1114 State St., 805/966-6634, www.laarcadasantabarbara.com, 10am-7pm daily) offers unique local boutiques, galleries, and specialty shops. Parking is free for the first 75 minutes, but don't expect easy or free beach parking.

Treasures abound at **Santa Barbara Arts** (1114 State St., 805/884-1938, www.sbarts.net, 11am-5:30pm daily), with an eclectic mix of artist-made creations from handmade jewelry to ceramics to paintings. For fine oil paintings and sculptures, explore the **Waterhouse Gallery** (1114 State St., 805/962-8885, 11am-5pm Mon.-Sat., 11am-4pm Sun.).

Browse artisanal food at the pop-up shop **Isabella Gourmet Foods** (602 Anacapa St., 805/585-5257, 8:30am-6pm Mon.-Thurs., 8:30am-2pm Fri.-Sat.) inside Honey B Kitchen, or French handmade chocolates at **Chocolats du CaliBressan** (1114 State St. #25, 805/568-1313, www.chococalibressan.com, 10am-7pm Mon.-Fri., 11am-6pm Sat., noon-5pm Sun.).

The Italian Pottery Outlet (929 State St., 805/564-7655, www.italianpottery.com, 10am-6:30pm daily) carries the biggest collection of Italian pottery and ceramics at affordable prices.

Mystique Sonique (1103 State St., 805/568-0473, www.mystiquesonique.com, 10am-7pm daily) has a great selection of all things vintage, hip, and chic for both men and women. **Fuzion Gallery & Boutique** (1115 State St., 805/687-6401, www.fuzionglass.com, 11am-7pm Sun.-Thurs., 11am-8pm Fri.-Sat.) stocks cutting-edge clothing from around the world, as well as from local start-ups. Hidden gem **Lovebird Boutique & Jewelry Bar** (535 State St., 805/560-9900, www.lovebirdsb.com, 9am-7pm Mon.-Fri., 9am-9pm Sat.-Sun.) has beautiful unique adornments.

Events

The biggest event of the year, **Fiesta** or **Old Spanish Days** (downtown Santa Barbara, 805/962-8101, www.oldspanishdays-fiesta.org, late July or early August, tickets: Carriage Museum, 129 Castillo St., $25) is a week-long celebration of the city's Spanish, Mexican, and Native American history. Events feature *folklórico*, flamenco, and Aztec music and dance, fantastic foods, and the amazing El Desfile Histórico (Historical Parade).

The Santa Ynez Band of Chumash Indians hosts the annual **Intertribal Pow-Wow** (Live Oaks, Los Padres National Forest, www.santaynezchumash.org/culture.html, late September/early October), where hundreds of tribes gather in honor of culture and heritage, with drummers from the United States and Canada, a variety of foods, and authentic handmade native crafts.

Hollywood notables gather for the annual **Santa Barbara International Film Festival** (805/963-0023, www.sbiff.org, $75 tickets), which includes tributes, movie screenings, and a gala.

The first Thursday of each month, the Santa Barbara Arts Collaborative curates **Art Crawl** (Del La Guerra St. and Anacapa St., www.sbartsblog.com, 5:30pm first Thurs. of the month, free), focusing on the best of the local art scene.

Accommodations

Santa Barbara is an expensive place to stay, regardless of time of year, weather, or even economic downturns. Most properties require a two-night minimum stay during the summer.

The ★ **Simpson House Inn** (121 E. Arrellaga, 805/963-7067, www.simpsonhouseinn.com, $325-400) features opulent rooms on an 1874 estate with a well-manicured and formal English garden. A vegetarian breakfast starts the day, afternoon tea and desserts are available at midday, and an evening wine-tasting brings the day to a close. It's a short walk to State Street.

In the Funk Zone, **The Wayfarer** (12 E. Montecito St., 805/845-1000, www.wayfarersb.com, $50-90 dorms, $150-350 private rooms) offers both dorm beds and private rooms, along with bikes, a communal kitchen, summer pool parties, and musical instruments for impromptu jam sessions in the lobby lounge.

The **Avania Inn** of Santa Barbara (128 Castillo St., 805/963-4471, $129-300) features pillow-top beds, a complimentary hot breakfast, free parking, and a steamy redwood sauna.

For beachfront stays, the dog-friendly **Hotel Milo** (202 W. Cabrillo Blvd., 866/547-3070, www.hotelmilosantabarbara.com, $200-360) features beautiful outdoor gardens, views of the wharf and harbor, and complimentary bikes for guests. On the higher end, mission-style resort **Fess Parker** (633 E. Cabrillo Blvd., 805/564-4333, www.fessparkersantabarbarahotel.com, $250-540) offers copious amenities and five on-site restaurants.

Intimate and elegant, the **Brisas del Mar Inn** (223 Castillo St., 805/966-2219, $200-320) is a Mediterranean-style villa just two blocks from the beaches and downtown, with spacious, comfortable rooms and complimentary bikes.

The nicest B&B for the price is **A White Jasmine Inn** (1327 Bath St., 805/966-0589, www.whitejasmineinnsantabarbara.com, $170-350), composed of three cottages, with richly decorated rooms and fragrant surrounding gardens.

The refined **Santa Ynez Inn** (3627 Sagunto St., 805/688-5588, www.santaynezinn.com, $270-550) rests in the foothills of wine country, offering a quiet retreat filled with luxury and warm hospitality.

Information and Services

The staff at **Santa Barbara Visitors Center** (1 Garden St., 805/965-3021, 9am-5pm Mon.-Sat., 10am-5pm Sun.) are available to assist visitors by answering questions and providing local area and service information. The center is centrally located in downtown inside a traditional adobe building.

The **Outdoors Santa Barbara Visitor Center** (113 Harbor Way 4th Fl., 805/884-1475, 11am-5pm daily) offers visitors exhibits and information about offshore destinations including Channel Islands National Park and Channel Islands National Marine Sanctuary.

⚓ Channel Islands National Park

Channel Islands National Park is made up of eight islands, though only five of those (Anacapa, Santa Cruz, Santa Rosa, San Miguel, and Santa Barbara) are within sight of the mainland. Since 1980 these areas have been federally protected. Long before they were tourist spots, they were ranch lands. And even longer before that, some 13,000 years ago, archaeological evidence suggests that they there were inhabited by indigenous people. Today, they're one of the last remaining wilderness spots in California.

Visiting the Park

Channel Islands National Park is one of the least-visited national parks in the United States, but it offers an array of outdoor activities, including backpacking, camping, scuba diving, kayaking, and surfing. The islands are most known for their high number of mysterious sea caves, arches, and abundant wildlife. A trip to the islands is an adventure into a solitary world, a hidden paradise for every outdoor adventurer.

The National Park Service authorizes a small number of guides and outfitter services. It is important to check with the **Robert J. Lagomarsino Visitor Center** (1901 Spinnaker Dr., Ventura, 805/658-5700, www.nps.gov/chis, 8:30am-5pm daily) and **National Park Service** (www.nps.gov) to plan your trip accordingly.

Getting There and Around

To access the islands by boat, the only ferry service leaves Ventura from **Island Packers** (1691 Spinnaker Dr., 805/642-1393, www.islandpackers.com), including day ($59-105 adults, $41-84 children) and overnight trips ($79-147 adults, $57-126 children). It offers transportation to five of the islands, including Channel Island whale-watching cruises and kayaking trips. Anacapa and Santa Cruz are about an hour each way by boat. The outer islands—Santa Rosa, Santa Barbara, and San Miguel—cost more to reach and take over two hours each way.

For groups, air travel is possible by charter from Camarillo Airport via **Channel Islands Aviation** (305 Durley Ave., Camarillo, 805/987-1301, $1,200 day trip up to 8 passengers, $1,760 camping up to 7 passengers) to Santa Rosa Island only.

Plan to walk or kayak your way around. There's no public transportation on any of the islands, and biking is not allowed.

Seasons

Temperatures average in the mid-60s to the low 50s year-round, but this is the coast, so be prepared for high winds and fog. The outer islands of Santa Rosa and San Miguel experience more frequent high winds, at times 30-knot winds. Other islands have more moderate winds. However, during the late spring and summer months, fog thickens, challenging visibility.

Park Entrances

Boaters must access Santa Barbara Island via the landing cove; dock access is limited. Access to Santa Rosa Island is permitted via coastline or beaches, and piers are available at Bechers Bay. Access to San Miguel Island is through Cuyler Harbor (beach only) or Tyler Bight. Access to Anacapa Island is at East Anacapa or Frenchy's Cove; however, a permit is required at Middle Anacapa, and visitors must be accompanied by a park ranger (access to West Anacapa is not allowed). Access to Santa Cruz Island is available via the pier at Scorpion Anchorage or Prisoners Harbor.

Visitors Centers

Robert J. Lagomarsino Visitor Center (1901 Spinnaker Dr., Ventura, 805/658-5700, www.nps.gov/chis, 8:30am-5pm daily) is located in Ventura and provides interpretive programs, tidepool displays, a bookstore, and island exhibits.

The small visitor contact stations on Santa Barbara and Anacapa Islands include resource displays and information on each island. Scorpion Ranch on Santa Cruz Island also houses information.

Information and Services

All information can be obtained via the visitors centers and through the **National Recreation Reservation Service** (888-448-1474, www.recreation.gov). There are no entrance fees, but a permit is required for camping and backcountry camping. Camping reservations can be made no more than five months in advance. Information required includes camping dates, transportation information, and number of campers.

Boaters should check with **The Nature Conservancy** (800/628-6860, www.nature.org) for landing information and permits. Private boaters must receive permission to land on certain islands, including Santa Cruz Island.

For weather reports, check the **Channel Islands Internet Weather Kiosk** (www.channelislands.noaa.gov/news/kiosk.html).

Sights and Recreation

All the islands offer hiking, water activities, and camping. Trails range from relatively flat trails to steep, rugged, mountainous trails. It is important to remember to stay within park boundaries and not hike on The Nature Conservancy property, which is clearly marked by a fence line.

Personal kayaks may be brought on the ferry, while rentals are available from **Channel Island Kayak Center** (1691 Spinnaker Dr., Ventura, 805/984-5995, www.cikayak.com, 10am-5pm Mon.-Fri., 10am-6pm Sat.-Sun., $35 single, 55 double kayak). For snorkel and scuba rentals, try **Ventura Dive & Sport** (1559 Spinnaker Dr. #108, 805/650-6500, www.venturadive.com, 10am-6pm Mon.-Fri., 8am-6pm

Sat., 8am-5pm Sun., $10-50 snorkel, $45-65 scuba).

On **Santa Cruz Island,** Scorpion Beach offers some of the best areas for water sports, with easy beach access and nearby sea caves for adventure exploration. Prisoners Harbor and Smugglers Cove also provide beach access; however, snorkeling and diving are not allowed. To access kelp beds, snorkelers and divers should explore near the pier and at the bay's eastern end. Kayaking at Scorpion Beach and sea caves is offered exclusively by **Channel Islands Adventure Company** (805/884-9283, www.sbadventureco.com, $149 adult, $139 children, plus ferry costs).

Santa Rosa Island offers sandy beaches, with easy access, and great opportunities for surfing. The north shore is best in winter and spring and the south shore is best in summer and fall.

Aggressive winds at **San Miguel Island** make water activities dangerous for the inexperienced. However, overnight stays offer time enough for an exceptional 16-mile ranger-guided hike to Point Bennett, where you can see one of the largest ensembles of wildlife.

Santa Barbara Island is a great place to see seals and sea lions from Landing Cove and from the overlook points of Sea Lion Rookery and Elephant Seal Cove. There are incredible stands of native vegetation and wildflowers. Kayakers can explore Sea Lion Rookery to the south, which offers a wonderland of wildlife, sea caves, and ocean arches.

The Landing Cove on **Anacapa Island** provides excellent swimming, diving, and snorkeling, but remember there are no lifeguards. Kayakers can head east toward Arch Rock or west toward Cathedral Cove for marine and wildlife viewing and sea caves. Hiking is limited on the island to only about two miles of trail.

There is no fishing allowed on any of the islands, and visitors are asked to stay on the trails and not disturb the flora or fauna. Visitors are asked to avoid animal nesting areas and to stay out of caves if not professionally guided. The park website contains a detailed list of restrictions.

Camping

Camping is available by **reservation only.** Campsites are primitive, with basic picnic tables and pit toilets. Trash containers are not provided; campers are expected to pack out their own garbage. Campsites are all close together, so don't expect a lot of privacy during high season. **Water** is available at the Scorpion Anchorage on Santa Cruz, at the Santa Rosa campground, and nowhere else. Due to the wind, San Miguel and Santa Rosa campgrounds have **windbreaks** for each campsite.

There are **no food venues, stores, or restaurants** on the islands. Santa Rosa Island campground and Scorpion Anchorage on Santa Cruz are the only sites for water. Plan accordingly and bring your own food and water.

Fires are not permitted except on eastern Santa Cruz Island, where there are fire pits and wood provided.

Camping on Santa Rosa Island beaches is for experienced kayakers and boaters on a seasonal basis, and a permit is required ($10-15 per night).

A **40-pound weight limit** restriction is imposed by the boat concessionaire. Bring the necessities, keeping in mind what is available on-site. Campgrounds are a half mile from the landings, except for Santa Rosa and San Miguel, where the campgrounds are 1-1.5 miles away. The eastern Santa Cruz site is an easy flat walk, while San Miguel and Santa Barbara require an uphill trek. Anacapa is uphill as well and includes stairs—a lot of stairs (approximately 156).

Ventura

About 35 miles southeast of Santa Barbara, **Ventura** (pop. 109,592) sits sandwiched between the American Riviera and Los Angeles. It's a beachy, surfer-friendly community with a cheerful, beer-and-tacos mentality. Its walkable Main Street, just three blocks from the beach, features eclectic small businesses and architecture, with art deco facades next to turn-of-the-20th-century structures next to polished tile-and-glass designs.

Sights

At the west end of Main Street, **Mission San Buenaventura** (211 E. Main St., 805/643-4318, www.sanbuenaventura-mission.org, 10am-5pm Mon.-Fri., 9am-5pm Sat., 10am-5pm Sun., $4 adults, $1 children) was the ninth mission in California, established in 1782. It is one of the few missions to still have wooden bells on display. From the gift shop, where the self-guided tour begins, the door opens to the courtyard, a beautifully landscaped area with a fountain in the center, surrounded by a few benches and interlocking short pathways. The church is across the courtyard. The church itself is long and narrow, a neoclassical-looking arch over the altar giving a more modern feel to the interior. The area behind the church is part of the original brick reservoir.

Recreation

Whatever your taste, Ventura has the beach for you. **San Buenaventura State Beach** (901 San Pedro St., 805/968-1033, www.parks.ca.gov, dawn-dusk daily) offers two miles of sea and sand for swimming, surfing, and picnicking. Accessed off Main Street, **Emma Wood State Beach** (W. Main St. and Park Access Rd., 805/968-1033, www.parks.ca.gov, www.reservecalifornia.com, dawn-dusk daily, $10 per vehicle) can be rocky but is a great spot for windsurfing or camping. Families flock to **Harbor Cove Beach** (1900 Spinnaker Dr., dawn-dusk daily), where the harbor's breakwaters provide relative safety from the ocean currents. Food and other amenities can be found across the street at Ventura Harbor Village. Farther north, **Faria Beach** (4350 W. US-101, at State Beach exit, 805/654-3951, www.ventura.org, dawn-dusk daily) is available for tent camping and has 15 RV hookups.

Ventura is also known for **surfing,** with **The Rincon** (Bates Rd. and US-101) its most famous landmark. Located between Santa Barbara and Ventura, The Rincon is a small cliffside cove between US-101 and the ocean. The intense swells make it a surfer's dream. Near the pier, **C-Street** is the nickname for another popular surfing spot, a mile-long stretch of sand at the end of California Street. Spectators gather along the concrete boardwalk to see wave-riders in action. For surf rentals, **Ventura Surf Shop** (88 E. Thompson Blvd., 805/643-1062, www.venturasurfshop.com, 9am-6pm Mon.-Sat., 9am-5pm Sun., $15-30 day) has been serving the area more than 50 years.

Food and Accommodations

If the margaritas and Mexican cuisine don't impress at **Limon y Sal** (589 E. Main St., 805/628-3868, 11am-11pm daily, $10-16), the decor will—the vast restaurant occupies a gorgeous 1928 bank building. For seafood fans, **Spencer Makenzie's Fish Company** (806 E. Thompson Blvd., 805/643-8226, www.spencermakenzies.com, 11am-9pm Sun.-Thurs., 10:30am-9pm Fri.-Sat., $8-12) has a reputation for great fish tacos and fish-and-chips.

Ventura is full of chain hotels and motels. For something different, downtown's **Bella Maggiore Inn** (67 S. California St., 805/652-0277 or 800/523-8479, www.bellamaggioreinn.com, $95-180) has a definite European feel. Just three blocks from the beach, the 32 rooms in this charmingly peculiar spot are all configured differently, and the inn almost feels more like a large bed-and-breakfast than a hotel. Or, stay in the cozy rooms of a converted Victorian church, complete with stained-glass windows, at the **Victorian Rose Bed & Breakfast** (896 E. Main St., 805/641-1888, www.victorianroseventura.com, $100-110).

Southern California Coast

Famous for its celebrity culture, laid-back beach vibes, and for being home to "the happiest place on Earth," Southern California lives up to the world's expectations.

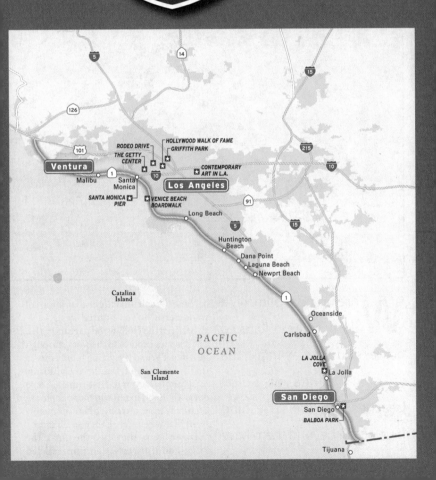

- RODEO DRIVE
- HOLLYWOOD WALK OF FAME
- GRIFFITH PARK
- THE GETTY CENTER
- CONTEMPORARY ART IN L.A.
- **Ventura**
- Malibu
- Santa Monica
- **Los Angeles**
- SANTA MONICA PIER
- VENICE BEACH BOARDWALK
- Long Beach
- Huntington Beach
- Dana Point
- Laguna Beach
- Newprt Beach
- Catalina Island
- Oceanside
- Carlsbad
- PACFIC OCEAN
- San Clemente Island
- LA JOLLA COVE
- La Jolla
- **San Diego**
- San Diego
- BALBOA PARK
- Tijuana

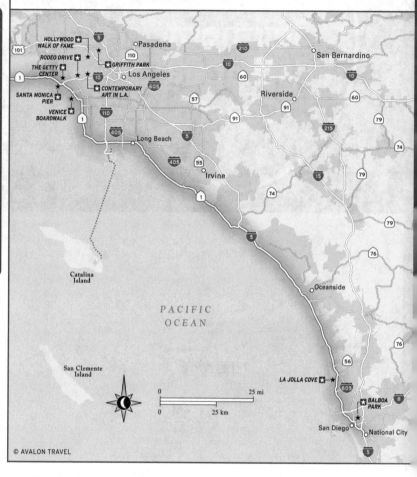

Southern California

© AVALON TRAVEL

While inland is primarily a dusty sprawl of stucco homes and freeway traffic, the sparkling sands of SoCal beaches and the refreshing blue ocean beyond them have become the spiritual home to millions of wanderers who've ventured west.

Between the Hollywood pageantry that Los Angeles exports to the world through film and TV, and the young family mecca that is Disneyland, Southern California feels familiar, even to first-timers. Some days, it's tough to tell whether people are genuinely more attractive here, or merely seem that way because they smile more.

Down here, they call the CA-1 the PCH, and it traverses an unparalleled

Highlights

★ **Santa Monica Pier:** Surrounded by a gorgeous beach and topped by a small amusement park, the pier is the center of attention (page 302).

★ **The Getty Center:** High on a hilltop above L.A., this free museum is home to eclectic art pieces and stunning views of the skyline (page 303).

★ **Venice Beach Boardwalk:** From the freaky to the fantastic, the Venice Boardwalk has it all. Prepare yourself for people-watching of fantastic proportions (page 306).

★ **Contemporary Art in L.A.:** Visit **The Broad** (page 310) and the **Los Angeles County Museum of Art** (page 311) to see why L.A. is the top contemporary art destination on the West Coast.

★ **Hollywood Walk of Fame:** Since 1960, entertainment legends have wished for a spot on this iconic three-mile sidewalk of the stars (page 313).

★ **Griffith Park:** A welcome expanse of greenery, "L.A.'s Central Park" includes the Griffith Observatory and the L.A. Zoo (page 314).

★ **Rodeo Drive:** Though the price tags along this famed Beverly Hills boulevard may be bigger than your zip code, window-shopping and celebrity-spotting are free (page 316).

★ **La Jolla Cove:** With its white sand and deep blue water, this beach north of San Diego is a refuge from the road, and its sea caves are a refuge for diverse marinelife (page 341).

★ **Balboa Park:** This sprawling urban park includes Spanish colonial architecture, lush gardens, multiple museums, and the world-famous San Diego Zoo (page 349).

Best Hotels

★ **Viceroy Hotel:** This ecofriendly Santa Monica hotel is a trendsetter (page 306).

★ **Ace Hotel:** This hip up-and-comer includes vibrant lounges, a cozy coffee shop, and an ornate theater—that's Hollywood style (page 325).

★ **Beverly Wilshire Hotel:** Even in Beverly Hills, this Italian Renaissance masterpiece stands out (page 325).

★ **Crystal Cove Beach Cottages:** Enjoy a peaceful retreat in a rustic cabin on

one of the last undeveloped beaches in Southern California (page 336).

★ **La Valencia:** This La Jolla villa is almost as beautiful as its views of the shimmering Pacific (page 346).

★ **Horton Grand Hotel:** The Gaslamp's most charming hotel happens to be ideally situated for exploring downtown (page 360).

★ **Hotel del Coronado:** This grand Victorian resort in San Diego is famous for celebrity guests like Marilyn Monroe and its resident ghost (page 361).

stretch of achingly beautiful beaches, from secluded, wealthy Malibu to eccentric, lively Venice Beach, and down farther to the 80 miles of surfable waves known to the world as San Diego.

Southern California is the perfect destination to eat delicate seafood, practice your water sports, and drive down the highway with the top down. It can be the perfect sunset ending to a Pacific Coast Highway road trip, or the perfect beginning.

Planning Your Time

Though seven days is adequate, give yourself extra time to explore. Copious sunshine and an abundance of activities make the Southern California coast a great place to get lost for a while.

That said, it may be necessary to make reservations at popular hotels more than a month in advance during summer months—especially in the top beach areas and cities with major attractions such as Los Angeles and San Diego. But the climate is welcoming most of the year—April and September in particular—and even the winter yields a few summery days, when it's possible to find great last-minute accommodations.

It's just over 60 miles from Oxnard to Los Angeles, and another 125 miles to San Diego. Driving times are dependent on the infamous Southern California traffic. Following scenic CA-1 is typically a much slower drive, but keep in mind that traffic can grind to a halt on the major freeways (US-101 and I-5) as well.

Getting There
Car

Southern California seems built for car travel. Major highways from the north include I-5 (southbound from Sacramento to San Diego), US-101 (southbound from Santa Barbara), and the coast hugger better known as Highway 1 (CA-1). From the east, I-15 connects Las Vegas to San Diego, and I-10 connects Phoenix to Los Angeles.

Air

Major airports are **Los Angeles International Airport (LAX)** (1 World Way, 310/646-5252, www.lawa.org/lax) and **San Diego International Airport (SAN)** (3225 N. Harbor Dr., 619/400-2404, www.san.org). The Los Angeles metropolitan area also offers several smaller, often less congested airports: **Bob Hope**

Best Restaurants

★ **Neptune's Net:** After a day riding waves, Malibu surfers sate their appetites with fresh seafood at the cliffside spot (page 299).

★ **Gjelina:** A short walk but a far cry from the Venice Boardwalk, this contemporary dining destination is all about the flavor (page 304).

★ **Guelaguetza:** L.A. puts Oaxaca on display at this experiential restaurant. Don't miss the mole (page 319).

★ **Zankou Chicken:** Delectable garlic paste and tahini add to the local lore

of L.A.'s storied Mediterranean chicken roaster (page 319).

★ **Musso & Frank:** For a taste of Old Hollywood, soak in the ambience at Tinseltown's oldest restaurant (page 319).

★ **Ironside Fish & Oyster:** Impressive interior design and amazing seafood make this San Diego spot a memorable experience (page 357).

★ **Las Cuatro Milpas:** Enjoy authentic Mexican cuisine made with the best flour tortillas in California—and possibly the world (page 357).

Airport (BUR) (also called Hollywood Burbank Airport), **John Wayne Airport (SNA)** in Orange County, and **Long Beach Airport (LGB).**

Train
Amtrak (800/872-7245, www.amtrak.com, $37 and up) offers service on the **Coast Starlight** to Seattle, Portland, Sacramento, Oakland, and Los Angeles. The **Pacific Surfliner** provides service from San Luis Obispo to Santa Barbara, Los Angeles, and San Diego. The **Sunset Limited** travels east-west between Tennessee and Los Angeles. International visitors can buy an unlimited travel USA Rail Pass, good for 15, 30, or 45 days.

Bus
Greyhound (800/231-2222, www.greyhound.com) offers special discounts to students and seniors with routes and stops sticking to major highways and cities.

Fuel and Services
Cars, and subsequently **gas stations** and other services, are ubiquitous in high-population Southern California.

Compared to most of the country, California typically has substantially higher gasoline prices because of its high taxes.

To receive reports on **road conditions,** call **511.** If your phone carrier does not support 511, call toll-free at 800/977-6368.

For **emergency assistance** and services, call **911.**

Oxnard

Oxnard (pop. 207,906) is the gateway to California's southern coast, the first place you hit when Pacific Coast Highway 1 (CA-1) splits from US-101. It's about 38 miles (45 minutes) away from Santa Barbara. The quiet beach town boasts a relatively uncrowded stretch of wide sandy beaches and marinas lining the **Channel Islands Harbor,** an exceptional place for diving, sea kayaking, sportfishing, and whale-watching. It's been ranked as one of the wealthiest and safest cities in America.

Downtown is liveliest around historic **Heritage Square** (715 S. A St.), a hub for shopping, community events, and wine-tasting at Rancho Ventavo Cellars Tasting Room. The open-air plaza features 15 restored Victorian mansions, fountains, and surrounding gardens. Guided **walking tours** (805/483-7960 ext. 3, by appointment, $5) provide an overview of the city's early farming roots and booming growth, attributed to the sugar beet industry.

Oxnard hosts the **California Strawberry Festival** (Strawberry Meadows of College Park, 3250 S. Rose Ave., $12 adults, $5 children, $10 parking) on the third weekend in May, featuring appropriately themed food items such as strawberry nachos, strawberry pizza, strawberry funnel cake, strawberry sundaes, and strawberry champagne.

At the **California Welcome Center** (2786 Seaglass Way, 805/988-0717, 9:30am-8pm daily), you'll find the most informative regional and state maps and brochures, as well as concierge services, souvenirs, food items, and special offers and attraction discounts.

Malibu

When Hollywood movie stars go to the beach, they go to **Malibu** (pop. 12,879), the exclusive community hugging Los Angeles's northwest coast. Rather than a centralized town, Malibu is a narrow strip of coastline stretching 27 miles along either side of the Pacific Coast Highway (CA-1), beginning just south of Oxnard. It's a gorgeous drive, as the highway winds between verdant mountain hillsides and sparkling ocean, with beachside colonies of multimillion-dollar homes scattered between state beaches and parks. It may not always seem like it, but there are no private beaches in Malibu. If you can find an access point without trespassing on clearly delineated private property, you may avoid paying for parking, and possibly catch some rays with a celebrity or two, watching surfers enjoy some of the area's celebrated point breaks.

beachfront homes in Malibu

Point Mugu State Park

Right where the Pacific Coast Highway comes back to the coast after Oxnard, you'll hit **Point Mugu State Park** (9000 CA-1 W., 800/444-7275, www.parks. ca.gov, 8am-10pm daily, $8-12), where 70 miles of hiking trails complement the waves, beach dunes, and campsites in remote country that seems much farther than a mere 50 miles from Hollywood.

Food

A few miles down the highway, ★ **Neptune's Net** (42505 CA-1, 310/457-3095, www.neptunesnet.com, 10:30am-8pm Mon.-Thurs., 10:30am-9pm Fri., 10am-8:30pm Sat.-Sun., $8-18) catches all kinds of seafood to serve to hungry diners, often in a fried form. Because it's adjacent to the County Line surf break, salt-encrusted local surfers often satisfy their enormous appetites here after hours out on the waves.

Leo Carrillo State Park

The beach at **Leo Carrillo State Park** (35000 CA-1 W., 310/457-8143, www. parks.ca.gov, 8am-10pm daily, $3-12 parking) offers more than just sunbathing and swimming. Caves, reefs, and tidepools make for an interesting stop. There is also a **visitors center** (10am-2pm Fri.-Sat.) and overnight camping.

Nicholas Canyon County Beach

Less crowded than other nearby beaches, **Nicholas Canyon** (33850 CA-1, http:// beaches.lacounty.gov, $3-10) offers one of several point breaks in Los Angeles County, making it a good spot for surfing, bodysurfing, bodyboarding, windsailing, and scuba diving. (It's often referred to as "Zeros.") Families enjoy nearly a mile stretch of sandy beach, with picnic tables and full bathroom facilities.

After exploring the beach, visit the fascinating **Chumash Discovery Village** (33904 CA-1, 424/644-0088, www.wishtoyo.org), which lies on a bluff overlooking the Pacific. Eight prehistoric (4000-6000 BC) sites have been found within a half mile of the current replicated village. Guided tours and presentations are available by appointment.

El Pescador State Beach

El pescador means "the fisherman" in Spanish. **El Pescador State Beach** (32860 CA-1, 310/457-1324, www.parks.ca.gov, 8am-sunset daily), a well-known spot for surf fishing, surfing, and bodyboarding, also offers good beachcombing, including tidepools rich with colorful sea anemones and starfish and small caves that can be explored at low tide.

El Matador State Beach

A rugged strip of white sand, steep cliffs, sea stacks, and incredible swells makes **El Matador State Beach** (32215 CA-1, 818/880-0363, www.parks.ca.gov, 8am-sunset daily, parking $8 all day) a favorite among surfers and body boarders. The natural splendor has made it a favorite backdrop for photo shoots as well. Park at the top of the bluff and follow the long staircase down the cliffside and onto the beach.

Zuma Beach

If you've ever seen the cult classic film *Earth Girls Are Easy,* you'll recognize legendary **Zuma Beach** (30000 CA-1, http://beaches.lacounty.gov, $3-12.50). This popular surf and boogie boarding break fills up fast on summer weekends. Crystal-clear water (unusual for the L.A. area) makes it good for swimming. Grab a spot on the west side of CA-1 for free parking, or pay a little for one of the more than 2,000 spots in the beach parking lot. Amenities include a snack bar, boardwalk, and volleyball courts, as well as restrooms and showers.

Point Dume State Beach

The crystal-clear water at **Point Dume State Beach** (Westward Beach Rd., 310/457-8143, sunrise-sunset daily), just two miles off of CA-1, makes it one of the best places in Southern California to scuba dive. The views from atop the coastal bluff are outstanding. It was named in honor of Padre Francisco Dumetz of Mission San Buenaventura by explorer George Vancouver, who made a spelling error.

Malibu Lagoon State Beach

Amid a row of beachfront mansions, **Malibu Lagoon State Beach** (23200 CA-1, 310/457-8143, www.parks.ca.gov, 8am-sunset daily, $12) offers easy public access. Malibu Creek runs into the ocean here, creating a unique wetlands ecosystem that's well worth exploring. The ancillary **Malibu Surfriders Beach** is a pretty stretch of sugar-like sand, offering a wealth of activities. Other park attractions include the 1929 **Adamson House and Malibu Lagoon Museum** (23200 CA-1, 310/456-8432, www.adamsonhouse.org, $7 adults, $2 children).

Santa Monica Beach

Malibu Pier

Malibu Pier (23000 CA-1, 888/310-7437, www.malibupiersportfishing.com) is busy in the summertime and lonely in the winter, when only die-hard surfers ply the adjacent three-point break and a few fisherfolk brave the chilly weather (which in Malibu means under 70°F). The pier hosts board rentals, sportfishing and whale-watching charters, restaurants, and food stands. Interpretive signs describe local history.

Food

Two sister restaurants sit on Malibu Pier. At the base of the pier is **Malibu Farm Restaurant & Bar** (23000 CA-1, www.malibu-farm.com, 310/456-8850, 7am-9pm Sun.-Fri., 7am-10pm Sat., $20-34), an upscale contemporary restaurant that takes reservations. At the end of the pier sits **Malibu Farm Café** (23000 CA-1, www.malibu-farm.com, 310/456-1112, 7am-9pm Sun.-Fri., 7am-10pm Sat., $12-18), a casual eatery that takes walk-in

guests only to dine with a panoramic rooftop view.

The Getty Villa

Perched on the cliffs just below Malibu in Pacific Palisades, **The Getty Villa** (17985 CA-1, Pacific Palisades, 310/440-7300, www.getty.edu, 10am-5pm Wed.-Mon., free but reservations required, $15 parking) is a lush estate, styled in the manner of an ancient Roman country home. The museum's immense, if at times controversial, collection of Etruscan, Greek, and Roman antiquities includes 44,000 pieces; only a small fraction are on display in its 23 galleries.

Santa Monica

Just five miles from Malibu, you'll hit **Santa Monica** (pop: 92,478). Born as a seaside retreat in the 1900s, the city was at one time home to silver-screen giants like Greta Garbo and Cary Grant. By the late 1960s, the Santa Monica Freeway brought new growth and an eclectic mix of families, free-spirited surfers, and business professionals. Today, Santa Monica plays home to moguls, tech geeks, starlets, yogis, musicians, self-styled gypsies, environmentalists, and creatives. With its fun-but-not-fancy pier, its inexpensive off-beach motels, and a variety of delicious inexpensive dining options, Santa Monica is a great choice for a road-trip stop.

Getting There and Around

CA-1 runs north and south along the coast traveling right through Santa Monica. The often congested I-10 freeway (also known as the Santa Monica Freeway) runs to the Santa Monica Pier from downtown Los Angeles; it's a rare day when traffic moves at the posted speed limit. If you are driving from Los Angeles, I-5 and US-101 join I-10 around downtown Los Angeles. This can be confusing if you're unaware, so keep your eye on the signs.

Not many places in Los Angeles can be accessed without a car, but Santa Monica is an exception. Many of the city's tourist destinations are within walking distance of each other. **Santa Monica's Bike Transit Center** (www.bikesm.com) provides bike rentals and two secured parking sites: at 320 Broadway and at 215 Colorado Avenue. A U-lock is recommended.

The **Big Blue Bus** (310/451-5444, www.bigbluebus.com, $1, free transfers) provides service both locally and throughout the Greater Los Angeles area. The Expo Line of the **Los Angeles Metro** (323/466-3876, www.metro.net, $1.75, 50 cent transfers), which opened in 2016, brought long-awaited commuter rail out of downtown to Santa Monica.

Sights
Santa Monica Beach

Santa Monica Beach embodies the city's history, scenic beauty, and active lifestyle with 3.5 miles of wide, sandy beach, perfect for sunbathing, biking, or roller blading. Known as "The Strand," this well-traveled path connects Santa Monica Beach to Will Rogers State Beach to the north and Redondo Beach to the south. Lifeguards keep watch over surfers, swimmers, and beach bunnies (much of the hit TV show *Baywatch* was filmed here). There are plenty of picnic areas and playgrounds.

★ Santa Monica Pier

The landmark **Santa Monica Pier** (Ocean Ave. at Colorado Ave., 310/458-8900, www.santamonicapier.org) has welcomed generations of families and out-of-towners since 1909. Today, highlights include a historical carousel, solar-paneled Ferris wheel, arcade games, and thrill rides at **Pacific Park** (310/260-8744, www.pacpark.com, $5-10 per ride, unlimited rides $30). Tucked beneath the carousel, the **Santa Monica Pier Aquarium** (1600 Ocean Front Walk,

310/393-6149, www.healthebay.org, 2pm-5pm Tues.-Fri., 12:30pm-5pm Sat.-Sun., $5 adults, free children 12 and under) includes touch tanks that allow for exploration of sea creatures like urchins, snails, and sea cucumbers, as well as worthwhile exhibits dedicated to jellyfish, leopard sharks, and stingrays. During the summer, the boardwalk becomes a stage for weekly outdoor concerts and free events. Historical **walking tours** (11am or noon Sat.-Sun., free) start at the **Pier Shop & Visitor Center** (310/804-7457); look for the tour guide in the blue shirt.

Palisades Park

Virtually nothing can escape the view of **Palisades Park** (851 Alma Real Dr., 310/454-1412, dawn-dusk daily), which lies atop sandstone cliffs overlooking Santa Monica Beach. Photographers, tourists, joggers, and yoga practitioners make use of the manicured lawns, benches, and pathway, appreciating the obscurely twisted trees, rose garden, artworks, and historical structures along the way. At the northern end of the park is a Chilkat Tlingit totem pole featuring a fish, raven, bear, and wolf. At the southern end, two cannons installed in 1908 point directly at the Santa Monica Pier, and a stone monument marks the 400th anniversary of explorer Juan Rodriguez Cabrillo's 1542 encounter of the bay. If you don't mind the park's resident homeless, who generally keep to themselves, Palisades is a good spot for watching the sunset.

Annenberg Community Beach House

In the 1920s, publishing bigwig William Randolph Hearst built the beachfront 100-room mansion that later became the **Annenberg Community Beach House** (415 CA-1, 310/458-4904, www.annenbergbeachhouse.com, 8:30am-5:30pm daily, free) for his mistress, actress Marion Davies. Today, modern additions to the historic estate include a play area, art gallery, and an array of recreational activities, including swimming in the marble and tile pool (June-Sept., $10 adults, $4 children 1-17).

★ The Getty Center

High on a hilltop overlooking both Santa Monica and Beverly Hills—most of the city, really—**The Getty Center** (1200 Getty Center Dr., 310/440-7300, 10am-5:30pm Tues.-Fri. and Sun., 10am-9pm Sat., free admission, $5 audio tour, $15 parking) is a fortress of travertine- and aluminum-clad pavilions, built to house the eclectic art collection of billionaire J. Paul Getty, which includes everything from Renaissance-era paintings to pop art. Getty opened a museum at his Malibu estate in the 1950s (The Getty Villa can still be visited today). After his death in 1976, an endowment was established to preserve his beloved collection and make it accessible to the public.

The center opened in 1998, welcoming visitors by way of a three-car, cable-pulled hover-train funicular (a large parking garage is at the base of the hill). Steps lead up to the main entrance of the rotunda building, which links all five of the art pavilions. Richard Meier's striking design includes fountains, glass windows several stories high, and an open plan that permits intimate vistas of the city below. A separate west building includes a cafeteria and restaurant. Stairs from the terrace lead down to outdoor terraces and gardens designed by Robert Irwin. The gardens and the views are as inspiring as the art. On a clear day, you can see the city skyline all the way west to the Pacific.

Admission is free; however you'll have to pay to park or take Metro bus 761. To take the free tram from the parking structure, ride the elevators up to the Lower Tram Station. The center is also

From top to bottom: the Getty Villa; rides on Santa Monica Pier; bike from Santa Monica to the Venice Beach Boardwalk via the Strand.

accessible by way of the 0.75-mile pedestrian path that is about a 20-minute walk from the parking structure.

Recreation

Beach volleyball is said to have been born in Santa Monica. A number of courts located north and south of the pier are available daily for public play on a first-come, first-served basis. Courts may be reserved in advance by calling 310/458-8300 and paying a required permit fee ($10-32).

Bike **the Strand** (40 miles), a popular and easily accessible bike path that gets busy in the summer; make sure to check with the local visitors center or bike rental shop for any safety requirements. You can ride to Will Rogers State Beach to the north and Redondo Beach to the south. There are many coastal communities in between, like Venice Beach (3 miles south) and Pacific Palisades (2.8 miles north). The bike path runs parallel to the **Oceanfront Walk** (a pedestrian walkway) until Bicknell Avenue (south of the pier), where it veers west, following the coastline north, passing under the Santa Monica Pier, and continuing on to Will Rogers State Beach. The Santa Monica portion of The Strand runs from Temescal Canyon in the north to Washington Boulevard in Venice in the south (8.5 miles/13.7 kilometers). **Santa Monica Bike Center** (1555 2nd St. Unit A, 310/656-8500, 7am-8pm Mon.-Fri., 8am-8pm Sat.-Sun.) rents bikes just off the pier.

Go Surf LA (2400 Ocean Front Walk, 310/428-9870, by appointment, www.gosurfla.com, $80) offers lessons to wannabe surfers (gear included).

Food

Reservations are required at **Melisse** (1104 Wilshire Blvd., 310/395-0881, www.melisse.com, 6pm-9:30pm Tues.-Thurs., 6pm-10pm Fri., 5:45pm-10pm Sat., $145 pp minimum). The two-Michelin-star restaurant caters to exclusivity,

furnishing a tasting menu of seasonal courses presented with world-class wines and classical French service. Chef Josiah Citrin's creation provides ambience as chic as such an incomparable meal deserves.

Tables are on the literal beach at **Back on the Beach** (445 CA-1, 310/393-8282, www.backonthebeachcafe.com, 8am-3pm Mon.-Thurs., 8am-4pm Fri.-Sun. Nov.-Apr., 8am-8pm daily May-Oct., $9-20). Classic American breakfast and lunch dishes are served year-round, plus dinner during the long summer months.

Bay Cities Italian Deli & Bakery (1517 Lincoln Blvd., 310/395-8279, www.bcdeli.com, 9am-6pm Tues.-Sun., under $10) has been whipping up authentic Italian pasta and sandwiches since 1925. Take a number; it's worth the wait.

For relatively affordable samplings of the current culinary moment in L.A., drop into Venice and check out the sister restaurants dominating the consciousness of west side foodies. If you can wrangle a spot at ★ **Gjelina** (1429 Abbot Kinney Blvd., 310/450-1429, www.gjelina.com, 8am-midnight daily, under $25), prepare to gorge on oysters, wood-fired pizza, or a litany of richly composed meat, seafood, and vegetable plates. If not, try its convenient takeaway component, or go browse the glass counter at **Gjusta** (320 Sunset Ave., 310/314-0320, www.gjusta.com, 7am-9pm daily, $6-18). The hard-working artisans of this standing-room-only deli either bake, cure, smoke, or roast everything to perfection.

The famed burger at the **Father's Office** (1018 Montana Ave., 310/736-2224, www.fathersoffice.com, 5pm-10pm Mon.-Wed., 5pm-11pm Thurs., 4pm-11pm Fri., noon-11pm Sat., noon-10pm Sun., bar open until 1am Mon.-Thurs., 2am Fri.-Sat., midnight Sun., $5-16) tops dry-aged beef with caramelized onions, gruyère and blue cheese, bacon, and arugula. It pairs perfectly with a world-class IPA or stout—for two decades, the gastropub has set the bar for local craft beer draft lists, featuring fresh kegs of the region's best.

Though local favorite **Santa Monica Seafood** (1000 Wilshire Blvd., 310/393-5244, www.smseafoodmarket.com, 9am-9pm Mon.-Sat., 9am-8pm Sun., under $25) is a retail fish market, it includes a café and oyster bar that serves fresh seafood with an Italian twist.

Fast food in Santa Monica means sunny, farm-sourced counter restaurants, and clustered around the Promenade area, you can take your pick of health-conscious sandwiches and salads at **Tender Greens** (201 Arizona Ave., 310/587-2777, www.tendergreens.com, 11am-9:30pm daily, under $12), or bowls and wraps at **Flower Child** (1332 2nd St., 310/382-2901, www.iamaflowerchild.com, 11am-9pm Mon.-Fri., 10am-9pm Sat.-Sun., under $12).

Nightlife and Entertainment

A half block south of the pier, **Chez Jay** (1657 Ocean Ave., 310/395-1741, www.chezjays.com) doesn't look like much, but the little nautical dive bar has been serving locals and celebrities for almost 50 years. Jay's peanuts are as famous as its clientele—ask them about the nut that made it to the moon! Open since 1934, **The Galley** (2442 Main St., 310/452-1934, www.thegalleyrestaurant.net, happy hour 5pm-7pm daily) is the oldest bar in town. Worth a visit for the kitschy nautical vibe alone—strong drinks don't hurt either.

Two well-established Brit pubs, **Ye Olde Kings Head** (116 Santa Monica Blvd., 310/451-1402, www.yeoldekingshead.com) and **Cock N Bull Pub** (2947 Lincoln Blvd., 310/399-9696), fill up for soccer and rugby games. Both offer a good range of brews and spirits, as well as fish-and-chips.

Literary fans will appreciate a bar dedicated to gritty poet and author Charles Bukowski. The aptly named **Barkowski** (2819 Pico Blvd., 310/998-0069, www.barkowski.com). The Buk himself preferred seedier locales, but the retro vibe and weary world outlook shared among his readers makes it work. If you prefer suds to cocktails, try the indoor/outdoor **The Library Alehouse** (2911 Main St., 310/314-4855, www.libraryalehouse.com, $5 after 11pm weekends), which has been deftly serving craft beer almost since there's been craft beer.

To be young and beautiful and in Santa Monica is to be drinking on the patio at **The Bungalow** (101 Wilshire Blvd., 310/899-8530, www.thebungalow.com). The stylish beachfront bungalow is the perfect spot to day drink, and becomes the perfect spot to night drink, right after being the perfect spot to toast the sun going down. You get the idea.

Shopping

Shopping on **Main Street** (www.mainstreetsm.com) may have you seeing stars. If you don't spot a celeb, you can settle for window-shopping. Main Street is the greenest street in Santa Monica, with earth-conscious boutiques like **Vital Hemp** (2305 Main St., 310/450-2260, 10am-6pm daily), a producer of quality hemp clothing for men and women that's friendly to the planet, and **Natural High Lifestyle** (2510 Main St., 323/691-1827, www.naturalhighlifestyle.myshopify.com), which features clothing and products made from hemp, organic cotton, buckwheat hulls, and FSC-certified plywood.

The eclectic **Mindfulnest** (2711 Main St., 310/452-5409, www.mindfulnest.com, 11am-7:30pm Sun.-Thurs., 11am-9pm Fri.-Sat.) features the works of nearly 100 contemporary artists. On Sundays, Main Street hosts the widely popular **Farmers Market** (2640 Main St., 310/458-8712, 8:30am-1:30pm Sun.), which features food booths, local retailers, arts and crafts, live music, and fun activities for the little ones, like face-painting.

The people-watching is magnificent at **Third Street Promenade,** a vibrant, pedestrian-only, outdoor shopping corridor northwest of Main Street. Expect great restaurants, movie theaters, street performers, and popular chain stores like Abercrombie & Fitch, Express, and Pottery Barn, with a few independent art galleries and specialty and vintage shops. On Wednesdays and Saturdays, it's home to another terrific **Farmers Market** (155-199 Arizona Ave., 310/458-8712, 8am-1:30pm Sat. and Wed.).

Adjacent to the Promenade, **Santa Monica Place** (4th St. and Broadway, 310/394-5451) is an open-air mall stocked with a collection of high-end retailers like Tiffany, Bloomingdales, and Kenneth Cole.

Events

Bring a blanket, find a spot on the beach, and watch the sun set while listening to Santa Monica Pier's summer **Twilight Concerts** (7pm-10pm Thurs. in summer). In the fall, the pier hosts **Front Porch Cinema** (Fri. nights), with music, films, and food and drinks. Rent a lawn chair for a few bucks or bring your own.

Accommodations

Ecofriendly trendsetter ★ **Viceroy Hotel** (1819 Ocean Ave., 310/260-7500 and 800/670-6185, www.viceroyhotelsandresorts.com, $300 and up) has been one of the top 50 hotels by *Condé Nast Traveler*, among others. Large airy cabanas with comfy couches and fluffy pillows provide shade from the sun and access to the pool. It's a block from the beach and a few blocks from downtown.

The green-certified **Ambrose Hotel** (1255 20th St., 310/315-1555, www.ambrosehotel.com, $175 and up) has a positive impact on its guests and the environment. Elegant rooms include cotton robes, bath linens, and natural bath products. Some have balconies and terraces; all come with a complimentary breakfast.

In the course of its history, the art deco 1933 **Georgian Hotel** (1415 Ocean Ave., 310/395-9945 and 800/538-8147, www.georgianhotel.com, $200 and up) has hosted stars and starlets. Today, it continues to please with stylish guest rooms and suites, boutique amenities, and a contemporary restaurant. It's just steps from the sand and close to shopping and restaurants.

Shutters on the Beach (Pico Blvd., 310/458-0030 and 800/334-9000, $575 and up) is a luxury hotel set right on the sand. Guest rooms are bright with hardwood floors, Tibetan rugs, spacious bathrooms, and balconies. The hotel houses a café, bar, and fine dining, as well as a spa.

HI Los Angeles/Santa Monica (1436 2nd St., 310/393-9913, www.hilosangeles.org, $50 dorm, $150 private) offers clean dorm-style and private rooms, and facilities that feature daily movies, Internet access, kitchen, laundry, and breakfast.

Information and Services

Free brochures and information on area attractions are available at the **Pier Shop & Visitor Center** (200 Santa Monica Pier, 310/804-7457, 11am-5pm Mon.-Thurs., 11am-7pm Fri.-Sun.). There is also a walk-in **Visitor Information Center** (2427 Main St., 310/393-7593, 9am-5:30pm Mon.-Fri., 9am-5pm Sat.-Sun.) that provides information resources, three computers with high-speed Internet access, and souvenirs. Tickets to area attractions are also available for purchase.

★ Venice Beach Boardwalk

The Venice Beach Boardwalk is just 2 miles, or about 10 minutes driving, from the Santa Monica Pier. Out of literally hundreds of beaches between San Diego and the Olympic Peninsula, you will not encounter another quite like Venice Beach. At times its 2.5-mile-long boardwalk seems like a circus on parade. While a steady stream of beach cruisers roll by on bikes, skateboards, rollerblades and skates to soak up the vibe, so too do hippies, oiled-up body builders, yoga acrobats, buskers, tarot readers, breakdancing b-boys, roller disco mavens, street hustlers, and every shade of exhibitionist.

Aside from the unusual beach life, you'll find cafés, souvenir shops, and recreational activities. For $4 you can pump iron at Muscle Beach. At 10:30am on Saturdays, take a free yoga class on the beach. There's also an outdoor roller rink and skate park.

The best time to visit is in the summer, mid-morning through the late afternoon. Venice Beach Boardwalk tends to feel a little safer in the light of day.

Los Angeles

America's second largest city, **Los Angeles** (pop. 4 million, 19 million metropolitan) has had its share of facelifts over the past two centuries, reinventing itself from Spanish military outpost to seaside playground to cinematic dream factory to super-suburbia. It's a city built on dreams, schemes, and intrigues, so it's no surprise that the movie industry found its home here.

Despite the constant arrival of new trends, L.A. has a soft spot for nostalgia, whether it's Old Hollywood glamour or greasy spoon food counters. The city's Mexican heritage is commemorated at Olvera Street, the very spot where the Pueblo de Los Ángeles was founded in 1781. After California became a U.S. state in 1850 and the railroad opened up the West to the rest of the country, film reels sent back east sold the city as a perennial sunny land where the American Dream comes true. And the city's tried to live up to that ever since.

While countless thousands of newcomers still arrive each year seeking fame and fortune, it's not all film industry making up L.A. culture: Art, theater, and food are thriving in Los Angeles these days. Of course, the city's notoriously bad traffic can slow down your efforts to enjoy it all. Fortunately, an ever-expanding metro rail system makes it easier

than ever to connect several of the city's prime destinations, such as Hollywood, downtown, and even the beaches of Santa Monica.

Getting There and Around
Car
Los Angeles is crisscrossed with freeways, providing numerous yet congested access points into the city. From the north and south, I-5 provides the most direct access to downtown. From I-5, US-101 South leads directly into Hollywood; from where Santa Monica Boulevard can take you west to Beverly Hills. Connecting from I-5 to I-210 will take you east to Pasadena. The best way to reach Santa Monica, Venice, and Malibu is via CA-1, also known as the Pacific Coast Highway. I-10 can get you there from the east, but it will be a long, tedious, and trafficked drive.

Traffic can be awful any time, even outside of typical rush hours. Local drivers accustomed to the conditions aren't always polite. Expect to be cut off by drivers paying attention to everything in the world but the road. Most road signs use numbers, but locals, including the radio traffic reporters, use names (e.g., Santa Ana Freeway, Santa Monica Freeway, etc.). There's no visible name-to-number translation on most maps, and names can change depending on which section of freeway you're driving.

Parking in Los Angeles can be challenging and expensive. You will find parking lots and structures included with many hotel rooms, but parking on the street can be difficult or impossible, parking lots in sketchy areas (like the Flower and Jewelry Districts) can be dangerous, and parking structures at popular attractions can be expensive.

Air
L.A. is one of the most airport-dense metropolitan areas in the country. **Los Angeles International Airport (LAX)** (1 World Way, Los Angeles, 310/646-5252,

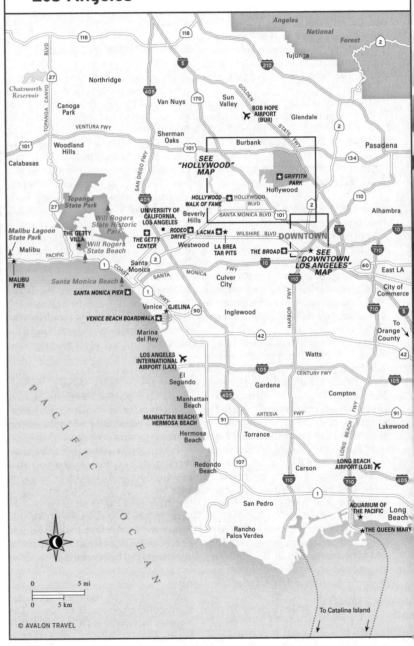

www.lawa.org) has the most flights, which makes it the most crowded of the L.A. airports, with the longest security and check-in lines. If you can find a way around flying into LAX, do so. One option is to fly into other local airports, including **Bob Hope/Hollywood Burbank Airport (BUR)** (2627 N. Hollywood Way, Burbank, 818/840-8840, www.burbankairport.com) or **Long Beach Airport (LGB)** (4100 Donald Douglas Dr., Long Beach, 562/570-2600, www.lgb.org). It may be a slightly longer drive to your final destination, but it can be well worth it. If you depart from LAX, arrive a minimum of two hours ahead of your domestic flight time (three hours on busy holidays).

Train
Amtrak (800/872-7245, www.amtrak.com) has an active rail hub in Los Angeles. Most trains come in to **Union Station** (800 N. Alameda St.). From Union Station, you can get to the San Francisco Bay Area, Portland, and eventually Seattle on the **Coast Starlight** train, or you can take the **Pacific Surfliner** south to San Diego. The **San Joaquin** runs out to Sacramento via the Bay Area. The **Sunset Limited** travels east-west between Tennessee and Los Angeles.

From Union Station, which also acts as a Metrolink hub, you can take the **Metrolink** (www.metrolinktrains.com) to or from various spots in Southern California, including Ventura and Oceanside.

Public Transit
The **Metro** (323/466-3876, www.metro.net, cash fare $1.75, day pass $7, seven-day pass $25) runs both the subway Metro rail system and a network of buses throughout the L.A. metropolitan area. You can pay onboard a bus if you have exact change. Otherwise, purchase a ticket or a day pass from the ticket vending machines present in all Metro rail stations. If you will be riding the Metro

often, consider purchasing a TAP refillable card ($1 plus regular fare); you must purchase a TAP card if you want to purchase the unlimited-ride day or seven-day passes.

Some buses run for 24 hours. The Metro rail lines can start running as early as 4:30am and don't stop until as late as 1:30am. See the website for route maps, timetables, and fare details on getting to and from downtown, Hollywood, Pasadena, Long Beach, South Bay, and Santa Monica.

Sights
Downtown
Downtown L.A. has tall, glass-coated skyscrapers creating an urban skyline, sports arenas, rich neighborhoods, poor neighborhoods, and endless shopping opportunities. Most of all, it has some of the best unique cultural icons in L.A. County.

Olvera Street
Bejeweled with history and culture, **Olvera Street** (125 Paseo de la Plaza, www.calleolvera.com, 10am-7pm daily) is at the historic center of L.A., where the "City of Angels" was born. At its south end, the tree-shaded **Old Plaza** (also known as El Pueblo de Los Ángeles State Historic Park) stands as a small gathering space for community events and pays tribute to the pueblo's 44 original *pobladores* (townspeople), who were of Spanish, Mexican, African, and Native American heritage. A few steps away, the **Mexican Cultural Institute** houses traditional and contemporary Mexican art. Two of L.A.'s oldest structures are found here. The **Old Plaza Church** was first built in 1784 but, due to floods and earthquake damage, was reconstructed in 1861. The oldest surviving building is the **Avila Adobe** (10 Olvera St., 213/485-6855, 9am-4pm daily, free). The walls are made of 2.5- to 3-foot-thick sunbaked bricks. A mixture of tar (brought from the La Brea Tar Pits), rocks, and horsehair was used to weatherize the

Two Days in Los Angeles

Day 1

Go Hollywood—Hollywood Boulevard, that is. Check out star footprints outside the **TCL Chinese Theatre** (page 311) and wander the **Hollywood Walk of Fame** (page 313). Poster and memorabilia shops abound, so pick up a still from your favorite movie.

For lunch, enjoy award-winning Mexican fare at **Yuca's** (page 319). Then head to **Griffith Park** (page 314) to enjoy the green space and the view of the **Hollywood Sign** from the Griffith Observatory. Then it's off to Beverly Hills for an afternoon of star-spotting and window-shopping on **Rodeo Drive** (page 316). See and be seen having dinner at the legendary **Spago Beverly Hills** (page 320).

After dinner, cruise the **Sunset Strip** (page 314), where revelers flock to legendary music clubs like the **Whisky a Go Go** and **The Viper Room** (page 321); or grab some laughs at **The Comedy Store** (page 321).

Day 2

After breakfast at **Original Pantry Cafe** (page 318), head to the birthplace of L.A.: **Olvera Street** (page 309). Tour the city's oldest structure, the **Avila Adobe,** and stroll the colorful marketplace. Spend some time enjoying art at **The Broad** (page 310) before browsing the food vendors at **Grand Central Market** (page 319) for lunch.

Hollywood's biggest stars have left their mark outside the TCL Chinese Theatre.

To explore much deeper into the city's past, spend the afternoon with the famous fossils at the **La Brea Tar Pits** (page 311) and checking the current exhibitions at **Los Angeles County Museum of Art** (page 311), then head back to Hollywood to sample the slices at **Pizzeria Mozza** or dine on pasta at sister restaurant **Osteria Mozza** (page 19).

After dinner, do the most Hollywood thing possible and go see a movie at one of the city's legendary movie palaces, either a new release at **TCL Chinese Theatre** or a classic film screening at **The Egyptian** (page 323).

---

cottonwood roof. A few exhibits include The History of Water in Los Angeles and a tribute to Christine Sterling, who is credited with preserving the Avila Adobe and creating the Mexican Marketplace. On the south side of Old Plaza, community group Las Angelitas del Pueblo offers 50-minute **tours** (10am, 11am, and noon Tues.-Sat., free). The on-site Mexican Marketplace consists of rows of clapboard stands selling souvenirs and Mexican imports at cheap prices.

★ **The Broad**

Contemporary art museum **The Broad** (221 S. Grand Ave., 213/232-6200, www.thebroad.org, 11am-5pm Tues.-Wed., 11am-8pm Thurs.-Fri., 10am-8pm Sat., 10am-6pm Sun., free entry, touring exhibitions require tickets) is beautiful to behold from the outside, but the architectural gem also houses a 2,000-piece collection of art by luminaries such as Cindy Sherman, Ed Ruscha, Andy Warhol, and Roy Liechtenstein. Exceptional visiting installations typically require tickets be purchased in advance.

Mid-City
La Brea Tar Pits

The **La Brea Tar Pits** (5801 Wilshire Blvd., 323/857-6300, www.tarpits.org, 9:30am-5pm daily, free) is one of the world's most renowned fossil sites. One hundred tons of fossilized bone have been discovered here; ongoing excavations of Pit 91 continue to unmask its victims. Among the fossils are a saber-toothed tiger, a giant sloth, bison, and six dire wolves. The most treasured find is "Zed," a nearly intact mammoth skeleton. A partial human skeleton, estimated to be 10,000 years old, has also been found.

Pit 91 has a viewing station, where docents explain how and why the bubbling asphalt has risen to the surface. The **George C. Page Museum** (5801 Wilshire Blvd., 323/857-6300, www.tarpits.org, 9:30am-5pm daily, $12 adults, $5 children, tours free with admission) features several excavated skeletons and other fascinating exhibits. Giant sculptures of mammoths and other prehistoric animals are often draped with climbing children. Wear a pair of cheap shoes—it isn't unusual to leave with tar in your footprints!

★ Los Angeles County Museum of Art

The 20-acre **Los Angeles County Museum of Art** (LACMA, 5905 Wilshire Blvd., 323/857-6000, www.lacma.org, 11am-5pm Mon.-Tues. and Thurs., 11am-8pm Fri., 10am-7pm Sat.-Sun., $15 general admission, $10 parking) holds the city's most impressive collections—120,000 works spanning human history. Covering three floors, the museum displays a selection of modern American art by artists that include Andy Warhol, Jasper Johns, and Robert Rauschenberg. The Art of the Americas Building includes an astounding display of 2,500 pre-Columbian objects, many excavated from burial chambers in Jalisco, Mexico. At the main level, the Ahmanson Building features a large staircase, reminiscent of Rome's Spanish Steps, while the plaza holds African art and modern works by greats like Picasso and Kandinsky. Classical Greek and Roman works are found on the second level. Admission is free every second Tuesday of the month, plus Martin Luther King Day, President's Day, and Memorial Day.

Hollywood

The world's movie capital earned its reputation during the boom of the 1920s when the entertainment industry cast Hollywood in its own opulent image. Today, the only "real" movie businesses remaining are the blockbuster premieres at the major movie theaters. Paramount Studios, at Melrose and Gower, is the last of the big five studios still active in Hollywood proper. But some of the old Tinseltown glitz remains. Fine restaurants draw glamorous crowds after dark, and celebrities still attend blockbuster premieres at the iconic movie theaters in Hollywood.

TCL Chinese Theatre

The most famous movie theater in the world literally made its mark with the handprints and footprints of silver-screen stars. Although official accounts say actress Norma Talmadge sparked a Hollywood tradition when she accidentally stepped into the wet concrete, the theater's owner, Sid Grauman, took credit for the idea. Today, millions of tourists visit **TCL Chinese Theatre** (6925 Hollywood Blvd., 323/461-3331, www.tclchinesetheatres.com)—historically known as Grauman's Chinese Theatre—to ogle the 200 celebrity prints and autographs immortalized in concrete. The first footprints belong to Mary Pickford and Douglas Fairbanks (1927); more recent additions include Robert De Niro and Sandra Bullock.

The theater's ornate architecture features a large dragon across the front, two

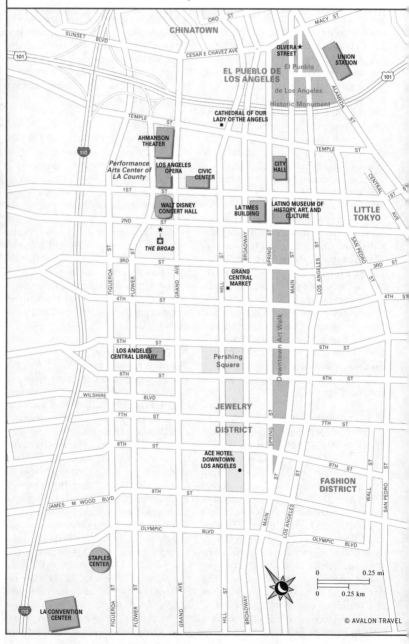

Downtown Los Angeles

stone Chinese guardian lions at the entrance, and etched shadow dragons along the copper roof. Inside, wall murals greet movie ticket holders. A glass case in the west wing displays three wax figures outfitted in authentic Chinese costumes.

★ Hollywood Walk of Fame

Nobody walks in L.A., so it's ironic the city would have the world's most famous sidewalk. Each year 10 million people visit the **Hollywood Walk of Fame** (Hollywood Blvd. from La Brea Ave. to Vine St., 323/469-8311, www. walkoffame.com), a 1.3-mile stretch that commemorates the entertainment industry's elite. Inspired by the handprints at Sid Grauman's Chinese Theatre, five-pointed terrazzo and brass stars are embedded into a charcoal background along Hollywood Boulevard and three blocks of Vine Street. Check the website to locate a specific star.

Though official groundbreaking did not occur until 1960, eight inaugural stars were temporarily planted on the northwest corner of Hollywood and Highland in 1958 to gain public attention. Contrary to popular belief, Joanne Woodward was not the first to be immortalized. The first permanent star is found at the intersection of Hollywood and Gower, and belongs to Stanley Kramer, director of *Guess Who's Coming to Dinner* and *It's a Mad, Mad, Mad, Mad World,* among others. Ms. Woodward, however, was the first to be photographed with her star. A circular, bronze emblem symbolizes one of five categories: motion pictures, broadcast television, music or audio recording, broadcast radio, and theater. Gene Autry is the only recipient with stars in all five categories.

Who deems Walk of Fame hopefuls "worthy" enough to join the more than 2,500 deified legends? A special

From top to bottom: a star in the Hollywood Walk of Fame; the TCL Chinese Theatre; Lucha Libre wrestling masks for sale at Olvera Street.

committee bound by rules, procedures, and financing selects the honoree. The price of a star is about $30,000 and is usually paid by the representing movie company or record label.

Sunset Strip

It's been the playground of mobsters, Hollywood celebrities, and rock stars: The **Sunset Strip** has a long, colorful history. The 1.5-mile portion of Sunset Boulevard stretches from Havenhurst Drive in West Hollywood to Sierra Drive near Beverly Hills. Infamous gangsters Bugsy Siegel, Micky Cohen (who was shot at what today is called the Key Club), Johnny Roselli, and Tony Comero were regulars at The Melody Room (a.k.a. The Viper), using it as a gambling den. Nightclubs and upscale restaurants attracted stars such as Clark Gable, Cary Grant, Fred Astaire, Jean Harlowe, and Lana Turner. Famed writers Dorothy Parker and F. Scott Fitzgerald lived at the Garden of Allah apartments that once stood between Crescent Heights and Havenhurst. Howard Hughes lived in the penthouse of the Argyle Hotel (known as the Sunset Tower Hotel, 8358 Sunset Blvd.), as did John Wayne, who kept a cow on his apartment balcony.

Decades worth of up-and-coming rock acts first made their names on the Strip and lived at the "Riot Hyatt." Today, you'll still find many of the Strip's legendary rock clubs here, such as **The Roxy,** the **Whisky a Go Go,** and **The Rainbow Bar & Grill.** At night, especially on weekends, no one is alone on the Strip. Don't plan to drive quickly or park on the street after dark; the crowds get big, complete with celebrity hounds hoping for a glimpse of their favorite star out for a night on the town.

★ Griffith Park

The 4,210-acre **Griffith Park** (4730 Crystal Springs Dr., 323/913-4688, 6am-10pm daily) is the largest municipal park in the country, with numerous opportunities for mingling with nature while enjoying some of the city's iconic sights. It's also recognizable from its role as the backdrop for many films, including *Rebel Without a Cause* and *Back to the Future.*

The cosmos come alive at **Griffith Observatory** (2800 E. Observatory Rd., 213/473-0800, noon-10pm Tues.-Fri., 10am-10pm Sat.-Sun., free), the park's most popular sight. Experienced stargazers help visitors explore the galaxies through demonstrations of powerful telescopes. At the entrance, a Foucault pendulum demonstrates the rotation of the Earth, while other displays focus on the moon and ocean tides. Planetarium shows ($7) occur daily.

The park has several fun activities for kids, including the **L.A. Zoo and Botanical Gardens** (5333 Zoo Dr., 10am-5pm daily, $20 adults, $15 children), the **Travel Town Railroad** (5200 Zoo Dr., 323/662-5874, www.traveltown.org, 10am-4pm Mon.-Fri., 10am-5pm Sat.-Sun., $3), pony rides, and a swimming pool. Educational sights include the **Autry National Center of the American West** (4700 Western Heritage Way, 323/667-2000, 10am-4pm Tues.-Fri., 10am-5pm Sat.-Sun., $14 adults, $10 students, $6 children 3-12, free children under 3), which holds an impressive collection of more than 500,000 Western and Native American artworks and artifacts.

A 53-mile network of hiking trails offers chances to spot local wildlife such as deer, coyotes, wild quail, and foxes. Many trails lead to viewpoints that include the Hollywood Sign; the most spectacular is from the observatory parking lot to Mount Hollywood. In a wooded canyon, the **Bird Sanctuary** (2900 N. Vermont Ave., 818/243-1145, 5am-10:30pm daily) provides the perfect spot for bird-watching, while the **Ferndell Nature Museum** (5375 Red Oak Dr., 6am-10pm daily), an outdoor exhibit, lets visitors explore native species of ferns, flowers, and plants. There is a snack stand and picnic area

Hollywood

0
0   0.5 mi

0.5 km

SUNSET
SAN VINCENTE BLVD
SUNSET STRIP
LA CIENEGA BLVD
West Hollywood
BEVERLY
CRESCENT HEIGHTS
FAIRFAX
SPAULDING AVE
ALTA VISTA BLVD
LA BREA AVE
HIGHLAND AVE
BLVD
SANTA
MONICA
VINE ST
ST
GOWER
BRONSON AVE
WESTERN
AVE
GOODWIN
HOLLYWOOD BLVD
SUNSET BLVD
VERMONT

Hollywood

MELROSE
Hollywood

PARAMOUNT PICTURES ★

MULHOLLAND
Laurel Canyon Park
LAUREL

NICHOLS CANYON RD
CANYON
Runyon Canyon Park

TCL CHINESE THEATRE ★
MAGIC CASTLE HOTEL ★
HOLLYWOOD BOWL ★
MUSSO & FRANK GRILL ★
HOLLYWOOD WALK OF FAME ★
PANTAGES THEATER ★

ZANKOU CHICKEN ▼
Los Feliz
FRANKLIN AVE
HOLLYWOOD AVE
SUNSET BLVD
Barnsdall Park

CAHUENGA
101
101
Universal City
UNIVERSAL CENTER DR
BARHAM BLVD
LAKE HOLLYWOOD DR
Lake Hollywood
LEDGEWOOD DR
HOLLYWOOD SIGN ★
Mt Lee
DERONDA DR
WESTERN CANYON RD
BEACHWOOD DR

GRIFFITH OBSERVATORY & SAMUEL OSCHIN PLANETARIUM ★
GREEK THEATER ★
GLENDOWER AVE
VERMONT CANYON RD
▲ Mt Hollywood
MERRY-GO-ROUND ■
✚ GRIFFITH PARK
COMMONWEALTH CANYON DR
RUSSELL AVE
COMMONWEALTH AVE

Forest Lawn Memorial Park-Hollywood Hills
FWY
VENTURA
170
134

TRAVEL TOWN RAILROAD AND MUSEUM ★
L.A. ZOO AND BOTANICAL GARDENS ★
THE AUTRY NATIONAL CENTER OF THE AMERICAN WEST ★
GRIFFITH
ZOO
PARK
CRYSTAL SPRINGS
VISITOR CENTER & PARK HEADQUARTERS ■
STATE
GOLDEN
5
SAN FERNANDO
Glendale
CHEVY CHASE
134
BRAND BLVD

SILVER LAKE BLVD
SUNSET BLVD
101
ALVARADO ST
MICHELTORENA ST
Silver Lake
GLENDALE BLVD
2
COMMONWEALTH AVE

Echo Park Lake
GLENDALE BLVD
FLETCHER
FWY
5
2

N
E
S
W

Welcome to Hollywood!

You'll know you've arrived when you see the **Hollywood Sign** (www.hollywoodsign.org). When it was erected in 1923 atop Mount Lee, it read "Hollywood-land." Twenty-six years later, "land" was removed and the 50-foot-tall letters that remained became a permanent feature of the Los Angeles landscape. Like all Hollywood stars, a bit of maintenance is required (the sign was made of wood). To ensure the sign's longevity, the original letters were auctioned off to the highest bidder (Hugh Hefner bought the "y" and Alice Cooper bought the "o" in memory of comedian Groucho Marx) and replaced with shiny new 45-foot-tall letters made of sheet metal; the refurbishment was completed in 2010. Access to the sign ain't what it used to be due to problems with vandalism and complaints from local residents. The area is now outfitted with high-security motion detectors, closed-circuit cameras, razor-sharp barbed wire, and Restricted Entry warning signs. Try to climb the fence and Los Angeles Police will have you cuffed quicker than you can say "tourist."

You can get a good look at the sign from the following places:

• **Griffith Observatory** (Griffith Park, 2800 E. Observatory Rd., noon-10pm Tues.-Fri., 10am-10pm Sat.-Sun., free)

• **Hollywood and Highland Visitors Center** (6801 Hollywood Blvd., 323/467-6412, 9am-10pm Mon.-Sat., 10am-7pm Sun.)

• **Lake Hollywood Park** (3160 N. Canyon Dr., 818/243-1145, 5am-sunset daily, free).

nearby to enjoy the cool shade along a babbling brook.

Paramount Studio Tours

For a most literal glimpse behind the scenes, take a guided tour of century-old **Paramount Studios** (5515 Melrose Ave., 323/956-1777, www.paramountstudiotour.com, tours 9am-4pm daily, $58), one of the original big five studios of old Hollywood. Countless films and television shows have been made here, ranging from Hitchcock movies to *Star Trek,* and the tour will take you by sound stages where hit films and shows are still shot today.

Beverly Hills

Thousands flock to Beverly Hills to get a glimpse of the stars and to browse the exorbitantly priced boutiques on Rodeo Drive. Five-star restaurants and chic hotels offer only the crème de la crème.

The three-block stretch of Wilshire Boulevard that runs through Beverly Hills from downtown to the ocean is known as "Museum Row," which includes the Los Angeles County Museum of Art at its far southeast corner. To the east, Beverly Hills links to West Hollywood via the Sunset Strip at Sierra Drive. At its northwest side, the world-famous Getty Center sits atop the Santa Monica Mountains.

★ Rodeo Drive

In the well-to-do neighborhood of Beverly Hills, the biggest celeb in town is the three-block hotshot known as **Rodeo Drive** (pronounced "ro-DAY-o," not like the bronco-riding cowboy event). Impressive boutiques and stylish shops abound with more than 100 of the most elite hotels and prestigious fashion retailers touting their "best in show" wearables. Though price tags may be bigger than your zip code, not everything is for sale. Take a walk along the palm-tree-lined drive to see the historic, iconic, and spectacular!

At the base of Rodeo Drive, the **Beverly Wilshire Hotel** (famous for the movie *Pretty Woman*) has been a fixture for over 100 years, lavishing the rich and famous in luxury. A newer addition, Rodeo Drive **Walk of Style** puts a twist on the Hollywood Walk of Fame by honoring fashion legends with bronze plaques (personal quote and signature included) embedded into the sidewalk. The first honoree inducted was high-fashion guru Giorgio Armani, whose quote reads: "Fashion and cinema together for life." Along the "Walk," look for other past winners, which include Princess Grace of Monaco, Salvatore Ferragamo, and Gianni and Donatella Versace.

Other sights include artist Robert Graha's *Torso*, a 14-foot aluminum sculpture that glistens under the Southern California sun at the intersection of Rodeo Drive and Dayton. Nearby stands Frank Lloyd Wright's last Los Angeles building project, The Anderton Court, a four-level shopping complex with an exposed, angular ramp, several circular windows, and a large geometric mast.

Although you won't see *The Beverly Hillbillies'* Oldsmobile spewing exhaust down Rodeo Drive, the black and yellow Bugatti Veyron and custom yellow Rolls-Royce of designer Bijan Pakzad (founder of the exclusive House of Bijan) have become big photo ops. To step into the House of Bijan ("the world's most famous store"), pay up. It's open by appointment only, catering to celebrities, movie moguls, and anyone willing to spend $15,000 or more on a single suit.

Recreation
Bicycling

One of Griffith Park's best features is its nine-mile **bike loop** (enter at Los Feliz Blvd. and Riverside Dr.). The route follows a tree-lined pathway and parts of the L.A. River Bike Path, forming a loop inside the park. Route information and

From top to bottom: gardens at the Getty Center; Griffith Observatory and downtown Los Angeles; Rodeo Drive in Beverly Hills.

bikes are available at **Coco's Variety Bike Shop and Prop Rental** (2427 Riverside Dr., 323/664-7400, www.cocosvariety. com, $10/hour), which also rents era-specific prop bikes to movie studios.

The seven-mile ride along the **Ballona Creek Trail** connects Ballona Creek in Culver City west to the Coast Bike Path in Marina del Rey. Access is at **Syd Kronenthal Park** (3459 McManus Ave., behind the ballfield bleachers). North of Inglewood the path is rough and you'll be working against the wind, but picturesque ocean views make it worthwhile. The path ends at Fisherman's Village in Marina del Rey but links to the beachfront **South Bay Trail,** which continues 22 miles along Santa Monica State Beach, north to Malibu and south to Torrance.

Expect twists, turns, and uphill insanity via **The Donut.** (The trail started 50 years ago at a doughnut shop.) This intense trail stretches 42 miles from Redondo Beach to Palos Verdes. Competitive cyclists train on the route. The views of Point Vice, Point Fermin, and Catalina Island are remarkable.

Spectator Sports

The **Los Angeles Dodgers** are the hometown baseball team. With L.A.'s perfect climate, **Dodger Stadium** (1000 Elysian Park Ave., 323/224-1471, www.dodgers. com) hosts some of the most beautiful outdoor games in the country.

Staples Center (1111 S. Figueroa St., 213/742-7100, www.staplescenter. com) doubles as a sports and entertainment venue. It's home to the **L.A. Kings** hockey team and the **Lakers, Sparks,** and **Clippers** basketball teams, while also hosting big-name performers like Katy Perry, Taylor Swift, and Madonna.

The St. Louis Rams brought NFL football back to Los Angeles in 2016, and the San Diego Chargers followed suit in 2017. Until construction is complete on a state-of-the-art stadium in Inglewood that will host both teams beginning in 2019, the **L.A. Rams** play at downtown's

Los Angeles Memorial Coliseum (3911 S. Figueroa St., www.therams.com). Meanwhile, the **L.A. Chargers** play in Dominguez Hills at the **StubHub Center** (18400 Avalon Blvd., 310/630-2000, www. chargers.com), also the permanent home of Major League Soccer team the **L.A. Galaxy** (www.lagalaxy.com).

Food

L.A.'s food landscape may have evolved over the past hundred years, but Angelenos have a soft spot for the classics, so many of its dining institutions remain as popular as ever—in most cases, the food even justifies their longevity! Beyond the beloved, vintage eateries, a wave of trend-setting restaurants have filled in a few foodie gaps.

Downtown

Serving breakfast 24 hours a day, the **Original Pantry Cafe** (877 S. Figueroa St., 213/972-9279, www.pantrycafe.com, 24 hours daily, $8-22 cash only) has been a fixture in Downtown L.A. since 1924, patronized by celebrities and politicians, and even owned by a former mayor. Join the lines under the red-and-white awnings. The classic American fare, served in huge portions, is worth it.

In-n-Out burger gets all the love in the movies, but in true L.A., a fondness for **Tommy's** (2575 Beverly Blvd., 213/389-9060, www.originaltommys. com, 24 hours daily, under $10) is practically hardwired. Maybe it's the 24-hour availability of its notorious chili burger that makes it so beloved. There are other locations throughout L.A., including a Hollywood location (5873 Hollywood Blvd.) with great people-watching.

It can be tough to find a way to squeeze into **Sqirl** (720 N. Virgil Ave. #4., 213/394-6526, www.sqirlla.com, 6am-4pm Mon.-Fri., 8am-4pm Sat.-Sun., $12-18), particularly on weekends, but if you're a fan of either organic food or creativity, you'll want to try. What started as a business to sell homemade jam has turned into a trendsetting artisan food and restaurant brand.

Restaurants serving Cali-Mex cuisine abound in Los Angeles, but since 1994, ★ **Guelaguetza** (3014 W. Olympic Blvd., 213/427-0608, www.ilovemole. com, 9am-10pm Mon.-Thurs., 9am-11pm Fri., 8am-11pm Sat., 8am-9pm Sun., $12-18) has blessed the city with authentic Oaxacan flavors. As you would in Oaxaca, you should go straight for the moles here—there are several, of various spice levels, and they're some of the best in the United States. Stick around for live music nightly at this large, colorful paean to Mesoamerica.

Plant-based cuisine is no longer just for vegans. As proof, consider Arts District spot **Café Gratitude** (300 S. Santa Fe Ave., 213/929-5580, www.cafegratitude. com, 8am-10pm daily, $10-16). Without meat, dairy, or synthetic ingredients, the restaurant creates healthful, balanced, organic, and above all flavorful dishes, including a pay what you can bowl of grains, kale, and beans.

A downtown landmark since 1917, **Grand Central Market** (317 S. Broadway, 213/624-2378, www.grandcentralmarket.com, 8am-10pm daily) is the oldest open-air market in the city, offering a wide variety of authentic dishes from around the world, from Mexican to Middle Eastern delights to Asian favorites. The market is often packed with locals grabbing a bite to go (Eggslut wins for longest line ever!) and tourists strolling about the food and gift shops. There is a parking garage ($2 for 90 minutes) on Hill Street (a one-way road).

Hollywood

With two locations, **Yuca's** (4666 Hollywood Blvd., 323/661-0523, and 2056 Hillhurst Ave., 323/662-1214, www.yucasla.com, 11am-6pm Mon.-Sat., $3-10) serves the best Mexican fare in L.A.—and that's saying something. They have the James Beard Award to prove it. There's not much dining space (the Hillhurst Ave. location is just a hut), but there's plenty of room for carnitas burritos, tacos, and tortas.

Eventually, everyone in L.A. eats at cultish chili dog spot **Pink's Hot Dogs** (709 N. La Brea Ave., 323/931-4223, www. pinkshollywood.com, 9:30am-2am Sun.-Thurs., 9:30am-3am Fri.-Sat., $4). It's been a late-night craving since 1939.

For a truly delicious lunch, ★ **Zankou Chicken** (7851 Sunset Blvd., 323/882-6365, www.zankouchicken.com, 10am-midnight daily, $8-14) slowly cooks chicken to perfection Armenian-style. Order a whole or half chicken, falafel, kebabs, or the miraculous marinated chicken *tarna*, and ask for extra garlic paste.

The wood-fired oven at **Pizzeria Mozza** (641 N. Highland Ave., 323/297-0101, www.pizzeriamozza.com, noon-midnight daily, $11-29) turns out rustic, blistered pizzas with luxurious toppings. Reservations are tough to get, but bar seats are available for walk-ins. Just as popular, **Osteria Mozza** (6602 Melrose Ave., 323/297-0100, www.osteriamozza. com, noon-midnight daily, $19-38) next door has a larger menu of luscious pastas and adventurous meat dishes.

If there's a kind of meat you've always wanted to try, chances are it will turn up at **Animal** (435 N. Fairfax Ave., 323/782-9225, www.animalrestaurant.com, 6pm-10pm Sun.-Thurs., 6pm-11pm Fri.-Sat., 10:30am-2:30pm Sat.-Sun., $20-40). A restaurant for the carnivore's carnivore, the trendsetting restaurant helped start a whole animal butchery renaissance with a minimalist menu that delves into game and specialty meats, including offal.

In steakhouse terms, ★ **Musso & Frank** (6667 Hollywood Blvd, 323/467-7788, www.mussoandfrank.com, 11am-11pm Tues.-Sat., 4pm-9pm Sun., $25-45) is Tinseltown to its core. It will be a century old in 2019, and while the Hollywood outside its front door has spun off into the future, timeless style pervades its leather booths and mahogany bar.

Beverly Hills

Nate 'n Al Delicatessen (414 N. Beverly Dr., 310/274-0101, 7am-9pm daily, $12-18) has been packing them in since 1945, with thick deli meat sandwiches, smoked fish bagels, and the signature Al's Chopped Salad. It's basically a traditional Jewish neighborhood deli, but it's Beverly Hills's neighborhood deli, so the conversation at the next table could clue you in to who's going to star in the next comic book movie blockbuster.

Entertainment bigwigs conduct business meetings at **The Grill on the Alley** (9560 Dayton Way, 310/276-0615, www.thegrill.com, 11:30am-9pm Mon., 11:30am-10pm Tues.-Thurs., 11:30am-10:30pm Fri.-Sat., 5pm-9pm Sun., $22-30), which pleases with all-American comfort food like meatloaf, its signature chicken pot pie, and generously portioned shortcake. Reservations are wise.

Wolfgang Puck's **Spago Beverly Hills** (176 N. Canon Dr., 310/385-0880, www.wolfgangpuck.com, noon-2:30pm Tues.-Sat., 6pm-10pm Mon.-Fri., 5:30pm-10:30pm Sat., 5:30pm-10pm Sun., $26-145) has earned its iconic status. The open kitchen crafts inspired dishes with the best locally grown ingredients, and the wine list is mind-boggling. Outside, the romantic patio is centered on a fountain etched with the word "passion" and two imported 100-year-old olive trees.

West Side

The fans waiting for counter space at old-school burger joint **The Apple Pan** (10801 W. Pico Blvd., 310/475-3585, 11am-midnight Tues.-Thurs. and Sun., 11am-1am Fri.-Sat., $7-8) make the case these are L.A.'s best hamburgers.

The huge sandwiches and heartwarming soups at **Canter's Deli** (419 N. Fairfax Ave., 213/651-2030, www.cantersdeli.com, 24 hours daily, $8-15) draw night owls to the heart of the predominantly Jewish Fairfax District.

Roy Choi become one of L.A.'s most famous chefs by driving his Kogi food truck to locations all over town. Fans tracked him on social media to line up and gorge on his tasty Korean-style tacos. These days, there's no need to check Twitter—a full time taqueria serves these tacos at **Kogi** (3500 Overland Ave. #100, 424/326-3031, www.kogibbq.com, 11am-11pm Tues.-Sat., 11am-9pm Sun., $7).

Nightlife
Bars and Clubs

The "sky party" at **The Rooftop** (550 S. Flower St., 213/892-8080, www.standardhotels.com/downtown-la, noon-2am daily, RSVP and guest list Fri. and Sat. after 8pm) in The Standard hotel comes complete with DJs, waterbeds, a heated pool, and, let's not forget, the stunning panoramic view. Non-hotel guests are welcome, but it's not so easy to get in. Even if you don't make it onto the roof, you can get a drink at the trendy ground-level bar—minus the pool, waterbeds, and view, of course.

The no-frills **Golden Gopher** (417 W. 8th St., 213/614-8001, 5pm-2am nightly) is the perfect downtown pit stop for a reasonably priced beer, but it isn't a typical dive bar; there's a dress code. If you prefer a froufrou drink, they'll mix, shake, and blend it up. Low-key entertainment options include a jukebox and Pac-Man arcade game.

Down the street, **Pattern Bar** (100 W. 9th St., 213/627-7774, noon-midnight Mon.-Thurs., noon-2am Fri., noon-2am Sat., noon-10pm Sun.) attracts a trendier crowd with its chic-meets-funky decor (vintage sewing stools line the bar). Tapas and cocktails named in honor of top designers lure in weekday fashionistas, but come the weekend, DJs draw a mixed crowd for dancing.

Cheap drinks and no fancy-schmancy business seems to be the motto at **The Dime** (442 N. Fairfax Ave., 323/651-4421, www.thedimela.net, 7am-1:30am daily). Nightly DJs spin a mix of old-school, hip-hop, and indie beats attracting unpretentious, hip crowds and the occasional celebrity. Just north of The Dime, **The Woods** (1533 N. La Brea Ave., 323/876-6612, 6pm-2am Mon.-Fri., 8pm-2am Sat.-Sun.) lives up to its name, decked out with rustic furnishings like antler chandeliers and tree stump tables.

Speakeasy survivor **Boardner's** (1652 N. Cherokee Ave., 323/462-9621, www.boardners.com, 4pm-2am daily, $3-20 cover) gives the fortysomething crowd a place to relive the 1980s every Monday night. "Bar Sinister" on Saturday nights lures Goths (black is required!). The rest of the week you'll find anything from aerialists and ribbon dancers twirling beneath the cathedral ceilings to *Beavis and Butthead* headbangers. Control freaks and minions take over the second floor for S&M role-playing.

Bar Centro (465 S. La Cienega Blvd., 310/246-5555, 5:30pm-midnight Mon.-Thurs. and Sun., 5:30pm-1am Fri.-Sat.) vibrates with the silk-stocking, upper crusters of Beverly Hills, nibbling caviar and sipping the latest martini concoction. The centerpiece is a long table with aqua orbs. There is plenty of seating for socializing and curtained hideaways to get cozy.

Live Music

A number of excellent outdoor venues make Los Angeles a favorite stop of the world's top musicians, but none more than the legendary **Hollywood Bowl** (2301 Highland Ave., 323/850-2000, www.hollywoodbowl.com, June-Sept.). It sets the bar for outdoor concerts, with a massive amphitheater built into the hills above the center of Hollywood. Its iconic stage shell projects music into the top seats, while luckier attendees picnic in private boxes surrounding the orchestra pit. All guests may and should bring wine and beer to drink on the premises during the venue's long summer season featuring world music, rock legends, special

performances by the L.A. Philharmonic, and sometimes a combination of all three. Stacked parking makes public transportation and ride share a good idea.

Two Sunset Strip legends mix celebrity with infamy. **The Viper Room** (8852 Sunset Blvd., 310/358-1881, www.viperroom.com, 8pm-2am daily, $8-25 cover charge) is where gangster Bugsy Siegel hung out in the 1940s, country giant Johnny Cash recorded his comeback album, and River Phoenix collapsed. Iconic bands like The Doors and The Byrds got their start at the **Whisky a Go Go** (8901 Sunset Blvd., 310/652-4202, www.whiskyagogo.com, no cover-$60 tickets). These days, both venues welcome local bands to play for boisterous young crowds each night.

For going on two decades, Los Angeles has nurtured a resurgent singer-songwriter scene focused around **Hotel Cafe** (1623 N. Cahuenga Blvd., 323/461-2040, www.hotelcafe.com, doors open 6:30pm, $10-30). The intimate dual venue hosts primarily acoustic music on a small main stage or smaller second stage, with shows nightly.

Laugh out loud at the **Groundlings Theater** (7307 Melrose Ave., 323/934-4747, www.groundlings.com, $10-20), which has been a fixture of L.A.'s improv and sketch comedy scene for 40 years. It's known as a proving ground for future *Saturday Night Live* stars (Will Ferrell, Kristen Wiig, and Phil Hartman all started here). The city's famous stand-up comedy circuit includes **The Improv** (8162 Melrose Ave., 323/651-2583, www.improv.com, $11-21), **The Comedy Store** (8433 Sunset Blvd., 323/650-6268, www.thecomedystore.com, free-$20), and **Laugh Factory** (8001 Sunset Blvd., 323/656-1336, www.laughfactory.com, $20-45 plus 2-drink minimum). Every night gets big laughs, some get big comics (like Chris Rock, Dave Chappelle, Jon Stewart, or Jerry Seinfeld), either in scheduled or surprise appearances.

Arts and Entertainment

The breathtaking stainless steel curves designed by acclaimed architect Frank Gehry make **Walt Disney Concert Hall** (111 S. Grand Ave., 323/850-2000, www.laphil.com) a must-see Los Angeles landmark. Never mind that the whole place was designed around creating a perfect acoustic space for musical performances by the Los Angeles Philharmonic and a litany of world music artists.

The glittering **Geffen Playhouse** (10886 Le Conte Ave., 310/208-5454, www.geffenplayhouse.com, $24-46) is home to a good-sized main stage, the Gil Cates Theater, and the cozier Skirball Kenis Theater. The company offers a mix of new work and local premieres, frequently with big-name talent. Special nights include Wine Down Sundays, Lounge Fridays, and Talk Back Tuesdays, where a special drinks or coffee reception is held before the performance. Saturday mornings often feature great kid-oriented shows.

Downtown's beloved 3,200-seat **Dorothy Chandler Pavilion** (135 N. Grand Ave., 213/972-7211, www.musiccenter.org) is a landmark performance center that boasts curving staircases, sparkling chandeliers, and grand halls draped in red and gold. The Pavilion is home of the Los Angeles Opera from September through June, as well as the Glorya Kaufman Presents Dance series.

The 2,600-seat art deco **Pantages Theatre** (6233 Hollywood Blvd., 323/468-1770, www.broadwayla.org) dates back to 1930. In its time it's shown movies, staged vaudeville acts, and hosted Oscars ceremonies. These days it brings touring Broadway musicals to town, including hits like *The Lion King*, *Book of Mormon*, and *Hamilton*.

Shopping

Where does L.A. go to shop? Downtown you may haggle in open-air markets or find cut-rate deals on designer (or mock-designer) fashions; Hollywood has everything from designer shops and lingerie boutiques to record stores and a farmers market; while Beverly Hills reigns as the queen of luxury shopping—for those with deep enough pockets.

Downtown

The 90 blocks of the **Fashion District** (between E. 8th St and E. 16th St., from Santee St. to Central Ave.) offer the best places to shop for wholesale clothing, shoes, accessories, and cosmetics. Among the crowded walkways and energetic price bargaining, the country's largest flower market also stocks scores of freshly cut bouquets.

Offering big discounts on precious stones and metals, the **Jewelry District** (Hill St., Olive St., and Broadway) gives those with an obsession for shiny things endless opportunities to hold on and not let go! Parking is available on Broadway.

The historic Mexican marketplace on **Olvera Street** (125 Paseo de la Plaza, 10am-7pm daily) includes dozens of vendor stalls selling leather items, sombreros, pottery, puppets, and handcrafted gifts.

Hollywood

Amoeba Records (6400 W. Sunset Blvd., 323/245-6400, www.amoeba.com, 10:30am-11pm Mon.-Sat., 11am-10pm Sun.) holds an impressive collection of new and used CDs, DVDs, and vinyl records covering a multitude of genres. When you're done browsing, stay for a live musical performance; sneaky good bands and artists play here regularly.

Hollywood style isn't all about the red carpet. Young stylish women in L.A. get their glamour shopping done at an array of **Melrose Avenue Boutiques** (Melrose Ave. between La Cienega and La Brea), finding fashionable accessories and attire fit for clubs, dates, and sun. The shops tend to get more upscale the farther west you go, anchored by the hip sportswear and high-end beauty products of the legendary **Fred Segal** (8100 Melrose Ave.,

Movie Night in Hollywood

In most of the road-trip destinations described in this book, your time will be better spent visiting historical landmarks than going to see a movie. But in Hollywood, several movie theaters are historic landmarks! Seeing a film on the big screen, here in the home of cinema arts, makes the act of going to a movie special.

Of course, the best-known historic movie palace is **TCL Chinese Theatre** (6925 Hollywood Blvd., 323/461-3331, www.tclchinesetheatres.com), originally known as Grauman's Chinese Theatre. Beyond the famous hand- and footprints out front, the original 1927 theater's ornate interior features a massive starburst ceiling medallion, and its new 94-foot screen is one of the world's largest, allowing IMAX as well as 70mm screenings. Buy tickets in advance for reserved seating.

The 86-foot curved screen inside Hollywood's acoustically rich **Cinerama Dome** (6360 Sunset Blvd., 323/464-1478, www.arclightcinemas.com) has also been given modern upgrades, so it may showcase premium sound along with large-format projection. Built in 1963, the iconic dome offers one of the world's unique film-going experiences. Buy tickets in advance for reserved seating.

Decorated with hieroglyphics and mummy masks, **The Egyptian Theater** (6712 Hollywood Blvd., 323/461-2020, www.americancinemathequecalendar.com) dates all the way back to 1922. It's been modernized, but under the ownership of film preservation nonprofit American Cinematheque, it primarily screens classic films from 100-plus years of Hollywood history, "as they were meant to be seen."

It's not a historic theater, but the hottest movie tickets in town are for films projected each summer onto the side of a large mausoleum at the **Hollywood Forever Cemetery** (6000 Santa Monica Blvd., 877/435-9849, www.cinespia.org). Founded in 1899, the cemetery makes a wonderful, if unlikely, setting for outdoor screenings, where you may watch while picnicking on blankets and (short) lawn chairs, while sipping on beer or wine you bring with you. You must buy tickets in advance for these incredibly popular screenings, but arrive early, because seating positions are first-come, first-served.

323/651-4129, 10am-7pm Mon.-Sat., noon-6pm Sun.).

Since 1934, the **Original Farmers Market** (6333 W. 3rd St., 323/933-9211, www.farmersmarketla.com, 9am-9pm Mon.-Fri., 9am-8pm Sat., 10am-7pm Sun.) has offered everything from gourmet foods to toys and gifts, with many local favorites among its 70 vendors. A trolley connects it to an upscale outdoor mall, **The Grove** (189 The Grove Dr., 10am-9pm Mon.-Fri., 10am-10pm Sat., 10am-8pm Sun.), which offers 575,000 square feet of boutiques and high-end department stores. A beautifully landscaped park features a "dancing" water fountain choreographed to music.

Beverly Hills

The five floors of **Barneys New York** (9570 Wilshire Blvd., 310/276-4400, www.barneys.com, 10am-7pm Mon.-Wed. and Fri.-Sat., 10am-8pm Thurs., 11am-6pm Sun.) are filled with enough designer clothing, cosmetics, and jewelry to put any fashion diva in a Prada coma. Get some air and a glass of wine at the rooftop restaurant.

MAC (363 N. Beverly Dr., 310/285-9917, www.maccosmetics.com, 10am-7pm Mon.-Sat., 11am-6pm Sun.) supplies beauty products that you can't find anywhere else. Displays of eye shadows and lipsticks are arranged like works of art, and professional makeup artists offer private lessons.

The eight-level **Beverly Center** (8500 Beverly Blvd., 310/854-0070, www.beverlycenter.com, 10am-9pm Mon.-Fri., 10am-8pm Sat., 11am-6pm Sun.) includes stores ranging from boutiques to big retailers. Altogether you'll find about 160 stores in which to spend your hard-earned dollars.

The rich and famous head to **Rodeo Drive** (between Santa Monica Blvd. and Wilshire Blvd.) to pick up their necessities, while everyone else settles for window-shopping. More than 100 boutiques along the three-block stretch include flagship stores for Chanel, Hermes, and Harry Winston.

Events

On New Year's Day, the **Tournament of Roses Parade** (www.tournamento-froses.com) takes place just northeast of downtown in Pasadena, primarily along Colorado Boulevard. Marching bands from all over the world come to join equestrians, more than 40 rose-covered floats, and the Rose Queen and her court. Bleacher seats are available and run $50-100. It's not unusual for people to camp out overnight for free curbside seating. If that doesn't sound appealing, try finding a spot early in the morning east of Lake Avenue.

Southern California's biggest LGBTQ+ celebration, the **LA Pride Festival** (www.lapride.org) attracts more than 400,000 people to West Hollywood each year for festivities surrounding a pridefully flamboyant parade along Santa Monica Boulevard beginning at Crescent Heights Boulevard.

Every second Thursday of the month, more than 25,000 visitors roam gallery open houses of the **Downtown Art Walk** (between 4th St. and 7th St., Spring St. and Main St., www.downtownartwalk.org). Maps are available online.

Accommodations
Under $150

Just outside of downtown, **Jerry's Motel** (285 Lucas Ave., 213/481-8181, www.jerrysmotel.com, $89-109) offers one of the best bang-for-your-buck stays in Los Angeles. Don't expect frills and you

won't be disappointed—it aims for clean, safe, and affordable, and hits the mark. For cheap digs close to the action, **USA Hostels Hollywood** (1624 Schrader Blvd., 323/462-3777 and 800/524-6783, www.usahostels.com, $43-55 dorms, $124-140 suites, includes breakfast) puts you right in the center of Hollywood's happening nightlife.

$150-250

With a retro-1960s vibe, **The Standard Downtown** (550 S. Flower St., 213/892-8080, www.standardhotels.com, $200-250) features platform beds, roomy tubs, peek-a-boo showers, and the world's coolest rooftop poolside bar.

On Hollywood's west side, **Farmer's Daughter Hotel** (115 S. Fairfax Ave., 323/937-3930, www.farmersdaughterhotel.com, $229-269, $18 parking) hosts *American Idol* contestants. In addition to urban cowboy decor, rooms feature rain showerheads, a refrigerator, hair dryer, and mini-bar. Strange but fun mutant-sized rubber duckies hang out at the pool.

A bastion of downtown, the **Millennium Biltmore** (506 S. Grand Ave., 213/624-1011, www.millenniumhotels.com/LA, $150-240) was a grand hotel that hosted celebrities and dignitaries in its 1930s heyday. The massive property is still a beaut, with its Roman exterior and ornate, cavernous public spaces that make staying there feel like a steal.

The 1927 art deco **Crescent Hotel** (403 N. Crescent Dr., 310/247-0505, www.crescentbh.com, $148-246) is just two blocks from famed Rodeo Drive. Rooms range from the 130-square-foot "Itty Bitty" to the 400-square-foot "Grand King." Beds are triple-sheeted in Turkish cotton. The Terrace offers classic breakfast and dinner menus, while The Lounge serves evening cocktails and small plates.

Just off Sunset Boulevard, the **Magic Castle Hotel** (7025 Franklin Ave., 323/851-0800, www.magiccastlehotel.com, $200-290) is two blocks from the Hollywood Walk of Fame and TCL

Chinese Theatre. Choose from standard, one-room, or two-room suites, each with complimentary breakfast and guest robes and cozy slippers. Guests also get free tickets to the Magic Castle, a private magic club.

Over $250

Located in the historic 1927 United Artists building, the hip ★ **Ace Hotel** (929 S. Broadway, 213/623-3233, www.acehotel.com/losangeles, $269-323) includes an ornate theater, vibrant lounges, and a cozy coffee shop.

The intricate design at Spanish-inspired **Hotel Figueroa** (939 S. Figueroa St., 213/627-8971 and 800/421-9092, www.hotelfigueroa.com, $329 and up) includes elegant arches and richly colored rooms. Its central location is close to great restaurants, clubs, and downtown attractions.

In the heart of Hollywood, the most happening stay is at **The Hollywood Roosevelt Hotel** (7000 Hollywood Blvd., 323/856-1970, www.thehollywoodroosevelt.com, $275-425), an elegant, old Hollywood rehab with well-furnished rooms built around a central courtyard, where drinks are served poolside and a party always seems imminent.

In the heart of West Hollywood, **Mondrian Hotel** (8440 Sunset Blvd., 323/650-8999, $375 and up) demonstrates luxury from the moment you open its mahogany doors and step into its modish lobby. Rooms feature 300-thread-count sheets, rain showerheads, bamboo floors, and floor-to-ceiling windows. The Lobby Bar offers a café menu, while the Herringbone restaurant serves fine seafood. The Skybar is an open-air poolside lounge, fully equipped with world-class DJs, celebrity guests, and stunning city views.

Even steps away from Rodeo Drive, the exquisite Italian Renaissance architecture of the ★ **Beverly Wilshire Hotel** (9500 Wilshire Blvd., 310/275-5200, www.fourseasons.com, $475 and up) stands out. Inside, marble crown moldings, dark woods, and crystal chandeliers continue the elegance. Three restaurants and two bars offer an array of dishes and drinks.

Information and Services

The **Los Angeles Convention and Visitors Bureau** (www.discoverlosangeles.com) maintains visitor information centers adjacent to two Metro stations: the **Hollywood and Highland Visitors Center** (6801 Hollywood Blvd., 323/467-6412, 8am-10pm Mon.-Sat., 9am-7pm Sun.) and the downtown **Union Station Visitors Center** (800 N. Alameda St., 9am-5pm daily). Maps, brochures, information, and advice about visiting the greater Los Angeles area are all available.

The South Bay

South of Venice, CA-1 zigs around Los Angeles International Airport before dropping due south to three beach cities that make up what is locally known as the South Bay: Manhattan Beach, Hermosa Beach, and Redondo Beach, all just over 20 miles from Los Angeles. All three destinations offer beach recreation, particularly surfing and volleyball, and all three feature piers open to fishing. Every August, Manhattan Beach is the site of the **Manhattan Beach Open volleyball tournament** (www.themanhattanbeachopen.com), while the cities take turns hosting the **International Surf Festival** (www.surffestival.org).

Home to wealthy sports and entertainment notables, **Manhattan Beach** is among the most desirable places to live in California, with homes selling for $1 million and up. It's also considered one of the top beaches in the state, its smooth sand attracting over 3.8 million visitors each year. Restaurants cluster around its pier, while sports bars populate the city's north end, around Rosecrans Avenue.

CA-1 runs down the middle of **Hermosa Beach,** which extends 15 blocks from east to west and 40 blocks from north to south. The beach is a hot spot for sunbathers, surfers, paddle boarders, and beach volleyball. At the end of Pier Avenue is an assortment of shops and eateries, as well as lively surf bars, clubs, and music venues.

Redondo Beach's stretch of sand gets crowded in the summertime, particularly near its pier, so if rubbing elbows with your fellow sun-worshippers doesn't work for you, you should head elsewhere. Surfers favor Manhattan and Hermosa, so there's more room for swimming in the water at Redondo. You'll also find the usual volleyball and other beach games, as well as restaurants on the pier.

Long Beach

CA-1 heads east and inland when it reaches the Palos Verdes Peninsula, which boasts an enclave of pricey cliff-top homes fronting the coast. The highway, however, shifts from commercial to industrial scenery as it enters **Long Beach** (pop. 470,130), about 17 miles from the South Bay beaches. Despite the name, Long Beach is less beach town than working port, the point of entry for international shipping coming into Los Angeles. To find the action, turn south on I-710 till it ends at Long Beach Harbor.

Sights

One of the most famous ships ever to ply the high seas, the magnificent *Queen Mary* (1126 Queens Hwy., 877/342-0738, www.queenmary.com, $28-75) now sits at permanent anchor in Long Beach Harbor, where it acts as a hotel, a museum, and an entertainment center with several restaurants and bars. You can book a stateroom ($120-570) and stay aboard, come for dinner, or just buy a regular ticket and take a self-guided tour. Explore many of the decks at the bow, including the engine room, which

the pier at Redondo Beach in the South Bay

still boasts much of its massive machinery, and see exhibits that describe the ship's history. The ship is also one of the most famously haunted places in California. Over its decades of service, a number of unfortunate souls lost their lives aboard the *Queen Mary,* and apparently some of them stuck around even after their deaths. To learn more, book a spot on one of the evening events, such as the Paranormal Ship Walk (8pm Sun.-Thurs., $44).

On the other side of Long Beach Harbor, the **Aquarium of the Pacific** (100 Aquarium Way, 562/590-3100, www. aquariumofpacific.org, 9am-6pm daily, adults $30, children $18) hosts animal and plant life native to the Pacific Ocean, from the local residents of SoCal's sea up to the North Pacific and down to the tropics. This large aquarium has far more than the average number of touch-friendly tanks, including the Shark Lagoon where you can "pet" a few of the sharks the aquarium cares for.

Food

They serve excellent smokehouse BBQ at **Beachwood Brewing & BBQ** (210 E. 3rd St., 562/436-4020, www.beachwoodbbq. com, 11:30am-midnight Tues.-Sun., $19-24), but that's not the top reason to visit. This champion brewpub makes some of the best beer in the state, especially stouts and IPAs, which happen to go pretty dang well with barbecue.

Accommodations

For a unique place to stay in Long Beach Harbor that isn't the Queen Mary, try the **Dockside Boat and Bed** (316 E. Shoreline Dr., Dock 5A, Rainbow Harbor, 562/436-3111, www.boatandbed.com, $260-330). You won't get a regular old hotel room—instead, you'll get a whole yacht. The yachts run 38-54 feet and can sleep 2-4 people. Unfortunately, you can't take your floating accommodations out for a spin; these yachts are permanent residents of Rainbow Harbor.

Catalina Island

For a slice of Greece in Southern California, take a ferry or a helicopter out to **Catalina Island** (pop. 4,096, www. catalina.com), a small populated island visible from many parts of the Southern California coast. The southern port town of Avalon welcomes visitors with European-inspired hotels, restaurants, and shops, while Two Harbors in the north provides an undeveloped gateway to nature, which includes a herd of wild roaming American bison.

Getting There and Around

Most folks take the ferry over from the mainland coast. The **Catalina Express** (800/613-1212 or 800/481-3470, www. catalinaexpress.com) departs from Long Beach (320 Golden Shore, $73.50 adults round-trip, $58 children round-trip) and Dana Point (34674 Golden Lantern St., $73.50 adults round-trip, $61 children round-trip, $17 parking), with boats going back and forth throughout the day, from 6am to just after sunset. San Pedro Port (Berth 95 at Swinford and Harbor Blvd., $75.50 adults round-trip, $58 children round-trip, $14 parking) is the only departure point for Two Harbors. The trip to the island takes about one hour.

You can also get to Catalina by air. **Island Express Helicopter Service** (310/510-2525, www.islandexpress.com, $250-390 round-trip per person) can fly you from Long Beach, San Pedro, or Santa Ana to Catalina in about 15 minutes.

Once you're on the island, the easiest way to get around is to walk. Some locals and visitors prefer golf carts, which can be rented at outlets, such as **Island Rentals** (125 Pebbly Beach Rd., 310/510-1456, www.catalinagolfcartrentals.com, $40/hour), near the ferry dock. Taxis hover near the ferry dock when the ferries are due in each day, and it's customary to share your ride with as many people as

can fit. To get a cab back to the ferry or the helipad when it's time to leave, call 310/510-0025.

Sights

When approaching Catalina on the ferry, you'll notice a round, white, art deco building on one end of town. This is the **Casino** (1 Casino Way, theater 310/510-0179). It's not a gambling hall, but rather harks back to the older Italian meaning of the word, "place of entertainment." It's used for movies and events.

Outside town, the coolest place to visit is the **Wrigley Memorial and Botanical Garden** (1402 Avalon Cyn Rd., 310/510-2897, www.catalinaconservancy.org, 8am-5pm daily, $7 adults, $3-5 children). Stroll through serene gardens planted with flowers, trees, and shrubs native to California—or even to Catalina specifically. At the center of the garden is the Wrigley Memorial, dedicated to the memory of the chewing-gum magnate who adored Catalina and used his

The retired *Queen Mary* is now a hotel, museum, and entertainment center in Long Beach.

sticky fortune to improve it. Most notably, he funded the building of the Avalon Casino.

Recreation

You'll find plenty of places to kick off into the water. The most popular spot is the **Avalon Underwater Park** (Casino Point). This protected area at the north end of town has buoys and markers to help you find your way around the reefs and keep safe. Not only will you see the famous bright-orange garibaldi fish, but you'll also get the opportunity to meet jellyfish, anemones, spiny lobsters, and plenty of other sea life. Out at the deeper edge of the park, nearly half a dozen wrecked ships await your examination.

Diving Catalina (34 Middle Terrace Rd., 310/510-8558, www.divingcatalina.com, $69-139) offers guided snorkel tours of the Casino Point Dive Park that include all equipment with the fees. Certified scuba divers can book a guided tour of Avalon Underwater Park. **Snorkel**

Catalina (107 Pebbly Beach Rd., 310/510-3175, www.snorkelingcatalina.com) specializes in deeper water excursions farther away from shore, taking guests out on a custom pontoon boat. Standard tours run 2-4 hours and let you check out the prettiest fish, sleekest seals, and friendliest dolphins around the island.

Kayaking is a popular way to see otherwise unreachable parts of Catalina. Rent a kayak, or if you're not confident in your own navigation abilities, take a tour with a reputable company. **Descanso Beach Ocean Sports** (5 St Catherine Way, 310/510-1226, www.kayakcatalinaisland.com) offers kayak tours to different parts of the island for a range of experience levels. All trips start north of Avalon and the Casino at Descanso Beach Club.

To rent kayaks, snorkel gear, or stand-up paddleboards, try **Wet Spot Rentals** (120 Pebbly Beach Rd., 310/510-2229, www.catalinakayaks.com, 9am-5pm daily Apr., May., and September, 8am-6pm Jun.-Aug.).

A great way to get around and beyond Avalon is on a bicycle. You can bring your own bike aboard the ferry, or rent a bicycle on the island at **Brown's Bikes** (107 Pebbly Beach Rd., 310/510-0986, www.catalinabiking.com, 9am-5pm daily, $8-18/hour, $20-45/day), which includes beach cruisers, mountain bikes, electric bikes, and tandems.

Catalina Adventure Tours (1 Cabrillo Mole, 562/432-8828, www.catalinaadventuretours.com, 8:30am-5pm Mon.-Fri., 8:30am-4pm Sat.-Sun., tours $28-159 adults) offers both land and sea tours, including underwater views from the semi-submersible Nautilus. Healthy adults can also try fly boarding—water jetpacks!

Food

So where do the locals go? Many of them crowd into **El Galleon** (411 Crescent Ave., 310/510-1188, www.catalinahotspots.com, 11am-9pm daily, $10-20), which features hearty American dishes with lots of aged steaks, chicken, and fresh fish.

It's part of the pedestrian-only stretch of Crescent Avenue, and the porch has a fabulous view of the harbor.

Steve's Steakhouse (417 Crescent Ave., 310/510-0333, www.stevessteakhouse. com, 11:30am-2pm and 5-9pm daily, $20-40) offers more than just steak; there are plenty of seafood options, too.

Accommodations

For inexpensive accommodations, your best bet is the **Hermosa Hotel & Cottages** (131 Metropole St., 310/510-1010 or 800/668-5963, www.hermosahotel.com, $150-350), which offers simple rooms about a block from the harbor beaches and a short walk from the Casino, shops, and restaurants.

The bright yellow **Hotel Mac Rae** (409 Crescent Ave., 310/510-0246, www.hotel-macrae.com, $179-349) has been in the Mac Rae family for four generations, and they've been running the hostelry since 1920. The rooms are right on the waterfront and have a Mediterranean flavor.

◆ Disneyland Resort

The "Happiest Place on Earth" lures millions of visitors of all ages each year with promises of fun and fantasy. During high seasons, waves of humanity flow through **Disneyland Resort** (1313 S. Disneyland Dr., Anaheim, 714/781-4565, www.disneyland.disney.go.com, Disneyland Park 8am-11pm daily, Disney California Adventure Park 8am-9pm daily, one-day ticket for one park $97-124 ages 10 and up, $91-118 ages 3-9, additional $60 for both parks), moving slowly from Land to Land and ride to ride.

Disney's rides, put together by the park's "Imagineers," are better than those at any other amusement park in the west. The technology of the rides isn't necessarily more advanced than other parks, but attention to details makes Disneyland rides more enthralling. Even standing in line becomes an immersive experience, with props and settings matching whichever Disney animation or film inspired the ride.

The Disneyland Resort is made of up of three main areas: Disneyland Park, the original amusement park that started it all in 1955; Disney California Adventure Park, a California-themed park that opened in 2001 with faster rides meant to appeal to older kids and adults; and Downtown Disney, a shopping and eating district outside the two parks. If you've got several days, try them all! If not, pick from the best of the best in each Land.

Getting There

Disneyland is located in Anaheim about 25 miles south of downtown Los Angeles and is accessible from I-5 South. Exit on Disneyland Drive toward Ball Road; stay in the left three lanes for **parking** (1313 S. Disneyland Dr., $20). From Long Beach, Disneyland can be reached via CA-22 East.

Disneyland Park

There are eight areas, or "Lands," of Disneyland Park: Main Street, U.S.A.; Tomorrowland; Fantasyland; Mickey's Toontown; Frontierland; Critter Country; New Orleans Square; and Adventureland.

You'll enter onto Main Street, U.S.A., which offers shops, information booths, and other practicalities. Your first stop inside the park should be one of the information kiosks near the front entrance. Here you can get a map, a schedule of the day's events, and the inside scoop on what's going on in the park during your visit.

Due north of Main Street is Sleeping Beauty's Castle and Fantasyland, with Mickey's Toontown beyond. To the east is Tomorrowland. Adventureland and Frontierland lie to the west of Main Street, with New Orleans Square to the west of Adventureland, and Critter Country in the far western reaches of the park.

The magical **FastPasses** are free with park admission. The newest and most popular rides offer FastPass kiosks near the entrances. Feed your ticket into one of the machines, and it will spit out both your ticket and a FastPass with your specified time to take the ride. Come back during your window and enter the always-much-shorter FastPass line, designated by a sign at the entrance. If you're with a group, be sure you all get your FastPasses at the same time, so you all get the same time window to ride the ride.

Adventureland

Adventureland is home to **Indiana Jones Adventure,** arguably one of the best rides in all of Disneyland. Even the queue is interesting: Check out the signs, equipment, and artifacts in mock-dusty tunnels winding toward the ride. The ride itself, in a roller-coaster style variant of an all-terrain vehicle, jostles and jolts you through a landscape that Indy himself might dash through, pursued by booby-traps and villains. Hang on to your hat—literally! It's also home to the kitschy, classic **Jungle Cruise,** where you'll encounter angry, angry hippos.

New Orleans Square

Next to Adventureland lies New Orleans Square and the **Pirates of the Caribbean** ride. Look for Captain Jack Sparrow to pop up among the other disreputable characters engaged in all sorts of debauchery. For a taste of truly classic Disney, line up in the graveyard for a tour of the **Haunted Mansion.** Concentrating more on creating a ghoulish atmosphere, rather than speed or twists and turns, it's less of a ride than a spooky experience.

Critter Country

Splash Mountain, Disney's take on the log ride, is the main attraction in Critter Country. The ride culminates in a long drop fashioned as if going over a waterfall. As the name suggests, it is possible that you'll get wet on this ride.

Frontierland

Take a ride on a Wild West train on the

Big Thunder Mountain Railroad. This older roller coaster whisks away passengers on a brief but fun thrill-ride through a "dangerous, decrepit" mountain's mine shafts.

Fantasyland

Fantasyland sits behind **Sleeping Beauty's Castle,** which itself is not a ride, but a walk-through attraction. Many of the rides here cater to the younger set, like the **carousel** and the flying **Dumbos.** The crazy fun of **Mr. Toad's Wild Ride** has appeal to all ages, with a rickety funhouse ride weaving a wacky, colorful narrative.

Tucked back in Fantasyland is what to many is Disneyland's quintessential ride: **It's a Small World.** With a constant soundtrack of the famous song in the background, the ride slowly tours an idealized vision of the world and introduces some favorite Disney characters.

If it's a faster thrill you're seeking, head for one of the most recognizable landmarks at Disneyland. The **Matterhorn Bobsleds** roller coaster looks like a miniature version of its Swiss Alps namesake. Bobsled coaster cars plunge down the mountain on a twisted track that takes you past rivers, glaciers, and the Abominable Snowman.

Mickey's Toontown

Set behind Fantasyland, Mickey's Toontown is the company town where Mickey, Donald Duck, Goofy, and other classic Disney cartoon characters make their residences. Wandering through it, you'll feel like you're inside a cartoon yourself. The main ride here is **Roger Rabbit's Car Toon Spin.**

Tomorrowland

Located toward the front of the park, Tomorrowland, despite its futuristic theme, is home to many classics, like **Star Tours** and perennial favorite, **Space Mountain,** a fast roller coaster that whizzes through an almost entirely darkened world.

Star Wars Land

Scheduled to open in 2019 is the highly anticipated new section of park devoted to the *Star Wars* movie franchise. Rumored rides and attractions include immersive space battle simulations, opportunities to mingle with robots and aliens, and the culmination of many a childhood dream—a chance to pilot the *Millennium Falcon!*

Food

The best areas of the park to grab a bite are Main Street, New Orleans, and Frontierland as they offer the most variety in concessions. But you can find at least a snack almost anywhere in the park.

For a sit-down restaurant meal inside the park, make reservations in advance for a table at the **Blue Bayou Restaurant** (New Orleans Square, 714/781-3463, $35-60), set in a dimly lit "swamp" overlooking the Pirates of the Caribbean ride. The Cajun and Creole cuisine matches the atmosphere, with large portions somewhat making up for overpriced meals.

Disney California Adventure Park

Disney California Adventure Park (8am-9pm daily) celebrates much of what makes California special. Like Disneyland Park, it's divided into thematic areas. Rides in California Adventure tend toward the thrills of other major amusement parks but include the great Disney touches that make it memorable.

You'll find two information booths just inside the main park entrance, one off to the left as you walk through the turnstile and one at the opening to Sunshine Plaza. This is where you'll get your park guide, Time Guide, and more information about what's going on in the park that day.

Hollywood Pictures Backlot

Celebrating SoCal's famed film industry, the Backlot holds the ultimate thrill ride: **The Twilight Zone Tower of Terror.**
Enter the creepy "old hotel," go through the "service area," and take your place inside an elevator straight out of your worst nightmares on this free-fall ride.

Less extreme but also fun, **Monsters, Inc. Mike & Sully to the Rescue!** invites guests into the action of the movie of the same name. You'll help the heroes as they chase the intrepid Boo. This ride jostles you around a bit but can be suitable for smaller kids as well as bigger ones.

A Bug's Land

Wanna live like a bug? Get a sample of the world of tiny insects on **It's Tough to Be a Bug!** This big-group, 3-D, multi-sensory ride offers fun for little kids and adults alike. You'll fly through the air, scuttle through the grass, and get a good idea of what life is like on six little legs. When they say this ride engages *all your senses,* they mean it.

Paradise Pier

Paradise Pier mimics the Santa Monica Pier and other waterfront attractions like it, with thrill rides and an old-fashioned midway. Most of the extreme rides cluster in the Paradise Pier area. The extra-long **California Screamin',** a high-tech roller coaster designed after the classic wooden coasters of carnivals past, includes drops, twists, a full loop, and plenty of screaming fun.

Golden State

For attractions styled after the Bay Area, Wine Country, and Cannery Row, head to the aptly named Golden State. For a bird's-eye view of California, try **Soarin' Over California.** This combination ride and show puts you on the world's biggest "glider," sailing over the hills and valleys of California. You'll feel the wind in your hair as you see the vineyards, mountains, and beaches you may have encountered on your road trip. If you prefer water to wind, take a ride down the **Grizzly River Run,** which turns white-water rafting into a Disney ride.

Cars Land

The high-powered characters from the 2006 hit film *Cars* populate rides like **Luigi's Flying Tires** and **Mater's Junkyard Jamboree**. The **Radiator Springs Racers** has park visitors racing through the film's Route 66-inspired setting in six-person vehicles.

Food

Most of the food is clustered in the Golden State area. For a Mexican feast, try **Cocina Cucamonga Mexican Grill** (Pacific Wharf, $10.50-14). If you're just dying for a cold beer, get one at the **Bayside Brews** (Paradise Pier, $6-8). If your thirst is for California wines, head for the **Mendocino Terrace** (Pacific Wharf, $9-15).

Downtown Disney

You don't need an admission ticket to take a stroll through the shops of Downtown Disney. In addition to the mammoth World of Disney Store, you'll find a Build-a-Bear Workshop and a Lego Store, among mall staples like Sephora. You can also have a bite to eat or take in some jazz or a new-release movie at Downtown Disney.

Disney Hotels

For the most iconic Disney resort experience, you must stay at the **Disneyland Hotel** (1150 Magic Way, 714/778-6600, http://disneyland.disney.go.com, $500-625). This nearly 1,000-room high-rise monument to brand-specific family entertainment has themed swimming pools, themed play areas, and even character-themed guest rooms that allow the kids to fully immerse themselves in the Mouse experience. The monorail stops inside the hotel, offering guests the easiest way into the park proper without having to deal with parking.

It's easy to find the **Paradise Pier Hotel** (1717 S. Disneyland Dr., 714/999-0990, http://disneyland.disney.go.com, $270-370); it's that high-rise thing just outside of the parks. This hotel boasts what passes for affordable lodgings within walking distance of the parks. Rooms are cute, colorful, and clean. You'll find a (possibly refreshing) lack of Mickeys in the standard guest accommodations at the Paradise, which has the feel of a beach resort motel.

Disney's Grand Californian Hotel and Spa (1600 S. Disneyland Dr., 714/635-2300, http://disneyland.disney.go.com, $540-740) lies inside Disney California Adventure Park, attempting to mimic the famous Ahwahnee Lodge in Yosemite. The hotel is surrounded by gardens and has restaurants, a day spa, and shops attached on the ground floors; it can also get you right out into Downtown Disney and thence to the parks proper. Guest rooms at the Californian offer more luxury than the other Disney resorts, with dark woods and faux-Craftsman detailing creating an attractive atmosphere.

Outside the Parks
Food

To escape the ubiquitous fast food and franchise restaurants immediately outside the park, head over to the **Anaheim Packing District** (440 S. Anaheim Blvd., 714/533-7225, www.anaheimpackingdistrict.com, 9am-midnight daily). It's kind of like a food court without the mall, featuring a diverse assortment of local food vendors serving decent food at reasonable prices, as well as coffee and drinks.

Accommodations

The massive park complex is ringed with motels, both popular chains and more interesting independent hotels. **The Anabella** (1030 W. Katella Ave., Anaheim, 714/905-1050, www.anabellahotel.com, $100-300) is a three-block walk to the parks. Guest rooms are furnished with an eye toward modern, stylish decor. You can get limited room service at the Anabella, and you can leave your car in their parking lot to avoid the expense of parking at Disneyland.

The **Desert Palms Hotel & Suites** (631 W. Katella Ave., 714/535-1133, www. desertpalmshotel.com, $180-250) is in walking distance of Disneyland. Regular rooms have one king or two queen beds, a TV, a phone, Internet access, and not a ton of room to walk around after all your luggage is crowded in with the furniture.

Huntington Beach

When CA-1 crosses the San Gabriel River coming south out of Long Beach, you'll have entered Orange County, the mostly suburban sprawl between Los Angeles and San Diego. After driving for about 15 miles and passing through Seal Beach, known primarily for its vast tidal wildlife refuge, you'll come across a long stretch of wide, flat, sandy beaches that continue virtually uninterrupted through the length of the county, beginning with **Huntington Beach** (pop. 200,652), a.k.a. Surf City USA.

At the north end is **Sunset Beach,** which is about wide as they come, with a grassy park and pedestrian path extending its 1.5-mile length, just behind a row of beachfront homes. Wild winds minimize good surfing days but provide the perfect fuel for windsurfing and kite surfing, plus fun bodysurfing and stand-up paddleboarding.

Southeast of Sunset Beach, three-mile-long **Bolsa Chica State Beach** (CA-1 in Huntington Beach, 6am-10pm daily, parking lot closes at 9pm) has smaller waves than beaches to the south, making it a popular spot for beginning surfers. Amenities include fire rings, volleyball courts, restrooms and showers, picnic ramadas (714/377-9422 for reservations), barbecue grills, basketball courts, and a paved bike path.

From top to bottom: Huntington Beach; catching waves at Huntington Beach; the historic Mission San Juan Capistrano.

Huntington City Beach (103 CA-1 from Beach Blvd. to Seapoint St., 714/536-5281, www.surfcityusa.com, 5am-10pm daily) constitutes. 3.5 miles of good surf, volleyball courts, and bike path. A pier in the center of the beach leads into Main Street, where you'll find the **Visitor Information Center and Kiosk,** as well as surf shops and rentals, restaurants and bars. Huntington Beach is home to the **International Surfing Museum** (411 Olive Ave., 714/300-8836, www.surfingmuseum.org, noon-5pm Sun.-Mon., noon-7pm Tues.-Fri., 11am-7pm Sat., free) and hosts late July's **U.S. Open of Pro Surfing** (www.vansusopenofsurfing.com).

Food and Accommodations

For quick vegetarian soups, salads, and sandwiches, stop at the **Bodhi Tree Café** (501 Main St., Ste. E, 714/969-9500, 11am-10pm daily, $10-20).

Across the highway from Huntington Beach, you can get ocean-view rooms and standard hotel furnishings at tiny **Sun 'N Sands Motel** (1102 CA-1, 714/536-2543, www.sunnsands.com, $139-289). Or try the larger and more stylish **Shorebreak Hotel** (500 CA-1, 714/861-4470, www.shorebreakhotel.com, $215-390), right in front of the pier; it's home to Asian-Mexican fusion restaurant **Pacific Hideaway** (714/965-4448, 7am-11pm Sun.-Thurs., 7am-midnight Fri.-Sat.).

Newport Beach

After passing over the Santa Ana River, CA-1 enters **Newport Beach** (pop. 86,688), 5 miles from Huntington Beach. Although Newport is a small affluent community built around a tiny bay protected by the Balboa Peninsula, it stays young and energetic by virtue of being the nearest beach for students of nearby **University of California Irvine.** Most of the activity will be found by exiting off CA-1 at Newport Boulevard and continuing onto Balboa Boulevard to enter the peninsula. Parking is limited, but the peninsula side features pretty beaches and shopping districts around two different piers.

Stretching southeast from the Newport Beach Pier (off 21st St.), **Newport Municipal Beach** is a beautiful and popular place to stretch out on the sand. Farther south, around Balboa Pier, you find restaurants and a small, open amusement park with a Ferris wheel, the **Balboa Fun Zone** (600 E. Bay Ave., 949/903-2825, www.balboaferriswheel.com, 11am-6pm Mon.-Thurs., 11am-9pm Fri., 11am-10pm Sat.).

A bike path runs along nearly the entire peninsula. You can rent a bike and surf boards at **20th Street Beach & Bikes** (2001 W. Balboa Blvd., 949/723-0043, www.beachandbikes.com, 9am-6pm Mon.-Fri., 9am-7pm Sat.-Sun., $10/2 hours).

Food and Accommodations

Local institution **The Crab Cooker** (2200 Newport Blvd., 949/673-0100, www.crabcooker.com, 11am-9pm Sun.-Thurs., 11am-10pm Fri.-Sat., $17-24) has been serving seafood since 1951. Looking for gourmet French cuisine with a hint of romance? **Pescadou Bistro** (3325 Newport Blvd., 949/675-6990, www.pescadoubistro.com, 5:30pm-9pm Tues.-Sun., $15-40) fits the bill.

Check into **The Island Hotel Newport Beach** (690 Newport Center Dr., 949/759-0808, www.islandhotel.com, $230-390) for perhaps the ultimate O.C. experience. The high-rise luxury hotel is situated in a giant shopping mall, a few minutes' drive from the beach. Expect cushy beds with white linens, private bathrooms, and all the best amenities.

Crystal Cove State Park

7 miles from Huntington Beach, **Crystal Cove State Park** (8471 CA-1 N., 949/494-3539, www.crystalcovestatepark.com,

Orange County

© AVALON TRAVEL

6am-sunset daily, $15) preserves one of the few stretches of undeveloped coastline in Orange County. Hiking through rolling hills, tidepooling, and bird-watching are a few of the activities that can be enjoyed here.

Accommodations

Restored historic cabins are available for overnight stays at ★ **Crystal Cove Beach Cottages** (35 Crystal Cove, 800/444-7275, www.crystalcovebeachcottages.

com, $169-249). The rustic accommodations are very popular; reservations can be made seven months prior to the time of your stay.

Laguna Beach

4.5 miles south, the town of **Laguna Beach** (pop. 23,190) has some of the nicest sands in the county, and it's one of the wealthiest communities. While this sometimes seems at odds with its historic surf culture, the dichotomy makes it interesting. Beach life extends among a dozen separate beaches. **Heisler Park** and **Main Beach Park** are most central, each offering amenities such as picnic tables and restrooms, with protected waterways, tidepools, water-based playground equipment, and scuba diving at several reefs right off the beach. If it's low tide, go south to search for the area's infamous Rapunzel-like tower, La Tour, nestled against a bluff just beyond the crags at the north end of Victoria Beach (2700 Victoria Dr., down the staircase)—just be careful not to slip on wet rocks.

For a taste of Laguna Beach glamour, browse the boutiques, galleries, and restaurants along Forest Avenue, just across the highway from Main Beach. More businesses are peppered north and south along CA-1—South Coast Highway, as it's known on this stretch.

Food and Accommodations

You'll find a variety of midscale bistros in Village Laguna, around Forest Street and CA-1. For the local mainstay, try the **Orange Inn** (703 CA-1, 949/494-6085, www.orangeinncafe.com, 5:30am-5pm daily, $5-10), which serves breakfast, burgers, and smoothies in a casual, surf shack-like space.

Laguna has developed a swanky reputation, and most of the hotels and resorts embrace that, with ritzy properties and sky-high rates. When it comes to location, the central (still pricey) midrange option would be **The Inn at Laguna Beach** (211 CA-1, 800/544-4479, www.innatlagunabeach.com, $460-550). Conversely, **Capri Laguna on the Beach** (1441 CA-1, 949/537-2503, www.caprilaguna.com, $280-650) puts you on the beach for less, if you don't request a view.

Loaded with framed decor, the **Art Hotel** (1404 N. Pacific Coast Hwy., 877/363-7229, www.arthotellagunabeach.com, $170-200) makes for Laguna's best budget option, with simple rooms and quick access to local beaches.

Dana Point

7.5 miles south of Laguna, the CA-1 ends where it meets the I-5 freeway, at the small harbor town of **Dana Point** (pop. 34,012). A bustling port between 1830 and 1840, today Dana Point offers a walkable marina with restaurants and shops. It also serves as departure point for visitors to **Catalina Island.**

Where CA-1 turns off to the freeway, the coast highway continues another 4.5 miles, passing through the pretty **Capistrano Beach** (35005 Beach Rd., 949/923-2280, www.ocparks.com, 6am-10pm daily), where you can catch a wave or a game of volleyball. Paths make biking, inline skating, and walking popular pastimes. You'll find a metered parking lot adjacent to the beach, plus showers and restrooms.

Accommodations

The **Blue Lantern Inn** (34343 Blue Lantern St., 949/661-1304, www.bluelanterninn.com, $200-350) offers beachfront elegance. Each of the 29 rooms boasts soothing colors, charming appointments, and lush amenities, including a spa tub in every bathroom.

I-5 North: Mission San Juan Capistrano

One of the most famous and beloved of all the California missions is **Mission San Juan Capistrano** (26801 Ortega Hwy., San Juan Capistrano, 949/234-1300, http://missionsjc.com, 9am-5pm daily, $9 adults, $6 children). From Dana Point, it's a quick 2.5-mile trip up I-5 to the mission.

This was the only one of nine California missions founded by Father Junípero Serra where he presided over

Sunday services. Today, this mission has a beautiful new Catholic church on-site, extensive gardens and land, and a museum, created within the old mission itself. Inside the original church, artifacts from the early days of the mission tell of its rise and fall. The graveyard outside continues that narrative, as do the bells and other buildings of the compound. In late fall and early spring, monarch butterflies flutter about in the flower gardens and out by the fountain in the courtyard.

These days, the mission may be most famous for the swallows that return every spring to the little town of San Juan Capistrano, and the celebrations that take place in their honor. These celebrations began during the mission's heyday in the 18th century and may have been started by Native Americans centuries before that.

Outside the mission, you'll find the town's main street, Camino Capistrano, which positively drips Spanish colonial history. Each old adobe building boasts a brass plaque describing its origins and use over the years.

North County Beach Cities

As the I-5 freeway continues south toward Mexico, the first thing you hit in San Diego County is the vast, inaccessible military base **Camp Pendleton**. At the first exit past the base, the Coast Highway officially picks up again as CA-101, which passes through the succession of charming beach cities of San Diego's North County. The I-5 moves much quicker than CA-101 through here, but even as they differ in character, each city has gorgeous coastline in common. A slow drive on the scenic highway can be fun, as evidenced by a steady stream of cyclists biking the 20-mile stretch of road.

Dana Point to Oceanside is 28 miles and takes about 30 minutes. From there,

The Mission San Luis Rey is the largest of California's historic missions.

Oceanside to Carlsbad is 3 miles and takes 10 minutes, Carlsbad to Encinitas is 10 miles and takes 15 minutes, and Encinitas to Del Mar is 6 miles and takes about 12 minutes.

Snug against the southern border of the base you'll find the military-friendly beach town of **Oceanside** (pop. 175,464), named for over three miles of flat beach extending south from a harbor and pier. It's home to the **Mission San Luis Rey** (4050 Mission Ave., 760/757-3651, www.sanluisrey.org, 9:30am-5pm Mon.-Fri., 10am-5pm Sat.-Sun., $7 adults, $3 children). Though not one of the missions founded by Junípero Serra, the size of the 1798 church earned it the nickname King of the Missions.

South of Oceanside lies **Carlsbad** (pop. 113,952), which features pleasant shops and restaurants around its charming **Carlsbad Village** (Carlsbad Village Dr. and State St.). There's free parking in the lot at **Tamarack State Beach** (101 Tamarack Ave.), which offers the county's

most consistent waves during the summer doldrums.

Carlsbad's main attraction is **Legoland** (1 Legoland Dr., 760/918-5346, www.legoland.com, 10am-6pm daily, $87 ages 13 and up, $81 ages 3-12). The amusement park for young children showcases what can be made from the iconic Danish building blocks, from dragons and pharaohs to miniature versions of major U.S. cities. An aquarium and water park are also part of this resort complex and cost an extra admission fee.

After crossing Batiquitos Lagoon, you'll wind up in **Encinitas** (pop. 63,131), a beautiful, artsy, and upscale beach community that meets the ocean at **Moonlight State Beach** (400 B St., 760/633-2740, www.parks.ca.gov, 5am-10pm daily, free parking). Pale sand and turquoise waters attract families, sunbathers, and surfers to a beach backed by sandstone bluffs in either direction. Boutiques, restaurants, and a small movie theater give the neighborhood a homey feel.

At the south Encinitas community **Cardiff by the Sea,** the campground at **San Elijo State Beach** (2050 CA-101, 800-444-7275, www.parks.ca.gov/SanElijo, dawn-sunset daily, $15 per vehicle) draws enough surfers and beach lovers that reservations fill up months in advance during summer months.

The posh community of **Del Mar** (pop. 4,365) is best known for its **Del Mar Race Track** (2260 Jimmy Durante Blvd., 858/755-1141, www.dmtc.com, $6), "Where the turf meets the surf." Horses race from mid-July through Labor Day, then again during the month of November. Popular, free concerts follow the races on Fridays (and some Saturdays) in the summer.

Locals love the beachfront dining room and patio at **Jakes Del Mar** (1660 Coast Blvd., 858/755-2002, www.jakesdelmar.com, 5pm-9pm Mon., 11:30am-9pm Tues.-Thurs., 11:30am-9:30pm Fri.-Sat., 10am-9pm Sun., $14-18). The restaurant sits right on the beach, close enough to hear the waves crash.

Torrey Pines State Reserve

Two miles south of Del Mar, Torrey Pines is on Coast Highway 101, west off the Carmel Valley Road exit on I-5. In addition to walks on the beach, the **Torrey Pines State Reserve** (12600 N. Torrey Pines Rd., 858/755-2063, www.torreypine.org, 9am-sunset daily, $15) offers unusually beautiful wilderness trails. Be sure to look for *Pinus torreyana,* the rarest species of pine tree in the United States. The shortest walk is the High Point Trail, only 100 yards up to views of the whole reserve, from the ocean to the lagoon to the forest and back. For an easy, under one-hour walk, take the Guy Fleming Trail for a level two-thirds of a mile through forest, wildflower patches, and views of the ocean.

Enjoy a picnic at **Torrey Pines State Beach,** which rests right below the reserve. At low tide, you can walk south to Black's Beach, at the northernmost point of La Jolla.

La Jolla

Torrey Pines is technically part of **La Jolla** (pop. 46,781)—literally "The Jewel"—a wealthy community stretching 10 miles between the coast and I-5 freeway. Along with public beach access and Torrey pine forests, its north end is home to the University of California San Diego, while its southern end furnishes upper-middle-class residential neighborhoods. The town center, officially called The Village of La Jolla, is famous for its high-end boutiques, ritzy hotels, renowned art galleries, and several of San Diego County's finest restaurants. Built on a rounded peninsula that plays home to both seals and sea lions, its business district abuts a rocky coastline and a smattering of tiny beaches, including its eponymous cove.

Getting There and Around
Car
La Jolla is off the I-5 freeway, just south of Del Mar and north of downtown San Diego. Northbound, take La Jolla Parkway to Torrey Pines Road via I-5 North. Southbound, take I-5 South and Torrey Pines Road to Fay Avenue. Parking is challenging and expensive ($12-15 per day).

Bus
San Diego's **Metropolitan Transit System** operates route 30, connecting to Pacific Beach, Old Town, and downtown to the south, and the University of California San Diego and University City to the east, stopping within walking distance of many local attractions. **North County Transit District**'s (760/966-6500) route 101 also serves UC San Diego and University City, running north on Torrey Pines Road to North San Diego County.

Sights
University of California San Diego
The **University of California San Diego** has earned a reputation as one of the world's top scientific research universities, but its 1,200-acre campus of sprawling lawns, trees, and architecture also features an abundance of art and cultural treasures.

Undoubtedly the most beloved structure is the postmodern **Geisel Library,** named for author Theodore Geisel, a.k.a. Dr. Seuss, creator of classic children's books *Cat in the Hat* and *Green Eggs and Ham.* Its unique, diamond-shaped tower stands over the wooded canyons forming the northeast corner of campus. A collection of the author's manuscripts, audio recordings, drawings, photographs, and other memorabilia are displayed within.

Eighteen commissioned art installations comprising the Stuart Collection appear throughout the campus, ranging

Wine-Tasting: Temecula

Horses and wine? Who knew these two would make a perfect pairing! In the Temecula Valley, renowned wineries and horse ranches share the rolling countryside, so wine-tasting via horseback makes perfect sense.

Saddle Up Tours (951/297-9196, www.saddleuptours.com) and **Wine Country Trails** (951/506-8706, www.winecountrytrailsbyhorseback.com) both offer packages that include tastings at 1-5 wineries and a gourmet meal ($115-415), with local wine history along the trail. Rides take place in the early morning when the air is crisp and in the evening just as the sun is setting, and generally last 90 minutes. If you've never been on a horse, don't worry. Rides are always led by a professional who provides instruction and horses are well-seasoned, so you don't have to be an experienced bronco-buster.

Out on the trail, you'll ride through open country, dotted with shrubbery and grapevines, with commanding views of the valley. Though you won't be sampling wine while riding through the vineyards (that's the reward at the end!), your horse will likely make a few stops to partake of the fruit.

The final destination is a tasting at some of the valley's best winemakers. **Wilson Creek Winery** (35960 Rancho California Rd., 951/699-9463) is home of the famous almond sparkling wine and lush 30-year-old cabernet grapevines. **Lorimar Vineyards** (39990 Anza Rd., 951/694-6699) features premium wines, live music, and a revolving art gallery. **Baily Vineyard** (33440 La Serena Way, 951/676-9463) is a master of the Bordeaux varieties. **Danza del Sol Winery** (39050 De Portola Rd., 951/302-6363) offers an incredible selection of both whites and reds.

GETTING THERE

Temecula lies 44 miles northeast of Oceanside. To get there, follow CA-76 East, then take I-15 North to Temecula Parkway. Take the CA-79 South exit toward Old Town Front Street.

from Tim Hawkinson's giant stone *Bear* sculpture to Terry Allen's *Trees,* which re-erects felled eucalyptus trees, encases them in metal, and rigs them to play recorded music and poetry. The collection's most visceral piece may be the tiny cottage that appears to have fallen from the sky to land at an awkward angle on the roof of Jacobs Hall. Unlike the rest of the collection, only limited viewings are available for Do Ho Suh's dizzying *Fallen Star* (9500 Gilman Dr., 858/534-2117, 11am-2pm Tues. and Thurs.), but the cottage's warped perspective promises to alter your perception like no other artwork.

Museum of Contemporary Art San Diego

The **Museum of Contemporary Art San Diego** (MCASD, 700 Prospect Ave., 858/454-3541, www.mcasd.org, 11am-5pm Thurs.-Tues., $10, $5 students, free with ID to students 25 and under, military) features 4,000 multifaceted artworks including painting, sculpture, photography, and video, with work by surrealist Joseph Cornell, minimalist Frank Stella, and pop artist Andy Warhol. The 1960s and '70s conceptual art collection includes art from Latin America, with an emphasis on the San Diego/Tijuana region. There is a beautiful sculpture garden outside the museum.

Beaches and Recreation
★ La Jolla Cove

Small but lovely, **La Jolla Cove** sits at the northern tip of La Jolla village, banked by a grassy park that's a perfect place to picnic or watch the sunset. Below the park, rocky outcroppings populated by vocal, sunbathing sea lions surround a small crescent of white sand, which accesses

La Jolla

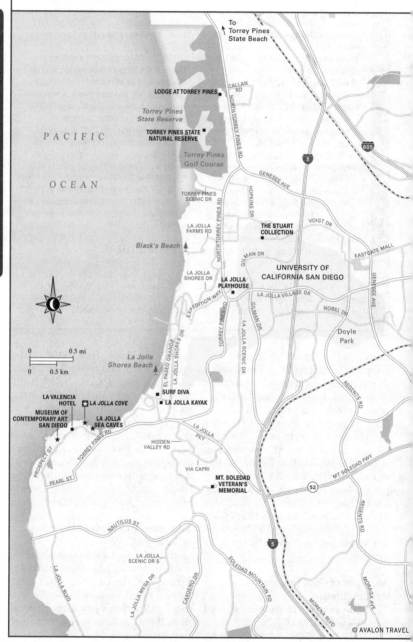

To Torrey Pines State Beach

CALLAN RD

LODGE AT TORREY PINES

Torrey Pines State Reserve

TORREY PINES STATE NATURAL RESERVE

NORTH TORREY PINES RD

Torrey Pines Golf Course

PACIFIC OCEAN

GENESEE AVE

805

5

TORREY PINES SCENIC DR

HOPKINS DR

VOIGT DR

THE STUART COLLECTION

LA JOLLA FARMS RD

Black's Beach

GILMAN DR

EASTGATE MALL

UNIVERSITY OF CALIFORNIA SAN DIEGO

LA JOLLA SHORES DR

LA JOLLA PLAYHOUSE

LA JOLLA VILLAGE DR

GENESEE AVE

EXPEDITION WAY

TORREY PINES RD

GILMAN DR

NOBEL DR

La Jolla Shores Beach

EL PASEO GRANDE

LA JOLLA SHORES DR

LA JOLLA SCENIC DR

Doyle Park

0   0.5 mi
0   0.5 km

SURF DIVA

LA JOLLA KAYAK

REGENTS RD

LA VALENCIA HOTEL

LA JOLLA COVE

MUSEUM OF CONTEMPORARY ART SAN DIEGO

LA JOLLA SEA CAVES

LA JOLLA PKY

TORREY PINES RD

HIDDEN VALLEY RD

VIA CAPRI

PROSPECT ST

PEARL ST

MT. SOLEDAD VETERAN'S MEMORIAL

MT SOLEDAD FWY

52

REGENTS RD

5

NAUTILUS ST

LA JOLLA SCENIC DR S

LA JOLLA BLVD

LA JOLLA MESA DR

CARDENO DR

SOLEDAD MOUNTAIN RD

MORENA BLVD

MORAGA AVE

© AVALON TRAVEL

the deep blue water of the protected La Jolla Underwater Reserve. Kayaks, surf boards, and rafts of any kind may not access the water here, but you'll often see scuba divers and snorkelers bobbing around the surface before descending into the water for a closer look at the colorful fish, coral, and sea kelp. Underwater snorkeling tours ($35 and up) and equipment rentals are provided by companies like **La Jolla Kayak** (2199 Avenida de la Playa, 858/459-1114, www.lajollakayak.com, 8am-6pm daily). Once or twice per winter, a massive wave called Sleeping Giant breaks across the cove, providing dazzling, up-close views of expert surfers slaying it.

La Jolla Sea Caves

At the northern end of La Jolla Cove are seven intriguing sea caves once popular among Prohibition-era bootleggers. The only way to see most of them is from the ocean, typically via kayak from La Jolla Shores. The exception is **Sunny Jim Cave.** Named by Wizard of Oz author L. Frank Baum for its resemblance to the world's first ever cereal box mascot, Sunny Jim may be reached through a manmade tunnel via a steep staircase inside snorkel and gift shop **The Cave Store** (1325 Coast Blvd., 858/459-0746, www.cavestore.com, 10am-5pm Mon.-Thurs., 10:30am-5pm Fri., 10am-5:30pm Sat.-Sun., $5 adults, $3 children 16 and under).

La Jolla Shores

La Jolla's best beach may be found a couple miles north of La Jolla village. **La Jolla Shores** (8300 Camino del Oro, 619/235-1169) offers a long, wide, family-friendly stretch of sparkling sand and mild water conditions throughout summer months. There's a playground for small children as well as swimming and bodyboarding areas designated by checkered flags. On the other side of those flags, beginner surfers may find open space to practice catching rides. More advanced riders tend to head for the north end of the beach, where the Scripps Pier adds size and structure to the waves. At the south end of the beach is the kayak launch, where paddlers access La Jolla Cove with rentals or sea cave tours from **La Jolla Kayak** (2199 Avenida de la Playa, 858/459-1114, www.lajollakayak.com, 8am-6pm daily).

Beach showers and bathroom facilities are available next to a sizable parking lot. For surf or stand-up paddleboard lessons or rentals—child or adult—inquire at **Surf Diva** (2160 Avenida de la Playa, 858/454-8273, 8:30am-6pm Sun.-Thurs., 8:30am-6:30pm Fri.-Sat., rentals $10-15/hour, lessons $65-75).

Black's Beach

On the other side of the cliffs framing the north end of La Jolla Shores, San Diego's best waves curl at **Black's Beach.** But unless you want to paddle the long way around from La Jolla Shores, you'll have to carry your board on a hike down the cliffside trail originating at the Torrey Pines Gliderport (2800 Torrey Pines Scenic Dr.) or down the steep, paved road descending from 9601 La Jolla Farms Road (gated to cars). Still, hundreds make the effort to ride almond-shaped barrels when the surf is up. Though gorgeous, the cliff-backed beach remains less populated, though you're likely to get an eyeful—its seclusion makes Black's a popular sunbathing spot for nudists.

As for **Torrey Pines Gliderport** (2800 Torrey Pines Scenic Dr., 858/452-9858, www.flytorrey.com, 9am-5:30pm daily, $175 paragliding, $225 hang-gliding), it offer a unique opportunity to paraglide or hang-glide on the eddies of wind blowing up the bluffs from the beach at Black's—beginners must start with a tandem flight.

Food

For authentic Mexican cuisine prepared with organic ingredients, try the tacos at **Puesto** (1026 Wall St., 858/454-1260, www.eatpuesto.com, 11am-9pm

Sun.-Thurs., 11am-10pm Fri.-Sat., $15), and save room for the exceptional flan dessert.

Known for its soufflé-style French toast, converted beach cottage **Brockton Villa** (1235 Coast Blvd., 858/454-7393, www.brocktonvilla.com, 8am-9pm daily, $10-14) makes a great ocean-view breakfast locale, especially on its deck.

To find respite from La Jolla's polished countenance without leaving the village, go to **Harry's Coffee Shop** (7545 Girard Ave., 858/454-7381, www.harryscoffeeshop.com, 6am-3pm daily) for old-school, American-diner breakfast.

La Jolla's **Burger Lounge** (1101 Wall St., 858/456-0196, www.burgerlounge.com, 10:30am-9pm Sun.-Thurs., 10:30am-10pm Fri.-Sat., $8-10) isn't the usual counter-service beef chain. Expect grass-fed beef with organic cheese and condiments. Albacore, lamb, and panko-crusted chicken round out the menu.

Two of La Jolla's finest contemporary chefs operate hotel restaurants. At the Grande Colonial Hotel, Jason Knibb shares his extraordinary mastery of flavors at **Nine-Ten** (910 Prospect St., 858/964-5400, www.nine-ten.com, 6:30am-9:30pm Mon.-Thurs., 6:30am-10pm Fri.-Sat., 7:30am-9:30pm Sun., $22-38), taking inspiration from seasonal ingredients—request a seat on the terrace for the ultimate experience. Over at the Lodge at Torrey Pines, chef Jeff Jackson spearheaded San Diego's farm-to-table movement, presenting seasonal menus that let his selection of high quality ingredients do the talking. Which may be responsible for the tranquil atmosphere permeating the dining room and deck of **A.R. Valentien** (11480 N. Torrey Pines Rd., 858/777-6635, www.arvalentien.com, 11:30am-2:30pm and 5:30pm-10pm Mon.-Fri., 7am-11:30am, noon-2:30pm, and 5:30pm-10pm Sat.-Sun., $30-40). Consider a tasting menu at both spots.

Seafood lovers in La Jolla have terrific options. For more than four decades, locals have lined up for fresh, local caught

La Jolla Cove

seafood sandwiches, salads, and plates at beloved **El Pescador Fish Market** (634 Pearl St., 858/456-2526, www.elpescadorfishmarket.com, 11am-9pm daily, $10-18). For fine dining with an ocean view, the seafood-centric California-modern tasting menu at **George's at the Cove** (1250 Prospect St., 858/454-4244, www.georgesatthecove.com, 11am-10pm Sun.-Thurs., 11am-11pm Fri.-Sat., $30-46) has long set the tone for beachside dining. Make a reservation for ocean terrace seating.

Nightlife and Entertainment

San Diego's first craft brewery, **Karl Strauss Brewing Company** (1044 Wall St., 858/551-2739, www.karlstrauss.com) operates a brewpub in the village, providing La Jolla's best stop to sample the region's celebrated beer culture.

Around sunset, live jazz music and cocktails grace the deck above **Eddie V's Prime Seafood** (1270 Prospect St., 858/459-5500, www.eddiev.com), which boasts a direct view of La Jolla Cove and tasty small plates to snack on.

Depending on the night, open-mic up-and-comers or big-name performers deliver punch lines with a two-drink minimum at the **La Jolla Comedy Store** (916 Pearl St., 858/454-9176, www.lajolla.thecomedystore.com, $5-20 tickets).

Plays and musicals grace the stage of world-class theater **La Jolla Playhouse** (2910 La Jolla Village Dr., 858/550-1010, www.lajollaplayhouse.org, $20 and up). Cofounded by Hollywood icon Gregory Peck, the Playhouse has been the birthplace of 26 Broadway productions, including Jesus Christ Superstar, Jersey Boys, and The Who's Tommy.

Shopping

San Diego's most fashionable upscale shopping (and window shopping) may be found at **Boutiques on Girard Avenue** (between Prospect St. and Kline St.). Individual boutiques come and go, and while top designer labels may have more staying power, the high rents here ensure that whatever you find will be current with international trends.

For designer wares at a reduced cost, a couple of gently used and vintage shops cater to fashionable men and women who don't mind looking great in yesterday's high fashions. Ladies should look a little south of the village to find **Take 2 Ladies Consignment Boutique** (6786 La Jolla Blvd., 858/459-0095, www.take2ladiesconsignor.com, 11am-6:30pm Mon.-Fri., 11am-5pm Sat.) and its collection featuring Jimmy Choo, Gucci, Prada, and more. For men, classy vintage attire and designer accessories cycle through **Le Chauvinist** (7709 Fay Ave., 858/456-0117, www.lechauvinist.com, 11am-5pm Mon.-Fri., 11am-4pm Sat., 9am-2pm Sun.), with accouterments ranging from dapper to hip.

Warwick's (7812 Girard Ave., 858/454-0347, 9am-6pm Mon.-Sat., 10am-5:30pm Sun.) is the country's oldest family-owned bookstore, with an eclectic collection of great reads and high-profile signings by beloved authors and entertainers.

La Jolla's history of supporting the arts has resulted in bringing several notable galleries to the village, as well as shops catering to arts, folk arts, and antiques along Prospect Avenue. The most heralded stop for contemporary art lovers would be **Madison Gallery** (1055 Wall St. #100, 858/459-0836, www.madison-galleries.com, 10am-6pm Mon.-Sat., noon-4pm Sun.). The renowned gallery routinely carries exciting works by artists living and dead, including Southern California favorites John Baldessari and Ed Ruscha.

Accommodations

A local fixture since 1926, ★ **La Valencia** (1132 Prospect St., 858/454-0771, www.lavalenica.com, $380 and up) invokes the breezy style of a Mediterranean villa. Centrally located near La Jolla village restaurants and shopping, it offers airy rooms (some with ocean views) and a heated pool that overlooks the shimmering Pacific.

The Bed & Breakfast Inn at La Jolla (7753 Draper Ave., 858/456-2066, www.innlajolla.com, $184-459) offers 13 uniquely styled rooms and two suites, some with fireplaces and ocean views but all elegant and comfortable. Close to everything, it's just a block from La Jolla Cove's cliffs and beaches and the Museum of Contemporary Art San Diego.

The most affordable option for a room with a view of La Jolla Cove may be found at **La Jolla Cove Suites** (1155 Coast Blvd., 858/459-2621, www.lajollacove.com, $250 and up). It's not fancy, but nearly all of its recently renovated suites face the ocean, and they feature small kitchens.

By staying just four blocks from the coast, you'll find a more affordable stay at **La Jolla Village Lodge** (1141 Silverado St., 858/551-2001, $170 and up). La Jolla's answer to a motel, its basic rooms are not without their charms, chief among them being free parking for guests.

The Craftsman-style **Lodge at Torrey Pines** (11480 N. Torrey Pines Rd., 858/453-4420, $400 and up) stands along an ocean bluff, fronted by not one but two world-class golf courses. Its commanding ocean views, spacious rooms, and shuttle service to La Jolla beaches and shopping make it well worth the steep price tag. Dining on-site includes a casual grill and A.R. Valentien, a high-end restaurant with exceptional farm-to-table cuisine and serene atmosphere.

Information and Services

Visit **La Jolla Village Information Center** (1162 Prospect St., 858/454-5718, 11am-5pm Tues.-Sun.) for assistance with local activities, dining, and shopping.

San Diego

San Diego (pop. 1.4 million) is the ideal destination for anyone whose idea of the perfect vacation is lying on a white-sand beach, looking out over the Pacific Ocean, and sipping the occasional cocktail. Resort hotels and restaurants perch along the seaside, beckoning visitors to the friendliest city in California.

Even though its urban area is small compared to other California metropolises, San Diego can't be beat for the combination of active lifestyles and culture. With a world-famous zoo, dozens of museums, a thick layer of military and mission history, and unmatched recreation, San Diego offers education, enlightenment, and fun. Urban explorers will enjoy the world-class beer scene as well as a thriving theater community.

Across the bay, the enclave of Coronado beckons, featuring one of the West Coast's finest beaches and the historic Hotel del Coronado, the world's second largest wood structure (after Oregon's Tillamook Air Museum).

Getting There and Around
Car
San Diego is 12 miles (about 15 minutes) from La Jolla and 124 miles (2-3 hours) from Los Angeles. Most visitors drive into San Diego via the heavily traveled I-5 from the north or south. I-805 runs parallel to I-5 at La Jolla and leads south through Mission Valley, though it experiences the heaviest rush hour traffic. To drive between the North County and San Diego, take I-15, which runs north-south farther inland. All three freeways cross I-8, which runs east-west through Mission Valley to the beaches. The smaller CA-163 cuts south-north through Balboa Park, connecting I-5 near downtown to I-15 by the Marine Corps air station in Miramar.

Parking is the hardest at the beaches in the summertime. In the various downtown areas, you'll find fairly average city parking issues. Happily, San Diego's major attractions and event venues tend to be accompanied by large parking structures. Just be prepared to pay a premium if you're doing something popular.

Air
The major-league **San Diego International Airport** (3665 N. Harbor Dr., www.san.org), a.k.a. Lindbergh Field, is stuffed right along San Diego Bay, convenient to downtown, Coronado, and almost every major San Diego attraction.

Train
Amtrak (800/872-7245, www.amtrak.com, $37 and up) runs the **Pacific Surfliner** a dozen times a day from San Luis Obispo to San Diego, with stops in Santa Barbara, Los Angeles, and Anaheim. Check into transfers from the **Coast Starlight** and the **Capitol Corridor** routes as well. Amtrak services the Santa Fe Depot (1050 Kettner Blvd.) and the Old Town Transit Center (4005 Taylor St.).

A reliable local commuter train, **The**

Coaster (www.sdcommute.com, $4-5.50 adults one-way, $2-2.75 seniors, free for children under 6) runs from Oceanside into downtown San Diego and back a dozen times a day Monday-Friday, with five trains running Saturday, plus special event and holiday service. Purchase tickets from the vending machines in every train station. In the North County, NCTD Coaster Connecter bus routes can connect to the train station. In San Diego proper, catch the trolley or the bus from either the Old Town Transit Center or the Santa Fe station.

Bus and Trolley
In downtown San Diego, Coronado, and La Jolla, the **MTS** (www.sdcommute.com or www.sdmts.com) operates both an extensive bus system and trolley routes. Trolley tickets cost $2.50. Bus fares are $2.25 for local routes and $2.50-5 for express routes. Use the vending machines at trolley stations to get a day pass ($5 regular day pass, $12 Rapid Express Routes day pass). If you plan to pay for your fare for buses or trolleys on board, have exact change available.

Sights
Downtown
Marina District and Gaslamp Quarter
San Diego got its start in historic Old Town, but it became a city due to its protected harbor. The **Marina District** (Harbor Dr. from Ash St. to Park Blvd.) sits where downtown hits the harbor, featuring several bayside parks, a collection of gift shops and restaurants at Seaport Village, large hotels, and boat slips for day cruises and the Coronado ferry. Pedicabs for hire offer rides in and out of **Gaslamp Quarter** (south of Broadway from 1st Ave. to 6th Ave.), the area where sailors historically came ashore to romp but which has been refashioned as a tourist shopping and entertainment district.

Maritime Museum of San Diego

The impressive collection of historical, restored, and replica vessels at the **Maritime Museum of San Diego** (1492 N. Harbor Dr., 619/234-9153, 9am-8pm daily, $16 adults, $8 children) is a must-see for seafaring enthusiasts. The prized relic is *Star of India,* the world's oldest active sailing ship. Built in 1863, of iron in a time when ships were made of wood, the *Europa* made 21 rugged voyages around the world, some lasting a year. The *Berkeley* is an 1898 steam ferryboat that operated for 60 years on San Francisco Bay. Purchased in 2004, the *HMS Surprise* is a 24-gun Royal Navy frigate built for the Academy Award-winning *Master and Commander: The Far Side of the World.* Other vessels include the *Medea,* a 1904 steam yacht; the *Californian,* a replica of a gold rush-era patroller; and the *B-39 Soviet,* one of the largest conventionally powered submarines ever built.

USS *Midway*

Follow the footsteps of the 225,000 sailors who served aboard **USS Midway** (910 N. Harbor Dr., 619/544-9600, 10am-5pm daily, $20, $10 children), America's longest-serving aircraft carrier. First launched in 1945, the ship today serves as a museum, offering an up-close look at life at sea. Real *Midway* sailors narrate a self-guided audio tour, and docents are available to answer questions. Explore the crew's sleeping quarters, the galley, engine room, even the ship's jail. The museum is also home to 29 restored aircraft and two flight simulators ($8 double, $16 single), which roll, spin, and loop during mock aerial combat missions.

Chicano Park

Tucked under the Coronado Bridge, this small Barrio Logan park boasts the world's largest collection of outdoor murals, mostly painted on the bridge's base supports. **Chicano Park** (1949 Logan Ave., Barrio Logan, 619/232-1930,

Spanish revival architecture abounds at Balboa Park.

www.chicanoparksandiego.com, open 24 hours) celebrates the community's Mexican heritage, and commemorates the 1970 protest of a highway patrol station on the site. Activists occupied the park for two weeks to preserve the green space for a neighborhood that had already been divided by freeways, and lost its waterfront access to port development.

★ Balboa Park

A sprawling 1,200-acre urban park with numerous open spaces, gardens, theaters, and the world-famous San Diego Zoo, **Balboa Park** (1549 El Prado, 619/239-0512, www.balboapark.org) is the cultural center of downtown. Many of the city's museums are found along Balboa Park's Prado, inside Spanish colonial revival buildings built for the 1915-1916 Panama-California Exposition.

Top museums include the **San Diego Museum of Art** (1450 El Prado, 619/232-7931, www.sdmart.org, 10am-5pm Mon.-Tues., Thurs., and Sat., 10am-9pm Fri.,

noon-5pm Sun., $15, children free), renowned for its Renaissance works, and **San Diego Air & Space Museum** (2001 Pan American Plaza, 619/234-8291, www.sandiegoairandspace.org, 10am-5pm daily, $19.75), fronted by a replica stealth bomber. Interactive exhibits make family learning fun at the **Fleet Science Center** (1875 El Prado, 619/238-1233, www.rhfleet.org, 10am-5pm Mon.-Thurs., 10am-6pm Fri.-Sun., $20, $17 children) and dinosaur-friendly **San Diego Natural History Museum** (1788 El Prado, 619/232-3821, www.sdnhm.org, 10am-5pm daily, $19, $12 children).

Balboa's gardens are a cultivated wonder of 350 species of plants and an estimated 1,500 trees, many selected by "the Mother of Balboa Park," Kate Sessions, who is credited with the park's rise to enchantment. The most photographed is the **Botanical Building** (1549 El Prado, 619/239-0512, 10am-4pm Fri.-Wed., free), an elegant lathe structure built in front of a serene lily pond. Walking paths meander through the colorful landscape of the ambrosial **Inez Grant Memorial Rose Garden,** with 130 species of the fragrant flower, and the fascinating **Desert Garden,** with 1,300 succulents and desert plants from around the world.

Ride the 1910 **Carousel** (2920 Zoo Dr., 619/239-0512, 11am-5pm Sun. and school holidays, 11am-5:30pm daily in summer, $2.50). All but two of the intricately hand-carved animals are original pieces. The model G16 **Miniature Railroad** (1800 Zoo Pl., 619/239-4748, 11am-4:30pm Sat.-Sun., 11am-6:30pm daily in summer, $2.50) takes a half-mile trip through four acres of the park.

San Diego Zoo

The biggest family attraction in Balboa Park, **San Diego Zoo** (2920 Zoo Dr., 619/231-1515, 9am-5pm daily Nov.-Feb., 9am-6pm daily Mar.-May and Sept.-Oct., 9am-9pm daily June-Aug., $52 adults, $42 children) showcases more than 4,000 endangered and exotic animals from

San Diego

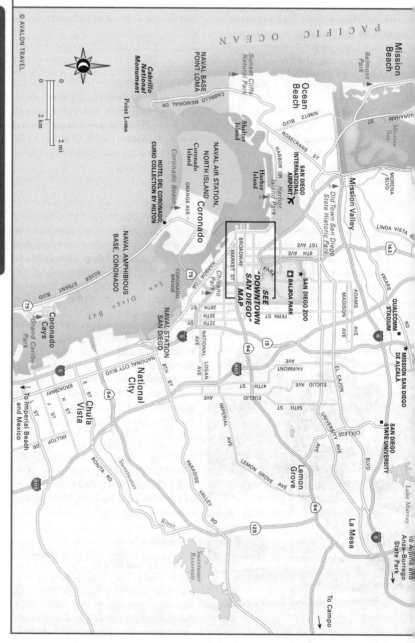

© AVALON TRAVEL

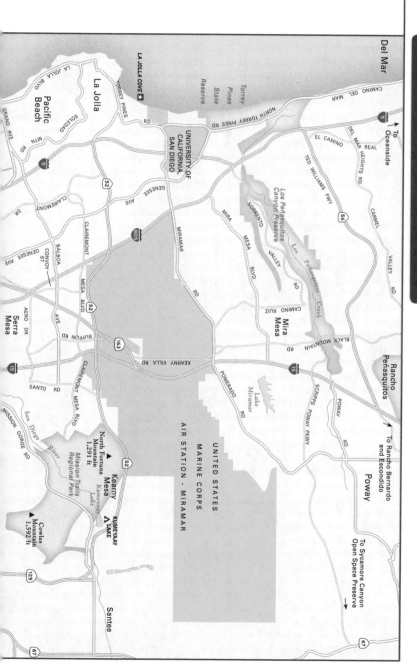

Downtown San Diego

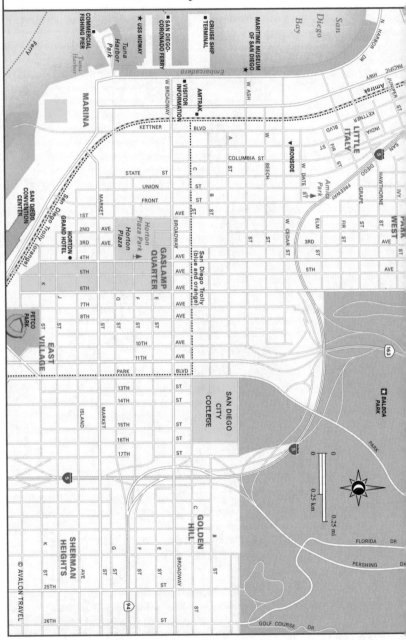

Two Days in San Diego

Balboa Park's beautiful Botanical Garden.

Day 1

Start your day admiring the exotic animals at the **San Diego Zoo** (page 349)—they're always most fun in the morning. Afterward, stroll through the cluster of culture in **Balboa Park** (page 349), beginning with lunch at **Panama 66** (page 357), the restaurant conveniently located in the sculpture garden of the **San Diego Museum of Art** (page 349). After eating, explore the diverse museums and art galleries within the park; wander its gardens, including the exquisite **Botanical Building** (page 349).

Continue your journey through the city's past in historic **Old Town** (page 354), where California's oldest city had its humble, adobe beginnings. Or, if you're feeling active, head to nearby **Mission Bay Park** (page 356) for an afternoon of paddle boarding, catamaran sailing, or Jet Skiing.

Whichever you do, set up your appetite for a seafood feast at Little Italy's exceptionally cool **Ironside Fish & Oyster** (page 357), followed by a sampling of San Diego craft beers at nearby **Bottlecraft** (page 358).

Day 2

Start with an authentic Mexican breakfast at **Las Cuatro Milpas** (page 357), then head to the harbor and the **Maritime Museum of San Diego** (page 348), which has one of the largest historical sea vessel collections in the nation. A half-mile south (just past the Broadway Pier), the **USS *Midway*** (page 348) is anchored in the harbor, waiting to be boarded and explored. Follow with lunch in the open air at meat-loving **Carnitas' Snack Shack** (page 357).

Drive across the two-mile San Diego–Coronado Bridge, or take the foot ferry from the Broadway Pier to the Coronado Ferry Landing (the ferry takes 15 minutes). After arriving in **Coronado**, rent a bicycle from **Bikes & Beyond** (page 356) and glide along the **Bayshore Bikeway** (page 356), just over two miles to **Hotel del Coronado** (page 355). (MTS route 904 also runs from the ferry landing to the hotel.) Put in some serious beach time or spend your afternoon strolling the Del's ornate lobby and grand decks, which look out across the Pacific—perfect for watching the sunset. End your day at the Del, or head back across the bridge for a casual meal of fish tacos at **Oscar's Mexican Seafood** (page 357), or pull out all the stops for upscale wood-fired fare at **Herb & Wood** (page 357), before partying at **Altitude Sky Lounge** (page 358), one of the rooftop bars of the **Gaslamp Quarter.**

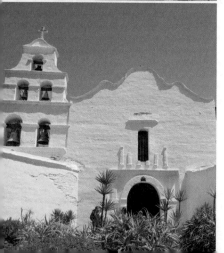

around the world, including polar bears, primates, elephants, and one of the largest populations of giant pandas. Walking paths connect all areas of the sometimes steep hillside park; guided bus tours, express buses, and an aerial tram provide faster transportation. Animals are more active during morning hours.

Old Town and Mission Hills
Old Town San Diego State Historic Park
The city's oldest standing structures are now historic landmarks preserved within **Old Town San Diego State Historic Park** (4002 Wallace St., 858/220-5422, www. oldtownsandiegoguide.com, 10am-5pm daily, free). A visit here gives a sense of what the original Puebla de San Diego settlement must have been like in the 1820s—a combination of Spanish colony and the American old west. Most buildings are old family residences, including the homes of Spanish soldiers. The **Mason Street Schoolhouse** depicts a reconstructed 19th-century classroom complete with desks and chalkboards. The **San Diego Union Building** features the typesetting tables and a printing press of the city's first newspaper. The Colorado House, site of the **Wells Fargo Museum,** invites guests inside an old bank vault.

Mission San Diego de Alcala
Just under 10 miles west of Old Town, Mission Valley is named for the first of 21 California missions established by Father Junípero Serra. **Mission San Diego de Alcala** (10818 San Diego Mission Rd., Mission Valley, San Diego, 619/283-7319, www.missionsandiego.com, Mon.-Fri. 8am-4:30pm, $3 adults, $1 children) remains an active Catholic parish while offering a small museum. First built on Presidio Hill in Old Town in 1769, it was moved in 1774 to its present location in

From top to bottom: Balboa Park; the *Star of India* at the Maritime Museum of San Diego; Mission San Diego de Alcala.

Mission Valley to make way for a Spanish military outpost. Prior to World War II, the crumbling buildings underwent reconstruction; their preservation continues today. Tour the bougainvillea-filled garden near a 46-foot-high bell tower and the museum, which holds old photographs and relics unearthed during excavations of the site.

Point Loma

Accessed by going to the western terminus of the I-8 freeway, the long peninsula responsible for shielding San Diego Bay from the Pacific Ocean is called Point Loma. With beaches on one side and marinas filled with fishing boats on the other, it combines natural scenery and plenty of places to eat.

Cabrillo National Monument

People have lived along the San Diego coastline for over 10,000 years, most notably the Kumeyaay nation. That's who Juan Rodríguez Cabrillo encountered when he became the first European to set foot on what is now the U.S. West Coast. A statue atop this hilltop peak of Point Loma reflects on that day in 1542, but that's not the reason to visit **Cabrillo National Monument** (1800 Cabrillo Memorial Dr., 619/557-5450, www.nps.gov/cabr, 9am-5pm daily, $10 per vehicle, $7 per motorcycle, $5 per person on foot). The panoramic view alone makes it worthwhile, gazing across the bay at the San Diego city skyline, Coronado, and the famous bridge connecting the two, plus the rocky Coronado Islands on the southwestern horizon of the expansive Pacific. You'll find two lighthouses on the 144-acre park, one being the **Old Point Loma Lighthouse,** put to use in 1855 but decommissioned 36 years later because it was too high up to be seen above San Diego's thick fog. The other is its modern replacement. The older lighthouse is open to visitors from 9am-5pm daily. Via a network of trails, it's a short hike down to sea level, where low tide reveals the unique tidepool ecosystem of fish and crustaceans that have adapted to life under only a few inches of water.

Coronado

The long, blue Coronado Bridge connects downtown San Diego to Coronado, an island-like enclave that beckons beach bums and film aficionados alike to the historic Hotel del Coronado. While the Del dominates the Coronado scenery, the island town also offers an array of other accommodations and restaurants. To get there, drive across the two-mile San Diego-Coronado Bridge, or take the foot ferry ($4.75 one-way) from the Broadway Pier to the Coronado Ferry Landing. The ferry takes only 15 minutes and departs every hour on the hour (9am-9pm Sun.-Thurs., 9am-10pm Fri.-Sat.).

Hotel del Coronado

For more than 125 years, **Hotel del Coronado** (1500 Orange Ave., 800/468-3533, www.hoteldel.com) has illuminated the shores of the Pacific Ocean with its majestic beauty. The "Grand Lady by the Sea" draws thousands each year to admire its pristine white Victorian architecture, crowned with a red roof and soaring towers. Notable guests have included Thomas Edison, Charlie Chaplin, Babe Ruth, Charles Lindburgh, and Marilyn Monroe (during filming of *Some Like It Hot*). *Wizard of Oz* author L. Frank Baum is said to have based the Emerald City on the hotel.

Like many old-world structures, Hotel del Coronado is haunted. In 1892, a young woman named Kate Morgan checked in and never checked out. She was found dead on a staircase leading to the beach, and no one ever claimed her body. Today, many believe Kate still occupies her former guest room.

Though the more lavish rooms cost a pretty penny, the hotel offers more affordable accommodations with no frills. You don't have to be a hotel guest to explore the property or enjoy its exquisite views.

Recreation
Beaches

Between the San Diego River and the hills of Point Loma, laid-back **Ocean Beach** (west of Abbot St. from Voltaire St. to Newport Ave.) is popular among surfers, swimmers, sunbathers, and volleyball players. At its north end, pets can run free along the sand and crashing waves at **Dog Beach** (end of Voltaire St.). At the foot of Newport Avenue, you can fish without a license off **Ocean Beach Pier** (end of Niagara Ave.)—size and catch limits still apply.

South of Ocean Beach, **Sunset Cliffs Natural Park** (700-1300 block of Sunset Cliffs Blvd.) sits atop sandstone bluffs overlooking the sparkling Pacific, proving a popular destination for scenic walks, especially at sunset. Surfers and sunbathers have forged steep, treacherous paths to access small beaches below, but locals know not to stand too close to the crumbling cliff edges.

A two-mile concrete boardwalk runs along the **Mission Beach** (1710 W. Mission Bay Dr.), populated by beach cruisers, skateboards, and bikini-clad sun seekers. The north end stays quiet relative to the south stretch of beach, which features a large parking lot and the Belmont Park complex of restaurants and carnival rides.

Coronado Beach (along Ocean Blvd.) is a gorgeous 1.5-mile stretch of sand set against the backdrop of the legendary Hotel del Coronado. The family-friendly beach is free to visit and has street parking.

Water Sports

Surfers can take a crack at some waves at **Mission Beach** (1710 W. Mission Bay Dr.) or the longboard-friendly **Tourmaline Surf Park** (Tourmaline St., west of La Jolla Blvd.). For daily surf conditions, call the recorded hotline of **San Diego Lifeguard Services** (619/221-8824, www.sandiego.gov/lifeguards)—anything over four feet will be too large for beginners.

You'll find 17 square miles of watery playground at **Mission Bay Park** (2688 E. Mission Bay Dr.). Protected from waves, this is where you'll find opportunities to play on the likes of Jet Skis, catamarans, kayaks, and stand-up paddleboards. Gear for these activities may be rented at **Mission Bay Sportcenter** (1010 Santa Clara Pl., 858/488-1004, www.missionbaysportcenter.com, Mon.-Fri. 10am-6pm, Sat.-Sun. 9am-7pm summer, 10am-5pm daily winter) or **Adventure Water Sports** (1710 W. Mission Bay Dr., 619/226-8611, www.adventurewatersports.com, 8am-5pm daily), or you may take classes at **Mission Bay Aquatic Center** 1001 Santa Clara Pl., 858/488-1000, www.mbaquaticcenter.com, 8am-6pm daily summer, 8am-5pm daily winter).

Bicycling

Open to bicycles as well as pedestrians, the **Bayside Walk** circumnavigates 27 miles of Mission Bay shoreline, where you'll pass quiet beaches and thrill-seeking boaters. If you tire of the bay, you can take your bike to the Mission Beach boardwalk, only two blocks west from the western shores of the bay. You'll find bikes for hire at **Ray's Rentals** (3221 Mission Blvd., 866/488-7297, www.rays-rentals.com, 9am-7pm daily).

A 25-mile ride around San Diego Bay, the **Bayshore Bikeway** begins at the Embarcadero downtown and loops around the bay, running along separate bike lanes. It passes numerous attractions, parks, and beaches, including Coronado, where riders have the option of turning around and following the trail back or taking the Coronado ferry back into downtown. At the Coronado Ferry Landing, **Bikes & Beyond** (1201 1st St., 619/435-7180, www.bikes-and-beyond.com, bikes $8/hour) rents bikes that can get you on your way.

Spectator Sports

From April to September, the **San Diego Padres** play major league baseball at Petco Park (100 Park Blvd., 619/795-5555, www.sandiego.padres.mlb.com, $18-250 pass), in the heart of downtown.

Food

Seafood and tacos rule in San Diego, so it stands to reason fish tacos are San Diego's signature street food. I recommend following any local to the nearest taco shop and ordering either carne asada fries—french fries topped with grilled meat, cheese, and guacamole—or a California burrito, which is effectively the same thing wrapped inside a flour tortilla. For the rest of your meals, consider these picks.

Downtown

Little Italy dominates upscale tastes. At **Herb & Wood** (2210 Kettner Blvd., 619/955-8495, www.herbandwood.com, 5:30pm-10pm Sun.-Thurs., 5:30pm-11pm Fri.-Sat., $28-38), Brian Malarkey uses a wood-fired kitchen to get the best out of the world's top ingredients. Right next door, Top Chef Richard Blais gets creative with technique at **Juniper & Ivy** (2228 Kettner Blvd., 619/269-9036, www.juniperandivy.com, 5pm-10pm Sun.-Thurs., 5pm-11pm Fri.-Sat., $18-30).

Around the corner, the city's best-looking seafood restaurant is also one of its best tasting: ★ **Ironside Fish & Oyster** (1654 India St., 619/269-3033, www.ironsidefishandoyster.com, 11:30am-midnight Sun.-Thurs., 11:30am-2am Fri.-Sat., $22-31). Don't let the wall of piranha skulls distract you from the raw bar or whole roasted fish.

San Diego's coffee scene has quietly become one of the nation's best, led by the award-winning beans of direct trade roaster **Bird Rock Coffee** (2295 Kettner Blvd., 619/272-0203, www.birdrockcoffee.com, 6am-6pm Sun.-Thurs., 6am-7pm Fri., 7am-7pm Sat., 7am-6pm Sun., $4-6). Nearby, on the Embarcadero, outdoor casual restaurant **Carnitas' Snack Shack** (1004 N. Harbor Dr., 619/696-7675, www.carnitassnackshack.com, 11am-10pm Mon.-Thurs., 11am-midnight Fri., 9am-midnight Sat., 9am-10pm Sun., $9-15) offers the city's best meaty sandwiches.

Mexican food definitely makes San Diego tick. For the locals' favorite authentic breakfast and lunch, head to Barrio Logan's ★ **Las Cuatro Milpas** (1857 Logan Ave., 619/234-4460, 8:30am-3pm Mon.-Fri., 6:30am-3pm Sat., $3-6). Don't mind the line to get in—it moves fast, and it's totally worth the short wait for the best flour tortillas in the world.

Fish tacos are viewed as a local delicacy, and great examples may be found at **Oscar's Mexican Seafood** (927 J St., 619/564-6007, www.oscarsmexicanseafood.com, 8am-9pm Sun.-Thurs., 8am-10pm Fri.-Sat., $4-8). Meanwhile, the taco has been elevated to gourmet—yet still affordable—status at Barrio Logan's **¡Salud!** (2196 Logan Ave., 619/255-3856, www.saludsd.com, 10am-9pm Tues.-Thurs., 10am-11pm Fri.-Sat., 9am-5pm Sun., $2.50-6).

Balboa Park

Set within the sculpture garden beside the San Diego Museum of Art you'll find **Panama 66** (1450 El Prado, 619/696-1966, www.sdmart.org/panama_66, 11am-5pm Mon.-Tues., 11am-11pm Wed., 11am-10pm Thurs.-Sun., $10-14). Hot and cold sandwiches, along with adult beverages, go well with picnic blankets among the sculptures.

In nearby Banker's Hill, you'll find local sea urchin and other fish at **Hane Sushi** (2760 5th Ave. #5, 619/260-1411, 11:30am-2pm Tues.-Fri., 5:30pm-10pm Tues.-Sun., $18-26). Word is, chef Ota, the owner, gets first pick of local fish.

Old Town and Mission Hills

Within Old Town San Diego State Historic Park, you'll find a half dozen touristy Mexican restaurants featuring colorful costumes and mariachis, but for

Craft Beer in San Diego

Craft beer has become a major tourist draw in San Diego, and most bars will have a terrific tap list. But the newest releases may be tasted at the breweries themselves. San Diego's must-visit craft destinations include reputation-establishing originals **AleSmith** (9990 AleSmith Ct., 858/549-9888, www.alesmith.com, 11am-10pm Mon.-Thurs., 11am-11pm Fri.-Sat., 11am-9pm Sun.), about 20 minutes out of downtown in Miramar, and the more central **Stone Brewing** (2816 Historic Decatur Rd. #116, 619/269-2100, www.stonebrewing.com, 11:30am-9pm Mon.-Thurs., 11:30am-10pm Fri., 11am-10pm Sat., 11am-9pm Sun.), which has a large restaurant and beer garden conveniently near the airport.

You may visit the city's first craft brewpub downtown. Established in 1989, **Karl Strauss** (1157 Columbia St., 619/234-2739, www.karlstrauss.com, 11am-10pm Mon.-Thurs., 11am-11pm Fri.-Sat., 11:30am-10pm Sun.) has since grown to include a dozen brewpub locations throughout Southern California.

The tops of the new breed are fresh IPA purists **Societe Brewing** (8262 Clairemont Mesa Blvd., 858/598-5409, www.societebrewing.com, noon-9pm Mon.-Wed., noon-10pm Thurs.-Sat., noon-8pm Sun.) and the quirky, endlessly creative **Modern Times** (3725 Greenwood St., 619/546-9694, www.moderntimesbeer.com, noon-10pm Sun.-Thurs., noon-midnight Fri.-Sat.).

But it's the well over a hundred ever-evolving small breweries that keep San Diego's reputation going. To get a proper sampling, go explore the craft-beer-rich urban neighborhood **North Park**, home to more than a dozen high-quality microbreweries.

---

the real OG spot, go outside the park to **El Indio** (3695 India St., 619/299-0385, www.elindiosandiego.com, 8am-9pm daily, $6-8). The family restaurant goes back to 1940 and claims to be the birthplace of the rolled taquito.

Point Loma-Ocean Beach

Dine on fresh catch dockside at **Point Loma Seafoods** (2805 Emerson St., 619/223-1109, www.pointlomaseafoods.com, 9am-7pm Mon.-Sat., 10am-7pm Sun., $10-14). The local mainstay offers no-frills sourdough sandwiches, seafood cocktails, grilled fish, and simple sushi. Not far away, former military base Liberty Station has been turned into a restaurant row of sorts, including diverse food stands at **Liberty Public Market** (2820 Historic Decatur Rd., 619/487-9346, www.libertypublicmarket.com, 11am-8pm daily, $7-25).

Nightlife
Bars and Clubs
For a quick sampling of the region's celebrated craft beers, visit taprooms such as Hillcrest's **Brew Project** (3683 5th Ave., 619/795-7890, www.thebrewproject.com), which curates an all-San Diego beer list; Little Italy's **Bottlecraft** (2252 India St., 619/487-9493, www.bottlecraft-beer.com), which doubles as a bottle shop; or South Park's **Hamilton's Tavern** (1521 30th St., 619/238-5460, www.hamiltonstavern.com), a divey beer mecca of sorts for craft enthusiasts, thanks to a steady rotation of world-class beers.

Ocean Beach offers a uniquely crusty brand of beach nightlife, with bars along Newport Avenue coming alive before the sun sets. **Wonderland Ocean Pub** (5083 Santa Monica Ave., 619/255-3358) offers the best view of the neighborhood's eponymous beach and pier, while the rooftop of **Sunshine Company Saloon** (5028 Newport Ave., 619/222-0722) manifests the surf- and yoga-friendly neighborhood's perennial happy hour vibe.

Downtown, rooftop bars offer escapist airiness for the urban set. Literally topping the list is **Altitude Sky Lounge** (660

K St., 619/446-6086, www.sandiegogaslamphotel.com, 5pm-1:30am daily). It sits 22 stories up, looking across the bay and into the Petco Park baseball stadium. Or, hang poolside at **Hard Rock San Diego's Float** (207 5th Ave., 619/764-6924, www.hardrockhotelsd.com, 11am-2am daily), a rooftop oasis with day beds, VIP cabanas, DJs, fire pits, and amazing views. Rooftop bars are summer favorites.

Vegas-style clubs bring a DJ-fueled, vibrant nightlife to the Gaslamp Quarter, including the state-of-the-art **Omnia San Diego** (454 6th Ave., 619/544-9500, www.omnianightclub.com) and **Fluxx** (500 4th Ave., 619/232-8100, www.fluxxsd.com), which features go-go dancers and constantly changing decor.

San Diego's gay scene centers around bars and clubs in the Hillcrest neighborhood. The festive **Baja Betty's** (1421 University Ave., 619/269-8510, www.bajabettyssd.com) is best known for late-night nachos, tequila cocktails, and friendly service. Down the street, **Urban Mo's** (308 University Ave., 619/491-0400, www.urbanmos.com) works hard to live up to its claim to be "The Best Gay Bar in the World."

Live Music

An outdoor music venue built adjacent to a hotel and a marina, **Humphreys Concerts by the Bay** (2241 Shelter Island Dr., 619/224-3577, www.humphreysconcerts.com) features popular music and comedy acts from April to September. The intimate outdoor stage is set up to entertain ticketed customers and guests of the hotel, but with a clear view from the marina, boats often gather stage right to catch a free show.

The hip **Casbah** (2501 Kettner Blvd., 619/232-4355, www.casbahmusic.com) is famous for showcasing rising stars, having hosted the likes of Nirvana and Smashing Pumpkins in an intimate dive bar space.

Popular music artists draw crowds nearly nightly to **The Observatory** (2891 University Ave., 619/239-8836, www.observatorysd.com), a former theater in the neighborhood of North Park turned concert venue.

Arts and Entertainment

San Diego's world-class theater culture includes productions at the **Civic Theatre** (1100 3rd Ave., 619/570-1100, www.sandiegotheatres.org), including touring Broadway musicals and productions by the California Ballet Company. The historic **Balboa Theatre** (868 4th Ave., 619/570-1100, www.sandiegotheatres.org) is a multi-performance venue featuring live music, modern dance, plays, and comedy acts.

The San Diego Symphony Orchestra takes the stage at the dazzling 2,200-seat **Copley Symphony Hall** (750 B St., 619/235-0804, www.sandiegosymphony.org). First opened in the 1920s, it's built in the French Renaissance style, with superb acoustics.

The Old Globe (1363 Old Globe Way, 619/234-5623, www.oldglobe.org) is the site of the popular Shakespeare Festival, as well as classics and Broadway productions.

Shopping
Downtown

Fronted by a newly remodeled public square, the mall at **Westfield Horton Plaza** (324 Horton Plaza, 619/238-1596, www.westfield.com/hortonplaza, 10am-8pm Mon.-Sat., 10am-6pm Sun., parking $8/hour after validation) offers top department stores, retail chains, and a movie theater.

Old Town and Mission Hills

Colorful gift and souvenir shops abound at Old Town's **Bazaar del Mundo Shops** (4133 Taylor St., 619/296-3161, www.bazaardelmundo.com, 10am-9pm Tues.-Sat., 10am-5:30pm Sun.-Mon.), a world market filled with international crafts and gifts. Shops include **The Galley Shop**, with authentic Native American jewelry,

Ariana (619/296-4989) for women's fashion, and **The Kitchen Shop** with hand-crafted Guatemalan pottery and carved kitchenware.

Balboa Park

The **San Diego History Center Gift Store** (1649 El Prado, 619/232-6203, 10am-5pm daily) features vintage reproductions of jewelry, pottery, and lamps, as well as art by local artists.

Mexican folk art inspires many of the crafts, jewelry, and decorative wares at **Casa Artelexia** (3803 Ray St., 619/501-6381, www.artelexia.com, 11am-6pm daily), including the skull-heavy styling of Día de los Muertos (Day of the Dead).

Point Loma-Ocean Beach

You'll find surf gear and surfwear at **South Coast Surf Shop** (5023 Newport Ave., 619/223-7017, www.southcoast. com, 10am-6:30pm Mon.-Sat., 10am-6pm Sun.).

With swimwear, towels, and more, **Wings Beachwear** (4948 Newport Ave., 619/224-2165, www.wingsbeachwear. com, 9am-7pm Mon.-Thurs., 9am-8pm Fri.-Sun.) has everything you need for the beach.

Events

Every July, **Comic Con** (111 W. Harbor Dr., www.comic-con.org) is San Diego's biggest event, drawing 125,000 sci-fi fans, cosplayers, video-game buffs, and celebrities. It sells out far in advance, as do most of the hotels anywhere near downtown (at triple their normal rates).

Also in July, Hillcrest comes alive with the three-day San Diego **Pride Festival** (619/297-7683, www.sdpride.org), which features a parade, a 5K run, and an enormous block party. It attracts nearly 300,000 people.

The second week of November, craft beer takes center stage for **San Diego Beer Week** (locations vary, www.sdbw.org). For 10 days, breweries, bars, and restaurants all over town offer special tap lists

and rare beer specials, making it a great time for beer tourists to sample the best of local brewing.

Accommodations

San Diego has acres of hotels, with a dense pack of standard chain hotels on the self-explanatory Hotel Circle in Mission Valley. The following have some beneficial combination of elegance, location, or character. Prices are at their lowest between September and June.

Under $150

The Pearl Hotel (1410 Rosecrans St., 619/226-6100, www.thepearlsd.com, $139 and up) is a retro-style abode with comfortable rooms. It offers film screenings by its pool in the summer.

Vintage Queen Anne bed-and-breakfast **Keating House** (2331 2nd Ave., 619/239-8585, www.keatinghouse.com, $109 and up) is within walking distance of all of the attractions in Balboa Park.

Budget accommodations begin with the **HI-San Diego** (521 Market St., 619/525-1531, www.sandiegohostels.org, $40 dorms, $130 private), in the middle of the Gaslamp Quarter. You can get just about anywhere from this almost-elegant youth hostel.

$150-250

Clean and stylish, **La Pensione Hotel** (606 W. Date St., 800/232-4683, www. lapensionehotel.com, $165 and up) is a four-story hotel in Little Italy offering a frescoed courtyard and good old-fashioned quiet.

Eco-chic **Hotel Indigo** (509 9th Ave., 619/727-4000, www.hotelinsd.com, $181 and up) is the first LEED-certified hotel in the city, with ecofriendly features, spacious rooms, floor-to-ceiling windows, and spa baths.

President Benjamin Harrison, King Kalakaua of Hawaii, and even Babe Ruth stayed in downtown's ★ **Horton Grand Hotel** (311 Island Ave., 619/544-1886, www.hortongrand.com, $179 and up), but its most famed guest was lawman Wyatt Earp, who took up residence for seven years! Its Victorian-era architecture and furnishings have been updated with all the modern comforts and conveniences to create a timeless experience.

Better than its rates suggest, **The Westgate** (1055 2nd Ave., 619/238-1818, www.westgatehotel.com, $179 and up) offers good rooms, a convenient location, plus a rooftop pool and track.

With spa service and a rooftop pool lounge, **Hotel Solamar** (435 6th Ave., 877/230-0300, www.hotelsolamar.com, $209 and up) touts itself as downtown's hip luxury hotel. Its location near the Gaslamp Quarter provides easy access to nightlife.

Over $250

Even in swanky Southern California, ★ **Hotel del Coronado** (1500 Orange Ave., 619/435-6611 or 800/468-3533, www.hoteldel.com, $250 and up) wins the prize for grandiosity. The white-painted, red-roofed mammoth sprawls for acres from the road to the sand. Inside, the Del

is at once a historical museum, shopping mall, food court—and hotel. It offers almost 700 rooms, plus another 70-plus individual cottages. Room sizes and decor vary, from smaller Victorian-decorated guest rooms to expansive modern suites.

The romantic **1906 Lodge at Coronado Beach** (1060 Adella Ave., 619/437-1900 and 866/435-1906, www.1906lodge.com, $250 and up) lavishes couples in luxury in quaint beachside suites featuring whirlpool tubs, cozy fireplaces, and patios.

Information and Services

The **San Diego Convention and Visitors Bureau** (SDCVB, www.sandiego.org) operates the downtown **San Diego Visitor Information Center** (996-B N. Harbor Dr., 619/236-1242, 9am-4pm daily Oct.-May, 9am-5pm daily June-Sept.). You can get help with everything from flight information to restaurant coupons to hotel reservations. To get a feel for the town before you arrive, check out the SDCVB website. Friendly folks can answer emails and phone calls about most anything pertaining to San Diego County.

Getting There

Air

The following West Coast airports offer the best access to major starting and ending points along the Pacific Coast Highway.

Seattle-Tacoma International Airport (SEA) (17801 International Blvd., 800/544-1965 or 206/787-5388, www.portseattle.org/seatac) is Washington state's main airport, and a major Northwest hub, served by a large number of domestic and international airlines.

Portland International Airport (PDX) (7000 NE Airport Way, 877/739-4636, www.pdx.com) is Oregon's largest airport, served by most major domestic airlines and several international providers.

San Francisco International Airport (SFO) (800/435-9736 or 650/821-8211, www.flysfo.com) is California's major northern hub, the largest airport in the Bay Area, and the second busiest in California.

Los Angeles International Airport (LAX) (1 World Way, 310/646-5252, www.lawa.org/lax) is Southern California's biggest and one of the world's busiest airports.

Bob Hope Airport (BUR) (2627 N. Hollywood Way, Burbank, 818/840-8840, www.hollywoodburbankairport.com), 35 miles from LAX, is much closer to Hollywood.

John Wayne Airport (SNA) (18601 Airport Way, Santa Ana, 949/252-5200, www.ocair.com), about 15 miles from Disneyland in Southern California's Orange County, connects to all the major West Coast cities.

San Diego International Airport (SAN) (3225 N. Harbor Dr., 619/400-2404, www.san.org) is a regional, single-runway commercial airport with domestic flights and limited international providers.

A valid photo ID (driver's license or passport) and boarding pass are required to pass through airport security checkpoints. Depending on the time of year and time of day, security wait times can take 30 minutes or more, and checked bags must be processed at least 45 minutes prior to scheduled departure time to ensure timely arrival at your destination. Consult your airline to monitor flight delays, cancellations, and other changes.

All airports provide assistance to the elderly and individuals with disabilities. Food, restrooms, rental car companies, and taxi and shuttle services are on-site.

Train

Amtrak (800/872-7245, www.amtrak. com) offers service throughout the West Coast on several lines. The **Coast Starlight** runs along the West Coast, connecting Seattle, Portland, and Los Angeles. The **Cascade** line travels from Vancouver, British Columbia, to Seattle and on to Portland. The **Pacific Surfliner** provides service from San Luis Obispo to Santa Barbara, Los Angeles, and San Diego.

Trains arrive and depart from Seattle's **King Street Station** (303 S. Jackson St.); Portland's **Union Station** (800 NW 6th Ave.); **San Luis Obispo** (1011 Railroad Ave.); **Santa Barbara** (209 State St.); Los Angeles's **Union Station** (800 N. Alameda St.); and San Diego's **Santa Fe Depot** (1050 Kettner Blvd.). No direct Amtrak service goes to San Francisco, but buses connect the city to other Northern California stations from the **Transbay Transit Center** (200 Folsom St.).

Bus

Greyhound Lines (800/231-2222, www. greyhound.com) serves major cities in Washington, Oregon, and California, with nationwide connections. Buses travel main interstates in both north and south directions (US-101, I-5), stopping in many small towns, including points along the coast. Buses do not stop in state or national parks or at tourist attractions.

BoltBus (877/265-8287, www.boltbus. com) is a fast and cheap way ($17-27) to travel I-5 (northbound and southbound) from Seattle to Portland, or San Francisco to Los Angeles. Both Greyhound and Bolt buses feature comfortable seating with extra legroom, Wi-Fi, and plug-in outlets. Bolt buses allow travelers to reserve their seats; however, Greyhound travelers should arrive early, as it is first-come, first-served. The best seats are from mid-center to the front, away from the bathroom. Buses can get cold, so bring something warm.

Urban bus stations are often located in areas where it may not be safe to walk to or from the station. Small towns don't always have dedicated bus stations, so contact the provider to locate curbside bus stop location.

Tickets may be purchased online with a credit card or at a station ticket window when available, using credit, debit, travelers checks, or cash. Be sure to bring photo ID. Smartphone users may download Greyhound's mobile app to manage trips, search schedules, and find terminal locations.

Car Rental & Share

Major international rental car companies are easily found at major airports, and most allow you to pick up a car in one location (Seattle, for example) and drop it off in another (like San Diego). Rentals require a valid credit card and driver's license for all registered drivers, with a minimum age requirement of 21. Expect to pay around $30 per day and up, plus taxes, fees, and insurance (optional), plus additional fees for drivers under the age of 25. If you are in the military or a member of AAA, AARP, or Costco, discounts may apply. For higher fees, most rental companies offer optional upgrades including alternative fuel and all-wheel-drive vehicles.

Rental car companies include:

- **Avis** (800/331-1212, www.avis.com)

- **Budget** (800/218-7992, www.budget.com)

- **Dollar** (800/800-3665, www.dollar.com)

- **Enterprise** (800/261-7331, www.enterprise.com)

- **Hertz** (800/654-3131, www.hertz.com)

- **National** (877/222-9058, www.nationalcar.com)

- **Thrifty** (800/847-4389, www.thrifty.com)

In addition to traditional car rental agencies, Internet-based car-sharing services offer short-term on-demand rentals for driving within some cities. **Zipcar** (866/494-7227, www.zipcar.com) rents by the hour, with cars picked up and dropped off at designated parking lot locations throughout Seattle, Portland, and most of the coastal cities in California. Smartphone-based **Car2Go** (877/488-4224, www.car2go.com), available in Seattle and Portland, charges by the trip, with smart cars accessible via smartphone that may be picked up and left behind at any legal parking spot. Both services require advance online member registration—including proof of driver's license—that should be completed a week or two prior to use.

Smartphone car-sharing services provide taxi alternatives, with on-demand door-to-door rides between specific destinations within a city. **Uber** (www.uber.com) is available in most large and mid-size West Coast cities, as well as a few smaller coastal towns, while **Lyft** (www.lyft.com) is primarily available in large cities. Both require credit card payment and downloading an app to your phone.

Driving Directions

The Pacific Coast Highway stretches 1,700 miles north to south, traveling on or near the coastline of Washington, Oregon, and California. For most of the route, the PCH follows U.S. Highway 101. However, at times, US-101 veers inland, and the coastal route splits off to U.S. Highway 1, including a long segment through Northern and Central California (from Leggett to San Luis Obispo) and a shorter stretch in Southern California (Oxnard to Dana Point). From Dana Point south into San Diego, I-5 joins the coast. To drive the entire length on US-101, plan on 30-32 hours of drive time. To include the more scenic Highway 1 portions, plan on 40 hours.

I-5 also provides a quicker, albeit significantly less scenic, inland route, passing through the major cities of Seattle, Portland, Los Angeles, and San Diego, and within 70 miles of San Francisco. I-5 travels roughly 1,300 miles overall, with 20 hours drive time direct from Seattle to San Diego. If you're following a shortened itinerary, accessing I-5 from various points along the coast may shave several hours of total drive time.

In Washington, two westbound routes connect Seattle to destinations on the northern Washington coast, a.k.a. the Olympic Peninsula. The quickest is the **Seattle-Bainbridge Island Ferry** (801 Alaskan Way, 888/808-7977 or 206/464-6400, www.wsdot.wa.gov/ferries, $18 per car one-way, $8 per passenger and walk-on, $4 children 6-18): From Bainbridge Island, follow WA-305 North to WA-3 North to WA-104 West to connect to US-101. A land route adds 75 minutes: Take I-5 south to connect with US-101 north at Olympia, where it traces a counter-clockwise loop around the entire length of the peninsula. To access the southern Washington coast from I-5, take WA-8 West at Olympia to meet the western loop of US-101 at Aberdeen (50 miles, 1 hour).

Oregon's north coast can be accessed from I-5 via US-30 West to US-101 at

Astoria, which can be accessed north of Portland at Longview (50 miles, 1 hour) or from Portland (97 miles, 2 hours). From Portland, US-26 West connects to US-101 at Cannon Beach (80 miles, 1.5 hours). Farther south, the quickest coastal access points from I-5 will be US-20 West at Albany, which goes to Newport (60 miles, 1.5 hours); OR-126 from Eugene to Florence (60 miles, 1.5 hours); and US-199, which connects Grant's Pass to US-101 at Crescent City, the northernmost coastal city in California (82 miles, 1.75 hours).

In Northern California, I-5 veers farther from the coast, and the best access to US-101 is Redding to Arcata via US-299 West (142 miles, 3 hours). At Sacramento, you can take US-80 West to San Francisco (90 miles, 2 hours).

In Central California, CA-152 West connects I-5 from Los Banos to US-101 at Gilroy (49 miles, 1 hour) or to CA-1 in Santa Cruz (85 miles, 2 hours); from Kettleman City CA-41 goes to CA-1 at Morro Bay (80 miles, 1.75 hours) or to US-101 at Paso Robles (56 miles, 1 hour).

In Southern California, I-5 and US-101 converge at Los Angeles, while CA-1 moves slowly along the coastal cities of Los Angeles and Orange Counties. CA-1 also converges with I-5 at Dana Point, then reappears in northern San Diego County, where I-5 is never more than 10 minutes from the coast.

Road Rules

Drivers and all passengers are required by law to wear a seat belt. Infant and child safety seats are required for children under 4 feet 9 inches (145 centimeters) and/or under the age of 8. It is illegal to operate a vehicle and a handheld device at the same time. All motorcyclists must wear a helmet. Don't litter; there are severe penalties ($1,000 or more) for throwing garbage of any kind from a vehicle. No drinking and driving; driving while intoxicated is extremely dangerous and highly illegal. Always abide by posted speed limits and other road signs.

Highway Safety

The highway has many sharp curves, steep ledges, and high cliffs that do not have guardrails. Drive as slowly as road conditions demand, even if that's slower than the posted speed limit; some routes have tree trunks or branches very close to the highway. The best advice is to take your time and enjoy the coastal scenery you came here for!

This road is quite isolated, especially in areas on Washington state's Olympic Peninsula, in Northern California, and at Big Sur, where there are no connecting routes to the interior for more than 90 miles. Make sure you have a full tank of gas, plenty of water, warm clothing, and snacks before traveling these sections of the coastal route.

Many sections of the Pacific Coast Highway are not lit by streetlights, making visibility difficult at night, especially when encountering the blinding headlights of oncoming cars. If you are not comfortable driving at night, plan your itinerary accordingly.

In case of an emergency, always carry flares, a spare tire, and a jack and wrench. Though on some parts of the road you may not receive cell phone service, carry a phone with you. Only pull over when absolutely necessary! Otherwise, wait until you reach a pullout or other safe area. When pulling over, get as far onto the shoulder as you can.

Road and Weather Conditions

With the exception of Southern California, weather conditions change rapidly along the Pacific Coast. Be prepared for extremes, from blustery rains to windstorms and hot sunny days. Fog is the most likely hazardous condition you will encounter. When warm inland air mixes with cool coastal temperatures, fog can get thick and linger. Use the pullouts if needed; otherwise, use low beams and drive *very* slowly.

In some areas, snow may also be a factor in winter. Be prepared with tire chains, and know how to install them. If bad weather is in the forecast, be aware some highways may be closed indefinitely, making some routes impassable.

Of particular concern within California are mudslides and rockslides. These typically follow heavy rains or snows, and may close highways for extended stretches. A series of slides in the winter of 2017 closed both the northern and southern CA-1 routes into Central California's Big Sur, making the area completely inaccessible to vehicles for most of the year. The same spring, another series of slides closed US-101 south of Humboldt Redwood State Park for over a week. In both cases, the closures resulted in three- to five-hour detours.

Check road condition updates when planning your route and again before hitting the road each day, and be prepared to take alternative routes in the event of a road closure. To check for road closures and conditions by state, consult the **Washington State Department of Transportation** (800/695-7623, www.wsdot.com/traffic/trafficalerts); **Oregon Department of Transportation** (800/977-6368, www.tripcheck.com); and **California Department of Transportation** (www.quickmap.dot.ca.gov). Within each state you may also access updated reports by dialing 511.

Wildlife on the Road
Domestic grazing animals and wildlife are both common sights on the Pacific Coast Highway, and it is highly likely you will cross paths with deer, elk, coyotes, raccoons, and other animals. Warning signs are usually posted in areas with higher animal crossing activity. If you come upon wildlife standing in the road,

come to a stop and honk your horn, but do not get out of the vehicle or attempt to pass. Wait until the road is clear, then be on your way.

Road Etiquette
The majority of the Pacific Coast Highway is two lane highway, meaning there are few opportunities for vehicles to pass slower traffic. The law requires slower vehicles to use turnouts or safely pull over when five or more cars line up behind them. If other drivers make it clear they want to pass, let them, and hope slower drivers will do the same for you. Do not jeopardize your safety by trying to navigate a winding, unfamiliar highway at an uncomfortable speed. It is imperative that you always leave at least three feet between your car and another vehicle, especially motorcyclists and bicyclists!

Parking
Most attractions, museums, parks, and beaches offer on-site parking, though many require a fee. When booking a hotel, ask if there is a secured parking garage or an open lot, and if there is a daily fee (parking fees can be up to $40 per day in cities). Some hotels offer free parking.

The Pacific Coast Highway serves as the major route of access to the many beaches and beachside towns. On-street parking within these communities can be hard to find during peak season when much of the road is congested with traffic. Parking garages, lots, and metered street parking are often available for a fee at popular destinations.

Fuel
Gasoline is difficult to come by on the more rural segments of the road, especially the farther north you are. Even in California, there will be long stretches where you may not see a gas station for miles. Know your mpg (miles per gallon) and fuel up whenever you have the

opportunity. Prices on the coast may be considerably higher. The GasBuddy smartphone app or website (www.gasbuddy.com) will guide you to fueling stations and sometimes highlight the cheapest rates. Note that in the state of Oregon, by law there is no self-service gas. Remain in your car and wait for an attendant to fill your tank.

Motorcycles

Motorcyclists are common along the coast, especially during the summer, so all drivers should keep a watch out for riders. For motorcycle riders, helmets are required by law, and it's recommended to keep at least three car lengths between you and other vehicles. Never use the shoulder (or fog line) to pass another vehicle! When necessary use pullouts, and watch for wildlife. Windstorms and rains can create difficult road conditions, such as fallen tree branches, debris, and standing water.

Bicycles

Experienced cyclists will find the Pacific Coast Highway a great way to travel. The shoulder (known as the fog line) can be hazardous due to gravel and road debris. Bicyclists are not legally required to stay on the shoulder, but many do as a courtesy to motor vehicles.

Take advantage of pullouts along the highway to allow vehicles to pass. Be cautious when riding cliffside in Big Sur. This part of the highway is extremely windy and rises high above the Pacific. To avoid pedaling against the wind, travel from north to south. Two other precautions: Watch for parked cars on the side of the road where the highway passes through coastal towns and watch out for redwood trees. As you wind your way through the redwood forest, you'll find that some trees sit very close to the edge of the road. Stay alert to avoid accidents. The Adventure Cycling Association offers resources at www.adventurecycling.org.

Visas and Officialdom

Passports and Visas

Visitors from other countries must have a **valid passport** and a **visa.** Visitors with current passports from one of the following countries qualify for the **visa waivers:** Andorra, Australia, Austria, Belgium, Brunei, Chile, Czech Republic, Denmark, Estonia, Finland, France, Germany, Greece, Hungary, Iceland, Ireland, Italy, Japan, Latvia, Liechtenstein, Lithuania, Luxembourg, Malta, Monaco, the Netherlands, New Zealand, Norway, Portugal, San Marino, Singapore, Slovakia, Slovenia, South Korea, Spain, Sweden, Switzerland, Taiwan, and the United Kingdom. They must apply online with the Electronic System for Travel Authorization at www.cbp.gov and hold a **return plane ticket** to their home countries within 90 days from their time of entry. Holders of **Canadian passports** don't need visas or waivers. In most countries, the local U.S. embassy can provide a **tourist visa.** Plan for at least two weeks for visa processing, longer during the busy summer season (June-Aug.). More information is available online: www.travel.state.gov.

Customs

Foreigners and U.S. citizens age 21 or older may import (free of duty) the following: one liter of alcohol (33.8 fluid ounces); 200 cigarettes (one carton); 100 cigars; and $800 worth of gifts.

International travelers must declare amounts that exceed $10,000 in cash (U.S. or foreign), travelers checks, or money orders. Meat products, fruits, and vegetables are prohibited due to health and safety regulations.

Drivers entering California stop at **Agricultural Inspection Stations.** They don't need to present a passport, visa, or even a driver's license but should be prepared to present fruits and vegetables, even those purchased within neighboring states just over the border. If you've got produce, it could be infected by a known problem pest or disease; expect it to be confiscated on the spot.

International Driving Permits

International visitors need to secure an **International Driving Permit** from their home countries before coming to the United States. They should also bring the government-issued driver's license from their home countries. They are also expected to be familiar with the driving regulations of the states they will visit. More information is available online: www.usa.gov/visitors-driving.

Travel Tips

Conduct and Customs

The legal **drinking age** in the United States is 21. Expect to have your ID checked not only in bars and clubs, but also before you purchase alcohol in restaurants, wineries, and markets. Recreational marijuana is legal to possess in amounts up to one ounce in California, Oregon, and Washington but may only be purchased by adults 21 and over, at licensed, dedicated retailers. Smoking marijuana in public is prohibited by law and not allowed at most hotels.

Smoking cigarettes is banned in many places. Don't expect to find a smoking section in restaurants or an ashtray in bars. Some establishments allow smoking on outdoor patios. Many hotels, motels, and inns are also nonsmoking. Smokers should request a smoking room when making reservations. Note that in Oregon and California, it's illegal to sell cigarettes to anyone under 21. In Washington, the age is 18.

Money

The currency is the **U.S. dollar ($)**. Most businesses accept the **major credit cards** Visa, MasterCard, Discover, and American Express—either with magnetic strip or chip technology. ATM and debit cards work at many stores and restaurants, and ATMs are available throughout the region. You can **change currency** at any international airport or bank. Currency exchange may be easier in large cities and more difficult in rural and wilderness areas.

Banking hours tend to be 8am-5pm Monday-Friday, 9am-noon Saturday. Never count on a bank being open on Sunday. There are **24-hour ATMs** not only at banks but at many markets, bars, and hotels. A **convenience fee** of $2-4 per transaction may apply.

Internet Access

While many hotels and B&Bs offer free Wi-Fi, some charge a fee of $6-12 per hour. Free Wi-Fi is becoming more and more available at cafés and public libraries. Do not expect to find Wi-Fi-friendly locations within rural areas, parks, or campgrounds. Likewise, cellular data transmissions may be unavailable at remote locations in all three western states.

Cell Phones

Several spots along the winding Pacific Coast Highway are dead zones. Cell service is simply unreliable even from the best carrier. Check your phone and make your calls on arrival or before leaving a travel hub or large town along the route.

Hotel and Motel Chains

Hotel and motel chains like **Best Western** (800/780-7234, www.bestwestern.com), **Motel 6** (800/557-3435, www.motel6. com), **Days Inn** (800/225-3297, www.days-inn.com), and **Super 8** (800/454-3213, www.super8.com) are easy to find along the coast. Many offer discount rates (depending on season) and reasonable amenities. Expect higher rates during the summer (June-Sept.).

High season is from June to August (although rates rise in spring, too), and you may find better deals as a walk-in guest during the off-season. The best tactic is to shop for deals and use any discount cards and auto-memberships that give you lower rates at participating hotels and motels. Stop at local visitors centers or pick up a complimentary ad magazine (which includes hotel and motel discount coupons) at local restaurants, convenience stores, and businesses.

Midweek rates are lower unless there is a special event taking place. Be sure to ask if the quoted rate includes tax, as this can add 10 percent or more to your final bill. If you find yourself without accommodations, many online travel apps, including **www.hoteltonight.com, www.hotwire. com, and www.priceline.com,** offer last-minute reservations.

Traveling with Children
Children will enjoy aquariums, amusement parks, and, perhaps most of all, the beach. Many beaches and parks are equipped with bathrooms. You'll also find several good family-friendly restaurant and hotel options. Generally hotels allow up to four in a room, so be sure to inquire about a suite if necessary.

The main concerns when traveling the highway with children are that the long drive can make them antsy and the twists and turns can cause nausea, even for moms and dads. Estimated drive times throughout the book may take longer with children, owing to restroom breaks and other stops. Bring plenty of car-fun activities to keep your kids busy, like books and travel games.

Parents should be wary of their children's activities, primarily at scenic lookout points and on trails. Many scenic pullouts do not have guardrails; it can be extremely unsafe to stand close to any cliff's edge, as loose earth can make it easy to slip and fall, and erosion may cause the ground to disappear beneath your feet.

Senior Travelers
If you are over 60 years of age, ask about potential discounts. Nearly all attractions, amusement parks, theaters, and museums offer discount benefits to seniors. Be sure to have some form of valid identification on hand or you'll end up having to pay full price. A driver's license or current passport will do.

Accessibility
Most public areas are equipped to accommodate travelers with disabilities, including hotels, restaurants, museums, public transportation, and several state and national parks where you'll find paved trails. That said, there are still some attractions that will pose challenges, such as certain historic sights and wildlife areas.

Those with permanent disabilities, including visual impairments, should inquire about a free **Access Pass** (888/275-8747, ext. 3, www.store.usgs.gov/access-pass) from the National Parks Service. It is offered as part of the America the Beautiful—National Park and Federal Recreational Lands Pass Series. You can obtain an Access Pass in person at any federal recreation site or by submitting a completed application by mail ($10 processing fee may apply). The pass does not provide benefits for special recreation permits or concessionaire fees.

Environmental Concerns
Each state has environmental concerns that involve water pollution, disruption of fish and wildlife habitat, and emissions. Washington, Oregon, and California have poured resources into conservation and preservation efforts, and have moved forward with renewable energy, recycling, and composting campaigns.

You can do your part as a visitor and protect the natural environment by doing the following: Stay on trails and do not step on plantlife; utilize pet waste receptacles in pet-friendly campgrounds; protect water sources by camping at least 150 feet from lakes and streams; leave rocks and plants as you find them; light fires only where permitted and use only established fire pits; pack it in, pack it out—check your campsite for garbage and properly dispose of it or take it with you.

Health and Safety

If immediate help is needed, always **dial 911;** otherwise, go to the nearest 24-hour hospital emergency room.

Carry your **medical card** and a list of any **medications** you are taking. Keep a **first-aid kit** in your car or luggage, and take it with you when hiking. A good kit should include sterile gauze pads, butterfly bandages, adhesive tape, antibiotic ointment, alcohol wipes, pain relievers for both adults and children, and a multi-purpose pocketknife.

Do not ignore **health or safety warnings!** Some beaches within California have health warning signs posted due to potential bacteria in the water. If you see such a sign, stay out of the water or risk getting sick.

With 1,700 miles of coastline, there may be plenty of other ocean dangers, including strong undercurrents, stingrays, jellyfish, sharks, sharp underwater hazards, and extreme cold. Inexperienced swimmers should only enter the water when and where a lifeguard is on duty, and that goes double for children. Experienced swimmers should take caution as well, as changing tides and rip currents may prove an invisible life-threatening risk at unfamiliar beaches.

Whether you're in a large city, resort area, small town, or even wilderness area, take precautions against **theft.** Don't leave any valuables in the car. If you must, keep them out of sight in the trunk or compartment with a lock if available. Keep wallets, purses, cameras, mobile phones, and other small electronics on your person if possible.

Crime is more prevalent in large cities. Be alert to your surroundings, just as you would in any unfamiliar place. Avoid using ATMs at night or walking alone after dark. Carry your car keys in your hand when walking out to your car. Certain **urban neighborhoods** are best avoided at night. Call a taxi to avoid walking too far to get to your car or waiting for public transportation.

Keep a safe distance from **wildlife.** Stay at least 300 feet away. Bring binoculars if you want an up-close view. If you encounter a bear or cougar, do not run or turn your back! Try to appear larger and bring pepper spray and a walking stick to use in defense. Stay in a group when hiking, as these animals typically target lone prey. Keep children close and where you can see them.

Be cautious at **viewpoints,** especially along coastal cliffs. Losing your footing in loose earth can be fatal, and erosion may cause cliff edges to drop away beneath your feet. Keep children from sitting on or climbing over railings.

Resources

Organizations
Washington
Olympic Peninsula Visitor Bureau (800/942-4042, www.olympicpeninsula.org): A regional organization that offers a synopsis of local destinations, access, fees, things to do, and transportation information.

Seattle B&B Association (206/547-1020, www.lodginginseattle.com): A member-based organization that provides a directory of local bed-and-breakfast venues.

Visit Seattle (866/732-2695, www.visitseattle.org): The official visitors guide to Seattle, with tips for dining, lodging, and activities.

Washington Lodging Association (800/225-7166, www.stayinwashington.com): A complete listing of member hotels, motels, lodges, and B&Bs.

Washington Tourism Alliance (800/544-1800, www.experiencewa.com): Find maps, guides, info, and recommendations on restaurants, lodging, and things to do throughout the entire state.

Washington Tribes (www.washington-tribes.org): Find info and resources relating to the Native American tribes and reservations within Washington state.

Oregon

Oregon Bed & Breakfast Guild (www.obbg.org): The professional association of Oregon's individually operated bed-and-breakfast inns, which provides a B&B directory and trip planner.

Oregon Coast Visitors Association (888/628-2101, www.visittheoregon-coast.com): A noteworthy guide to all the cities, stops, lodging, and activities along the coast.

Travel Oregon (www.traveloregon.com): The state's main tourism entity offers complete resource information for visitors.

Travel Portland (www.travelportland.com): The city's official online guide to local art, food, hotels, and lifestyle.

California

Access Northern California (925/283-0111, www.accessnca.com): This organization helps individuals with disabilities navigate their way through Northern California by providing wheelchair-friendly trails and locations for a better experience.

California Association of Boutique & Breakfast Inns (www.cabbi.com): The state's only association of member B&Bs and boutique lodging, from the redwood coast to San Diego.

Discover Los Angeles (www.discoverlos-angeles.com): The official guide to the Los Angeles area, where you can learn about the city's neighborhoods, culture, attractions, restaurants, events, and nightlife.

San Diego (800/350-6205, www.sandi-ego.org): The city's web-based travel guide, where local area information and special offers on area attractions and activities are provided, including trip planners.

San Francisco Travel (415/391-2000, www.sftravel.com): Features trip ideas, tickets to area attractions, and downloadable visitor guides.

Visit California (www.visitcalifornia.com): This California Tourism Industry-run site offers detailed information on Northern, Central, and Southern California travel offerings.

Visit Santa Barbara (805/966-9222, www.santabarbaraca.com): Find info on Santa Barbara, including history, food and shopping guides, events, and lodging.

Newspapers and Magazines
Washington

Seattle Magazine (www.seattlemag.com): This sophisticated publication keeps readers in the know about the sparkly Emerald City's hip restaurants and hangouts.

Seattle Weekly (www.seattleweekly.com): Filled with local events and reviews of local eateries and nightlife venues, this paper is available at no cost.

The Stranger (www.thestranger.com): A free weekly paper filled with "things to do" in Seattle, including great suggestions on restaurants, bars, and music venues.

Oregon

Oregon Coast Magazine (www.oregon-coastmagazine.com): A colorful and engaging resource with local area history, photos, and highlighted information about area sights, such as lighthouses.

Oregon Coast Today (www.oregoncoast-today.com): Published in Lincoln City, this free weekly features current information on arts, entertainment, and activities.

The Oregonian (www.oregonianlive.com): This is Portland's daily newspaper, which has an entertainment section and events calendar.

Portland Mercury (www.portlandmercury.com): Free alt-weekly magazine is a guide to Portland's hip happenings, including music, food, and culture.

Willamette Week (www.wweek.com): A freely distributed alt-weekly covering local news, dining, culture, and nightlife.

California

Los Angeles Times (www.latimes.com): A longstanding news publication with a fantastic *Arts & Culture* section.

LA Weekly (www.laweekly.com): Los Angeles's key alt-weekly news source and guide to local culture and events.

San Diego CityBeat (www.sdcitybeat.com): A weekly guide to San Diego's eclectic mix of food, music, art, and culture.

San Diego Reader (www.sandiegoreader.com): This free alt-weekly magazine provides insights into local food, theater, and events.

San Diego Union-Tribune (www.utsandiego.com): This is the daily newspaper for the San Diego metro area.

The San Francisco Chronicle (www.sfgate.com): This is the daily newspaper for the City by the Bay.

San Francisco Weekly (www.sfweekly.com): A good resource for news, art, film, and local happenings.

Santa Barbara Independent (www.independent.com): Packed with information on visual arts, galleries, theater, food venues, and hotels.

Travel Guidebooks
Washington

Alden, Peter, and Dennis Paulson. *National Audubon Society Field Guide to the Pacific Northwest.* Knopf Doubleday Publishing Group, 1998. A pocket field guide that covers habitats of more than 1,000 of the most common species found in the Pacific Northwest, with additional coverage on the region's topography and geology.

Burlingame, Jeff. *Moon Olympic Peninsula.* Avalon Travel Publishing, 2015. An extensive journey through the mountain meadows and temperate rainforests of Washington state's magnificent Olympic Peninsula, with recommendations on hiking, birding, camping, and exploration.

Rudnick, Terry, and Craig Schuhmann. *Moon Pacific Northwest Fishing.* Avalon Travel Publishing, 2012. A guide to fishing the plentiful waters of the entire Pacific Northwest.

Oregon

Henderson, Bonnie. *Day Hiking Oregon Coast.* Mountaineers Books, 2015. A user-friendly trail guide with grids, charts, and useful information.

McRae, W. C., and Judy Jewell. *Moon Coastal Oregon.* Avalon Travel Publishing, 2016. Filled with information on dining, accommodations, and recreation along Oregon's coastal regions.

California

Brown, Ann Marie. *Moon Bay Area Biking.* Avalon Travel Publishing, 2012. The perfect complement to a coast trip for avid cyclists, *Moon Bay Area Biking* is filled with rides in and around the Bay Area and alongside the Pacific Coast, outlining a wide variety of scenic roads and trails.

Brown, Ann Marie, and Tom Stienstra. *Moon California Hiking.* Avalon Travel Publishing, 2016. The complete guide to 1,000 of the best hikes in the Golden State.

Linhart Veneman, Elizabeth. *Moon Napa & Sonoma.* Avalon Travel Publishing, 2017. An immersion into Northern California's wine country from the coastal mountains of Santa Cruz to the hot, windy hills of Sonoma.

Stienstra, Tom. *Moon West Coast RV Camping.* Avalon Travel Publishing, 2015. The complete guide to more than 2,300 RV parks and campgrounds in Washington, Oregon, and California.

Thornton, Stuart. *Moon Coastal California.* Avalon Travel Publishing, 2016. A focus on California's diverse coastline, with information on hiking trails, surfing spots, and recommended stops along the way.

History and Culture
Washington

Frye Bass, Sophie, and Florenz Clark. *Pig-Tail Days in Old Seattle.* Binford & Mort Publishing, 1973. A fascinating account of Seattle's early days as told by the granddaughter of Seattle founder Arthur A. Denny, with stories about some of the city's famous streets.

Halliday, Jan, and Gail Chehak. *Native Peoples of the Northwest.* Sasquatch Books, 2002. The only guide that introduces readers to contemporary Northwest Native cultures.

Mapes, Lynda. *Native Peoples of the Northwest.* Mountaineers Books, 2013. An exploration into one of the largest dam removal projects in the world, and the efforts to save the Northwest ecosystem.

McNulty, Tim. *Olympic National Park: A Natural History.* University of Washington Press, 2009. A look at the heart of the Olympic Peninsula's ecosystems, wildlife, and current archaeological discoveries.

Oregon

Blakely, Joe R. *Building Oregon's Coast Highway 1936-1966: Straightening Curves and Uncorking Bottlenecks.* CreateSpace Independent Pub, 2014. An epic journey of how Oregon's spectacular coast highway was built across a steep basalt cliff, through Arch Cape, bridging Thomas Creek gorge and leveling mountains.

Clark, Ella E. *Indian Legends of the Pacific Northwest.* University of California Press, 2003. Native American myths that tell the story of their link to the mountains, lakes, and rivers, and of the creation of the world.

Gulick, Bill. *Roadside History of Oregon.* Mountain Press Publishing Company, 1991. The book follows Lewis and Clark's journey along the Columbia River to pioneer town-builders at the end of the Oregon Trail, from the lighthouses off the storm-ridden coast to the Chinese who helped shape Oregon's early fishing and mining industries.

California

Estrada, William D. *Los Angeles' Olvera Street.* Arcadia Publishing, 2006. A historical look at El Pueblo de La Reina de Los Angeles—where the city was born in 1781—and its evolution.

Henson, Paul, and Donald Usner. *The Natural History of Big Sur.* University of California Press, 2007. An ecological look at the diversity of Big Sur's many species of marine wildlife, as well as the impact of developers. The book provides excellent information for visitors, bringing greater awareness to the importance of preserving the region's natural resources.

Scheffler Innis, Jack. *San Diego Legends: Events, People, and Places That Made History.* Sunbelt Publications, 2004. Everything you'd want to know about San Diego—a fantastic historical account of the rise of the seaside city, including stories about the infamous "nudist invasion" of the 1935 California-Pacific Exposition, the murder of the first mayor, and more.

Outdoor Recreation

National Park Service (www.nps.gov): Provides detailed information for all national parks on the West Coast, which includes fees, hours, trails, fishing regulations, and more.

Recreation.gov (www.recreation.gov): Provides national parks and forests campground information with options to reserve campsites.

U.S. Forest Service—Pacific Northwest Region (503/808-2468, www.fs.usda.gov/r6): Information on Oregon and Washington National Forests with external links and resources.

Surfline (www.surfline.com): A fantastic website that provides current surfing conditions along the entire coast.

Trail Link (www.traillink.com): A national database of hiking and biking trails.

Washington

The Mountaineers (206/521-6000 main line, 206/521-6030 emergency line, www.mountaineers.org): A Seattle-based nonprofit organization that helps people explore, conserve, and learn about the lands and waters of the Pacific Northwest through sponsored excursions, books, and magazines.

Olympic National Park (360/565-3130, www.nps.gov/olym): Targeted information about access, camping, hiking, and more.

Washington Department of Fish & Wildlife (360/902-2200, www.wdfw.wa.gov): A complete online guide to fishing and hunting regulations, including seasonal and permit information.

Washington State Parks & Recreation Commission (360/902-8844, www.parks.wa.gov): Details Washington's diverse parks and provides access to campground information and reservations.

Oregon

Oregon State Parks (www.oregonstateparks.org): Provides camping information within Oregon state parks.

Portland Hikers (www.portlandhikersfieldguide.org): A great website

provided by Trailkeepers of Oregon with a list of winter, spring, and backpacking trails to explore.

California

California Department of Parks & Recreation (www.parks.ca.gov): Provides camping, off-highway-vehicle, and boating information, including fees and regulations.

Redwoods National and State Parks (www.nps.gov/redw): Complete information on visiting the largest trees on Earth, such as park fees, hours, seasons, transportation, trails, and available campgrounds.

Reserve California (www.reservecalifornia.com): Offers online reservations for California state parks and campgrounds.

Sports
Washington

Seattle Mariners (www.mlb.com/mariners): Official Mariners Major League Baseball website, providing schedule and ticket information.

Seattle Reign FC (www.reignfc.com): The official site for Seattle's professional women's Major League Soccer team.

Seattle Seahawks (www.seahawks.com): Schedules and tickets for Seattle's NFL football team are available here.

Seattle Sounders (www.soundersfc.com): Seattle's Major League Soccer team's official website, featuring schedules, ticketing, and more.

Seattle Storm (http://storm.wnba.com): The official site for Seattle's WNBA professional women's basketball team.

Oregon

Portland Timbers & Thorns (www.timbers.com): The site contains seasonal schedules for both of Portland's professional soccer clubs: men's Timbers and women's Thorns.

Portland Trail Blazers (www.nba.com/blazers): Blazer basketball fans can check for game information and ticket availability.

California

Anaheim Ducks (www.nhl.com/ducks): The official site for Anaheim's NHL pro hockey team.

Golden State Warriors (www.nba.com/warriors): These five-time basketball champions represent all of the Bay Area and were scheduled to move from Oakland to San Francisco by the beginning of the 2019 NBA season.

Los Angeles Angels of Anaheim (www.mlb.com/angels): The official site for Anaheim's Major League Baseball team.

Los Angeles Chargers (www.chargers.com): A second Los Angeles NFL team moved from San Diego in 2017 and will move into a new stadium in Los Angeles in 2019.

Los Angeles Clippers (www.nba.com/clippers): The official site for Los Angeles's second NBA team.

Los Angeles Dodgers (www.mlb.com/dodgers): The official website of the six-time World Series Champion Major League Baseball team.

Los Angeles FC (www.lafc.com): The official team site for the Major League Soccer team playing in Los Angeles beginning in 2018.

Los Angeles Galaxy (www.lagalaxy.com): The official team site for U.S. Major League Soccer's five-time champions.

Los Angeles Kings (www.nhl.com/kings): The official team site for the NHL pro hockey team playing in Los Angeles.

Los Angeles Lakers (www.nba.com/lakers): The official team site of the 16-time NBA champions.

Los Angeles Rams (www.therams.com): The longtime NFL franchise returned to Los Angeles in 2015 and is expected to play in a new stadium in 2019.

Los Angeles Sparks (http://sparks.wnba.com): Official site of the professional women's basketball team representing Los Angeles in the WNBA.

San Diego Padres (www.mlb.com/padres): The official team site for San Diego's Major League Baseball team offers schedules and tickets.

San Francisco 49ers (www.49ers.com): The official NFL team site of the five-time Super Bowl champions, offering schedules and tickets.

San Francisco Giants (www.mlb.com/giants): The official team site of San Francisco's three-time champion Major League Baseball team, offering schedules and tickets.

INDEX

INDEX

INDEX

LIST OF MAPS

PHOTO CREDITS

MAP SYMBOLS

═══ Expressway	○ City/Town	✈ Airport	⚲ Golf Course
─── Primary Road	◉ State Capital	✗ Airfield	🅿 Parking Area
─── Secondary Road	⊛ National Capital	▲ Mountain	⛭ Archaeological Site
┄┄ Unpaved Road	★ Point of Interest	✚ Unique Natural Feature	⛪ Church
─── Feature Trail	• Accommodation		⛽ Gas Station
------ Other Trail	▼ Restaurant/Bar	☂ Waterfall	◯ Glacier
············ Ferry	■ Other Location	⚑ Park	◯ Mangrove
═══ Pedestrian Walkway	Λ Campground	🚩 Trailhead	◯ Reef
▥▥ Stairs		⛷ Skiing Area	◯ Swamp

CONVERSION TABLES

°C = (°F - 32) / 1.8
°F = (°C x 1.8) + 32
1 inch = 2.54 centimeters (cm)
1 foot = 0.304 meters (m)
1 yard = 0.914 meters
1 mile = 1.6093 kilometers (km)
1 km = 0.6214 miles
1 fathom = 1.8288 m
1 chain = 20.1168 m
1 furlong = 201.168 m
1 acre = 0.4047 hectares
1 sq km = 100 hectares
1 sq mile = 2.59 square km
1 ounce = 28.35 grams
1 pound = 0.4536 kilograms
1 short ton = 0.90718 metric ton
1 short ton = 2,000 pounds
1 long ton = 1.016 metric tons
1 long ton = 2,240 pounds
1 metric ton = 1,000 kilograms
1 quart = 0.94635 liters
1 US gallon = 3.7854 liters
1 Imperial gallon = 4.5459 liters
1 nautical mile = 1.852 km

°FAHRENHEIT	°CELSIUS
230	110
220	
210	100 WATER BOILS
200	
190	90
180	80
170	
160	70
150	
140	60
130	
120	50
110	
100	40
90	
80	30
70	20
60	
50	10
40	
30	0 WATER FREEZES
20	-10
10	
0	-20
-10	
-20	-30
-30	
-40	-40

MOON PACIFIC COAST HIGHWAY ROAD TRIP

Avalon Travel
Hachette Book Group
1700 Fourth Street
Berkeley, CA 94710, USA
www.moon.com

Editor: Rachel Feldman
Series Manager: Sabrina Young
Copy Editor: Deana Shields
Graphics and Production Coordinator: Lucie Ericksen
Cover Design: Erin Seaward-Hiatt
Interior Design: Darren Alessi
Moon Logo: Tim McGrath
Map Editor: Albert Angulo
Cartographer: Brian Shotwell
Indexer: Greg Jewett

ISBN-13: 978-1-63121-892-7

Printing History
1st Edition — 2016
2nd Edition — April 2018
5 4 3 2 1